Shamans, Prophets, and Sages

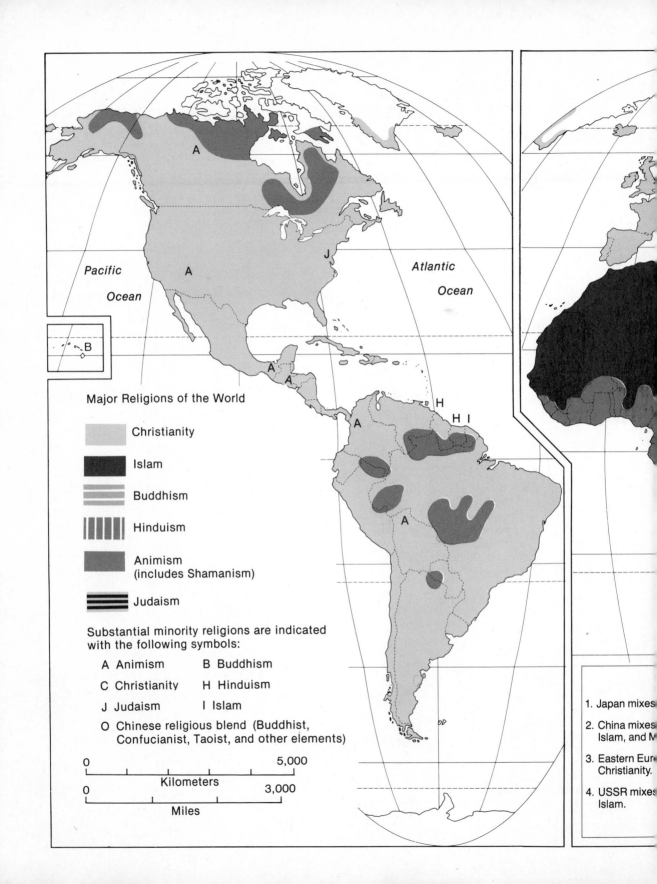

Pacific

Ocean

Atlantic

Ocean

B

Major Religions of the World

Christianity

Islam

Buddhism

Hinduism

Animism
(includes Shamanism)

Judaism

Substantial minority religions are indicated
with the following symbols:

A Animism   B Buddhism

C Christianity H Hinduism

J Judaism   I Islam

O Chinese religious blend (Buddhist,
   Confucianist, Taoist, and other elements)

0   5,000
      Kilometers
0   3,000
         Miles

1. Japan mixes

2. China mixes
   Islam, and M

3. Eastern Eur
   Christianity.

4. USSR mixes
   Islam.

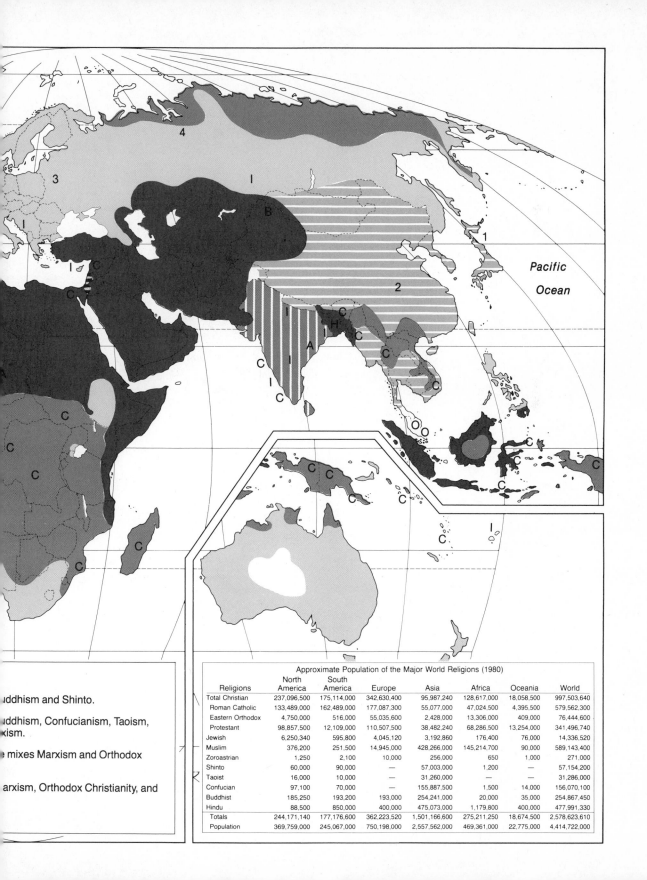

Pacific

Ocean

...ddhism and Shinto.

...uddhism, Confucianism, Taoism,
...xism.

...e mixes Marxism and Orthodox

...arxism, Orthodox Christianity, and

Approximate Population of the Major World Religions (1980)							
Religions	North America	South America	Europe	Asia	Africa	Oceania	World
Total Christian	237,096,500	175,114,000	342,630,400	95,987,240	128,617,000	18,058,500	997,503,640
Roman Catholic	133,489,000	162,489,000	177,087,300	55,077,000	47,024,500	4,395,500	579,562,300
Eastern Orthodox	4,750,000	516,000	55,035,600	2,428,000	13,306,000	409,000	76,444,600
Protestant	98,857,500	12,109,000	110,507,500	38,482,240	68,286,500	13,254,000	341,496,740
Jewish	6,250,340	595,800	4,045,120	3,192,860	176,400	76,000	14,336,520
Muslim	376,200	251,500	14,945,000	428,266,000	145,214,700	90,000	589,143,400
Zoroastrian	1,250	2,100	10,000	256,000	650	1,000	271,000
Shinto	60,000	90,000	—	57,003,000	1,200	—	57,154,200
Taoist	16,000	10,000	—	31,260,000	—	—	31,286,000
Confucian	97,100	70,000	—	155,887,500	1,500	14,000	156,070,100
Buddhist	185,250	193,200	193,000	254,241,000	20,000	35,000	254,867,450
Hindu	88,500	850,000	400,000	475,073,000	1,179,800	400,000	477,991,330
Totals	244,171,140	177,176,600	362,223,520	1,501,166,600	275,211,250	18,674,500	2,578,623,610
Population	369,759,000	245,067,000	750,198,000	2,557,562,000	469,361,000	22,775,000	4,414,722,000

Shamans, Prophets, and Sages
An Introduction to World Religions

Denise Lardner Carmody
Wichita State University

John Tully Carmody
Wichita State University

Wadsworth Publishing Company
Belmont, California
A Division of Wadsworth, Inc.

Religion Editor: Sheryl Fullerton
Production Editor: Vicki Friedberg
Managing and Text Designer: Cynthia Bassett
Print Buyer: Karen Hunt
Cover Designer: Diane Hillier
Copy Editor: Susan Thornton
Endpaper maps are adapted from Ismael R. al-Faruqi and David E. Sopher,
Historical Atlas of the Religions of the World.
Copyright 1974 © Macmillan Publishing Co. Used with permission.

Printed in the United States of America

2   3   4   5   6   7   8   9   10 — 89   88

ISBN 0-534-04263-5

Library of Congress Cataloging in Publication Data

Carmody, Denise Lardner, 1935–
Shamans, prophets, and sages.

Bibliography: p.
Includes index.
1. Religions   2. Religion, Primitive.   I. Carmody,
John, 1939–   II. Title.
BL80.2.C338   1985   291   84-17434
ISBN 0-534-04263-5

For Roslyn Pope-Sturgis

Contents

Contents

Contents

Contents

Contents

Contents

Preface

This is a core textbook for introducing the world religions. It provides a central orientation to the major traditions around which one may build various fuller treatments by adding primary source materials, contemporary materials, films, and the like. Two features of the book are distinctive. First, it focuses on the personality types that (arguably) have dominated the nonliterate, Western, and Eastern strands of the world religious heritage. Second, it has a moving point of view.

By *personality types* we mean the sorts of characters and functionaries that have stood at the centers of the three strands of the world religious heritage. The distinction between *character* (how the person actually is formed in his or her selfhood) and *function* (how the person serves a social group and is regarded by them) is not sharp for our purposes. Almost all the shamans, prophets, and sages with whom we shall be dealing both identified themselves with their roles (that is, thought of their core character in terms of their shamanism, prophecy, or sagehood) and were so identified by their social group. Within and without, therefore, they were people who centered their social groups by their visions, revelations, wisdoms, powers, and performances. When one looks at the history of religions, they are (in our opinion) the most significant characters and functionaries.

To call these personalities "types" is to admit that we are dealing with generalizations or abstractions. When we describe shamans as specialists in archaic techniques of ecstasy, or as people who ride their imaginations to the worlds of the gods, we are speaking of a general tendency, a pattern that holds by and large. We believe that the pattern will be more verified than not in the case of a specific American Indian, Eskimo, Japanese, Nepalese, or other sort of shaman, but we are not saying that all the details of the type will fit exactly or be the same. The shamanic type is like a piece of off-the-rack-clothing: Frequently it needs al-

terations, large or small, to fit the particular person under discussion.

The same with the prophetic and sapiential types. Although we would argue that almost all prophets stress will and ethical imperatives (in contrast to shamans who stress imagination and ecstatic experiences), we do not mean to cram any given prophet into our typical mold. The mold is more forged from past individual cases than designed to stamp out new ones. Similarly, although typically the sage stresses the intellect and a comprehensive worldview, Hebrew sages may shade this quite differently than Greek; Muslim philosophers may sketch quite a different world than Buddhist. The type is a tool, not a straitjacket. It should be a means, not something to fixate upon as an end in itself. So we urge that it be taken lightly but seriously as a generalization rather than an unfailing law.

Our moving point of view is necessary because although the three strands—nonliterate, Eastern, and Western—of the world religious heritage are dominated by different types, no type is ever completely in charge. Thus nonliterate peoples show prophetic and sapiential figures, in addition to the predominant shaman. Eastern peoples show shamanic and prophetic figures, in addition to the predominant sage. Western peoples show shamanic and sapiential figures, in addition to the predominant prophet. As we move from strand to strand, we have to fill in the nuances that this complicated reality demands. We have to point out, for example, that although biblical Judaism seems clearly dominated by the prophetic type, rabbinic Judaism may well have favored the sapiential type. In the same way, periods of Christian and Islamic history have made the sage a strong competitor to the prophet.

Thus we have found it necessary to have supplementary sections in each of our three parts. Part I on the shaman comments on prophecy and wisdom among nonliterate peoples. Part II on the prophet discusses shamanism and wisdom among prophetic peoples. And Part III on the sage relates the themes of shamanism and prophecy to sagacious peoples. The result is that the point of view keeps moving: adding qualifications, filling in subtler colors. By the end, we hope, students will be able to hold in mind this important point: both the three central types, well defined, and a good sense of how the types overlap, interact, are as much different emphases as radically different orientations.

Our thanks to Sheryl Fullerton of Wadsworth Publishing Company, Karla Kraft of Wichita State University, and the following scholars who reviewed the manuscript and offered helpful suggestions: Gary T. Alexander, Pennyslvania State University; Frank Burch Brown, Virginia Polytechnic Institute and State University; Robert Cohn, Northwestern University; and Miriam Levering, University of Tennessee.

1

Introduction

DINAH HOWELL

Dinah Howell, the heroine of Robb Forman Dew's excellent novel *Dale Loves Sophie to Death,* has nerve problems, deep fears, and lingering uneases. In her mid-thirties, married, the mother of three, she can't seem to find the things for her peace. During the academic year she lives in western Massachusetts, where her husband teaches English literature. Each summer she returns to her home town in Ohio, half-consciously looking for the clues that might solve her problem of nerves. We, the readers, are **Freudian** enough to agree with Dinah that the clues she seeks probably lie back "there," in the place her home town occupies on the map of her mind. Robb Forman Dew knows this map very well. Taking us through a summer of Dinah's self-reflection, Dew creates for Dinah parents, children, a husband, and girlhood friends who make the nerve problems plausible. Dinah remains a distinct individual; her troubled insides stay somewhat the product of her own bad choices and self-indulgences; but any one of us might have made similar choices. Any one of us might one day have nerves equally high strung.

This catholic, universal quality of a hero's or heroine's character is, of course, essential for effective literature. If we, the readers, are going to identify with a character, we have to see in her traits we can find in our own mirrors. So too with effective books on **religion**, even undergraduate texts. However generous students may be in granting textbook authors special indulgence, not expecting anything very interesting or personal, the enterprise still finally fails if nothing in the three hundred pages strikes a familiar note, brings the subject right home. Until a **shaman** becomes someone we might conceivably have known, shamanism will remain an exotic mystery. Unless a **prophet** can speak from lips just like ours, prophecy will remain quite bizarre.

Since Robb Forman Dew knows her business, Dinah Howell's troubles could be yours or mine. Somehow her parents never made her feel either fully loved or fully distinct, just this particular self. Somehow her children frighten her terribly, because she realizes she can never fully please them. Is Dinah then condemned to continue the cycle of misfiring, the generational gap of miscommunication, that she and her own parents created? Will her children, when they reach their mid-thirties, be as disaffected from her as she is from her parents? There is a real chance they will be just as disaffected, and so a real basis for her fears.

None of us is so secure, so sure we will succeed at basic tasks such as child rearing, that our nights can't be threatened with bogies, our days now and then break down. If our own childhood memories are not sunny, how can we predict fair sailing for our children? And even if our own childhood memories are quite sunny, how can we be sure we know exactly why, exactly how to reproduce the recipe? So we stumble ahead cautiously, trying to cope by not looking too closely. We distract ourselves, keep very busy, and gratefully notice that most kids seem to survive. Still, when an artist like Dew grabs our attention, we realize that our strategy is very vulnerable. Wise as we have been to keep from paralyzing ourselves with over-reflection, full maturity can demand that we face our fears directly, confront our deeper selves.

One of the central ironies in Dew's novel is that Dinah's father is a psychiatrist, a man supposed to know the backwaters of the psyche. Toward the end of the book, he shows Dinah that neither his learning nor his wide experience has exempted him from parental pains: "It's not easy, either, to know that you can't love your children the way they want to be loved. You can only love people however you happen to love them. I *did* always know that you weren't happy and that it would be hard for you, but I always thought that you understood that I don't ... *enjoy* life either. I hoped you'd give me credit for my own misery. And I hoped you'd know that I wished you well."[1] So Dinah and her father stand together as fellow sufferers, and we put the book down, thinking that maybe their future will hold more reciprocal understanding. The novel has impressed us with the trials of every day, the many ways all of us are struggling not to go under, so we put it down more compassionate than we were at its beginning.

Religion deals with compassion and the struggles not to go under. It deals with other things too, of course—God, justice, and ecology, for instance—but inner turmoil is part of its regular fare. Indeed, none of the religious figures we study in this book would have gained their stature or influence had they not had helpful things to say about coping. Neither shamans nor prophets nor **sages** would have retained their influence if their people's indices of inner turmoil had kept rising. Like good psychiatrists, all of these traditional religious functionaries have had to help their people adjust. Like mature people anywhere today, they have had to face life's irreducible mysteries. None of us has ever seen God, ever died knowing exactly what would befall her. Like Dinah Howell, all of re-ligion's heroes have learned their wisdom through suffering. Like the way for you and me, their way up to **wisdom** has been their way down to the center of themselves.

PEACE OF MIND

Nearly without exception, the religions of the world try to fill their followers with the **hope** that the center of themselves can prove beautiful and trustworthy. "If you can find the place where your whirling world stops," they have said, "you can gain a rich measure of peace." In this instance, **peace** is not the absence of armed conflict, the lack of armies marching down darkened plains. It is the tranquillity of order, the quiet that comes when all things stand in place. A person may find peace living in a grand mansion, with many objects of art. Another may find peace living in a grass hut, with only the birds and stars for treasures. Either way, peace will not depend upon external things. No possessions will secure an individual order. Either way, peace will depend on the quality of a person's thoughts, how the mind situates an individual in the world.

The *Dhammapada,* a Buddhist text that millions have found helpful, puts this thesis about peace quite forcefully:

All that we are is the result of what we have thought: it is founded on our thoughts, it is made up of our thoughts. If a man speaks or acts with an evil thought, pain follows him, as the wheel follows the foot of the ox that draws the wagon. All that we are is the result of what we have thought: it is founded on our thoughts, it is made up of our thoughts. If a man speaks or acts with a pure thought, happiness follows him, like a shadow that never leaves him. "He abused me, he beat me, he defeated me, he robbed me,"—in those who harbour such thoughts hatred will never cease. "He abused me, he beat me, he defeated me, he robbed me,"—in those who do not harbour such thoughts hatred will cease. For never does hatred cease by hatred here below: hatred ceases by love; this is an eternal law.[2]

The leading Buddhists, whom we will describe as sages, were much interested in peace of mind. As the verses from the *Dhammapada* suggest, they tended to approach the problem of suffering by trying to re-orient the sufferer. If a person were less inclined to *desire* so many things—money, security, good repu-tation, other peoples' gratitude and love—she prob-ably would suffer considerably less. If she did not have so many false expectations, she would not be disappointed so often.

Take Dinah Howell, for example. One of the golden moments in her past that she tries to reassess during her visits back home was her day as high school homecoming queen. From the time of her selection, she expected that to be driven around the football field, surrounded by her court, and kissed by the captain of the football team would fulfill her richest fantasies. In reality, the evening was a thorough disaster. Dinah was so numb from overexcitement that she felt virtually nothing, and her older brother, who had been forced to escort her (because her father considered the whole affair beneath him), became so irritated by her airs that he left her stranded at a grimy pizza parlor, humiliated and utterly confused.

In her returns to such memories, Dinah tends to focus on all the injuries people did her. Focusing on her father or her brother, she tends to say, "He abused me; he defeated me; he robbed me of my shining hour." Until she is willing to lance these boils, the student of the *Dhammapada* might suggest, Dinah will continue to suffer unhappiness. Similarly, until she better focuses her relations with her children, they will continue to cause her much pain.

This is not to say, of course, that Dinah's father or brother acted honorably. It is not to say that her children don't sometimes act like the Devil's own whelps. It is only to say that Dinah, and any one of us, has to learn a measure of detachment and dispassion, if she is to find an inner tranquillity. For the Buddhist sage, such inner tranquillity, leading to behavior that profits both the individual and other members of society, is most likely to come from meditation and wisdom studies. In the Buddhist scheme, ethics or living well depends on (and reinforces) two other main pillars, meditation and wisdom studies. By meditation, people can learn the patterns of their minds, where the consciousness might come to rest. By wisdom studies, they can learn how the world actually hangs together, what objective views are realistic. With a calm mind and a realistic outlook, a person has a good chance of living well. With a distressed mind and a faulty outlook, a person already is sunk.

Sages like the Buddhist masters have tended to specialize in the requirements of the good (satisfying, tranquil, socially helpful) life. They have tended to specialize in peace of mind. From the traditions of their tribe, or the revelations of their God, or their sense of nature's way, wise elders East and West have pointed their people toward happiness. In terms of its discipline, their guidance has been sober and demanding. In terms of its best results, their guidance has brought thousands to great joy.

When our mind stands in perfect balance, our spirit is open and free; the joy that wells up tells us we have found our inmost vocation, are living as we were made to live. Presently, Dinah Howell is but a poor, wayfaring stranger. Were she to take up the *Dhammapada,* however, or the similar teachings of other sages, she might leave her world of woe. Were she to learn to love as they instruct her, she might find measures of joy she never suspected.

JUSTICE

Where sages tend to focus on the mind, prophets tend to focus on the will. Where sages labor to bring peace, prophets labor to bring justice. And where sages generally look to meditation, prophets generally look to God's Word. So sages and prophets show some differences, as do the religions they have historically centered. For example, there are important differences between the sagacious traditions of India and East Asia and the prophetic traditions of the Near and Middle East. Hinduism is not the same as Judaism, and Buddhism stands off from Christianity. In significant part because of the different emphases of their founding figures, the wisdom traditions and the prophetic traditions conceive the world differently. To a sufferer such as Dinah Howell, they therefore offer different medications.

We do not mean, of course, that the medications prescribed by sages bear no similarities to those prescribed by prophets. We do not mean that India and Israel have no more in common than the initial letter of their names. The sages credited with the **Vedas**, the Hindu Scriptures, have a great deal in common with Israel's biblical prophets. The Buddha and Jesus probably would dialogue quite profitably, as would Confucius and Muhammad. However, one maxim of philosophical study directs scholars to distinguish among ideas so that later they might unite them. In due course, we hope to point up the similarities among these traditions, underscore the possibilities for dialogue. Right now, however, we are just beginning our overview of the world religions, merely making the first markings on the map. We need first to stress some distinctions that separate sages and prophets.

Let us pursue the matter of justice, taking it as both a constant concern of most religious prophets and a major source of human healing, strong medicine for troubled souls like Dinah Howell. Doing so, we notice that Dinah's life is very insular, a little world almost completely isolated from community or global affairs.

Her husband, who remains in Massachusetts, is mesmerized and paralyzed by the plight of the Cambodian refugees, but she and her friends in Ohio move in very constricted circles, think very circumscribed thoughts. They enjoy a great many parties, go swimming each day at the club, and seem mainly concerned with the weather, the heat outside and the more dangerous chills within. Thus Dinah's troubles appear somewhat superficial, afflictions of the leisurely and wealthy class. In many parts of the world, and in most prior periods of world history, a thirty-five-year-old woman would have been too busy constantly to rake over her adolescent hurts, too harried by brute problems of survival.

Prophecy tends to concern itself with the larger picture of things, the overall social situation. In this sense, prophecy is not so much a preview of the future, a prediction of what soon will occur, as a judgment about present disorders, a diagnosis of present social ills. From the perspective of the Word of God (**Adonai**, the Father, **Allah**), the prophet finds present times wanting—lacking the fairness and compassion they should have. Until the people of a present time repent, throwing off their injustices and returning to God's strict standards, the prophet can give them no rest. For there will be no good life for any of us, the prophet believes, until justice rolls down like a mighty stream. One cannot serve God and mammon. One cannot claim to love God while closing one's heart to a brother or sister in need. If Dinah had eyes to see with, ears to hear, she would be more concerned with trying to succor and reform the world around her than with trying to minister to her own little affronts and bruises. Cut free from her consuming self-centeredness, she would go out to greater problems and truths that might set her free.

Perhaps the foremost of our recent American prophets was Martin Luther King, Jr., and a recent analysis of the difficult last year of his life strikes many of the chords that religious prophets usually are playing:

By the end of 1967, King himself had moved beyond a narrow approach to the war in Vietnam and had long before rejected a single narrow focus on black rights in the U.S. By the end of that crucial year King was openly declaring that "the dispossessed of this nation—the poor, both white and Negro—live in a cruelly unjust society. They must organize a revolution against that injustice, not against the lives of ... their fellow citizens, but against the structures through which the society is refusing ... to lift the load of poverty." By then he was vaguely but courageously advocating campaigns of "massive civil disobedience ...
to compel unwilling federal authorities to yield to the mandates of justice." Originally that was supposed to be the purpose of the Poor People's Campaign: the opening of a nationwide movement of "massive civil disobedience" on behalf of radical, humanizing change in America.[3]

The great prophets, then, make vast demands on us. Like Moses, Jesus, and Muhammad, they want to create entirely new social structures. From the strength of their union with God, they see the injustices of present times as terribly ungodly, blasphemies against the Creator. So, many of them die relatively young, murdered or completely worn out. Their justice is a most demanding taskmaster. Their religions often seem to ask too much. But the love they have fostered has transformed the world, keeping much evil and darkness at bay.

ECSTASY

The third of our major religious personality types, the shaman, predominates in **nonliterate** and small-scale societies. As we shall see, there are good grounds for thinking that shamans have served human tribes since prehistoric times and for correlating their work with imaginative **ecstasy** and healing. Shamanism has continued into the present in many tribes of American Indians, Eskimos, Africans, and Australians, as well as in hamlets of India, East Asia, and other locales. Focusing on shamanism therefore will allow us to deal with many of the themes that used to be treated under the rubric of "primitive religion," before Western scholars realized how condescending and culture-bound that rubric was. In addition, our interest in the shaman, like our interest in the sage and the prophet, will focus on the way that the shaman actualizes a part of the human personality we all can actualize, a part human beings have long enjoyed and used for survival.

Referring again to Dinah Howell, let us ask what prescription a shaman's traditions might suggest. If a typical shaman were to come upon Dinah, how would his background likely dictate trying to bring her out of her doldrums? Mainly through exercises that would stir her imagination, put her in closer touch with her body, and bring her to a richer appreciation of the natural world. For thousands of years, shamans have used trances and quasi-hallucinatory states to heal illnesses of both body and spirit. Tapping the powers of the psyche and powers they have found in animal nature, they have made thousands of people more whole.

Recently Michael Harner, an anthropologist working out of Columbia University in New York, has described the nonordinary, shamanic state of consciousness that healers have long used in small-scale societies:

In engaging in shamanic practice, one moves between what I term an Ordinary State of Consciousness (OSC) and a Shamanic State of Consciousness (SSC). These states of consciousness are the keys to understanding, for example, how Carlos Castaneda [a bestselling anthropologist, or novelist, who works with the shamanic traditions of the Yaqui Indians of Northern Mexico] can speak of an "ordinary reality" and a "nonordinary reality." The difference in these states of consciousness can perhaps be illustrated by referring to animals. Dragons, griffins, and other animals that would be considered "mythical" by us in the OSC are "real" in the SSC. The idea that there are "mythical" animals is a useful and valid construct in OSC life, but superfluous and irrelevant in SSC experiences. "Fantasy" can be said to be a term applied by a person in the OSC to what is experienced in the SSC. Conversely, a person in the SSC may perceive the experiences of the OSC to be illusory in SSC terms. Both are right, as viewed from their own particular states of consciousness. The shaman has the advantage of being able to move between states of consciousness at will.[4]

Dinah Howell might not find the shamanic exercises that Harner proposes compatible with her ordinary state of consciousness, but she probably could agree that one of the major gaps or lacks in her life is a consuming passion that takes her out of herself and gives the world a glow. Very seldom does she ride her imagination like an eagle or travel her mind as though mounted on Pegasus, the winged horse of Greek mythology. So she lies in bed late into the morning, chronically depressed. So she reduces the physical world to a cozy little garden and string of weather reports. Dinah needs a massive infusion of imaginative energy, to see the world as vast and beautiful. She needs, through science, or art, or shamanic practices, to take flame with images of creative power. Standing out from herself, ecstatic, she could gain both more energy and better perspective. Actualizing the shamanic part of her potential, she could drown her unhappiness in a great love of the world.

That is the way that don Juan, Carlos Castaneda's central hero, speaks about his life, as a love affair with the physical world:

"Only if one loves this earth with unbending passion can one release one's sadness," don Juan said. "A warrior [don Juan's term for a shaman] is always

joyful because his love is unalterable and his beloved, the earth, embraces him and bestows upon him inconceivable gifts. The sadness belongs only to those who hate the very thing that gives shelter to their beings." Don Juan again caressed the ground with tenderness. "This lovely being, which is alive to its last recesses and understands every feeling, soothed me, it cured me of my pains, and finally when I had fully understood my love for it, it taught me freedom."[5]

Shamans learn to use their imagination to gain powers of healing and freedom. Shutting down "ordinary reality" (which, for all its solid anchoring of our sanity, can be constricting and enslaving), the shaman finds more energy within, and more splendor without, than most industrialized people can imagine. Is it possible to tap these shamanic resources, without losing the great gains of industrialization? Is it possible to regain a healing and energizing relation with the earth? For the sake of Dinah Howell, and all the rest of us who are underdeveloped, let us give an open mind to the shamanic traditions that say it is.

THIS BOOK

The first thing that we, the authors, ask of you, the reader, is an open mind. If the sages, prophets, and shamans whom we shall display are going to show you even a fraction of their treasures, you will have to open the eyes of your mind. Some of what they describe will be quite familiar, and some may seem quite strange. Some of their prescriptions for living a good life will be quite acceptable, but others may put you off. You have the right to your own convictions, of course, and we don't demand that you try to become a shaman, or a prophet, or a sage. But the only way that you can know whether shamanism, or prophecy, or wisdom even *might* make sense of past human history, and even *might* still be valuable today, is to give it a fair hearing. We shall try to keep our part of the bargain, which is to present each tradition as sympathetically and enthusiastically as we can, stressing the rich resources we find in it.

Another thing to keep in mind as you work your way through this text is the materials and methods we do *not* emphasize, the other approaches one might take. By focusing on key personality types and functionaries, we do not, for instance, give much space to each religion's history. From time to time we will indicate how a given tradition arose and developed, but such historical information will only supplement our central focus (see appendixes). Similarly, we will not attempt a full analysis of the **belief system** of any of the traditions, although regularly we shall have to erect some of the intellectual scaffolding by which a shaman's or a prophet's, or a sage's convictions hang together. Third, the *rituals* or ceremonies that the traditions have developed could be given more attention than we shall give them here. If one asks how central functionaries such as shamans have reached the common people with their messages, ritualistic studies can be very illuminating. So we shall use ritualistic studies from time to time, but again only as a subordinate focus. As a result, such other important religious functionaries as priests and kingly rulers will not receive the attention they might elsewhere.

There are liabilities, then, in focusing on only three main religious types, ways that our approach may skew the data. Nonetheless, we think that shamans, prophets, and sages have been the most important repositories of religious wisdom and power, and so studying them can get one to the heart of the world religions' matter. And just what might the heart of the world religions be? It just might be enough light and warmth to make it through one's years, enough power to live and die well.

Were an evolutionist, a student of the human species' march through the long history of our planet, to summarize the impact of religion, that light and warmth probably would be the gist.[6] Seeing itself fenced in by death, disease, suffering, ignorance, madness, and other threats, the human species has found in itself, or discovered in its environment, spiritual forces, psychosomatic disciplines, ultimate images and thoughts that have kept it struggling for survival, endowed it with meaning and hope. As a simple matter of evolutionary fact, our strange species, which alone has the power to anticipate and reflect, has needed intellectual or spiritual resources just as much as it has needed food, shelter, and procreation. The fact that we have survived for hundreds of thousands, perhaps more than a million, years is a strong testimony to the evolutionary utilities of religion. That today, when some people find genuine religion to be on the wane, our species faces threats to its survival more terrible than any it has ever faced in the past strongly suggests that even industrialized people cannot live by technology alone.

Herewith, then, a long look at attitudes, mind-sets, and convictions that pertain to the present as much as the past. If it is true that shamans, prophets, and sages have drawn most of the map of human history, it is equally true that their explorations of the human condition apply to all of our central problems today. Have we staggering problems with an increasingly polluted environment? Shamans have taught millions of people to love the world well. Have we economic injustices and military aggressions that place the entire globe in nuclear bondage? Prophets have opened ways of justice and love that have freed hundreds of generations from slavery. And do most of us still wander in dark nights of ignorance, still not know the things for our joy and peace? Sages like the Buddha and the great rabbis have worked on detachment and commitment for centuries, found renewable resources of light and warmth.

SUMMARY

We began with Dinah Howell, a fictional sort of everywoman, whose fears and uneases express much of the human condition. Dinah's particular problems focus on the relations between parents and children, the difficulty of loving well those whom fate has placed closest to us. Because of her deep-seated confusions, Dinah seems destined for years of suffering. Even her psychiatrist father can only offer her the consolation that he, too, suffers and is unhappy.

In other times or cultures, sages like the author of the *Dhammapada* would have had a great deal more to offer. The peace of mind that Dinah seeks was for them a matter of what one thinks. If one thinks evil thoughts, one is bound to find unhappiness. If one thinks pure thoughts, one is sure to come to peace. Meditating on such propositions, Buddhist sages have taught their disciples detachment. If Dinah were to give up her worst cravings, she might learn to enjoy her life.

The prophet likely would approach Dinah's problems quite differently, stressing their social side. Having her concentrate on justice, the reform of her society's inequities, the prophet would give her egocentricity a body blow, exercise her spirit in practical love. The typical shaman would largely agree but likely would shift Dinah's focus to the natural world, helping her to develop a wider imagination. In shamanic perspective, the power we need to live life well is a function of nonordinary awareness.

In this book, we shall try to give all these prescribers—shamans, prophets, and sages—a fair and sympathetic hearing. Realizing that there are many other ways of approaching the world religions, we shall try to use our concentration on the leading personality types to focus on the heart of the religious matter: the traditions' resources for bringing human beings to a peace and joy that fulfill.

STUDY QUESTIONS

1. Why do you think we chose Dinah Howell to begin our Introduction?

2. What was your reaction to the quotation from the *Dhammapada*?

3. What is the usual link between the prophet's focus on justice and her loyalty to the Word of God?

4. How does shamanism depend on special states of consciousness?

5. When one looks back over human evolution, what is the likely heart of the religious matter?

NOTES

1. Robb Forman Dew, *Dale Loves Sophie to Death.* New York: Penguin, 1982, p. 215.

2. *The Dhammapada,* verses 1–5, trans. Irving Babbitt. New York: New Directions, 1965, p. 3.

3. Vincent Harding, "The Land Beyond," *Sojourners,* 12/1 (January 1983), p. 21.

4. Michael Harner, *The Way of the Shaman.* San Francisco: Harper & Row, 1980, p. xiii.

5. Carlos Castaneda, *Tales of Power.* New York: Simon and Schuster, 1974, p. 285.

6. See John Bowker, *The Sense of God.* Oxford: Clarendon Press, 1973, pp. 44–65.

I

Shamans

The word shaman *comes from Tungus, a Siberian language, where it is the name given to the central religious figure of most Siberian and Central Asian tribes. In his famous study of shamanism, Mircea Eliade stresses the ecstatic quality of the shaman's powers: "A first definition of this complex phenemenon, and perhaps the least hazardous, will be shamanism = technique of ecstasy."*[1]
To heal his tribe's sick members, or guide its dead to their rest, or champion his people against evil spirits, the Siberian shaman goes out of himself, in what a modern Western observer might call a trance or a hallucination, and journeys in spirit to another realm, where most of the crucial battles of sickness and health, death and life, evil and good are waged.

We shall consider shamanism in this strict sense, detailing how the Siberian shaman, who has become for scholars the prime exemplar of humanity's ancient techniques of ecstasy, tends to function. However, we shall also consider the (similar) ways that prehistoric religious functionaries appear to have served their people, and the (similar) ways that East Asian, African, Australian, and American Indian religious functionaries have used ecstasy right down to the present. Following this survey of contexts in which the shaman appears to have been the principal religious figure, we shall consider contexts in which another figure (the prophet or the sage) has pre-

dominated but the shaman has continued to be significant.

Let us now set the stage for these studies by indicating a kinship that we contemporary Westerners retain with the classical shamans, even though our social circumstances differ greatly from theirs. As we suggested earlier, the shaman's rich imagination *might heal many people like Dinah Howell, who don't know how to picture alternatives to their patterns of pain and defeat. When Eskimo shamans become ecstatic in order to journey to the bottom of the sea, where Sedna, the goddess of the animals, has fenced in the seals, they exercise a vivid imagination. Producing pictures of what Sedna looks like, how they must make their way past the fierce dogs guarding her door, what the seals say to them about their imprisonment, and the like, the shamans tells their breathless audience how the mission is going, what life beyond the audience's ordinary range is like. Because they and the audience tend to equate what is real with what is vividly experienced, both the shamans and their audience take their descriptions seriously. Like the message that any Central Asian might receive from a departed parent in a dream, the shaman's ecstatic experience is one of the important things that every sober person takes seriously.*

The modern West has brought human imagination under scientific control, with many ben-

eficial results. Defining reality as what can be experienced through the senses and tested through dispassionate judgments, it has revolutionized humanity's understanding of the natural world and produced enormous advances in health care. But sometimes this scientific disciplining of our imaginations can constrict our feelings, so that reality becomes less vivid, challenging, and satisfying than it might be. Sometimes the mental world of the modern Westerner is arid and thin, compared to the lush poetry that ancient peoples have had in their heads. The limits of our imaginations are the limits of our worlds. When a shaman pictures our relation to the game on which we depend for food as decisively influenced by our relation with ultimate powers such as Sedna, he or she may be speaking a richer, more poetic truth than our scientifically disciplined minds can handle.

For example, the shaman may be telling us, in his own peculiar way, that animals, human beings, and the holy power at the source of all things are so bound together ecologically that any push on one is felt by all the others. How we treat the rest of creation colors all our relations with our God or highest value, and how we conceive God or our highest value colors all our relations with the rest of creation. To break one of Sedna's laws would put the Eskimo shaman out of phase with the rest of nature. Thus the rules about when a shaman may eat seal meat, what a hunter has to give back to the ocean, how women are to sew the seal skins, and the like express the Eskimo's profound appreciation of the fragility of human life, its intense dependence on the game, the weather, and good fortune.

Slowly, we in the modern West are regaining some of the classical shaman's ecological instinct. Step by step, we are realizing that in all sectors of our life we are tied to other creatures. When we cause acid rain to fall on lakes and forests, we taint our food, drink, and raw materials for housing. When our leaders make a decision about the flow of money, the stock market jumps, the housing industry is affected, factories open

Figure 1   Alaskan house post, Haida, Sukkwan Island, ca. 1950. Nelson Gallery—Atkins Museum, Kansas City, Missouri (Nelson Fund).

and close, and unemployment rises or falls. Since unemployment affects a state's income, which in turn affects state institutions such as universities, a change in federal banking can determine whether or not students study phenomena like shamanism, learn the power of their imaginations, and increase their ability to picture creation as a very complex web.

The limits of our world are the limits of our imaginations.

NOTE

1. Mircea Eliade, *Shamanism: Archaic Techniques of Ecstasy*. Princeton, N.J.: Bollingen/Princeton University Press, 1972, p. 4.

2

Shamanism in Prehistoric Cultures

THE DANCE OF THE TIGER

Putting their trained imaginations to work on the data gathered in a century of archeology, prehistorians have been trying to picture the first periods of truly human existence. They wonder what the Ice Age cultures might have been like that produced the splendid paintings found in the caves of France and Spain. One of the most respected of these prehistorians, Bjorn Kurtèn, has written a fascinating novel about a crucial period in human evolution, when Neandertals and early members of our modern species (*Homo sapiens sapiens*) may have interacted.

The Neandertals were the older line, perhaps dating back 250,000 years. From excavations at sites such as Shanidar in Iraq, we know that they were "human" enough to have buried some of their dead with flowers and to have cared for a disabled member of the group who could not fend for himself. Our new species, better equipped for speech and foresight, eventually

proved the more fit for evolutionary survival. But Kurtèn captures a time when the two lines may have shared the same physical area, sometimes in peace and sometimes in conflict. Using his scientific knowledge, he carefully depicts the intimacy with nature that prehistoric humanity's artistic remains show it to have possessed, making his central figure, Tiger, an artist who identified closely with animals (as the classical shaman frequently does).

Tiger's family is killed and he is wounded by Shelk, another *Homo sapiens sapiens*. Tiger is nursed back to health by a Neandertal tribe. When he finds that Shelk (whose name means "large elk") has also killed his Neandertal friends, Tiger vows to avenge both of his "peoples." This passion for revenge takes shape as Tiger watches two magnificent black tigers outwit a family of huge mammoths. Burning into his imagination the memory of the black tiger's patience and power, Tiger imagines himself as cunning and destructive as a hunting tiger and sets out to draw a scene that will prefigure his destruction of Shelk:

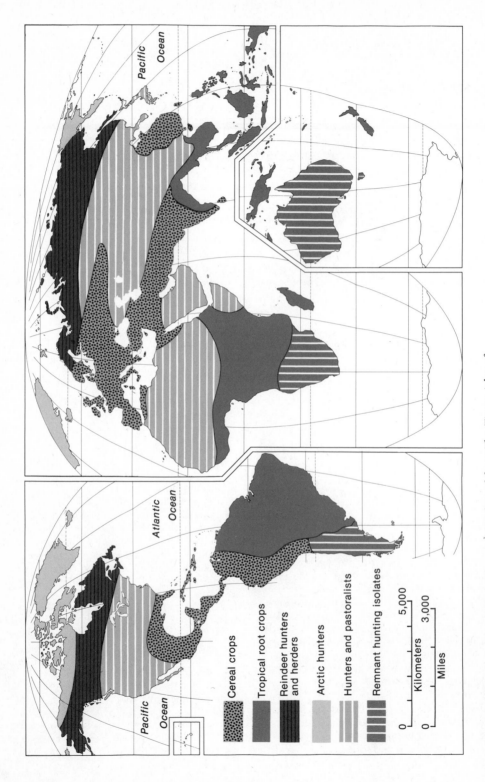

Figure 2 *Original economies of the world. Adapted from* The Times Atlas of
World History, *edited by Geoffrey Barraclough, 1979. © Hammond, Inc. Reprinted
with permission of Times Books Limited, England.*

Cereal crops

Tropical root crops

Reindeer hunters
and herders

Arctic hunters

Hunters and pastoralists

Remnant hunting isolates

Kilometers

Miles

0   3,000   5,000

Pacific
Ocean

Atlantic
Ocean

Pacific
Ocean

The Ancient Religious Mind: Twenty-Five Key Dates

4.6 BILLION YEARS AGO   Formation of the Earth

3.6 BILLION YEARS AGO   Rise of Life

4 MILLION YEARS AGO   *Australopithecus,* Advanced Hominid in Africa

2 MILLION YEARS AGO   *Homo Habilis,* Stone Tools

1.5 MILLION YEARS AGO   *Homo Erectus,* More Sophisticated Tools

500,000 YEARS AGO   Use of Fire

100,000 YEARS AGO   *Homo Sapiens,* Ritual Burial

75,000 YEARS AGO   Mousterian Cave Dwellers; Clothing to Survive Northern Winters

40,000 YEARS AGO   *Homo Sapiens Sapiens,* "Modern Man," Full Hunting Culture

35,000 YEARS AGO   Clothing Adequate for Life in Siberia

30,000 YEARS AGO   Prehistoric Painting and Sculpture

30,000–25,000 YEARS AGO   Migrations Across Bering Strait to New World

20,000 YEARS AGO   Colonization of Europe, Japan

15,000 YEARS AGO   Extensive Cereal Collecting

10,500 YEARS AGO   Humans Throughout South America

9,500–6,500 YEARS AGO   Cereal Cultivation, Domestication of Animals

8,000 B.C.E.   Full Withdrawal of Glaciers

8350–7350 B.C.E.   Jericho, First Walled Town (10 Acres)

6250–5400   Catal Huyuk (Turkey), Large City (32 Acres)

CA. 6000   Rice Cultivation in Thailand; Pottery and Woolen Textiles in Catal Huyuk

CA. 5000   Irrigation of Mesopotamian Alluvial Plains

CA. 4000   Bronze Casting in Middle East

CA. 3500   Megaliths in Brittany, Iberian Peninsula, British Isles; Invention of Wheel

CA. 3100   Pictographic Writing in Sumer

CA. 3000   Spread of Copper Working

He would appear gentle and innocent, but behind that mask he would be as swift and deadly as the tigress. . . . He sketched out a great picture of the scene he had witnessed. The immense black mammoths took shape under his hand. Then came the tigers. He worked in ecstasy to reproduce in sensitive lines the flow of power, the clownish insolence, the mastery of the male tiger; to catch the urgency and precision of the female, her single, high-rising attack, the one unerring stroke of violence in the whole combat . . . [then] he drew a different image, which came from another secret place in his mind. There were only two figures here: one, a majestic shelk; the other, a black tiger moving in to attack. The shelk, for all its glory, was touched by the premonition of death, while every line in the tiger was alive with implacable anger.[1]

This is the moment of decision in the novel, when Tiger finds in himself the scenario or story that may solve his conflicts. As Kurtèn describes it, his artistic work is ecstatic, welling up from depths in himself that he had never visited before, and projecting him into an enlarged, new set of possibilities. True, Tiger is an artist, a man of special skills. But all of his people, both his fellow *Homo sapiens sapiens* and his adopted family of Neandertals, apparently rode their imaginations freely to consort with animals, birds, and spirits. What archaic shamans did in formal ceremonies ordinary individuals likely did in less dramatic ways. The point was to connect oneself to the splendors of the surrounding natural world and tap its special powers. Tiger would have known the difference between the shelk of his picture and the man who was his hated enemy. He would have known the difference between himself and the black cat that was to take the shelk down. But he saw the dance of the magnificent black tigers around the mammoths as a clue to his own situation, made the wonderful scene of the cats' hunting prowess a symbol of his own ability to muster his utmost skill.

Animating Kurtèn's novel is the conviction that Ice Age humans such as Tiger, and Neandertals such as his lover Miss Angelica, were much more like us twentieth-century people than unlike us. For all the immense differences in physical and cultural circumstances, a similar body and brain gave them a consciousness similar to ours. So the imaginative ecstasies of their artists and shamans, in which they probably identified with animals and spirits, were both functional and liberating, as our imaginative flights can be. So such ecstasies helped them cope with their environment and gave them peak moments of fulfillment, as our ecstasies might.

THE ROOTS OF CIVILIZATION

When prehistorians first started to study the remains of Ice Age human beings, some of which go back as much as forty thousand years, they hypothesized that nonliterate peoples of the present (for example, Australian aborigines) probably had retained Ice Age or Paleolithic modes of thought. This led to an interpretation of Paleolithic remains in terms of hunting magic, fertility worship, and other theories that anthropologists working with present-day nonliterate peoples had developed.

Following these first interpretational flurries, sexual theories had much vogue. Influenced by psychoanalysis, prehistorians noted the many masculine and feminine features one might see in Paleolithic art, the plethora of possible phallic and vulva symbols.

With the use of closer, microscopic analyses, however, prehistorians have become more cautious. Viewed close up, many of the Paleolithic remains show notational schemes, probably related to a lunar calendar, and complex juxtapositions of animals, plants, and human figures who may, together, compose "time-factored" scenes.

Probably the leading champion of this newer interpretational focus is Alexander Marshack, whose hefty volume *The Roots of Civilization*[2] narrates both how he stumbled onto the significance of notational marks and the growing evidence for the sophistication of Ice Age humanity's cognitional processes. When Marshack began to verify his hunch that the strange cuts on Paleolithic bones from many European excavations might be records or calculations based on the phases of the moon, he found a whole new vista opening up. In this new vista, Ice Age human beings shared one of our own most determining characteristics, a self-conscious positioning in time. For if early humans did have the ability to calculate the phases of the moon, they necessarily also had the basic wherewithal to tell stories, placing their experiences in a dramatic frame of past beginning, present middle, and future end.

This is what Marshack means by the terms *time-factored* and *time-factoring*. If one's consciousness is shaped by a sense of the seasons, down to the considerable detail that a careful observation of the phases of the moon can bring, then one stands above the perceptual level of animals that can merely sense, above even the perceptual level of animals that can make tools, organizing reality much more panoramically. In essence, all one's cognitional apparatuses, all the results of the brain work one does, factor experience in temporal terms, giving one a "historical" sense of the world. Thus, long before they had the ability to write, and so verbally record their sense of time's passage, human beings probably thought in terms of stories, probably lived with an explicit, reflex sense of spring, summer, fall, and winter that made them actors in the dramas of nature's seasons.

This hypothesis, which Marshack first derived from very old bones, seemed to grow richer and more confirmed when his microscopic analyses of animal figures on later and larger art works showed more time-factored details. For example, regularly he would find not simply a salmon or a reindeer but a salmon with details specific to the spring time of the salmon run or a reindeer with details specific to the fall time of the reindeer rut. When he discovered similar scenes showing flowers in spring bloom or trees in fall fruitfulness, such data helped support his time-factoring hypothesis. The result was a wider context for Paleolithic art and ceremonies. Hunting magic and fertility worship may well have occurred, as may dramatic expressions of sexual differentiation, but one could now place them in the broader horizon of a consciousness probing the flow of nature's seasons, factoring the sense of being immersed in nature's ongoing story.

As a result, older interpretations of Paleolithic cave art, which centered on supposed hunting rituals (in which the leading figures would act out the coming hunt, so as to assure, by what scholars called *sympathetic magic,* a successful kill), have become more dubious. If one approaches this art with Marshack's sensitivity to temporal factors, the seasonal dimensions of the art stand forth. Then hunting magic may be less prominent than seasonal celebrations:

It is interesting that of the many human figures found with animals in Upper Paleolithic art none have weapons in hand, whereas many do have ceremonial and symbolic dress or objects. It is only later, after the Upper Paleolithic is ended, when the ice is gone and the culture changes, that we get images of hunters at the chase with weapon in hand, and even here we cannot be sure that the hunt is not ceremonial and that the animals hunted and represented are not symbolic of seasonal rites. The Upper Paleolithic image is usually of a man naked, or robed in animal skins, often with body and hand attitudes that seem to stress the ritual, ceremonial nature of the relation.[3]

Is it then likely that human cognition really caught fire, taking the first giant steps that would one day lead it to explore the moon and outer planets, when our brain gained the capacity to factor time and we began to celebrate rites of spring and fall? Further, is it because they were the prime seers in a storied or mythological existence that the archaic shamans were so important? Do their ecstasies, their imaginative journeys, represent some of the mind's earliest, most creative efforts to order a flow of experiences not only felt but reflexively known to participate in the time of the cosmos, the seasons that all other creatures obeyed unknowingly? If so, the archaic shamans were at the crux of the evolutionary drives that eventually led not only to written history but to all our later conceptions of the intimate bonds between space and time.

HUNTING

The peoples of the Ice Age lived by hunting game and gathering edible vegetation. This "economy" made them both nomadic, since they had to follow the game on which they lived, and sensitive to the seasons, since both animals and plants manifest important seasonal changes. Granting a time-factored and story-making consciousness, it is likely that the prehistoric hunting populations created many tales about the animals and plants that were the main agents or factors in their life situation. Today we tend to call such stories **myths**, meaning by this term tales that go beyond what one can know with certainty (from observation), stories about the mysterious origins and ends of things.

Among the many students of myth, Mircea Eliade has probably been the most influential theoretician of the religious or ultimate dimension of humanity's primal stories. Early in his masterwork, *A History of Religious Ideas,* Eliade speculates on the stories that probably riveted the early Ice Age hunters:

It seems plausible to state that a certain number of myths were familiar to the Paleolithic populations, first of all the cosmogonic [birth of the world] myths and the myths of origin (origin of man, of game, of death, etc.). To give only one example, a cosmogonic myth

brings on the stage the primordial Waters and the Creator, the latter either as anthropomorphic [in human form] or in the form of an aquatic animal, descending to the bottom of the ocean to bring back the material necessary for the creation of the world. The immense dissemination of this cosmogony and its archaic structure point to a tradition inherited from earliest prehistory. Similarly, myths, legends, and rites related to ascent to the sky and "magical flight" (wings, feathers of birds of prey—eagle, falcon) are universally documented, on all continents, from Australia and South America to the Arctic. Now these myths are bound up with certain oneiric [dream] and ecstatic experiences specifically characteristic of shamanism, and their archaism is indubitable.[4]

This paragraph demands a little interpretation. First, Eliade is trying to perform the delicate task of correlating evidence from the Paleolithic period with data about "archaic" peoples that exist today, uninfluenced by writing and Western critical reason. He is aware of the dangers in attempting such a correlation (imagine the changes that could have occurred in the course of forty thousand years, even when both prehistoric and recent groups share the important characteristic of nonliteracy), but the light that more recent data *might* shed on much earlier times tempts Eliade to project recent religious experiences back to Paleolithic times. Thus, he is willing to conjecture that certain Paleolithic data (for example, paintings in which a human figure wears the head of a bird) represent states of consciousness like those of recent shamans, who frequently describe trances in which they fly like birds.

Second, Eliade stresses the *cosmogonic* myth, in which a people tells the story of how the whole world began. The logic here is simple enough. Once human beings reached the stage of a time-factored consciousness, they must have tried to picture how the story of the world began. Seeing that human beings, animals, and plants all came into being and then passed out of being, the first humans surely must have played with the notion that the whole world had a birth or time of origin and perhaps would have a death or time of ceasing as well. Recent nonliterate peoples usually have had such myths, and Paleolithic peoples would have had all ingredients necessary for them.

By *oneiric* experiences Eliade means things that occur in dreams. In most shamanic tribes, dreams are very important, not at all the "unreal" happenings that modern Western common sense implies that they are. As though they instinctively knew much of what Freud and later psychoanalysts have discovered, shamans have long been convinced that dreams can be revelations, sources of important guidance. As well, shamans have long put into their reports of their ecstatic experiences things that do not occur in ordinary reality but may well occur in dreams: flying like a bird, swimming down to the bottom of the sea, talking with animals, and the like. It would seem that the earliest shamanic experience probably also used a freer imagination than that of modern Western common sense, an imagination that many of us now only exercise while dreaming.

Among other symbolic realities that may well have preoccupied the early hunters are the rainbow, which seems to be a bridge to the heavens (the place to which many shamans "fly"); the Lord of the Beasts, a figure who presides over the movements of the game; fire, which humanoid creatures had been using for perhaps half a million years; sex; birth; death; and killing, by which hunting peoples survived. Each of these primal entities, and of course many others, begged a storied explanation. Each was something that early peoples would have had to get their minds around, if they were to cope with their environment successfully. Thus each probably preoccupied shamans, as they tried to put together a view of the whole, and probably preoccupied the people who participated in the Paleolithic ceremonies that acted out the tribe's fears, hopes, and deepest convictions. As the art left behind in the European caves suggests, the storied combinations into which these primal entities might enter are beyond calculation. Thus we can be quite confident that the early hunters had a complex, richly imaginative world, heightened by shamanic ecstasy.

AGRICULTURE

Thirty thousand years ago people like Tiger and Eliade's shamans were following game that traveled routes determined by Europe's Ice Age and painting wonderful scenes of animal life like those that adorn the walls of the caves at Lascaux in France.[5] They had brought to its peak a way of life that had been evolving for hundreds of thousands of years. Ten thousand years ago the discovery or invention of agriculture began to change this mental world the hunters had developed. Thenceforth greater stability, more wealth, larger social units, and more elaborately organized religions would provide human consciousness with a basis for new stories and, with the advent of writing, a new way to collect them.

The climatic change that set the scene for agriculture was the melting of the glaciers. In the new, warmer era (often called the Mesolithic), the Paleolithic abundance of game may have seemed a paradise lost. Hunt-

ing instincts remained and may finally have led to corps of guards or soldiers, but gradually a new focus on crops took center stage. By the time that agriculture had become firmly rooted, in what archeologists call the Neolithic period, humanity was decisively altering its ancient patterns of behavior. Above all, human beings now were applying their time-factoring skills with much greater precision, searching out the time to plant and the time to reap, calculating when to store seeds and how much harvest to place in storage. Humanity's interest in fertility also shifted focus, from the fertility of animals to the fertility of plants. The ancient division of labor between men and women shifted as well, women's "gathering" becoming more important.

With all these changes, it is highly likely that human beings' stories about the world also changed. Not only would it have been necessary to explain the origin of specific plants and of plant cultivation in general, it also would have been necessary to realign cosmogonies and myths about sex, death, and other primal entities. For if a people changes its economy, it changes its entire culture. The ecology of human life is such that central features such as an economy—the way people obtain the goods necessary for survival—tie into all other central features: religion, politics, family life, art, and the like.

Many students of archaic myths feel that the stories they find in recent primitive agricultural societies may well reflect conceptions that go back to the early Neolithic times, when agriculture began in the Near East. For example, the Hainuwele story from New Guinea, one of the most famous agricultural myths, says that the plants the people now cultivate first sprang up from the murder of a semidivine maiden (Hainuwele). Consequently, every time they celebrated their festival rites, the cultivators of New Guinea reminded themselves that their food came from a bloody act back at "the beginning," an act that forever linked the source of life to death. In some early agricultural societies this link apparently led to ritual sacrifices: shedding the blood of consecrated victims, so as to renew the force of the power that started agriculture. In other early societies the emphasis apparently was on participating in the sacred power and reality of the god or goddess whose death had begun the agricultural process. This one did by eating the foods in which the divinity now was present.

Thus, whereas hunting had stressed the bonds between human beings and animals, agriculture tended to stress the bonds between human beings and vegetation. As well, it tended to spotlight the feminine side of the mystery of life, for many stories about vegetation likened the earth to a fertile mother. The farmer would sow seeds in the womb of the earth, and after gestating they would come forth like new children. Moreover, the periodicity of the fertile earth was like the periodicity of women. Thus one finds a proliferation of Neolithic artifacts that suggest a cult of a Mother Goddess. Whereas Paleolithic art represented the fertility of woman and man rather equally, the art of the early agricultural cultures began to subordinate the male principle to the female. Both remained represented, and their correlation remained strong, but the male figure became secondary and the female primary. This is true, for example, of the artistic remains from Catal Huyuk in Turkey, an excavation site about nine thousand years old. There the central Goddess is represented in three ways—as a young woman, a fertile mother, and an aged crone—while her rather peripheral male companion is represented as either a young boy or a young man.

Interestingly, symbols of both fertility and death abound in the various shrines of Catal Huyuk. We see how agriculture reset the terms of male-female polarity, and how it sharpened the interrelation of life and death. We do not know precisely what rites occurred in these shrines to act out these new emphases, but we do know that by about 4500 B.C.E. (before common era) agricultural societies were building large-scale temples and exhibiting a highly developed priesthood. Probably, therefore, the more settled and wealthy conditions that agriculture produced led to a group of professionals who organized complex religious rites in honor of the Goddess. Probably the age of the individual shaman was giving way to the age of the group of priests.

Whatever the particulars, the overall result was clear. Through agriculture humanity stepped away from shamanistic tribal religion, stepped toward the priestly religions of the later civilizations. Human social units grew in size, had more leisure, and developed religious rites and mythologies considerably more intricate. Older "masculine" hunting ways did not disappear completely, but newer "feminine" farming ways came to predominate.

NEOLITHIC RELIGION

The agricultural practices that first took hold in the Near East spread into Europe only slowly, for several reasons. First, the climate in central and western Europe remained sufficiently cool to host a considerable number of game animals and fish. Second, the farming techniques developed in the Near East had to be adapted to the forest-covered areas of Europe.

Between 6500 and 5300 B.C.E., vigorous cultural activities in the Balkan Peninsula laid down remains that allow archeologists to reconstruct something of what "Old Europe" was like when it stood on the threshold between hunting and agriculture. The remains indicate widespread ritual activities, in which animal-shaped vessels and masks of spirits or gods were used. In terms of social organization, tribes were merging into larger units, making villages with as many as a thousand inhabitants. The walls and ditches of these villages suggest that they needed defenses against other merged tribes.

At one of these Old European Neolithic sites, south of Bucharest, excavations have uncovered a fine temple, with walls painted in red and green spirals. A sizeable column suggests rites in which the people venerated the **axis mundi**, the pillar that stabilized the earth and linked it with heaven. Since this pillar figures in many shamanic systems of thought, one can suspect a holdover of ideas from the previous hunting culture.

If we apply what we know about the archaic agricultural societies that were still in bloom at the beginning of the twentieth century, we can make further inferences about the religions of Old Europe. In this light, the remains from Neolithic sites suggest cults of the dead, of fertility, and of vegetation, with woman and the soil tied closely together. The overall **cosmology**, or view of the world, might have stressed an *axis mundi,*[6] and the people might have hoped for an existence after death, perhaps on the model of the "resurrection" of crops in the spring.

If this picture is accurate, the infiltration of agricultural ideas considerably enriched and complicated the Neolithic peoples' thought world. By the time that we find written texts (around five thousand years ago), such further cultural developments as metallurgy, an urban way of life, kingship, and a well-organized priesthood show an accelerated pace of change, in which the old ways of the Paleolithic hunters were being left further and further behind. Still, even before writing, agriculture had led to fairly elaborate sacred buildings that were ritual centers, to funeral rites that likened human life to the cyclical life of plants, and to ceremonies designed to ensure the fertility of the crops. Certainly there were vestiges of the older identification with animals. The domestication of some animal species, such as the dog and the pig, kept people close to animal symbols. But Neolithic religion increasingly was shaped by a greater social organization, making ritual activities more specialized and more predictable.

Further, through the mastery of nature that agriculture represented, humanity took a big step away from its earlier awe of nature. To be sure, agriculture was a fragile venture, dependent on sun, rain, and protection against pests. And agriculture certainly had mysteries of its own, new reasons to venerate fertility and regeneration. Nonetheless, the world of the farmer became considerably more secure than that of the hunter, considerably more circumscribed and controlled. With such an increase in security or order, a more orderly religion emerged. The full rosters of agricultural gods that we later find in the civilizations of Mesopotamia and Egypt, which came hard on the heels of the new agricultural settlements, reflect this increased orderliness. So do the complex ceremonies and large-scale temples. Soon the priesthood that managed this more orderly religion became a special class, with full-time professional duties. After that, the leading religious figure no longer was just a gifted member of the tribe, sharing the tribe's common duties and fears, but a functionary set apart. When priestly ways of thought came to power, shamanic imagination no longer painted most people's pictures of reality.

Thus Neolithic religion was a thing of transition, a passenger between small-scale tribal life and large-scale civilization. By the time of metallurgy (six thousand years ago), when bronze and iron began to be worked and mined, the shamanic heritage began to pass to smiths, guards, and idiosyncratic healers, who worked on the fringes of agricultural society. Their lives were individualized enough, or precarious enough, to depend on a personal vision. In the mainstream, however, imagination could become more routinized and doctrinal, less spontaneous and poetic.

This was both a loss and a gain. The gain, clearly, was in clarity. More people knew where they stood, could think of a world full of gods who were giving them an increasing prosperity. The loss was in many personal freedoms, for agricultural societies gradually became quite hierarchical and quite dependent on slavery. Striving to develop the order suggested by their detailed agricultural calendars and systems of theology, kingly and priestly rulers often became very cruel. The Neolithic era shows us humanity at a crossroads, making choices that would prove to be decisive for the rest of history. Because of agriculture, there could be no going back to the unmediated mysteries of the forest primeval, no continued dominance of the hunters' culture, with its raw sufferings and raw ecstasies. The population would grow, medicine and education would develop, and religion would generate full theologies and **liturgies**.

THE LEGACY OF SHAMANIC DOMINANCE

Although shamanism was later to lose its status as humanity's most central and directive set of experiences, by the Ice Age it had such momentum that it continued to dominate groups who lived apart from agriculture, as well as individual healers and seers in agricultural societies who treasured its imaginative ecstasies. Thus, few cultural groups ever completely lost the early shamanic heritage, because few cultural groups ever were without poets, healers, alchemists, and the like, who kept the shamanic legacy.

But how should we regard the spiritual achievements of the prehistoric eras that shamanism dominated? What profits might a fair account of history enter in its ledger? First, there is the great profit of the Intellectual powers that shamanism nourished. Without the shamans' strivings to expand ordinary consciousness and synthesize the ingredients of human experience in new combinations, there would be no human race such as we have today. True enough, the disciplined intellectual searches of the science and technology that shape so much of our current culture owe their rise to the classical Greeks' explorations of reason twenty-five hundred years ago. Nonetheless, free imagination remains the clue to creativity of all sorts, so the imaginative forays of Paleolithic peoples prove, in retrospect, to have been warm-up exercises even for modern science.

Second, the prehistoric shamanic cultures bequeathed their successors at least a hope, and probably a confidence, that human beings have the resources to get themselves through most crises. The practical problems of early human living were formidable enough, but the first hard look at human mortality and evil must have been even more formidable. By discovering ways to step out of ordinary states of awareness and become more intimate with the powers of life and death, the early shamans released humanity from its first, most restrictive prisons. As the nineteenth-century German philosopher Nietzsche put it, when human beings have a *why* they can put up with almost any *how*. Suffering, deprivation, and even death become bearable, when someone gives them a plausible meaning. The mere fact that there *may* be life beyond the grave, may be a Master of the Animals who can turn friendly, may be a way to bring the forces of procreation to one's side opens the windows of the soul and lets in a blessed light. The worst human state is the despair that paralyzes all action, puts all thought in a straitjacket. Without images of hope, human beings give up on their humanity, forfeit the struggle to go on.

Not only did the early shamans create many images of hope, they summoned many forces for healing. In part because of their imaginative dealings with animals and plants, they became keen students of animal and plant life. Thus they often gathered an impressive pharmacy of roots, berries, and juices that trial and error proved healing. Even more significant, however, were the shamans' abilities to muster a sick person's faith, enlist a sick person's will to live. Five thousand years after the invention of writing, we still are far from knowing all the implications of faith and the will to live.[7] For instance, empirically, as a matter of observation, we have good grounds for thinking that laughter is often healing. Scientifically, as a matter of experimental testing, we still don't know why. However, as our biochemical studies become more sophisticated, we realized that changes in our states of consciousness lead to changes in our levels of hormones, enzymes, and the like. Thus laughter, joy, and peace may lead to chemical states that help our tissues to heal, just as stress and anxiety may lead to chemical states that cause our tissues to fray.

Shamans of recent small-scale societies have shown themselves almost geniuses at exploiting the human being's psychosomatic sensitivities, mustering very deep psychic forces to fight disease. Like a coach who coaxes a runner to a state of fitness and exertion in which he or she transcends ordinary thresholds of pain, the Paleolithic shaman may have brought people to remarkable levels of concentration, unpredictable feats of endurance. The only "proof" we have for any of this is that the human race survived tens of thousands of very difficult years. Based on what we know about modern-day shamans, we can infer that prehistoric shamans were a major reason for that survival. To have people who can go out of themselves, travel to the gods or ultimate forces, represent the people's needs, and tap the people's inmost psychic powers has proved remarkably useful to nonliterate peoples of today. There is every reason to think it proved just as useful to peoples of the Ice Age.

From shamans, therefore, our species got much of its initial spiritual thrust. Through their trances, visions, artworks, and feats of endurance these first religious leaders set the human imagination burning. Ever since, members of our species have been invited to ponder, meditate, go into themselves for crucial answers. Ever after, the physical world has had an aura of holiness, of being a mystery both awesome and fascinating. If a main mark of human success is the ability to find the world to be such a mystery, the early shamans were remarkably successful. Because of them, we, too, might risk flights of creativity and healing.

SUMMARY

We began our look at prehistoric shamanism by considering Tiger, a fictional member of our species from the time that we and the Neandertals shared Old Europe. In both Tiger's close identification with animals and his creative work as an artist, we saw features that Paleolithic shamans probably brought to heightened clarity. Also, we saw features, suggested by remains from Paleolithic sites, that confirm Ice Age humanity's kinship with our own.

In recent interpretations of Ice Age humanity, "time-factoring" has come to the fore. At the roots of civilization seems to lie a capacity to compute cycles such as those of the moon and so orient oneself in the world of nature's ebb and flood with increasing understanding. If so, the vivid scenes of Paleolithic art probably represent more than a simple hunting magic or a simple concern with sexual differentiation. More likely, they reflect sophisticated stories of human beings' immersion in a world of complex temporal processes.

For hunting peoples, myths of origin no doubt played a central cultural role, as did the shaman's use of images from dreams. From their shamans' ecstasies, hunting people probably got notions of a heaven to which they might fly and animals with whom they might commune. Agriculture slowly overturned this world of the hunters' shamans, placing more emphasis on the cycles of plants, the interactions of life and death, and the feminine forces of generation. Together, the dying images of hunting cultures and the growing images of agricultural cultures made the Neolithic a complicated era. Temples grew in size, rituals probably became more complex, priests supplanted shamans, and revolutions such as the development of metallurgy and writing glimmered on the horizon.

Nonetheless, the shamanic heritage did not completely die, either in the Neolithic or in any of humanity's subsequent eras. What the first seers had done for the human imagination, the human sense of hope and instinct for psychosomatic healing continued, paying rich dividends. Thus, despite the fact that modern culture has brought a strict disciplining of the shamanic imagination, the creativity of humanity's first great religious figures still has a great deal to teach us.

STUDY QUESTIONS

1. What are some of the advantages in Tiger's ability to identify with animals?

2. Why is the ability to factor time so significant?

3. Compose a simple myth to explain the origin of hunting.

4. How did agriculture change the human imagination?

5. Why was Neolithic religion able to become more complex and ritualistic?

6. What are some of the major dangers in a shamanic approach to healing?

NOTES

1. Bjorn Kurtèn, *Dance of the Tiger*. New York: Berkeley, 1981, pp. 197–98. See also Jean Auel, *The Clan of the Cave Bear*. New York: Bantam, 1981.

2. Alexander Marshack, *The Roots of Civilization*. New York: McGraw-Hill, 1972.

3. Ibid., p. 272.

4. Mircea Eliade, *A History of Relgious Ideas,* vol. 1. Chicago: University of Chicago Press, 1978, p. 26.

5. See Annette Laming, *Lascaux*. Baltimore: Penguin, 1959.

6. See Eliade, *History,* p. 50.

7. See Norman Cousins, *Anatomy of an Illness*. New York: Bantam, 1981.

3

Shamanism in Recent Small-Scale Societies

The Classical Siberian Shaman
African Shamanism?
Australian Shamanism
South American Shamans: The Iticoteri
South American Shamans: The Conibo and the Jivaro
North American Shamans: Characteristics of Tribal Cultures
North American Shamans: Unity of Natural Cycles
Beyond the "Primitive"
Analysis: The Shamanistic Core
Summary
Study Questions
Notes

THE CLASSICAL SIBERIAN SHAMAN

As we mentioned earlier, recent Western studies of shamanism have tended to take the shamanism of Siberia and Central Asia as a prototype. This bent was exhibited in the first comprehensive study of shamanism, Mircea Eliade's *Shamanism: Archaic Techniques of Ecstasy*, and the great influence of Eliade's work has stamped most subsequent studies. Therefore we begin our survey of the shamanism of recent small-scale societies with this prototype.

Shamans of Central and North Asia may come to their work either through heredity or through a spontaneous calling. Regardless of how they are recruited, however, in most tribes they gain respect and status only by having appropriated two kinds of teaching. The first is ecstatic and personal: information or rev-

elations that come through the individual's dreams, trances, or other sorts of extraordinary personal experience. The second is traditional: the techniques and lore that past shamans of the tribe have amassed.

Before an Asian shaman becomes "accredited," he (almost all Siberian shamans are male) usually must pass an initiatory test. Sometimes this test takes the form of a sickness, other times the form of a dream journey. The Yakut of eastern Siberia have a legend that shamans are born in the north, where they live in the branches of a giant fir tree. The greatest shamans live in the top branches, the middling shamans live in the middle branches, and the weakest shamans live in the lowest branches:

Some informants say that the Bird-of-Prey-Mother, which has the head of an eagle and iron feathers, lights on the tree, lays eggs, and sits on them; great, middling, and lesser shamans are hatched in respectively three

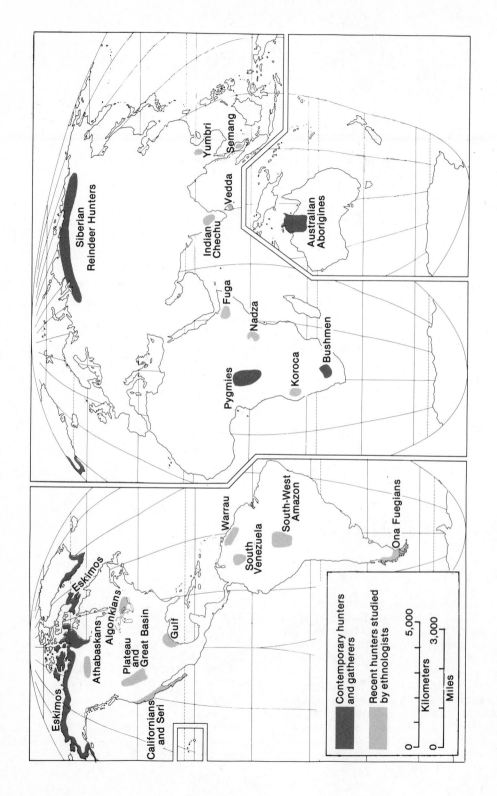

Figure 3 Modern hunters. Adapted from The Times Atlas of World History, edited by Geoffrey Barraclough, 1979. © Hammond, Inc. Reprinted with permission of Times Books Limited, England.

years, two years, and one year. When the soul comes out of the egg, the Bird-Mother entrusts it to a devil-shamaness, with only one eye, one arm, and one bone, to be taught. She rocks the future shaman's soul in an iron cradle and feeds him on clotted blood.[1]

After this dramatic beginning, three black devils come for the initiate, cut his body to pieces, thrust a lance into his head, and throw bits of his flesh in different directions.

Other Asian tribes have similar myths of shamanic initiation, most of them concerned with showing the initiate's interactions with the fearsome forces that will shape his future vocation as a healer. Because his initiation has taken him to the realms of sickness and death, upon his return, the shaman will be thought capable of helping his tribe battle these arch-foes. The candidate may have his bodily parts scattered to the winds as a sacrifice to all the spirits concerned with disease. He may have to spend long hours contemplating his own skeleton, so that he can get to the very bone of the human condition. Frequently he will be led by animal spirits and tossed about by demons. Almost always a motif of death and resurrection will shape his experiences of suffering and triumph.

Among the Goldi, a Tungusic tribe, a shaman may have a sexual relation with the spirit that instructs and guides him. Thus one Goldi shaman reported that a spirit approached while he was sleeping and took him as her husband. She had intercourse with him and taught him what he needed to know for his work. The spirit was very small, yet very beautiful. She lived alone in a mountain hut, and sometimes she came to him in the form of an old woman or a wolf. The shaman really had no choice in the matter of becoming the spirit's husband, since she told him that if he refused she would kill him.[2]

In the thought systems of many Asian tribes, shamans have numerous helping spirits and do a lot of business with the souls of the dead. Since guiding the souls of the dead to the land of their rest is an important shamanic function, familiarity with departed souls obviously is very helpful. The other helping spirits, many of which have an animal form, may assist the shaman in healing rites or in matters related to the tribe's hunting of game. Birds are especially appropriate helping spirits, since in many tribes the shaman does his work by taking magical flights to the realm of the gods, demons, or departed ancestors. This practice correlates with the North and Central Asian cosmology, in which the world has three zones: heaven, earth, and under-earth. The shaman frequently works in all three. Usually heaven and earth are connected by a pillar, the *axis mundi*, up which the shaman may climb or fly. Regularly the shaman also assembles a costume and equipment (cap, drum, mask) whose symbolism represents the three zones of his world.

AFRICAN SHAMANISM?

Most studies of African religion do not deal with shamans, because there are few similarities with the pattern of ecstatic flights and initiatory dismemberment that one associates with the Siberian prototype. So, for example, Evans-Pritchard's well-known study of Nuer religion shows us an African people of the Sudan whose main religious figures are priests and prophets. Let us consider these two functionaries, and then see what sort of "shamanism" they suggest.

Each Nuer family has a lay master of ceremonies, who functions at weddings, funeral rites, initiations, and other ritual occasions that invoke the clan solidarity of the people involved. In ceremonial sacrificing for sin, however, the master of ceremonies gives way to the priest. Most Nuer priests wear a leopard skin over their shoulders, and they are intimately associated with earth.

It is said that a leopard-skin priest ... will not approach people when they are making pots lest the pots crack; and in this sense he may be said to respect ... the earth. If anything goes wrong with the standing crops he may be asked to anoint ... the earth with butter. He may also be asked to anoint seed and digging-sticks with butter before sowing. When a priest is buried, his corpse, so that it will not be in contact with the earth, is placed between hides on a light platform erected in the grave. ...[3]

The respect that Nuer priests receive rests in large part on this association with the earth. In the Nuer scheme of things the earth is the context or stage for all human activities, so the priest, as the functionary most closely associated with "here below," shares that importance. The significance of the earth does not, however, amount to a **cult**, as it does among some West African tribes, nor do the Nuer greatly esteem farming, since their chief economic interests are the husbandry of cattle and fishing. Rather, the priest stands for the entire human realm, representing the earth and sacrificing on behalf of human beings to the divine forces located in the sky above. Most priests claim a descent from Gee, the first man and priest, and receive their power through hereditary lines. On the other hand, it is also possible to become a priest

Figure 4   Sacred Ashanti stool, Ghana. According to tradition, the power and well-being of the Ashanti state were vested in a stool thrown down from the heavens. Nelson Gallery–Atkins Museum, Kansas City, Missouri (Nelson Fund).

simply by being asked to function as one. Only Nuer men can be priests, since Nuer women do not sacrifice.

The Nuer priest's most important function is to preside at the ceremonies that can free people who have committed homicide from the dangers to which that act exposes them. Therefore a Nuer who kills another person hurries to a priest, who sacrifices a cow on the killer's behalf. A slayer who eats or drinks anything before this ceremony, the Nuer think, will surely die. The priest also offers the slayer sanctuary from the blood feud that homicide often precipitates. Once at the house of a priest, a person who has killed usually will not be molested. Stopping blood feuds obviously is of urgent importance to the whole tribe, but the priest's offices have the further importance of pacifying the ghost of the slain person. Without the ritual ceremonies, the ghost would almost be bound

to cause much mischief. Also, without the ritual ceremonies the murderer would remain in a state of *nueer* (grave sin), as would any people who broke the prohibition against contact between the kin of the slayer and the kin of the slain.

The Nuer prophet is someone who has a familiar spirit. The possession of this spirit, who often takes the form of a **totem**, or animal helpful to the tribe, gives the Nuer prophet powers that ordinary people, including priests, do not have. The role of Nuer prophets seems to be of relatively recent vintage (the last century), in contrast to the long-standing tradition of sacrificial priests. The prophet's powers are quite personal, a matter of individual **charisma** rather than hereditary power, and the Nuer view them as communicating the voice of God. Whereas the priest is a personage of the earth, one who speaks in the name of the people and represents them before heaven, the prophet is a source of heavenly revelation, a conduit of the divine speech.

Thus it is protocol for a Nuer prophet to begin his address with an identification of who he is: what heavenly spirit is possessing him. (Most prophets actually are inspired by "spirits of the air" or "children of God," lesser heavenly entities. The Nuer do not think that God himself, with a capital *G*, enters into human beings or directly inspires them.) Many Nuer prophets have behaved very strangely. For example, perhaps the first and certainly the most famous of the Nuer prophets, Ngundeng, who died in 1906, would go off alone for weeks at a time to live in the bush. For extended periods he would eat only the excrement of humans or animals and would sit atop his *kraal* (pen) with one of its posts penetrating his anus. Often he would fast for long periods and fall into a trance. Deng and his son Gwek finally built a huge mound of earth, sixty feet high with a base diameter of one hundred feet, to honor *deng*, his possessing spirit. This mound became a famous Nuer landmark and cult center. Some Nuer prophets seem to have sought personal gain from their powers, and European colonial administrators usually considered them troublemakers, but prophets like Ngundeng show how powerful the African sensitivity to spirits could become.

Although African priests and prophets, like most of the Nuer, do not display the ecstatic flights characteristic of the Siberian shaman, nor the initiatory death-resurrection, they are like the classical shaman who is extremely sensitive to the kinship of all creatures. As well, their interest in spirits, possession, and violations of taboos is characteristic of many shamanic figures. So perhaps we should think of the leading African religious figures as broadly shamanic in type. Insofar as their world is alive with spiritual forces, ecological interactions that have religious overtones, it is quite like the world of most shamans.

AUSTRALIAN SHAMANISM

In contrast to Africa, native Australia does have an overall pattern of religious thought and action that fits the classical shamanic model. For example, the central religious figure in most native Australian tribes was the medicine man (male), who basically received an initiation and performed curing rites like those of the classical shaman.[4] One of the distinctive features of Australian shamanism, however, was the importance of the medicine man's ability to regain the condition of the "ancestors" who lived on the earth at the time it gained its present form. All archaic Australians had the capacity and calling to return to the aboriginal time through a sort of "dreaming," but the medicine man was most perfect in this skill—most able to reproduce humanity's original powers. A medicine man who showed prowess as a healer was considered able to fly to heaven, descend to the underworld, talk with the ancestors, and see spirits.

To gain such powers, an Australian medicine man passed through an initiatory death and resurrection, at the hands of other medicine men or through the agency of spirits. Among the Aranda, when spirits were to accomplish the initiation the candidate would go to sleep at the mouth of a cave. A spirit would come and pierce his tongue with an invisible lance. People would know that this had happened because they would be able to see the hole in the initiate's tongue. Then a second spirit would come and cut off the initiate's head. He would die and be taken deep into the initiatory cave, to a realm of perpetual light and springs—a paradise. There the spirit would tear out his internal organs and give him new ones, which would help him in his work as a healer. The candidate would return to life but would behave like a lunatic for a transition period. After a year, if the opening in the candidate's tongue had not healed, he would be thought fit to begin a healing practice. This year of probation would be given over to studying with other medicine men, who would teach him how to use his new internal organs.

Many tribes' initiations were led by other medicine men and included a ritual operation in which the candidate's skin was abraded, his tongue incised, and his scalp filled with rock crystals. With these faculties changed, the initiate was able to sense the spirits, speak the words, and think the thoughts necessary for his work of healing. For example, he became able to perceive the magical objects that many tribes think cause illness and to know where to suck them out of the sick person's body. As well, he could sing poison into the tribe's enemies or fly to the heavens to find rain.

Among the Wiradjuri the medicine man often had an animal spirit that helped him in his work. Thus one boy being initiated by his father saw a tiger snake, the same totem that the father himself used. Taking the string that trailed from the snake's tail, the father and son followed their totem down into the ground, up the inside of a hollow tree, and finally through the air to the great ancestor Baiame. Passing through the door that all healers must pass, they saw Baiame sitting in his camp. He was a very old man with a long beard. From his shoulders extended two great quartz crystals, and surrounding him were all the people he commanded, in the form of birds and beasts.

The myths of most Australian tribes provide pictures of creation that shape the medicine man's sense of the spirits of his initiation or the ancestors to which his dreams return him. The Aranda, like people of other continents, associate the primordial time of creation with a state of darkness, out of which the animals and other features of the present come at the volition of a primal personage:

In the very beginning everything was resting in perpetual darkness: night oppressed all the earth like an impenetrable thicket. The gurra ancestor—his name was Karora—was lying asleep in everlasting night, at the bottom of the soak of Ilbalintja; as yet there was no water in it, but all was dry ground. Over him the soil was red with flowers and overgrown with many grasses; and a great tnatanja [ceremonial pole] was swaying above him. This tnatanja had sprung from the midst of the bed of purple flowers which grew over the soak of Ilbalintja. At its root rested the head of Karora himself: from thence it mounted up toward the sky as though it would strike the very vault of the heavens. It was a living creature, covered with a smooth skin like the skin of a man. And Karora's head lay at the root of the great tnatanja: he had rested thus ever from the beginning. And Karora was thinking, and wishes and desires flashed through his mind. Bandicoots began to come out from his navel and from his armpits. They burst through the sod and sprang to life.[5]

The myth goes on to describe the origin of other creatures from Karora, concluding with the pleasant thought that Karora continues to sleep under the Ilbalintja Soak. Men and women of the tribe who come to it to quench their thirst can make him smile in his sleep, if they bring an offering of green inuruna boughs. He is their great chief, and their approach in homage pleases him.

SOUTH AMERICAN SHAMANS: THE ITICOTERI

American Indian tribes, north and south, have pivoted their cultures on their shamans. No doubt this reflects the ancient Siberian origin of most native Americans, who probably began to cross the land bridge of what is now the Bering Strait ten thousand years ago. Anthropologists who have had the opportunity to live with American tribes have characterized the thought world of their leading healers and wise men as generally shamanic. Florinda Donner's very readable account of her stay with the Iticoteri of the Venezuelan jungle illustrates this analysis.

During Donner's stay, the local *shapori*, whom her glossary defines as "a shaman, witch doctor, sorcerer," decided to initiate an apprentice. The candidate was seventeen or eighteen, with a slight, agile body; a narrow, delicately featured face; and deep brown eyes that were large and glowing. To begin his initiation, he moved out of the general compound into a small hut that was set apart. The tribe believed that this separation was necessary because they thought that the *hekuras* (tiny humanoid spirits) that a shaman tries to lure into his chest to give him power flee from women and dislike the general compound. The candidate was given a helper (a youth who had never been with a woman) to guard his fire and give him each day his ration of water and honey, the only food he was allowed. The helper also blew into the candidate's nostrils the hallucinogenic snuff that Iticoteri shamans use to secure their visions of the hekuras.

The initiate followed rather strict rules, which were apparently designed to tire him, break down his ordinary perceptions, and increase his susceptibility to visions. He had to lie in his hammock most of the day, could not sit on the ground, and became more and more haggard.

Within a week, Xorowe's face had darkened from the epena *[snuff]. His once glowing eyes were dull and unfocused. His body, dirty and emaciated, moved with the clumsiness of a drunkard. Life went on as usual in the* shabono *[compound], except for the families living closest to Xorowe's hut, who were not allowed to cook meat on their hearths. According to Puriwariwe [Xorowe's teacher],* hekuras *detested the smell of roasting meat, and if they so much as caught a whiff of the offensive odor, they would flee back to the mountains. Like his apprentice, Puriwariwe took* epena *day and night. Tirelessly, he chanted for hours, coaxing the spirits into Xorowe's hut, begging the* hekuras *to cut open the young man's chest.*[6]

After a week Xorowe himself began to chant, at first very tentatively, then more and more confidently. He began with the hekura songs of the armadillo, tapir, jaguar, and other animals thought to be masculine and so easy to entice. Then came the songs of plants and rocks. Last came the songs of the difficult female spirits, including the spider, the snake, and the hummingbird. Near the end of the second week Xorowe's arduous labors paid off. He cried out with joy that the hekuras were come to him, humming and buzzing, opening his chest and his head, coming through his fingers and feet. When the spirits began to enter his eyes and nose, his cries turned to panic. Later he shouted that he must never find a woman near his hut, a ritual exclamation almost expected of a shaman dealing with the most treacherous female spirits. Jealous of their relationship with the shapori, the female spirits wanted no competition from earthly women.

Toward the end of his initiation, Xorowe traveled to the depths of the earth, going through cobwebs of darkness, across rivers and mountains. His teacher described these trials:

Women, women, do not despair. On his path he will meet those who have withstood the long nights of mist. He will meet those who have not turned back. He will meet those who have not trembled in fear by what they have witnessed during their journey. He will meet those who have had their bodies burned and cut up, those who had their bones removed and dried in the sun. He will meet those who did not fall into the clouds on their way to the sun.[7]

When the time of trial ended, Xorowe emerged hollow-eyed and melancholy, but with a new aura of strength, as though his experiences had given him a new core. The boy who had been attending him washed his body, dried him with fragrant leaves, and painted wavy lines from his forehead to his cheeks and shoulders. Then his teacher took him away to the forest for more training. With time he would become a healer, powerful in the measure that he controlled the hekuras. When he became fully mature in his art, he would even be able to send hekuras against his compound's enemies. The Iticoteri are a very aggressive, warring people, who constantly raid one another's compounds. Having a powerful shapori to help in such fighting makes a group feel confident they will hold their own.

On several different levels, therefore, the spirit world to which the shaman has the widest access shapes the Iticoteri world. Sickness comes when one has lost personal power or been set upon by the hekuras of an enemy. Good hunting, successful childbirth, and victory in battle also involve the spirit world. Thus Xorowe's initiation was fraught with social significance. As he battled to see the hekuras, he was shaping the future fate of his people.

SOUTH AMERICAN SHAMANS: THE CONIBO AND THE JIVARO

The Conibo Indians of Peru and the Jivaro Indians of the Ecuadorean Andes are other South American tribes with a strong shamanistic tradition. From them Michael Harner, whose distinction between the ordinary state of consciousness and the shamanic state of consciousness was discussed in our introduction, got his start on a personal journey into the shamanic world.[8] When the Conibo accepted Harner's petition to learn about their shamanism, they first insisted that he drink a brew made from local vines. Tossing it down, Harner lay in wait for dramatic effects. They were not long in coming.

It was night, and he was outside. As he stared up at the dark sky, faint lines of light appeared. They grew sharper, became more intricate, and then burst into bright colors. Slowly a sound gathered force and came close to him, like the roar of an advancing waterfall. His jaw became numb. The lines of light became more complicated and the sound of the waterfall grew louder. Then dim figures began to move in the darkness. As the scene came into focus, they became like a carnival of demons. At the center was the head of a giant crocodile. Then the carnival scene dissolved and a huge boat, like a Viking galley ship, came into view. Beautiful singing waved forth from the large number of people on board. Under closer inspection, these people seemed to have heads of blue jays and bodies of human beings, like gods of ancient Egyptian tomb paintings. Harner thought that they had come to take his soul away.

The numbness spread throughout Harner's body, and he had to muster all his will power simply to keep his heart beating. Then he became aware of four distinct levels of activity in his brain: a superficial level of observation; a level put out of commission by the drugs he had taken; a third level that was the source of his visions; and a deepest level, at which giant reptiles started mustering revelations reserved for the dying. These reptiles projected a synopsis of cosmic history, in which huge prehistoric birds arrived on the planet earth to escape from their enemies. The birds created the myriad forms of life on the earth, in order to disguise their presence. Thus the whole of the evolution of life on earth unfolded before Harner as a panorama directed by the birds; a panorama of great scale and vividness. Struggling wildly, Harner finally was able to muster the strength to ask for the antidote to the drugs he had taken and so to escape the grip of these death-door visions. As the Conibo attendants gave him the antidote, a giant defender arose from his depths to protect him from the reptiles and birds. Then the antidote took effect and the fantastic creatures faded away.

Relating this experience to an old Conibo shaman, Harner realized that his visions fit an accepted pattern. The shaman told him that the vividness of his ordeal, however, was remarkable, and that it bespoke a great natural talent for shamanism. Among the Jivaro he developed this talent, going on an extremely arduous initiation walk through the forest. The high point of the initiation was the time he spent behind a wondrous waterfall. It was like being inside a glittering cathedral of liquid light and sound. Wrapped around by the flowing light and noise, Harner first felt soothed and then as if he were flying. The waterfall became stationary and he became the one who moved. The next night a powerful thunderstorm lashed the forest. Awakened, he saw in its flashing light a huge snake, one of the dangerous spirits against whom his teachers had warned him. Harner summoned his courage and rushed the snake. An earsplitting scream filled the night and then the monster was gone. All was peaceful, and Harner fell to the ground unconscious.

After this initiatory experience, Harner studied with several Jivaro shamans, laboring to acquire the magical darts that are their main instruments for healing. These darts, or spirit helpers, are invisible, perceptible only to those in an altered state of consciousness. Enemies can manipulate them to cause illness, and the shaman must suck them out of the sick person's body to effect a cure. To guard themselves, Jivaro shamans constantly work to attract spirits and mold them into a shield. The drink the shamans take helps them see their magical darts. It also helps them see the body of their patient as though it were transparent glass. The usual hour for curing is the setting of the sun, and the shamans alert their spirit helpers by singing songs of power. Generally the helpers have an animal form, and serious shamans work hard to acquire a great variety of them. The more helpers they have, the stronger will be their power and the wider the range of illnesses they can cure.

From these and other experiences with American Indian shamans, Michael Harner became convinced that the key to the shamanic worldview and powers is an altered state of consciousness that makes the spiritual forces of both the psyche and the outside natural world vivid and controllable. With or without drugs, the shamans he studied used their spirit helpers to protect their people and battle their enemies. The helpers therefore were the prime players in a wildly imaginative second world that the shamans inhabited, a world they often considered more valuable than the world of ordinary consciousness.

NORTH AMERICAN SHAMANS: CHARACTERISTICS OF TRIBAL CULTURES

Thus far we have discussed the vividness of the typical American shamans' experiences, the dramatic quality

of their visions and spiritual techniques. Åke Hultkrantz, one of the leading authorities on American Indian religions, sees such shamanism as a feature of almost all the American tribal cultures (although he cautions that the Siberian prototype is not always completely fulfilled). Beginning with South American tribes and moving north, Hultkrantz summarizes the situation as follows:

Among the technically more advanced groups in the tropical forest area shamanism seems to have a stronger hold, and the guardian spirits of the medicine men, seldom observed among the marginal peoples, are here more distinctly outlined. The Tulpi chief is often a medicine man as well and in this function he takes on an actual cult after his death. Within the Andean high culture the shaman performs with healing methods inherited from more primitive times. Similarly, shamanism lives on as a primitive undercurrent in the Mexican and Mesoamerican high cultures. In North America it is predominant within the primitive hunting cultures, in the east partly in communal forms (the shaman societies), in the west with a more individualistic bent, for here the influences from the collectivistic agrarian cultures are less apparent. Ceremonial societies may replace the shaman in his medicinal functions within the extreme agrarian cultures, especially among the Pueblo Indians. Among the Hopi he is all but an outcast and the borderline here between medicine man and dreaded black magician is vague.[9]

Thus one who studies the tribal societies of North America, or any other geographic area, soon becomes aware of the various implications of the term *shamanism*. Shamans are both ordinary tribal members and extraordinary functionaries who sometimes must segregate themselves. At the deepest levels of the tribal cultures of the Americas seem to lie many holdovers from the Siberian past, and throughout these cultures an ecstatic use of the imagination is important, but priestly (sacrificial) and sapiential (wisdom) features often intrude to disturb any simplistic interpretation of the American religious patterns. For example, shamanic healing may be supplemented by a more empirical approach that emphasizes the wisdom of the person who has experimented with many different drugs and physical techniques rather than ecstatic powers and spiritual helpers. As a result Hultkrantz prefers to reserve the term *shaman* for the person who goes out of his body in order to obtain the help of supporting spirits.

Nonetheless, in our broader focus, which contrasts the shaman's imagination with the prophet's will and the sage's intellect, many of the American religious

Figure 5 Indian Boy *by George Catlin (1796–1872). Nelson Gallery–Atkins Museum, Kansas City, Missouri (Nelson Fund).*

functionaries remain shamanic. From the individual vision quest that many tribes made part of the male passage into adulthood, to the healing activities of the medicine man or woman, American Indians exploited the ways that images can muster psychosomatic powers and the forces of the plant and animal kingdoms can be personified. The vision of Lame Deer, a famous Sioux holy man, exemplifies this imaginative exploitation.

The vision came to Lame Deer when he was sixteen, in the midst of his passage into adulthood. Left alone in an isolated place for four days without food or water, he finally heard voices that changed all his later life:

Slowly I perceived that a voice was trying to tell me something. It was a bird cry, but I tell you, I began to understand something of it. That happens sometimes. I know a lady who had a butterfly sitting on her shoulder. That butterfly told her things. This made her become a great medicine woman. I heard a human voice

too, *strange and high-pitched, a voice which could not come from an ordinary, living being. All at once I was way up there with the birds. The hill with the vision pit was way above everything. I could look down even on the stars, and the moon was close to my left side. It seemed as though the earth and the stars were moving below me. A voice said, "You are sacrificing yourself here to be a medicine man. In time you will be one. You will teach other medicine men. We are the fowl people, the winged ones, the eagles and owls. We are a nation and you shall be our brother. You will never kill or harm any one of us. You are going to understand us whenever you come to seek a vision here on this hill. You will learn about herbs and roots, and you will heal people. You will ask them for nothing in return. A man's life is short. Make yours a worthy one."*[10]

After this experience, Lame Deer lost his sense of fear. All sense of time departed, and he sat as though in a trance. Then his great-grandfather came to him in a vision, dripping blood from the white soldier's wound that had killed him. His great-grandfather asked him to take the name *Lame Deer*, the great-grandfather's own name. At that moment the *nagi*, or spiritual essences, within Lame Deer surged like a river in a flood, filling him with power that convinced him he would become a successful medicine man. This made him weep for happiness. Finally the old man who was in charge of his vision quest came for him. The four days of trial were over, and he had passed successfully. The old man asked for the details of Lame Deer's visions and then made a first intepretation, assuring him that all the implications would only unfold slowly. Still, from that day Lame Deer knew he had been set on the path to becoming a holy man and healer.

NORTH AMERICAN SHAMANS: UNITY OF NATURAL CYCLES

Shamans use several different methods to obtain their ecstatic visions. Using hallucinogenic drugs and fasting are common, as are dancing and singing. Among the Kwakiutl of the Pacific Northwest coast a winter ceremonial uses the rituals of a shamanistic men's society to actualize the tribe's myths. These myths depend upon a fundamental division of the year into two parts, summer and winter, during which the basic relationship between human beings and animals shifts dramatically:

Throughout the summer portion of the year, the relationship between human beings and animals is that of hunter and hunted. The hunter kills and eats the flesh of animals. Eating of the animal flesh causes the animals to become one with human beings but in human form. It is during the long, elaborate Winter Ceremonial that this relationship is reversed, in order to regain the primordial identity of human and animal in animal form. Human beings take up the masks of animals in ceremonial dances, thus becoming animals. They return to the original conditions so as to engender the supernatural powers of creation that may benefit the community. Thus a relationship of reciprocity lies beneath the interdependence of human beings and animals. This reciprocity is completed by the role reversal of hunter and game animals as the seasons change. In summer the animals undergo death. In the winter, by means of the Winter Ceremonial, it is the human beings who descend into darkness and death, thus restoring the animal spirits. In this ceremonial process, human order must often pit its strengths against supernatural antagonists who devour humans. This amounts to a shamanic effort to recover the humans devoured by these deities. The pervasive use of cannibalistic and flesh-eating symbolism appropriately expresses the Kwakiutl recognition of the basic identity of humans and animals.[11]

Notice how this description gathers together a number of shamanic themes already discussed. First are the roots of the shamanic "philosophy" in the ancient relation of the hunter to the game. Second is the vast significance given to the changes of the seasons (which of course shape this relation). Third is the interplay of life and death: The death of animals is necessary to the life of human beings, but in eating animals human beings merge with them. The renewal of animal life therefore is important to human identity as well as human survival, so in their ceremonies hunters mask themselves as animals and participate in the animals' descent into the nether world of death and darkness. Imaginatively, death and darkness are represented as spiritual forces or deities threatening human existence and so requiring the shaman's protective powers. The shaman fights against the sickness that causes death, going to the land of the dead to retrieve souls on the verge of leaving sick bodies or to guide the souls of those who have died to a peaceful rest.

In the shamanic world, therefore, the natural order that humans and animals share, in which life and death contest, brings all the participants into a certain unity. The force of the cosmos pulsates in the rhythms of life and death; humans and animals connect, identify, and are interchangeable at many points in these rhythms. It is important that hunting tribes restore the power balance among animals and humans—keep the rhythms of death and life, fertility and destruction going.

This support of cosmic rhythms seems to be a major function of elaborate tribal ceremonies like the Sioux Sun Dance. Uniting themselves to the power of the sun, using tokens of such fellow creatures as trees and eagles, the Sioux sun dancers honor the circle of life. As Joseph Epes Brown has summarized it:

Through rich and varied means specific forms of life are celebrated and honored within the lodge. Decorated trees may be planted, pine trees perhaps for the dancer's arbor; moisture-bearing cattails are offered by friends and relatives for the dancer's bed, or chokecherry bushes are planted in conjunction with sacred rites and altars. High in the fork of the sacred tree there is an offering nest for Thunderbird. Some form or aspect of the bison, and an eagle or a rawhide effigy of a human being, is hung upon the tree. Small children sometimes fashion and bring into the lodge pairs of little clay animals: elks, deer, rabbits, kitfoxes, dogs, otters, even grasshoppers. Thus present within the lodge is that which grows from the earth and those who live in the water, who walk on the earth, and who fly in the air. The powers of all things and all beings are present in the holy place. The Sun Dance is thus not a celebration by humans for humans; it is an honoring of all life and the source of all life that life may continue, that the circle be a cycle, that all the world and humankind may continue on the path of the cycle of giving, receiving, bearing, being born in suffering, growing, becoming, returning to the earth that which has been given, and finally being born again.[12]

Immersed in nature, shamanic peoples have looked beyond nature's cycles to see the forces of life and death as they are: both enemies and allies, both antagonists and friends. The dance of life includes both; with this vision the dance is beautiful, harmonious, a reason for loving one's time as a human being.

BEYOND THE "PRIMITIVE"

Although Åke Hultkrantz characterized as "primitive" some of the strata in which American Indian shamanism appears to lodge, most anthropologists and students of religion have rejected the term *primitive religion*.[13] On close inspection, the lives, thought systems, rituals, and efficacies of the tribal religions show them to be sophisticated and admirable to a degree that renders the term most inappropriate. In some cases the technologies of these tribes are much simpler than those that have developed in the modern West, and certainly the nonliteracy of many traditions differentiates them significantly from peoples whose religious relations with the world have been mediated by writing. But the richness of many tribes' mythologies, the sophistication of their symbol-systems, and their ability to bring their people peace and prosperity argue against the facile assumption that life apart from modern technology is less than fully human.

Indeed, when an anthropologist such as Florinda Donner lets herself enter into the life of the people she is studying, so that she really is shaped by their rhythms and convictions, a great many attractions may appear. In a society like that of the Iticoteri there is time to savor the beauties and vagaries of nature, time to enjoy intimate bonds with family members and friends. Life yields up many impressive individual moments for leisurely contemplation. The relative poverty of the material culture can leave "space" for a holistic spirituality, making it possible to consider which values and achievements make human beings most human. Just what are all the suffering and striving supposed to attain?

Questions such as these are challenging, humbling, and disorienting. Any facile notion of arranging cultures on a scale of one to ten vanishes as soon as one pursues it. Some cultures, for example, are more warlike than the most militant arms-building Western powers. If their frequent battles employed nuclear arms, their land might soon be smoking and charred. But of course the very small scale of their weapons and wars makes for qualitative differences. Among small-scale societies a hair-trigger temper does not endanger a whole ecology, put into peril millions of lives.

On the other hand, the lack of critically developed reason, as it is applied, for instance, in science and philosophy in the modern Western sense, makes the worldview of nonliterate societies comparatively underdeveloped, makes intense presence in the moment the obverse side of a dim sense of the future and the past. Among some peoples sense of time, nature, and "reality" is more fluid than those of modern Westerners, although their history, science, and picture of the world's scale are considerably more constrained. If they were to make the transition to modern Western culture that many previously nonliterate peoples have made in this century, one would expect a complicated set of cultural transactions, a complex accounting of profits and losses. The price for the material possessions and technological power that modern Western society has generated usually is a loss of intimacy with nature and one's fellow tribal members.

To drive one's mind with scientific precision, to calculate one's reality with a computer's control usually puts premodern science, medicine, and psychology under a cloud of suspicion. Usually the old ways become bits of nostalgia that technological progress shunts to the side. The fundamentalisms of Islam, Christianity, Judaism, Hinduism, and other literate traditions that have grown in influence recently are in part an effort to try to have things both ways. With one foot in modernity the fundamentalist reaches back in search of a time, a way of thought and life, that allowed her people to feel the world to be a whole, to experience life as ordered and welcoming. Such efforts pinpoint much of the spiritual challenge facing the twenty-first century. How can we make a world for five or more billion people that is hospitable to life? What worldview would be both efficient enough to answer our basic material needs and spiritual enough to give our lives a deep meaning?

One sees efforts to have both from time to time in movements for a holistic medicine, a physics aware of the Tao, an economics in which people really mattered. One also sees individuals able to span broad cultural distances and keep their footing in both the shamanic and the modern Western worlds: visionaries such as Castenada's don Juan, anthropologists such as the African specialist Colin Turnbull.[14] And then there are statements from tribal people who are in the midst of cultural transition yet are fighting to keep the best of their past. Such a person is Lorna, a contemporary Alaskan Eskimo woman fighting to retain some of her people's shamanic sensitivity to nature, despite the inrush of soft drinks and television:

> *Often it was the natural world that prompted reflections or observations from her: a change in the weather, such as a heightening of winter or summer; the appearance of spring; the ebbing of short-lived warmth. She did not need a listener. She was not given, even with a listener present, to extended conversation. She had things on her mind, from time to time, and she delivered herself of them—in the presence of a person, or in the presence of (she believed) attending spirits. These spirits might respond—a gust of wind, an agitation of the ocean, a movement of animal life.*[15]

ANALYSIS: THE SHAMANISTIC CORE

A shaman is a person sensitive to the presence of attending spirits. We may describe these spirits literally or metaphorically. If we take them literally, we have the style of speech that many nonliterate ecstatics themselves use and the (futile) sort of interpretation of tribal consciousness that some scholars make. By discussing them metaphorically we may assimilate them to contemporary Western culture, so that they make more sense to us, but we risk closing outselves to what tribal peoples themselves may have been experiencing. This sort of interpretational dilemma is inevitable, since all interpretation flows between the poles of "them" and "us." Realizing that there are both a false objectivity and a false subjectivity to be avoided, let us conclude by risking a summary interpretation of the kinds of experiences that seem to lie at the heart of many tribal cultures. Insofar as the shaman has been the central figure for many tribes (not the only religious or spiritual figure, and not the central figure for all tribes), what do shamanic ecstasy, imagination, intercourse with spirits, and the like tell us about preliterate, precivilizational religion, the kind that has dominated most human beings through most of our race's history?

These aspects of shamanic religion tell us, first, that human beings everywhere are engaged in the business of making sense of their experience, constantly trying to construct a "world," an interconnected whole. Second, we see that certain mediating features of our contemporary Western culture are unrepresentative of human history as a whole. Having no written language and being in rather direct contact with physical nature, most human beings have lived with an immediacy, a vividness of perception and response, that is quite rare in contemporary Western life. We speak, think, work, and regard the physical world more abstractly than most other peoples have. We stand apart from the rhythms of nature, conceive ourselves as nonnatural, different in kind from other aspects of nature. In the master story of most other peoples, human beings have been a fractional part of a cosmic whole. They have shared the bounties of Mother Earth and Father Sky with inanimate beings, plants, and other animals with more equality. This is not to say that tribal peoples see no difference that human thought brings into the animal kingdom or that tribal peoples have no sense of how their conceptions of things dictate a great deal of what things can be and "say" to them. It is simply to say that no geology, biology, astronomy, critical history, scientific medicine, critical philosophy, and the like constantly hammered home to nonliterate tribal peoples the fact that worldviews are human artifacts, "reality" is to a great extent a matter of social conventions and consensuses.

Third, many of the people whom the shaman epitomizes have had **transcendent** experiences, have expanded their world, by *ec-stasis*: standing out from their "ordinary" consciousness. By drugs, dancing, or simple shifts in perception, they have gained a different kind of awareness, with different relations to nature, animals, and other people. In this different, ecstatic awareness, the forces and features of nature have been personified. Thus the vitality of a tree, power of a big cat, mobility of a bird, and the like have taken shape as essences or realities to be reckoned with somewhat independently of their "containers" or embodiments as birches, tigers, and eagles. So Eskimo shamans speak of how dangerous the world can be, since everything is made of souls. American Indian shamans such as Lame Deer hear people of the fowl nation speaking to them.

In such speaking, the metaphoric weight of natural things becomes very heavy. Everything can symbolize, move away from its physical presence or literal meaning, quite easily. Then the world outside comes to teem with significance, so one tries to quiet one's senses and mind, the better to receive such significance, appreciate it, dwell within it. The inside world of memory, imagination, unfocused desire, and the rest becomes equally potent. Dreams, semiconscious images, shifts in perception caused by fasting or sleeplessness, and the like allow one to meet great-grandfather, or reptiles from the deepest stratum of one's mind, or fantastic creatures like gorgons and one-eyed goddesses.

Fourth, it seems to us that this ecstatic consciousness has made shamanic peoples' worlds frightening but also very beautiful. Beyond the pragmatic uses to which shamans have put their ecstatic powers—healing, seeking out game, comforting the dead—have lain the beauty, joy, and power of ecstasy itself. Typically, therefore, tribal shamans have come to *need* to shamanize. Unless they sang and traveled in spirit, they would grow sad and lethargic. Shamanizing was a creative way to paint the world afresh, recompose the world's stories, fit old tunes together into new symphonies. Thus shamanizing often gained the force of an artistic vocation, in which the artist and the work fuse into one. Painting, performing music, writing, and other forms of art are ways of being, modalities for developing a self. So is shamanizing: traveling to the gods, mastering the powers of healing, protecting one's people against meaninglessness, finding stories and images to recreate the world. The "archaic techniques of ecstasy" that Eliade and others have stressed therefore have a personal as well as a social dimension. Socially, they have served many group needs and attracted many marginals.[16] Individually, they have been powerful ways of expanding reality and becoming more alive.

SUMMARY

We began our overview of shamanism in recent small-scale societies with Mircea Eliade's analysis of the Siberian patterns that have become classical or prototypical. Although Siberian shamans may inherit their role or receive a special calling, they only become accredited through an initiatory death and resurrection. Regularly they draw upon the powers of animal or other familiar spirits, and their work of healing, representing the tribe before the gods, guiding the souls of the dead, and the like usually takes place through "magical flights" to the heavenly or underworld portions of the threefold shamanic universe.

Among most African tribes one does not find this classical Siberian pattern. Thus the Nuer, a tribe who have become famous through anthropological studies like those of Evans-Pritchard, focus much of their cultural life on priests and prophets. Priests are especially necessary for the sacrifice necessary to settle blood feuds, and prophets are charismatic personalities thought to give voice to one of the gods. However, the sensitivity of both priests and prophets to spirits makes them broadly shamanic.

Australian tribes usually do fit the shamanic prototype. More often than not, the Australian medicine man comes to power through an initiatory death and resurrection in which he receives new organs and spiritual helpers.

American Indian tribes, south and north, also reflect much of the Siberian pattern. A contemporary *shapori* of the Iticoteri learns to go out of himself to contact helping spirits from different animals, and the visions of the Conibo and Jivaro deal with similar spirits. Scholars of North American Indian cultures frequently make careful distinctions between shamans and other sorts of medicine women or wise men, but the visions of North American holy men such as Lame Deer clearly reflect the classical shamanic heritage. Similarly, the Winter Ceremonial of the Kwakiutl and the Sun Dance of the Sioux reflect the ancient shamanic identification of human beings with animals, and the ancient sense that the cosmos comprises one integrated circle of life (and death).

When one steps back to try to see these tribal patterns whole, their considerable sophistication becomes manifest. No responsible observer can call them "primitive" in a pejorative sense. There are profits and losses in the move from tribal culture to modern technology, but any thorough evaluation of these profits and losses forces the evaluator to make his or her criteria very clear. Intuiting this, people in transition, such as the Alaskan Eskimo woman Lorna, often fight to retain the best parts of their tribal past. In our view, the shamanic core of much tribal consciousness is a sensitivity to the presence of attending spirits. Through their ecstatic dealings with these spirits, shamans have made new worlds of great vividness and power. Thus their lives have not only been socially useful; they have been personally gratifying as well, like the lives of artists everywhere.

STUDY QUESTIONS

1. Why does the classical Siberian shaman have to "die"?

2. How is the Nuer leopard priest associated with the earth?

3. What is the significance of the story of the Wiradjuri father and son being led by a snake to the ancestor Baiame?

4. How did the Iticoteri candidate Xorowe gain his visions of the hekuras?

5. How might one explain Michael Harner's vision of huge prehistoric birds directing the evolution of life on earth?

6. What was the signficance of Lame Deer's taking his great-grandfather's name?

7. Explain the reciprocity between human beings and animals that the Kwakiutl try to maintain.

8. What would the Iticoteri lose were they to take on a modern Western mentality?

9. How is the world different when one sees it unmediated by writing?

NOTES

1. Mircea Eliade, *Shamanism: Archaic Techniques of Ecstasy*. Princeton, N.J.: Bollingen/Princeton University Press, 1972, p. 37.

2. Ibid., p. 72.

3. E. E. Evans-Pritchard, *Nuer Religion*. New York: Oxford University Press, 1974, p. 291.

4. See Mircea Eliade, *Australian Religions*. Ithaca, N.Y.: Cornell University Press, 1973.

5.   Barbara Sproul, *Primal Myths*. San Francisco: Harper & Row, 1979, p. 321.

6.   Florinda Donner, *Shabono*. New York: Delacorte, 1982, p. 183.

7.   Ibid., p. 188.

8.   See Michael Harner, *The Way of the Shaman*. San Francisco: Harper & Row, 1980, especially pp. 1–19.

9.   Åke Hultkrantz, *The Religions of the American Indians*. Berkeley: University of California Press, 1979, p. 86.

10.   Joan Halifax, *Shamanic Voices*. New York: E. P. Dutton, 1979, pp. 74–75.

11.   Sam D. Gill, *Native American Religions*. Belmont, Calif.: Wadsworth, 1982, p. 126.

12.   Joseph Epes Brown, *The Spiritual Legacy of the American Indian*. New York: Crossroad, 1982, pp. 104–5.

13.   See, for example, Sam D. Gill, *Beyond the Primitive*. Englewood Cliffs, N.J.: Prentice-Hall, 1982.

14.   See, for example, Colin Turnbull, *The Forest People*. New York: Simon and Schuster, 1962.

15.   Robert Coles and Jane Hallowell Coles, *Women of Crisis*. New York: Delta, 1978, pp. 187–88.

16.   See I. M. Lewis, *Ecstatic Religion*. Baltimore, Penguin, 1971.

4

Shamanism Within Prophetic Societies

Hebrew Ecstatics
Kabbalists and Hasidim
Christian Charismatics
Christian Visionary Mystics
Muslim Healers
Sufi Saints
Summary
Study Questions
Notes

HEBREW ECSTATICS

Within the scope of this text, we will emphasize the prophetic societies generated by Judaism, Christianity, and Islam. All of these societies have looked back to formative figures (Moses, Jesus, Muhammad) who seem best fitted to the type of the prophet. Thus prophecy has played a formative role in the evolution of all three of these world religions, and it has continued to shape them even when such other religious types as the teacher (**rabbi**), priest, and religious lawyer have assumed major powers.

For Israel, prophecy seems to have had its origins in ecstatic experiences widespread throughout the ancient Near East. In ancient Syria, Phoenicia, and Babylon, for instance, local gods used diviners and people possessed as their oracles. Thus around 1100 B.C.E. Wen-Amon, an official of an Egyptian temple on a journey to Phoenicia, found himself at the whim of

the ecstatic experiences of a retainer of the local Phoenician prince.

> *While he [the prince] was making offering to his gods, the god seized one of his youths and made him possessed . . . and while the possessed (youth) was having his frenzy on this night, I had (already) found a ship headed for Egypt and had loaded everything I had into it.*[1]

Wen-Amon knew enough about the ecstatics of the ancient Near East to get moving when one of their gods gained the ear of a powerful prince.

Early Hebrew prophecy probably shared much of this prevailing Near Eastern tendency to consider ecstasy or seizure a mode of divine communication. Thus texts of the Hebrew Bible such as 1 Sam. 10:5–11 show vestiges of a tradition of bands of ecstatic prophets. In this text Samuel is telling Saul what to expect after being anointed and proclaimed prince of Israel:

"After that you shall come to Gibeath-elohim, where there is a garrison of the Philistines; and there, as you come to the city, you will meet a band of prophets coming down from the high place with harp, tambourine, flute, and lyre before them, prophesying. Then the spirit of the Lord will come mightily upon you, and you shall prophesy with them and be turned into another man. Now when these signs meet you, do whatever your hand finds to do, for God is with you. And you shall go down before me to Gilgal; and behold, I am coming to you to offer burnt offerings and to sacrifice peace offerings. Seven days you shall wait, until I come to you and show you what you shall do." When he turned his back to leave Samuel, God gave him another heart; and all these signs came to pass that day. When they came to Gibeah, behold, a band of prophets met him; and the spirit of God came mightily upon him, and he prophesied among them. And when all who knew him before saw how he prophesied with the prophets, the people said to one another, "What has come over the son of Kish? Is Saul also among the prophets?"

According to biblical tradition, prophecy went back to Moses. Commenting on this tradition, one scholar summarizes the general picture of early Hebrew ecstaticism as follows:

If there is no reason to question the tradition that traces the nebiim *[prophets] to Moses, we must admit that we do not hear much about them before the late period of the judges and the early monarchy, when they are mentioned in connection with the Philistine wars. This circumstance is not surprising, because a major function of these ecstatic prophets, as also of the Nazirites [a group consecrated to God by vow], seems to have been to stimulate patriotic and religious fervor. Usually these men prophesied in groups whose communal experiences are described in such passages as I Sm 10:6–8, 10–13. Hence, they are often given the generic name "sons of the prophets" . . . which has been variously interpreted "members of prophetic guilds," "professional prophets," and "prophetic disciples." All of these interpretations may be justified. The ecstatic experience that served as the climate for prophecy often was induced by mutual contagion through dance and music.[2]*

Prophets such as these ecstatics apparently lived alone or worked as apprentices to a powerful leader. They could be attached to cult centers or the court of the king. They often wore haircloth, and sometimes they had their hair tonsured. Their ecstatic experience largely isolated them from the rest of society, which regarded them as a species of the mad, and on balance their utterances seem to have been an ambiguous mixture of delusion and genuine contact with the divine.

Compared to the classical Siberian prototype, the early ecstatic Hebrews lack a clear initiatory paradigm of death and resurrection, are less concerned with healing (exceptions might be Elijah and Elisha), and have no animal spirit helpers. On the other hand, Saul is transformed into a new man (with another heart) when the divine spirit comes upon him, and the dances and songs of the Hebrew ecstatics show parallels with many classical shamans. Thus we may suspect that some similar psychological faculties are involved in both cases.

KABBALISTS AND HASIDIM

In the **Common Era,** Judaism came to be dominated by rabbinic scholars. The main interest of these scholars was **halakah,** legal lore, although they did also concern themselves with **haggadah,** concrete materials intended to edify. Certainly the rabbinic scholars who pored over the **Talmud** developed powerful imaginations, but *ecstatic* is not an apt word to describe them. The more vivid Jewish imaginations, by contrast, belonged to the Kabbalists and Hasidim: semiecstatics who exerted a great influence in medieval European Judaism. Both groups had antecedents among Jews of the biblical and early Common periods, especially those who lost themselves contemplating the **merkabah,** or divine chariot, described in the first chapter of the book of Ezekiel.[3] But with the secret teachings of the Kabbalists an imaginative flight to the recesses of the divine nature unfolded very broad wings.

The most famous work of the Kabbalist movement was the *Zohar,* or Book of Splendor. Most likely it was written by a Spanish Kabbalist, Moses de Leon, who died in 1305 c.e. The method of the Zohar is to take a biblical text and produce a **midrash,** or explanatory commentary, on it. Often this midrash takes the form of a visualization that expresses convictions held by Kabbalists somewhat secretly (apart from the talmudic mainstream). This method is ecstatic in an accommodated sense, since it tries to draw the devotee out to a vision of the divine nature and work. Consider, for example, the Zohar's comments on the first verse of Genesis:

"In the beginning" (Gen. 1:1)—when the will of the King began to take effect, he engraved signs into the heavenly sphere (that surrounded him). Within the most

hidden recess a dark flame issued from the mystery of eyn sof, the Infinite, like a fog forming in the un-formed—enclosed in the ring of that sphere, neither white nor black, neither red nor green, or no color whatever. Only after this flame began to assume size and dimension, did it produce radiant colors. From the innermost center of the flame sprang forth a well out of which colors issued and spread upon everything beneath, hidden in the mysterious hiddenness of eyn sof.[4]

If one compares this commentary with the biblical text itself, one sees what imaginative license the Kab-bala could take. Drawing upon what it thought of as oral tradition, each generation tended to amplify what the long stream of previous contemplators of Gen. 1:1 had envisioned. When one became adept in this tra-dition, accustomed to viewing the biblical texts with the eye of a Kabbalist, reality itself took on a new appearance. Although K. P. Bland chooses to stress the inward focus of this Kabbalistic eye, he agrees with us that Kabbalistic imagination amounted to a trans-formed consciousness, and that the Kabbalists' con-ception of God's realm was transcendental (beyond-going and outward, we would say):

The agent of this transforming reinterpretation of rabbinic Judaism is the human capacity or appetite for locating the sacred, the real, or the divine in the inward depth of all things. By using a wide variety of ascetic or contemplative techniques that alter ordinary modes of perception, the Jewish mystic claims to pierce reality and thereby gain insight into, and various de-grees of attachment to, the ultimately unified and har-monious source of all being. Except for the radically transcendental concepts of God's realm elaborated in the first stage of Jewish mysticism, the perspective of Kabbala is inward.[5]

Inward or outward, the gaze of the Kabbalist was fixed on unusual or supernormal scenes, much as was Michael Harner's gaze, whether he looked outward at a ferocious serpent or inward at the prehistoric birds cavorting in his depths. In the mystical life, the life where the spirit is raised and intensified by direct dealings with the divine, "up" and "down," "inward," and "outward" are not to be taken literally. One finds ecstasy sharpening sensitivity to the divine or spiritual force deep within everything, introversion making the outer world appear more sacramental. This is true for the Hasidim, whose founder and most eminent figure, the **Baal Shem Tov** ("Master of the Good Name"), lit up Eastern Europe both during his own lifetime (1700–1760) and for 150 years after. Indeed the visions and wonder workings of the *Besht* (acronymn for *Baal*

Shem Tov) became the prime examples of how the **zaddick** (the charismatic saint whom the Hasidim ven-erated) stepped forth from ordinary human limitations to converse with God and battle the Evil One.

In one story typical of the tales the Hasidim created, the Baal Shem Tov saved his people and their Torah by journeying in spirit to heaven, where Satan and his evil minions had shut the gates and were keeping the Jews' prayers from getting through to God. On earth hateful Christians were threatening another persecu-tion of the Jews, with book burnings that destroyed both bibles and talmudic volumes. On the Day of Atonement (**Yom Kippur**), at the holiest part of the ceremony, the Besht threw himself on the ground in prayer and roared like a wounded lion. For two hours he struggled visibly in front the people, until finally he raised himself from the ground, his face aglow, and pronounced the catastrophe averted. Later it became known that during those two hours he had met his heavenly double and traveled to the gates of paradise:

They went to the palace, where the Messiah sits wait-ing for the day when he may go down to earth. As soon as they entered, the Messiah told them, "Be joyous! I will help you." and he gave the Baal Shem Tov a token. The Baal Shem Tov took the token back to the heavenly gate. When he brandished the token, the heav-enly portals swung open, as wide as the earth is large. So all the prayers entered, going straight to the throne of the Name. Heaven fell to ecstatic rejoicing, and all the angels sang hymns of praise. But the dark angels fled back to their hellish dungeons, routed and fearful again.[6]

As with the early biblical prophets, there are sim-ilarities to the psychodynamics of classical shamanism, but no exact replications. Kabbalists and Hasidim were not initiated in ceremonies of dying and rising. They had some dealings with good and bad spirits, and in a broad sense their ecstasies were therapeutic (healing people's bruised hopes), but a strong faith in a sov-ereign creator God made their reality discernibly dif-ferent from that of most tribal shamans. It is in the power of their imaginations, therefore, that they sug-gest a Jewish shamanism. When the *eyn sof* (depths of divinity) or gates of heaven became fully real, the Jewish adept was quite akin to an ecstatic brother or sister in a nonliterate tribe.[7]

CHRISTIAN CHARISMATICS

In the New Testament the term *charism* has both a broad and a technical sense: "The broad sense: the free gifts given by God—generally a spiritual gift, the Holy Spirit, salvation in Jesus Christ, eternal life, the privileges of Israel, liberation from a danger. The technical sense: a free gift appropriated by one person or another, which allowed him to accomplish through the Spirit activities suited to the community's good."[8] Among the several descriptions of such gifts, 1 Cor. 12:28 is quite representative: "God has appointed in the church first apostles, second prophets, third teachers, then workers of miracles, then healers, helpers, administrators, speakers in various kinds of tongues." The closest correlations between Christian charismatics and the shamanic ecstatics we have been studying probably occur among the prophets, workers of miracles, healers, and speakers of tongues.

Christian prophecy built upon the prophecy of the Old Testament (Hebrew Bible). Inheriting this tradition, the first Christians thought of Isaiah, Jeremiah, Ezekiel, and the other prophets as heroes of faith whom God had inspired with visions of the future and courage to denounce the injustices of their times. Jesus fit many of the outlines of the Old Testament prophet, and after his death the early Christian community seems to have included numerous people thought to have gifts for revealing divine secrets, exhorting, consoling, and generally building up the community by flights of spiritual inspiration.

Miracles also had both Old Testament precedent and Jesus' personal example. Among the extraordinary accomplishments that the Christian scriptures attribute to Jesus are miraculous healings of fever, leprosy, paralysis, deafness, muteness, blindness, epilepsy, rheumatism, hemorrhage, and demon possession, as well as resuscitations from death. In addition, Jesus is said to have changed the course of nature by calming a storm, multiplying loaves of bread, walking on water, changing water into wine, and withering a fig tree. The point in these stories seems not so much the literal reality of what happened (which today's historians simply cannot determine) but the way that the followers of Jesus used his extraordinary deeds as images of God's power, signs of why Jesus should be thought worthy of wholehearted faith. In the imaginations of Jesus' followers, these unusual occurrences were an invitation to step outside ordinary perceptions of reality, contemplate a world fraught with the power of a God to whom Jesus had special access.

In the footsteps of Jesus, many Christian saints became associated with miracles and healings. By the time of the Middle Ages, Christian imagination had dozens of *thaumaturges* (wonder-workers) to contemplate. Later these wonder-workers even assumed a certain bureaucratic orderliness: people prayed to St. Blaise about disease of the throat, to St. Anthony for lost articles. People went on pilgrimages to shrines of such saints, often hoping for cures or special favors. This tradition continues today at such shrines of the Virgin Mary as Lourdes in France, Fatima in Portugal, Chestochowa in Poland, and Guadalupe in Mexico.

The gift of tongues (*glossolalia*) seems usually to have occurred in an ecstatic state. One of the problems it raised was interpreting what the strange speech might mean, since the person uttering it usually was not conscious of its significance. Today one can find this phenomenon in Pentecostal churches, along with such related ecstatic happenings as "slaying in the Spirit."[9]

As Christian charismatics—Jesus, the healer saints, and some contemporary ecstatics—have gone about their work, they have sometimes thought themselves in combat with Satan or other evil forces. For example, the New Testament portrays a dramatic encounter between Jesus and Satan during Jesus' sojourn in the wilderness. In this encounter Jesus thwarts Satan's tempting will, prefiguring the victory over Satan that Christian faith has seen in the resurrection:

Then Jesus was led up by the Spirit into the wilderness to be tempted by the devil. And he fasted forty days and forty nights, and afterward he was hungry. And the tempter came and said to him, "If you are the Son of God, command these stones to become loaves of bread." But he answered, "It is written, 'Man shall not live by bread alone, but by every word that proceeds from the mouth of God.'" Then the devil took him to the holy city, and set him on the pinnacle of the temple, and said to him, "If you are the son of God, throw yourself down; for it is written, 'He will give his angels charge of you,' and 'On their hands they will bear you up, lest you strike your foot against a stone.'" Jesus said to him, "Again it is written, 'You shall not tempt the Lord your God.'" Again, the devil took him to a very high mountain, and showed him all the kingdoms of the world and the glory of them; and he said to him, "All these I will give you, if you will fall down and worship me." Then Jesus said to him, "Begone, Satan! for it is written, 'You shall worship the Lord your God and him only shall you serve.'" Then the devil left him, and behold, angels came and ministered to him. (Matt. 4:1–11)

Throughout subsequent history, Christian healers and reformers often have used texts such as these to bolster their confidence as they fought against "principalities and powers." Thus Martin Luther, the father of the sixteenth-century Protestant Reformation, saw his struggle as in part a battle against Satan. Christianity, therefore, has kept something of the classical shaman's spiritual warfare.

CHRISTIAN VISIONARY MYSTICS

Partly due to charismatic movements, there is now a revived interest in Christian mysticism.[10] When we interpret this interest in the light of a solid acquaintance with the history of Christian attempts to gain union with God, we find that Christians probably have had as many different methods for unifying the human spirit and opening it to God as have other meditative religions. Among the *hesychasts*, practitioners of **hesychaism**, in Eastern Orthodox Christianity, for example, one finds breathing disciplines much like the **pranayama** regimes of Hinduism. Among "negative" Christian mystics such as Denis the pseudo-Aeropagite and John of the Cross one finds a denial of the imaginability of the divine as ruthless as Hinduism's *neti, neti* ("not this, not that"). Yet the central doctrine of Christianity, the belief that God's Word took flesh in Jesus Christ, has assured that all aspects of Christianity, mysticism included, would have a material or sacramental focus. Thus respected teachers of mystical lore such as Teresa of Avila have insisted on retaining the humanity of Jesus. For them not even the highest flights toward union with God ought to leave behind the flesh of the earthly Jesus.

One of the most beautiful ways that Christian mysticism has incorporated the symbol of the Incarnation and lured its common people as well as its adepts out of the ordinary perceptions is through its sacred art. Above all, the iconography (sacred printing) of Eastern Christendom has set before the Christian faithful alluring portraits of Jesus, Mary, and the saints. Contemplating these at the weekly liturgy, the devout faithful have felt a pull to consider the whole world filled with the force of the Holy Spirit, sensing how the grace of God might make any life powerful with love like the saints'. This iconographic tradition had to withstand fierce challenges within Eastern Christianity (**iconoclasm**), and Protestant Christianity has always feared that iconography would compromise the transcendence of the one God, but the intimate ties of iconography with the Incarnation of God's form make it a good example of how the general Christian imagination has been ecstatic.

To appreciate such classical iconographic achievements as those of Orthodox Russia, one must understand the conventional quality of the iconographer's trade.

There is no reason to doubt that in ancient Russia icons were regarded as sacred, meriting reverence regardless of their artistic quality—an attitude that undeniably affected the approach painters took to their

subjects. ... Religious artists did not usually invent their own subjects, as secular painters did. They followed an iconographical convention established and developed by custom and the church authorities. Only the choice of colors was at their discretion; in everything else they were supposed to be governed by the traditional canons. That is why icons representing the same subject, even when painted centuries apart, can be so alike that historians may find it impossible to differentiate them.[11]

For the Russian faithful themselves, the icon often was considered a window to the world of Christian spirituality. Thus a famous twelfth-century icon, "Christ of Veronica," takes the legend of Veronica (that while Jesus was carrying his cross a kindly woman, Veronica, gave him a towel on which to wipe his face and received it back imprinted with his visage) and renders it as a striking portrait of Jesus.[12] (El Greco has a similarly striking rendition, perhaps inspired by his days of apprenticeship as an icon painter.) Jesus has a long, narrow face; a long, thin nose; thick, braided hair; and a full, reddish beard. As in many Orthodox icons, the eyes are especially arresting. Under heavy brows, his large eyes stare forcefully, not directly at the viewer but slightly to the viewer's left. This is a man with whom you would not trifle, a figure of great alertness and power. The implication is that whatever sufferings Jesus endured while carrying the cross have taken away none of his self-possession. He remains a stern master, before whom an unprofitable disciple would be bound to quake. He remains a sovereign king, clear-eyed, realistic, and dominating.

What happened when a person took pictures such as these seriously, using them as the focus of a personal prayer to God? How were the senses and ideas of devout traditional Christians educated? Ecstatically, we would say. The person contemplating the traditional icons was called to go out of herself, focus on another, put off self-concern for the sake of a concern with a God of flesh and blood. The Jesus of "Christ of Veronica" is fully a man but one imbued with special energy and clarity. "That is what human nature can become," the docile worshipper of such an icon likely heard the icon imply. "That is the way your gracious God has chosen to appear." Similar icons of Mary, John the Baptist, the apostles, and famous saints implied similar messages. If the believer gained eyes to see, ears to hear, the world could be transformed. Change the manner of perception, substitute faith for ordinary sensing, and gospel scenes, scenes of nature, and scenes of family life might all become "sacramental." At that point the traditional Christian would have drawn close to Carlos Castaneda's don Juan, become a lover of the beautiful creation God had vouch-safed to make, especially the human portions.

On the way to such a transformed perception Christians did begin with an initiatory motif of death and resurrection, as St. Paul's explanations of baptism (e.g., Rom. 6:3–4) show. They did not, however, try to gain animal spirits as helpers, nor use their perceptual changes as shamanic healers did (seeing the body of the patient from a new angle, so as to be able to remove the objects causing its disease). They did not legitimately develop trances for travel to the heavens or guidance of the souls of the dead. But they did work for a transformation of the senses, were engaged in battles against evil spirits, and did include in their saintly ideal an ecstatic pursuit of a vividly imagined Savior.

MUSLIM HEALERS

The Muslim God, like the God of Jews and Christians, is the sovereign creator of the world. His divinity reaches into every corner and his power severely delimits all lesser spirits. The Muslim natural world therefore is not the world of the **cosmological myth** that dominates many tribal peoples. It is something created and not in the ultimate analysis capricious or impenetrable.[13] Nonetheless, Islam has left considerable space for *jinns* (spirits), and Muslim folk healing has made the battle between possessing spirits and the power of Allah a central concern. Without going through the classical shaman's sort of initiation, and often without employing ecstasy in the sense of trance, many Muslim healers yet have developed thought worlds akin to the shaman's. At the least, they have worked in a world populated with numerous nondivine, less-than-ultimate spiritual powers.

Sudhir Kakar, an Indian trained in Western psychoanalysis, has written a fascinating account of Indian folk medicine, both Muslim and Hindu, that shows the complexity that major concerns like healing usually develop in "the little tradition" (life among the masses). In the course of observing the healing practices of an eighty-seven-year-old Muslim *pir* (wise elder), Kakar came to appreciate the strong influence of the jinns. The pir, whom people addressed by the respectful title *Baba*, told Kakar:

Each human being has its own jinn . . . who is born with him and stays with him till he dies. When the angels come to take away the soul of a good man, they kill the jinn. This is the reason why we Muslims bury a

*dead body and you Hindus cremate it—to ensure the death of a man's jinn. Sometimes, however, especially in the case of a sinful man, it happens that the jinn escapes by hiding in the organs of elimination, which are impure and cannot be reached by the angels. He then becomes a demon (*bala*) and is on the lookout for a victim in whose body he can find a home and whose blood he can drink.*[14]

Baba went on to say that the bad jinns, or demons, are all around us, flying in the air, creeping on the ground. Only the person of knowledge, however, can see them. When illness or other upset occurs, one should always suspect the influence of a bala. A sorcerer may have sent the bala against us, or the restless demon may simply have spied us on its own and thought we would make a good victim. Since they like fresh blood the best, balas tend to favor young girls. There are different kinds of balas, though, and one of the most terrifying is the *jaljogini*, who will suck all the blood out of a person leaving a wretched shell. Kakar's psychoanalytic bent leads him to interpret the jaljogini as follows:

Fascinated, I had listened to Baba describe one of the core fantasies of Indian culture (common, it now seems, to both the Hindus and Muslims), namely the horrific vision of an overpowering feminine sexuality that exhausts, sucks and drains even the most powerful male to death. I have described this fantasy in detail elsewhere, relating it to the Indian male child's dread of the mother's "demonic" eroticism so that later for many who fall ill and suffer from acute anxiety—become possessed by the jaljogini, *as Baba would say—the orgasmic act of love can become a dreadful affair, transformed from a normal "little death" into the dread of a permanent annihilation and emptying of the self.*[15]

To try to cure his patients of their demonic possessions, Baba basically would invoke the presence of Allah. He saw himself as a conduit between the victim and Allah, a channel of the healing power that Allah can unleash. Thus the success or failure of any therapy lay out of Baba's hands. He only knocked at Allah's door on his patient's behalf. Whether Allah chose to open the door and let the patient in was a matter between Allah and the patient. Baba's skill lay in his ability to connect the case at hand to the power of Allah. He had apprenticed himself to a teacher and spent long years learning what sorts of balas cause what sorts of sicknesses and which of Allah's ninety-nine names is the most appropriate to invoke in each case. He had also learned the Koranic verses containing the ninety-nine names and so was able, for example, to produce a verse with the name *al-Hefiz*, "the Guardian," on behalf of a patient possessed by a jinn that caused great fear. Were the patient to be in the throes of distress and anxiety, *al-Qadri*, "Lord of Power," would be the appropriate invocation.

Additionally, Baba would prepare **talismans** (charms or objects thought to be filled with power) to guard his patients. This preparation involved a complicated symbolism mixing the twenty-eight letters of the Arabic alphabet, the twelve signs of the zodiac, and esoteric astrological lore. Magical circles, the positioning of the talismans, and other occult knowledge rounded out Baba's professional expertise. The core of his efficacy, though, was what he thought of as soul force: the power of the divine that he was able to transmit. This only comes to a pir after years of service to a guru and devotion to God. Then the healer finally starts racing toward Allah and Allah starts pulling him heavenward. When the two forces combine, one has the connection that makes the pir an effective healer. The soul force of Baba's teacher was such that Baba was convinced his teacher never really died. Even now Baba could close his eyes and visualize the teacher, who would tell him what to do for each victim.

SUFI SAINTS

The basic creed of Islam rivets human beings to Allah and the prophecy of Muhammad: "There is no God but God, and Muhammad is His prophet." The record of Muhammad's prophecies is the Koran (or Qur'an), and within a short period of time after Muhammad's death (632 C.E.) the study of the Koran and Muhammad's own religious practices became the mainstay of Islamic law or guidance (**Shariah**). By and large, this law has centered the lives of orthodox (**Sunni**) Muslims, much as **Torah** has centered the lives of orthodox Jews. Heterodox Muslims, such as the Shiites who came to dominate Persia, have developed their own law and rituals, some of which are quite ecstatic (in the sense of intensely emotional). The closest Muslim equivalents to tribal shamans, however, probably have occurred among the Sufis, the imaginative or mystical adepts who parallel the Jewish Hasidim and the Christian charismatics.

The early Sufis probably got their name from the Arabic word for wool, the material from which they wove the simple garments they wore as a sort of uniform. In the wake of its rapid expansion after the Prophet's death, Islam had come into great wealth and power. To the Sufis such prosperity was threatening

true religion. So, somewhat as the early Christian monasticism of the Egyptian desert arose in part as a protest against the worldliness that threatened Christianity after Constantine made it the favored religion of the Roman Empire, the Sufis separated themselves from ordinary social life and pursued what they hoped would be a purer Islam. In so doing they activated many of the psychodynamics that we have already seen: exercises to heighten or change consciousness, efforts to accumulate personal soul force, sensitivity to surrounding spirits (both helpful and malign), and a tendency to perceive the world as replete with symbolic significance.

Sufism has continued to be influential into the twentieth century, as Martin Lings's interesting book, *A Sufi Saint of the Twentieth Century*, shows. The book deals with the life and teaching of Shaikh (an Arabic title of respect, usually given to an elder) Ahmad Al'Alawi of Algeria. The Shaikh became friendly with a French doctor called in to treat his influenza. Over the course of some years the doctor came to know the Shaikh as a friend and to learn about Sufism. Sufis consider their interpretation of Islam to be entirely orthodox (others disagree). It stresses the divinity of the prophet Muhammad's revelations and underscores the five "pillars" on which orthodox Islam rests: the creed ("There is no God but God, and Muhammad is His prophet"), prayer five times a day, almsgiving to the poor, fasting during the month of Ramadan, and pilgrimage to Mecca at least once in one's lifetime. But the Sufi brotherhoods cluster around their Shaikhs in an effort to realize the inner force of Islamic faith. Like the Christian writer Thomas à Kempis, they think it better to *feel* compunction (or love, or hope, or faith) than to know its definition. This effort to feel, see, experience the spiritual realities of Koranic religion has led the Sufis to develop the ecstatic dances of their whirling dervishes, rhythmic recitations of the names of Allah, and teaching stories that are like the puzzling **koans** for which Zen Buddhists are famous.

Arresting as they may be to the outward eye, such Sufi practices still are not the core of the brotherhoods' life:

The subjection of the body to a rhythmic motion is never, for the Sufis, any more than an auxiliary; its purpose is simply to facilitate **dhikr** *in the fullest sense of remembrance, that is, the concentration of all the faculties of the soul upon the Divine Truth represented by the Supreme Name or some other formula which is uttered aloud or silently by the dancers. It was explained to me by one of the Shaikh's disciples that just as a sacred number such as three, seven or nine, for example, acts as a bridge between multiplicity and*

Unity, so rhythm is a bridge between agitation and Repose, motion and Motionlessness, fluctuation and Immutability. Fluctuation, like multiplicity, cannot be transcended in this world of perpetual motion but only in the Peace of Divine Unity; and to partake of this Peace in some degree is in fact that very concentration which the dhikr *aims at. Knowledge of this virtue of rhythm is part of man's primordial heritage, and all men possess it instinctively whether they are aware of it or not.*[16]

So dance and the other Sufi practices aim at transforming the disciple's consciousness in the direction of remembrance, concentration, and peace. Sufism is a mystical movement in the sense that it strives after an experiential union with the divine. In orthodox Islam this union can never become an identity. Such **pantheism** has led to mystics such as al-Hallaj being killed for blasphemy. But close union with the divine and a heightened awareness of the divine presence in all things are both legitimate and highly desirable.

Other good things—healing, personal peace, social order—may follow from Sufi piety, but its strongest engines seem to be the felt goodness of remembrance itself. Just as the advanced shamans sing and dance for the intrinsic value of what happens to them in ecstasy, so the advanced Sufi dances and prays for the truth, the vision of Allah, that these exercises bring. The Sufi does not die and rise like the classical shaman. He does not traffic with the world of animal spirits. But his imagination is transformed, his world does come alive with spiritual powers, and he is taken out of himself, made ecstatic, by the splendor of the Koranic God, the beauty of the sovereign "Lord of the Worlds."

Tov make the traffic between heaven and earth quite dramatic.

Christian charismatics of New Testament times used the Hebrew prophetic background and the example of Jesus to interpret their ecstatic seizures and wonder-workings. Jesus had been a great healer and a fighter against Satan, so it was natural for the Christian saints to exhibit similar qualities. The imaginative flights of the visionary mystics of the Eastern iconographic tradition show still another face of Christian ecstaticism, one both beautiful and perceptually transforming.

Muslim healers and Sufis manifest more ways in which a prophetic tradition may share some of the psychodynamics that manifest themselves most strikingly in tribal shamanism. The interest of a healer such as Baba in demonic forces and the ways that the Sufi Shaikhs try to bring their disciples to union with God parallel some of the demonology and ritualism we have seen in the classical shamans.

The strong monotheism of each of the prophetic traditions sharply distinguishes it from tribal shamanism, but the sense that the world is alive with spiritual forces and the need to step outside ordinary consciousness keep each of the prophetic traditions somewhat connected to what has gone on in many shamanic tribes.

SUMMARY

To sketch the analogues to shamanism that one finds in prophetic societies such as Judaism, Christianity, and Islam, we sought religious types in each of these traditions who have shown a markedly ecstatic character. For example, we began with the early Hebrew prophets, the forerunners of the great writing prophets. As portrayed in the Bible, these wandering bands of ecstatics sang and danced themselves into states where they felt seized by the power of God. Later Jewish ecstatics such as the Kabbalists and Hasidim focused on imaginative interpretations of the Bible. The sort of midrash one finds in the Zohar brings the whole world afire with the divine presence, and the Hasidic tales of the powers of saints like the Baal Shem

STUDY QUESTIONS

1. What is the relationship between Saul's receiving a new heart and the spirit of God coming mightily upon him?

2. In what sense was the Baal Shem Tov's journey to heaven a work of healing?

3. How might Jesus' miraculous healings have employed dynamics similar to those of classical shamans?

4. How could the contemplation of an icon such as "Christ of Veronica" take the Christian worshipper out of herself and transform her consciousness?

5. Where does Sudhir Kakar's interpretation of the jaljogini locate the reality of the Muslim jinns?

6. How does the Sufi desire to gain "the peace of the divine Unity" differ from the classical shaman's intercourse with the spirit world?

NOTES

1. James B. Pritchard, ed., *Ancient Near Eastern Texts*, 3d ed. Princeton, N.J.: Princeton University Press, 1969, p. 26.

2. Bruce Vawter, "Introduction to Prophetic Literature," *The Jerome Biblical Commentary*, vol. 1. ed. Raymond E. Brown et al. Englewood Cliffs, N.J.: Prentice-Hall, 1968, p. 225.

3. See Gershom G. Scholem, *Major Trends in Jewish Mysticism*, 3d ed. New York: Schocken, 1961, pp. 40–79.

4. Gershom G. Scholem, ed., *Zohar: The Book of Splendor*. New York: Schocken, 1963, p. 27.

5. K. P. Bland, "Kabbala," *Abingdon Dictionary of Living Religions*, ed. Keith Crim. Nashville: Abingdon, 1981, p. 395.

6. Denise L. Carmody and John T. Carmody, *Western Ways to the Center*. Belmont, Calif.: Wadsworth, 1983, p. 74. See Meyer Levin, *Classic Hasidic Tales*. New York: Penguin, 1975, pp. 125–131.

7. See Arthur Green, "The Zaddiq as *Axis Mundi* in Later Judaism," *Journal of the American Academy of Religion*, 45/3 (September 1977), 327–47.

8. Xavier Léon-Dufour, *Dictionary of the New Testament*. San Francisco: Harper & Row, 1980, p. 131.

9. See Morton Kelsey, *Discernment*. Ramsey, N.J.: Paulist, 1978, pp. 10–50.

10. See Harvey Egan, *What Are They Saying About Mysticism?* Ramsey, N.J.: Paulist, 1982.

11. Mihail Alpatov, "The Icons of Russia," in Kurt Weitzmann et al., *The Icon*. New York: Alfred A. Knopf, 1982, pp. 237–38.

12. Ibid., p. 259.

13. See Isma-il al-Faruqi, "Islam," in W. T. Chan et al., *The Great Asian Religions*. New York: Macmillan, 1969, p. 310.

14. Sudhir Kakar, *Shamans, Mystics & Doctor*. New York: Alfred A. Knopf, 1982, p. 25.

15. Ibid., p. 28. The "elsewhere" to which Kakar refers is his book *The Inner World*. New York: Oxford University Press, 1978, pp. 87–103.

16. Martin Lings, *A Sufi Saint of the Twentieth Century*, 2d ed. Berkeley: University of California Press, 1973, p. 92.

5

Shamanism Within Sagacious Societies

Hindu Folk Religion
Tibetan Buddhist Demonology
Chinese Exorcism
Chinese Spirtualism
Japanese Folk Religion
Greek Ecstaticism
African Ecstaticism
Summary
Study Questions
Notes

HINDU FOLK RELIGION

In the previous chapter we considered indications that shamanism has had analogous forms in societies dominated by prophecy. In the present chapter we consider analogues in societies dominated by wisdom. And just as certain aspects of the Jewish, Christian, and Muslim imaginations seemed to show parallels with shamanic fantasy, so do certain aspects of the imaginations of the sapiential societies. India, for example, has for millennia housed a great variety of religious allegiances and orientations. The main forces, historically, have been the *Vedic* orientations brought by the **Aryans** who invaded India four thousand to thirty-five hundred years ago and the orientations of the *Dravidian* natives who have remained strongest in the south. Between them, these two sets of orientations have produced a dazzling **pantheon** of gods, rarefied speculation like that of the Upanishads and philosophical schools, and

many of the ecstatic, nature-oriented concerns prominent in the classical shamanic societies. It is these latter concerns that beg attention here.

Two hundred fifty miles directly south of Delhi, in the town of Bharatpur, is a famous temple, the Balaji, to which many Indians come for the cure of psychosomatic illnesses. The main assumption behind the healing rituals of the temple is that most petitioners are possessed by a destructive spirit. Usually the destructive spirit has suggested its presence through symptoms such as stomach pains, headaches, or fits of uncontrollable rage. To relieve the patient of such afflictions, the priests of the temple have developed formalized processes focused on a warfare between the offending spirit and one of the protector deities resident in the temple. The formalized process or ritual ordinarily begins with the patient's overt possession by a demon, the clearest evidence of which is a rhythmic swaying of the upper half of the body and a violent sideways shaking of the head. The demon may also manifest its presence by making patients beat the floor with their hands, hit their backs against the wall, or lie down on the floor with heavy stones piled on their backs. Patients enter a trancelike state (what a psychoanalyst might call a *dissociation*). They are able to carry on a conversation but generally will not remember what went on during the ritual.

The center of the process usually is a struggle between the demon and the protector god who is invoked by the priest. The demon shouts, curses, and makes accusations or complaints through the mouth of the patient, while the onlooking crowd (the family of the patient or other pilgrims) berates the offending spirit. Generally the demon finally agrees to leave the patient, after greater or lesser struggle, and the temple priests ensure continuing protection by the helpful deity by giving the patient talismans or the protection of a good possessing spirit. In the latter instance, the good spirit usually manifests itself through a shorter and calmer trance, during which the patient offers prayers and prostrations to the protector deity. A Western psychoanalyst might attribute the patients' pains to sexual inhibition or repressed anger resulting from Indian ideals of self-control and family peace, but the framework in which the patients and priests view the sicknesses is the folk Hindu conviction that the world is populated with many spirits, both good and evil.[1]

Among Hindus of the Himalayas one finds a deep stratum of folk religion that also shows shamanistic traits. For instance, when a village family suffers a misfortune its first tendency is to consult the local ecstatic, whom they consider their contact with the powers of the spiritual world: "Most supernatural beings make their presence felt by imposing difficulties or troubles upon people—usually disease or death to people or animals, and sometimes other troubles such as hysteria, faithless spouses, sterility, poor crops, financial loss, or mysterious disappearance of belongings."[2] The ecstatics whom the family consults may come from any caste, and their work usually consists of going into trances so as to become the *medium* (mouthpiece) of a particular god. They may gain these trances by singing songs to the god, beating a drum, or using other techniques that alter their consciousness.

While in trance ecstatics may be impervious to pain, and the god who speaks through them usually will not use the ecstatic's ordinary voice. The voice of the god may reveal the cause of the illness, name the thieves responsible for the loss, or provide other explanatory information. Then the god is likely to prescribe a *puja*, or short devotional ceremony, to placate the spiritual powers at the root of the troubles. This puja also may involve ecstatic trances, in which the god can dance and receive offerings. Other popular prescriptions are pilgrimages to the temple of a powerful god and removal of objects in the patient's body or surroundings disclosed to have caused the problem.

TIBETAN BUDDHIST DEMONOLOGY

Buddhism began in India twenty-five hundred or so years ago, but over time it was largely transplanted to countries east of India. The three major families of Buddhism—**Hinayana**, **Mahayana**, and **Vajrayana**—agree on essentials such as Buddha's Four Noble Truths: All life is suffering. The cause of suffering is desire. If desire is removed suffering will cease. The way to remove desire is the eightfold path of right views, right intention, right speech, right action, right livelihood, right effort, right mindfulness, and right concentration. In addition, the ritualistic forms that Buddhism has taken in each of the three major families show several shamanic features: flights of imaginative ecstasy, battles with demons, exercises to change ordinary perception. Let us exemplify this claim by examining the *chöd* ritual of traditional Tibetan Buddhists, those of the Vajrayana school.

The *chöd* ritual, which only males participated in, usually took place in a desolate spot such as a cemetery or the site of a terrible tragedy. Such a site was thought to stir up the occult forces thought to exist there. The main actor learned a ritual dance involving geometrical figures, stamping, and leaping. He also had to learn to handle the bell, drum, dagger, trumpet, and other implements that usually were involved. The principal point to the ritual was a self-offering to the hungry demons that haunt our minds. Monks in training therefore would use the *chöd* as a way to increase their progress in self-denial, their removal of the barriers to enlightenment.

Alexandra David-Neel, who observed many *chöd* rituals during her long stay in Tibet early in this century, describes the ceremony as follows:

The celebrant blows his bone trumpet, calling the hungry demons to the feast he intends to lay before them. He imagines that a feminine deity, which esoterically personifies his own will, springs from the top of his head and stands before him, sword in hand. With one stroke she cuts off the head of the naljorpa [ascetic celebrant]. Then, while troops of ghouls crowd round for the feast, the goddess severs his limbs, skins him and rips open his belly. The bowels fall out, the blood flows like a river, and the hideous guests bite here and there, masticate noisily, while the celebrant excites and urges them with liturgic words of unreserved surrender.[3]

These liturgic, or ritual, words draw on the Buddhist convictions that (1) we are involved in a cycle of rebirths and (2) we sentient beings live off one another. The self-offering that the celebrants make is therefore an act of repayment. They are making retribution to all the creatures from whom they have taken sustenance, pleasure, the things needed to clothe and house themselves during all their lives in the cycle of **transmigration**. As well, they are actualizing the notion that the Buddhist adept should generously give all that he or she has to relieve the sufferings and fulfill the needs of other sentient beings.

As the *chöd* ritual progressed, the ghouls faded away. In the utter desolateness of the lonely site, celebrants finally focused on their wretchedness, their physical, moral, and **ontological** nothingness. To do this they might, for example, imagine themselves as heaps of charred human bones emerging from a lake of black mud. The goal of immersing themselves in such imagery was to reach a state of mind in which they felt they really had nothing to sacrifice. It was an illusion even to think that they were something that could be given back to those from whom they had profited. Better for them to sink into the lake of black mud, extinguish the false notion that they were selves of substance and worth.

Tibetan **lamas**, or monks, would sometimes undertake pilgrimage tours, trying to perform the *chöd* near 108 lakes and 108 cemeteries. This could send them wandering for years over Tibet, India, Nepal, and China. Once David-Neel watched a lama perform the *chöd* near the corpse of a person recently deceased. He beat a drum, sang, danced through the ritual diagrams, and invited the attending gods and demons to join in. In his dancing he shouted that he would "trample down" the evil passions within himself, the evil forces surrounding him. Howling, moaning, alternately challenging the demons and recoiling from them in fear, this monk offered a striking illustration of the *tantric* (based on a **tantra**) effort to call all the powers of the imagination and the unconscious into the struggle after liberation. In fact, the monk's howls and moans so moved David-Neel that she feared for his health and sought to shake him from his trance. But he was so lost in the imaginative theater of the ritual that he saw David-Neel as another of the demons. When she went to the monk's teacher to warn him that his disciple seemed on the verge of doing himself injury, the teacher calmly pointed out that the disciple

had had the dangers pointed out to him before he began, and that no price was too high to pay for **enlightenment**.

The Tibetan Buddhist tradition owes some of its imagery and ritual to the native tradition that preceded the arrival of Buddhism in Tibet (around 800 C.E.). This native tradition focused on the **bon**, a shamanic practitioner who fought against demons. Tibetan Buddhism seems to have joined the bon background to the tantric inclinations of the Indian teachers who tutored it, producing a profound religion in which the native tradition of demons and trances was made to serve the Buddhist struggle for liberation from the realm of desire and suffering. Using the natural fears, suggestions, and conditionings that exercises such as spending the night in a desolate cemetery would arouse, and playing on the belief that the world is filled with occult forces, the Tibetan masters offered their disciples a powerful "shock therapy."

CHINESE EXORCISM

We have been describing layers or dimensions of traditional Asia religions in which similarities to shamanic ecstasy, shamanic concern with good and evil spirits, and the powerful shamanic imagination stand forth. Hinduism and Buddhism both have a deep layer in which such similarities occur, and so does traditional Chinese religion. Buddhism, of course, had a great influence on pre-Communist China, so the Buddhist theories of **karma**, transmigration, and ghosts and spirits shaped the imaginations of most traditional Chinese. However, China also retained shamanic features from native sources. Long after the sober wisdom of Confucius had become the formative ideal of the educated classes, and the poetic insights of Taoists such as Lao-tzu and Chuang-tzu had beguiled the intelligentisia, a concern with **divination**, the fate of ancestors in the afterworld, and the exorcism of malign or even diabolical spirits influenced the general populace.

Taoist priests seem to have been popular exorcists, but the ritual materials they employed show the influence of such "Confucian" notions as *yin* and *yang*. In a **dualism** that actually predates Confucius, traditional China had expressed the intuition that reality is composed of two opposed sets of forces. The **yin** forces were associated with what was considered dark, passive, and feminine. The **yang** forces were associated with what was considered light, active, and masculine. One of the ways a person could fall into a state of possession that necessitated exorcism was by having the yin forces overpower the yang. Consequently, the ritual of exorcism was replete with such yang symbols as burning candles, incense sticks, peach wood, cash coins, swords, invocations, gongs, crackers, and freshly killed cocks. According to convention, these were elements opposed to the yin side of reality and so able to bring the patient back to a balance that would oust the possessing forces.

These possessing forces were demons or evil spirits. The function of the priest performing the exorcism was to confront them and cast them out of the patient by his superior will power and the force of the symbols he wielded. Notice in the following description how the directions of the compass (a shamanic theme especially prominent in American Indian religion) come into play:

He [the priest] then picks up a sprig of willow which he dips in the cup, and sprinkles first the east, then west, north and south corners of the house. To reenforce the spell he fills his mouth with water, and spurts it against the east wall with the invocation: "Slay the azure spirits of the east, spawn of unlucky stars, or let them be expelled to a distant country." The red demons of the south, the white in the west, and the yellow in the centre, are similarly banished to the accompaniment of gongs and crackers whose efficacy is commensurate with the riot of sound they create. When the pandemonium is at its height, the exorcist raises his voice to be heard above the din and screams: "Evil spirits of the East get you back to the East, of the South return thither. Let all demons seek their proper quarters and vanish forthwith.[4]

Obviously, people who feared the powers of demonic forces would find an exorcism ritual like this quite impressive. As the colors assigned to the demons of the different directions and the noise of the gongs and crackers suggest, Chinese folk imagination pictured the warfare between the forces of good and evil with considerable flair. It is not difficult, moreover, to suspect parallels with the Hindu cases of possession and affliction that we contemplated previously. The pressures of traditional Chinese family life were as intense as those of traditional Hindu family life, and the expressions of the psychic distresses those pressures could cause (using Western terms) might conveniently be attributed to a malign spirit. In casting out such a spirit, the Taoist priest would embody the community's resources against evil and disorder, much as the classical shaman did. Although the priest's training might not include a ritual death and resurrection, he would know the various gods of the body, forces of the compass, and yin/yang powers of foods and implements, so as to be able to muster the many energies of health and peace. Like Baba, the Indian Muslim pir whom we studied earlier, the traditional Taoist priest employed ritual techniques designed to give the patients' pains and fears a tangible, attackable form and to bolster the patients' confidence that they could be healed.

In extreme cases, Chinese demonic possession could take the form of the bizarre effects and diabolical threats popularized recently in the American film *The Exorcist*. Thus a generation ago Peter Goullart described an exorcism he had witnessed in which the possessed person howled, gave bestial whoops, uttered incredible obscenities, convulsed, and had his body swell to grotesque proportions and then release malodorous excreta from all its orifices. The hatred and venom of the possessed man's outcries, his thrashing efforts to injure the attending priest and onlookers were a sobering display of the malice that "demonic" powers can manifest, their Satanic dimension.[5] The world of the human personality is such that love of evil and hatred of goodness occasionally break out in naked self-exposure. What some people express through the butcheries and massacres all too frequent in our recent headlines other people express through diabolical possession. Obviously both types of people cry out for exorcism, by whatever fair means possible.

CHINESE SPIRITUALISM

The spiritual world continued to be a lively part of Chinese reality well into the twentieth century, influencing even medical students exposed to Western science. This is clear in the dazzling account that Maxine Hong Kingston, an American of Chinese extraction, has written of her mother's training as a doctor in pre-Maoist China. Western medicine had begun to take over the curricula of Chinese medical schools, but most medical students remained fully convinced of the reality and power of ghosts. Kingston's mother was older than the rest of the students, however, and not about to be intimidated by their fear of ghosts. When the other students began to speak of one particular room in the dormitory as being haunted, Kingston's mother decided to sleep there. That night she encountered a sitting ghost, who pressed down on her chest heavily.

Rousing her spirit of resistance, Kingston's mother faced the ghost down:

I do not give in. . . . There is no pain you can inflict that I cannot endure. You're wrong if you think I'm afraid of you. You're no mystery to me. I've heard of you sitting ghosts before. Yes, people have lived to tell about you. You kill babies, you cowards. You have no power over a strong woman. . . . You cannot even assume an interesting shape. Merely a boulder. A hairy butt boulder. You must not be a ghost at all. Of course. There are no such things as ghosts. Let me instruct you, Boulder. When Yen, the teacher, was grading the provincial exams one year, a thing with hair as ugly as yours plopped itself on his desk. (That one had glaring eyes, though, so it wasn't blind and stupid like you.) Yen picked up his ferule and hit it like a student. He chased it around the room. (It wasn't lame and lazy.) And it vanished. Later Yen taught us, "After life, the rational soul ascends the dragon; the sentient soul descends the dragon. So in the world there can be no ghosts."[6]

Now, Kingston is a creative writer, working on the border between journalism and fiction. Her intent is not a literal report of what her mother told her, let alone what her mother experienced as a medical student, but an impressionistic retrieval of what a traditional Chinese mother put into the imagination of a child of the new world. When Kingston asked her mother what life had been like, how things used to be done in the old country, her mother answered in tales of spirits and dragons. This was the thought world of the traditional Chinese. In the midst of making flat statements denying the existence of ghosts her mother would recount an adventure with a sitting ghost. Probably the mother herself no longer remembered or could fathom what had "really" happened. After many tellings a dream of the night or a dream of the day passed for a solid occurence. Still, clearly it was important to take the **occult** seriously. Clearly talismans and a strong will were necessary protections.

Throughout much of Chinese history what C. K. Yang has called "diffused religion" wove its spiritualistic way through family and political life.

The presence of symbols of gods and spirits and the performance of religious rituals in all major aspects of organized social life created a general feeling of awe and respect for institutionalized practices. Enter a house, participate in the ceremonial activites of any group, walk through a neighborhood or a public square, look at a memorial arch, go through a city gate, climb a large bridge, view a sizable public building of any nature, and one would nearly always see an altar, an idol, the picture of a god or spirit, a magical charm, or some mythological lore of the gods and spirits connected with the nature and history of the object.[7]

Among the major agents of this diffusion of religion were the various Chinese priests. Prior to the rise of Confucianism to cultural predominance in the late centuries B.C.E., the *wu*, or shaman, exerted a strong influence. With the advent of Confucian rationalism power shifted to the cultic functionary who performed the public rites. Later Buddhist and Taoist priests took over many of the temples. Still, shamans, practitioners of **geomancy**, diviners, and similar ecstatics always remained a strong influence in the private sphere. When people were down on their luck, sick, or afraid, they often consulted a "priest" of a less ritualistic, more ecstatic character. One could easily find such a priest in the market place, sitting behind a little table, ready to diagnose one's troubles or tell one's fortune. In addition, shamans worked both the urban and the rural neighborhoods, offering to pray for people's well-being, make contact with the dead, cure stubborn sicknesses, and exorcise evil spirits. The geomancers, whose skill lay in determining the propitious directions for building sites, exerted a sizable influence on all construction. (In the 1940s the Communists initiated a special campaign against **sorcery** in the rural areas of the north, charging the traditional ecstatic healers with swindling. The most telling argument in this campaign was the Communists' charge that when the sorcerers themselves took ill they went to doctors trained in modern medicine.)

In traditional China spiritualism therefore was a permanent feature of the mental landscape. Across all the major traditions—Confucian, Taoist, and Buddhist—an alertness to spiritual influences characterized most of the citizenry. The mercantile guilds had their defending deities. The individual peasants had stores of **amulets**. Even the popular literature joined to "high" religious notions such as karma "low" notions of animals who could talk and make mischief.[8]

JAPANESE FOLK RELIGION

The native religious culture of Japan also was spiritualistic. Shamans, mediums, **soothsayers**, and the like traditionally had a wide influence, much of it involving ecstatic trances and warfare in the spirit world. When this native tradition was forced to articulate itself, because of competition from Buddhism and Taoism, it took the name **Shinto**. Just as Buddhists followed the way of Gautama, Shintoists followed the way of the **kami**, the native gods who were the focus of anything vivid or powerful in nature. Confucian mores came to dominate Japanese family and social life, Buddhism and Taoism furnished the educated classes their philosophies, but Shintoist sensibilities never left the Japanese mainstream. Deeper than any identification of the people with the deified emperor or the formalized rituals of the Shinto priesthood lay the ancient sense that nature is alive with spiritual powers, the kami are as close as a striking rock or arresting tree.

Ichiro Hori has written one of the best-known works on Japanese folk religion, in the midst of which occurs a full chapter on Japanese shamanism. Hori notes that shamans continued to function in parts of Japan into the mid-twentieth century. At one time wandering female shamans were probably the predominant force on the level of popular religion, but even in recent times villages in the northeast of the island of Honshu were likely to have resident female shamans who kept alive the old services of communing with spirits, deities, ghosts, and the dead. They also divined the future and told fortunes through trance, offered prayers for the recovery of the sick, and purified new buildings.

Of special interest to us is the initiation that recent-day female shamans have undergone, since in northeast Honshu they follow a quite formal training regime:

The novices undergo training disciplines such as cold-water ablution, purification, fasting, abstinence, and observance of various taboos. They are taught the techniques of trance, of communication with superhuman beings or spirits of the dead, and of divination and fortune-telling; they also learn the melody and intonation used in the chanting of prayers, magic formulas, and liturgies, and the narratives and ballads called saimon. *After three to five years' training, they become full-fledged shamanesses through the completion of initiatory ordeals and an initiation ceremony which includes the use of symbols of death and resurrection.*[9]

The initiation ceremony is quite dramatic. The novice dons a white death robe and sits face to face with her teacher. Several shamanic elders chant the names of deities, buddhas, and magical formulas. The novice begins to tremble, and at just the opportune moment the teacher cries, "What is the name of the deity possessing you?" The novice gives the name and falls over in a dead faint. When the novice is revived from this faint (which is taken to be her death), she changes into a colorful wedding garment and offers nine toasts of sake, the most important part of the traditional Japanese wedding ceremony. Hori does not fully expand on this symbolism, but it would seem not only to conform to the classical shamanic initiation in many motifs but also to add an espousal of the candidate shamaness to her possessing deity. Thereafter the shamaness tends to call to her possessing spirit at the beginning of a session of divination or other work, using poetic songs much like love ballads.

The tradition of women being special conduits of the spirits continues in some of the so-called New Religions that have proliferated in Japan in the past century. Many of these new religions derive from a charismatic founder; commingle elements of Confucianism, Buddhism, and Shinto; and offer their adherents healing for mental and physical pains. In such healing women frequently play the role of medium to a spirit who will diagnose the patient's problem and offer a suitable therapy. Frequently this spirit is ancestral, a member of the family or clan. In the cosmology of many New Religious groups such ancestral spirits are thought of as yin. Since women too are yin, they are better conduits of the ancestral spirits than men. Men, who are yang, are better in the role of ascetics. Generally, their yang makes men better positioned for enlightenment, but if a woman works hard to overcome her presumed karmic hindrances to enlightenment, taking on austerities and disciplines, she can shoot ahead of a man, attaining greater heights of spiritual power. Thus the prominence of women in the New Religious healing rites has a twofold justification. In Confucian terms, women are good mediums by virtue of their yin character. In Buddhist terms, their skill is evidence of the struggle to gain spiritual powers that their sex makes a great challenge. Either way, they often are the main point of contact between earth and the spiritual world.[10]

In the more refined portions of Japanese religious culture, where Mahayana Buddhist philosophy has made a great impact and **Zen** discipline has deeply impressed itself, the ecstatic tendencies of the folk heritage often transform themselves into an aesthetic or sacramental sensitivity. The advanced Buddhist does not deny the realm of the spirits, nor the psychic powers available to shamans, but his or her concentration on the **emptiness** of all things leaves both spirits and psychic powers behind. The Zen adept, for example, strives mightily to realize the simple is-ness (or being) of everything, its **suchness** and dancing flow. Ecstasy then comes to flame in the experience of **satori**: enlightenment, seeing everything bright and clear.

GREEK ECSTATICISM

In the terms of our typology, Greece is the land where Western rationality came to birth: Philosophy and science, in their Western senses, originated in the labors of the Greeks who, both before and after Socrates, studied nature, society, human psychology, and the relation of all three to the divine. Because of this epochal achievement, the golden age of Greece in the fourth century B.C.E. stands as a landmark of sapiential progress. Nonetheless, most of ancient Greek religion was less refined than the theologies of Plato and Aristotle: closer to the earth, the mythology, the ecstasy that the religion of nonliterate peoples generally has spotlighted.

Overall, the religion of ancient Greece, prior to Christianity, is a complicated tapestry, woven of many strands. The cultures of the prior Minoan and Mycenean civilizations left their mark on classical Greece, as did the cultures of such invaders as the Dorians of Macedonia. In the deepest strata lie elements of a fertility worship focused on a Great Goddess figure, although the host of Olympian gods led by Zeus magnified many human skills and traits. Both the powers of the earth and the powers of the sky received full attention. Indeed, one may speculate that the skyward orientation of the Olympian religion (which orientation the Greeks shared with such other Indo-Europeans as the ancient Iranians and the Vedic Aryans) ultimately led to Platonic philosophy, the upward ascent of the mind toward the sources of its intellectual light. Balancing this was a concern with the mysterious depth of things that flowered in the Orphic and Eleusinian mysteries, both of which prepared initiates for death and a happy afterlife.

For the average Greek of that period, the world was alive with fates, furies, and other spiritual forces. Shrines to various gods dotted the landscape, and at many of them one would find an ecstatic attendant, priest or priestess, who could be consulted as an oracle. The attendant would go into trance, become the medium of the god, and declaim a cryptic response to the petitioner's inquiry. Even the famous oracle of Apollo at Delphi operated in this fashion, although Apollo was the god of balance, reason, and order. Amulets, prayers, sacrifices to the numerous gods, and rituals for the removal of the **pollution** that one could incur by transgressing social or religious taboos were features of the popular religion.

One of the most famous evidences of the ecstatic quality of ancient Greek religion comes from the *Bacchae*, a play by the noted tragedian Euripides (480–406 B.C.E.). The play describes the cult of Dionysius or Bacchus, a foreign god of fertility imported by the Greeks, that attracted many female devotees called *Bacchae* or *Bacchantes*. Behind the plot lies the myth that Dionysius was the son of Zeus and Semele, a Theban princess. Hera, the wife of Zeus, was jealous of Semele and tricked Zeus into killing her with a thunderbolt.

In the Bacchae, *the sisters of Semele deny the divinity of Dionysius, are driven mad by him, and dance in frenzy on the mountains. . . . The play, while set in the remote past, naturally reproduces aspects of the Dionysiac cult known in Euripides' own day, and later. Dancing on the mountains—in the depths of winter— whether in a maddened ecstasy like that of the Theban women [the sisters of Semele], or with a joyous sense of release, such as that evinced by the Bacchantes who are the chorus of the play, is characteristic. So is the* omophagia, *the tearing to pieces and devouring of an animal raw: the women of Thebes merely tear Pentheus [another character in the play] to pieces, but the joyous Bacchantes of the chorus speak of the delight in eating the raw flesh of a goat during their rites.*[11]

Dionysius was the god of wine, as well as fertility in general, and a counterpart to the rational Apollo. He stood for passion, spontaneity, and emotional release. To gain his great powers, one entered into communion with him by eating raw flesh, drinking, and dancing frenziedly in his honor. The power of the god was ecstatic, took worshippers out of themselves. On the other hand, the power of the god also entered, making worshippers *entheos*, or possessed by the god. This experience of ecstasy and possession seems to have been its own reward, for little in the Dionysian cult suggests such social services as divination or healing. One might say that the cult symbolized the need all people have to express their strongest emotions (including their need to step outside of "ordinary" reality) if they are to be completely whole.

The cult of Dionysius therefore parallels the function of **orgiastic rites** among many peoples: an opportunity to lay aside daily conventions and restraints, so as to give vent to pent-up aggressions and desires. More personally, it parallels the orgasmic function of sexual love, art, and mystical prayer. Precisely because the Greeks made such monumental contributions to the discovery of the human mind, the appreciation of the rational human self, their close attention to the emotional needs of the psyche stands out in clear relief. The ancient Greek rituals, festivals, dramas, and the like provided marvelous avenues to ecstasy, sublime invitations to imaginative release. Classical shamanic features may have lain underground, or flourished only in the little tradition, but the great Greek tradition was sufficiently ecstatic to show parallels with the psychodynamics of shamanism.

AFRICAN ECSTATICISM

As we have already noted, traditional African religion is hard to typify. The nonliterate character of many groups leads one to anticipate shamanic patterns, but these generally do not occur, at least not in the Siberian mode. African initiation ceremonies may play out a theme of death and resurrection. African diviners may work in trance. But priestly rites, sacred kingship, and wisdom concerns seem at least as prominent as a shamanic interest in a transformed perception. Although shamanism may not be the pivotal element in African religion, taken as a whole, that does not mean that such African phenomena as possession by a deity or attending spirit do not beg connection with shamanic psychodynamics.

For example, one finds ecstatic features in the (sapiential) divination practices of the Ndembu, a people of northwestern Zambia. Among them the diviner tends to come to that role by being afflicted by the divination spirit Kayong'u. This affliction amounts to a sign that the god has chosen him. Thus when he was about thirty-five one future diviner named Muchona became seriously ill. People thought he was going to die but a diviner diagnosed his illness as an assault of Kayong'u. The sickness itself involved asthmatic attacks and fits of trembling. The only way Muchona could find a cure was by becoming a diviner and turning his fits to good use. To divine he would employ the god's possession of him in a controlled way, making himself a conduit of the god's knowledge and power.

To make the transition to the public status of "diviner" Muchona had to pass through an initiatory rite. At night he was taken to a hut and washed with water and medicines. Near daybreak he heard the sound of drums starting up and was seized by spasms of shaking. This meant that Kayong'u had seized him. The attendants marked his body with red clay, to denote the power of Kayong'u to destroy witches (whom the Ndembu consider the source of many evils). When the drums again played Muchona fell into a second seizure. The attendants held before him a red cock, symbolizing Kayong'u's awakening within him, and Muchona bit off the cock's head. Then the attendants led forward a goat and beheaded it. Muchona lapped up the goat's blood, further expressing Kayong'u's power within him.

Kayong'u having shown himself present in full strength, the time had come to test Muchona's potential to be a diviner. The attendants put him astride a clay alligator containing several hidden objects. His task was to divine where the objects had been hidden. This Muchona did with remarkable success, so he was con-

sidered to have passed his test and shown a good aptitude for divination. Consequently he was put to study basket divination for several months and then began a professional career.

Among the Ndembu the diviner focuses mainly on descrying the causes of misfortune and death.

His job is not to foretell the future, but rather to scrutinize the past in order to identify the spiritual and human agents responsible for personal misfortunes. Since all human problems, such as infertility, illness, and trouble in hunting, are ascribed to moral conflicts within the human community, the diviner's task is to disclose acts of immorality which have provoked the vengeance of the ancestors, and to reveal the destructive hand of witches and sorcerers.[12]

To determine such acts of immorality, the Ndembu diviner often employs basket divination. Going into a mild trance, so that he can be taken over by Kayong'u, the diviner shakes his winnowing basket and reads out the patterns that emerge among its ritual pieces. The pieces or objects that rise to the top of the heap after the shaking are the most important. Each object has a symbolic message, and the combination of the several top objects becomes a cipher or interpretational key to the source of the misfortune in question. There are twenty-odd objects in the basket, representing various misfortunes, social classes, and evil motives. For example, a piece of red clay signifies enmity or holding a grudge. A piece of wood tied with bark string represents a corpse. A piece of white clay stands for the absence of witchcraft. The diviner uses these symbols to compose a story giving the etiology or causality of the misfortune. In practice this amounts to a shrewd set of guesses about the current psychological state of the patient, the current social interactions in which she is involved, the influence of past conflicts, and so forth. The objects in the divining basket become a sort of Rorschach blot, a medley begging decipherment in terms of what the patient and the community have invested in the situation.

The parallels between the Ndembu ritual and rituals of typically shamanic societies include not only the ecstatic quality of the diviner, who works by going outside normal consciousness, but also the reading of the community's psychodynamics. For example, the work of the Eskimo shaman often includes bringing the community to confess its breaches of tribal taboos, which are thought to influence the state of the game, the state of individuals' health, and the like. "Healing" is a holistic matter in most traditional societies, so healing techniques such as divination embrace social and psychological factors as much as physical and theological.

SUMMARY

To suggest the analogues to shamanism in societies dominated by sapiential concerns, we looked mainly at the folk stratum, or "little tradition" within the major sapiential complexes. Within Hinduism, for example, we found folk healing, at temples such as the Balaji, that depends on the patient's being diagnosed as possessed by an offensive spirit. Similarly, we saw among Hindus of the Himalayas divination rituals that employ an ecstatic possessed by a god. The Tibetan Buddhist ritual of the *chöd* illustrates how the tantric tradition has tried to bring occult forces to the aid of the enlightenment process. When the lama performs *chöd* he brings his faith in spiritual forces to bear on the karmic debts he owes, making the forces help him advance toward a true estimate of his own nothingness.

Chinese exorcism shows how possession by malicious spirits has been treated in yin/yang terms. When the Taoist priest sends the demons of the various directions back to their proper haunts, he reasserts human control over the psyche. Extreme cases of diabolical possession reveal the depths of evil that ecstaticism may on occasion encounter, reminding us that the shamanic imagination encounters both sides of the personality. Less dramatically, the ghosts that Maxine Hong Kingston's mother met, and the diffused quality of spiritualistic concerns that C. K. Yang reported, show a China filled with otherworldly images.

Japanese folk religion has had a strong shamanistic center, with many of the classical Siberian motifs clearly in view. Women have predominated, going through initiatory rituals of death and resurrection and contracting "marriages" with possessing gods. For the ancient Greeks, the world was alive with spiritual powers, and most shrines had attendant diviners. The *Bacchae* of Euripides suggests the wild, orgiastic forms that Greek ecstaticism occasionally would take, as well as the Greek recognition that human beings are seldom purely rational. Many traditional African tribes have used divination for diagnosis and healing. The experience of the Ndembu diviner Muchona suggests how an African diviner would become possessed by a spirit such as Kayong'u, and the Ndembu practice of basket divination hints at the psychological shrewdness of many shamanic rituals.

STUDY QUESTIONS

1. What probably is the role of the onlooking crowd in the healing rituals of the Balaji temple?

2. Why would a Tibetan lama want to undertake the *chöd* ritual?

3. What does an exorcist offer a religious community?

4. Does the diffused character of traditional Chinese religion distinguish it from the culture of twentieth-century America?

5. Why is the Japanese shamaness taught the techniques of trance?

6. What does Dionysius seem to have represented to the ancient Greek psyche?

7. What is the genius of Ndembu basket divination?

NOTES

1. See Sudhir Kakar, *Shamans, Mystics & Doctors*. New York: Alfred A. Knopf, 1982, pp. 53–88.

2. Gerald D. Berreman, *Hindus of the Himalayas*, 2d ed. Berkeley: University of California Press, 1972, p. 89.

3. Alexandra David-Neel, *Magic and Mystery in Tibet*. New York: Dover, 1971, p. 150.

4. V. R. Burkhardt, *Chinese Creeds and Customs*, vol. II. Hong Kong: South China Morning Post, 1958, p. 142. Quoted in Laurence G. Thompson, *Chinese Religion: An Introduction*, 3d ed. Belmont, Calif.: Wadsworth, 1979, p. 31.

5. See Peter Goullart, *The Monastery of the Jade Mountain*. London: John Murray, 1961, pp. 86–89.

6. Maxine Hong Kingston, *The Woman Warrior: Memoirs of a Girlhood Among Ghosts*. New York: Alfred A. Knopf, 1977, pp. 70–71.

7. C. K. Yang, *Religion in Chinese Society*. Berkeley: University of California Press, 1961, p. 298.

8. See Arthur Waley, trans., *Monkey*. New York: Grove Press, 1958.

9. Ichiro Hori, *Folk Religion in Japan*. Chicago: University of Chicago Press, 1968, pp. 203–4.

10. See Helen Hardacre, "The Transformation of Healing in the Japanese New Religions," *History of Religions*, 21/4 (May 1982), 305–20.

11. A. W. H. Adkins, "Greek Religion," *Historia Religionum*, vol. 1, ed. C. J. Bleeker and Geo Widengren. Leiden: E.J. Brill, 1969, p. 396.

12. Benjamin C. Ray, *African Religions*. Englewood Cliffs, N.J.: Prentice-Hall, 1976, p. 104.

PART

II

Prophets

By now it should be clear that the world religions resist any overly neat typology. Useful as it is to focus on the central functionaries, whose experiences have deeply stamped most of the traditions, we must always remember that typologies are somewhat abstract, never completely adequate to the profusion of concrete data. Concretely, the distinctions among shamans, prophets, and sages are seldom razor-sharp. Not only do priests, saviors, diviners, and other functionaries intrude, shamans, prophets, and sages themselves break out of our restrictions of their roles. Because they are all human beings possessed of imagination, will, and intellect, they all project symbols of hope, issue cries for justice, ponder the deep structure of things. So the descriptions we make are only approximations. They more resemble the truth than distort it, but they are not photographic reproductions. Rather they are sketches, emphases, broad strokes—outlines to get the beginning student oriented. The advanced student will need more categories and distinctions, but that is beyond the scope of an introduction to comparative religion.

In beginning perspective, the shaman stands forth as an ecstatic. Through such techniques as fasting, isolation, dancing, and taking hallucinogenic drugs, the shaman gains access to a nonordinary reality. In this reality the forces of the spiritual side of life gain an unaccustomed viv-

idness and power. Both good and bad, these forces are personified, magnified, invested with intelligence and voice. So the shaman leaves his body, flies to the gods, and has dramatic interviews with strange overlords, mortal combats with fierce foes. So the shaman sees spirits that are potential allies, becomes intimate with a god who gives her insight, and learns to make contact with the ghosts of the departed and relay their messages to the living. The shamanic initiation, with its dying to ordinary life and rising to new modes of perception, makes all this flight and extraordinary communication possible. It so transforms the candidates' imagination and perception, so draws out their special potentialities, that they are now citizens of two worlds, adventurers able to trek through several wildernesses.

The prophet has an imagination, of course, and a need to handle the ultimate themes of life and death. Among the prophet's people, as well as the shaman's, friends die, children grow ill, the ultimate mystery of things threatens to swamp the psyche. But the prophet tends to have a different sort of response to the common human condition. Where the shaman stresses a transformed imagination, the prophet stresses a transformed will or heart. Where the shaman has intercourse with nature's spirits, the prophet has intercourse with nature's Creator. Where the shaman frequently is a healer of humanity's physical ills, the

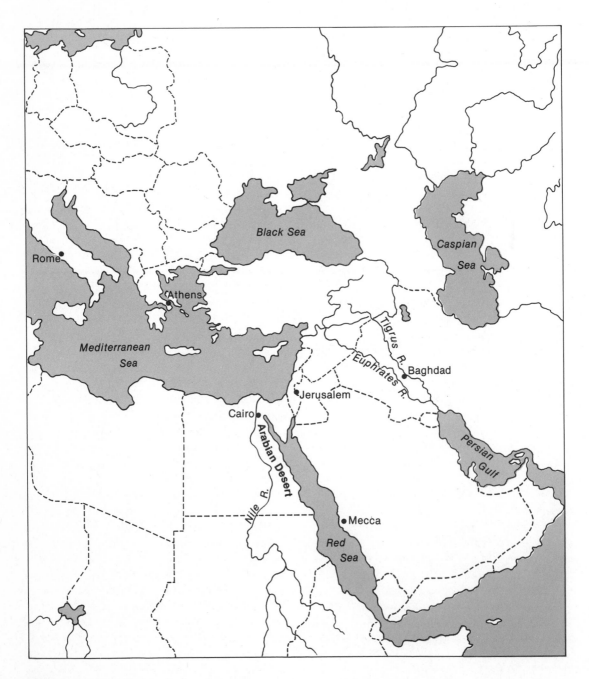

Figure 6   The Near East.

prophet frequently is a healer of humanity's social ills. While hope lures the shaman's imagination, justice lures the prophet's will. If the shaman undergoes an initiatory death and resurrection, the prophet receives new lips, cleansed as with a burning coal, to transmit the new, overwhelming reality: the Word of God.

In Part II we mainly deal with the Word of the God of the Middle Eastern patriarchs: Abraham, Isaac, and Jacob. When Moses, Jesus, and Muhammad uttered the prophecies that came to shape the Western half of the globe, it was the will of this God that they declaimed. Their Torah, Gospel, and Koran are so many versions of the revelation or self-disclosure of the new, true, singular God of their common father: Abraham, the man of faith. *Although at first Abraham saw only barrenness, faith led him to await progeny as numerous as the stars in the heavens, the grains of sand along the sea. Although ordinary perception found only injustice and wickedness, faith showed Abraham enough justice to make him plead for Sodom and Gomorrah, make his singular God a power one could forthrightly address.*

We modern people may take these prophetic features for granted, consider them staples of an old Western mythology. In their day, however, they were blazing bursts of newness, leaps of being without historical precedent. The heavens had parted. The source of things had struck humans dumb. Where shamans had found many spirits to battle and enlist, prophets had been riveted to an inexplicable One. Where shamans had sought new eyes to see with, new ears to hear, the transformed senses of prophets took their people into unknowing: No one could ever see God. So the wonder of the shaman's world gave way to the holiness of the prophet's. The blazing, communicating mystery became pure, just, loving—so much so that it convicted all humans of sin. *The recipients of God's Word felt they had to start a new venture, cleansed of the old uncleannesses.*

This is also true of prophecy outside the Middle East. In fifteenth century C.E. India, Nanak, the

founder of Sikhism, *found revelations of the True Name taking him beyond the age-old divisions between Muslims and Hindus. In sixth century B.C.E., Iran, Zoroaster, the founder of* Zoroastrianism, *had to cleanse his people with the holiness of the one Wise Lord: "As the holy one I recognized thee, O Wise Lord, when I saw thee at the beginning, at the birth of existence, appoint a recompense for deed and word: Evil reward to the evil, good to the good, through thy wisdom, at the last turning-point of creation."[1] In the prophetic strands of the shamanic and sapiential cultures, things were much the same. A prophet is a person charged to bring society under the will of the holy ultimate powers.*

NOTE

1. *Gathas*, 43:5, in the Hymns of *Zarathustra*, trans. Jacques Duchesne-Guillemin. Boston: Beacon, 1963, p. 135.

6

Judaism

MOSES

The central figure behind the Hebrew Bible and Judaism as a whole is Moses, who lived around 1300 B.C.E. Because he was the figure whom the biblical authors associated with the Exodus from Egypt and the giving of the Torah on Mount Sinai, Moses may be considered Judaism's "founder." This does not mean that Moses began the tradition that grew into "Judaism." Abraham, who lived around 1800 B.C.E., deserves that honor. But Moses delivered the Hebrews from their first great ethnic oppression, and his reception and promulgation of God's Law made him the personage held responsible for the code that defined later Jewish life. Further, by leading the Hebrews in the wilderness, taking them to the verge of the promised land, Moses opened for them the chance to become a kingly nation. Thus later generations thought of

Moses as the prophet through whom God had made the Jews his chosen people.

Among the biblical chapters that establish Moses' prophetic primacy are Exodus 19 and 20. After the Exodus, when God had parted the waves of the sea and freed the Hebrews from the Egyptians, Moses went up Mount Sinai and heard God say:

Thus you shall say to the house of Jacob, and tell the people of Israel: You have seen what I did to the Egyptians and how I bore you on eagles' wings and brought you to myself. Now therefore, if you will obey my voice and keep my covenant, you shall be my own possession among all peoples; for all the earth is mine, and you shall be to me a kingdom of priests and a holy nation. These are the words which you shall speak to the children of Israel. (Exod. 19:3–6)

Note, first, that the God with whom Moses deals is self-disclosing. He has a personality, speaks of an "I,"

Judaism: Twenty-Five Key Dates

CA. 1200 B.C.E.   Exodus from Egypt

CA. 1013–973   David

722   Fall of Northern Kingdom to Assyria

586   Fall of Southern Kingdom to Babylon

331   Alexander Conquers Palestine

168   Maccabean Revolt

63   Romans Conquer Jerusalem

70 C.E.   Romans Destroy Jerusalem

80–110   Canonization of Hebrew Scriptures

CA. 200   Promulgation of Mishnah

CA. 500   Babylonian Talmud Complete in Rough Form

640   Muslim Conquest of Middle East

1041   Death of Rashi, Bible and Talmud Commentator

CA. 1135   Birth of Maimonides

1187   Muslims Reconquer Jerusalem from Christians

1290–1309   Expulsion of Jews from England and France

1492–1496   Expulsion of Jews from Spain and Portugal

1516   Introduction of Ghetto in Venice

1521   Jewish Migrations to Palestine

1648   Massacre of Polish and Ukranian Jews

1654–1658   Jewish Communities in New Amsterdam and Rhode Island

1760   Death of Baal Shem Tov

1897   Founding of Zionist Movement

1938   Every Synagogue in Germany Burned

1948   Creation of State of Israel

and relates himself to the history of Israel. The miraculous escape from Egypt is a proof of his power. If the Hebrews choose, they can have a special relation with him. Though all the earth is his by right, he wants Israel to be special, what he calls his "own possession." The condition for this special relation is obedience to what he says. The **covenant**, or contractual bond, between Israel and God depends on Israel's obedience. If the people obey, they can expect all to go well, for they will be pleasing to the maker of all things, the ruler of all times. As the person who represents Israel and mediates this speech, Moses is the singular prophet. Later Judaism interpreted his speaking with God person-to-person as the peak of intimacy with the divine.

After hearing these words, Moses descended Mount Sinai and prepared the people for God's coming in a cloud to address them. The biblical text emphasizes the awesome power of this coming:

On the morning of the third day there were thunders and lightnings, and a thick cloud upon the mountain and a very loud trumpet blast, so that all the people who were in the camp trembled. Then Moses brought the people out of the camp to meet God; and they took their stand at the foot of the mountain. And Mount Sinai was wrapped in smoke, because the Lord descended upon it in fire; and the smoke of it went up like the smoke of a kiln, and the whole mountain quaked greatly. And as the sound of the trumpet grew louder and louder, Moses spoke, and God answered him in thunder. And the Lord came down upon Mount Sinai, to the top of the mountain; and the Lord called Moses to the top of the mountain, and Moses went up. And the Lord said to Moses, "Go down and warn the people, lest they break through to the Lord to gaze and many of them perish. (Exod. 19:16–21)

The result of God's coming, as Exodus 20 portrays it, was the Ten Commandments that came to epitomize the Torah. At the head of these commandments lay the first principle of right order: worship of the God who had led the people out of Egypt. There was only one God. The Sabbath was to be set aside as a day of rest in his honor. Because this God was holy, his people were to live in holiness, honoring their parents, not killing or committing adultery or stealing or lying.

In retrospect, we can say that the Word of God given to Moses on Mount Sinai laid out a charter that directed much of Western history. The Ten Commandments, notion of chosenness, and sense that all life passes under the review of a holy God made the people who embraced biblical religion different from their counterparts in the shamanic tribes. There are analogues, to be sure, but the covenant between Israel and God is distinctive. Despite the fact that chosenness often has been abused, the notion of intimacy with God, sharing time with God, retains a breathtaking boldness. In the history of all the religions, the Mosaic prophecy is singular.

TORAH

The Torah is the "teaching" or "instruction" necessary to keep the covenant and be God's people. As one might expect, this makes it both a powerful notion and one capable of considerable development. Within the Hebrew Bible itself, the idea that Israel was to be a "kingdom of priests" (Exod. 19:6) seems to have authorized the development of ritual legislation for the conduct of sacrifices and festivals that would answer the call to be a "holy nation." After the biblical period, the rabbis' reflections on scriptural Torah became very important, since such reflections were thought to represent an oral tradition that ran alongside of the biblical writings.

So *Torah* came to have both narrow and expansive connotations. It could be the simple path of living with the God of the fathers in faith; it could also be the etailed path of applying the Ten Commandments and other laws to all the minutiae of daily life. In either connotation, however, it was sacred and precious. God had done astounding things on Israel's behalf, the most overwhelming of which was choosing Israel's people to be his own. Guidance as to the proper response to this divine magnanimity therefore became all-important. From outward protocol to inward dispositions of the deepest heart, wise Jews wanted to respond as fully as they could.

The prophetic character of Torah shows in its emphasis on **revelation** and **morality**. The teaching that

Moses promulgated was not human legislation of his own contrivance. To the pious Jew, it was God's legislation, the expression of the divine will. The initiative was thought of as God's. The end was God's own mysterious purposes. Israel's part was not so much to understand (although of course understanding was desirable) as to obey.

When the accent of a teaching is on obedience or performance, one has a strong moral instruction. Although not denigrating the mind, the biblical and rabbinic authors favored the will. So Judaism became a rather practical religion: how one congregated with one's fellow Jews, the laws one fulfilled. By congregating loyally and fulfilling generously, one kept the human part of the bargain. If one glimpsed something of the order and reason behind the entire plan of the Creator, so much the better. It was not necessary to understand, however, in order to obey and perform.

There is a holistic or prudential quality to Torah, therefore, and this quality seems typically prophetic. The prophet aims obliquely at the minds of his hearers, but directly at their hearts. So Moses' problem with his contemporaries was their "stiff-neckedness" or grumbling refusal to obey. So the prophet Jeremiah saw that his contemporaries would only fulfill the covenant if it were renewed deep within them, as though hearts of flesh had replaced their hearts of stone. A prophetic "education," it follows, was more than data for the mind. It rather emphasized symbols for the imagination and affections, stories the whole people might indwell. What the prophetic teachers hoped to accomplish was justice: right order between the people and God, right order among the people as a community. If the people would *do* justice, live fairly and piously, Israel would prosper. Indeed, prosperity *was* little more than social fairness and pious religion. The God so generous in the past would respond to social fairness and pious religion generously. (And if he did not, Jewish sapiential authors such as Job finally concluded, that was his business.) The business of Israel, defined by the Word of God, the Torah from Sinai, was to hear and obey.

Through later history Torah became virtually synonymous with Jewish religion, as a recent short introduction to Judaism suggests.[1] Indeed, meditating on God's law became one of Judaism's primary religious practices. Rabbis were esteemed in the measure they had mastered and penetrated Torah, and the *zaddikim*, or saints, whom Hasidic Judaism revered were considered incarnations of the Torah's teaching, living manifestations of the ideas of Torah.

From the time of the destruction of the Temple in Jerusalem (70 C.E.), the veneration of Torah became central to the Jewish mainstream. Indeed, when Jews no longer sacrificed as they had in the Temple, immersion in Torah became rather ritualistic. Of course this increased the intellectual appeal of the Law, as we shall emphasize when considering the sapiential features of Judaism in Part III. Here, however, we must stress that even the very detailed study of Torah, down to the smallest jot and tittle, retained a prophetic thrust toward performance. The orthodox rationale for the ardent study of Torah was the making of holy lives. God was holy. To respond to God in a worthy fashion the faithful Jew also had to be holy: one who knew what God wanted and did it generously.

Over the years, faithful observance would make the Torah congenial. If people apprenticed themselves to the Law, the Law would finally become a source of freedom. As Confucius could say of himself that when he was seventy he could do whatever he pleased, for his will and the Way were one, so might many pious Jews have said, were their humility to have allowed it. Having a good conscience before God, enjoying a good reputation in the community, and feeling that the world made considerable sense, many traditional Jews found Torah a beloved discipline, a harness grown supple and light from long years of obedient wearing.

BIBLICAL PROPHECY

Granted the foundational primacy of Moses and the centrality of Torah, how do the most famous prophets, those whose writings are a high point of the Hebrew Bible, factor in? Most persuasively. The descriptions of their callings and the contents of their proclamations underscore the revealed and moral emphases that we have placed at the core of the prophetic type.

One of the most famous accounts of a prophetic calling occurs in Chapter 6 of the book of Isaiah. Isaiah first gives the time of his vision (the year that King Uzziah died: 742 B.C.E.). He saw the Lord sitting upon a throne up high, the extended part of His robe filling the Temple. The highest angels, the seraphim, stood above Him, covering their faces with two wings, their feet with two wings, and using two wings to fly. The seraphim called out to one another, proclaiming the holiness of the Lord. The foundations of the Temple shook and it filled with smoke. Isaiah's response stresses the sublimity of the sight: "Woe is me! For I am lost; for I am a man of unclean lips, and I dwell in the midst of a people of unclean lips; for my eyes have seen the King, the Lord of hosts." (Isa. 6:5) Then one of the seraphim flew to Isaiah and touched his

mouth with a burning coal taken from the altar. This took Isaiah's guilt away.

Then Isaiah heard the voice of the Lord:

And I heard the voice of the Lord saying, "Whom shall I send, and who will go for us?" Then I said, "Here am I! Send me." And he said, "Go, and say to this people: 'Hear and hear, but do not understand; see and see, but do not perceive.' Make the heart of this people fat, and their ears heavy, and shut their eyes; lest they see with their eyes, and hear with their ears, and understand with their hearts, and turn and be healed." (Isa. 6:8–10)

This is a very interesting commission. The prophet volunteers, is accepted to represent the Lord, but is given a puzzling, paradoxical message to proclaim: "Hear and hear, but do not understand; see and see, but do not perceive." What can this mean?

Most likely, it expresses the frustration that the prophetic vocation (or the fate of being God to wayward human beings) often entails. When the prophet gives voice to the divine Word, he or she regularly meets active resistance. People are far from overjoyed at receiving a call to justice. The divine holiness is too demanding, too insistent that people change, for the messenger of God to be welcome. Only the few who have pure hearts welcome the speech of the pure God. The majority would rather not hear, prefer to keep on with business as usual. People love their sins, the prophet learns. A large part of many souls wants the division and suffering sin brings. There is no understanding this phenomenon. It is an absurdity or irrationality stuck deep in the human heart.

For prophetic religion, as the last verse (Isa. 6:8) shows, understanding is a matter of the heart. Were the people to open their hearts, grasp the divine Word, they would have to turn: repent, be converted, make a new beginning. This would heal them of their pains and sorrows. It would take away their remorse and guilt. But many people will not bear it, strangely want their moral misery, so they choose to keep their hearts closed. Revelation and morality go together in prophetic religion. Proclaim the Word of God and you ask people for a change of heart.

Jeremiah, who worked a century after Isaiah, also reported that his prophethood began with a dramatic calling:

Now the word of the Lord came to me saying, "Before I formed you in the womb I knew you, and before you were born I consecrated you; I appointed you a prophet to the nations." Then I said, "Ah, Lord God! Behold, I do not know how to speak, for I am only a youth." But the Lord said to me, "Do not say, 'I am only a youth'; for to all to whom I send you you shall go, and whatever I command you you shall speak. Be not afraid of them, for I am with you to deliver you, says the Lord." Then the Lord put forth his hand and touched my mouth; and the Lord said to me, "Behold, I have put my words in your mouth. See, I have set you this day over nations and over kingdoms, to pluck up and to break down, to destroy and to overthrow, to build and to plant." (Jer. 1:4–10)

The implication of this calling is that God had predestined Jeremiah to prophethood, despite Jeremiah's reluctance or sense of not being fit, and that God would stand by his prophet. Years later, after many encounters with kings and commoners, most of whom had resisted his preaching, Jeremiah ventured into the same paradoxical region of the human heart that Isaiah had had to visit. People need new faculties, he realized, if they are to see what they should see, hear what they ought to hear, have the understanding that a covenant relationship with God entails. In fact, the only way that Jeremiah could see his mission's succeeding would be if God were to redo the covenant, reach into Israel's heart and forgive its iniquity: "This is the covenant which I will make with the house of Israel after those days, says the Lord: I will put my law within them, and I will write it upon their hearts; and I will be their God, and they shall be my people. And no longer shall each man teach his neighbor and teach his brother, saying, 'Know the Lord,' for they shall all know me, from the least of them to the greatest, says the Lord; for I will forgive their iniquity, and I will remember their sin no more.' " (Jer. 31:33–34)

MEDIEVAL JUDAISM

What we are calling *medieval Judaism* is the talmudic religion that flourished between the biblical period and the modernization of Judaism in the nineteenth century. The Talmud is a collection of the rabbis' interpretations of Torah. It has roots in the legal materials of the Bible that became increasingly important after the time of Jeremiah, when some of the people returned to Israel from their captivity in Babylon. The wisdom portions (the "Writings") of the Hebrew Bible also contributed to the rabbis' sober style. But the special catalyst in the development of the Talmud was the dispersion, or **diaspora**, of the Jews that occurred after the fall of Jerusalem and the destruction of the Temple in 70 C.E. Among the diaspora communities the need grew to adapt Torah to different circumstan-

ces. The synagogue became a house of study as much as a house of prayer, and the rabbis who interpreted the Law sought the counsel of the most eminent teachers, both present and past. With time this counsel became a great corpus of interpretation and teaching that begged codification. Around 200 C.E. Rabbi Judah compiled the *Mishnah* ("teaching"), which collected much oral teaching, and around 500 C.E. the Babylonian *Talmud* ("learning"), composed of the Mishnah and the *Gemara* (debates on the Mishnah), gave Judaism a sort of encyclopedia of Torah interpretation.

The prophetic strains of Jewish religion manifest themselves in the Talmud's continuity with scripture. As a collection of the oral Torah thought to have been parallel with the Hebrew Bible, the Talmud was, in a sense, revealed. As a body of legal and edifying material directly aimed at enabling Jews to live a holy life, it was thoroughly moral and practical. This shows in the *Pirke Aboth*, a short ethical tractate of the Mishnah much beloved by traditional Jews. The very first verses of the first chapter are replete with the sense of carrying on a Word of God or teaching that calls the chosen people to holy living:

Moses received Torah from Sinai and delivered it to Joshua, and Joshua to the Elders, and the Elders to the Prophets, and the Prophets delivered it to the Men of the Great Synagogue. These said three things: Be deliberate in judging, and raise up many disciples, and make a hedge for Torah. Simeon the Just was of the survivors of the Great Synagogue. He used to say: Upon three things the world standeth: upon Torah, upon worship, and upon the showing of kindness. Antigonos of Socho received from Simeon the Just. He used to say: Be not like servants who serve the master for condition of receiving a gift, but be like servants who serve the master not on condition of receiving a gift. And let the fear of Heaven be upon you.[2] (Pirke Aboth 1:1–3)

Torah, the beloved focus of the rabbis, goes back to Moses. Moses handed it on (the basic meaning of *tradition*). What the rabbis of the diaspora and later medieval Jewish life did therefore had ancient precedent. They were followers in the footsteps of the biblical heroes. Their communities depended upon them for guidance just as the communities of Moses and the biblical prophets had depended upon Moses, Isaiah, and Jeremiah. If the rabbis seemed to live in tamer times, without the callings from God that Isaiah and Jeremiah received and with less resistance to their message, the core of their task remained that of their predecessors. They were to center the people in God's words, the worship of God, and fraternal charity. The people would survive, keep the covenant, fulfill their divine destiny in the measure they retained these three foci.

The notion that Talmud was a "hedge for Torah," providing protection, explains much of the medieval rabbis' motivation. The further they could extend what a holy life entailed, the more precisely they could specify it, the better their people's chance of pleasing God. So they developed detailed rules for how to keep the Sabbath; how to maintain a **kosher** (fitting, pure) diet; how to deal with irregularities in ritual; how to deal with civil disputes; and the like. Of course this involved a delicate balance, since preoccupation with detail could obscure the spirit. But the desire to keep the people as far from laxity as possible drove the rabbis to broader and broader legislation, deeper and deeper pursuit of the heart of the Torah's matter.

A good illustration of this development, and of the way that rabbinic interests could become encyclopedic, is what happended in the case of bodily care:

There is a Rabbinic saying, "Physical cleanliness leads to spiritual purity" (A.Z. 20b), and the cleanliness referred to is internal, not external, and means regular purgations. We shall see below that great importance was attached to regular motions as a rule of health, because they had moral reactions. That is why it is remarked: "Who delays answering nature's call is guilty of transgressing the command, 'Ye shall not make yourselves abominable' (Lev. xx. 25) (Mak. 16b); and "A disciple of the sages should not reside in a city in which there is not a privy" (Sanh. 17b). Without such purgation the mind is unable to concentrate on the devotion which should be offered to God in the morning. Therefore it was taught: "Whoever wishes to receive upon himself the yoke of the kingdom of heaven in perfection should first have evacuation, then wash his hands, put on the phylacteries, and offer his prayers" (Ber. 15a).[3]

The material content of the text speaks for itself. The form of citing previous authorities (the abbreviations list the places in the Talmud or Scriptures from which the quotations come) shows the traditional quality of premodern Judaism. The overall goal—the pious life, defined in terms of proper reverence for God, prayer, and justice toward one's neighbor—shows the prophetic stamp.

MODERN JUDAISM

The Talmud remained the font of Jewish life well into the nineteenth century. Indeed, it continues to shape Judaism today, but since the nineteenth century the tenets of modern European science have influenced most educated Jews away from the unquestioned acceptance of talmudic authority that prevailed in medieval times. As the new science uncovered the antiquity of the earth, the old view that the earth was about six thousand years old came into crisis.[4] As the new philosophy stressed the autonomy of human nature, its need to take charge of its own affairs, the traditional reliance on an ancient legal code came in for serious questioning. This did not mean that, prior to World War II, most European Jews did not center their lives in Torah. Rather, more and more Jews found themselves having to contend with ideas the Babylonian Talmud never entertained.

The Jews who struggled to retain the old ways came to be called *Orthodox*. No doubt many different opinions and practices were comprised by this umbrella, but common to them all was the instinct that in any confrontation between Torah and modernity, Torah deserved one's first loyalty. Still, few people refused to open Orthodoxy to the changing times. Indeed, in a "challenge" to Orthodoxy Emanuel Rackman has stressed the diversity that traditionally has been allowed:

Orthodoxy is not monolithic: it requires acknowledgment of the divine origin of the commandments and firm resolve to fulfill them; however, it also permits great latitude in the formulation of doctrines, the interpretation of Biblical passages, and the rationalization of mitzvot [obligations]. It is not difficult to demonstrate that the giants of the Tradition held widely divergent views on the nature of God, the character of historic revelation, and the uniqueness of the Jewish faith. Not all of these views could possibly be true, and yet not one of them may be deemed heretical, since one respected authority or another has clung to it. The only heresy is the denial that God gave the Written and Oral Law to His people, who are to fulfill its mandates and develop their birthright in accordance with its own built-in methodology and authentic exegesis.[5]

If Orthodoxy, the most cautious of Judaism's subtraditions, has allowed great doctrinal latitude, centering itself in fulfilling the mandates of Torah rather than in imposing a single understanding of those mandates, all the more so have Reform and Conservative Judaism tried to accommodate Judaism to modernity. In fact, they have stressed that Jewish practice (ritual life, concrete ethics, relations with the surrounding Gentile environment) should be more realistic than Orthodox practice often seemed to be. As Abraham Feldman has described it:

Reform is classical Judaism asserting anew the right and the duty of accelerating the process of progress and change where changes seem to be necessary. If some customs and practices are no longer meaningful, then they are no longer useful, and to cling to them mechanically or to acknowledge them as valid whilst they are largely neglected is to endanger the very survival of Jews and Judaism. In the absence of an authoritative legislative body continuing to function, and thus to be compelled to wait for the slow progress of Halachic change through responsa *[answers from distant authorities], which often takes generations, is to expose the patient to danger. Therefore, Reform's principal contribution is the decision to keep Judaism forever contemporary, and to keep it responsive to the religious needs of successive generations. Its purpose is not to preserve, let us say, in Hartford, or in Brooklyn, or in Chicago, or even in the United States of America, all the forms of the Judaism of Poland, of Galicia, Hungary, Rumania or Lithuania, but to keep Judaism* Jewish *in content whilst adapting the traditional forms to contemporary life, and creating new forms as needs require. Some day, Judaism in the State of Israel might become adapted to the new life and challenge of its needs and ways.*[6]

Between Orthodoxy and Reform lies Conservative Judaism, which like them is not a monolith but a cluster of like-minded people who retain considerable individual variety. In terms of the patterns of religious tradition developed in our discussion, the distinguishing feature of Conservative Judaism is a veneration of *halakah* (talmudic law) that is tempered with an emphasis on making it flexible enough to serve local conditions effectively. The veneration of halakah places the Conservative Jew close to the Orthodox, as the desire to adapt the traditional law to local conditions places him or her close to the Reform. One method that some Conservative Jews have advanced for adapting halakah is *takkanah*: "ordinance promulgated by local Rabbinic authorities in post-talmudic times, meant to bolster religious and moral life, and supplementing a Torah regulation."[7] Insofar as takkanah allowed for local adaptations, it might be progressive. Insofar as it tried to keep Torah the regulatory force organizing daily life, it might be traditional.

Throughout modernity, then, Judaism wrestled with the question of how to adapt the Torah. Apart from a minute group of extremists on both the left and the right, the mainstream tried to make the traditional legislation pertinent to changed modern times. Almost always, however, the old prophetic ideals kept most religious Jews pursuing a discipline, a cod-

ified way of life, that would make them faithful to God's choice of them. Almost always, doing the will of the Holy God remained the high goal.

JEWISH SOCIAL THOUGHT

By social thought here we mean the general understanding of society that Judaism has shown over the centuries. In this meaning, perhaps the first thing to be said is that Judaism has been a matter of the community more than a matter of individuals. For example, most Jewish prayer is in the plural number, something uttered on behalf of the whole group. Most understandings of Jewish law, divine revelation, and the purpose of human life have stressed the collectivity. In contrast to Christianity, Buddhism, and several other world religions, Judaism has not developed a celibate or solitary pathway for inward individuals. In common with Islam and Christianity, it has made social justice and almsgiving strong obligations, ordinary virtues and expectations. Traditional Jewish perusal of the Talmud took place in groups, rather than in solitary studies; the synagogue was much more a place for social acts of worship than a place for lonely private vigils.

This is not to say, of course, that Judaism has had no place for individual differences or needs, nor that Jews never sought peace and quiet for personal perusal of their faith. The Jewish God was thought to have chosen the Jews as a people, to have made a convenant with a group; therefore, the existence and needs of the people took precedence over the existence and needs of the individual. Relatedly, the immortality that most Jews conceived was the continuance of the community line, rather than the continuance of the individual personality. Not surprisingly, therefore, justice bulked large in Jewish social thought. As a heritage from the biblical prophets, Jewish thinkers received a mandate to urge their people toward fairness, equity, mutual considerateness, and mutual support. Let us consider some of the implications of the Jewish understanding of justice.

"It has been widely stated that justice is the moral value which singularly characterizes Judaism both conceptually and historically. Historically, the Jewish search for justice begins with biblical statements like 'Justice (Heb. *zedek*), justice shall ye pursue' (Deut. 16:20). On the conceptual side, justice holds a central place in the Jewish world view, and many other basic Jewish concepts revolve around the notion of justice."[8] Theologically, the main attribute of God's action is justice (Gen. 18:25, Ps. 9:5). The purpose of the divine commandments to human beings is the establishment of justice (Ps. 119:137–44). When people obey the divine laws, and show one another justice, they help to fulfill the divine plan. When the Messiah comes, universal justice finally will reign.

So basic is justice in the Hebrew Bible that it is virtually synonmous with holiness, very often is paired with "grace." Later the rabbis associated justice with charitable works, linking it with the trust and integrity that doing good creates. When people do works of justice, they become builders of peace, agents of redemption. Thus there is little virtue that Judaism does not instinctively connect with zedek. Were people to stand in the proper relations that justice implies— obedient to God, fair to one another—most of our social problems would melt away. The biblical prophets saw this and prayed that justice would roll down like a mighty stream. True religion, the rabbis also saw, means embodying in one's rituals and neightborly dealings the truth, the simple rightness, that "justice" best connotes.

In modern times, the justice of God continued to be urgent, as Jews suffered special persecutions in Eastern Europe (*pogroms*) and then the "holocaust" of six millions by the Nazis during World War II. In the Bible Job had sketched some of the issues in the question of God's justice, but the sufferings of Jews in modern times (which built on medieval precedent) sharpened this question to a razor's edge. Indeed, for some contemporary Jewish thinkers, the Nazi holocaust has circumscribed the notion of God.[9] In the wake of the death camps of Auschwitz, Dachau, Belsen, and the rest, what sense does it make to speak of a God who cares for the Jewish people, a God capable of guiding history? A terrible dilemma seems to have arisen: Either God is powerless to change the course of history, or God doesn't care that his people suffer. Perhaps the most eloquent spokesman on this issue has been the novelist Elie Wiesel. Himself a prisoner in the death camps, one of the millions who lost family and friends, Wiesel has slowly worked his way back from an initial despair and loss of faith. Resetting himself in his Hasidic roots, he seems recently to have been trying on the notion that we can place God on trial, even find God guilty, and still continue to pray and do justice.[10]

On the more horizontal, simply human level, Torah of course has always sought justice. The halakic laws were intended to make people observant of the commands that would bring the community prosperity and peace. Many of the rabbis' judgments and teaching stories illustrated the kindness, concern, and restraint that pious faith ought to generate. If the people were to walk the way of life, reject the way of death, they

had to render one another justice. So justice has been at the center of traditional Jewish social thought.

JEWISH PERSONAL THOUGHT

By personal thought here we mean a sense of the self, an understanding of the personal drama. Thus the question before us is, How has Judaism tended to regard the individual's journey through time? The answer, mainly shaped by the prophets, seems to be: as an invitation to love God, and so find the world to be good. For the prophets, human beings are most essentially defined by their inner connectedness to God. It is in knowing God that individuals learn how things hang together. One therefore could say that traditional Judaism depends less on psychology than on theological anthropology. Its knowledge of the soul did not come by studying the soul in isolation, but by studying the soul in relation to God.

Leo Baeck has put the matter this way:

To know the nature of God means to the prophets to know that he is just and incorruptible; that he is merciful, gracious and long-suffering; that he tries the heart of man; and that he has destined man for the good. Through knowledge of God we thereby learn what man should be, through the Divine is revealed the human. The ways of the Lord are the ways which man should follow—"and they shall keep the way of the Lord, to do justice and judgment" (Gen. 18:19). Hence a prerequisite to the understanding of man is an understanding of what God gave to him and commands him to do.[11]

When the individual set to putting the knowledge of God into practice, the tradition offered him or her considerable guidance. Among the pivotal matters this guidance spotlighted were the Sabbath, Torah, good deeds, and marriage.[12] The Sabbath periodized the individual's time. Even more incisively than the way the annual festivals took the individual through the year, the Sabbath was the peak and central reference for each week. The days prior to the Sabbath were for preparation, both practical and spiritual. The days after the Sabbath carried the Sabbath's glow and depended upon its recharging of the individual's faith. No matter how poor or pressured the individual's circumstances, the Sabbath offered a zone of respite. It was a time for the family to cease its busyness, leave off its squabbling, even cede its worrying to the peace of its Lord. Like a bride adorned for her husband, the Sabbath came majestically each Friday at sundown. When the mother of the family lit the Sabbath candles, and the family sat down to the special meal, things for once were as faith said they should be. God was in his heaven, taking care of what finally mattered, so all was right with the world.

One of the customary occupations of the Sabbath was studying Torah. Another was setting aside time for conjugal lovemaking. Torah housed all the treasures of Jewish faith, so what better way to use God's pre-scribed rest than by immersing oneself in the books that praised God's goodness, recalled God's bounty to Israel? All work was to fall away. Sabbath was time for feeding the spirit. The great food for the Jewish spirit was the Torah, so in synagogue and home alike Torah was the main fare. By and large, women did not study Torah. In each home the father was the local rabbi. But if men were thought of as representing the Torah's mind, women were thought of as representing the Torah's heart. So women sacrificed themselves that their husbands and sons might study. They cooked, cleaned, and often ran businesses. Maintaining the good health of their families and making good mar-riages for their children were constant concerns.

Marriage was the normal estate in Judaism, so much so that being single was a cause for pity. Both un-married men and unmarried women figured among the stories of the misfortunate, those whom life had denied a chance to be fully human. The greatest bless-ing of a home was its children. The later Jews always retained the biblical command to increase and mul-tiply. To raise up children who were learned and pious was to fulfill one of the Lord's primary expectations. The satisfactions of the spouses in marriage were im-portant, but in some ways secondary. The tradition realized that unhappy, frustrated spouses were not likely to raise happy children. It realized that work and sexual love are primordial human needs. But it expected both work and sexual love to be fitted to the frame sketched in the Torah, subordinated to the de-mands and joys of generous faith.

Among the demands and joys of generous faith were good deeds. To be a good Jew meant assuming one's share of the community's burdens. On the whole, most Jews could not avoid these burdens. They tended to live in homogenous groupings, whether ghettoes or towns freely formed, that made little place for the individualist, the semiparticipant or marginal member. Neighbors tended to overflow one another's homes, overflow one another's lives. News and gossip flew back and forth constantly. The wealth of the fortunate exposed them to demands for generous almsgiving. A birth, marriage, or funeral was something to cele-brate in the whole. So the individual worked out his or her Godward definition quite socially. The Sabbath,

the Torah, marriage, and good deeds joined the knowl-edge of God to the knowledge of one's neighbor.

JEWISH ECOLOGY

By ecology here we mean a people's relation to nature, its sense of the physical world. All traditional peoples have had an implicit ecology, since all have interacted with the floods and the fields, the sources of their food and the sources of their weather. Only in recent, sci-entific times, however, has ecology become under-stood. As biologists and naturalists have studied the interactions among living things, they have seen more and more connections. Gradually it has dawned that nature groups things in ecosystems: dynamic yet hom-eostatic wholes composed of functionally interrelated parts. As pollution has come to blur the postmodern horizon, people at large have come to sense that some-thing ecological has gone very wrong.

Looking backward at the roots of Western tech-nology, some scholars postulate that much of the prob-lem lies in the Old Testament. The reception given to texts such as Gen. 1:28, where human beings are told to "be fruitful and multiply, and fill the earth and subdue it," might look like a mainspring of the recent technological rapaciousness of the West. If the biblical God is understood as having placed the natural world before human beings as raw material for them to de-velop at their good pleasure, the biblical God becomes indictable for a great deal of ecological devastation.

The main response of scripture scholars to this sort of charge has been defensive.[13] As they read the He-brew Bible, the Genesis account made human beings stewards of creation, not entrepreneurs set loose to exploit nature as they would. Granted the anthropo-centricity of the Bible, in which the drama of human beings is more central than the fate of cosmic evo-lution, it remains true that the Lord of Israel was also the Lord of nature, the God of history was the beautiful source of the restful waters and everlasting hills. The Psalms are replete with natural imagery. Job has the morning stars sing together and the beasts of the deep witness to God's power. For Jeremiah the fate of the land is linked with the fate of the people, so the des-olations of the people show in the untended land. For the Pentateuchal writings, the first five books of the Bible attributed to Moses, the land is God's special promise to Israel, an inalienable part of the covenant.

In the biblical period, therefore, Israel came to realize that people were separate from nature.[14] The land was beautiful, and a gracious gift of God, but the land was of lesser interest and importance than the people. Space went together with time. Nature was God's province as much as history. But time and history predominated over space and nature. Human beings, creatures a little less than the angels, were players in a theater of sin and grace, loss and redemption, that nature only shaped peripherally. The greater religious significance of nature was the way it relativized human affairs. Time and tide, waiting for nothing human, put a wide border around human pretentiousness. If people lost perspective, the everlasting hills could put them back into line. Ultimately, of course, only God gave true perspective. The grass withered, the flowers faded; only the Word of the Lord endured forever. But nature lasted longer than mortal humans, so nature helped mortal humans take the long view, estimate things under the aspect of eternity.

Medieval Judaism was less interested in nature than was biblical religion, since by late medieval times many Jews had moved away from land-owning and land-working. Scholarship, medicine, and commerce regularly had more prestige. The talmudic authors divided on both the general question of manual labor and the specific question of working the land. Some praised manual labor as a defense against devilish idleness and a fulfillment of the Lord's command to earn one's bread by the sweat of one's brow. Others thought that manual labor developed the animal side of human nature, in contrast to the spiritual development that Torah or even profane studies brought. There was no question of condemning work as such, including the work of farming. There was no question of withdrawing the land from the covenant or forgetting the assertion of Genesis that God saw that his creation was very good. But there was a question of what emphasis the pious Jew ought to place, had he the choice, and the weight of the rabbinic tradition fell on the side of culture, away from the side of nature.

Even through modern and contemporary times, the old battles of the biblical prophets with the nature deities of Israel's Caananite neighbors seem to have retained a residual hold on the Jewish psyche. When Yahweh separated himself from the **baals** and **astartes** of Israel's neighbors, the cycles of nature fell into some disrepute. The prophets lashed the people for recidivism (going back to the old nature religion), and the rabbis were sons of the prophets enough to fear too close an absorption with nature. So the rabbis' God, too, was as far from the nature deities as the heavens from the earth.

Today Judaism continues to take a complex position toward nature. At its best, this position is beautifully balanced: Nature is very good, but not the first arena of God's revelation. Abraham Joshua Heschel recently expressed this view admirably:

Biblical thinking succeeded in subduing the universal tendency of ancient man to endow nature with a mysterious potency like mana and orenda by stressing the indication in all of nature of the wisdom and goodness of the Creator. One of the great achievements of the prophets was the repudiation of nature as an object of adoration. They tried to teach us that neither nature's beauty nor grandeur, neither power nor the state, neither money nor things of space are worthy of our supreme adoration, love, sacrifice, or self-dedication. Yet the desanctification of nature *did not in any way bring about an alienation of nature. It brought man together with all things in a fellowship of praise. The Biblical man could say that he was "in league with the stones of the field" (Job 5:23).*[15]

JERUSALEM

Probably the single place that best focuses Jewish social thought, personal thought, and ecology is Jerusalem,[16] capital of the contemporary state of Israel. When the Jews gained a new national homeland in 1948, fulfilling decades of longing focused on **Zionism**,[17] Jerusalem again became the real center of Jewish geography. All the biblical overtones of the City of David lie inside the old walls. Outside the old walls lie the demographics of the new situation in the midst of a hostile Arab population. Historically, Jerusalem summons images of kingship, prosperity, a golden age, a pawn of Christians and Muslims. Sociologically, Jerusalem gives the Jewish people a realized dream, a place of their own to which next year the Messiah just might come.

Psychologically, contemporary Jews are apt to overflow with feelings about Jerusalem, some of them quite conflicting. On the one hand, there is a pull to support the powers in the new capital trying to promote Israel's survival and prosperity. On the other hand, there are the facts that the majority of Jews still live outside Israel, quite often more prosperously than they would live inside Israel, and that not all the things done in the Knesset (parliament) in Jerusalem merit full support. Ecologically, the policies emanating from the Knesset have made much land that had been barren spring back to green life. Yet on the West Bank the policies of intruding into the land have become so mixed with political and religious aims that agronomy can seem a military weapon. Very tangled, then, the web woven from Jerusalem. Very much a patchwork, the many materials of contemporary Israelite morality.

Figure 7   Jerusalem: The Western Wall, with the Dome of the Rock in the background. Photo by J. T. Carmody.

In prophetic perspective, Jerusalem is almost bound to be an ambiguous symbol. The classical prophets often found themselves pitted against kings ensconced in Jerusalem, as spiritual spokesmen opposing worldly powers. Typically, the prophets feared that worldly reliances, above all military recourses, would keep the people from pure religion, weaken Israel's firm faith in God's provision. Equally typically, the kings rejected the prophets' perspective, preferring to play power politics. The resultant split of the Kingdom, and then fall of the southern portion of Babylon, stands in biblical history as a great vindication of the prophets. Through the many centuries when Jews had no dominant power over their ancestral land, and the many more centuries when they mainly lived outside it in the diaspora, the priests and rabbis could deal with questions of power politics rather distantly, as theoretical more than practical issues. Today, however, the religious and secular sides of Jewish faith again have come to swords' point in Jerusalem, as the report

of the Special Commission of Inquiry into Israel's responsibility for the 1982 slaying of hundreds of Palestinian refugees in Lebanese camps suggested.

The commission worked in the context of a Jewish law and tradition whose roots extend back to the Bible. Modern jurisprudence was the dominant idiom, but the talmudic heritage was never far away. The result was an arresting confluence of democratic self-criticism and religious sensitivity. For although the proximate blame for the massacre fell squarely on non-Jewish shoulders (the actual murderers were right-wing Christians), the commission found leading Jewish military and political officials guilty of indifference and imprudence. Because the highly developed traditional moral code held that one who is able to avert an evil and does not do so is somewhat responsible for that evil, leading generals, the defense minister, and even the prime minister came in for the committee's blame. The matter of the findings was deeply disturbing to many Jews, since it confirmed their suspicions that the aggressive war in Lebanon, with its terrible destructive bombings, had been pitting the nation's soul. But the form of the findings, their deep and honest self-criticism, was an act of healing, a step of therapy and hope. As many commentators the world over pointed out, there are only a handful of other nations in the world where such a public self-criticism would be conceivable, and few if any of them are in the Middle East.

So the prophetic emphases on justice, conversion to God, and walking in the ways of truth continue to shape daily life on the streets of Jerusalem. Down those streets hurry bearded Hasidic Jews and visiting Americans, devout religionists and Jews nearly completely secularized. The land and the ethnic solidarity have become lodestones to chosen people all over the globe. The Jews of European origin (Ashkenazim) who have been our main reference point increasingly find they must accommodate to the Jews of Iberian and Oriental origin (Sephardim). Within a small country, an amazing variety obtains. Fundamentalists going out to establish new settlements think they are fulfilling a biblical mandate. Twenty miles away in the Hebrew University professors teach that such fundamentalism is foolish. Meanwhile, the specter of the death camps hovers outside Jerusalem at Yad Vashem, the memorial set in the nearby hills. The intransigence and militarism of the Israeli hawks is inconceivable without this specter, which has led many to vow "Never again!"

It would be presumptuous for us to venture an opinion about how an Isaiah or a Jeremiah likely would respond to the new Israel. Times change and prophetic judgments with them. Still, the words of Second Isaiah seem wholly relevant: "Thus says the Lord: 'Keep justice, and do righteousness, for soon my salvation will come, and my deliverance be revealed. Blessed is the man who does this, and the son of man who holds it fast, who keeps the sabbath, not profaning it, and keeps his hand from doing any evil.'" (2 Isa. 56:1–2)

SUMMARY

We began our study of Judaism with Moses, the personage whom Jewish tradition came to consider the archetypal prophet. By serving as the spokesman for the awesome deity portrayed in Exodus, Moses mediated the covenant, Torah, and passage to the promised land, as he had led the Exodus from Egypt. Through Moses, the people received a spectacular invitation to live with a holy God. The basis for such living was the Torah, the teaching that elaborated the Ten Commandments and rest of God's guidance. Torah was both revealed and moral: the Word of God and an instruction demanding enactment. From its prophetic origins, Torah expanded to become a full legislation for all of daily life.

The biblical exponents of Torah include the famous writing prophets. For many of them prophecy came as a disturbing call. Isaiah saw the holy God surrounded by the Seraphim and found that his lips had to be purified. Jeremiah was pushed forward despite his youth. Both bore down on the moral dimension and so encountered the paradoxes and turnings of the human heart. For the rabbis who dominated medieval Judaism, the heart remained the crux. Still, the rabbis were convinced that their legal labors built a necessary hedge for Torah, to keep the actions the heart prompted in check. Modern Jews had to contend with ideas and forces that neither the biblical prophets nor the medieval rabbis had conceived. The Orthodox, Reformed, and Conservative responses to the modern situation hint at the variety in the Jewish tradition.

As a worldview, Judaism has developed rich sociological, psychological, and ecological notions. Social thought has been to the fore, since the basic instinct has been to think first of the group, and the primary virtue has been social justice. Jewish psychology has rooted the self in its connection to God. Through observing the Sabbath, studying Torah, marrying generously, and devoting oneself to good deeds, the individual Jew could grow mature and fulfilled. Relations with the land were always resonant with the biblical promises, but the biblical anthropocentrism meant that the land was somewhat peripheral to the major Jewish interests. In itself the land was God's good creature and gift, but not a place intrinsically divine.

Today much of the prophetic tradition remains visible in Jerusalem. The land is again in Jewish hands, Jewish psyches again look to the ancient capital, and the fifteen Jewish millions worldwide center their collective body where David ruled. The pressures of recent Jewish experiences, from the World War II death camps to the recent Middle Eastern wars, show how demanding the prophetic tradition can be. Even when rulers in Jerusalem fail the stringent biblical standards, however, the old prophetic proclamations inspire other Jews to judge them correctly.

STUDY QUESTIONS

1. How do the verses from Exod. 19:16–21 paint the Jewish God?

2. In what sense is Torah holistic or prudential?

3. Explain the paradoxical message Isaiah was given to proclaim.

4. Why did the rabbis want to make a hedge for Torah?

5. What is the main inspiration of Reform Judaism?

6. What does the Jewish insistence on justice say about Jewish social thought?

7. How did Sabbath observance shape the Jewish psyche?

8. Is the Bible part of the cause of our current ecological problems?

9. How valid is the traditional Jewish notion that one who can help avert an evil and does not is guilty of that evil?

10. Describe a prophetic personality.

NOTES

1. See Jacob Neusner, *The Way of Torah: An Introduction to Judaism*, 3d ed. Belmont, Calif.: Wadsworth, 1979.

2. R. Travers Herford, trans., *The Ethics of the Talmud: Sayings of the Fathers*. New York: Schocken, 1962, pp. 19–23.

3. Abraham Cohen, *Everyman's Talmud*. New York: Schocken, 1975, p. 239.

4. See Emanuel Rackman, "A Challenge to Orthodoxy," in *The Life of Torah: Readings in the Jewish Religious Experience*, ed. Jacob Neusner. Belmont, Calif.: Wadsworth, 1974, p. 161.

5. Ibid., p. 162.

6. Abraham Feldman, "What is Reform Judaism?", in Rackman, *The Life of Torah*, p. 169.

7. Ben Isaacson, *Dictionary of the Jewish Religion*. New York: Bantam, 1979, p. 157.

8. Steven S. Schwarzschild, "Justice," in Geoffrey Wigoder et al., *Jewish Values*. Jerusalem: Keter, 1974, p. 194.

9. See Richard L. Rubenstein, *After Auschwitz*. Indianapolis: Bobbs-Merrill, 1966.

10. See Robert McAfee Brown, *Elie Wiesel*. Notre Dame, Ind.: University of Notre Dame Press, 1983.

11. Leo Baeck, *The Essence of Judaism*. New York: Schocken, 1961, pp. 35–36.

12. See Mark Zborowski and Elizabeth Herzog, *Life Is with People*. New York: Schocken, 1962.

13. See, for example, James Barr, "Man and Nature: The Ecological Controversy and the Old Testament," in *Ecology and Religion*, ed. D. Spring and E. Spring. New York: Harper & Row, 1974, pp. 48–75.

14. See Walter Brueggemann, *The Land*. Philadelphia: Fortress, 1977.

15. Abraham Joshua Heschel, *God in Search of Man*. New York: Farrar, Straus and Giroux, 1977, pp. 90–91. *Mana* and *orenda* are Polynesian and Algonquin words for the sacred power that may manifest itself anywhere in nature.

16. See Michael Avi-Jonah et al., *Jerusalem*. Jerusalem: Keter, 1973.

17. See Getzel Kressel et al., *Zionism*. Jerusalem: Keter, 1973.

7

Christianity

Jesus
Gospel
Evangelical Prophecy
Medieval Christianity
Modern Christianity
Christian Social Thought
Christian Personal Thought
Christian Ecology
Geneva
Summary
Study Questions
Notes.

JESUS

Christianity derives from the prophecy and person of Jesus, even more directly than Judaism derives from the prophecy and person of Moses. Jesus, of course, is mediated to us by the New Testament, just as Moses is mediated by the Hebrew Bible. In both cases, many hands have worked over the biographical materials, and much faith has poured into the casting of the founder's image. Nonetheless, if Jesus seems less legendary than Moses, it is because the New Testament more directly reflects his personality than the Hebrew Bible reflects the personality of Moses. In the case of Jesus, the principal accounts were written within a generation of his life and death. In the case of Moses, tens of generations intervened. However, in both cases a striking God directed an exceptional man to recast a people's faith. Moses mediated a covenant that used the aura of the Exodus from Egypt to bind the people

to their holy God. Jesus used a sense of filial intimacy with God to proclaim the dawn of a new era, the Kingdom of God, in which all people might respond to the divine as to their father and might respond to one another as siblings.

Mark, chronologically the first gospel of the Christian **canon**, shows us the specialness of Jesus' relation to God: "In those days Jesus came from Nazareth of Galilee and was baptized by John in the Jordan. And when he came up out of the water, immediately he saw the heavens opened and the Spirit descending upon him like a dove; and a voice came from heaven, 'Thou art my beloved Son; with thee I am well pleased.'" (Mark 1:9–11) For primitive Christianity, therefore, Jesus did what he did, preached and healed as his contemporaries remembered him to have done, because of a special opening of the heavens, a special descent of the divine Spirit. Like the prophets of old, he had received a commission and guidance from the divine. What he preached and enacted was not from

Christianity: Twenty-Five Key Dates

CA. 30 C.E.   Death of Jesus of Nazareth

CA. 65   Death of Apostle Paul

CA. 95   Last of New Testament Writings

CA. 100–165   Justin Martyr, Leading Apologist

CA. 185–254   Origen, Leading Theologian

313   Christians Freed of Legal Persecution

325   First Council of Nicaea

354–430   Augustine, Leading Theologian

451   Council of Chalcedon

CA. 480–550   Benedict, Founder of Western Monasticism

CA. 540–604   Pope Gregory I, Founder of Medieval Papacy

787   Second Council of Nicaea [Last One that the Orthodox Church Considers Ecumenical]

869–870   Rome Declares Photius in Schism

1054   Mutual Anathemas between Rome and Constantinople

1096–1099   First Crusade

1225–1274   Thomas Aquinas, Leading Theologian

1369–1415   John Hus, Bohemian Reformer

1517   Luther's Ninety-Five Theses

1509–1564   John Calvin, Leading Theologian

1545–1563   Council of Trent

1620   Mayflower Compact of the Pilgrims

1703–1791   John Wesley

1869–1870   First Vatican Council

1910   Beginning of Protestant Ecumenical Movement

1962–1965   Second Vatican Council

himself, a matter of his own creativity or genius. It was a gift, a charge, a manifestation of the God in him, the divine power filling his soul.

Like the Hebrew prophets, Jesus preached a Word thought to be revealed and demanded its generous enactment. His message came from on high and it targeted justice, mercy, faith, and love. A parable recorded in Matthew shows how Jesus would concretize his prophetic demand for performance:

"What do you think? A man had two sons; and he went to the first and said, 'Son, go and work in the vineyard today.' And he answered, 'I will not'; but afterward he repented and went. And he went to the second and said the same; and he answered, 'I go, sir,' but did not go. Which of the two did the will of his father?" They said, "The first." Jesus said to them, "Truly, I say to you, the tax collectors and the harlots go into the kingdom of God before you. For John came to you in the way of righteousness, and you did not believe him, but the tax collectors and the harlots believed him; and even afterward when you saw it, you did not afterward repent and believe in him." (Matt. 21:28–32)

The first part of the parable is common prophetic moralism: *do* what is right! The second part shows the innovations that Jesus and Christianity worked on Jewish prophecy. For them the time of Jesus, inaugurated by the preaching of John the Baptist, was the zero hour, the age of the Messiah. Despised people such as the tax collectors and harlots could be saved, if they believed. On the other hand, people who saw John's righteousness and would not repent lost their golden chance. Jesus was a crux, a stumbling block, a sign of judgment. In him the prophetic call became so personalized that to reject him was to cut oneself off from the covenant, mercy, and grace. Things had heated up since the time of Jeremiah. The Spirit was poised to make the new alliance, written in hearts of flesh, if people would give Jesus their allegiance.

This Christian view of Jesus soon deepened to the point where Jesus was much more than a prophet. For the theologies of John and Paul, Jesus was the Word of God incarnate, the eternal divine speech come in human form. The opening verses of John set the matter plainly, interpreting the drama of the Baptist and Jesus:

There was a man sent from God, whose name was John. He came for testimony, to bear witness to the light, that all might believe through him. He was not the light, but came to bear witness to the light. The true light that enlightens every man was coming into the world. He was in the world, and the world was made through him, yet the world knew him not. He came to his own home, and his own people received him not. But to all who received him, who believed in his name, he gave the power to become children of God; who were born, not of blood nor of the will of the flesh nor of the will of man, but of God. And the Word became flesh and dwelt among us, full of grace and of truth; we have beheld his glory, glory as of the only Son from the Father. (John bore witness to him, and cried, "This was he of whom I said, 'He who comes after me ranks before me, for he was before me.' ") And from his fulness have we all received, grace upon grace. For the law was given through Moses; grace and truth came through Jesus Christ. No one has ever seen God; the only Son, who is in the bosom of the Father, he has made him known. (John 1:6–18)

The Gospel of John probably reflects influences from the Greek culture (Hellenism) to which Christianity early had to adapt itself. This culture seems the likely cause of Christianity's early use of the title *savior* for Jesus. It is one of the clearest indications of why Christianity soon came to think of Jesus as more than a prophet, and of how the long Christian interest in salvation got its start.

Johannes Bauer has summarized the New Testament situation nicely:

In hellenistic circles gods, heroes, and rulers are regarded as saviours in cases in which they have supplied some kind of need. The "saviour" Asklepios brings healing from sickness. The divinised ruler acts as "saviour" when he creates peace and order. The deity who breaks the power of death and matter in the mystery cults is likewise saluted as "saviour." Jesus was probably never called "saviour" (soter) during his lifetime. Nevertheless this honorific title seems to have been employed at a very early stage, as we can gather from Acts 5:31 and 13:23, and also Phil 3:20. In Lk 1:47

this title is used to designate God. But in Lk 2:11 it is Jesus Christ who is the "saviour."

In the same way, too, in the Pastoral Epistles both God and Christ are designated by the title of soter. *When this* soter *title is applied to Jesus it is chiefly as the deliverer of the people from sin and death; in other words on the basis of his work of redemption. In addition to this there is an* eschatological element *[concern with the last days] (absent from the hellenistic concept of* soter*) in the "epiphany in glory" which is still awaited, and in which the work of redemption will finally be completed (Tit 2:13; Phil 3:20). It may be that John deliberately chooses a mode of designation which closely resembles the formula employed in the cult of the emperor as* soter *(formulae of this description are applied to Hadrian), or alternatively he may even be reacting against the idea of Asklepios as "saviour" (his sanctuary at Pergamum is referred to as the "throne of Satan" in Rev. 2:13).*[1]

GOSPEL

The Christian equivalent of Torah is **Gospel** (*evangelion*). Etymologically, it means "glad tidings" or "good news." Within the New Testament we can discern two different strata of the gospel, both of which are thoroughly prophetic. First, there is the gospel of Jesus himself. This pivoted on the notion of the Kingdom or Reign of God. The glad tidings that Jesus had to announce was the dawning of God's Kingdom. This is the major motif of the preaching we see in the **synoptic** gospels (Mark, Matthew, Luke). Jesus came, like a prophet, with a divine message to utter.[2] He was to herald the new age, the time of fulfillment, that God had long been preparing. His audience knew about such a time, because they were mainly Jews versed in the notion of a messianic age. The **Messiah**, or anointed king, whom prophets such as Isaiah had foreseen, would bring the people prosperity and peace. He would be their defender against surrounding foes, their guide to justice and joy. Judaism has kept the notion of the Messiah down to the present, still hoping for a golden age.

For Jesus, the age had come. For Jesus' followers, the master soon took on the outlines of the Messiah. Jesus' own self-conception is less certain.[3] He spoke of himself most often as the Son of Man, which could mean either a simple human being or the heavenly figure described in the biblical book of Daniel. As the synoptic gospels portray it, Jesus was leery of the political overtones that the traditional Israelite notion of the Messiah usually carried. His own understanding of the Kingdom of God had political implications, but its core was prophetically religious. God, whom Jesus knew intimately as a Father, was offering his people a new opportunity for close relationship and fulfillment. In contrast to the division between God and the people, and the divisions among the people themselves, the Father was calling for repentance, reconciliation, and close familial sharing. Out of this might come the sort of political implications that Paul found—for example, a people in whom there would be strict equality: neither Jew nor Greek, slave nor free, male nor female (Gal. 3:28)—but the first import was religious: Repent and believe.

The first denotation of the gospel, then, is the good news that Jesus himself heralded. Saying that God's Kingdom was at the threshold, Jesus called for conversion and faith. The second denotation or stratum in the New Testament shifts the good news so that the person of Jesus becomes the main focus. As some New Testament scholars have put it, the proclaimer became the proclaimed. When the early Christians came to understand Jesus as the Word of God incarnate (largely because of his resurrection from the dead), the great happening of their recent history became the presence and fate of Jesus himself. For the Johannine communities (those whose faith shaped the gospel of John and John's epistles), the simple presence or being of Jesus was the main miracle. As we saw in the opening verses of John, Jesus as the Word become flesh was full of grace and truth. Like the **Shekinah**, or presence of the Israelite Lord, the body of Jesus shone with a holy power. Simply to be near this power and accept its authenticity made one a new being, a convert and person saved. So in John the sayings and doings of Jesus are so many signs of what God is like when he comes into human form, and Jesus' death on the cross is a moment of high victory in which Satan is crushed.

For the Pauline communities, the main panel of the gospel is the death and resurrection of Jesus. Like a new **Passover** (the Israelite feast celebrating the Exodus from Egypt), Jesus was to be celebrated with a great sense of freedom. The Pauline good news was that Jesus had taken humanity from bondage to liberation, sin to grace, the letter of the law to the spirit. In the resurrection of Jesus, Paul saw the beginnings of a new creation, a whole fresh order of humankind. Jesus was for him a second Adam: like the first human being in standing at the head of many descendents, unlike the first human being in being obedient rather than wayward, a source of friendship with God rather than wrath. The resurrection, which Paul attributed to the power of the Father, showed the rightness of Jesus' message and ministry. It was the authentication by God

of his prophet's work, his Son's goodness, and the outpouring of the divine Spirit.

From his faith in Jesus' passover to resurrected life, Paul derived a particularly explosive and joyous interpretation of the gospel. His sense of the good news made the believer in Jesus impervious to any threat life could throw up:

What then shall we say to this? If God is for us, who is against us? He who did not spare his own Son but gave him up for us all, will he not give us all things with him? Who shall bring any charge against God's elect? It is God who justifies; who is to condemn? Is it Christ Jesus, who died, yes, who was raised from the dead, who is at the right hand of God, who indeed intercedes for us? Who shall separate us from the love of Christ? Shall tribulation, or distress, or persecution, or famine, or nakedness, or peril, or sword? As it is written, "For thy sake we are being killed all the day long; we are regarded as sheep to be slaughtered." No, in all these things we are more than conquerers through him who loved us. For I am sure that neither death, nor life, nor angels, nor principalities, nor things present, nor things to come, nor powers, nor height, nor depth, nor anything else in all creation, will be able to separate us from the love of God in Christ Jesus our Lord. (Rom. 8:31–39)

EVANGELICAL PROPHECY

From its conviction that a new age had come, in which Jesus offered a new beginning and fresh divine life, the New Testament's prophecy emphasized the paradoxes that Christian faith could entail. Building on themes of the Hebrew prophets, it made the poor and dispossessed the special objects of God's care, in contrast to most human beings' tendency to laud the rich and well established. We see this paradoxical sort of prophecy in *Luke*, the book that one recent study of the New Testament calls "the gospel of the poor and outcast."[4]

For example, the "Magnificat" that Luke puts in the mouth of Mary, the mother of Jesus, both reflects the Old Testament faith of Hannah (1 Sam. 2:1–10) and makes the anticipated birth of Jesus an act of a God wholly on the side of the lowly and hungry:

My soul magnifies the Lord, and my spirit rejoices in God my Savior, for he has regarded the low estate of his handmaiden. For behold, henceforth all generations will call me blessed; for he who is mighty has done great things for me, and holy is his name. And his mercy is on those who fear him from generation to generatiion. He has shown strength with his arm, he has scattered the proud in the imagination of their hearts, he has put down the mighty from their thrones, and exalted those of low degree; he has filled the hungry with good things, and the rich he has sent empty away. He has helped his servant Israel, in remembrance of his mercy, as he spoke to our fathers, to Abraham and to his posterity for ever. (Luke 1:47–55)

In this passage, Luke expresses the early Christian prophetic conviction that the God of Jesus is a God of justice, a deity whose heart goes out to society's victims and defenseless sufferers. Placed in the context of Mary's conception of Jesus by the Holy Spirit, the Magnificat implies that the birth and life of Jesus are God's overthrow of earthly establishments, God's decisive shaking of the foundations of injustice. This theme later issues from Jesus' own mouth, in Luke's version of the "Beatitudes": " 'Blessed are you poor, for yours is the kingdom of God. Blessed are you that hunger now, for you shall be satisfied. Blessed are you that weep now, for you shall laugh. Blessed are you when men hate you, and when they exclude you and revile you, and cast out your name as evil, on account of the Son of man! Rejoice in that day, and leap for joy, for behold, your reward is great in heaven; for so their fathers did to the prophets.' " (Luke 6:20–23; also see Matt. 5:3–12.)

The new age come with Jesus therefore upsets many preconceptions. Evangelical prophecy is comfort for the afflicted, but also affliction for the comfortable. We see this second, balancing part of Jesus' prophetic message in the "Woes" that follow directly on the Lukan beatitudes: " 'But woe to you that are rich, for you have received your consolation. Woe to you that are full now, for you shall hunger. Woe to you that laugh now, for you shall mourn and weep. Woe to you, when all men speak well of you, for so their fathers did to the false prophets.' " (Luke 6:23–26) In rather **apocalyptic** (relating to the concept of the **apocalypse**) speech, the Lukan Jesus makes the gospel a revolutionary proclamation. According to the standards of his loving Father, the age-old inequities among the social classes and between individuals will have to go. The justice of this holy God demands the alliance of true, genuine prophecy with the victims of "man's inhumanity to man." As the false prophets of the Hebrew Bible prostituted themselves, becoming the mouthpieces of the powerful, so only a false follower of the gospel would curry favor with an oppressive establishment.

Latter-day **evangelicals** have been formed by Jesus' prophecies. Taking the gospel as their prime (for many, sole) authority, they have struggled to bring their audiences the comforts of the Kingdom, the new beginnings opened up by the Incarnate Word. Sometimes they have remembered both sides of Jesus' preaching, the beatitudes and woes alike. Sometimes they have lost the full balance, offering only the comforts ("pie in the sky") and forgetting the social reforms. Recently, however, more evangelicals seem to be accepting the proposition that the Christian gospel always has a dimension of social justice. Letting all the New Testament texts sink in, more have been allying themselves with groups defending the rights of the poor both at home and abroad.

Robert Linder has documented this shift among American evangelicals, noting such examples as the "Affirmation of God's Mission" approved by the Missouri Synod Lutherans in 1965, the "Statement Concerning the Crisis of our Nation" of the Southern Baptists in 1968, the Wheaton Declaration of the Congress on the Church's Worldwide Mission in 1966, and the statements of the United States Congress on Evangelism in 1969.

But the climax to growing evangelical social re-awakening came with the Thanksgiving Workshop on Evangelical Social Concern held in Chicago in November, 1973, and the Declaration of Evangelical Social Concern subsequently issued by its participants. Taken in context and remembering how difficult it has been in the past to secure agreement among evangelicals on controversial issues, the promulgation of the Declaration was nothing short of a miracle. In brief, the 473-word social action statement made clear the evangelical faith of the signers, confessed past sins, emphasized that God requires both love and justice, pointed out that the Christian life demands total discipleship, and proclaimed: "So we call our fellow evangelical Christians to demonstrate repentance in a Christian discipleship that confronts the social and political injustice of our nation." The only question that remains is: For how many of the country's more than 40 million evangelicals did the 45 original signers speak?[5]

MEDIEVAL CHRISTIANITY

Medieval Christianity never lost the prophetic thrust toward social justice (Jesus' own message was too clear for that), but frequently medieval Christians understood the gospel more privately that the early Christians had. As well, frequently their understanding of prophecy stressed its predictive aspect. To be sure, if by medieval Christianity we mean the span from the **Fathers** of the third century to the reformers of the sixteenth century, we have a lot of time about which to generalize. Still, one can see an individualistic emphasis as early as Athanasius, the great champion of orthodoxy at the Council of Nicaea (325). Athanasius wrote a life of Antony, the desert hermit, that made lonely struggles against the demons a paradigm for the Christian's religious progress. He also wrote an endorsement of the Psalms that took Hebrew prophecy mainly as the prediction of the coming of the Savior:

The books of the Prophets contain foretellings about the sojourn of the Saviour, admonitions concerning divine commands and reprimands against transgressors, as well as prophecies for the gentiles. . . . The pronouncements of the Prophets are delared in nearly every Psalm. About the visitation of the Saviour, and that we will make his sojourn as one who is God, so it says in the forty-ninth psalm: The Lord our God shall come manifestly, and shall not keep silence, *and in the one hundred and seventeenth:* Blessed is he that comes in the name of the Lord.[6]

By Athanasius' time, Christians felt the need to make the Hebrew Bible a type or forecast of the New Testament. Indeed, their very name for the Hebrew Bible, the "Old Testament," suggests a before-and-after mentality. Before Jesus, the Christian God Incarnate, there were the preparations God worked through Israel. High among these were the predictions of the prophets that a messianic age would dawn in which people would find forgiveness and justice. After Jesus, Christians found the fulfillment of these preparations. For them the life of God made available through Jesus' death and resurrection was a new, interior covenant, and the preaching, miracles, sufferings, death, and resurrection of Jesus fulfilled the prophets' forecasts of the Messiah. That Jews did not accept these interpretations of the Hebrew Bible only increased the vehemence with which Christians of the **patristic** age proposed them. Through the later Middle Ages it became standard to attribute Jews' objections to blindness and bad will.

In the later medieval period the tradition continued to say that Jesus was a prophet, but this was a somewhat minor emphasis, usually supplemented by the quick addition that Jesus was more than a prophet. Further, there was an implicit contrast between Jesus and Moses, such that Jesus was viewed as having brought a new law:

The conception of the gospel as a new law, which had come from the early church, continued to be a way to describe the commandments of Jesus as a ful-

Figure 8 Madonna with the Child Jesus, *late fifteenth century, Nelson Gallery—Atkins Museum, Kansas City, Missouri (Nelson Fund).*

fillment or an amendment of the old law. Although he was not merely a prophet, Christ as teacher of the new law could be identified as a prophet, too, and this in a treatise addressed to Jews. When Christ had said of himself, "I am the truth," this pertained not only to "the confession of Christ" as such, but *"the truth of justice"* as it affected one's neighbor. It followed that anyone who denied the truth in the case of his neighbor for fear of offending those in power was "undoubtedly denying Christ" as truth incarnate.[7]

More powerful than social questions in medieval theology, however, was the **scholastics'** concern with **metaphysics**. For the great scholastics such as Anselm, Albert, Thomas, and Bonaventure, the truth of God implied an objective ordering of reality that the intelligent, persistent inquirer could discover. Behind this conviction lay the medieval faith in the revelation of the Creator, and from this conviction flowed the tight scholastic analyses of the virtues and ethical entailments of Christian faith. But front and center stood the analysis of how the mind related to the objective order of reality, what the hierarchy of being itself was. Among the leading scholastics, prophetic concerns intruded less than wisdom concerns. Thus the predominant mode was rather dispassionate, not at all the angry style of an Elijah or a Jeremiah.

Nonetheless, the medieval Christians read the Bible honestly enough to balance the pursuit of truth with the need to do the truth in love. What Paul had laid out in 1 Cor. 13, his hymn to love, commanded the assent of all the orthodox. In fact, such influential Western medieval movements as the Franciscan and Dominican renovations of monasticism strike the comparativist as prophetic revivals. In the East, the battles about the status of icons could also be read as a prophetic matter. Was the concern of the classical prophets for a pure, unidolatrous faith to mean stripping the altars of all images, or was the equally classical prophetic concern for a humane, merciful faith to mean visual helps for the ordinary person's piety?

The Protestant Reformers of the sixteenth century inherited these earlier medieval issues, and the Protestant return to the Bible can be interpreted as another prophetic revival. For example, when Luther attacked the concern with "works" that he found rampant in early-sixteenth-century Christian faith, demanding instead faith in the Word of God, he reiterated a strong Old Testament theme (although perhaps somewhat individualistically):

Let us then consider it certain and firmly established that the soul can do without anything except the Word of God and that where the Word of God is missing there is no help at all for the soul. If it has the Word of God it is rich and lacks nothing since it is the Word of life, truth, light, peace, righteousness, salvation, joy, liberty, wisdom, power, grace, glory, and of every incalculable blessing. This is why the prophet in the entire

Psalm (119) and in many other places yearns and sighs for the Word of God and uses so many names to describe it. On the other hand, there is no more terrible disaster with which the wrath of God can afflict men than a famine of the hearing of His Word, as He says in Amos (8:1). Likewise, there is no greater mercy than when He sends forth His Word, as we read in Psalm 107 (20): "He sent forth his word, and healed them, and delivered them from destruction." Nor was Christ sent into the world for any other ministry except that of the Word.[8]

MODERN CHRISTIANITY

The Protestant Reformers' principles of the primacy of individual conscience and the legitimacy of individual interpretation of Scripture were important roadmarks on the way to modernity. By the eighteenth century, when a new science and philosophy suggested the clear demise of the medieval period, **autonomy** was the watchword in progressive European religious circles. In fact, the breakdown of the medieval synthesis between faith and reason had become almost glaring. Those who followed such modern philosophers as Immanuel Kant (1724–1804) largely rejected faith, in favor of an independent critical reason quite suspicious of all traditional authorities. Those who still loved biblical religion or the old rituals of faith tended toward **pietism**, a religious stance that gave primacy to devotional feelings. As nineteenth-century science led to an evolutionary perspective, and the philosopher Karl Marx (1818–1883) shaped nineteenth-century social thought, traditional Christian faith became something of an intellectual backwater in Europe. Recent Christianity has been deeply stamped by this sense of history's having threatened to pass it by.

In the early twentieth century Albert Einstein (1879–1955) and Sigmund Freud (1856–1939) were prime movers in new theories of nature and the human psyche that forced Christianity to still further reassessments. The Freudian revolution is still being pondered, but the Einsteinian revolution seems to have chastened Christian speculation and helped it realize that the biblical pictures of the world are only commonsensical portraits in the service of deep *mythic* (storied) truths. Thus many Christian theologians have come to believe that one will not find in the Bible scientific cosmology in anything like the modern sense of the term. Genesis, Psalms, John, and Colossians all speculate about the world not on the basis of empirical experimentation but on the basis of their religious experience of God or Christ.

The Marxist program has probably become the principal modern challenge to Christianity's prophetic role. By highlighting the place of wealth in social relations, and analyzing the **ideology** stemming from the disparities in wealth among the different social classes, Marxist thinkers have sharpened the biblical prophets' concern for justice and fair dealing. However, the Soviet, Chinese, and other Marxist regimes that have butchered millions and repressed individual liberties suggest the problems with prophetic regimes that have cast out God. In the name of progress or the preservation of the state, Marxist-Leninist prophets have done things that biblical heralds would have considered unthinkable, diabolical. The challenge to recent Christians in many geographic areas has been to restore a genuine prophetic tradition, cut their ties with oppressive political regimes, and make themselves competitive with Marxist movements to aid the poor.

We shall see more of this challenge when we consider Christian social thought, and we shall see more of the Freudian challenge when we consider Christian personal thought. Here let us update the Christian development of the prophetic tradition by studying some reflections of the contemporary Protestant theologican Dorothee Sölle. An adolescent during the height of Nazism, Sölle has used the evil and suffering she's seen to develop a mordant insistence on justice:

I've heard that Saint Thomas recommended three ways to combat melancholy: sleeping, bathing, and study of the sufferings of Christ. I've noticed that my friends advise in such cases sleeping with someone, drinking, and the study of one's own suffering. I imagine other of my friends, if I could ask them, would recommend watchfulness, work, and study of a world map pinpointing illiteracy and the manufacturers of arms. But those friends whose advice could help set me right live far away behind walls.[9]

The recommendation of Saint Thomas is medieval wisdom: common prudence combined with a sober assessment of what Christ went through. Contemporary recommendations are self-centered: sex, drink, scraping one's innards. Yet, Sölle suggests, the melancholy that threatens to overwhelm us today responds to neither of these prescriptions. Like a soldier poised for battle, the faithful person today must watch, labor, and never forget the sufferings of the world's underdeveloped billions, the evils of the world's destructive technologists. The best recommendations, though, are not even available to us. In prisons, torture cells, and mental hospitals the prophets and sages who know

contemporary melancholy in their bones give an eloquently silent witness. Our greatest hope is the fear they inspire in those responsible for the world's great systems of evil. If we would know the contemporary dimensions of prophecy and so break through to a genuinely religious joy, we must study the people who suffer most from today's injustices, the prime victims of today's irreligion.

Harkening back to another medieval paradigm, Sölle uses Saint Francis of Assisi to clarify our current ecological and spiritual disorders:

Blessed saint francis, pray for us, now and in the time of despondency. Your brother the water is poisoned. Children no longer know your brother the fire. The birds shun us. They belittle you, popes and czars, and the americans buy up assisi, including you. Blessed saint francis, why did you come among us? In the stony outskirts of the city I saw you scurrying about, a dog pawing through garbage, even children choosing a plastic car over you. Blessed saint francis, what have you changed, whom have you helped? Blessed saint francis, pray for us, now and when the rivers run dry, now and when our breath fails us.[10]

CHRISTIAN SOCIAL THOUGHT

Historically, Christianity has retained its prophetic form. Now more sharply, now less, its preaching of Jesus' good news has kept it emphasizing justice, good will, and the Word of God. If we move from the horizontal perspective of history to the vertical perspective of structural analysis, we also find the persistence of a prophetic form. Sociologically, for example, the Christian notion of the Church has spurred Jesus' followers to institutionalize justice and love. Even though Christians have been far from fully successful in this effort, the pressures of such an ideal have led to many of the West's greatest social achievements: widespread education, health care, democratic politics, and legal fairness. The cracks and failings in each of these systems does not gainsay the great good they have brought. In terms of global history, the yield of the biblical prophetic energies has been handsome and distinctive.

Central to this evangelical vision is the sense that Jesus' followers make with him a single organism. In the Johannine writings, the operative figure is that of branches joined to a vine. In the Pauline writings, the main metaphor is that of a mystical body. For both portions of the New Testament, the divinity of Christ has meant the divinization of his followers. Eastern Christianity most fully developed this conviction, and so most fully exploited the New Testament sense of **grace**. The "favor" of God that grace connotes expanded in the East to become a share in the divine life itself. The trinitarian God, Father-Son-Spirit, came to the believer in baptism and dwelt in her heart. The consolations of the Spirit during the believer's earthly life were a pledge of the eternal joy she would have with God in heaven. Thus the Christian body social had a mysterious depth and a most helpful future. The Church suffering on earth was supported by the Church triumphant in heaven.

Often this hopeful future kept Christians from full attention to life in the present. The **alienation** that Marxist and Freudian critics have found in Christian political and psychic life are a species of immaturity often caused by "pie in the sky." On the other hand, the restrictions of the Marxist and Freudian visions, their despair before radical evil, have made mature Christians their strong critics. If the Marxist "classless society" or the Freudian "good adjustment" is the best future for which human beings can hope, ours is of all species the most to be pitied. Compared with the promises of the Johannine Jesus, such latter-day religions have seemed to most Christians pale and puny.

Consider, by contrast, the commandment of love and promise of intimacy that the New Testament records, the incarnate God having left his Church:

This is my commandment, that you love one another as I have loved you. Greater love has no man than this, that a man lay down his life for his friends. You are my friends if you do what I command you. No longer do I call you servants, for the servant does not know what his master is doing; but I have called you friends, for all that I have heard from my Father I have made known to you. You did not choose me, but I chose you and appointed you that you should go and bear fruit and that your fruit should abide; so that whatever you ask the Father in my name, he may give it to you. This I command you, to love one another. (John 15:12–17)

One does not have to be cynical to see that, granted such high ideals, the history of Christian wars and depredations has given the Church a major credibility problem. Insofar as most of the modern colonialists have come from Western countries nominally Christian, the subjugation of American, Indian, African, and Asian natives has besmirched the original gospel. In the United States, the enslavement of blacks and the ravishing of Indians have made white Christianity a scandal. Sociologically, a religion is only as good as

the practical justice, the operative charity, that it nourishes. True enough, none of the world religions can pass a stiff scrutiny by such standards. All have failed their own best ideals. By having claimed to inherit Jewish chosenness, however, Christians set themselves up for a singularly mighty fall.

That is not to say, of course, that all modern Christians have been colonizers or slavers. Some, like the Quakers, have produced splendid works of service. Taking the "friendship" theme of passages such as John 15 seriously, they have sought to bind up wounds, enlighten minds, and reconcile enemies. A good recent example of this sort of service shines forth in *A Compassionate Peace*, a report of the American Friends Service Committee on how the Middle East might move from conflict to justice and tranquillity. The Preface of the report shows that the prophetic portion of the Christian tradition continues to inspire a profound social vision:

More recently, the committee has gone beyond only providing immediate aid in the wake of war to try to deal with the roots of violence, which lie in injustice and the denial of human rights and the terrible poverty that afflict so many millions at home and around the world. To change these conditions is to build the foundations of peace, which must be the concern of all men and women of goodwill. In these difficult enterprises, we have often known disappointment. Our workers have provided food, comforted the homeless, marched for justice, and stood beside the outcast, but they have failed to reach to the hatreds and the despair that corrode the soul and alienate the human family across neighborhoods and across nations. But we have also seen miracles, where humanity and caring were reborn and compassion returned, where hatred has given way to forgiveness and where community has been rebuilt. These miracles happened because special individuals dared to live as if change was possible, and it became possible. They were competent people; able to understand difficult problems, able to find places to take hold, and able to discover what tasks needed to be done. But competency wasn't enough, it had to be undergirded with the certain faith that human beings can rise above their baser natures and respond to stimuli other than fear and threat and naked power.[11]

CHRISTIAN PERSONAL THOUGHT

Ideally, the Christian church was supposed to afford individuals a favoring climate for personal growth.

Through most of Christian history personal growth largely meant progress in the love of God, but human nature was intractable enough to ensure that the other foci of maturity—competence in one's work, warmth in one's family circle, usefulness to one's community—came in for due consideration. Still, the person's greatest dignity, in traditional Christian perspective, came from being an image of God. By reason and love, the human person was an icon of the divine. As the Logos was the Reason of the Father, and the Spirit was the Father's Love, so the development of the human icon meant progress in wisdom and charity. One sees these orthodox themes in the Greek and Russian traditions of the spiritual master, the *staretz* who gave many Orthodox Christians personal counsel in how to mature in the life of faith.

One of the popular themes of such counsel, as a devout Christian would have received it from a wise elder in many periods of Church history, was distancing the soul from worldliness, opposing the values of secular life. Many personalities occupied with **contemplation** and thirsty for deep communion with God, would retire from worldly occupations, taking themselves to lonely fastnesses such as the Siberian north. This is how such a twentieth-century contemplative spoke about the dangers of life in the world:

Father John was, like a true son of the Far North, radostopechalie—joyous, calm, contemplative. He was not a great talker, immersed as he was in prayer and contemplation. Once, I asked him: "Father, tell me, is it true that in order to be 'saved,' to 'live in God,' we must live away from crowds, as you do here in the North?" He answered, "I believe it is true, man of God. It is very difficult to live a holy life in the world. There is so much activity and so much vanity. When the devil wants to detach someone from the one thing necessary, he occupies him with a lot of work which does not leave him a free moment for meditation or for deepening his interior life. As a result, the prayer of one who lives in the world is full of distractions, dry, and tedious. He may even give up prayer altogether. Such a man is 'drowned' in the world. Of course, men can be saved in the world, but it is so much more difficult. The early monks went to the desert in order to be alone with God. It is very difficult indeed to serve God and the world at the same time, but such is unavoidable when one lives in the world."[12]

The contemplative side of the personality, its need to commune deeply with God, ruminate, and enjoy interior quiet, stands to the fore in monks such as Father John. The active side of the personality, its need to work and build, stands to the fore in the Christians who raised families, ran institutions, and called their times to account. And although one can document prayerful withdrawal in the lives of the classical prophets, as one can document it in the life of Jesus, the active pursuit of justice seems the more direct expression of the prophetic personality. The Word of God that seizes the prophet impels him or her to judge and reconcile current times by the standards of the divine holiness. So doing, the prophet confounds the secular analysts who find religion to be sheer alienation. If late-nineteenth- and early-twentieth-century European society provided Freud many examples of neurosis abetted by religion, the work of nineteenth-century Methodists to combat the wretched conditions brought by English industrialization, the work of twentieth-century proponents of the "social gospel" on behalf of the American poor, and the work of recent American Catholic bishops in opposing the arms buildup show an impressive prophetic maturity.

Some of the perceptions and decisions ingredient in such a maturity appear in Robert McAfee Brown's autobiographical book *Creative Dislocation—The Movement of Grace*. In the following passage, Brown is reflecting on his growing appreciation, in the late 1960s and early 1970s, of the institutional props to the Vietnamese War:

My appreciation to Stanford for protecting my freedom of conscience and expression remained, but it began to be balanced by a recognition that Stanford and places like it were part of the huge military-industrial-educational complex that was not only supporting the war but profiting from it. Research in some areas of the sciences was contributing to the war, Defense Department contracts were helping support other departments, and many members of the Board of Trustees were associated with industries lavishly rewarded for designing or making instruments of human destruction. Stanford, I came to realize, could tolerate a certain amount of offbeat protest without any fundamental challenge to its place in our society. It would not, nor would other universities, become a catalyst for social change. Its role would increasingly be that of a conserver, a very good one, of the status quo. Was that institutional direction the one I wanted to endorse with my own future?[13]

In the measure that they have studied the prophetic Jesus, Christians through the centuries have found that a prophetic psychology meant ambiguity toward their present times. The prophetic sense that only God commands the believer's full loyalties laid a foundation for criticizing their nations, local communities, and local churches, when these seemed worldly or given over to war making. As a result, the mature Christian has not had an easy time in larger society, as mature Jews and Muslims have not. To follow the prophetic vocation very far usually has meant encountering strong resistance and backlash.

CHRISTIAN ECOLOGY

The Christian view of nature has varied through the centuries, of course, but throughout a biblical anthropocentrism has been significant. As Genesis laid things out, human beings had a mandate to subdue the earth. Like the Hebrew Bible, however, the Christian Scriptures balanced this anthropocentrism with a strong sense that nature came from the creative hand of God. Paul, for example, taught that when one considered the world the divine power behind it ought to be manifest:

For the wrath of God is revealed from heaven against all ungodliness and wickedness of men who by their wickedness suppress the truth. For what can be known about God is plain to them. Ever since the creation of the world his invisible nature, namely his eternal power and deity, has been clearly perceived in the things that have been made. So they are without excuse; for although they knew God they did not honor him as God or give thanks to him, but they became futile in their thinking and their senseless minds were darkened. Claiming to be wise, they became fools, and exchanged the glory of the immortal God for images resembling mortal man or birds or animals or reptiles. (Rom. 1:18–23)

In both Paul and the Synoptics the Jewish sense of the land underwent considerable change due to the Christian conviction that faith in Jesus meant a new convenant, no longer tied to either the land or the people of Israel. Still, Jesus seems to have been a person sensitive to his environment, and this sensitivity entered into his preaching:

A number of Jesus' parables employ natural symbolism, however, so we should not take Jesus' and the Synoptics' indifference to geographic locale as a general blindness to nature's significance. Pheme Perkins has considered several of these nature parables under the heading "Parables of Growth," and she suggests that natural processes generally provided Jesus with analogies to the processes of human beings' religious growth. In addition, Jesus drew metaphors from nature to make his teaching more vivid and pointed. For
example, he used the weather we share in common to sharpen his exhortation that we love our enemies (Matthew 5:45). He pointed to the birds of the air and the flowers of the field to allay our anxieties about food and clothing (Matthew 6:25–33). Behind this tendency Perkins sees the instinct of the Hebrew Bible to assimilate the workings of God's word to a fruitful harvest. Thus Isaiah 55:10–11 has God eloquently proclaim: "For as the rain and the snow come down from heaven, and return not thither but water the earth, making it bring forth and sprout, giving seed to the sower and bread to the eater, so shall my word be that goes forth from my mouth; it shall not return to me empty, but it shall accomplish that which I purpose, and prosper in the things for which I sent it."[14]

Through the patristic and medieval periods, creation continued to serve as a stimulus to praise the Creator. We have mentioned Athanasius' reverence for the Psalms, and the development of ordered monastic prayer meant the daily use of the Psalms to praise the Creator of the universe. When the Protestant Reformation took up prophetic biblical themes, it too underscored the importance of natural revelation. John McNeill, in fact, has spoken of a twofold **Calvinist** revelation:

God makes Himself known to man in a twofold revelation. He is known as Creator, both through the outward universe and through Holy Scripture: He is known as Redeemer through the Scripture alone. This distinction had such growing importance for Calvin that . . . it controlled the structure of the Institutes in the final Latin edition. Man is himself a part of that created world through which God is made known. The ordered array of the heavenly host, the symmetry and beauty of the human body, the versatility and inventiveness of the mind are testimonies of God, and His acts of justice and mercy in experience and history invite us to acquire a knowledge of Him. Yet through the perversity of our natures we "turn upside down" these intimations of God and set up as the object of our worship "the dream and phantom of our own brain." Not on the basis of the light of nature but through the revelation of the Word we gain a true and saving knowledge of God. Yet Calvin's world, from stars to insects, from archangels to infants, is the realm of God's sovereignty. A reverent awe of God breathes through all his work.[15]

Insofar as redemption struck many Christians as more marvelous than creation, and the work of Christ predominated over the movements of the stars, Christians had an inclination to subordinate nature to Scripture. This inclination came home to roost in modernity when natural science began to describe a creation at variance with the pictures of Genesis. Indeed, fundamentalist Christians were only being consistent when they turned their backs on modern science and insisted that creation had to have occurred as Genesis portrayed it. Today the majority of Christians seem to dissolve this conflict by relegating theological and scientific reflections to different orders of discourse. The two must relate, if the contemporary Christian is not to be schizophrenic, but each is said to have its own methods and ends. The end of theology is the clarification of faith. The method of theology is reflection on the data of revelation, many of which are cast in symbolic or storied form. Thus contemporary Christians who wish to bring their faith to the aid of ecological reform have to penetrate the Genesis account and reach the core of the Creator's work. When the Christian God looked upon his creation and proclaimed it very good, he probably cast a veto against environmental pollution and abuse.

GENEVA

In dealing with Judaism as a prophetic religion, we brought our sketch to rest in Jerusalem, the city most central to Jewish understandings of the Word of God and Jewish demands for justice. Today the Christian analogue to Jerusalem probably is Geneva, the home of the World Council of Churches. Historically, Rome and Constantinople, the homes of Catholicism and Orthodoxy, have strong claims to the title of being Christianity's center. Presently, Rome presses forcefully for social justice, as the recent popes' encyclicals eloquently demonstrate; Orthodoxy, largely under the restraints of Communist regimes, witnesses to prophetic themes mainly by suffering. But Geneva, one of the key cities of the sixteenth-century Protestant Reformation, is the focus of perhaps the largest Christian effort to reshape the world's economic, political, technological, and religious systems in the direction of divine justice. (Orthodox and Roman Catholic Christians participate in most of these efforts, making them truly ecumenical.) Let us consider some of the translations of the prophetic Word of God that agencies of the World Council of Churches recently have been suggesting for the year 2000.

First, the World Council has opened itself wide to third world peoples in the last decades, and their voices now ring in its assemblies eloquently. From the surging native churches of Africa, Asia, and Latin America representatives of the poor describe a world that many citizens of the affluent northern nations never glimpse:

I should like to start by stating some very well known facts which give shape to our own debate. If no major event happens, the population of the earth, which in 1850 was 1,262 million, and in 1975 was 3,968 million, will in the year 2000 probably be 6,254 million. Of this population, in 1950 34% were living in developed regions; in 1975 that figure went down to 29%; and in 2000, it is expected to go down to 22%. The population in less developed regions, therefore, was 66% in 1950 and 71% in 1975; in the year 2000, it is expected to be 78%. It is quite clear that the minority, living in the developed parts of the world, at this stage consume about 75% of the world's resources. They control about 88% of the gross world product, 80% of world trade and investment, 93% of its industry and almost 100% of its scientific and technological research.[16]

Obviously enough, the combination of rising population in the underdeveloped countries and high consumption of the globe's resources in the developed countries puts the nations on a collision course. We shall consider the military and political aspects of this collision course momentarily. The author of the figures cited above, however, riveted his exposition to the most basic injustice they produce, the proliferation of world hunger. Nowadays, perhaps 1 billion people are in danger of not getting enough sustenance to meet their energy needs. About 450 million people suffer serious malnutrition, many of them living in rural parts of East Asia. Every year about 50 million children die of malnutrition in the developing countries, compared to only 0.5 million in the developed countries. This would be a tragic situation whatever its causes. The fact that so many go hungry when food is available and only needs redistribution makes the situation outrageous: "Raising the food intake of the over 450 million severely undernourished to the level of their nutritional requirements would involve the equivalent of 40–60 million tons of wheat per year. This is no more than 3–5% of present world cereal consumption, or 10–15% of the cereals now being fed to livestock in the developed countries."[17]

Christians associated with the World Council, as humanists of several stripes, have concluded from figures such as these that the world's economy needs a serious overhaul. Further, it seems patent to most of them that the nations' arms buildup is a major culprit in the present dysfunctions, since it siphons off so many resources that might go into the agricultural, educational, medical, and other programs that could help the poor down from their cross. Equally patent are the political consequences of these figures: a world always on the edge of massive conflict, if not nuclear conflagration, as around the globe severe poverty tempts group after group to violent revolution. Indeed, the wracking social structures of Latin America, South Africa, and Asia give many young people the feeling that they have nothing to lose by attempting to revolt. The World Council has tried to face these feelings honestly and help to change the structures making so many so miserable. Predictably, this effort has brought considerable criticism from the right, perhaps most popularly in early 1983, when the television program "60 Minutes" devoted two segments to the complaints of conservative Christians against the politics of the World Council.

In rebuttal, defenders of the World Council have honed the classical Protestant propheticism to a razor's edge:

What is forgotten in the sort of analysis of violence that pervaded the "60 Minutes" segment is something that the WCC itself, along with the Latin American Catholic bishops, has begun to bring into the public discussion. This is the ongoing reality of what is usually called the "hidden" violence already at work in our society—the violence embodied in injustice, unemployment, starvation and all the other social ills that destroy and demean and kill human beings just as decisively as bullets or bayonets. As Phillip Potter [General Secretary of the World Council] said in one of the few comments Morley Safer [the "60 Minutes" interviewer] permitted him to complete, providing "soup and soap" is not enough. It is the causes behind the lack of soup and soap that are the problem.[18]

SUMMARY

We began our delineation of the prophetic mentality shaping Christianity by studying Jesus, the Christian founder. As presented in the New Testament, the book he imprinted with his lively personality, Jesus came on the Israelite scene with a divine commission. His preaching demanded enactment: The time of the Kingdom was at hand, people had to repent and believe in his good news. By the end of the New Testament era, this prophet had become divine, the eternal Son of God. Thus the gospel of the early Christians celebrated both Jesus' joyous preaching of the Kingdom and the good news that in His divine Son God had conquered death. As Messiah, Son of Man, and Incar-

nate Word, Jesus had put into the world of space and time the healing love of the Father. The believer who clung to Jesus in faith could stand against all enemies and onslaughts.

Evangelical prophecy, proposed in the light of Jesus' having made all things new, put a fine point on the paradoxes of the Hebrew prophets. As the "Magnificat" of Mary and the "Beatitudes" of Jesus show, the poor and outcast had become the apple of the Father's eye. Latter-day evangelicals have been returning to this early perception, slowly taking up the themes of radical justice. Medieval Christianity never lost such themes, but often it placed them second to monastic solitude or metaphysics. Jesus continued to be a prophet, but the ways in which he was more than a prophet (divine) struck medieval people as more interesting. The Protestant Reformers returned to the biblical Word of God and so to many demands of the Hebrew prophets.

Modern Christianity saw the deepening of the split between faith and reason that some versions of Protestantism had encouraged. By the time that new science, philosophy, economics, and psychology had definitively separated Europe from medieval convictions, Christianity was on the defensive. Nowadays prophetic theologians such as Dorothee Sölle find the most burning Christian faith to be behind walls: in those people suffering from injustice the world over.

Christian social thought, rooted in the Church, places a high premium on justice and love. The union of the branches in the vine means the subordination of all members to God's grace. The tragedy of modern Christian history is the rapacious conduct of the colonizers and slavers who belied the Christian sociological ideal. Psychologically, the basis of the person's great dignity has been the notion that he or she is an image of God. Contemplative personalities sought to burnish this image and keep it free of worldly taints by withdrawing into quiet. Active personalities sought to make the gospel a goad to social justice and peacemaking. Ecologically, the biblical themes of human beings' privileged place in creation and creation's manifestation of God have shaped most of the Christian traditions. Jesus clearly saw nature as a gift and lesson from God, Paul found the Creator manifest in creation, and Athanasius and Calvin sensed God in the stability of the mountains or the movement of the stars. But redemption often bulked larger than creation, so nature easily could be abused.

Today the city of Geneva is to prophetic Christianity much as Jerusalem is to prophetic Judaism. In the programs of the World Council of Churches to combat world hunger, deescalate the arms race, and lessen the structural causes of violence, the prophetic Word continues to demand justice. Predictably this raises opposition, reminding Christians that their leader paid dearly for his prophecies.

STUDY QUESTIONS

1. How does John the Baptist function in the New Testament proclamation of the Kingdom of God?

2. Why could Paul write that nothing could separate Christians from the love of God?

3. What is the relation between the Lukan beatitudes and the Lukan woes?

4. Why might one interpret the Eastern Church's controversy over icons as a prophetic issue?

5. Explain Dorothee Sölle's references to Saint Francis of Assisi.

6. How does *A Compassionate Peace* bring the Christian prophetic tradition up to date?

7. What is the valid point in Father John's description of life in the world?

8. Are the nature parables of Jesus prophetic? Why?

9. What would a biblical prophet likely make of today's figures on world hunger?

NOTES

1. Johannes B. Bauer, "Saviour," in *Encyclopedia of Biblical Theology*, ed. Johannes B. Bauer. New York: Crossroad, 1981, p. 813.

2. See Geza Vermes, *Jesus the Jew*. London: Fontana/Collins, 1973.

3. See Edward Schillebeeckx, *Jesus*. New York: Seabury, 1979.

4. Norman Perrin and Dennis C. Duling, *The New Testament: An Introduction*, 2d ed. New York: Harcourt Brace Jovanovich, 1982, p. 313.

5. Robert D. Linder, "The Resurgence of Evangelical Social Concern (1925–75)," in *The Evangelicals*, rev. ed., ed. David F. Wells and John D. Woodbridge. Grand Rapids, Mich.: Baker, 1975, pp. 224–25.

6. Athanasius, "A Letter to Marcellinus," sec. 2, 5, in *Athanasius*, trans. Robert C. Gregg. Ramsey, N.J.: Paulist, 1980, pp. 102–3.

7. Jaroslav Pelikan, *The Christian Tradition,* vol. 3. Chicago: University of Chicago Press, 1978, p. 120.

8. Martin Luther, "Treatise on Christian Liberty," in *The Protestant Reformation*, ed. Lewis W. Spitz. Englewood Cliffs, N.J.: Prentice-Hall, 1966, p. 62.

9. Dorothee Sölle, *Revolutionary Patience*. Maryknoll, N.Y.: Orbis, 1977, pp. 27–28.

10. Ibid., pp. 40–41.

11. American Friends Service Committee, *A Compassionate Peace*. New York: Hill and Wang, 1982, p. vi.

12. Sergius Bolshakoff and M. Basil Pennington, *In Search of True Wisdom: Visits to Eastern Spiritual Fathers*. Garden City, N.Y.: Doubleday, 1979, p. 41.

13. Robert McAfee Brown, *Creative Dislocation— The Movement of Grace*. Nashville: Abingdon, 1980, p. 37.

14. John Carmody, *Ecology and Religion*. Ramsey, N.J.: Paulist, 1983, pp. 96–97. See Pheme Perkins, *Hearing the Parables of Jesus*. Ramsey, N.J.: Paulist, 1981, pp. 76–89.

15. John T. McNeill, *The History and Character of Calvinism*. New York: Oxford University Press, 1979, p. 209.

16. Diogo de Gaspar, "Economics and World Hunger," in *Faith and Science in an Unjust World*, vol. 1, ed. Roger L. Shinn. Philadelphia: Fortress, 1980, pp. 225–26.

17. Ibid., p. 227.

18. Robert McAfee Brown, "The Gospel According to Morley Safer," *The Christian Century*, 100/6 (2 March, 1983), p. 185.

8

Islam

MUHAMMAD

As Moses and Jesus are the preeminent figures in the origins of Judaism and Christianity, so Muhammad is the personality who inspired Islam. And whereas Moses is shrouded in historical obscurity, since he lived about nineteen hundred years before Muhammad, and Jesus is shrouded in the controversy surrounding Christian claims that he was divine, Muhammad is a relatively straightforward historical figure. To be sure, his life and thought are not fully documented from modern historical perspectives, and the **hagiography** of his followers has colored many of the reports about him. Still, Islam's insistence that Muhammad was merely a man and that the Koran represents God's communications to him (often through the angel Gabriel) provide a comparatively objective context in which to examine Muhammad's life and thought.

Muhammad probably was born before 570 C.E. near Mecca. Practically orphaned from the start, since his father died before his birth and his mother shortly after it, he was raised by an uncle in circumstances that some Koranic passages suggest were at least moderately well off. For example, Surah 93, verses 6–8 says, "Did he not find thee an orphan, and shelter thee? Did he not find thee erring, and guide thee? Did he not find thee needy, and suffice thee?"[1] In maturity Muhammad worked in commerce for a rich widow named Khadija, whom he later married. "She was related to the Christian scholar Waraqa ibn Nawfal, but it is not clear whether she or her family provided any religious inspiration or instruction for Muhammad. She did, however, give him social standing and personal support during the initial crises of his religious experiences, and she was the mother of all his children except Ibrahim."[2]

When Muhammad, for whatever combination of personal needs and social circumstances, began to

Islam: Twenty-Five Key Dates

570 C.E.   Birth of Muhammad
609–610   First Koranic Revelations
622   Hejira [Flight to Medina]
630   Conquest of Mecca
632   Death of Muhammad
636–640   Conquest of Damascus, Jerusalem, Egypt, Persia
CA. 650   Establishment of the Canon of the Koran
661–750   Umayyad Caliphate
680   Murder of Husain, Shiite Saint
711   Muslim Entry into Spain
713   Muslim Entry into Indus Valley
750–1258   Abbasid Caliphate
762   Foundation of Baghdad
909   Rise of Fatimids in North Africa
956   Conversion of Seljuk Turks
966   Foundation of Cairo
1099   Christian Crusaders Capture Jerusalem
1111   Death of Al-Ghazali, Leading Thinker
1258   Sack of Baghdad by Mongols
1453   Ottoman Turks Capture Constantinople
1492   End of Muslim Spain
1707   Decline of Mogul India
1803–1804   Wahabism Victorious in Mecca and Medina
1924   Secularization of Turkey
1947–1948   Creation of Pakistan and Israel

seek spiritual sustenance, he had available the polytheistic traditions of most of the Arab tribes of his day, a thin strain of monotheistic tradition among the few Arabs who had broken with polytheism, and the influences of neighboring Jews and Christians. Following the custom of his own Arab tribe, the Quraish, Muhammad took to withdrawing for a month each year to give himself to religious devotions. During one of these withdrawals, on the mountain of Hira near Mecca about 610 C.E., he had the first of his vivid religious experiences. Some commentators think that Surah 74:1–5 is the best Koranic text from which to conjecture what that first experience was: "In the name of God, the Merciful, the Compassionate. O thou shrouded in thy mantle, arise, and warn! Thy Lord magnify, thy robes purify, and defilement flee!" For others Surah 96:1–5 offers the best clues to the first revelations Muhammad received: "In the name of God, the Merciful, the Compassionate. Recite: In the Name

of thy Lord who created, created Man of a blood-clot. Recite: And thy Lord is the most generous, who taught by the Pen, taught Man that he knew not."

We shall deal with the content of these passages in the next section. Here we should note the familiar prophetic features: A person receives a special calling, is told to announce a divine message, and is overwhelmed by the holiness of the God, the Creator and Lord, who sends that mission. Slowly Muhammad's mission clarified, until he became convinced that God was asking him to announce a new set of ideals to the Arab people. They initially rejected these ideals, since conversion would have entailed such steps as withdrawing from their polytheism and the religious business (for example, the selling of amulets) it generated in Mecca. By the time that Muhammad's followers became a significant number, opposition to his message had led to persecution. Thus he accepted an invitation to go to nearby Medina, where he raised an army, formed a Muslim community, and dominated the scene from 622 C.E. on. By 630 he was strong enough to return, conquer Mecca, and cleanse it of its pagan statues. However, the Meccan triumph proved short-lived, for he unexpectedly died in 632 C.E.

According to the traditions (**hadith**) that developed after Muhammad's death, he was a man of great humanity. The traditions picture him as sympathetic to the weak, gentle, slow to anger, and somewhat shy in crowds. They also attribute to him a rich sense of humor. Thus in one story the Prophet's associate Abu Bakr starts to beat a pilgrim for letting a camel stray. Muhammad begins to smile and then shows Abu Bakr the irony that a pilgrim such as Bakr (on his journey through life) should divert himself to beat a pilgrim on the way to Mecca (to perform one of the key Muslim obligations). Later Islam embellished this simple portrait, attributing miracles to Muhammad or placing him at the beginning of creation, but the official Muslim theology keeps him as simply the Prophet: the man God chose to announce the divine Word.

KORAN

The Koran (or Qur'an) is the collection of the "recitals" that Muhammad received, the revelations he was to declaim to his people. It is the Muslim equivalent to the Jewish Torah and the Christian Gospel (or Christ as the Word behind the Gospel). As the verses we have already quoted show, the Koran has the form of speeches from God to Muhammad and his audience. Our first quotation, dealing with Muhammad's own life, suggests that Allah (Arabic term meaning "God") had a providential care for the Prophet. The second and third specimens, which may represent Muhammad's first revelations, sound many of the central Koranic themes: Muhammad is to *warn* his people of the pending judgments of Allah; he is to *magnify* the goodness and holiness of his God; he must *purify* himself in the presence of this holiness; he must flee any *defilement*. Further, his recital to the people will be in the name of Allah, stressing that Allah is Lord and Creator. Finally, the verses proclaim that Allah is the generous teacher of human beings, giving them scriptures that reveal his mysteries. Even these brief verses therefore show the Koran to be a prophetic work burning with such lofty themes as judgment, creation, and revelation.

Materially, the Koran consists of 114 chapters, or surahs, and is roughly the length of the New Testament. The surahs are arranged by length rather than date, the longest being found at the beginning and the shortest at the end. Islamic tradition assigns the surahs to Mecca or Medina, depending upon where the Prophet is thought to have been when he received their contents. On the whole the shorter surahs are considered Meccan and the longer surahs Medinan. In style, the Koran is passionate, poetic, very moving. Indeed, Muslims have long argued from the sublimity of its Arabic to the divinity of its source.

In addition to the themes we have already noted, the following also weave through the Koran: praise for the one God and his many signs in the natural world; warnings about the final day of resurrection and judgment; exhortations to piety and good works; reminders of the long history of prophecy, which includes Abraham and Jesus; statements about social and personal morality; and comments on contemporary problems. Most of these themes recur often, since the Koran does not unfold in a logical, deductive fashion but keeps circling back and interweaving. The collection of Muhammad's revelations that we now have most likely dates to the third **caliph**, Uthman, around 650 C.E. It includes the passages then being used by the best "reciters" among the Prophet's companions. From the beginning to today the Koran has been more oral than written, in that throughout Muslim history emphasis has been on speaking and hearing the Koran, rather than reading it.

Theologically, the Koran is absolutely central to Islam. The basic creed of Islam ("There is no God but God and Muhammad is His Prophet") shows why Muhammad's recitals quickly came to be considered God's own Word. As Muslim theologians further reflected on the matter, the Koran became eternal: something with God as part of his divine existence. God's prior revelations through Moses, Jesus, and the rest were good enough in their day, but the Koran is the last, summary revelation. Thus Muslims speak of Muhammad as the "seal" of the prophets, the one who brings prophecy to its consummation. The highest Muslim learning has been the interpretation of the Koran, and traditionally the devout Muslim would memorize all the holy verses.

In Islamic usage, the chapters of the Koran have individual names, usually taken from their first words or most prominent images. One of the most beloved surahs is "Light" (Surah 24), whose poetic depicting of God suggests something of the Koran's power: "God is the Light of the heavens and the earth; the likeness of His Light is as a niche wherein is a lamp (the lamp in a glass, the glass as it were a glittering star) kindled from a Blessed Tree, an olive that is neither of the East nor of the West, whose oil well nigh would shine, even if no fire touched it; Light upon Light; (God guides to His Light whom He will.)" (verses 35–37)

The image of God as the light of the world portrays him as the source of vision, sense, and beauty. That God's likeness burns like the flame of an oil lamp (in dark night) makes him the difference between safety and threat, security and desolation. And that God guides to his Light whom he will suggests the priority of the divine in all human affairs. There is no wisdom or goodness that Allah does not supply, no human achievement that can boast of being independent.

One of the last surahs (107) is called "Charity." It suggests the social demands of Koranic faith: "In the Name of God, the Merciful, the Compassionate. Has thou seen him who cries lies to the Doom? That is he who repulses the orphan and urges not the feeding of the needy. So woe to those that pray and are heedless of their prayers, to those who make display and refuse charity." (verses 1–6) The clear message is that one cannot pray sincerely to Allah and neglect society's marginal people. One cannot pray insincerely to Allah and avoid his doom. Thus Islam has made the *zakat*, or obligatory alms, one of its five central pillars. The prophetic word come to Muhammad, like that to Moses and Jesus, demanded performance: justice and helpfulness.

KORANIC PROPHECY

The other pillars of Islam, in addition to almsgiving, are recitation of the creed, prayer five times a day, fasting during the lunar month of Ramadan; and pilgrimage to Mecca at least once during one's life. Let us reflect on the prophetic character of these other four pillars, to condense the Koran's omnipresent concern with doing the will of the holy God.

The creed boils Muslim faith down to its quintessence. If there is no God but God, all other gods are idols, false pretenders. To "associate" anything with God therefore is the worst of sins. Indeed, idolatry, or **shirk**, flies in the face of the overwhelming impression recorded in the Koran: only Allah is fully real, wholly important, worth a life's dedication. As Surah 4:51 puts it, "God forgives not that aught should be with Him associated; less than that He forgives to whomsoever He will. Whoso associates with God anything, has indeed forged a mighty sin." When scholars of comparative religion speak of Islam's "absolute monotheism," they draw on this impassioned hatred of idolatry. For such rigorist Muslims as the Wahhabis, any veneration of saints, or even excessive devotion

to Muhammad, is forbidden on pain of condemnation as *shirk*. Islam's prohibitions concerning representations of God or even of human figures stem from its deep regard for the sovereign uniqueness of the "Lord of the Worlds." Thus one finds no statues, icons, or portraiture in mosques. Only the Word of God given to Muhammad is to dominate. Muhammad's grandeur and poverty alike stem from the fact that he is simply God's **rasul**: his messenger, spokesperson, apostle.

What is prophetic about the injunction to pray five times each day? The sense that one's vision and work depend utterly on the holy Creator, and the form in which Islam casts this prayer. Concerning the sense, one notes that the prophet's entire meaning depends upon the Word of his or her God. All that the prophet proclaims comes from the revealing Source. In the Muslim view of things, the Creator is omnipotent and omniscient, the creature but a drop of sperm and a clot of blood. One must never try to bridge the chasm between the two (that would be *shirk*), and the true believer always fears the possibility of wandering away from its importance. Regular prayer therefore tries to make the sentiments of the first surah of the Koran habitual: "In the name of God, the Merciful, the Compassionate. Praise belongs to God, the Lord of all Being, the All-merciful, the All-compassionate, the Master of the Day of Doom. Thee only we serve; to Thee alone we pray for succor. Guide us in the straight path, the path of those whom Thou hast blessed, not of those against whom Thou art wrathful, nor of those who are astray." The form in which Islam casts its daily prayer, the bowing, kneeling, and prostration that places one's forehead on the ground, shows the submissiveness and humility that true faith inculcates. Before the Lord of all Being the only proper posture is prostration. Five times each day, the devout Muslim incarnates this belief: acts it out, sends it running along sinews and nerves so that it teaches the back, the knees, the forehead, the whole being.

Fasting is similarly physical. Abstaining from food and drink from dawn to sunset, as strict interpretation demands, the Muslim teaches the body, and through the body the spirit, that Allah is demanding, faith entails sacrifice. So for one month each year observant Muslims are ascetic. (Ramadan is also a joyous time, however; after sunset there is feasting.) Whether Ramadan occurs in the short days of winter or the long days of summer (as a lunar month it moves), the body must hallow it. The prophetic aspect of this practice is its willfulness and performative character. The prophet is less concerned with considering than with acting. The prophetic goal is not clear thoughts so much as individual and social reform.

The last of the five pillars, the **hajj**, or pilgrimage,

is also a practical observance. Ideally it takes place during the twelfth month of the Islamic year. Ten miles outside Mecca all pilgrims change into a two-piece robe, and female pilgrims must completely veil themselves. In Mecca all parade seven times around the Ka'ba, the shrine to which worldwide Islam turns in prayer, if possible touching the Black Stone in its wall. They also run seven times between the two hills of Safa and Marwa and go to the plains of Arafat and Mina to cast stones at cairns. (These rituals reflect pre-Muslim practices incorporated into the *hajj*.) At the end of the pilgrimage is a great animal sacrifice, which Muslims all over the world replicate at the same hour. Thus many aspects of *hajj* strengthen the bonds among all believers. The coincidence of the sacrifices, similarity of the pilgrims' garb, and reinforcement of the centrality of Mecca help to retie all Muslims to the city of their religion's birth.

Ingenious in their simplicity and practicality, the five pillars prop a faith that would clear the world of ambiguities and make devout living blessedly clear. With One Sole God, the source of the world and all human meaning becomes obvious. With one Prophet, and from God's speech to him one book, the map for life's way becomes equally obvious. Of course Islam has sent out many branches and evolved to considerable complexity. But at its center has always lain the two ruthless, riveting propositions of the creed. For those brought up on the haunting Arabic verses of the Koran, life could be as clear as a cloudless day in the desert.

MEDIEVAL ISLAM

Muhammad died in 632 C.E. By 636 C.E. his successors had unified Arabia and poised Islam on the threshold of rapid expansion. Thus in 636 C.E. they took Damascus and Jerusalem, and by 640 parts of Egypt were in their hands. In 643 they were taking charge in North Africa. The year 648 gave them Cyprus. By 649 they had conquered all of Persia. In 655 C.E. they took control of the waters around Greece and Sicily. And so it went, like wildfire. By 700 Afghanistan was Muslim and by 800 Armenia, Iraq, and eastern India were in the fold. The eighth century also brought Muslims into France; by the ninth century, Switzerland. After 1050 C.E. their European presence faded, but virtually all parts of southern Europe had been deeply stamped.

For the Muslims themselves, this expansion was a natural outlet for many energies. Demographically, it meant more room for a pent-in population. Econom-ically, it meant a great increase in wealth. The military expeditions goaded Muslim males to prowess. The religious imperatives were to spread the Prophet's message. Among the peoples whom the Muslims conquered, often there were complementary motivations. Some were chafing under oppressive Christian rule. Others were looking for a new cause, energetic and challenging, into which they might pour their religious and military energies. The result of this match between Arab energies and neighboring peoples' ripeness was a burst of expansion, and then cultural flowering, with few parallels in world history.

We shall deal with several aspects of the cultural flowering momentarily. To paint the picture of expansion faithfully, however, we must also note the tragic divisions that crippled Islam from well nigh its beginnings. Most of the early caliphs were murdered while in office, and Ali, the fourth caliph, lost office to another dynasty. This loss led to the division between Sunni and Shia Muslims that has persisted to this day. The **Shia** have been partisans of Ali, believing that Muslim rule ought to descend along the blood lines of the Prophet's family. (Ali was the cousin and son-in-law of Muhammad.) The **Sunnis** have accepted the caliphs who preceded and followed Ali. ("According-ing to the Shi'a, the 'followers' of 'Ali,' he was the first legitimate caliph or iman, 'spiritual leader' after the Prophet. He is called the 'friend of God,' a title which the Shi'a add to the regular confession of faith in God and in Muhammad. He is in particular the ideal warrior and saint and many legends are told of his miracles and holiness, while judgments and maxims attributed to him are widespread.")[3]

The golden civilization of medieval Islam that accompanied its geographical expansion reached into science, art, architecture, poetry, law, philosophy, theology, and mysticism. The Umayyads (the dynasty deriving from the man who ousted Ali) were patrons of Hellenistic science, so by 700 C.E. there was an officially sponsored astronomical observatory in Damascus. The successors of the Umayyads, the Abbasids (eighth through thirteenth centuries), preferred Persian science, so from their center in Baghdad spread support for Persian medicine and astronomy. The Abbasids also sponsored the translation of many Greek materials and imported mathematicians from India. In the West Muslims dominant in Spain patronized scientific centers in Cordoba and Toledo.

In art Muslim beliefs led to abstract styles, including a lovely calligraphy to ornament copies of the Koran. The peak centuries in architecture were the sixteenth and seventeenth, when builders in Ottoman Turkey, Safavid Persia, and Mughal India erected gorgeous mosques and mausoleums (for example, the Taj Ma-

*Figure 9   Courtyard of Cairo Mosque, with purification fountain.
Photo by J. T. Carmody.*

hal). The thirteenth century was a high point for Muslim poetry. At that time Ibn al-Khabbaza expressed the Arab ideal in an elegy: "Your life was of the true order of Arab eloquence; the Tale was brief, the words were few, the meaning was immense."[4] In Persia Rumi consummated a line going back to the woman Rabia and the man Junaid, making Persian poetry Islam's most honored.

Overall, however, law became the dominant intellectual activity, since **shariah** (religious guidance) became a jurisprudential affair (quite parallel to the rabbinic development of Torah). Using the Koran, the hadith, and the growing number of documents dealing with the community's consensus and analogical reasonings, the Muslim lawyers developed quite comprehensive codes. These tended to outweigh the influence of philosophy and theology, since the codes were more practical. Islamic philosophy showed the influence of Greek sources, but it was suspect of following an authority (reason) that might be at odds with the Koran. Although theology accepted the supremacy of the Koran and then tried to reason out the views of God, human nature, the structure of the cosmos, and the like that the Koran implied, it also suffered the restraints of **shariah**.

No doubt the greatest of the medieval Muslim intellectuals was the Persian al-Ghazali (1058–1111 c.e.), who was a lawyer, philosopher, theologian, and mystic. He followed Sunni doctrine, finally trying to unite all his studies in the mystical experiences of the Sufis. Al-Ghazali's regard for the Sufis can be gleaned from the following famous endorsement: "I learnt with certainty that it is above all the mystics who walk on the road of God; their life is the best life, their method the soundest method, their character the purest character; indeed, were the intellect of the intellectuals and the learning of the learned and the scholarship of the scholars, who are versed in the profundities of revealed truth, brought together in the attempt to improve the life and character of the mystics, they would find no way of doing so."[5] True to the prophetic sources of his faith, al-Ghazali favored the people who had developed the best practice, the most impressive results.

MODERN ISLAM

Sufism declined after the thirteenth century, becoming rife with abuses and superstitions. As well, Arab influence declined, as Turkish and Persian rulers took over more and more of the Muslim empire. From the sixteenth century European expansion took the political and cultural play away from Islam, and Napoleon's easy conquest of the Turks at the end of the eighteenth century dealt Islamic military might its final blow. Early in the nineteenth century, however, the rigorist Wahhabis, centered in Arabia, catalyzed a reform movement designed to counter both Sufi and European influences. Many Muslim countries, finding themselves ill-equipped to compete with the new science, industrialization, and political thought emanating from Europe, suffered severe questions about their future. Ought they to take up the new ideas, or would the new ideas prove ruinous to their traditional cultures? Above all, were the new ideas compatible with Koranic religion and shariah?

To the present, Islam continues to struggle with these questions. On the one hand, such occurrences as the discovery of oil in the Middle East have brought some of the money necessary for the education, health care, and industrialization that might change the fate of the millions of Muslim poor. On the other hand, the history of the Shah of Iran, whose modernizations, as well as cruel tyrannies, proved unpopular with many of his people, shows the strength of the traditional religious ways. Saudi Arabia, the largest of the Islamic oil producers, recently has been dominated by the Wahhabis, who came to control Mecca in 1924. They have determined that Saudi Arabia should be quite conservative in religious matters. The new Iranian regime begun by the Ayatollah Khomeini represented a Shiite (Shia) form of conservatism, more volatile and bloody. How money, technology, and faith will mix in the Islamic twenty-first century is anybody's guess.

Common to the many Muslim regimes of modern times has been the problem of correlating the traditional prophetic insistence on faith and devout practice with an intellectual openness to the political institutions that modernity has developed. V.S. Naipaul, a not very sympathetic critic of Islam (and Hinduism), has reported on this problem in contemporary Iran, Pakistan, Malaysia, and Indonesia. In each country he found a strong inclination to try to achieve progress and prosperity by passionate belief, rather than sober intellectual analysis. Representative of Naipaul's experiences with the **mullahs** (religious teachers) of Iran was the following:

I asked whether history—the history of Islamic civilization—was something he had studied. He misunderstood; he thought I was asking a question about Muslim theology, and he said of course he knew Islamic history: when the Prophet first gave his message the people of his village didn't want it, and so he had to go to the next village. And always—whether I attempted to get him to talk about the scientific needs of Muslim countries, or about his ideas for Iran after the revolution—we slid down his theology to the confusion of his certainties. With true Islam, science would flourish; the Prophet said that people should go out and learn. With true Islam, there was freedom (he meant the freedom to be Islamic and Shia, to be divinely ruled); and everything came with freedom (this idea of freedom quite separate from the first).[6]

More representative of infra-Muslim opinion is the volume *Islam in Transition: Muslim Perspectives.* In it one finds reflections such as the following by Najib Mahfuz, an eminent Egyptian novelist:

But there is some general research concerning a full application of the Shari'a; *I believe that every Muslim welcomes this and considers that its execution will accomplish his most cherished dream. This true Muslim persevering in his duties often finds himself perplexed. He leads a contemporary life. He obeys civil and penal laws of Western origin and is involved in a complex tangle of social and economic transactions and is never certain to what extent these agree with or contradict his Islamic creed. Life carries him along in its current, and he forgets his misgivings for a time until one Friday he hears the* imam *[prayer leader in the mosque] or reads the religion page in one of the papers, and the old misgivings come back with a certain fear. He realizes that in this new society he has been afflicted with a split personality: half of him believes, prays, fasts and makes the pilgrimage. The other half renders his values void in banks and courts and in the streets, even in the cinemas and theatres, perhaps even at home among his family before the television set. . . . The wise men entrusted with looking into the application of Islamic legislation must (1) produce a thorough interpretation of how these principles should be understood (today); (2) provide a profound interpretation which will help us to understand the reality of our present lives; and (3) maintain wholehearted respect for the principles to which political organizations are bound, namely, the inevitability of the socialist solution, social peace and national unity.*[7]

One senses the author's profound sympathy for the sufferings of conscientious Muslims caught between the old and new portions of their culture. His desire to update the shariah testifies both to his own religious loyalty and to his honesty about the needs of present-day Islam. He is an eloquent spokesman.

ISLAMIC SOCIAL THOUGHT

As the final imperative listed by Najib Mahfuz shows, the "socialist solution" ranks high on the agenda of many contemporary Muslim intellectuals. This is a malleable phrase, hammered into different shapes by different groups, but its usual import is producing forms of government that serve the people as a whole, in contrast to forms that advance the interests of only certain classes. Insofar as populist movements seek or have found power in numerous Muslim lands, some form of "socialism" often is proposed. How this is compatible with the iron rule that has obtained in such lands as Iran and Egypt, or with the overall Islamic tradition, is the sort of question dominating much current Islamic sociology.

Traditionally, Muslims have felt that society exists in order that human beings might realize the divine "pattern" the Creator has set them. One of the most central elements in this pattern is the family. However, Islam has not made marriage a sacrament, and it has allowed a man to marry more than one woman, so long as he is able to provide all his wives justice, equity, and loving care. Concerning property, the tradition has been that private property is an inviolate right. As well, one naturally has the right to pursue wealth. With wealth, however, one's social obligations are increased, and one is expected to care for society's deprived. Islam has also considered the right to life inviolate: "The life of one's fellowman is inviolate, except by due process of law. Nothing may henceforth be decided by force or violence. Such recourse is legitimate only in self-defense and in the safeguarding of the security of missionaries. For the Muslim is duty-bound to bring his faith to the knowledge of mankind with sound preaching and wise counsel, to convey the warning and command of his Lord."[8]

The broadest Muslim political unit is the *Ummah,* which is roughly equivalent to the Christian Church or the Buddhist *Sangha.* Usually Muslims have interpreted the Koran as teaching that Muhammad and his successors form a **theocracy** in the Ummah; their rule has been a divinely sanctioned fusion of the secular and the religious. Indeed, it is extremely important to realize that Islam does not separate the secular and the religious spheres. Traditionally, Muslim culture is a unitary whole, and one of the chief conflicts of Islam with modern Western culture has been the West's tendency to separate the secular and the religious spheres or even to make the religious sphere purely private. The ties of the Muslim community, by contrast, all fold into the perspective of God's will. Indeed, because they have shared membership in the single House of Islam, Muslims even have felt an obligation to fight on one another's behalf. (Koran 4:75) Overall, members of the Ummah have felt they should be to one another as "brothers and guardians."

In almost all traditional societies, women have been second-class citizens, considered ineligible for enlightenment, or incapable of political rule, or simply the weaker vessels. The traditional subjugation of women one finds in Islam therefore has parallels in Christian and Eastern societies. In the darker strains of the Muslim tradition, however, one meets subjugation in an especially stark form. The result has been **purdah** (subjection to seclusion and veiling), polygyny, concubinage, and the harem. Frequently the popular view was that women were not to be taught to read and to write, and that they were morally crooked because they came from Adam's bent rib. Thus one finds such grim epithets as: "It were best for a girl not to come into existence, but being born she had better be married or buried."[9] As Christianity has had its misogynistic horrors of witch burning, Hinduism has had **suttee** (widow burning), and China has had foot binding, so Islam has had the horror of clitoridectomy, or female circumcision. The traditional rationale for this practice has run something like this: "Circumcision of women releases them from their bondage to sex, and enables them to fulfill their real destiny as mother."[10] On the other hand, Muhammad considerably raised the status of women from what it had been in pre-Islamic Arabia, and there are widespread changes afoot in the current Muslim world.[11]

In many parts of the current Muslim world, of course, Islam sits atop an older sociology and religion. Thus in Indonesia the pre-Muslim Hindu influence remains strong, even in the lives of those who are nominally Muslims, because it is part and parcel of the Indonesian culture. Still, the official prominence of Islam causes most of the strongest movements for social change to speak in Islamic accents:

You ask me the situation of the farmers today and how the kiyai *[commune leader] can change this unjust society? The farmers today do not receive justice. Most of them are poor because they have no land. There are more farmers now who have no job. The landlords use machines, instead of the farmers, in their farms. The farmers receive very low prices for their products. Meanwhile, the rich in our society are so rich. They get their wealth from the money that is given or lent to our country by the very rich nations. Now, how can a* kiyai *help in the changing of this kind of society? How can he make the landlords and the rich give up their properties which, according to Islam, belong to Allah and must be given back to the people who are creatures of Allah?*[12]

ISLAMIC PERSONAL THOUGHT

The orthodox conception of the self began with the notion of creation. In Surah 96 the self is described essentially as a small thing that God made from a blood clot or a drop of sperm. The essence of Islam and of being a Muslim was to recognize the creator-creature relation: a sovereign God who is completely the Lord of a very insignificant vassal. The basic scriptural message of Islamic anthropology is submission, even a certain holy slavery. This attitude was no false humility. Rather, it was the bare truth of the human condition. Human beings came from God, and their destiny depended on living out the pattern that God had in making them. Thus, they had no basis for self-glorification.[13]

On this theological foundation, Islam built its notions of personal dignity and maturity. As to how Muslims conceive adulthood, the stage of personal maturity, the following is a representative example:

Islam has a conception of adulthood. Though Muslim tradition is not self-consciously occupied with it, especially as opposed to childhood or youth, it does provide a notion of what the fully matured person should be. A Muslim legal concept that is close to our own sense of adulthood defines the mukallaf—*the legally and morally responsible person—as one who has reached physical maturity, is of sound mind, may enter into contracts, dispose of property, and be subject to criminal law. Above all, he is responsible for the religious commands and obligations of Islam, for bearing the burden (*taklif*) laid upon him by God.*[14]

This description better applies to Sunni personal thought than to Shiite, since Sunni Islam lays more emphasis on the legalistic, Shiite on the charismatic.

In representing the socially minded side of Muslim personal thought Sunni lawyers sometimes were polar opposites to Sufi masters, who stressed individuality, parable, and paradox. While the lawyers tended to prescribe for the external and general side of things, the Sufis focused on the relativity most events bear when seen from the inside. This is the message of the following Sufi story:

Teaching, as was his custom, during the ordinary business of life, Sheik Abu Tahir Harami rode his donkey one day into a marketplace, a disciple following behind. At the sight of him, a man called out: "Look, here comes the ancient unbeliever!" Harami's pupil, his wrath aroused, shouted at the defamer. Before long there was a fierce altercation in progress. The Sufi calmed his disciple, saying: "If you will only cease this tumult, I will show you how you can escape this kind of trouble." They went together to the old man's house. The sheik told his follower to bring him a box of letters. "Look at these. They are all letters addressed to me. But they are couched in different terms. Here someone calls me 'Sheik of Islam'; there, 'Sublime Teacher.' Another says I am the 'Wise One of the Twin Sanctuaries.' And there are others. Observe how each styles me in accordance with what he considers me to be. But I am none of these things. Each man calls another just what he thinks him to be. This is what the unfortunate one in the market place has just done. And yet you take exception to it. Why do you do so—since it is the general rule of life?"[15]

Through observing the five pillars and the other prescriptions of religious law, the Muslim could hope to mature, become fully adult, feel at home in the world Allah had made. By attending to Sufi wisdom, he or she could balance this external goal with an inner sense of the relativities that meditation and prayer spotlight. Feeling the dependence of everything on God, the world's thorough **contingency**, the Sufis would have one take a skeptical view of human assumptions, swallow both praise and abuse with several grains of salt.

In Shiite Islam ritual has tended to be dramatic, making self-conceptions vibrant. One sees this in a recent description of the personal cult of the Ayatollah Khomeini:

If one could analyze this persona (the image projected by Khomeini, including the legends that have been built up around him) sociologically by asking to whom its different parts appeal, two classes would likely be most engaged: the subproletariat of unemployed new urban migrants and the traditional petit bourgeoisie, classes whose traditional religious imag-

ination has been formed around the drama of the tragedy of Karbala, the martyrdom of the third Iman, Husain, at the hands of the archtyrant, Yezid. Khomeini's persona draws on a similar emotional configuration, one that generates a stoic determination in the face of overwhelming odds in a world of injustice and corruption. Several elements in the persona contribute to this image.

First, a legend of distress has been cultivated about his person. Like Husain, his father is said to have been unjustly slain, he was deprived of his rightful possessions (land, position), and he lost an infant daughter and a grown son. Second, and deeper, is his asceticism and eschewing of humor or lightheartedness. Unlike other ayatullahs who use humor to bind followers, Khomeini plays upon the notion that control of knowledge, especially that gained through gnostic exercise, is a dangerous enterprise, one that requires self-discipline. Asceticism is not turning away from the world, but a refusal to be seduced by the concerns of materialism and hedonism. This play on asceticism serves two related functions: it is a mark of courage in a corrupt and seductive world, and it wards off the suspicion of being self-seeking in those who exercise power.[16]

ISLAMIC ECOLOGY

If Muslim psychology proposes an asceticism that does not turn away from the world, Muslim ecology proposes an interlocking assertion that the world is essentially good. No matter how human beings may abuse it, creation itself is the work of the holy and merciful God. Indeed, the Muslim conception of the paradise that will bring the mature believer eternal happiness abounds in natural images. Thus Surah 55 speaks of the garden of paradise having fountains of running water, green pastures, palm trees, pomegranates, and cool pavilions. By contrast, the fiery place of hell has molten brass, a heaven split asunder and turned crimson like red leather, and boiling water. Natural appetites for food and sex will find rich satisfaction in the garden: all sorts of fruits, maidens untouched by man or jinn. One reason that Islam did not separate the religious and secular spheres, therefore, is that it did not spiritualize religion. Religion was something for the body as well as the spirit, something woven through the world of space and time as well as something entailing timeless thoughts and mystical loves.

Nonetheless, Islam makes it very clear that nature does not participate in the divinity of Allah. The Muslim insistence on monotheism has led to a dim view of fertility gods and goddesses, as it did for the biblical prophets. Indeed, it is characteristic of the Jewish, Christian, and Muslim prophets alike to restrain any strong emotional attachments to nature. Many of these prophets do strike off lovely naturalistic poetry, but almost always in the service of praising God, showing the Creator's splendid distance from the creature. Insofar as the stars of the heavens or the sands of the desert restore a proper perspective, they are very useful to prophetic religion. Insofar as they threaten to attract worship to themselves, they are potentially idolatrous.

The Ayatollah Khomeini notwithstanding, the Muslim mainstream does not appear markedly ascetic, does not deny to human beings the enjoyment of nature's fruits. Nor have ecological sensitivities, in the today's connotation of conservative and gentle dealings with nature, been the rule. Just as the biblical account of creation exalts the place of human beings, so does the Muslim understanding. Islam has no **Tao** or **Buddhanature** inextricable from physical nature. Nature is not a form or body of Allah. The Muslim garden, with its fountains and shading trees, has become a beautiful art form. The adornments at such sites as the Alhambra in Granada, Spain, is all that an ecologist could wish. But the cars of Cairo are woefully unmuffled, and the hills of Tehran have become a basin for heavy smog. Environmental ecology, therefore, may soon be a major problem in Muslim countries.

By way of solution, the Muslim notion of creation provides many incentives to work with nature, appreciating its bounties and applying new technologies carefully. As Isma'il al-Faruqi has summarized it:

Islam regards the whole of nature as profane (that is, other than sacred), an innocent creature which God created out of nothing for the enjoyment and use of humanity. Nature, Islam asserts, is a great, positive blessing, whose joys are advance payments on the rewards of Paradise. It is an orderly cosmos created by God as the theater where humanity is to do good deeds. Nature is perfectly fitted and equipped by the Creator according to the best measurement, the best form, the best pattern, and is hence absolutely free of any flaws. . . . humans are capable of altering its forms to what ought to be. Agriculture, horticulture, engineering, and architecture—in short, civilization itself—have their basis precisely in such alteration. But no alteration performed out of vengeance or resentment against nature, or without responsibility to the Creator of nature, can remain innocent for long. For if nature is not used as a gift from God given for moral purpose, its abuse is certain. If the moral purpose of God is denied, may nature not be abused? In Islam, no such abuse of nature is possible. For the secret working of nature is God's pattern and will, and the utility of nature is a divine gift meant soley for fulfillment of the moral law.[17]

One sees, then, a solid basis for a Muslim ecological sensitivity. If this basis is less respectful of nature in its own right than many Western ecologists now would wish, it does make solid provision for respecting the Creator's will in structuring nature as he has.

Islam's ecological problems therefore likely will come from another direction, as American Christianity's have: the legitimacy of subjugating nature to the pursuit of wealth. Thus al-Faruqi, in dealing with the Muslim view of wealth, goes on to add:

Many Puritans overexerted themselves to become rich and succeeded in winning both wealth and, supposedly, divine blessing. For they believed in the Puritan doctrine. The more they prospered, the more their faith encouraged them to press harder; and the more they exerted themselves and produced, the more they succeeded. Muslims share this belief and strengthen it with the faith that people are obliged to remold nature and the world, if the meaning of their viceregency is to be fulfilled.[18]

MECCA

The Muslim city parallel to Jerusalem and Geneva is Mecca. Traditionally Mecca has been the Islamic *omphalos* (navel) and lodestone. Today worldwide Islam has many economic and political subcenters, but the *hajj* and the practice of facing Mecca at daily prayer ensure that Mecca continues to be the orientation point of the Muslim world. Through history Medina and Jerusalem also have been venerated because of their importance in the Prophet's life; Baghdad, Cairo, Istanbul, Damascus, and Delhi have been important cultural or political centers. Mecca, though, has been in a class by itself, because it was *the* city of the Prophet.

Muhammad was born in Mecca, a member of the Quraish tribe that dominated the Meccan area. Pre-Islamic Mecca became prominent as a station on the spice-trade route to the West from the south of Arabia and the East, and it was important to pre-Islamic Arab religion because of the Black Stone (most likely a meteorite) that had been venerated for centuries. Because of the wealth brought by trade and the wealth brought by the religious businesses that flourished

around the Black Stone, sixth-century Mecca was a prosperous place. A dozen or so subclans of the Quraish tribe divided governmental powers. Since Muhammad was a member of one of the weaker clans, his relatively low status may have been a secondary reason for the Meccans' resistance to his prophecies and efforts to gain political power. (The primary reason, as we noted, was the conversions Muhammad demanded.) Although Muhammad gave Islam its political shape while in Medina, his incorporation of the Black Stone into Islamic ritual and his journey from Medina to Mecca on pilgrimage several months before his death ensured that Mecca would be the spiritual center of his new religion.

After the Prophet's death, Mecca continued to be mainly a religious center. The early caliphs ruled from Medina, so it was the *hajj* that sustained Mecca. When the Umayyad dynasty made its capital in Damascus, it took pains to preserve Mecca, seeing to it that the religious center stayed in good repair and the city remained livable. The Umayyads also enlarged and enhanced the Ka'ba, the shrine containing the Black Stone. In 930 C.E. a heretical sect called the *Qarmatians* scandalized the Muslim world by sacking Mecca and carrying off the Black Stone. It was returned twenty years later, but the injury lingered on long after. The Ottoman Turks captured Mecca in 1517, and it remained under Turkish control until 1924. In 1925 the current monarchy of Saudi Arabia took power, bringing both Mecca and Medina under its control.

Religiously, recent Meccan policy has been shaped by the Wahhabis (who call themselves "Unitarians," because of their stress on the divine unity and their corresponding opposition to all idolatry). The eighteenth-century founder of this sect, Muhammad Ibn 'Abd al-Wahhab,' was born near Riyadh in central Arabia. He studied with the Sufis but was more influenced by the strict legal school of the Hanbalites. His conservative theology soon shaped the prevailing Arabian dynasties and so dominated Saudi Arabia and Mecca when freedom from Turkish rule came.

The Wahhabis have been reformists, trying to root out the excrescences, as they have seen them, that developed after the pristine early period. Especially, they have opposed the cults of the saints and Sufism. As well, they have impressed upon Arabia a moral fervor to purify society of all behavior not showing proper respect for the holiness of Allah. Thus modern Mecca has been the center of a strict, rigorist form of Islam.

Ritualistically, Mecca remains dominated by the Ka'ba, which is not only the center of the pilgrimage ceremonies but also the focal point of all Islamic geography. Called the House of Allah, the Ka'ba physically is a cube of Meccan granite about forty feet long, thirty-three feet wide, and fifty feet high. It stands at the center of the great open-air Mosque of Mecca and is regarded as the *Quiblah*, the specific place to which Muslims turn in daily prayer. (In each mosque the world over is a *mihrab*, a niche marking the direction of the Qiblah.) In Muslim mythology, the Ka'ba is the center of the world, the naval of the living earth that Allah created. When this mythology developed a celestial geography, the earthly Ka'ba was located on an axis with the seven Ka'bas of the seven celestial spheres, all eight Ka'bas standing directly below the throne of Allah. As humans circumambulate the Meccan Ka'ba, so angels process around the throne of Allah.

The Black Stone, which is in the southeastern corner of the Ka'ba, is the "cornerstone" and "foundation" of the Ka'ba, its holiest part. An important part of the *hajj* ritual is kissing or touching the Black Stone, "the right hand of God on earth." Worshippers also press close to a section of the Ka'ba wall near the Black Stone called the *multazam*, from which the sacred power of the Ka'ba is said to emanate. Outside the Ka'ba is a broad pavement for circumambulation; across from it is the sacred well of Zamzam, where Hagar and Ishmael (Surah 2:119, 125) are said to have drunk; near the face of the Ka'ba is a stone said to preserve the footprint of Abraham. Thus the Ka'ba has several neighboring sites that pilgrims usually visit, as they strengthen their ties not only to Muhammad's prophecy but to all the prophecy derived from Abraham.

SUMMARY

The dominant personality behind Islam is Muhammad (ca. 570–632 C.E.). Born in Mecca, raised an orphan, Muhammad began receiving revelations when he was about forty. The theme of these revelations was that he should warn his compatriots of Allah's coming judgment and impress upon them the holiness of the sole Creator. This message met with initial resistance, but eventually Muhammad came to power in Medina and two years before his death took complete control of Mecca. His great dignity in Islam comes from the divine messages he received, which made him the seal of the prophets. In Muslim memory Muhammad was very humane: gentle and humorous, a holy man and great leader.

The Koran is the collection of the messages, or "recitals," that Muhammad received. Usually its various surahs are assigned to Mecca or Medina, depending upon their likelier place of origin. The corpus we now possess dates from around 650 C.E. and arranges the surahs roughly in terms of their length. The Koran is absolutely basic to Islam, being considered the eternal Word of Allah. In such chapters as "Light" (Surah 24) and "Charity" (Surah 107), one sees the poetry at the Koran's core and its demands for social justice.

The practical gist of the Koranic prophecy is the Five Pillars that have long structured Muslim faith. The creed that exalts the one God and the prophecy of Muhammad rivets Islam to a strict monotheism, and prayer five times each day enables the believer to embody the submission that the divine Lordship warrants. By fasting during the month of Ramadan, making pilgrimage to Mecca at least once during his or her lifetime, and being generous in almsgiving, the devout Muslim fulfills the other cardinal duties of Islam.

On the foundation of Koranic prophecy medieval Islam built a military empire with amazing rapidity and then a golden civilization. Although the early division between Sunnis and Shiites helped fragment the empire, in less than two hundred years Islam stretched from the western Mediterranean to eastern India. Science, art, architecture, philosophy, and mysticism all flourished in the first five hundred years, as did poetry and theology. Still, the dominant influence was Muslim law (shariah). Nonetheless, al-Ghazali, the greatest of the medieval Muslim thinkers, most praised Sufi mysticism.

Modern Islam has tried to reconcile its traditional faith with the new Western sciences and political ideals. Today this struggle continues to preoccupy Muslim intellectuals, from Iran to Indonesia. The general social thought of Islam has stressed the wholeness of human culture, resisting any split between the sacred and the secular. Women have not fared very well, by today's standards, as they have not in most traditional religions. Psychologically, the central Muslim notion has been the person's complete dependence on the Creator for being and breath. Sunnis, Sufis, and Shiites have all accented the notion of Muslim maturity differently, stressing respectively legal capacity, an inward awareness of relativities, and dramatic asceticism. Ecologically, Islam makes nature the good gift of God, which human beings may exploit in pursuing wealth, so long as they obey God's laws and remember the needs of society at large.

Historically, Mecca has been Islam's emotional center. As the city of the Prophet's birth and the place to which Muslims all over the world make prayer and pilgrimage, Mecca dominates the Muslim mind even today. The Wahhabi rigorism that has ruled recent Arabia now gives Meccan religion a rather strict tone, but the hajj rituals take the pilgrim all the way back to Abraham.

STUDY QUESTIONS

1. What is the likely content of Muhammad's first revelations?

2. How does the Koran make Muhammad the "seal" of the prophets?

3. In what sense is the injunction to pray five times each day prophetic?

4. What was the central cause of the split between the Sunnis and the Shiites?

5. Why do some Muslim observers today speak of their contemporaries as having split personalities?

6. What is the significance of Islam's refusal to separate the sacred and the secular?

7. Explain the Sunni view of adulthood.

8. How does Islam take nature into the afterlife?

9. Explain the likely impact of Mecca's being the *Qiblah*.

NOTES

1. Koranic translations are from A. J. Arberry, *The Koran Interpreted*. New York: Macmillan, 1973.

2. G. D. Newby, "Muhammad," in *Abingdon Dictionary of Living Religions*, ed. Keith Crim. Nashville: Abingdon, 1981, p. 499.

3. Geoffrey Parrinder, *A Dictionary of Non-Christian Religions*. Philadelphia: Westminster, 1971, p. 16.

4. A. J. Arberry, *Aspects of Islamic Civilization*. Ann Arbor: University of Michigan Press, 1967, p. 257.

5. W. Montgomery Watt, *The Faith and Practice of al-Ghazali*. London: Allen & Unwin, 1953, p. 162.

6. V. S. Naipaul, *Among the Believers*. New York: Vintage Books, 1982, p. 51.

7. John J. Donohue and John L. Esposito, eds., *Islam in Transition: Muslim Perspectives*. New York: Oxford University Press, 1982, p. 240.

8. Isma'il al-Faruqi, "Islam," in W. T. Chan et al., *The Great Asian Religions*. New York: Macmillan, 1969, p. 359.

9. Kari Ka'us Iskander, *A Mirror for Princes*. London: Cresser, 1951, p. 125.

10. George Allgrove, *Love in the East*. London: Gibbs & Phillips, 1962, p. 128.

11. See *Women in Contemporary Muslim Societies*, ed. Jane I. Smith, Lewisburg, Pa.: Bucknell University Press, 1980.

12. Naipaul, *Among the Believers*, p. 334.

13. Denise L. Carmody and John T. Carmody, *Ways to the Center*. Belmont, Calif.: Wadsworth, 1981, p. 325.

14. Ira N. Lapidus, "Adulthood in Islam," in *Adulthood*, ed. Erik H. Erikson. New York: W. W. Norton, 1978, p. 97.

15. Idries Shah, *The Way of the Sufi*. New York: E. P. Dutton, 1970, p. 174.

16. Michael M. J. Fischer, "Islam and the Revolt of the Petit Bourgeoise," *Daedalus*, 111/1 (Winter 1982), p. 119. On the need to control the great power that sainthood brings, and the evils that can result when one does not, see Robert C. Neville, *Soldier, Sage, Saint*. New York: Fordham University Press, 1978, pp. 89–91.

17. Isma'il al-Faruqi, *Islam*. Niles, Ill.: Argus, 1979, pp. 55–56.

18. Ibid., p. 57.

9

Prophecy in
Shamanic Societies

Eskimo Views of Death
Eskimo Views of Birth
Pygmy Ecology
Ik Degeneration
The Goals of Shamanic Rituals
Images and Words
Summary
Study Questions
Notes

ESKIMO VIEWS OF DEATH

The Eskimos of far North America relate closely to the Siberian peoples who have furnished scholars the shamanic prototype. Thus one finds among both the fishing peoples of coastal North America and the hunting peoples of the inland areas visionary initiations, flights to the gods, and impressive psychosomatic healings. These shamanic activities, as well as the mythological lore of the Eskimo shamans, are intrinsic to the general culture. Not surprisingly, therefore, they weave into what we might call the shamanic "morality," which is full of demanding taboos. This demanding character of their moralities brings the shamanic tribes close to the prophetic people we have studied.

Among the Eskimos, the *angakog*, or shaman, protects the tribe against famine and disease. To counteract famine, which usually the tribe attributes to the wrath of the gods, he or she (most Eskimo shamans are male) goes to the gods in trance and tries to determine what violations of the tribal taboos have

caused the gods to withhold the game. These taboos include strict regulations against hunting or fishing out of season, the seclusion of women during menstruation, and avoidance of contact with death. (Other typical sources of the gods' wrath are such wrongdoings as murder, incest, and infanticide.) Clearly therefore, the Eskimo culture, like that of most shamanic peoples, derives a strict morality from the shaman's visions and worldview. Clearly it has a large ingredient of willpower. Just as the prophet often has a dazzling imagination, as well as an intense will, so the shaman often has a powerful sense of the upright behavior that contact with ultimate realities demands, as well as intense images of these realities.

One of the classical anthropological treatments of Eskimo culture is Franz Boas's late-nineteenth-century study, *The Central Eskimo*. In its description of Eskimo customs regarding death, we glimpse the deep feelings that death regularly evoked:

If it is feared that a disease will prove fatal, a small snow house or hut is built, according to the season, into which the patient is carried through an opening at the back. This opening is then closed, and subsequently a door is cut out. A small quantity of food is placed in the hut, but the patient is left without attendants. As long as there is no fear of sudden death the relatives and friends may come to visit him, but when death is impending the house is shut up and he is left alone to die. If it should happen that a person dies in a hut among its inmates, everything belonging to the hut must be destroyed or thrown away, even the tools . . . lying inside becoming useless to the survivors, but the tent poles may be used again after a year has elapsed. No doubt this custom explains the isolation of the sick. If a child dies in a hut and the mother immediately rushes out with it, the contents of the hut may be saved.

Though the Eskimo feel the greatest awe in touching a dead body, the sick await their death with admirable coolness and without the least sign of fear or unwillingness to die. I remember a young girl who sent for me a few hours before her death and asked me to give her some tobacco and bread, which she wanted to take to her mother, who had died a few weeks before.[1]

Such an attitude toward death is common among nonliterate peoples. Living close to the elemental forces of nature, they tend to treat the great mysteries of birth and death both more dramatically and more realistically than do people of the modern West. Death occurs in the midst of the tribe, not in distant hospitals, and burial rites take place with few of the softening effects of funeral parlors and churches. Shamans often contemplate a skeleton, skull, or bones, to impress upon the psyche the significance of death. The tribe as a whole develops a mixture of pragmatism (trying to minimize the disruption to ordinary life) and awe. The awe is for life's most fearsome yet inevitable event. No one knows what happens after death, but Eskimos, like many other peoples, believe in an afterlife. Thus the young woman anticipated seeing her mother and expected that her mother would continue to have needs and likes similar to those she had had while alive.

Because of the ultimacy of death, the Eskimos have made it taboo. This again is not unique to shamanic tribes, but perhaps among shamanic tribes taboos are more vivid than they are in prophetic or sapiential societies. Thus the following definition of *taboo* would apply among almost all nonliterate peoples: "A strong prohibition backed by sanctions, often of a sacred or supernatural character. Taboos may attach to persons (for example, lepers in the OT [Old Testament]), to objects, to places, to activities, or to words and expressions."[2] The author goes on to note that taboos may apply to all people at all times or only to some people at some times, and that the violation of a taboo may be punished automatically, as a sort of natural law, or may entail social sanctions.

ESKIMO VIEWS OF BIRTH

Boas's informants provided him with details of Eskimo birth customs that suggest parallels with the death taboos. When a woman is about to deliver, the tribe builds her a small hut or snow house, which she enters to await her pangs. The woman may have only a limited number of attendants, and the community at large does not witness the birth. The mother must herself cut the navel cord. The baby is then cleansed with bird skin and clothed in a little bird skin gown. Among some groups a female shaman comes to the mother and child as soon as the mother is able to walk and leads them through rites apparently designed to safeguard the child. The ritual basically involves walking in circles on the ice or snow and then later washing the baby in urine. The bird skin gown of the child is changed several times in the first months, to accommodate the early growth. The kind of skin depends upon the month in which the baby is born. At the end of the first year the child's several gowns are fastened to a pole and placed on the roof of the hut. Then the family takes a small piece from each gown, which it regards as a powerful amulet, and throws the rest into the sea. People wear their amulets at the annual festival of Sedna, the chief goddess, and men born abnormally (for example, in breech birth) must wear women's clothing at this feast.

Boas did not learn the reasons for all of these Eskimo customs, but it seems clear that many of them are ways of insuring that the birth and early months of the child go according to tribal convictions about the fateful significance of birth, the tabooed quality of blood, and the need to bring both mother and child back into "normal" contact with the rest of the tribe and the deities of the snow, ice, and other elements. Among tribes of the Cumberland Sound area a new mother cannot eat raw meat for a year after the birth, and two months after it she must visit each hut in the village. Prior to that visit she cannot go into any hut but her own. At the two-months period she also must throw away all her old clothing. If an infant dies, the mother must cover her head for a year whenever she is outside her hut. When the group catches a seal, she must throw her hat away and make a new one. The parents of the dead infant must carry its boots with them when they travel, and when they stop they must bury these boots in the snow.

The force of life, therefore, like the force of death, is so significant that Eskimos handle it carefully. Birth seems to be what some theorists call a "liminal" time: a sort of threshold. New forms of life are beginning, death is always a close possibility, and many strange things might happen. The connection between birth and hunting seems to be that the guardians of the lives of both humans and animals demand a reverence for the miracle they bestow. As the tribe depends upon seals for its livelihood, so it depends upon births to replenish its human numbers. Perhaps a "quantitative" notion creeps in, suggesting that after birth the guardians or gods of life want a special appreciation shown, without which they will not further extend themselves and provide game. Newborn children tend to be named for people who have died within the past year, and many tribes believe that reality most basically is composed of souls. Trees, rocks, fish, and animals all have souls, as do human beings. "Life" therefore encompasses much more than what meets the eye. All around are the souls of past living things, and one must apologize to the soul of any animal one has to kill.

The dominant influence upon Eskimo culture, obviously enough, is the severe cold that holds Eskimos in its grip most of the year. Robert Coles has described the disciplined, restrained behavior that this environment tends to develop in Eskimo children:

Eskimo children are masters of the faint smile, the slight grimace that never goes any further. They are usually quiet children, more controlled than Indian or Chicano children. Often in an Arctic village a small child is discouraged from talking too much—by parents who may strike a visitor as taciturn, even forbidding or surly, but who have their own reasons to distrust words and more words, or "emotional" people. In the clutch, when the weather is worst and the danger of starvation, illness, death the greatest, the person who is moved to talk a lot, move around a lot, become demonstrative and excited, may well be the person who misses whatever chance there is for survival. One must learn to be careful, controlled—able to husband emotional as well as physical energy, able to sit and wait, or move at all costs. A fierce outer world is resisted successfully only by a finely regulated inner world, wherein words and the emotions that generate them are watched as closely as the next blizzard, days or weeks long, that may at any moment make comment, conversations, expressions of "feeling" a dangerous indulgence at best.[3]

The shamanic imagination of the Eskimo cultural leaders therefore is quite compatible with a highly disciplined, tightly controlled child rearing and set of customary practices. Like the biblical prophet, the Eskimo shaman can focus on doing to the subordination of talking or even feeling.

PYGMY ECOLOGY

The Pygmy people of the Congo area of central Africa (in present-day Zaire) show little of the dramatic ecstasy that marks the shamanic prototype. Their place among "shamanic" peoples therefore derives more from their nonliteracy and intimate ties with nature than it does from trance. Because their dealings with nature have not been mediated by traditional texts, they demonstrate the integration with the demands of the environment that one finds among some of the tribal groups. Imaginative and cooperative, the Pygmies have worked out a happy interaction with their forest surroundings, a distinctive **ecology** characterized by reverent concern to get along with their environment, draw it into their personal and tribal lives. One sees this in various parts of Colin Turnbull's account of the many months he spent with the Pygmies.

Turnbull's informants were completely formed by their life under the huge trees of the Congo rain forest. Indeed, many of their perceptions were limited to what the shortened perspectives of the forest allowed. Thus when Turnbull took his friend Kenge outside the forest, Kenge had a big adjustment to make:

Kenge first began to realize that there really was another world, beyond the forest. He had often heard people talk about it, and up at Paulis the forest was thinned to the merest savannah; but nowhere had he really seen beyond the forest. The mission was built on a high hill, cleared of vegetation so that crops could be planted to supply the mission school and hospital with food. Usually the distant horizons were hazy, and everywhere we looked down only on a sea of trees. Several times I tried to tell Kenge that beyond this lay another world, a world of lakes and mountains and open plains, but he just nodded disbelievingly. He had never seen even a hill, as such. He had climbed up them, inside the forest, and had seen small hills such as the one on the far side of the Epulu, the one on which the Nduye mission stood, but that was all. One evening, however, we were both sitting on a boulder at the highest point of the Biasiku mission, looking over the forest. To the east the sky was becoming less and less hazy, and gradually out of the haze a great black mass began to form. Kenge saw it before I did, and asked if it was a black storm cloud. It was the vast bulk of the Ruwenzori, the Mountains of the Moon. We never saw the peaks, but even the lower ranges towered so far above the forest that Kenge was almost frightened. He asked me about them, and I did my best, but it was next to impossible to describe things of which he had no experience, and for which there were not even any appropriate words in his language.[4]

The Pygmies might sometimes be cruel to the animals they hunted, but on the whole they impressed Turnbull with their love for the forest and all its other inhabitants. In contrast to the villagers who lived outside the forest, the Pgymies practiced few magical rites, harbored few superstitions. Whereas the villagers inhabited a world filled with malign spirits, and so constantly were fearful, the Pgymies looked upon the forest as their loving parent. As they took pains to care for their children, surely the forest would take pains to care for them. So whenever things went badly in the Pygmy world, the people would gather at night to sing the *molimo*, a chorus of songs and haunting pipings offered to the forest. As one elder Pygmy put it, the only reason things could go wrong in the forest was if the forest had fallen asleep. The molimo was an effort to awaken the forest gently, so that it would feel good and resume its care of its children.

Behind the molimo lay a general theology that stressed the goodness of the forest and was quite clear that the forest represented God. The same elder pointed out that different people call God different names, but nobody really knows what God is like. God must be good, however, because so many good things exist. God must be like the forest, giving his children all they need and want. From this very positive view of ultimate reality, the Pygmies drew interesting ethical consequences. One was not to injure the life of the tribe in the forest, by selfish or uncooperative acts. Apart from this general injunction, however, daily life was rather casual. Certain customs provided the order necessary for peace around the fireplace and cooperation in hunting. Certain occasions, such as puberty, led to happy celebrations. But the dominant motif of Pygmy life was a day-by-day enjoyment of existence in and with the forest.

Thus work and play, child rearing and hunting, unfolded with little pressure. People could be noisy, giving one another little time for sleep. The rain could become oppressive. But birth and death, puberty and marriage went their way positively, naturally, without a lot of tension and worry. With enough food to eat and a hut in which to live, a Pygmy family usually was

happy. A lot of time went into singing and telling stories. Both fathers and mothers took a hand in child care and child raising. The Pygmies worked to survive, and their community customs demanded enough discipline to make any solid member quite mature. But the "prophetic" dimension of Pygmy life came through not as a set of external commandments but as a positive call to enjoy life in the present, by living ecologically. Indeed, the ecological satisfactions of Pygmy life seemed to soothe away most anxieties. At bottom, few Pgymies doubted that their forest existence was very blessed.

IK DEGENERATION

In contrast to the Pgymies, the Ik, a mountainous people of Uganda living near the Kenyan border, show how morality breaks down when dealings with nature are disrupted. Because the traditional patterns of Ik hunting life had broken on the stones of modern African politics, Turnbull found them a people of fractured culture. Family life, friendship, and even basic relationships had gone into abeyance. Mothers and children fought each other for food. Old people expected no help or loyalty. It was dog eat dog, the survival of the wiliest, because people had been brought to a state of desperate hunger. Clearly, therefore, the prophetic, will-directed side of peoples' lives may depend on a minimal ecological flourishing. Clearly it is hard for them to honor cooperative customs when nature is not a benevolent parent, fruitful and provident like the Congo forest.

Turnbull himself heightened the horror of the lives of the Ik by setting them alongside the Pygmies:

[The Pygmies] have a communal spirit that is difficult to define without either seeming like a wooly-minded romantic or reducing it to terms that are both unromantic and inadequate. It is, let us say, centered on a love for and devotion to their forest world, and results in their wholehearted, unquestioning identification with it. And what more powerful force toward social unity and cohesion can there be than such a deep-rooted sense of identity? All this the Ik lack, and more besides.

When the Pygmies, who are no angels, become involved in disputes, they manage to settle them without stigmatizing anyone as a criminal, without resort to punitive measures, without even passing judgment on the individuals concerned. Settlement is reached with one goal in mind, and that is the restoration of har-

mony within the band, for the good of the whole. If there is one thing that is surely wrong in their eyes, it is that the dispute should have taken place to begin with, and to this extent both disputants are to blame and are held in temporary disfavor. All this, too, the Ik lack, for while their disputes rarely reach the stage of physical violence, their violence is there, deep and smoldering, scarring each man and woman, making life even more disagreeable and dividing man against his neighbor even further. There is simply no community of interest, familial or economic, social or spiritual. With the Ik the family does not even hold itself together, much less serve as a model for a wider social brotherhood of Ik. Economic interest is centered on as many individual stomachs as there are people, and cooperation is merely a device for furthering an interest that is consciously selfish.[5]

In the memories of present-day Ik lie scenes of a better time. Before their migratory hunting life was disrupted, they managed a decent living. Thus the sight of Mount Morongole, previously their most revered site, brings a wave of nostalgic peace. Once Mount Morongole centered a tribal existence with enough food to eat, sufficient help from nature and freedom from subjection to other human beings, to permit laughter and cooperation. A generation of hunger, however, has cast Mount Morongole in the role of a throwback. Recent Ik have had little reason to cheer the goodness of life, and so little reason to be reverent toward nature or one another. Without a solid ecological foundation, social justice—the prophet's great concern—has withered away.

The anthropologist Margaret Mead, commenting on Turnbull's study of the Ik, noted that it emphasizes how fragile the structure of a society is.[6] In prophetic cultures, the leading spokespersons protect this fragility by grounding the group's customs in the divine will. The Ten Commandments, for example, are not simply a short code worked up so that people will get along. They are the Word of God, the expression of the divine will. Thus biblical law, like the traditional law of most literate peoples, is seen as written at God's behest, expressing something heavenly.

Nonliterate peoples tend not to have a single heavenly deity like the biblical God, and their law usually is informal, a matter of customs transmitted orally. These customs connect closely with the particular environment that a given people indwells. For example, Eskimo customs are full of taboos concerning seals and reindeers, the prime animals upon which Eskimos depend. The rupturing of a people's relations with its accustomed environment sends shock waves throughout the whole culture. It is as though a main wall had

collapsed, a central pillar had fallen. The Ik culture presents an especially striking instance, but there are parallels wherever technological or political changes have overthrown age-old patterns of social life. Many Eskimos of Alaska, for example, are even now caught between the technological culture of the lower forty-eight states and the prehistoric ways of their own people. They may not suffer famine as the Ik have and so come to a complete social breakdown, but their social and psychological sufferings can be severe. For them, too, social justice and the other prophetic themes tend to grow muted, further confirming the fragility of communal human existence, the dependence of all communities upon such minimal goods as food and shelter.

THE GOALS OF SHAMANIC RITUALS

Most nonliterate peoples, whether or not they have given a central place to shamanic ecstasy, have pivoted their cultures on significant rituals. The overall impetus to these rituals and their overall goal are prophetic in the sense of integrating community behavior with the norms of the holy cosmos. One sees this in the rites that many archaic peoples have celebrated in honor of Mother Earth. Even when such rites take the form of sanctioned orgies, to stress the theme of fertility, they have a dimension of reenforcing the (generally rather strict) tribal morality. Mircea Eliade has made this point cross-culturally:

But the meaning of the orgy is not difficult to understand; the orgy is a symbolic re-entry into chaos, into the primordial and undifferentiated state. It re-enacts the "confusion," the "totality" before the Creation, the cosmic Night, the cosmogonic egg. And one can guess why a whole community should re-actualise this regression into the undifferentiated. It is to remove the original wholeness out of which sprang differentiated Life, and from which the Cosmos emerged. It is by such symbolical and lurid reintegration into the pre-cosmological state that they hope to ensure an abundant harvest. For the harvest represents the Creation, the triumphal manifestation of a young, rich and perfect form. "Perfection" is produced in the beginnings, ab origine. They hope, therefore, to recover the vital reserves and the germinal riches which were made manifest for the first time in the majestic act of the Creation.

But all this, let us repeat it, has religious significance. It must not be assumed that the cults of the

Earth-Mother encourage immorality in the profane sense of the term. Sexual union and the orgy are rites celebrated in order to re-actualise primordial events. The rest of the time—that is, apart from the decisive moments of the agricultural calendar—the Earth-Mother is the guardian of the norms: among the Ya-hengo of the French Sudan she is the champion of morality and justice; among the Kulango of the Ivory Coast, the goddess hates criminals, thieves, magicians and malefactors. In Africa in general, the sins most abhorred by the Earth-Mother are crime, adultery, incest and all kinds of sexual misdemeanour; in ancient Greece, both bloodshed and incest rendered the Earth barren.[7]

The rituals of nonliterate peoples therefore serve many of the same ends that rituals of literate prophetic peoples serve. The integration of the tribe with the cosmic powers is quite parallel to the relation of the House of Islam or tribe of Israel with the One God. If the stress of the nonliterate tribe tends to be more on the *being* of the people than their doing, this does not exclude doing or performance. The nonliterate sense of the unity of the cosmos, the way that a single power pervades all that lives, leads to a stronger desire to gain harmony with this power. The source of cosmic order is less personified, more diffuse, so "harmony" takes the place of the prophetic "obedience." In the prophetic case obedience often leads to the proliferation of law, so that the people become followers of a detailed scriptural path. Thus one sees Jewish ritual interwoven with *halakah*, Islamic ritual connected to *shariah*, Christian ritual directed by **canon law** or **synod** discipline. The willful accents of the prophet lead to the intellectual rigors of the lawyer and the emphasis on **rubric** of the priest. While these help mightily to focus people's obedience, they run the risk of obscuring the more holistic goals that nonliterate tribes such as the Pygmies often realize quite beautifully. As St. Paul put it, the letter (of the law) kills; only the spirit quickens.

Most significant prophets themselves, of course, have realized this. Thus most significant prophets have been opponents of legalism. Insofar as legalism frequently has taken a ritualistic turn, expressing itself in highly regularized ceremonies, prophecy has often appeared antiritualistic. This is true, for example, in Protestant Christianity, which owed much of its birth to Martin Luther's opposition to Roman Catholic ritualism. Luther himself retained sacramental forms, so his antiritualism was more a matter of degree than something absolute. Still, one seldom finds in the successors of the major prophets, Christian, Jewish, or Muslim, the freedom that marks such nonliterate rituals as the Pygmy *elima*.

The *elima* is the female puberty rite, and it amounts to a great celebration of women's life power. Little in the *elima* is fearful or surrounded by taboo, as so many other peoples' reactions to blood have been. Little is ashamed of sexuality or ambiguous about menstruation. Better than most prophetic sexual moralities, the Pygmy has integrated sexual power with the generative cycles of the cosmos. Puberty is personal and tribal, yes, but even more it is a manifestation of the fecund goodness of the whole forest. The end of the *elima* is the reaffirmation of the goodness of the whole forest, the wonder and sacredness of all life. One might say, in fact, that many nonliterate peoples' sense of social justice has been cosmic rather than societal. Rites such as the *elima* have hymned the flourishing of the whole living earth.

IMAGES AND WORDS

Our descriptions of shamans and prophets have characterized shamans as imaginative and prophets as messengers of a divine word that demands action. This is a fair enough general description, we believe, yet it begs qualification and nuance as soon as one tries to move to particular cases. For example, we have already seen that prophets such as Isaiah and Muhammad have received striking visions, dazzling pictures, during their prophetic calls. And, we have suggested that the rituals of nonliterate peoples, for all their grounding in colorful myths about the origin of the earth and the patterns of creation, follow through to make strong demands for moral living. No strong division exists, therefore, between images and words. Because both shamans and prophets have been fully human, they have all experienced things, stored the images of such experiences in their memories, striven to interpret new situations in the light of these stored images, had flashes of insight by grasping the meaning of a new configuration of the images, and expressed such insight in concepts and words. Although it is characteristic of shamans to focus on the early stages of this process, enjoying its dazzing images and entertaining stories, it is not characteristic of shamans to neglect the ethical, active follow-through. Similarly, although prophets may strike us as people given a word that demands obedient execution, people who stress the later stages of the movement from experience to action, many prophets have begun their careers by receiving startling visionary scenarios.

This was the case with Wovoka, the Paiute Indian of Nevada responsible for the Ghost Dance that seized the imagination of many tribes during the last decade of the nineteenth century. The following description of his visionary commission comes from Hartley Burr Alexander's famous study of Amerindian rituals:

To complete the picture I would cite one final ritual which perhaps best of all images the red man's poetic philosophy. It was probably on January 1, 1889, on the occasion of an eclipse of the sun visible in the western states, that a Paiute sheepherder in Nevada beheld the great vision which made of him the Messiah of the Indian race. "When the sun died," he said, "I went up to heaven and saw God and all the people who had died a long time ago. God told me to come back and tell my people they must be good and love one another, and not fight, or steal, or lie. He gave me this dance to give to my people." These were the commands. The people were to dance five days at a time, and they must wait patiently on this earth, for in a near time the old life of the Indian, as it was before the coming of the white man, would be restored. This was God's promise, and the restoration was near. The souls from beyond were already at the door. For the dead were to be restored to life; the sick and decrepit were to be healed; the old were to be given their strength once more; the herds of the buffalo would return; game would be plentiful. The white men would disappear, drowned in a great flood which God would send to overwhelm them.[8]

The Ghost Dance, as the ritual derived from Wovoka's vision was called, spread rapidly among the tribes of the West. Those who danced it were seeking a vision. They would dance until they fell into a trance in which they would see their dead relatives returning to the earth, along with vast numbers of buffalo, great herds such as had existed before the coming of the white settlers. The songs that the dancers composed poured out both their heartbreak at the passing of their tribal culture and their hope that somehow the old days might return. When the Ghost Dance reached the warlike Sioux, who had only been at peace with the whites for a few years, the whites became alarmed and had troops sent to the Sioux reservation to keep the Indians controlled. "It was at the end of the year, amid snows, that the conflict at Wounded Knee took place, needless, with misunderstanding, and cruel. It was the last act in the tragedy of the encounter of the races, and it bloodily marked the setting of the Indian's sun. Mainly it was Indians who were killed. Many of the dead wore "ghost shirts" which marked them as followers of Wovoka. The medicine men had assured them that these were impervious to bullets."[9]

One sees, then, how the prophet's hard criterion of effective action can break the shaman's imagery. One sees that images and action-oriented words have to cooperate, not compete. Still, the glory in the encounter between the Ghost Dancers and the white soldiers probably lay with the dancers, who only wanted the return of their basic rights, a chance to live with their gods in the good natural world. The "manifest destiny" of the white prophetic peoples, who pushed forward relentlessly and rapaciously, proved too strong for the visionary Indians. Might lay with the rifles and efficiency that the prophetic will to action had spawned in Europe. But that might, as in so many other instances in the long centuries of world history, was clearly far from right. The vision of the dancers probably had a strong case in terms of justice and beauty. The tragedy, of course, was that the different religious slants could not be reconciled, the different images and words could not become mutually expanding and fulfilling.

SUMMARY

The prophetic aspect of nonliterate peoples' religions is expressed in their firm moral codes. Among the Eskimos, who are close to the ecstatic prototype of the Siberian shamanic peoples, both birth and death provoke a concern for order, an obedience to holy laws, like that of the classical prophets. The Eskimo taboos surrounding death, for example, stress the transitional character of this event. It is a nonordinary, special time, so the tribe must carefully hedge all contacts with it. To be in the presence of the dead is to become nonordinary oneself, "polluted" even. Yet among the Eskimo dying seems quite peaceful, as though death finally fits, becoming appropriate if not ordinary. Eskimos have similar taboos about birth, suggesting that birth also focuses the tension between the ordinary and the extraordinary for them. Children usually are named for relatives recently deceased, and the clothing of infants becomes the source of powerful amulets. Beyond these special demands that times of death and birth call forth, Eskimo life as a whole begets a strong disciplining of the emotions. The severe cold that obtains through most of the year requires a self-control that is similar to that of the prophet.

In great contrast to the cold environment of the Eskimos is the tropical milieu of the Congo Pygmies. In their case the surrounding environment seems friendly, a good symbol of a benevolent god. Much of Pygmy morality therefore involves interacting with the forest gratefully and trying to make tribal life harmonious. The Ik, on the other hand, show the social disintegration that occurs when ecological circumstances grow grim. For lack of good and comfortable traditional ways, the Ik turned their will toward cruel competition, seemed no longer able to summon the images and agreements necessary for cooperation.

Generalizing from these and other nonliterate people, one might suggest that the rituals of shamanic tribes usually target such prophetic goals as firm adherence to the tribal morality. Thus even the orgies that many groups have celebrated are not so much times of moral breakdowns as parts of an ongoing effort to situate the tribe harmoniously in the creative cycles of nature. Where the shamanic peoples somewhat differ from the prophetic is in the cosmological accent of their rituals. They are more concerned with being in harmony with nature than doing the will of a God who stands outside nature. The Pygmy *elima*, for example, celebrates sexual maturity with a naturalness and joy that few prophetic moralities have managed to develop. The Ghost Dance that led to the crowning tragedy of white-Indian relations in the United States further suggests that shamanic images and prophetic words could complement one another. What Wovoka wanted for his people was not essentially different from what white settlers wanted for themselves. Just as Pygmy emphasis on being complements prophetic emphasis on doing, so the imagery of the Ghost Dance might have complemented the western migration of the settlers.

STUDY QUESTIONS

1. Why do traditional Eskimos express little fear of natural death?

2. Why does birth take the Eskimo mother apart from ordinary social contacts?

3. In what sense did the forest promote Pygmy cooperativeness?

4. Contrast the Pygmy and Ik senses of morality.

5. Why does Eliade judge that the orgiastic cults of Mother Earth do not encourage immorality?

6. What was the ethical content of Wovoka's vision?

NOTES

1. Franz Boas, *The Central Eskimo*. Lincoln: University of Nebraska Press, 1964, pp. 204–5.

2. C. R. Taber, "Taboo," in *Abingdon Dictionary of Living Religions*, ed. Keith Crim. Nashville: Abingdon, 1981, p. 730.

3. Robert Coles, *Eskimos, Chicanos, Indians*. Boston: Little, Brown, 1977, pp. 190–91.

4. Colin Turnbull, *The Forest People*. New York: Simon & Schuster, 1962, pp. 247–48.

5. Colin Turnbull, *The Mountain People*. New York: Simon & Schuster, 1972, pp. 156–57.

6. Margaret Mead, from the back cover of *The Mountain People* (paperback edition).

7. Mircea Eliade, *Myths, Dreams, and Mysteries*. New York: Harper Torchbooks, 1967, pp. 186–87.

8. Hartley Burr Alexander, *The World's Rim*. Lincoln: University of Nebraska Press, 1967, p. 225.

9. Ibid., pp. 226–27.

CHAPTER

10

Prophecy in Sagacious Societies

Hinduism
Buddhism
China
Japan
Greece
Understanding and Will
Summary
Study Questions
Notes

HINDUISM

In official Hinduism the truth by which society coheres and individuals find fulfillment reposes in the Vedas, the ancient scriptures derived from the Aryan invaders who came to power in India about thirty-five hundred years ago. The Vedas, in turn, derive from the visions of the seers (**rishis**) to whom ultimate reality disclosed itself. These seers probably were **yogins**, people expert in interior disciplines designed to quiet the senses and free the human spirit. In all likelihood their focus was internal, a state of **enstasis**, in contrast to the outgoing, ecstatic character of the shaman. Similarly, their concentration on visionary truth distinguishes them from the Near Eastern prophets who concentrated on social justice.

As with all generalizations, this characterization of the Vedic rishis must be qualified. The truth that the classical Hindu seers recorded was dazzling and brought the world to light, as much shamanic expe-

rience has. It was a truth inseparable from a holy life, so it demanded a moral discipline similar to that demanded by the classical prophets. This discipline, both social and personal, enables us to speak of a "prophetic" strain in Hindu religious culture.

The most celebrated disciplinary code of ancient India was the *Laws of Manu*, a collection assembled between the second century B.C.E. and the second century C.E. The name *Manu* calls to mind the primal man, Adam in Old Testament terms. The Rig Veda regards Manu as the instigator of the sacrifices that formed the center of *brahmanic* culture, although according to other Hindu scriptures he was the counterpart of the Old Testament Noah, the sole survivor of a universal flood. The code attributed to him outlines the major duties of the different classes in society and has been a great influence down the centuries.

The basic presupposition of the authors of Manu was the doctrine of karma, that our actions determine our character and social class from one stage to the next in the cycle of **transmigration**. Thus in XII. 3 Manu

104

gives a karmic interpretation of action: "Action, which springs from the mind, from speech, and from the body, produces either good or evil results; by action are caused the (various) conditions of men, the highest, the middling, and the lowest."[1]

The highest condition is that of the priest, or **brahman**, whose original duty was performing sacrifices to the various Vedic gods. The midding social condition belongs to the warriors and merchants (or farmers). The lowest social condition belongs to the manual laborers and outcastes, whose situation seems to bespeak bad karma left over from previous lives. In urging people to live virtuously, Manu was promising that they could alter the quality of their karma, and so the direction of their transmigration. Were they to discipline their mind, speech, and body, they could hope to be reborn in a higher social condition, nearer to achieving **moksha**: full release from the cycle of transmigration.

The social consequences of Hindu codes such as Manu differed little from the consequences of the codes developed after the Near Eastern prophets. The Jewish and Muslim lawyers, for example, sought to order society by what they thought of as divine imperatives, written by God into human nature and the cosmos. The same applies to the Hindu codifiers. Manu taught that the social divisions of Hinduism went back to the creational sacrifice of a primal giant, whose head became the brahmanic class, middle portions became the middling classes, and feet became the lowest classes. The various duties of these classes also were part of the divinely ordered system of things and so were not something that human initiative could change. From time to time reformers and innovators came onto the Indian scene, but they seldom did more than dent the immemorial system of karma and the four classes. Despite wars and cultural evolution, there was little clamor for a religious revolution aimed at a new social order.

The Bhagavad-Gita, Hinduism's most popular religious text, illustrates the Hindu control of potential social change. In dealing with action, its main counsel is discipline and detachment:

If a man is trained in a discipline, becomes wholly purified, learns to control himself and his senses, his own individual existence now being the existence of all—even when he acts, he is not stained. Disciplined, knowing the nature of things, he will think: "I don't do anything!" When all the while he sees, hears, touches, smells, eats, goes about, sleeps, breathes, talks, voids, grasps something, opens and shuts his eyes; he knows full well that the senses merely play on the objects of sense. Resting his acts in God, he has lost his attachment.

He acts, but evil clings to him no more than water to a lotus leaf. Disciplined men do act with their body, thought, meditation, or even their senses alone, but they do so to purify themselves, and without attachment. The disciplined man gives up the results of his acts and attains perfect peace. The undisciplined man acts out of desire; he is attached to the results; his acts imprison him. (5: 7–12)[2]

BUDDHISM

The Buddhist scheme of things configures religion as a trinity of approaches to human perfectability. By wisdom, meditation, and morality the devout Buddhist can hope to approach **nirvana**, release from karma and entry into fulfillment. Wisdom and meditation intertwine, much as for the Hindu rishis. The devout Buddhist pursues a philosophy that is more personal than academic, striving to become illumined by a truth that can reset the entire personality. On the way to such an illumination he or she usually both studies key traditional texts and engages in some form of meditation. Many forms are yogic in character, quieting the mind and integrating the different layers of awareness or consciousness.

Morality, the third leg of the tripod, focuses on the active or behavioral side of both personal and social life. On the one hand, it should express the wisdom and calm that the devout Buddhist is trying to develop through philosophical studies and meditation. On the other hand ethical striving gives the aspirant practical experience of the difficulties lying in the way of enlightenment, the resistances one must overcome. Thus the precepts of traditional Buddhist morality resemble the precepts of the prophetic ethicians. The way to enlightenment and nirvana, like the ways of Torah, Gospel, and Koran, is demanding and imposes discipline. One does not reach the Buddhist goal without a strong will, a firm resolve.

The centerpiece of traditional Buddhist morality, or **sila**, is the five precepts that are incumbent on all members of the **Sangha** (community): abstention from taking life, theft, sexual or sensuous disorders, lying, and intoxicants. If we embroider this centerpiece, following the commentary of the famous master Buddhaghosa (fifth century C.E.), we can gain a good sense of Buddhist discipline.

Taking life refers to murdering anything that is alive. It is the act that expresses the will to terminate the life force of someone or something else. The most blameworthy murders are of human beings. Next come the murders of large animals. To Buddhaghosa's mind, the effort the murderer must expend, the intensity of his or her will, is a main index of the heinousness of the crime. Another index is the virtue of the human being killed. Thus it is much worse to kill a saint than a criminal.

Theft, or "taking what is not given," varies in seriousness according to the value of what is stolen. In his analytical style, Buddhaghosa distinguishes five factors involved in any theft: "someone else's belongings, the awareness that they are someone else's's, the thought of theft, the action of carrying it out, the taking away as a result of it."³ Buddhaghosa also lists the several different kinds of unlawful acquisition: theft, robbery, underhanded dealings, stratagems, and casting lots. This tendency to divide up different stages and kinds of moral acts probably stems from the practice of Buddhist meditation. Through their serious meditation, many Buddhist masters have come to see the various stages of intention, desire, and action with unusual clarity. Enlightenment is largely a matter of perfecting one's awareness, and with such perfecting comes a huge clarification of how one is thinking and feeling.

The third precept mainly targets sexual misconduct. Grossly, it forbids "going into" many classes of sexual partners: men and twenty kinds of women. Buddhaghosa obviously handles the precept from a heterosexual male point of view. Ten of the kinds of women are protected by family, kinship, or customary law, which declares sexual relations with them forbidden. The flavor of Buddhaghosa's religious style and the customs of his time seep through his list of the other ten kinds of forbidden women: "women bought with money, concubines for the fun of it, kept women, women bought by the gift of a garment, concubines who have been acquired by the ceremony which consists in dipping their hands into water, concubines who once carried burdens on their heads, slave girls who are also concubines, servants who are also concubines, girls captured in war, temporary wives."⁴ Once again, a main index of the seriousness of the offense is the dignity of the person offended.

Buddhaghosa finds lying reprehensible both because it deceives others and because it obscures the truth. The seriousness of such falsehood depends on the circumstances. If it causes great harm or greatly misrepresents reality, it is a major offense. If it is merely a convenience, like lying to avoid lending some possession to a friend, it is a minor offense.

The main problem with intoxicants is their tendency to cloud the mind. Such clouding can result in serious harm to other people, but it is also reprehensible in itself, since it abuses the most central part of the personality. Any devout Buddhist, trying to bring the mind to full light, would consider becoming intoxicated senseless, an action diametrically opposed to his or her religious strivings.

These five traditional precepts have been at the heart of Buddhist morality. Insofar as they direct the will to a serious, energetic rejection of evil, they are like the prophet's stony "thou shall not's." Insofar as they only target social justice indirectly and do not come as the commands of a willful God, they stand at some distance from the prophetic prototype.

CHINA

The paramount teacher of traditional China was Confucius, who was a sage rather than a prophet. Confucius neither saw visions nor proclaimed the Word of a transcendent God. He did, however, prescribe rules for virtuous conduct. In his opinion these rules distilled the wisdom of the great personalities to whom China owed its civilization. The Way that these ancients had taught and modeled was the straight path to social prosperity. As well, it was the pattern for a life in harmony with nature. Thus the human Way of the ancients and the natural Way of the cosmos stood in a benign symmetry. If people began to get their personal lives in order, by appropriating the ancients' teachings, they could contribute mightily to political peace. At the same time, they could integrate themselves with the ordered cycles of the stars and the seasons. Confucius' hierarchical thinking therefore reached out toward what we have been calling a prophetic goal. Thinking that people could mold their human natures largely as they wished, Confucius urged a strong will to virtue, a disciplined action to make the self integral with the hallowed Way.

One of the works most influential in traditional China was the *Great Learning*, which was attributed to Confucius. Wing-Tsit Chan has summarized the importance of this Confucian classic as follows:

The importance of this little Classic is far greater than its small size would suggest. It gives the Confucian educational, moral, and political programs in a nutshell, neatly summed up in the so-called "three items": manifesting the clear character of man, loving the people, and abiding in the highest good; and in the "eight steps": the investigation of things, extension of knowledge, sincerity of the will, rectification of the mind, cultivation of the personal life, regulation of *the family, national order, and world peace. Moreover, it is the central Confucian doctrine of humanity (*jen*) in application.*[5]

In the mid-thirteenth century C.E., on the eve of the Mongol invasions, China definitely adhered to the hierarchical ideals laid out in the Great Learning. However, Jacques Gernet, who has studied this period in some detail, projects the Confucian concern for order all the way back to the formation of the Chinese state:

The political structure of the State as it had continued to exist in China since it was first established in the third century B.C. is perhaps not unconnected with the concepts and attitudes that most strikingly characterized the Chinese. The order that reigned in imperial China was a moral order *which an autocratic State had been able to impose step by step, until it reached the smallest social unit: the individual family. The lack of any sharp dividing line between a man's private and his public life, between his duties to the family and his duties to the State, lay at the basis of the Chinese concept of government: morals and politics were one.*[6]

If the Confucians furnished Chinese society the orderly part of its politico-moral scheme, the Taoists furnished the poetic, in some ways disorderly part. Thus in general the Taoists fostered political eruptions, sometimes in the name of religious visions and ideals:

Today the most vital element in Taoism, apart from the philosophy of Lao-Tzu, is the lay societies and sects. Often secret, they have flourished in China since the days of the Red Eyebrows, who overthrew Wang Ming in 25 A.D. They might be compared to the Continental—in contrast to the Anglo-Saxon—Freemasons. One of their goals has been to foster charity and asceticism on the part of their members; another has been to organize opposition against "too much government." Their secrets include everything from passwords to charms and spirit-writing. Thus, although their function is partly secular, they owe many of their ideas to Buddhism and especially to Taoism. Since the beginning of the Ming Dynasty such groups have led at least eight rebellions against the central government, in two of which they probably came as close to conquering China as the Yellow Turbans did in 184 A.D. Because they represent a two-thousand-year old tradition of individualism and of revolt against tryanny, they have been vigorously suppressed since the Communists came to power.[7]

Whether orderly or disorderly, the Chinese shared the Near Eastern prophets' concern for social questions. In contrast to the Hindus and Buddhists, they focused on the consciousness of the group rather than the consciousness of the individual. Whether they sought social justice, in today's sense of equalizing the rights of the poor and marginal people, is debatable, Probably they did not. Overall their society was too hierarchical to be persuaded by democratic or egalitarian ideals. Thus overall their slant was not prophetic, did not feel a great pressure toward radical fairness in matters of wealth and power.

JAPAN

Buddhism and Confucianism furnished Japan most of its formal ethics, so a concern with such fundamental matters as the five precepts of Buddhist morallity marked many individual lives, as the hierarchical style of Confucian thought dominated Japanese social ethics. One sees both the Confucian and the Buddhist influences in so early a Japanese document as the *Constitution* of Prince Shotoku, who guided imperial policy in the early seventh century C.E.

The Prince's Constitution contains seventeen articles, the first of which clearly is Confucian and the second of which clearly is Buddhist:

I. *Harmony is to be valued, and an avoidance of wanton opposition is to be honored. All men are influenced by partisanship, and there are few who are intelligent. Hence there are some who disobey their lords and fathers, or who maintain feuds with neighboring villages. But when those above are harmonious and those below are friendly, there is concord in the discussion of business, right views of things spontaneously gain acceptance. Then what is there which cannot be accomplished?* II. *Sincerely reverence the three treasures. The three treasures, viz. Buddha, the Law, and the Monastic orders, are the final refuge of the four generated beings [those born from eggs, from a womb, moisture-bred, or formed by metamorphosis], and are the supreme objects of faith in all countries. Few men are utterly bad. They may be taught to follow it. But if they do not betake themselves to the three treasures, wherewithal shall their crookedness be made straight?*[8]

The Prince goes on to promote obedience to the imperial commands, decorum among ministers and functionaries, impartial adjudication of law suits, opposition to such evils as flattery and sycophancy, entrusting offices to wise men, diligent attention to matters of state, good faith, restraint of anger, fair reward and punishment, a single ruler in each province, faithful performance of civic duties, restraint of envy, preference for the public over the private, forced labor at seasonable times, and consultation rather than private judgment in all matters of importance. These promotions all bear a markedly Confucian tone, and in them one can see the seeds, maybe even the stalks, of the social ethic that has dominated recent-day Japan.

Analyzing recent-day Japanese society, Chie Nakane has stressed that a fierce competition often develops between companies or neighboring villages. Further, she has underscored the sharp awareness of hierarchical rating that prevailed in the traditional Japanese village:

This rating protocol is exemplified in its traditional form by the ranking of households in a village community. There have been numerous studies of hierarchy in village politics by rural sociologists in Japan; indeed, the villagers' sharp awareness of it compares with the caste-consciousness in a Hindu village. The ranking hierarchy was normally determined by the relative length of establishment of each household in the village. Thus the older tended to be ranked higher, but wealth was an additional factor (though never the primary one) in determining rating. Along with this fairly stable ranking, there was a custom by which every village community made an annual roster ... in which all households of the village were listed in order from top to bottom, with an internal grading into several classes, according to actual wealth and income, and efficiency in handling money. ... Such rankings, which were of great weight in the establishment of the social order, stimulated competition among households with relatively similar standing. Aged farmers can still recall today stories and anecdotes relating to such competition. For example, they would try their best to get up earlier than their neighbours, for it was thought that the actual number of work hours paralleled the volume of production. So, to forestall neighbours from being up as early as themselves, they would open their sliding doors very quietly, and carry any noisy farming tools, such as rollers, so as to avoid making any sound when they passed the neighbours' houses. The degree reached by such competition even prompted inhumane excesses. I was told by one old woman in a comparatively poor village that it was the greatest pleasure of her life when her neighbour's store building caught on fire.[9]

One sees, therefore, that the Confucian promotion of hierarchical thinking did not always achieve harmony. In fact, in Japan it often has promoted fierce competition between parallel businesses, teams, or villages. No doubt this competition, as well as certain kinds of harmony, could enter the service of productivity. No doubt it could be a useful way of harnessing social energies. Seldom, however, does it seem to have been a way of mobilizing social change, promoting egalitarian movements. Prior to the rather recent influx of Western political ideas, Japan was quite content with its traditional social patterns. One was born a peasant or a monarch and generally lived within that happenstance. True, Buddhist organizations sometimes wiped away social distinctions. Talent occasionally would leap over all barriers. But both Buddhist notions of karma and Confucian concerns for rank and harmony were strong hedges against social flux. Thus in Japan prophetic concern for social justice has been less prominent than sagacious concern for social order. Ideally, of course, the two would go together, as we shall see below. Ideally a society would order itself by aiming at a fundamental social justice.

GREECE

Ancient Greece owes its cultural distinction to the burst of creativity that lit up the sky in fourth century B.C.E. Athens. If Socrates, Plato, and Aristotle were the most luminous sages, they had prior stimulus from the great tragedians and collateral stimulus from many fine artists. Among the tragedians Aeschylus (525–456 B.C.E.) stands out for his impassioned, prophetic concern for social justice. It will serve our purposes here to condense Eric Voegelin's analysis of Aeschylus' early play *Suppliants*, since the play was a landmark in the classical Greek clarification of justice and righteous political action.[10]

The tension in the play emanates from the desire of the fifty daughters of King Danaus to avoid marriage to the fifty sons of King Aegyptus, brother of Danaus and victor over him in a struggle to gain rule of the Nile valley. The daughters flee to Argos in Greece and request sanctuary from Pelasgus, King of Argos. Pelasgus is displeased, for the daughters are not entitled to sanctuary rights (since they are not Greeks) and custom dictates that they should submit to those who have conquered them. On the other hand, the suppliant daughters can claim the protection of Zeus, have distant blood ties to Argos, and threaten to commit suicide rather than submit to the sons of Aegyptus. Since their suicides would bring Pelasgus and Argos under a cloud, the king has to consider their petition carefully. At first glance, then, the conflict is between the customary rights of victors in war and the equally customary notion that women do not have to enter marriages abhorrent to them but can claim the protection of the god Zeus and their kinsmen.

Further complicating the drama, however, is the daughters' overall resistance to marriage. For although one might reject a particular marriage as abhorrent, to reject marriage in general would completely violate Greek custom. Against this debit, however, stands the credit that the daughters are relatives of the king, through their common ancestor Io. Their suicide therefore would bring the pollution of familial guilt to Argos and thoroughly blacken its name. On the other hand, the king fears that if he grants the daughters' petition he will offend the Aegyptians and risk their going to war against his city-state. Justice, the playwright is teaching, often is a very difficult matter. Until the mind is clear, it is nearly impossible to bring the will to convinced action. The king therefore waves back and forth in indecision, well aware of the deep counsel he needs: "There is need of deep and saving counsel, like a diver, descending to the depth, with keen eye and not too much perturbed." (Lines 407 ff.) Custom, he slowly comes to see, sometimes must yield to the justice one only finds in the depths of the human spirit.

Interestingly, however, the king does not undertake the descent toward justice alone. Since the welfare of all the people of Argos is involved, all must participate in the struggle to determine what is right. The political implications of this participation are enormous. Aeschylus is saying that the only sort of decision from which social justice and political health arise is that in which the citizenry have opened their souls to the persuasion of heroic figures, like the king, who are willing to suffer the tortures of descending to their own spiritual depths.

Aeschylus' focus is prophetic in the sense that he suggests that the spirit must adhere to the search for what is just. Theologically, his prophethood is less clear. The gods figure in his narrative only externally or symbolically. There is no serious question of a revelatory word from on high. Rather, the king must take counsel with his own innermost sense of what is fair, and then he must draw the people into his consultation. Unless he can persuade them that his sense of justice is accurate, he will not be able to act effectively on their behalf. Equally, he will not have the comfort of their support of his judgments. Thus the dramatic beginnings of the Greek tradition of intellectual analysis show a quite political orientation. In Aeschylus one sees an early form of the concern for the health of the *polis*, or city-state, that preoccupied Socrates, Plato, and Aristotle. In contrast to the outward orientation of the classical prophets, who experienced the demands of justice as the Word of a divine Creator, the Greek philosophers and playwrights tended to focus on the inner weighings and turmoil of the human mind. Not from "out there" but from "in here" would the answers to the decisive problems of justice and action come.

The king is able to persuade his fellow citizens of Argos. His own sense that the suppliant daughters deserve sanctuary wins the approval of the people as a whole. Below the level of customary law, the community comes to a shared conviction about a more basic justice. It is not clear from the play that this conviction will lead to the overthrow of the traditional customs. Certainly the descent to a deeper justice need not depreciate the ordinary uses of less reflective customs. But it does spotlight the heart of the prophetic matter. This is the primacy of justice, its high status as a pressing matter of individual and group conscience. Too often we forget that conscience was something the human race had to discover. The prime place individual conscience has come to hold in Western culture only clarified gradually, through the tremendous labors of poets such as Aeschylus, philosophers such as Socrates. In these labors, the Greeks bequeathed us a legacy quite like that of the biblical prophets.

UNDERSTANDING AND WILL

The sage emphasizes the understanding. The prophet emphasizes the will. For the sage the pearl of great price is the new being that comes with understanding. For the prophet the desire of God is that people do what is just. As we have seen, these distinctions are not dichotomies. To say one does not deny the other. Thus it is not surprising that sages have sketched rigorous social codes, in hopes of guiding their people to inspired living. Similarly, it is not suprising that prophets have bemoaned the lack of understanding among their people, correlating it with a lack of good will. The prophetic instinct, in fact, is to suspect that only those who do the truth will come to the light. The sapiential instinct, by contrast, is to think that the light will draw people of good will to works of justice and love.

Were the religions detached, purely academic or social affairs, they might be willing to recognize the distinctions between prophets and sages and let each sort of personality live as it wished. Sages probably would have neat green lawns, their edges well trimmed, with no dandelions allowed. Prophets probably would have unruly plots of roses, violets, and crabgrass. The way of the prophet would lead to the hurly-burly of the marketplace and the courtroom. The way of the sage would lead to the serenity of mountain streams and ivied classroom buildings.

But the religions are not detached or pure. They are interested, involved, committed. Because the ultimate mystery of life has grabbed them by the throat, they pursue wisdom and justice with passion. Indeed, when a religion has no passion, it has ceased to be alive. When an individual has no passion, she or he has ceased to be religious. Yet the antidote to the poison of passion, the potential for passion to dement and warp, is nothing other than wisdom. If the eye of the mind is clear and calm, the heart will not love bloodshed and strife. If the eye of the mind is confused, the heart will be a seat of emotion on the verge of tipping and crashing.

In the *Laws*, Plato created one of the most famous symbolisms for the way divinity would draw the full human being, mind and heart, toward truth and justice:

We may imagine that each of us living creatures is a puppet made by the gods, possibly as a plaything or possibly with some more serious purpose. That, indeed, is more than we can tell, but one thing is certain. These interior states are, so to say, the cords, or strings, by which we are worked; they stand in opposition to one another, and pull us with opposite tensions in the directions of opposite actions, and therein lies the division of virtue from vice. In fact, so says our argument, a man must always yield to one of these tensions without resistance, but pull against all the other strings—must yield, that is , to that golden and hallowed drawing of judgment which goes by the name of the public law of the city. The others are hard and ironlike, it soft, as befits gold, whereas they resemble various substances. So a man must always co-operate with the noble drawing of the law, for judgment, though a noble thing, is as gentle and free from violence as noble, whence its drawings needs supporters, if the gold within us is to prevail over the other stuff. In this wise our moral fable of the human puppets will find its fulfillment. It will also become somewhat clearer, first, what is meant by self-conquest and self-defeat, and next that the individual's duty is to understand the true doctrine of these tensions and live in obedience to it, the city's to accept this doctrine from a god, or from the human discoverer just mentioned, and make it a law for her converse with herself and other societies.[11]

The resolution of the tensions between sages and prophets, between the mind and the will, and even between virtue and vice, Plato suggests, lies in a careful attention to the "drawings" that we experience. What leads toward the light and is obedient to noble law is a drawing we may attribute to divinity. What leads to unruly darkness and is violent we must deeply suspect. Our interior states therefore become a crucial testing ground. As Aeschylus prefigured, the way to a justice that is more profound than custom passes through the depths of the individual soul and demands a communal discernment.

All the more reason, then, to correlate injustice and destructiveness with distraction. People with little sense of what is stirring within them are always liable to act foolishly and hurtfully. True, one does on occasion find an agent of evil who has a deep interiority, but such a case is rare. Most evil, the religious sages tell us, comes from distraction and superficiality. The great font of foolishness and disorder is not knowing oneself. The prophet does not disagree, but she rather stresses how the evil-doer, the sinner, averts herself from the law of God, the Word that would make her free.

Is the "Athenian stranger" who dominates the *Laws* and speaks in the passage we have quoted therefore a prophet? That is not the first name he would give himself, nor the first name we would give him, but it is a name that could open to embrace him. For the law he promotes is inward and nonviolent, a guidance that would take both the mind and the heart into the gentle play of the divine puppeteer.

SUMMARY

To hint at the prophetic elements at work in sagacious societies, we surveyed several religions and lands. In Hinduism we found a discipline, enshrined in legal codes such as Manu, that seemed to accord with the prophetic concern for holy deeds, righteous action. Central to this code and all Hindu thought about action is the concept of karma, as well as the sense of social class. The Bhagavad-Gita illustrated the changes that yoga tends to ring on "action," especially the call for detachment from any concern about an action's fruits.

To suggest a Buddhist form of prophetic concern we analyzed the five central precepts of Buddhist sila. Using Buddhaghosa's commentary, we glossed the proscriptions against murder, theft, sexual disorder, lying, and taking intoxicants. Buddhaghosa's remarks displayed the keen analytic talent that meditation tends to develop but also the distance at which Buddhist morality stands from the **theocentric** and social imperatives of the Near Eastern prophets. The Chinese case we studied was the *Great Learning*, a text that the *Neo-Confucians* made part of the Confucian canon.

This text well displayed the Confucian concern with rank and harmony, as did the brief description we gave of the overall political structure of the Chinese state. Not surprisingly, we found the less-ordered side of Chinese social dynamics largely to repose in Taoist energies. Both Confucians and Taoists, however, were keenly interested in social questions, an emphasis that makes them cousins of the biblical prophets. Their lesser concern for a radical social justice, on the other hand, distinguishes them from the biblical prophets.

Japanese social ethics derived from both Buddhist and Confucian notions (largely mediated by China). This is clear from so early a document as the early seventh century C.E. *Constitution* of Prince Shotoku. In more recent times, Japanese businesses and villages have taken the Confucian sensitivity to rank as a stimulus to intense competition. Indeed, when an aged woman can say that the greatest pleasure in her life has been watching her competitor neighbor's house burn down, one can speak of sensitivity to rank that has burned to the very quick.

Classical Greek "prophecy" such as that of the playwright Aeschylus took the form of a dramatic and highly moral reading of the spiritual states necessary for political order. In *Suppliants* King Pelasgus becomes a heroic figure because he is willing to dive down to the depths of his spirit in search of a justice more profound than customary law. By showing that Pelasgus draws his people into the search for just order, Aeschylus sketches the ideal social dynamics of the *polis.* Were people to open their spirits to the adventurers who try the depths of conflict resolution and justice, the political process would become a matter of great, even truly religious, dignity. Thus the overlap of the sage's concern for understanding and the prophet's concentration on will suggests a holistic ideal. As Plato hinted in the *Laws,* the paramount task is learning to discern the pull of God on the golden cord that leads to *both* truth and justice.

STUDY QUESTIONS

1. Why does the Bhagavad-Gita focus on acting without attachment?

2. Why does Buddhist morality make so much of avoiding intoxication?

3. What is prophetic about the Confucian emphasis on conscientiousness and altruism?

4. How has the Confucian emphasis on hierarchy bred strong competition in Japan?

5. Did the king of Argos make the right decision? Why?

6. What could be noble about being a puppet of the gods?

NOTES

1. Sarvepalli Radhakrishnan and Charles A. Moore, eds., *A Sourcebook in Indian Philosophy.* Princeton, N.J.: Princeton University Press, 1957, p. 173.

2. Kees Bolle, trans., *The Bhagavadgita.* Berkeley: University of California Press, 1979, p. 65.

3. Edward Conze, trans., *Buddhist Scriptures.* Baltimore: Penguin, 1959, p. 71.

4. Ibid.

5. Wing-Tsit Chan, *A Source Book in Chinese Philosophy.* Princeton, N.J.: Princeton University Press, 1969, p. 84.

6. Jacques Gernet, *Daily Life in China.* Stanford, Calif.: Stanford University Press, 1970, pp. 244–45.

7. Holmes Welch, *Taoism: The Parting of the Way.* Boston: Beacon, 1966, p. 157.

8. Ryusaku Tsunoda et al., eds., *Sources of Japanese Tradition,* vol. 1. New York: Columbia University Press, 1958, p. 48.

9. Chie Nakane, *Japanese Society.* Berkeley: University of California Press, 1972, pp. 88–89.

10. See Eric Voegelin, *Order and History,* vol. 2. Baton Rouge: Louisiana State University Press, 1957, pp. 247–53.

11. Plato, *Laws,* 644d–645c, trans. A. E. Taylor, in *Plato: Collected Dialogues,* ed. Edith Hamilton and Huntington Cairns. Princeton, N.J.: Princeton University Press, 1963, pp. 1244–45.

III

Sages

Sages are people who are wise. With or without the acclaim of their contemporaries, they are people able to set human affairs in order. Usually they insert present human events into a bigger scheme of things. Usually they make the age-old ways of nature or the human family a frame or border that places present human events in perspective and proportion. The sage is not visionary as the shaman is. His or her wisdom is not a matter of striking images or dazzling entranced flights. But the sage is "visionary" in the sense of seeing the bigger picture, looking beyond present times and taking a longer view. Sometimes this longer view depends upon the Word of God, as in the case of Jewish, Christian, and Muslim sages. For them the Torah, Gospel, or Koran provides the border and perspective. Other times the longer view comes from mythic figures of the distant past and merges with a primal sense of the vastness of the cosmos. This is the way the ancient Hindu and Chinese sages appear, as venerable ponderers of the venerable past, the time when humanity was more at home in the world.

Whatever their ways to wisdom, the sages whom humanity has most venerated all stand against short-sightedness and opportunism. Like the prototypical shaman, they have died to ordinary, here-and-now sorts of judgments and live beyond the distraction and selfishness of the common herd. With the classical prophet, they sense the sacredness of the origin of things and the need for social order. But the distinguishing feature of the sage, East or West, is an intellectual grasp of reality's whole. The sage is learned in the knowledge that brings peace, because she or he has studied physical nature, or the sacred books, or the wiles of human nature and has gained an intuitive sense of their whole. As a result, nothing is so new to the sage that it cannot be correlated with previous experience. Nothing is so distinct from the basic forces of creativity and destruction, life and death, that the sage cannot categorize and handle it.

To be sure, a great deal of the authentic sage's wisdom is a confession of ignorance. Socrates stands as the prime Western model of this confession, but he has many brothers and sisters in the East. Thus the Hindu sages who shouted, neti, neti ("not this, not that") taught India that ultimate reality could never be captured in human speech or imagery. Thus the Buddhist sages who focused on nirvana point beyond the realm of perception and karma, hushing their students to silence. The "whole" with which sages become familiar is more than ordinary human perception can embrace. The cosmos, or God, or Buddhanature is complete and simple, as we human perceivers are limited and mortal. So the unknowing or ignorance of the sage is a testimony to the priority and overflowing fullness of ultimate reality. The sage is not agnostic in the cynical, narrowing sense. Her or his reluctance to speak is not an implicit confession that the world is unspeakably chaotic or ugly. Rather it is a tribute to the ineffable richness and power of ultimate reality. Abiding mind to mind with the mystery of Being, heart to heart, the sage prefers the purer language of silence, the more fitting speech of still attunement.

Still sages do speak, and the reason is mainly their compassion. Left to their own inclinations, sages typically would commune directly on the mountain top or burrow deeper into the sacred texts. But the glaring spiritual needs of humankind force the sages to try to communicate their sense of the whole. The myriads who suffer because they lack even an elementary glimpse of truth are petitioners the sage cannot ignore. Were most people to have a sense of why their lives are as they are, they might be able to endure the way they presently must suffer. All life is suffering, the

Buddha saw. The greatest compassion one can muster is to ease this suffering by explaining how it arises and how it may be undercut. So the sage typically addresses her speech to the core of human intelligence, where the intellect, will, and imagination conjoin. This "place" is the heart, the central seat of reason and love. The heart has its reasons, the Western sage Pascal knew, which often the mind doesn't grasp. Thus the midmost mind, as Confucius called it, is the faculty most in need of conversion.

In Part III we mainly deal with the Eastern forms of wisdom, since they have best delineated the sagacious prototype. In India, China, Japan, and ancient Greece, the sage has been the dominant cultural hero. True enough, Judaism, Christianity, and Islam also have venerated the sage and sometimes have canonized sagacious learning. But the component stressing will in these cultural complexes and their huge debts to founding prophets make it less clear that wisdom has been their prime treasure. So it will be the

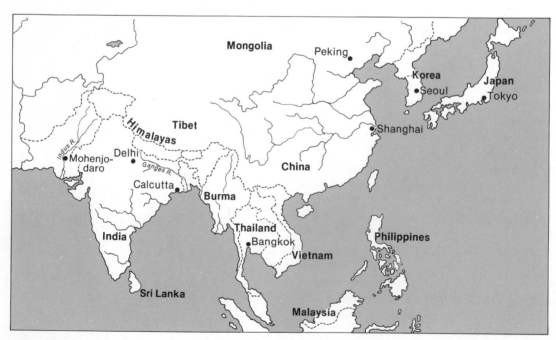

Figure 10   Asia.

Religious Wisdom: Twenty-Five Key Dates

CA. 1500 B.C.E. Vedas
CA. 1360 Hymns of Akhenaton
1000–500 Redactions of Pentateuch
800–400 Upanishads
750–550 Hebrew Prophets
550 Oldest Parts of Zoroastrian *Avesta*
500 Oldest Parts of *Analects*
400–250 Job; Ecclesiastes; *Bhagavad Gita*
CA. 350 Plato's *Laws; Tao Te Ching*
CA. 330 Aristotle's *Metaphysics*
CA. 160 Buddhist *Prajna-Paramita*
CA. 80 *Lotus Sutra*, Key Buddhist Text
CA. 50 Buddhist *Dhammapada*
CA. 50–90 C.E. New Testament Writings
413–426 Augustine's *City of God*
425 Buddhist *Visuddhimagga*
CA. 500 Babylonian Talmud
CA. 650 Canonization of the Koran
712–720 Shinto Chronicles
CA. 1100 Al-Ghazali's *Revivification of the Sciences*
1175 Chu Hsi's Neo-Confucian Synthesis
1190 Maimonides' *Guide for the Perplexed*
1270 Aquinas' *Summa Theologica*
1536 Calvin's *Institutes*
1581 Compilation of *Adi Granth*, Sikh Scripture

East that furnishes us our major studies in wisdom. After looking at the Hindu, Buddhist, Chinese, Japanese, and Greek traditions stressing wisdom, we will also study shamanic and prophetic parallels.

Since perhaps half the world's population now lives in cultures influenced by the sages we will study in this section, this focus offers some pregnant opportunities. For instance, it sketches some of the main things one must appreciate if one is to grasp the basic culture of today's 1 billion Chinese or 650 million Indians. If the world is becoming smaller, drawing all 4.5 billion of us human beings closer together, it is obviously important for Western people to understand the ideas of the Eastern sages.

CHAPTER

11

Hinduism

The Vedas
The Upanishads
The Gita
Shankara
Nature
Society
Self
Ultimate Reality
Gandhi
Summary
Study Questions
Notes

THE VEDAS

As we have noted, the origins of Hindu wisdom extend back to the Aryan seers responsible for the Vedas. The root of the word *Veda* (*ved-*) means "to know" and is cognate to the English *wit*. So the seers responsible for the Vedas were sages to whom the gods or ultimate reality had granted visions of how things are, what the truth of life actually is. Many of the Vedic hymns and reflections deal with these gods, who in the earliest period seem mainly to have been personifications of forces of nature. Thus Agni was the god of fire, Varuna the god of the sky, Rudra the god of the storm. At times the Vedas deal with such gods almost commercially, promising them sacrifices and gifts in return for their favors. At other times the attitude is reverent and praising, the response of an appreciative spirit to the wonders of fire, the sky, or the storm.

Within the Vedas themselves, however, one sees probings that reach beyond the multiplicity of the many gods. Searching for the origin of the world, some rishis pondered in a deeper and simpler vein. Rig Veda X:129 is one of the most famous texts they have left us:

Then there was not nonexistent nor existent: there was no realm of air, no sky beyond it. What covered it, and where? and what gave shelter? Was water there, unfathomed depth of water? Death was not then, nor was there aught immortal: no sign was there, the day's and night's divider. That One Thing, breathless, breathed by its own nature: apart from it was nothing whatsoever. Darkness there was: at first concealed in darkness this All was undifferentiated chaos. All that existed then was void and formless: by the great power of Warmth was born that One. Thereafter rose Desire in the beginning, Desire, the primal seed and germ of Spirit. Sages who searched with the heart's thought discovered the existent's kinship in the non-existent. Transversely was their severing line extended: what was above it then, and what below it? There were

116

Hinduism: Twenty-Five Key Dates

CA. 2750 B.C.E. Growth of Civilization in Indus Valley
CA. 1500 Aryan Invasions; Vedic Literature
800–400 Upanishads
600–500 Challenges of Mahavira and Buddha
CA. 500 Aryans as Far South as Ceylon
500–200 Epic Poetry: *Mahabharata, Ramayana, Bhagavad Gita*
322 Chandragupta Founds Mauryan Empire
100 B.C.E.–100 C.E. Rise of Bhakti Literature
480 C.E. Fall of Gupta Empire
680 Flourishing of Tamil Bhakti Movement
788–820 Shankara, Leading Philosopher
800–900 Rise of Hindu Orthodoxy
1017–1137 Ramanuja, Leading Philosopher
1175 First Muslim Empire in India
1485–1533 Chaitanya, Leader of Krishna-Bhakti
1498 Vasco da Gama Visits India
1526 Beginning of Mogul Dynasty
1653 Completion of Taj Mahal
1690 British Found Calcutta
1707 Decline of Mogul Power
1818 Beginning of British Rule
1869–1948 Mahatma Gandhi
1885 Founding of Indian National Congress
1947 Indian Independence; Partition of Pakistan
1971 Founding of Bangladesh

begetters, there were mighty forces, free action here and energy up yonder. Who verily knows and who can here declare it, whence it was born and whence comes this creation? The Gods are later than this world's creation. Who knows then whence it first came into being? He, the first origin of this creation, whether he formed it all or did not form it, Whose eye controls this world in highest heaven, he verily knows it, or perhaps he knows not.[1]

This is a remarkable text and a good preview of later Hindu tendencies. First, it senses that the origin of the universe stands outside, beyond the states of the universe as we now know it. Thus at the origin there was neither nonexistence, or existence but something that synthesized or went beyond these alternatives. By questions, the author probes the ground of that zero time imaginatively: Was there air, sky, shelter, water, death, or immortality? How were things marked? How did day divide itself from night? Like

the authors of Genesis, the writers of the Rig Veda were puzzled and intrigued: In what ways did this present creation come to be? The option of this poet was for a primal One Thing, apart from which there was nothing at all. This One Thing surely was different from anything we know. Surely it was paradoxical, breathless yet breathing in a way all its own. Probably the original state of things was darkness, undifferentiated chaos, void. For something like the One Thing to arise, warmth and desire must have come along. Desire, will, is the primal seed of everything we know, so we can assume it was there when creation began to take shape. The sages have drawn their diagrams and thought their thoughts. They have pinpointed existence, nonexistence, begetting, free action, and energy, both above and below the line between heaven and earth.

Yet who really knows? Even the existence of the gods followed the primordial act of origination. He who was there, the One Thing, probably knows. If he did it, or was a part of it, he must understand it. Now he watches over this world from the highest heavens, so it would be comforting to think that he understands the whole. But we cannot be sure. Maybe even he doesn't truly know. Maybe it is a mystery no eye has ever seen, no ear ever heard. The mind travels, the imagination pictures, but neither can find a sure result. The origin of things is wonderfully obscure. Perhaps it is wonderful because it is obscure. Our spirits love to journey toward it. Our hearts open in its direction. But we don't know, never grasp it. So we must live wayfaringly, continuing to search yet reconciling ourselves to never finding as we initially wish.

THE UPANISHADS

Among the Hindu scriptures the Upanishads hold an especially important place. They are the end of the Vedic materials and therefore are considered scriptural. Yet they have been the wellspring of much later Hindi wisdom writing, because their probing of ultimate questions has seemed to license investigations into the final stuff of the world and the soul. The word *Upanishad* itself denotes something secret and mystical. By the eighth century C.E. the late Vedic texts (the Upanishads) constituted a discernible corpus. About that time the paramount Hindu philosopher Shankara focused on the Upanishads in developing his profound view that all reality constitutes a simple oneness.

Although the canonical Upanishads differ considerably among themselves in doctrine and imagery, they tend to agree on certain main themes. Among these are the superiority of the spiritual to the physical, the value of knowledge in contrast to ignorance, the necessity of a disciplined life for attaining spiritual goals, the importance of certain rituals, the derivation of the physical world from a single divine cause, the necessity of both good works and right knowledge, the link between ignorant action and repeated rebirths, and the primacy of knowing one's innermost spiritual being.[2]

In the Brihad-aranyaka Upanishad, one of the most important, occurs an interesting discussion between the thoughtful woman Gargi and the sage Yajnavalkya about the ultimate "warp" of reality. (The relevant definition of *warp* is "the basic foundation or material of a structure or entity").[3] Gargi has pressed the sage to tell her about the weave of reality: "That, O Yajnavalkya, which is above the sky, that which is beneath the earth, that which is between these two, sky and earth, that which people call the past and the present and the future—across what is that woven, warp and woof?" The sage answers that she is asking about space. Sensing that she still has not gained the final goal of her inquiry, Gargi presses one further question: "Across what then, pray, is space woven, warp and woof?" This is the capital question, eliciting from the sage the capital answer: the Imperishable.

To describe the Imperishable, Yajanavalkya launches into a long list of negatives: "It is not coarse, not fine, not short, not long, not glowing, not adhesive, without shadow and without darkness, without air and without space, without stickiness, odorless, tasteless, without eye, without ear, without voice, without wind, without energy, without breath, without mouth ... without measure, without inside and without outside." The Imperishable does not consume anything and no one consumes it. It is the commander of the sun and the moon, the earth and the sky, and all other things. Without the knowledge of the Imperishable, other religious attainments are of little worth: "Verily, O Gargi, if one performs sacrifices and worship and undergoes austerity in this world for many thousands of years, but without knowing that Imperishable, limited indeed is that [work] of his." For the Imperishable is the unseen Seer, the unthought Thinker, the only One that understands. "Across this Imperishable, O Gargi, is space woven, warp and woof."[4]

The Imperishable, then, is the Upanishadic sage's ultimate wisdom. When pressed for the material cause of things, the "that from which" everything is made, Yajnavalkya can only say, Something that is of itself, something that does not perish. This is a characteristic answer, one that many sages, Western as well as Eastern, have fashioned. Pushing off from the perishable nature of the things of sensory experience, they have conceived of the ultimate foundation of reality as other than sensible things, other indeed than anything within the range of human experience. The best we can say of the origin of the universe, the final reason of everything that exists, is that it *is* independently, in a mode that does not perish, pass away, or suffer change. To uphold the world it must be different than the world. Either in the midst of worldly flux or apart, it must surpass the "world," the mental construct of the material and spiritual whole that we limited humans fashion.

On the other hand, the ultimate material cause of things must be enough like us, discernible by us, to warrant our giving it negative names and seeking to know it. Were it absolutely other, completely apart from our human realm, we could not even discuss it negatively. Pondering this equally primordial fact, the Upanishadic seers came to focus on the human spirit or soul as the best analogue or presence of the Ultimate. This spirit or soul (**atman**) seemed the best focus for the inreach of the Ultimate that makes human beings exist. While they live, human beings are imperishable: Something keeps them from total change and decay. Thus while they have a given identity they draw upon the Imperishable, depend upon It and express It. Between It and them there must be a connection, maybe even an identity. Certainly the most real part of them is the presence of the Imperishable, without which they would actually perish. So perhaps the best way to regard them (ourselves), or anything, is as a form of the Imperishable, one of its myriad extrusions or expressions. If so, one can say that, in the last analysis, only the Imperishable is real or actual or existent. Everything else at best receives a passing reality from the temporary presence to it, presence in it, of the Imperishable. For that reason, Yajnavalkya can rightly call it that across which even space is woven, warp and woof.

THE GITA

The Upanishads depict the mind's ascent to the ultimate principle that might unify the plurality of human experience. They imply that careful questioning, with special attention to the spiritual component of the questioner, can bring into view the Imperishable. The Bhagavad-Gita, which is part of the great Hindu epic called the *Mahabharata*, was probably composed shortly after the last of the principal Upanishads (about 300 B.C.E.). It has become India's most beloved spiritual work, largely because of its catholic character. In the Gita one finds such a variety of paths of salvation that no personality need feel without hope. Be the reader an intense scholar or a humble worker, an accomplished yogin or a poor householder, the Gita lays before her or him an attractive path.

Indeed, the most dazzling revelations of the Gita suggest that God is eager to help, to labor on behalf of, the person desiring salvation. This is a dramatic teaching, for the great self-disclosure of Krishna in Chapter 11 shows that the power of divinity is awesome:

Then, O King, when he had spoken thus, Hari, the great lord of mystery, revealed to the son of Pritha his supreme form as god. With a multitude of mouths and eyes displaying wonders, adorned with the very heavens, with divine weapons raised as for battle; crowned with the skies, in ethereal raiment scented with divine

perfumes and balms, made of all wonders was this limitless god, and his face looked in all directions. If a thousand suns should at once blaze up in the sky the light of that mighty soul would equal all their brightness.[5]

This is what scholars of religion call a **theophany**: a manifestation of divinity. Where the Gita advances beyond the Upanishads is in the personal quality of its theophanies. The great force being revealed is not merely imperishable. It is the light within all light, the power within all creativity, taking a personal face and form. In large part because he dominates the Gita, Krishna has become the most beloved **avatar**, or manifestation form, of the Hindu divinity. (Specifically, he is an avatar of Vishnu, who stands in the Hindu Trinity for the powers of preservation, the energies that conquer evil, perishing, and death. If Brahma is the creator and Shiva is the destroyer, Vishnu-Krishna is the kindly, close deity who cares for human life.) The main burden of Krishna's advice to Arjuna, the prince whose moral conflicts the Gita sets out to solve, is the primacy of Arjuna's spirit (atman) and the care divinity has for the spirits of all its people. Arjuna must do what he has to do, fulfill his caste responsibility (*dharma*) as a warrior by fighting, but he can do this calmly, without inner perturbation, because he can repose his spirit in Krishna.

Toward the end of the Gita, in Chapter 18, Krishna discloses his fullest secret, which sets a seal on his advice that Arjuna should detach his spirit from worldly worries and trust in Krishna's provision:

Arjuna, the lord of all beings abides in their hearts and through his mystic power they turn round fixed to a turning wheel. Take shelter in him alone with all your being, son of Bharata. Through his grace you will win the peace beyond and the eternal home. So I have told you wisdom of all secrets the most hidden. Ponder it carefully then act as you will. Listen again to my highest word, the most secret of all. You are loved by me surely and I will tell you for your good. Set your mind on me, belong to me, worship me and bow before me. You shall come to me alone. Truly I promise you. You are dear to me. Forsaking all things of the law, come to me as your single shelter. Do not be sad, I will save you from all evil.[6]

This possibility of a personal love relation to the god has endeared the Gita to the Hindu masses. Through **bhakti**, devotional love, millions have made Krishna their soul mate and support. With more emotion or less, the typical devotee to Krishna has prayed, sacrificed, performed rituals, and generally sought to make her or his life coincide with the god, fill with an awareness of the god's presence and love. For the last thousand years, *bhakti* has probably been the most influential religious orientation in India. People with no education or status have found it especially ennobling, for it says that one need only be able to love.

A second teaching of the Gita that has assured its popularity concerns **karma-yoga**. A yoga is a sort of discipline, so karma-yoga is a discipline concerning action or work. Essentially the Gita, as we saw in the last chapter, teaches that one can live in the world, work and act, without accruing bad karma, as long as one does not become involved emotionally in the fruits of one's work, its successes or failures. When work is a pure form of self-expression, done only for its own sake, with no ulterior motives, it can purify the self of the fear and desire that bind the atman to the cycles of rebirth.

Sensing the aptness of this teaching for a political movement based on the power of truth (**satyagraha**), Mahatma Gandhi warmly embraced the Gita's karma-yoga. In fact, he made the spinning wheel the symbol of his movement, for it seemed a beautiful illustration of how work can purify the worker of all base attachments. Going round and round, with no anxiety about what it produces, the wheel conjured the free, unconcerned workers whom Gandhi hoped would liberate India from British rule.

SHANKARA

In Hindu tradition six orthodox schools of philosophy have taken the teachings of the Vedas, the Upanishads, the Gita, and other venerable early writings in different directions. Each school has had its own special emphases, but all the schools have pursued moksha, liberation from the samsaric world of death and rebirth.

The luminary of Hindu philosophy, however, is Shankara, leader of the Nondualist (*advaita*) sect of Vendanta. The eminent scholar Heinrich Zimmer has spoken of Shankara as follows:

The most important name in this surprising development is that of the brilliant Sankara, the founder of the so-called "Nondualist" (advaita) school of Vedantic philosophy. Little is known of his brief career, which is now supposed to have endured for but thirty-two years, somewhere around 800 A.D. Legends credit his conception to a miracle of the god Shiva, and state that the child was at an early age a master of all the sciences; he is declared to have caused a river to come closer to his mother's door so that she should be saved the

trouble of going to fetch water. At an extremely early age he retired to the forest, where he met the sage Govinda and became his pupil. And thereafter he wandered throughout India, engaging everywhere in victorious arguments with the philosophers of the day. Shankara's commentaries on the Brahmasutra, Bhagavad Gita *and the* Upanishads, *and his original philosophical works (such as the* Vivekacudamani, *"The Crown Jewel of Discrimination"), have exercised an incalculable influence on the history of philosophy throughout the Far and Middle East.*

Basing his reasoning on the Vedic formula, tat tvam asi, *"That art thou," he developed with unwavering consistency a systematic doctrine, taking the Self (at-man) as the sole reality and regarding all else as the phantasmagoric production of nescience (avidya). The cosmos is an effect of nescience, and so also is the interior ego (ahankara) which is everywhere mistaken for the Self. Maya, illusion, mocks the perceiving, cogitating, and intuitive faculties at every turn. The Self is hidden deep. But when the Self is known there is no nescience, no maya [illusory quality of "reality"], no avidya; i.e., no macrocosm or microcosm—no world.*[7]

The legends that grew up around Shankara derive as much from the sanctity of his life as from the power of his thought. His main intuition, as Zimmer notes, was the nondual, unitary character of all reality. Only the Self, with a capital *S*, is actually and fully real. (Thus for Shankara the Self is much like Yajnavalkya's Imperishable.) The plurality we find in the world comes from our ignorance. Both the notion of a cosmos and the notion of a personal, individual self result from ignorance of the great Self. Indeed, the ordinary person lives completely immersed in illusion, distracted from the primary reality of what makes existence possible. To know the Self therefore is to do away with the ordinary world that most people inhabit. Within and without, the insight that Shankara holds out would turn a person topsy-turvy. For that reason, relatively few people have gone the full way of Vedanta and completely routed all their ignorance. But a great many Indians have followed Shankara's nondualism some of the way, sharpening their sense that ordinary perception is at best provisional; true realization would show the world to converge at, or rest upon, or manifest a single center.

One of Shankara's secondary contributions to Hinduism was a strong rebuttal of Buddhist philosophy. After the Buddha many impressive thinkers developed a philosophy that challenged the **monism** of the Upanishads. In place of the single reality, Imperishable or Self, that the most speculative parts of the Vedas proposed, the Buddhists taught that the ultimate or **tran-**

scendent (that which goes beyond) is a Void. In the wake of Shankara, Vedanists have countered this Buddhist position:

One view is that the transcendent is the Void itself. Properly grasped, it can be the object of ultimate spiritual concern and hence the saving truth, as powerfully demonstrated by Buddhism. The Buddhists see all things, including consciousness itself, as being of the nature of flux. There is no place other than the whirling flux from whence to survey consciousness. Others, however, chiefly the Vedantists, view the nature of the transcendent as substantial. According to the Vedanta, consciousness' orientation to the transcendent itself reveals the transcendent as an eternal and unchanging entity. Consciousness is oriented as it is because its essence is the self (atman) that struggles to be free from the bondage of phenomena. Therefore, in the very orientation of consciousness the self serves as its own bridge leading to the far shore or the ground beyond the abyss. In fact, the far shore, consciousness, the bridge (i.e., the self), and the abyss all get welded into one homogenous and self-identical reality.[8]

The author is saying that Shankara and his followers have sensed that the world has a simple and solid ultimate reality. By contrast, the Buddhists have sensed that the world is essentially in flux. Both schools have proposed their senses of reality as more than an academic construct. Both truths can orient a life toward salvation, free people from samsara and rebirth. To reach Shankara's self and dissolve the world of phenomena or multiplicity would be to reach moksha. To move through the flux completely detached would be to reach nirvana. An outside observer therefore might say that the two paths converge toward the same goal: the complete freeing of the human personality.

NATURE

Shankara stands at the acme of Hindu sagehood, honored as the philosopher who has developed the most rigorous expression of the religious core of the Vedas. Obviously other holy people have greatly influenced Hinduism, however, and their wisdom usually has embodied the detachment and the sense of union with the whole of reality that the Upanishads, the Gita, and Shankara have encouraged. Because of such an ideal, most of the Hindu sages have downplayed nature. As a result, many Hindus have dealt with nature ambiguously or distractedly.

This is not to say that many Hindus did not farm, hunt, and fish. It is not to suggest that most Hindus thought their physical surroundings unreal or untrustworthy. It is only to suggest that the core of most of the Hindu subtraditions has stressed the spiritual side of human nature and correlated it with the "inner" side of physical nature, the *being* or more-than-physical source of the world.

Still, the Vedic notion of **rita** (order, duty, or ritual) and the later notion of karma helped Hindus find the natural world quite orderly. Rita presided over such phenomena as sunrise, sunset, and the seasons. Karma expressed the Hindu conviction that things in the cosmos are as they are because of previous causes or choices. As well, all cosmic actions have sure effects. Thus the world usually seemed patterned, regular, dependable. Of course, flood, famine, earthquake, sickness, or war could upset the Hindu's confidence in the regularity of the cosmos. Even then, however, the doctrine of karma whispered that all events had their reasons; nothing happened without a purpose.

Karma connects with the doctrines of transmigration and rebirth. For Hinduism the life force passes over to new forms at death, and these forms are determined by the dead entity's karma. Rita is aligned with the vast scheme of space and time that Hindu cosmology developed. Time, for instance, came to be measured by the **kalpa**, the great cycle that stretched 4,320,000 human years (12,000 divine years, each of which was 360 human years). Each *kalpa* had four stages, two of which were a golden age at the beginning and a degenerate age at the end. Almost always sages spoke of present times as part of the degenerate age and so perhaps on the brink of a rebirth of the whole process. A thousand kalpas composed what was called a *Brahma Day*, the span from the creation of the universe to its destruction. Following a Brahma Day came a Brahma Night, a period of universal rest equal in duration to a Brahma Day (i.e., a thousand kalpas). Thus the Hindu universe had an enormous rhythm of day and night, life and death. If a person situated herself in the midst of this enormous rhythm, the troubles of present times might dwindle considerably. Indeed, even if it took many lifetimes to break the hold of karma and enter into moksha, there was no need for anxiety. One had plenty of time, so the only requisite was to do the best one could in one's present existence.

Nature in these terms was a wide border giving the Hindu spirit space to breathe and gain perspective. It could also become allegorical, as it does in the following story adapted from the Mahabharata:

Once there was a brahmin [priest] who wandered into a dark forest filled with wild animals. Indeed, so ferocious were the lions, elephants, and other great beasts of this forest that even Yama, the god of death, would only enter it when absolutely necessary. The brahmin only came to sense the wicked nature of the dark forest gradually, but then he grew more and more fearful. Panicking, he found himself running in circles, becoming more and more confused.

Finally the brahmin looked about on every side and saw that the forest was caught in a huge net held by a giant woman with outstretched arms. There were five-headed serpents everywhere, so tall that their heads nearly reached the heavens. Then the brahmin came to a clearing, with a deep well covered by vines and underbrush. Running frantically from a wild elephant that was pursuing him, he stumbled into the well, fell through the brush, and lodged halfway to the bottom, held upside down by a few vines.

At the bottom of the well was a huge snake. Above him waited the great elephant, which had six faces and twelve feet. To the side, in the vines that held him, were many bees that had built hives and filled them with honey. When the honey dripped toward him, the brahmin reached out to catch it in his mouth. The more honey he ate, the more he could not satisfy his thirst for it. Meanwhile, black and white rats gnawed at the vines holding him. Though the elephant stood guard above, the serpent stood guard below, the bees buzzed on all sides, and the rats gnawed at his lifeline, the brahmin continued to grope for more honey.[9]

As the commentators make clear, the forest is the limited sphere of our life: dark and filled with dangers. The woman holding a net over it is the process of aging. The beasts are the diseases and other forces that seek to destroy us, and the huge snake is time. The elephant is the year, with its twelve months. The rats are day and night. The honey, sadly enough, is the pleasures of life, for which our thirst seems unslakable. Faced with such a situation, wise people would not stumble into the forest carelessly or let themselves panic and rush about pell-mell. They would realize that the only way to pass through life successfully, slip away from the beasts, or out-duel time is to keep one's wits and practice a stern detachment. Any attached, ignorant way of handling nature or human affairs will only bring one to disaster. The best way to deal with nature or time is with hands off.

SOCIETY

In the mid-1970s Indira Gandhi, head of the Indian government, imposed a state of "Emergency" to try to get her country's political and social problems under control. V. S. Naipaul, a journalist of Indian ancestry, has ruminated on the underlying causes of such problems as follows:

In a speech before the Emergency, Jaya Prakash Narayan, the most respected opposition leader, said: "It is not the existence of disputes and quarrels that so much endangers the integrity of the nation as the manner in which we conduct them. We often behave like animals. Be it a village feud, a students' organization, a labor dispute, a religious procession, a boundary disagreement, or a major political question, we are more likely than not to become aggressive, wild, and violent. We kill and burn and loot and sometimes commit even worse crimes."

The violence of the riot could burn itself out; it could be controlled, as it now was, by the provisions of the Emergency. But there was an older, deeper Indian violence. This violence had survived untouched by foreign rule and had survived [Mahatma] Gandhi. It had become part of the Hindu social order, and there was a stage at which it became invisible, disappearing in the general distress. But now, with the Emergency, the emphasis was on reform, and on the "weaker sections" of society; and the stories the censored newspapers played up seemed at times to come from another age. A boy seized by a village moneylender for an unpaid debt of 150 rupees, fifteen dollars, and used as a slave for four years; in September, in Vellore in the south, untouchables forced to leave their village after their huts had been fenced in by caste Hindus and their well polluted; in October, in a village in Gujarat in the west, a campaign of terror against untouchables rebelling against forced labor and the plundering of their crops; the custom, among the untouchable men of a northern district, of selling their wives to Delhi brothels to pay off small debts to their caste landlords.

To the ancient Aryans the untouchables were "walking carrion." Gandhi—like other reformers before him—sought to make them part of the holy Hindu system. He called them Harijans, *children of God. A remarkable linguistic coincidence: they have remained God's chillun. Even at the Satyagraha Ashram [community] on the riverbank at Ahmedabad, which Gandhi himself founded after his return from South Africa, and from where in 1930 he started on the great Salt March.* Son et Lumière *at night these days in the ashram, sponsored by the Tourism Development Corporation; and in the mornings, in one of the buildings, a school for Harijan girls. "Backward class, backward class," the old brahmin, suddenly my guide, explained piously, converting the girls into distant objects of awe.*

The antique violence remained: rural untouchability as serfdom, maintained by terror and sometimes by deliberate starvation. None of this was new; but suddenly in India it was news.[10]

There are some qualifiers one should place on Naipaul's observations. First, although born in Trinidad (of Indian parents) and educated at Oxford, Naipaul brings to India the sort of special sensitivity that an American of Irish extraction might bring to "the troubles" of Northern Ireland. Because the country he is observing has swum in his own blood, he sees its failures with a special acuteness. Second, one could document the failures of other religio-cultural systems as graphically as Naipaul has documented the Hindu failures. His own later work, *Among the Believers*, is a scathing indictment of the foibles and horrors of the fundamentalist Islams of Pakistan, Iran, Malaysia, and Indonesia. Nazi, Soviet, Latin American, Cambodian, Chinese, African, and other failures, atrocities, and inhumanities blot the social records of the religions that have held sway in those areas. The treatment of Amerindian tribes and black slaves in the United States raises similar hackles and cautions.

Still, it remains that Hindu caste has been a powerful ingredient in what to the outsider looks like the nearly unrelieved misery of millions of Indian poor. Among all classes, but especially the poor, Indian women have suffered the worst burdens. For to the general tendency of the religions to stigmatize women as second-class citizens and dangers to the virtue of men, one must add the special Hindu twists: A woman could not attain moksha without first being reborn as a man, and a devout widow was expected to throw herself on her husband's funeral pyre.

The poverty, slavery, and general abuse into which the untouchables often have fallen, simply because they had been born into a certain social stratum, calls into question all the religions' tendency to justify the status quo as a matter of divine ordinance. One need not employ Marxist analyses of ideology and class conflict to clarify the self-advantage that the upper classes have pursued through the Hindu caste system. Common sense will do. So Hinduism, like most of the other world religions at too many times and places, calls into question the humaneness of religion as a whole. While its ideals are blazing achievements of the human spirit, some of its practices are the devil's own handiwork.

Sometimes writers of textbooks in world religion are criticized for sugar-coating the traditions' dark features. By quoting Naipaul, and assuring the reader that Hinduism is by no means the only religio-social system that deserves biting criticism, we hope to suggest a sobering balance. All things can be abused, even those supposed to be pure and holy.

SELF

As we have seen from Shankara, the self is a special concern of Hindu wisdom. Specifically, the relation between the human personality and the inmost force of the world has preoccupied the Indian sages. Ma Jnanananda, a contemporary *guru* living in Madras on the southeast coast of India, illustrates the personal experiences through which many sages have solved the main problems of the self. Since she stands in the *advaita* tradition of Shankara, she also shows the current relevance of Vedanta, as well as the current ability of exceptional Hindu women to break through the social restraints that bound most of their foremothers.

Ma Jnanananda is the only woman ever allowed by her eminent *advaita* teacher to take the *sannyasi* vows that mean a formal renouncing of all worldly life, including family ties and possessions. She owes this distinction, as well as her honorific title **guru** (religious teacher) to the understanding of the deepest *advaita* truths that she has gained through her intense mystical experiences. That she had these experiences while married and the mother of five children testifies to the extraordinary force of her religious energies, as well as to the empirical fact that grace pervades the world and the divine has not left itself without witness anywhere.

An American professor interviewed Ma Jnanananda in the late 1970s:

At another interview—in fact nearly the last I had with her—Ma Satguru [true teacher] talked more about the trance state of **samadhi***, which was such an important ingredient in her role as guru. When I came to see her on April 4, 1979, her elder son told me that she had been in* samadhi *more or less continuously for the past few days. He said that I might find she was having difficulty answering questions. When I sat down in front of her for* darshan *[blessing], I could sense the difference, so to speak, in her level of consciousness. With a kind of sympathetic response, I even felt myself carried away by her self-absorption and did not much want to pursue a conversatiion. But we both made an effort, and I was able to gather a few comments.*

She said that she had experienced this deep absorption many times ever since she was a child. She added that when one is finally fixed in it, there is no more ego. Now that absorption is always the background of her consciousness. Samadhi *is an experience without content and yet it is not empty. It is complete fullness. "In that state I used to ask myself, 'Where am I?' Then I would try to think of myself at some point, but I immediately felt myself to be at the opposite point. In short, it is a feeling of being simultaneously everywhere. But there is no perception of the physical world. The physical world is dissolved in unity.*[11]

For much of Hinduism, bringing the self to a sense of union with ultimate reality has been the great psychological ideal. Nonetheless, Hinduism has made ample provision for the other needs of the self and for the typical stages in the self's unfolding. The other needs of the self, in addition to moksha, have traditionally been enumerated as pleasure, wealth, and duty. Pleasure (*kama*) means sexual fulfillment and all the joys of culture. Wealth (*artha*) means the material well-being necessary for good health, solid family life, and a prosperous society as a whole. Duty (*dharma*) means the general responsibilities one has to follow in the hallowed teachings of the Hindu mainstream and the special responsibilities of one's caste. Thus brahmans would have special responsibilities to offer sacrifices and give good example, warriors would have special responsibilities to provide political leadership and military defense, merchants and farmers would have special responsibilities to be honest in their business dealings.

Salvation (*moksha*) was the highest of the four life goals, and so the most influential in structuring the classical Hindu life cycle. In childhood the upper-class Hindu male (women were seldom considered qualified for the life-cycle scheme) would apprentice himself to a guru to learn the tradition. Practicing celibacy and obedience, he would try to lay the foundation for a life that ultimately would culminate in moksha. The second stage of the life cycle entailed marriage and secular responsibilities. Hinduism overall has had a high respect for the benefits of marriage; Indians have tended to enjoy their children (and rely on them to offer sacrifices to ensure their peace in the afterlife, as well as provide material support in their old age); and Indian secular life has been busy with the trading, warfare, state-craft, and the other concerns of any great culture. In the second state, therefore, one was to experience what the traditional truths might mean, flesh out the venerable maxims so that they became concrete and prudential.

When his hair had turned gray and he saw his children's children, the Hindu was supposed to enter the third life-cycle phase. This entailed retiring from active life to the "forest" (either the real forest or some less rugged retreat) for meditation and an intense, full-time pursuit of enlightenment. The fourth life-cycle stage was that of a wandering holy man (*sanyassin*). In it the person would travel as light as possible, beg his food, and try to become a living symbol of the paramount significance of the Hindu spiritual truths, the surpassing value of the self's union with **Brahman**, the holy ultimate reality. Moksha would finalize this union, taking the self outside the realm of karma, into a definitive fulfillment.

ULTIMATE REALITY

The Imperishable, the Self, and Brahman have been prominent among the designations of ultimate reality preferred by the Hindu philosophers. Overall, Brahman, the impersonal ground of both nature and human personalities, probably has predominated. Brahman has had both a hidden and a manifest aspect. Hidden, it passes beyond all human imagination, conception, or experience. Manifest, it appears as the depth of the physical world, the deep mystery that now and then may become perceptible anywhere. For the Hindu yogins and philosophers, wisdom has been the vision and power to unite oneself with such an ultimate reality. Throughout the high, intellectualist part of Hindu culture, the Upanishadic call to identity ("that art thou") has been a major refrain.

This has not meant, however, that Hindus, whether intellectuals or uneducated, have not pictured ultimate reality in personal terms. On the contrary, the Hindu pantheon has been replete with striking gods and goddesses. We have mentioned the trinity, or *trimurti*, of Brahman, Vishnu, and Shiva, as well as the old Vedic gods such as Agni, god of the fire, and Indra, god of the storm. In later Hinduism Vishnu, especially in the avataric form of Krishna, and Shiva probably have been the dominant masculine faces of the ultimate. (Shiva, however, often appears as hermaphroditic—male and female.) The dominant goddesses have been variations of the Great Mother, often given their particular coloring by local legends and customs. One of the major goddesses of pan-Hinduism, however, has been Kali, the wife of Shiva, who has been especially prominent in eastern India, with a strong cult centered in Calcutta. In considering the fearsome and motherly features of Kali, we will be dealing with aspects of ultimate reality that have absorbed millions of Hindus through the centuries.

David Kinsley has written an interesting comparison of Krishna and Kali that stresses, among other things, the goddess's connection with **maya**, ordinary reality as illusory and deceptive:

Kali is a Hindu goddess; she is a being who has revealed herself to the Hindu tradition and whose popularity suggests that she typifies in some way the Hindu vision of the divine. In trying to understand Kali, the place to begin, it seems to me, is with a consideration of the Hindu vision of reality and the ways in which Kali either embodies elements of this vision or dramatically illustrates them. . . . Ramakrishna [an influential modern Hindu saint] once had a vision of maya. *In this vision he saw a beautiful young woman, pregnant and about to give birth, emerging from the Ganges [India's most sacred river]. She lay down on the bank and soon gave birth to a son. She suckled him and caressed him fondly. Suddenly she was transformed into a terrible hag. She grasped the infant, crushed him in her mighty jaws, and returned into the waters of Ganges. The world of "my" and "me" is alluring, bewitching, and fleetingly beautiful. For him who sees truly, however, such a world is seen as a narrow, binding, petty world of self-centeredness. The man who truly sees has torn the veil of* maya; *he is able to focus on the flux of all things, the inevitable decay of sensual beauty, the futility of worldly security. He is able, that is, to discern the shrew who lurks behind the beautiful mask.*

Kali quite clearly conveys maya *as seen from the "other shore." She illustrates strikingly what the world of appearance looks like to the one who has been beyond. She may be voluptuous and smiling in her later representations, suggesting the dark allure of the world based on not-knowing, but her overall presence, which is frightening, and her dwelling place in the cremation ground clearly mock the ultimate significance of a world grounded in the ego.*[12]

In other representations, Kali stands for time, death, and the wild creativity that India has associated with female fertility. She is the womb from which all life issues and the grave to which all life returns. Since it has been India's custom to equate male perfection with a quiet intellectualism, and to counterpose to this a female nature especially energetic and generative, Kali and other of the great goddesses have been active, excited forces that their male consorts have sought to control. True, other Hindu goddesses have been represented in the arts similarly to the Pietas and Mona Lisas of Western Christianity. But the main image of divinity that the *Mahadevi*, or Great Goddess, has displayed in India is maternal creativity. Sometimes comfortingly, sometimes with horrid destructiveness, the goddess has allowed the Indian psyche to confront the power of life-death quite directly.

The god Shiva, with whom Kali sometimes is paired, represents divine energy in a masculine or androgynous mode. Shiva is the destroyer, the negative energy necessary for change and newness. He is both ascetic (a yogin with matted hair and contemplative posture) and erotic (ithyphallic, or portrayed with an erect penis).[13] The devotees of Shiva have been more fearful than the devotees of Krishna. Where Krishna represents a playful and romantic side of ultimate reality, Shiva is the Lord of the dance of Life and Death.

Overall, then, India has insisted that all aspects of ultimate reality—creative and destructive, male and female, ascetic and erotic—must receive their due. In India the religious arts have striven to be holistic: as complete as experience and imagination suggest the Ultimate must be.

GANDHI

Probably the man who most personified Hindu wisdom to the twentieth century was Mohandas Gandhi (1869–1948), the Mahatma, or great soul, who led India to freedom from British rule. Gandhi was born into the third caste (traders), studied law in London, and then went to South Africa to defend Indian rights. Back home in India he put together a political movement based on nonviolence (**ahimsa**) and the power of truth. In Gandhi's view, if people would confront their antagonists directly, relying not on physical force but the rightness of their claims, they would take the first step on the path to political sanity. The further steps would include coming to see their adversaries as brothers and sisters, purifying their own hearts of violent emotions, and discerning the presence of God in all truth-filled situations. Since Gandhi's combination of nonviolence and pursuit of God as truth has been so influential, it offers a portrait of the powers of the saintly Hindu sage.

Mahatma Gandhi's autobiography, *The Story of My Experiments With Truth*, shows how his personal strivings for purity of spirit intertwined with his leadership of a political movement rooted in nonviolence. Gandhi fasted, followed a vegetarian diet, and practiced celibacy in order to free his spirit from bodily constraints, prepare a vessel fit for the inspiration of God. He studied nonviolence in the intuitive conviction that that part of the Indian religious tradition held the key to humanity's future survival. Among his many reflections on *ahimsa* the following is typical:

Ahimsa is a comprehensive principle. We are helpless mortals caught in the conflagration of himsa *[vio-*

Figure 11   Raj-ghat, memorial to M. K. Gandhi in Delhi. Photo by J. T. Carmody.

lence]. *The saying that life lives on life has a deep meaning in it. Man cannot for a moment live without consciously or unconsciously commiting outward* himsa. *The very fact of his living—eating, drinking, and moving about—necessarily involves some* himsa, *destruction of life, be it ever so minute. A votary of* ahimsa *therefore remains true to his faith if the spring of all his actions is compassion, if he shuns to the best of his ability the destruction of the tiniest creature, tries to save it, and thus incessantly strives to be free from the deadly coil of* himsa. *He will be constantly growing in self-restraint and compassion, but he can never become entirely free from outward* himsa.[14]

Violence, Gandhi admits, is part of the evolutionary and political structure of reality. Insofar as species live off one another, violence is a law of life that we cannot avoid. Nonetheless, we can strive to minimize our violence and destructiveness, not injuring any fellow creature needlessly. By a vegetarian diet, we can minimize our injury to fellow animals. By such traditions as the protection of the cow, India has long tried to focus nonviolence on a highly visible symbol of animal vitality. Such practices foster self-restraint and compassion, virtues especially needed in modern social affairs. The phenomenon of war, which for Gandhi probably reached its most tragic expression in the bloody conflicts between Indian Hindus and Muslims that followed upon independence from Britain, depends upon our lack of restraint and compassion. Surely a sagacious society, one that listened to the wisdom of its elders and traditions, would be able to muster the minimal spiritual power needed to keep itself from civil war. That India could not muster such minimal virtue sickened Gandhi's spirit. As a final irony, he ended his life the victim of a Hindu assassin, a fellow religionist so unwise that he thought killing a champion of peace would advance the Hindu cause.

Erik Erikson, whose psychoanalytic study of Gandhi won great praise a generation ago, has described the Mahatma as a "religious actualist":

If, for the sake of the game, I should give his unique presence a name that would suit my views, I would call him a religious actualist. *In my clinical ruminations I have found it necessary to split what we mean by "real" into that which can be known because it is demonstrably correct (factual reality) and that which feels effectively true in action (actuality). Gandhi absorbed from Indian culture a conception of truth (sat) which he attempted to make actual in all compartments of human life and along all the stages which make up its course. . . . While he learned to utilize craftily what was his first professional identity, namely, that of a barrister English style, and while he then became a powerful politician Indian style, he also strove to grasp the "business" of religious men, namely, to keep his eyes trained upon the all-embracing circumstance that each of us exists with a unique consciousness and a responsibility of his own which makes him at the same time zero and everything, a center of absolute silence, and the vortex of apocalyptic participation. A man who looks through the historical parade of cultures and civilizations, styles, and isms which provide most of us with a glorious and yet miserably fragile sense of immortal identity, defined status, and collective grandeur faces the central truth of our nothingness—and, mirabile dictu [marvelous to say], gains power from it.*[15]

Such a sage was Mahatma Gandhi. Looking through the nothingness of human pretense and violence, he found the power of divine truth.

SUMMARY

In the Vedas we found the beginnings of a Hindu wisdom that consistently has sought the explanatory foundation of the cosmos. Rig Veda X:129 showed us that quite early Indian sages wondered who, if anyone, knows the origin of the world. In the Upanishads this restless quest for an ultimate explanation zeroed in on the relation between the ground of the self and the ground of the world. Thus the sage Yajnavalkya, pressed by the inquisitive Gargi, found the ultimate warp and woof of reality to be the Imperishable, that which exists of itself. The Bhagavad-Gita meditated on the personal side of ultimate reality, displaying the grandeur of Krishna as the deepest reality of all things. That Krishna loves those devoted to him and will care for them promoted *bhakti* to the status of a major religious path. Similarly, the Gita's teaching about *karma-yoga* afforded the average person a way to remain in the workaday world and still strive for religious purity. Shankara, the philosopher who most rigorously

exploited the Upanishadic teachings about the identity of the self and the ground of reality, suggested to the Hindu intelligentsia that ordinary perception finds only a world of illusion. From the standpoint of enlightened wisdom, only the Self is fully real. In contrast to the Buddhist promotion of emptiness, Vedantists have taught that reality forms a primal unity.

The Hindu attitudes toward physical nature have ranged from seeing it as a web of illusion to sensing that it composes a vast, well-ordered expanse of space and time. Allegorically, nature often furnished religious sages sharp images for teaching the futility of spending life on external objects of desire. As stern critics such as V. S. Naipaul have emphasized, the Hindu social order, so strongly molded by caste, often has perpetrated great cruelties, especially upon its outcasts or untouchables. As well, women have suffered special burdens in Hindu society, as they have in most traditional societies. Still, women such as Ma Jnanananda show the fulfillment that the individual self can find when it reaches the *samadhi*, the deep trance that the philosophers and yogins have lauded. By losing her ego in the unity of the physical world, Ma Jnanananda approached the verge of moksha. The other legitimate goods that Hinduism has allowed the self—pleasure, wealth, and duty—pale before moksha, so moksha has determined the structure of the ideal Hindu life cycle. Thus the upper-class male traditionally has been expected to study, live as a householder, retire to the forest, and then wander the world in pursuit of, or witness to, moksha.

Hindu ultimate reality has had both impersonal and personal forms, the impersonal probably predominating in sagacious circles and the personal probably predominating among lay persons. Kali shows the striking form that ultimate reality could assume when its destructive feminine qualities came to the fore, and Shiva shows a masculine form of destructiveness. Brahma and Vishnu, however, balance these wild aspects of divinity, suggesting that the Hindu instinct has been holistic. In Mahatma Gandhi, such holism underscored ahimsa and Truth. Were human beings to deal with one another and nature nonviolently and to conceive the divine as the Truth that may appear anywhere, they would halve their destructive conflicts and realize the best of India's age-old wisdom.

STUDY QUESTIONS

1. What role does Rig Veda X:129 assign to desire?
2. How can the Imperishable answer Gargi's question about space?

3. How might *bhakti* become a way of detachment and salvation?

4. Is the Vedantin teaching about the transcendent more persuasive than the Buddhist? Why?

5. Why does the brahman caught in the well continue to thirst for honey?

6. How could any religious tradition support the concept of untouchability?

7. What is the difference between the phase of studenthood in the classical Hindu life cycle and studenthood in contemporary America?

8. Explain the symbols of Kali as *maya.*

9. Why would the Mahatma Gandhi allow a person to take part in war?

NOTES

1. Rig Veda, X:129, trans. Griffith; in Ainslie T. Embree, ed., *The Hindu Tradition.* New York: Vintage, 1972, pp. 26–27.

2. See James Helfer, "Upanisad," in Keith Crim, ed., *Abingdon Dictionary of Living Religions.* Nashville: Abingdon, 1981, p. 778.

3. *Webster's Third International Dictionary*, Unabridged, Springfield, Mass.: G. & C. Merriam Co., 1971.

4. Robert Ernest Hume, trans., *The Thirteen Principal Upanishads*, 2d ed. rev. New York: Oxford University Press, 1971, pp. 118–19.

5. Bhagavad-Gita, 11:9–12; in Ann Stanford, trans., *The Bhagavad-Gita.* New York: Seabury, 1970, pp. 82–83.

6. *Bhagavad-Gita*, 18:61–66; in Stanford, pp. 130–31.

7. Heinrich Zimmer, *Philosophies of India.* Princeton, N.J.: Princeton University Press/Bollingen, 1969, p. 414.

8. J. G. Arapura, "Transcendent Brahman or Transcendent Void: Which is Ultimately Real?," in Alan M. Olson, ed., *Transcendence and the Sacred.* Notre Dame, Ind.: University of Notre Dame Press, 1981, pp. 86–87.

9. Denise L. Carmody and John T. Carmody, *Eastern Ways to the Center.* Belmont, Calif.: Wadsworth, 1983, p. 33.

10. V. S. Naipaul, *India: A Wounded Civilization.* New York: Vintage Books, 1978, pp. 42–43.

11. Charles S. J. White, "Mother Guru: Jnanananda of Madras," in Nancy Falk and Rita Gross, eds., *Unspoken Worlds: Women's Religious Lives in Non-Western Cultures.* San Francisco: Harper & Row, 1980, pp. 26–27.

12. David R. Kinsley, *The Sword and the Flute.* Berkeley: University of California Press, 1975, pp. 134–35.

13. See Wendy Doniger O'Flaherty, *Siva: The Erotic Ascetic.* New York: Oxford University Press, 1981.

14. Mohandas K. Gandhi, *An Autobiography: The Story of My Experiments With Truth.* Boston: Beacon, 1957, p. 349.

15. Erik H. Erikson, *Gandhi's Truth.* New York: W. W. Norton, 1969, pp. 396–97.

CHAPTER

12

Buddhism

BUDDHA: ASHVAGHOSA'S ACCOUNT

Like most of the great religious founders, Buddha early became the object of veneration that led to legend. The earliest Buddhists stressed his humanity, but as the community developed, it increasingly saw his life as an archetype. Since the Buddha lived about 560–480 B.C.E., and the earliest texts we have come from about 80 B.C.E., the first Buddha we meet in literary form is four hundred years old. By the time of the famous biography by Ashvaghosa, around 100 C.E., "Buddha" is nearly six hundred years old. It is not surprising, therefore, that Ashvaghosa's work is highly imaginative, paralleling Christian lives of Jesus from the early medieval period, or thirteenth-century Muslim lives of the Prophet.

Still, the *Buddhacarita*, as Ashvaghosa's life is called, gives a good picture of how Buddhist conviction had come to regard the Enlightened One. First, there is the depiction of Gautama's birth. His father Buddhodana was king of the tribe of the Shakyas, and his mother was called Maya, because of her resemblance to the Goddess of that name. Just before her conception of the Buddha she had a dream in which a white elephant seemed to enter her body. The pregnancy was tranquil and the queen loved to withdraw into the forest to practice deep meditation. The birth itself was marvelous: The Buddha emerged from Maya's side, without causing any pain, as though he had descended from the sky. He was fully aware, having practiced meditation through many lives, and he shone like a young sun. He took seven strides, surveyed the four corners of the earth, and proclaimed: "For enlightenment I was born, for the good of all that lives. This is the last time that I have been born into this world of becoming."[1]

The Buddha's birth brought to the palace the great

Buddhism: Twenty-Five Key Dates

536–476 B.C.E.   Buddha
519   Gautama's Enlightenment
473   First Buddhist Congress
363   Second Buddhist Congress
273–236   Reign of Buddhist Emperor Asoka
236   Rise of Mahayana Tradition
160   *Prajna-Paramita* Literature
80   Lotus Sutra; Buddhist Decline in India
CA. 200 C.E.   Nagarjuna, Leading Philosopher
220–552   Missions to Vietnam, China, Korea, Burma, Java, Sumatra, Japan
430   Buddhaghosa, Leading Philosopher
594   Buddhism Proclaimed Japanese State Religion
749   First Buddhist Monastery in Tibet
805–806   Foundation of Japanese Tendai and Shingon Sects
845   Persecution of Chinese Buddhists
1065   Hindu Invasions in Ceylon
1175   Honen; Japanese Pure Land
1193–1227   Rise of Japanese Zen Sects
1260–1368   Tibetan Buddhism Influential in China
1360   Buddhism Becomes State Religion in Thailand
1543–1588   Final Conversion of Mongols
1603   Tokugawa Government Begins Domination of Japanese Buddhism
1646–1694   Basho, Great Japanese Buddhist Poet
1868–1871   Meiji Persecution of Buddhism in Japan
1954–1956   Sixth Buddhist Council in Rangoon, Burma

---

sage Asita, who predicted that the babe would discover the extinction of all birth. Queen Maya, being unable to bear the joy she felt at the young child's majesty, went to dwell in heaven. Thus Buddha was raised by his aunt. His childhood passed peacefully and gloriously, and he was betrothed to Yashodara, renowned for her beauty and goodness. The king surrounded his son with all pleasures and sensual delights; Yashodara bore a son, Rahula; and the Buddha passed thirty years enjoying all that the senses can afford. One day, however, he ventured outside the palace and saw an old man. This was the first time he had met with aging and it shocked him deeply. Then he saw a diseased man, and finally a corpse, who plunged him further into disquiet. So he withdrew from his women, his parties, and his pleasures to contemplate the impermanence that was stealing his joy. Like a lion pierced by a poisoned arrow, he paced hither and yon, puzzled over this and that. Meeting a religious beggar, he con-

ceived the idea of pursuing liberation. Finally he left the palace and began his quest for the path to peace.

The first stage of healing came when Gautama sat and thought about the origination of things. This led to the first stage of trance and the beginning of tranquillity. Studying with various yogic teachers and practicing fierce austerities brought further progress, but something still was lacking. When he realized that starving the body was not the best way, he departed from his ascetic teachers. Nourished by the maiden Nandabala and encouraged by the serpent Kala, he went forward to a final battle with Mara, the Evil One. Neither Mara himself, nor his sons (Flurry, Gaiety, and Sullen Pride), nor his daughters (Discontent, Delight, and Thirst) could deter the Enlightened One, whose avowed intent to gain full freedom had now intensified.

At the climactic point, Buddha sat under a pipal tree and vowed that he would not leave until he had won the final victory. He mounted the various steps of trance, first recollecting all his former births, then realizing the connection between beings' states and their prior deeds, and then seeing that desire and ignorance hold the key to the chain of conditioned co-production, the mesh of the mutual influences that keep the samsaric world going. Finally Buddha reached the point where he could see no self anywhere. He remained in this exalted state, which not only brought him full bliss but made the earth sway in joy, for seven days, completely aware.

After enlightenment the question became, What was he to do with his liberating knowledge? The low-mindedness of the world, the passions in which most people lose themselves, and the subtlety of the truth led the Buddha to despair of communicating the **dharma**. Because he felt an obligation to enlighten all beings, not only those people who are not deeply mired in passion, Buddha proclaimed the Path to Peace, the path that made the great gods Indra and Brahma shine with joy.

BUDDHA: THE NOBLE EIGHTFOLD PATH OF DELIVERANCE

Early in his teaching, the Buddha met some of his prior companions, ascetics whom he had scandalized by stopping his severe fasting and returning to a middle way of moderation. The former companions were of two minds, nursing a grudge because he had broken with them yet attracted by his manifest peace. After pointing out that none of them could give him an instance in which fasting alone had produced enlightenment, the Buddha told his former companions the secrets he had discovered:

Listen carefully and I will explain to you the mysteries of the path to deliverance, and when you understand these, then your quest will be ended and you too will find deliverance. Now this, monks, is the noble truth of pain. Birth is painful. Old age is painful; sickness is painful; death is painful; as is sorrow, lamentation, dejection, depression and despair. All are painful. Contact with any of these unpleasant objects, ideas or sensations is painful. In short there are five relationships which when we grasp them are painful. Know this: the ceaseless cycle of births and death is painful. Therefore the first Noble Truth is that existence is painful.

Now that you have heard the first Noble Truth, Oh monks, listen to the second: the cause of pain, of suffering, is found in desire. It is the craving, combined with pleasure and lust, which leads to rebirth. It is the search for pleasure here and now. This is the second Noble Truth: unhappiness is caused by selfish craving. Now, monks, you know the first two Noble Truths: existence is full of pain and that pain is caused by selfish craving. Listen now, Oh monks, to the third Noble Truth: the end of pain is found in the end of desire, the end of craving, the ending which comes without a twinge of appetite. This is the third Noble Truth: deliverance from pain is found through non-attachment.

Thus, monks, you have heard the first three Noble Truths: existence is full of pain, pain is caused by selfish desire, and deliverance from pain comes through non-attachment to the things of this world. Listen now to the fourth Noble Truth: there is a way which leads to the cessation of pain, and wise are those who walk in that way. The way is simple if one but follows the Noble Eightfold Path. This Eightfold Path is so-called because there are eight steps to be taken; namely, right views, right intention, right speech, right action, right livelihood, right effort, right mindfulness, and right concentration. These are the eight stages of the Noble Eightfold Path of Deliverance.[2]

To stop desire, the Buddha tried to bring before his hearers the same impermanence that originally had impressed itself upon him. As though realizing that his own shock before the onslaught of age, disease, and death could be generalized, he would contrast the ignoble desire for impermanent things of the world with the noble desire for nirvana, the state of permanent freedom beyond the world of samsara:

There are two cravings, O priests; the noble one, and the ignoble one. And what, O priests, is the ignoble craving? We may have, O priests, the case of one who, himself subject to birth, craves what is subject to birth; himself subject to old age, craves what is subject to old age; himself subject to disease, death, sorrow, corruption, craves what is subject to corruption. And what, O priests, should one consider as subject to birth? Wife and child, O priests, are subject to birth; slaves, male and female, goats and sheep, fowls and pigs, elephants, cattle, horses and mares, gold and silver are subject to birth. All the substrata of being, O priests, are subject to birth; and enveloped, besotted, and immersed in them, this person, himself subject to birth, craves what is subject to birth.

And what, O priests, should one consider as subject to old age, disease, death, sorrow, corruption? Wife and child, O priests, are subject to corruption; slaves, male and female, goats and sheep, fowls and pigs, elephants, cattle, horses and mares, gold and silver are subject to corruption. All the substrata of beings, O priests, are subject to corruption; and enveloped, besotted, and immersed in them, this person, himself subject to corruption, craves what is subject to corruption. This, O priests, is the ignoble craving.

And what, O priests, is the noble craving? We may have, O priests, the case of one who, himself subject to birth, perceives the wretchedness of what is subject to birth, and craves the incomparable security of a Nirvana free from birth; himself subject to old age, disease, death, sorrow, and corruption, perceives the wretchedness of what is subject to corruption, and craves the incomparable security of a Nirvana free from corruption. This, O priests, is the noble craving.[3]

The repetitious style of these discourses suggests the oral character of early Buddhist studies. Probably the early preachers developed stereotypic phrases and groups of ideas—old age, disease, death, sorrow, corruption—that their hearers came to accept and use as a matter of habit. The pivotal point in this sermon, therefore, is the contrast between the noble, wise regard of all the negative aspects of ordinary, pain-laden existence and the ignoble. The ignoble, foolish person lusts for what is fleeting and is bound to give pain. Contrary to all reason, he or she chases after money, sexual pleasure, or social status, even though fully aware that they are intrinsically passing. By contrast, wise people set their hearts on what is permanent, the goodness of nirvana. Detaching themselves from temporal things, they desire only the unconditioned, the state of the flame when the candle has burned out. That noble desire, the Buddha promises, leads to peace, happiness, and freedom.

THE DHAMMAPADA

The way of the noble desire that leads to nirvana is the path of the Buddha's Teaching. This path, or *dhammapada*, stresses that the quality of our lives mainly depends upon how we regard the situations in which we find ourselves. For example, the difference between the wise person, well on the way to nirvana, and the fool, immersed in **samsara**, is their varying attitudes toward subjection to birth, corruption, old age, and the rest. The wise person is as subject to these conditions or forces as the foolish person. Both are mortal, fragile, shaped by karma, sure to encounter suffering. But the wise person takes this suffering condition to heart and strives to extinguish all desire for it. Foolish people, contrary to their own best instincts, continue to lust after pleasures that are bound to fade.

We have already made use of the opening verses of the *Dhammapada*, the beloved Buddhist text that takes its name from "the path of the teaching," but they are worth a second look: "All that we are is the result of what we have thought: it is founded on our thoughts, it is made up of our thoughts. If a man speaks or acts with an evil thought, pain follows him, as the wheel follows the foot of the ox that draws the wagon. All that we are is the result of what we have thought: it is founded on our thoughts, it is made up of our thoughts. If a man speaks or acts with a pure thought, happiness follows him, like a shadow that never leaves him."[4] Unlike the prophet, the sagacious author of the Dhammapada speaks little of changing society directly. It is not our outer circumstances, the injustice or justice of our milieu, that rivets the Buddhist interest. It is the inner attitudes we bring to the deepest, most constant factors in our human condition. These, the Buddhist is convinced, most shape who we are, whether we enjoy life or find it a dour misery.

To free suffering people from their mental binds, texts such as the Dhammapada would almost push their faces in the muck of painful reality. Do your neighbors bother you? Do they abuse you, beat you, rob you, speak ill of you? Pay them no mind. As long as they preoccupy your thoughts, foment a desire for revenge, fan flames of hatred, you are their slave. As surely as if you bound yourself to the wheel of rebirth with cords of leather, your thoughts of hatred and revenge will keep you tied to samsara. The only way to break the slavery your wretched neighbors would inflict upon you is to clear them from your head. When you don't care how they treat you, no more hate them than you would hate a rainy sky, you have become free.

So too with the positive desires that bind you. As long as food, money, sexual pleasure, achievement at work, the good opinion of your friends, or any other passing, this-worldly goods preoccupy you, you are not free. The slightest wind of temptation will defeat you. The smallest tear in your plans will throw you into depression. Sensuality and this-worldliness account for the vast majority of the many walking wounded. By and large, the worst enemy of the man in the street is himself. Because he is so underdeveloped spiritually, a thousand trifles can upset or wound him. True, by the end of his life he may have matured, made of his scars something honorable. With the Greek poet Aeschylus, the Buddhist can agree that much wisdom comes through suffering. But the compassion behind the original Teaching makes the Buddhist sage want to undercut the unnecessary suffering that causes so many people to writhe. If they would only realize that everything temporal comes to an end, nothing worldly is to be trusted, millions could change their lives from sadness to peace.

So the Dhammapada beats a steady tattoo on such themes as detachment, moral earnestness, striving for virtue. Convinced that people willing to take themselves in hand can dramatically improve the quality of their lives, it attacks sloth, sensuality, hopelessness, and the other main enemies of spiritual progress. The Dhammapada assumes the canonical Buddhist faith that wisdom and meditation must buttress morality. It is no opponent of deep study or peaceful sitting. But its own predilection is ethical, active, pragmatic. "Get off your backside," the Dhammapada urges. "Think the thoughts, do the deeds, that can give you back your life. Take a positive attitude, setting your sights on Buddhahood and nirvana. Look beyond this-worldly grief. If you do, you will distinguish yourself from the crowd of the unthinking, the mediocre, the sensual. If you wish, you can live in the midst of the muck and not be tainted. Were your mind to be pure and your body disciplined, you could begin a happy life this very hour."

Verse after verse, this beloved little manual urges the faithful on:

Let us live happily then, not hating those who hate us! Among men who hate us, let us dwell free from hatred! Let us live happily then, free from ailments among the ailing! Among men who are ailing, let us dwell free from ailments! Let us live happily then, free from greed among the greedy! Among men who are greedy let us dwell free from greed! Let us live happily then, though we call nothing our own! We shall be like the bright gods, feeding on happiness. Victory breeds hatred, for the conquered is unhappy. He who has given up both victory and defeat, he, the contented, is happy. There is no fire like lust; there is no losing throw like hatred; there is no pain like this body; there is no happiness higher than peace.[5]

Nirvana is consummate peace. Nirvana is the end of all suffering. The path of the Teaching goes straight toward nirvana.

NAGARJUNA

The Dhammapada has been especially influential in lands dominated by the Theravada Buddhist sects. Buddhaghosa, the sage whose analysis of morality (*sila*) we discussed earlier, was a philosopher and meditation master complementary to the Dhammapada and so perhaps Theravada Buddhists' most revered thinker.

Mahayana Buddhism took a more speculative and lay direction. In both philosophy and devotional life, it tried to widen what it took to be the narrownesses of the early tradition. Thus in its image of the perfected life it filled out the social dimension, speaking of the **bodhisattva**, or enlightened being, as one whose compassion reaches out to save all fellow creatures. Philosophically, the Mahayana sutras that focused on the *Prajnaparamita* (wisdom-that-has-gone-beyond) ruminated deeply about the presence of nirvana in the midst of samsara and also about the profound emptiness that wisdom finds at the core of all things. For Mahayana, the most revered thinker probably has been Nagarjuna (ca. 250 C.E.). Somewhat parallel to the way the Shankara furnished speculative Hinduism a profound analysis of ultimate reality, Nagarjuna furnished Mahayana Buddhism deep ruminations about relativity and emptiness.

Nagarjuna's basic method for clarifying the nature of ultimate reality was to show the erroneousness of "reification." *Reification* (from the Latin *res*, "thing") is the tendency to treat as separate, independent, and substantial that which is only relational, dependent, and fleeting. It is the tendency to "thing-ify" all the matters of our experience. Because of this fallacious tendency, we miss the "three marks" that Buddhism has found characteristic of all that we experience: all is painful, fleeting, and selfless. By missing the three marks, we think of the matters of our experience as full rather than empty, desirable rather than of little account. By removing the errors of reification, Nagarjuna hoped to complement the moral exhortations of texts such as the Dhammapada. If he could bring people to understand that all the matters of human experience are empty, he might stop at the source: people's tendency to desire such things. The philosophy or wisdom study of Nagarjuna therefore was thoroughly religious. In assaulting the way that most people spontaneously think about what they experience, he was trying to free them to think bigger and deeper thoughts, thoughts leading to nirvana.

The following analysis of time will illustrate Nagarjuna's style and profundity:

If the present and future exist presupposing the past, the present and future will exist in the past. If the present and future did not exist in the past, how could the present and future exist presupposing that past? Without presupposing the past, the present cannot be proved to exist. Therefore neither present nor future time exist. In this way the remaining times can be inverted. In the same way we should regard highest, lowest, middle, oneness and difference. A non-stationary time cannot be grasped, and a stationary time which can be grasped does not exist. How, then, can one perceive time if it is not grasped? Since time is dependent on a thing, how can time exist without a thing? There is not any thing which exists; how, then, will time become something?[26]

The key to the passage is the play on the words *exist* and *thing*. Nagarjuna is trying to show the logical muddles we fall into when we reify time or any other matter of our experience. Time is not a simple, stationary thing. It is thoroughly relational. Break it into its popular triad, past-present-future, and you will see that each part supposes the others. Moreover, in a real sense neither time as a whole nor any of its three parts exists: stands forth in reality as something independent and unchanging. What, in fact, do we know that stands forth in reality wholly independent in its arising or its functioning, wholly resistant to change or development? If we know nothing of such a nature, then none of our experience yields "things" that "exist." All of our experience suggests that reality is relational, mutually conditioned, interdependent, and on the move. All that we experience is "empty," possessing no own-being, pointing toward the Void.

Yet there is a sense in which our experience does yield realities, beings, existents. Passing though they be, while they impinge upon us or one another they are. If their passingness is their samsaric side, their "areness" is their nirvanic side. To *be* in their passing, conditioned ways, they must depend upon or manifest the unconditioned, the nirvanic. Ineffable as this unconditioned is, we can intuit that it is inseparable from samsaric existence. Though we cannot name it and must not think of it as a thing or solid entity, we can reason that nirvana is in our midst; freedom grounds even our constraints.

Using such dialectical, back-and-forth thoughts of Nagarjuna and his followers, Mahayana Buddhism developed a rationale for life in the world. When disciples purify themselves of attachments to samsara, live flowingly and relationally rather than statically and reifyingly, they can sense how nirvana and samsara are one. Before such enlightenment, rocks are just rocks and trees are just trees. When such enlightenment begins to dawn, rocks and trees turn over: They are not independent but related, not solid but empty. After such enlightenment, rocks are again rocks, and trees are again trees, but their unconditioned, ultimate aspect is to the fore. Thus the rocks of the famous Zen Rock Garden in Kyoto have become symbols of wisdom. Jutting out of a bare raked sand, they suggest that any item of experience can conjure the relational, nirvanic whole because any item of experience expresses the ultimate reality and interconnection of all items.

NATURE

As discrete, changing, and empty, nature has no special value. The philosophical analyses of deep thinkers such as Nagarjuna gave Buddhists no reason to desire nature, cling to its potentialities or beauties. On the other hand, the integrity of nature, its ability to be what it is without striving or strife, has appealed to many Buddhists, especially those of East Asia. One sees this, for example, in the poetry that Buddhism has shaped in Japan, a good illustration of which is the work of the monk Saigyo (1118–1190 C.E.).

Among the better-known poems of Saigyo is one in which the monk stops for a moment in the shade of a willow tree alongside the road. He is on a journey, and the pause is only for a moment of refreshment. By the willow flows pure water from a fresh spring. The monk's time in this perfect spot flows like the water. The "stop" has become an arrival. William LaFleur interprets this imagery in Mahayana terms:

The imagery and emotions of the poem are subtle, but so too is the value attributed in it to nature. The poet has found in the stream and the willow a "given" world of religious meaning. We find in this verse a conception of pilgrimage by implication, but it is one which coheres precisely to that found in other of his poems, one which suggests that the goal of pilgrimage is often found within the natural world through which the pilgrim-poet travels rather than at some distant place deemed and designated as "sacred" by the consensus of the cultus-concerned religious community. In finding the way as equivalent to the goal, Saigyo, in addition, gives expression to a common notion in Mahayana Buddhism. We find frequently in his verses the phrase yukue mo shrianu, *words which mean "and not knowing the destination." In many ways this phrase encapsulates this poet's view of pilgrimage, for he discovers the realm of sacrality along the way rather than at its end. Because of this his wandering can be comparatively aimless and destinationless. Because in the thought of Mahayana Buddhism the goal of nirvana is to be found within the world of samsara, the postulation of distant goals is, theoretically at least, redundant. Saigyo seems to have translated this principle into a peculiar mode of pilgrimage for himself. In his case, however, it had special value inasmuch as this enabled him to find "the sacred" in natural contexts and phenomena met by him and entered into by him as he went along the road. Although theoretically in Mahayana all things in the samsaric realm are sacred, experientially men find that "although all things are sacred, some things are more sacred than*

Figure 12   Moss Temple Grounds, Kyoto. Photo by J. T. Carmody.

others." In Saigyo's case this was the way in which he experienced the natural world and its forms.[7]

Indian Mahayanists might have followed the theoretical argument that all things are equally sacred and so nature can be one's privileged entrée to nirvana, but they were not pushed to a naturalistic focus as East Asian Mahayanists were. Indian culture, deeply rooted in the Hindu concepts of karma and maya, tended to look through nature in search of a Brahman without natural limitations. Karma, maya, samsara and the rest of the Buddhist conceptual repertoire came to East Asia, but the pre-Buddhist cultures of China, Japan, and the other East Asian lands forced the Mahayanists to concretize their teachings, make them enhance here-and-now existence close to the soothing, challenging, absorbing world of nature that East Asia long had loved. So the old East Asian esthetico-religious approach to nature tended to fuse with the new Buddhist views. In painting and poetry, trees remained simply trees, mountains stood simply for themselves; yet all the

while they expressed ultimate reality, the sacredness of nirvana.

Chinese landscape painting, for example, expressed the agreement of Taoists and Buddhists that the empty can be more significant than the full. In Buddhist terms, the emptiness of things testifies to their fleeting, nonnirvanic character, pointing the observer away from desire. Aesthetically, emptiness works on the viewer's inner spirit to suffuse a sense of peace. Not among the myriad hurrying things of secular life will one find the way, but in retreats from busyness, in lonely vigils and rugged natural woods. During the Sung Dynasty (960–1280 c.e.) landscape painting reached sublime heights, developing away from details, toward empty space:

Later there arose a general movement away from explanation to mere hinting, from the crowded canvas to the sparse. It is illuminating to see the later Sung masterpieces with large areas of empty space occurring as part of the composition, while only the topmost peaks of a few mountains are limned in, or a single leafy spray of peach blossom or other flower. Ever since, space has been the most outstanding characteristic of our landscape painting.[8]

In the space emphasized by a perceptive artist, nature's rugged, arresting facets could stand forth. Mi Fei, some of whose paintings present marvelous mountain peaks and grizzled pine trees, exemplifies the strong personal character that the East Asian love of nature could nurture:

Mi's character, in particular, was well in harmony with the strength and rigidity of towering peaks—he was deeply in love with the rugged aspects of nature. A story is told of him that when he was once walking in the Wu-Wei district of Anhui, he saw a very large rock in his pathway; it was grizzled, strangely shaped, quite ugly to look at, but Mi suddenly felt his heart go out to it, and, finely robed as he was, knelt down in the dust and called it "My elder Brother!" For this he became known as "Mad mi," but now we understand that kind of witlessness.[9]

SOCIETY

For scholars of religion, one of the most interesting conflicts is that between what society at large considers witless and sages consider wise. Generally, society at large wants people to stay in line, play their assigned roles, not stir up trouble by eccentric behavior. Many Buddhist sages have contradicted such social expectations, preferring quite idiosyncratic paths. Thus in Buddhism the term *society* could connote "inhibiting," "constraining," or even "herdlike." Often the sages' first move has been to cast off the usual, largely unthinking mores of their fellows. One sees this move defended in a traditional text from the Pali Canon of Buddhist scriptures:

Fear is born from intimacy, passion is born in company, so the sage wanders without company, without intimacy, and cuts down what usually occurs, does not let it grow again, does not feed what usually happens. People call him a sage because, wandering alone, he has seen the state of peace and considers things. Casting aside the seeds of things, not feeding desire, he sees the end of birth and death, throws away thought, goes beyond definition. The sage knows all clinging and wants none of it. He is free of greed, ungrasping. He makes no effort, for he has gone across (the stream of life). The wise call him a sage because he conquers

all, knows all, lets no event touch him, has abandoned all craving. . . . He wanders alone, unshaken by praise or blame, like a lion unafraid of any noise, the wind not caught in any net. . . . He takes alms from high and low, accepting whatever they give, neither reproaching nor praising. . . . The crested blue-necked peacock cannot fly like the ruddy goose, and the householder cannot equal the monk, the solitary sage meditating in the forest.[10]

However, through the Mayayana development of such early sagacious instincts, the sage could leave the forest and come back to society at large. This seems the implication of the last of the famous Zen teaching pictures on "Oxherding." The ox stands for the original nature or Buddha-mind that the zealous disciple is trying to achieve. The pictures depict religious progress as a development through the following stages: seeking the ox, finding the tracks, first glimpsing the ox, catching the ox, taming the ox, riding the ox home, forgetting the ox so that self alone predominates, forgetting self as well as the ox, returning to the source, and (as the climax) "entering the market place with helping hands." In explicating the climactic phase the sources say:

The gate of his cottage is closed and even the wisest cannot find him. His mental panorama has finally disappeared. He goes his own way, making no attempt to follow the steps of earlier sages. Carrying a gourd, he strolls into the market; leaning on his staff, he returns home. He leads innkeepers and fishmongers in the Way of Buddha. Barechested, barefooted, he comes into the market place. Muddied and dust-covered, how broadly he grins! Without recourse to mystic powers, withered trees he swiftly brings to bloom.[11]

These verses and, even more, the humorous picture of the sage swinging home, show how the tensions between society and the sage can turn over 360 degrees and come to rest in a perfect balance. As a fully realized human being, a sage come into full possession of his Buddha-mind, the pilgrim of the last picture is completely at home in the "ordinary" world of social affairs, the marketplace with its drinking, innkeeping, and fishmongering. The mud and dust of the road neither mar nor bother him. He is completely at ease wherever he finds himself. More, wherever he finds himself he helps other people prosper, brings out the best in those around ("withered trees he brings swiftly to bloom").

The implication is that society urgently needs free, uncoopted sages for its vitality. Unless some people have left the common way, trekked off and found their original minds, society at large will choke on its laws and conventions, be crushed by its masses of mindlessness. Wandering Buddhist pilgrims deserve the pittance of food and aid they beg because their quests prevent society from slumbering. The chance that a sage may arise and give shopkeepers and merchants a justification for their lives makes the quirks of all pilgrims bearable.

The Buddhist Sangha, which has paid special honors to monks seeking full enlightenment, therefore has developed an instinct to respect both the eccentric and the ordinary. The tie between the two is the service the genuine eccentric renders the community at large. Because of the *bodhisattva* vow to labor for the enlightenment of all, the eccentric does not wander selfishly but to pursue a light that would enhance the community as a whole. The Buddha broke with the conventions of his day, both those of the court and those of the band of ascetics he first joined. The Dharma says one must stop desiring, come to wander free. So the third of Buddhism's jewels, the Sangha, has protected full-time pursuers of sagehood, even when the common populace considered them witless. If only by praising celibacy and poverty, the monastic community has been a strong countercultural force. By stressing spiritual freedom, the monk or pilgrim has opposed the materialistic presuppositions of the majority. Therefore Buddhist society usually has pivoted on a healthy tension between banking and meditation, the needs of the ordinary many and the hopes of the exceptional few.

SELF

The center of Buddhist psychology is the teaching that there is no self. When we dispel the illusion that something permanent and solid, a perduring "I," stands at the center of our lives, we cut through the tangled knots of samsara with a mighty sword.

As they meditated on this teaching, Mahayana Buddhists came to see that enlightenment and nirvana are independent of any particular caste or station. As the Dhammapada had transported the notion of the brahman, making the highest caste that of the spiritually advanced rather than the high-born, so the Mahayana texts transposed Buddhist practice into lay keys. Thus one of the most famous and influential of these Mahayana texts, the *Vimalakirtinirdesa Sutra*, makes a householder the epitome of enlightened virtue:

At that time there dwelt in the great city of Vaisali a wealthy householder Vimalakirti. Having done homage to the countless Buddhas of the Past, doing many good works, attaining to acquiescence in the Eternal Law, he was a man of wonderful eloquence . . . residing in Vaisali only for the sake of the necessary means for saving creatures, abundantly rich, ever careful of the poor, pure in self-discipline, obedient to all precepts. . . . Though living at home, yet never desirous of anything; though possessing a wife and children, always exercising pure virtues; though surrounded by his family, holding aloof from worldly pleasures; though using the jeweled ornaments of the world, yet adorned with spiritual splendour; though eating and drinking, yet enjoying the flavour of the rapture of meditation; though frequenting the gambling house, yet leading the gamblers into the right path. . . . Thus by such countless means Vimalakirti, the wealthy householder, rendered benefit to all beings.[12]

Clearly, Vimalakirti was able to be in the world but not of it. Clearly, the core of Buddhist perfection had little to do with station as a monk or celibate. If the eye of the mind were simple, the mind could think on anything. If the purity of the heart were advanced, the heart could embrace anything. And the key to such simplicity and purity? Most likely the grasp of **anatman**: having no self. When people came to realize not only that all external things are painful, fleeting, and selfless, but that these marks equally applied to their own "I," they were on the verge of enlightenment, stood well across the border into freedom. Like the happy oxherder come home to the marketplace, Vimalakirti no longer cared about goals or strivings. Even finding the ox of Buddha-mind had passed from his ambition. There was no fixed, graspable "I" to attain enlightenment. Neither enlightenment nor nirvana was a full, tangible thing. Rather all was empty and dancing. Anything—gambling, eating, making love—could be used for good or for ill. If he had given up egocentricity and selfish desires, the householder could be as saintly or wise as the monk. To the pure, all things are pure. The point was not position or station but inner purity.

In the devotional Buddhism that developed in Japan, self-loss reached the point where simple faith in Amida, the Buddha of light, sufficed for salvation. Thus a poem of Shinran, one of the most profound of the Japanese saints who stressed such faith, reads like the confession of the famous New Testament publican (Matthew 18:10): "Shameless though I be and having no truth in my soul, yet the virtue of the Holy Name, the gift of Him that is enlightened, is spread throughout the world through my words, although I am as I am. There is no mercy in my soul. The good of my fellow man is not dear in mine eyes. If it were not for the

Ark of Mercy, the divine promise of the Infinite Wisdom, how should I cross the Ocean of Misery?"[13]

The self, therefore, could gain a personal relation with a Buddha such as Amida, or even with one of the Bodhisattvas (such as Kuan-yin, a motherly figure greatly beloved in East Asia). Although Buddhists tend to shy away from the romantic or sexual overtones that bhakti carries in Hinduism, the fervor of their devotions often has matched the fervor of the Hindu bhaktas. In both cases, devotional love can become a path to loss of self. Casting aside any concern for merit, placing all his hopes in the virtues of Amida, a saint such as Shinran lost all self-concern. Amida was great and he was inconsequential. What mattered was magnifying Amida, spreading the gospel of salvation by faith. All personal gain or glory shrank to insignificance. In the degenerate present age, few people could grasp the austere teachings of the profound sutras, follow through on the strict ethics required to be morally advanced. But all people could sense the graciousness of Amida, respond to the offer of his care and concern. Thus all people were apt candidates for Shinran's preaching. Those whom the elitists had written off could be the most honored of the congregation. Chanting to Amida was utterly egalitarian. If done with full faith and love, a single recitation could bring the chanter to Amida's Western Paradise, the Pure Land where there would be no pain.

From strong artists such as Mi Fei to the humblest devotée of Shinran's flock, Buddhists could become very much their own people. The doctrine of *anatman* meant neither uniformity nor blandness. In fact, having nothing inert, fixed, or worth clinging to at one's center often meant gaining great freedom to be as one wished, create as one's muses dictated. When that happened, the Buddhist personality overflowed with energy and grace.

ULTIMATE REALITY

The question of how Buddhism regards ultimate reality implies several subquestions: Which Buddhists? At which times? Literally or metaphorically? Depending upon the sect, historical period, and level of discourse one is studying, the answers can vary considerably. Nonetheless, it seems clear that mainline Buddhism has wanted to say several things about ultimate reality. First, it exists and is the basis of ordinary reality, but it does not constitute a separate, nonempty thing. Second, it is the source of full bliss and peace. Third, it is most efficacious to approach it negatively, by casting

off desire and freeing our minds from reifications. Fourth, we may symbolize it by personifying divinities or imagining paradises filled with light. Fifth, it is more mental than physical, better reached by silence than speech or action. Let us expand on these five points.

First, ultimate reality (nirvana) is the basis of ordinary reality because Buddhists, like most other philosophically minded religionists, have felt that ordinary reality, with its marks of pain, fleetingness, and selflessness, does not explain itself. Yet, quite distinctively, Buddhists have refused to reify nirvana. It is not beyond samsara in the sense of constituting another realm. We are wrong to seek a solid ultimate like the Hindu Brahman. The reality of changing entities, the being of all becoming things, shows us nirvana but not apart from change or becoming.

Second, to grasp the ultimate character of ordinary reality and to let one's spirit be ordered by it is to be drawn toward full bliss and peace. Nirvana is not inert, apathetic, or dismal. Those who enjoy it are not repressed but fulfilled. The Buddha preferred not to talk about the ultimate, because he feared such talk would distract people from the process of attaining the ultimate. It little profits a person struck by a poisoned arrow to ask where the arrow came from or what the final form of the poison will be. The intelligent move is to remove the arrow, begin the process of healing. The same principle applies to spiritual wounds: The important thing is to grasp the cause of suffering and start to rid oneself of desire. That is the way to start toward full bliss and peace.

Third, nirvana remains negative, ineffable, the far side of this painful, limited reality we know experientially. When we calm the mind by meditation, organize the will by morality, dispel the shadows of the intellect by wisdom, we open ourselves to the influences of nirvana. Of itself, ultimate reality is full of light; uncorrupted, human nature glows with brightness. The shields between us and ultimate reality are the desires and reifications we impose. Strip away desire, and reality can begin to be for the individual as it is in itself. Stop reification and no things will interpose themselves. The way to the fullness of nirvana is emptying the mind and heart. The way to wandering freely in unconditionedness—escaping the limits of space, time, and human imperfection—is following the eightfold path.

Fourth, these rather sober assessments of nirvana represent the older Buddhist traditions.[14] The developments in the Mahayana and Vajrayana (Tantric) traditions allowed for more personification of ultimate reality and more imaginative depictions of its paradisial side (or anteroom). Thus the *Lotus Sutra*, perhaps the most beloved text of devotional Buddhists, multiplies the figures and powers of the Buddha, picturing him presiding over a paradise sensually dazzling:

And instantly the Lord darted from the circles of hair on his brow a ray, which was no sooner darted than the Lords, the Buddhas stationed in the east in fifty hundred thousand myriads of kotis *of worlds, equal to the sands of the river Ganges, became all visible, and the Buddha-fields there, consisting of crystal, became visible, variegated with jewel trees, decorated with strings of fine cloth, replete with many hundred thousands of Bodhisattvas, covered with canopies, decked with a network of seven precious substances and gold. And in those fields appeared the Lords, the Buddhas, teaching with sweet and gentle voice the law to creatures; and those Buddha-fields seemed replete with hundred thousands of Bodhisattvas.*[15]

Relatedly, the tantric approaches to liberation and ultimate reality that have flourished in Tibet sometimes employ personifications of ultimate reality ("deity yoga"): "The supreme method is cultivation of deity yoga within the context of realizing emptiness of inherent existence. The wisdom consciousness understanding emptiness and fused with emptiness appears as a deity, and within this state what formerly bound one in cyclic existence can be used as aids to liberation."[16]

Fifth, ultimate reality has tended to impress Buddhists as more mental than physical, a reality more like thought than anything else. One sees this most clearly in groups such as the Yogacarins, who taught that true reality is "mind-only." In ultimate perspective, only the intelligibility of experience is fully real. Only the mental or ideational side fully counts. Indeed, to be and to be mind-ordered are interchangeable. Ultimately, reality is wholly mental, completely full of light. The best path to ultimate reality, it follows, is dispelling our darkness through meditation and study, changing distracting chatter into silent attention. If we do not block it out with chatter, do not cloud it over with desire, ultimate reality will surface in our spirits and flood us with light.[17]

SHUNRYU SUZUKI

There is no Buddhist sage quite parallel to the Hindu sage Mahatma Gandhi, no recent exemplar of the Buddhist tradition who has seized the imagination of the entire globe. Still, many gurus have renovated the Buddhist tradition for modern times, and high among

those to whom Americans have been much attracted stands Shunryu Suzuki, a Japanese guru, or *roshi*, instrumental in the development of the Zen Center in San Francisco. Some talks that Suzuki-roshi gave to a Zen group in Los Altos, California, shortly before his death in 1971 express the beauty of the Soto Zen approach to ultimate reality. This approach allows one's buddha-nature gradually to ripen, stressing poise in the present, attention to what occurs moment by moment.

Suzuki-roshi, like many of his predecessors in the Zen lineage, had a gift for concrete stories and examples. So, for instance, he could make failure, the difficulty of picking oneself up and continuing through mistake after mistake, a way into a helpful groove:

We say, "A good father is not a good father." Do you understand? One who thinks he is a good father is not a good father; one who thinks he is a good husband is not a good husband. One who thinks he is one of the worst husbands may be a good one if he is always trying to be a good husband with a single-hearted effort. If you find it impossible to sit [meditate] because of some pain or some physical difficulty, then you should sit anyway, using a thick cushion or a chair. . . . When you are sitting in the middle of your own problem, which is more real to you: your problem or yourself? The awareness that you are here, right now, is the ultimate fact. This is the point you will realize by zazen [meditational] practice. In continuous practice, under a succession of agreeable and disagreeable situations, you will realize the marrow of Zen and acquire its true strength.[18]

One of the main strengths of Zen is its concreteness. Zen does not ask people to remove themselves from their present, here-and-now circumstances but to attend to these circumstances, meditate in the midst of them. Be times good or bad, zazen is appropriate. In good times, zazen can express one's joy and clarity, deepening them. In bad times zazen can bring one back together, pick up the pieces. The concrete situation in which one finds oneself is always relevant. The depths of the personality are always in play. Regular sitting therefore becomes an ongoing instruction in realism. The time one puts in, morning or night, is a healing by reattunement to the way things are. Unless we are attuned to the way things are, we cannot expect to live peacefully. Unless we meet our environment with collected, open spirits, we cannot expect to grow realistic. Zen is no more than sitting one's way to realism. It is no less than letting the deep orientation of one's central being toward light and peace take over and increasingly purify.

Suzuki-roshi also displayed the Zen love for simple gestures:

When you practice Zen you become one with Zen. There is no you and no zazen. When you bow, there is no Buddha and no you. One complete bowing takes place, that is all. This is Nirvana. When Buddha transmitted our practice to Maha Kashyapa, he just picked up a flower with a smile. Only Maha Kashyapa understood what he meant; no one else understood. We do not know if this is a historical event or not, but it means something. It is a demonstration of our traditional way. Some activity which covers everything is true activity, and the secret of this activity is transmitted from Buddha to us. This is Zen practice, not some teaching taught by Buddha, or some rules of life set up by him. The teaching or rules should be changed according to the place, or according to the people who observe them, but the secret of this practice cannot be changed. It is always true. So for us there is no other way to live in this world. I think this is quite true; and this is easy to accept, easy to understand, and easy to practice. If you compare the kind of life based on this practice with what is happening in this world, or in human society, you will find out just how valuable the truth Buddha left us is.[19]

In perfected living, gestures express the self. In the kind of living that helps us perfect ourselves, gestures mold the personality usefully. As we mature, our gestures, words, thoughts, and personalities grow more integral. Like the imprint of an artist on her paintings, they become more original and distinctive. Actually, everything about a significant artist's work is distinctive. No one else has quite the same brush strokes, perspective, or colors. The same is true of individual personalities, as they mature in the art of living. No one else walks, talks, thinks, speaks, or looks at the world quite the same way.

The positive yield in such maturity is the wholesale beautification it brings. As one integrates a personality, both meditates and acts more and more deeply, the whole of life becomes more ordered; more and more times become valuable. For more and more times fit into the flux of the dharmas, the dance of the constituent elements of reality. Although in the beginning only times of meditation may be integrating, with practice, eating, drinking, study, and work join the dance. Toward the end, close to nirvana, there is only eating, drinking, study, and work—no eater, drinker, student, or worker. In the nirvana of Zen, action and actor are one, self is gone and gesture is whole.

SUMMARY

The life of the Buddha exemplifies the teaching that centers the Middle Way. Raised a prince, possessed of all this world's goods, Gautama came into crisis when he met old age, sickness, and death. Resolving to find a peace that would undercut these dark threats, he left palace, wife, and child to pursue salvation. When he found that severe austerities did not bring him to his goal, he broke with severe austerities. When he found that meditation quieted his agitations, he pressed on toward a deeper interiority. Reaching enlightenment, he saw the omnipresence of suffering and its cure. His Four Noble Truths, which are the core of all Buddhist Teaching, spell out the Enlightened One's great illumination. To crave this-worldly pleasures is the way to bondage; to break with desire is the way to full peace or nirvana.

Traditional texts such as the Dhammapada have amplified the Four Noble Truths, urging readers to take themselves in hand and seize the opportunities the Buddha's wisdom has opened. If we will, we can live among the ailing free of ailments, among the greedy free of greed. Nagarjuna, penetrating the causes of this possibility, argues that nothing really is worth desiring; everything we experience is intrinsically empty. He therefore urges a routing of reification parallel to the routing of desire urged by the Dhammapada. Reality is painful, fleeting, and selfless. Nowhere is there anything independent or substantial enough to merit clinging.

East Asian Buddhists have focused much of the Dharma on nature, finding its flux and serenity a sweet inducement to interiority. Thus the monk Saigyo applied the Mahayana conviction that nirvana is in the midst of samsara to the natural scenes one may meet while journeying. For him the stages of the process could meld with the term. Chinese landscape painting expressed the same idea, stressing the emptiness that gives any scene its spiritual significance. Sociologically, Buddhism promoted the rights of pilgrims and monks to wander in solitude, seek an eccentric way, for from their searches would come the wisdom needed to keep society spiritually alive. Further, the Mahayanists painted an ideal development that brought the sage back into the market place. When one has herded the ox back home, the mud and dust of ordinary living do not matter. The psychological correlative to this sociological emphasis has been the doctrine of selflessness. When the individual makes anatman a personal truth, the purity of mind and heart necessary to find all places sacred comes close to hand. Thus Vimalakirti could display the highest virtues in the householder state, and Shinran could make devotion a straight path to salvation.

Ultimate reality, nirvana, has had several overtones through Buddhist history, the principal of which underscore the nonobjectivity or no-thingness of the final truth. The ultimate is not apart from the ecology of nature, society, and the self; it is their depth and being. It shows in the happiness that comes when we free ourselves from desires, play our roles selflessly. We may imagine it as a personal deity or connect it with the many fields of paradisial bliss. We may stress its mentality and connect our own-beings to its light. Whatever our way, roshis such as Shunryu Suzuki assure us that the way things are is beautiful. We can mature into integral, graceful personalities. We can make human living a high art. Striving, studying, and sitting, we can find the Middle Way clear-eyed and lovely.

STUDY QUESTIONS

1. Why did the Buddha's first healing come from thinking about the origination of things?

2. How can the craving for nirvana be noble?

3. How practical is the teaching of the Dhammapada?

4. How does Nagarjuna's stress on emptiness relate to the traditional three marks?

5. Explain Saigyo's sense of the relation between stations such as the roadside willow and the goal of his pilgrimage.

6. How does the ox herder who "enters the market place with helping hands" express the Mahayana understanding of enlightenment?

7. What nuances did Shinran place on "selflessness"?

8. Why can we reach nirvana by deity yoga?

9. Why did Suzuki-roshi love the image of the Buddha just picking up a flower with a smile?

NOTES

1. Ashvaghosa, *Buddhacarita*, sec. 1, in Edward Conze, trans., *Buddhist Scriptures*. Baltimore: Penguin, 1959, p. 36.

2. George N. Marshall, *Budda: The Quest for Serenity*. Boston: Beacon, 1978, pp. 75–76.

3. *Majjhima-Nikaya*, Sutta 26, in Henry Clarke Warren, trans., *Buddhism in Translations*. New York: Atheneum, 1973, p. 333.

4. *The Dhammapada*, verses 1 and 2; trans. Irving Babbitt. New York: New Directions, 1965, p. 3.

5. Ibid., verses 197–202, p. 32.

6. Nagarjuna, *Mulamadhyamakakarikas*, 19:1–6; adapted from Frederick J. Streng, *Emptiness*. Nashville, Abingdon, 1967, p. 205.

7. William R. Lafleur, "Saigyo and the Buddhist Value of Nature," *History of Religions*, 13/2 (November 1973), pp. 115–16.

8. Chiang Yee, *The Chinese Eye*. Bloomington: Indiana University Press, 1964, p. 157.

9. Ibid., p. 158.

10. *Suttanipata*, sec. 12, 1:298–300; adapted from Stephen Beyer, ed., *The Buddhist Experience*. Belmont, Calif.: Dickenson, 1974, pp. 236–38.

11. Philip Kapleau, *The Three Pillars of Zen*. Boston: Beacon, 1967, p. 311.

12. Ninian Smart and Richard D. Hecht, eds., *Sacred Texts of the World*. New York: Crossroad, 1982, pp. 273–74.

13. Ibid., p. 265.

14. See Edward J. Thomas, *The History of Buddhist Thought*, 2d ed. New York: Barnes & Noble, 1951, pp. 191–32.

15. Saddharmapundarika, 11; in H. Kern, trans., *Saddharmapundarika or the Lotus of the True Law*. New York: Dover, 1963, pp. 231–32.

16. Jeffrey Hopkins, "Supplement," in Tsong-ka-pa, *Tantra in Tibet*, vol. I. Boston: George Allen & Unwin, 1977, p. 198.

17. See Ashvaghosa, *The Awakening of Faith*, trans. Yoshito S. Hakeda. New York: Columbia University Press, 1967.

18. Shunryu Suzuki, *Zen Mind, Beginner's Mind*. New York: Weatherhill, 1970, pp. 39–40.

19. Ibid., p. 64.

13

Chinese Religion

CONFUCIUS: GOODNESS

Confucius (551–479 B.C.E.) has been the most influential sage in east Asian history. Both in China and beyond, the essential structures of social relations—family life, government, public ceremonies—have derived from this master. What, then, did Confucius teach? Let us consider a few representative texts and then generalize about his message.

The Master said, It is Goodness that gives to a neighborhood its beauty. One who is free to choose, yet does not prefer to dwell among the Good—how can he be accorded the name of wise? The master said, Without Goodness a man cannot for long endure adversity, cannot for long enjoy prosperity. The Good Man rests content with Goodness; he that is merely wise pursues Goodness in the belief that it pays to do so. Of the adage "Only a Good Man knows how to like people,

knows how to dislike them," the Master said, He whose heart is in the smallest degree set upon Goodness will dislike no one. Wealth and rank are what every man desires; but if they can only be retained to the detriment of the Way he professes, he must relinquish them. Poverty and obscurity are what every man detests; but if they can only be avoided to the detriment of the Way he professes, he must accept them. The gentleman who ever parts company with Goodness does not fulfill that name. Never for a moment does a gentleman quit the way of Goodness. He is never so harried but that he cleaves to this; never so tottering but that he cleaves to this.[1]

"Goodness" is Arthur Waley's translation of **jen**, probably the most important word in Confucius' lexicon. It has overtones of "humaneness," "sympathy," and "unselfishness." The person who attains Goodness becomes fully human, lives as human beings were intended to live. He or she is innately attractive and

---

Chinese Religion: Twenty-Five Key Dates

CA. 3500 B.C.E.   Earliest Chinese City

CA. 1600   Shang Bronze Age Culture

551–479   Confucius

520   Traditional Date for Death of Lao-Tzu

403–221   Warring States Period

206   Han Dynasty Reunites China

CA. 200   Rise of Religious Taoism

CA. 112   Opening of "Silk Road" Links China with West

CA. 150 C.E.   Buddhism Reaches China

304–589   Huns Fragment China

607   Beginning of Chinese Cultural Influence in Japan

658   Height of Chinese Power in Central Asia

700   Golden Age of Chinese Poetry

CA. 730   Invention of Printing in China

845   Great Persecution of Buddhists

1000   Flourishing of Painting and Ceramics

1130–1200   Chu Hsi, Leading Neo-Confucian Thinker

1234   Mongols Destroy Empire

1275   Marco Polo in China

1585   Matteo Ricci in China

1644   Manchu Dynasty; Confucian Orthodoxy

1850   Taiping Rebellion

1893–1977   Mao Tse-Tung

1900   Boxer Uprising

1949   Communist Victory

---

powerful, influencing others simply by example. Thus a neighborhood depends upon Goodness, for without it no locale can be human or desirable. Thus we should want to live with good people, for otherwise we would forfeit our humanity, perhaps even turn criminal. Only Goodness keeps a person stable in hard times. Lose faith in Goodness and hard times will sweep you under. On the other hand, without Goodness good times equally will sweep you under, take away your peace. So those who are fully human, deeply advanced, satisfy themselves with Goodness alone. They do not pursue Goodness or take refuge in it as a means to an end. They know that goodness is its own reward, an end in itself.

From the vantage point of Goodness, no one is unattractive. Loving the beauty of human achievements, the good person rejoices in anyone's success. Knowing the difficulties on the way to Goodness, the good person has compassion for anyone's failure.

Goodness makes the sage so appreciative of the human enterprise that, succeeding or failing, any other member of the tribe solicits benevolence. The Way, or *Tao*, that Confucius taught aimed directly at Goodness. Through ritual, study of the ancient models, and persistent self-control, the student strove to become wedded to Goodness as the Master had been. By the end of his life, the Master felt that if he heard the Way in the morning, in the evening he could die content. He felt that he could do whatever his heart prompted, for the prompting of his heart had become identical with the dictates of the Way.

Thus the Way to Goodness became the great Confucian treasure. If wealth and high station became impediments to the Way to Goodness, they had to be relinquished. If poverty and obscurity were essential to becoming a gentleman true to this Way, poverty and obscurity it would have to be; Confucius himself never gained the political office he desired. More of his fame came after his life than while he could have enjoyed it. So he learned that following the Way has to be its own reward. Virtue has to be an end in itself.

Most likely, therefore, "virtue" was nothing moralistic or narrow-minded. To support the life structure Confucius erected it had to be free and broad. The commentators who constrict Confucius to the purely secular, pragmatic realm seem to miss this psychological truism. Through his studies, rituals, and strivings to walk the Way, Confucius found the fullness of humanity, human capacity opened wide and being filled. His Goodness was a synonym for godliness, sacredness, the ultimate in moral reality. Attaining Goodness was his peak experience, the consummation of what he had been made to feel.

CONFUCIUS: RITUAL

The outer form of jen is li: ritual, ceremony, prescribed behavior. For Confucius only the long, patient observance of society's rituals could make people apt for Goodness, formed so that they might be fully human. Thus li was no perfunctory or casual matter. The ceremonies that Confucius loved—the bowings, music, and formulaic words—had been fashioned in the venerable past and served a crucial function in his own present. Through ritual people could render one another justice and humaneness. Subjects could honor rulers and rulers could properly rule. Children could honor parents and parents could properly educate. To Confucius' mind, a social body well educated in what li entailed and well motivated to enact it was almost bound to be in good health. Li therefore was sacramental, a sacred fitting of interior disposition to exterior form. Were a ruler to realize its power, li would accomplish far more than harsh compulsion.

This seems to be the import of *Analects* 2:3: "The Master said, Govern the people by regulations, keep order among them by chastisements, and they will flee from you, and lose all self-respect. Govern them by moral force, keep order among them by ritual and you will keep their self-respect and come to you of their own accord."[2] Now, there are several levels at which one can interpret this text. On the level of common sense or ordinary human experience, the point seems to be that people do better when they are not compelled but attracted. If social ceremonies, the ritualized ways of conducting human affairs, are graceful, meaningful, honestly performed, then most people will play their parts as good citizens, feel pride in their community and serve it well.

On a middling level, the text probes the relation between self-respect and good citizenship. People treated well by their leaders, not patronized or brutalized, tend to have a healthy self-love, a salutary freedom from fear, and so to respond positively and energetically. In making this assumption, Confucius was opposing those whom China has called *Legalists*, philosophers who thought harsh law and order were the only way to run a state. Neither Confucius nor the Legalists thought in terms of sin, had the biblical sense that human nature has been unintelligibly weakened. Both argued from outer performance, what they observed to work. That Confucius has won the greater honors throughout Chinese history suggests the broad acceptance of the possibly for human perfectibility. "Give people a fair deal, a fair chance," the majority seem to have felt, "and most organizations will at least muddle through."

On a profound level, Confucius probably was drawing on the ancient notion of sacred kingship, according to which rulers mediate to their people the powers running the cosmos. In this context, state rituals are fraught with ultimate significance and affect the fertility of the crops, the good fortune of the coming year, the favor or disfavor of the deities. The final meaning of li, then, would be a way to harmony with the whole or foundation of reality. Not to know the sacred ceremonies, not to enact them well, would be to court disaster, miss or distort the *Te* (power) necessary to keep life harmonized with its source.

Rejecting what he interprets as the tendency of most Western translators to project subjectivist views onto Confucius, Herbert Fingarette has argued that almost all of Confucius' interests were outer-directed. This leads Fingarette to lay great stress on li and to configure li and jen as follows:

In short, where reciprocal good faith and respect are expressed through the specific forms defined in li, there is jen's way. Thus li and jen are two aspects of the same thing. Each points to an aspect of the action of man in his distinctively human role. Li directs our attention to the traditional social pattern of conduct and relationships; jen directs our attention to the person as one who pursues that pattern of conduct and thus maintains those relationships. Li also refers to the particular act in its status as exemplification of invariant norm; jen refers to the act as expressive of an orientation of the person, as expressing his commitment to act as prescribed by li. Li refers to the act as overt and distinguishable pattern of sequential behavior; jen refers to the act as the single, indivisible gesture of an actor, as his, and as particular and individual by reference to the unique individual who performs the act and to the unique context of the particular action.[3]

Thus the Goodness that Confucius hymned had in li an outer training ground and area of expression. Were the "gentleman" to develop fully, follow the Way faithfully, maturity would find him both graceful and good. In all situations he would know how to conduct himself. Each meeting would be a humane affair. Confucius sensed that the quality of our meetings largely determines the quality of our common life. When we make contact, exchange our best, cooperate and mutually edify, we promote peace and prosperity. When we miss one another, through either a lack of decent social forms or such social forms' neglect, we invite enmity and ruin. Both foreign wars without and domestic injustices within depend upon people missing one another, finding no social forms through which they can bridge their differences, knit together their fortunes, make common cause. From the simple handshake we use to initiate polite meetings to the subtle rituals between parent and child, friend and friend, spouse and spouse, li permeates our lives. We either learn to make li authentic, deep, and beautifully expressive, or we come to lack an essential limb, deprive society of a full member.

One does not find in Confucius much criticism of the social order that the rituals of his day were supposed to promote. Few comments suggest how women, peasants, and others marginal to the centers of power might share in the common weal more equitably, also enjoy a sense of grace. Elitist as well as profound, satisfied as well as sapiential, Confucius stands at some remove from the archetypal prophet. In his defense one might say that ritual should assure all people a kindly hearing, Goodness make the sage do his best for whoever comes along.

LAO-TZU: THE TAO

Mainly because Confucian thought provided the clearest rationale for social relations and made the most persuasive case that it carried forward the traditions of the model gentleman of old, Confucian thought became the backbone of Chinese culture. Taoist thought, as we shall see, was more poetic and personal. Buddhist thought was more analytic and metaphysical. Over the course of time, the Confucians opened their system to accommodate Taoist and Buddhist insights. China, and East Asia as a whole, has not been a cultural area in which distinctions between different traditions

have been hard and fast. Historically, one did not have to opt for either Confucianism or Taoism, Confucianism or Buddhism. Social matters could go forward in a Confucian spirit and metaphysical speculation be Buddhist. Public matters could follow the Confucian classics and private reading favor the Taoist classics. In fact the popular saying arose, "In office a Confucian, in retirement a Taoist." For the workaday world, Confucius provided the patterns. For the life of the individual spirit, Lao-tzu was the master.

The classic attributed to Lao-tzu, the *Tao Te Ching*, opens with a famous and characteristic passage:

The way that can be spoken of is not the constant way; the name that can be named is not the constant name. The nameless was the beginning of heaven and earth; the named was the mother of the myriad creatures. Hence always rid yourself of desires in order to observe its secrets; but always allow yourself to have desires in order to observe its manifestations. These two are the same but diverge in name as they issue forth. Being the same they are called mysteries, Mystery upon mystery—the gateway of the manifold secrets.[4]

Like Confucius, Lao-tzu is wedded to a Way, a Tao. Although he is less insistent than Confucius that this Tao is the wisdom handed down by the great worthies of the past, there is no indication that he thinks his ruminations about it novel. The Way that Lao-tzu lauds is firmly rooted in Chinese culture. It differs from the Way of Confucius not in its ancestry but in its naturalism. Confucius speaks of a Tao for running human affairs. In the background are the ultimate patterns of the cosmos. Lao-tzu speaks of a Tao to integrate the individual with the ultimate patterns of the cosmos. To the side are political questions. If people collectively open themselves to this Tao, human affairs may begin to heal, the body politic cast off its gray pallor.

Lao-tzu is more mystical than Confucius, more drawn to the ineffable side of nature's Way. People truly wise do not prate about the Tao. People who prate about the Tao are not truly wise. For the Tao recedes into mystery. No one can sound its depths, measure its outreach. At the beginning of heaven and earth stands a primal power that escapes human ken. Only when creation began to differentiate did something nameable show its face, the mystery take definite forms.

If we are to handle this twofold character of the Way, we must get our desires under control. The only way to approach the ultimate, ineffable side of the Tao is desirelessly—with completely empty spirits. On the other hand, to observe the manifestations of the Tao we need to sharpen our spirits, become involved with creation, desire to understand and manipulate the world in which we live. Yet the final word about the Tao is its mysteriousness. It is a fullness we shall never plumb or exhaust, a gateway to marvelous secrets. The most primordial fact about human existence is its condemnation to mystery, its chance to stretch out "unknowingly" to the All, contemplate the Whole wordlessly.

Sages who give their lives over to the Tao find themselves cut adrift from the common populace. No more in Lao-tzu's day than in our own were most people interested in ultimate mysteries. Thus one hears a plaintive tone in some of Lao-tzu's passages:

The multitude are joyous as if partaking of the t'ai lao *offering [a great feast] or going up to a terrace [on an outing] in spring. I alone am inactive and reveal no signs, like a baby that has not yet learned to smile, listless as though with no home to go back to. The multitude all have more than enough. I alone seem to be in want. My mind is that of a fool—how blank! Vulgar people are clear. I alone am drowsy. Vulgar people are alert. I alone am muddled. Calm like the sea; like a high wind that never ceases. The multitude all have a purpose. I alone am foolish and uncouth. I alone am different from others and value being fed by the mother.*[5]

The mother is Tao, the nourishment of the mystic's spirit. To contemplate Tao, the End and Way of things, feeds what Lao-tzu considers our deepest humanity. But it also alienates him from people at large, who do not contemplate the End and Way of things. Sufficient for them is the joy or pain of the present moment. Using that simple rule, they find life uncomplicated, bustle about trying to accomplish clear goals. Nothing is clear in the mystic's life. All is clouded by the omnipresent Mystery. The unknowing that afflicts mystics is a purification from the certainties of the multitude, the at-home-ness and familiarity of the workaday world. Enter the depths of the Tao, the mysteries of why and how there is something rather than nothing, and you will lose your bearings, find your mind becoming blank. Only a blank mind can mirror the impenetrable richness of the Tao. Only difference from the man in the street can make a sage.

LAO-TZU: POLITICS

From his immersion in the Way, Lao-tzu sometimes lashes out at the conventions of his time. To his mind, the sagehood of the Confucians cannot do the political job; it is not sufficiently in tune with the ultimate Tao fully to profit the people: "Abandon sageliness and discard wisdom; then the people will benefit a hundredfold. Abandon humanity and discard righteousness; then the people will return to filial piety and deep love. Abandon skill and discard profit; then there will be no thieves or robbers. However, these three things are ornaments and are not adequate. Therefore let people hold on to these: Manifest plainness, embrace simplicity, reduce selfishness, have few desires.[6]

The reputed sageliness of the Confucians, the public sense of wisdom ruling the day, seemed to Lao-tzu impotent. Dealing mainly with the surface, it could provide only a veneer of virtue and order. Were one to take a hard look at the state of society, the Confucian models might come into focus as a prime obstacle. Radical surgery, a genuine cure, would require lopping them off. Since they were a powerful cause of the social disease, their simple removal would benefit the people a hundredfold. So too with the "humanity" and "righteousness" currently holding sway. Because those notions took people away from their spontaneous instincts, interposed themselves between family members and friends, they were impediments to filial piety and friendship. Dropping them, too, would be a positive move, a way to revitalize older, more trustworthy instincts.

One of the main symbols Lao-tzu uses to express this sense of "back to basics" is the uncarved block. Lacking the adornments of culture, human nature is rough but healthy. It knows directly the requirements of justice, the warmth of familial love. The Tao moves it easily, for it has few shields to deflect the Tao's touch. Insofar as culture entails artifice, convention, and role playing, culture is replete with shields. Thus culture consistently deadens people's sensitivities to the Tao, makes justice and family relations complicated or recondite. When laws and customs multiply, the instincts that make people most human tend to rust. Banditry becomes legal or worth risking. Tyranny finds justifications; haughtiness holds degrees. If we would get back to the uncarved block of human nature, let go of our supposed skill, our relentless concern for profit, we would have a simpler but more vigorous society. Thieves and robbers would dwindle, either because there would be less incentive to steal or because the general populace would mete out a justice very effective and swift. Plainness, simplicity, selflessness, and desirelessness are the ways to civic prosperity. When people deal with one another directly and covet few of one another's goods, they can enjoy their here-and-now situations and savor a contented ambitionlessness.

If the leading symbol of the Tao Te Ching is the uncarved block, the leading prescription is *wu-wei.*

Wu-wei is actionless action, effortless doing, attentive going with the flow. It is the opposite of violent force, calculated manipulation, aggressive ambition to bend nature or other people to one's will. Nature moves by wu-wei: The water laps away the rock, the baby dominates the household, the female outlives the male, the valley survives the storm. Wisdom attuned to nature would run affairs indirectly, nudge things along with a gentle touch. It would realize that the key to good politics is winning people's hearts; the central victory is getting people to want to do what they should.

Chapter 63 is pregnant with wu-wei:

Act without action. Do without ado. Taste without tasting. Whether it is big or small, many or few, repay hatred with virtue. Prepare for the difficult while it is still easy. Deal with the big while it is still small. Difficult undertakings have always started with what is easy. And great undertakings have always started with what is small. Therefore the sage never strives for the great, and thereby the great is achieved. He who makes rash promises surely lacks faith. He who takes things too easily will surely encounter much difficulty. For this reason even the sage regards things as difficult. And therefore he encounters no difficulty.[7]

We have met paradoxical speech such as this before. Almost always it represents the sage's effort to grab people's attention and to stir up the minds of the audience. Sages usually gain their station by going apart from common opinion, offering a fresh and personal point of view. All around him Lao-tzu saw people striving, pushing, using force. Clearly this was not nature's way, and clearly it was not succeeding. The hair trigger of human relations, he observed, goes off destructively every time someone tries to force it, whenever a leader forgets its sensitivity. The way to get things done is not-doing. The way to permanent results is indirection, example, persuasion. Of course, one also needs doses of common prudence. The keen sailor sees the storm brewing and heads back to port. The alert politician senses trouble beginning and moves before the riot starts. Most disasters occur because leaders do not know group dynamics. Most states fail to flourish because their leaders ignore the Tao.

NATURE

Confucianism, Taoism, and Buddhism all influenced the traditional Chinese view of nature. Confucianism took over some of the ancient cosmological notions, such as the interaction of yin and yang, and by the time of the Neo-Confucian Chu Hsi (1130–1200 C.E.) had developed a quite sophisticated philosophy of nature. Taoism remained the inspiration of poets and painters; the seminal works of Lao-tzu and Chuang-tzu continued to have great influence even after much "Taoism" had become concerned with alchemy or regimes for gaining immortality (see appendixes). Chinese Buddhism took many of its terms from Taoism but made metaphysical contributions all its own. As we saw in the case of classical landscape painting, the notion of emptiness developed by Nagarjuna and other Mahayana thinkers furnished Chinese aesthetics a persuasive rationale. Other schools, such as Hua-yen, which stressed the interconnectedness of all realities, married Buddhist convictions about change to the Chinese love of concretenesss. The result was a view of nature that encouraged people to find nirvana in the midst of samsara, and to see physical change as the flux of the dharmas.

The theory that nature is governed by the bipolarity of yin and yang had quite ancient roots:

In traditional China, expressed through the concepts of yin *and* yang, *bipolarity constituted the specific characteristic of Chinese metaphysics. Once this principle had suggested itself, perhaps as early as 1000–500 B.C.E., the Chinese were able to develop a perfectly coherent theory of the cosmos. Nature was seen to operate through the interplay of light and darkness, heat and cold, male and female, and so forth. The* yang *(represented by the first of each pair) and* yin *(the second of each pair) were not in absolute and permanent opposition to each other. They might best be described as definable phases in a ceaseless flow of change. . . . As a consequence of the principle of constant transformation embodied in the* yin-yang *theory, the Chinese concept of the primary elements focused on the fundamental* qualities *observed in things. These qualities were not static but were ceaselessly interacting, transforming, and replacing each other. The chinese word* hsing, *which has customarily been translated as "element," is actually a verb meaning "to walk, to go, to act." There were five* hsing . . . *water, fire, wood, metal, and earth [their order and mutual reactions differ in other texts]. Thinking of* hsing *as verbal will help us to keep in mind their active nature (water overcoming fire, fire burning wood, and so forth); while thinking of* hsing *as adjectival will help us to understand their elemental nature (that is, all things may be categorized as either "watery," i.e., liquid; "fiery," i.e., gaseous; and so forth).*[8]

Around the fifth century B.C.E. arose what came to be known as *The Book of Changes (I Ching),* a text

*Figure 13   Fishermen (handscroll detail) by Hsu Tao-ning, about 970–1051.
Nelson Gallery-Atkins Museum (Nelson Fund).*

that eventually gained the high status of being enlisted in the Confucian canon. Employing the notion of yin-yang bipolarity, and stressing nature's constant change, the I Ching lays out a number of pictures in which an adept can read the signs of the changing times. The patterns are based on eight main trigrams (figures with three lines) featuring broken and unbroken lines. In their different combinations, the three trigrams become sixty-four hexagrams, which are considered to represent all the possible forms that nature's yin and yang may assume. As a result, the sixty-four hexagrams can stand for all possible situations and institutions. In germ, therefore, the hexagrams represent a basis for an objective analysis of natural change. Against the powerful Chinese tradition of trying to divine which

spirits were capriciously determining events, the expert in the new cosmology of the I Ching groped after an understanding of the laws by which nature combined its essential ingredients and so constantly changed. This move toward a more rational analysis of change impressed the Neo-Confucians, who made the I Ching a very influential text.

A third Chinese approach to nature developed into what became known as *feng-shui* (or *fung-shui*): geomancy, using and guiding the forces thought to emanate from the earth.

The essence of this idea is that the configurations of land forms and bodies of water on the face of the earth direct the flow of hey shae *[primordial energy]*

and that this has great implications for the fate of the world's human inhabitants. . . . Fung shui is the source of all luck and efficacy. A successful man, family, or lineage is successful because they have "good fung shui"; if they are not successful, it is because they have "bad fung shui." Fung shui can be a beneficial force if handled properly, but it can also be an extremely dangerous and destructive force if improperly dealt with. If one gets too large a dose of fung shui it may cause disease or even death, not only for an individual family, but an entire village or an entire lineage group. . . . In the New Territories, and probably in Kwangtung Province as a whole, entire villages were set up according to fung shui prescriptions to ensure the pros-

perity and safety of future generations. Villages had to be constructed at the foot of a hill if possible so that the fung shui could flow gradually from the higher mountains along the crests of smaller hills to concentrate on the village. Village sites had to have bodies of water standing in front of them to balance the flow of fung shui coming down from the mountains.[9]

SOCIETY

An important part of traditional Chinese sociology has been a great effort to fit the main social units—family, state—to nature's patterns. Both Confucius and Lao-tzu urged the people to follow the Way because they thought the Way would make people harmonious with nature. In less philosophical circles, however, "harmony with nature" was a quite fearsome matter. To fail the family's mores and so bring the clan into disgrace, was much more than a social faux pas. Rather it was a crack in the wall that defended the clan from a nature either ruthlessly indifferent or downright malign. Through thousands of years of traditional Chinese history, the formal rituals of li and the bedrock ethics of not shaming one's clan dominated the mainstream social thought because they seemed the best way to avoid chaos, a society out of harmony with nature.

One sees the dramatic form this social thought could assume in the story with which Maxine Hong Kingston begins her fascinating book *The Woman Warrior*:

"You must not tell anyone," my mother said, "what I am about to tell you. In China your father had a sister who killed herself. She jumped into the family well. We say that your father has all brothers because it is as if she had never been born. . . . I remember looking at your aunt one day when she and I were dressing; I had not noticed before that she had such a protruding melon of a stomach. But I did not think, 'She's pregnant,' until she began to look like other pregnant women, her shirt pulling and the white tops of her black pants showing. She could not have been pregnant, you see, because her husband had been gone for years. No one said anything. We did not discuss it. In early summer she was ready to have the child, long after when it could have been possible.

"The village had also been counting. On the night the baby was to be born the villagers raided our house. Some were crying. Like a great saw, teeth strung with lights, files of people walked zigzag across our land, tearing the rice. . . . At first they threw mud and rocks at the house. Then they threw eggs and began slaughtering our stock. We could hear the animals scream their deaths—the roosters, the pigs, a last great roar from the ox. . . . They smeared blood on the doors and walls. One woman swung a chicken, whose throat she had slit, splattering blood in red arcs about her. We stood together in the middle of our house, in the family hall with the pictures and tables of the ancestors around us, and looked straight ahead. . . . When they left they took sugar and oranges to bless themselves. They cut pieces from the dead animals. Some of them took bowls that were not broken and clothes that were not torn. Afterward we swept up the rice and sewed it back up into sacks. But the smells from the spilled preserves lasted. Your aunt gave birth in the pigsty that

night. The next morning when I went for the water, I found her and the baby plugging up the family well.

"Don't let your father know that I told you. He denies her. Now that you have started to menstruate, what happened to her could happen to you. Don't humiliate us. You wouldn't like to be forgotten as if you had never been born. The villagers are watchful."[10]

"Don't humiliate us. . . . The villagers are watchful." How much fear, pathos, and destiny lurk in those phrases? How many women and children drowned, how many men suffered killing jobs or military service because humiliation was ever to be avoided, and the watchful neighbor always to be appeased? But more than clan custom, neighborhood habit stalked the villages of traditional China. Ghosts and demons prowled, projected outward from intense, troubled psyches.

Traditional societies have a dark, shocking side counterbalancing their apparent peace and consistency. Often the price of their harmony has been severe inner repression. When life is so hard physically that people have no alternative to cooperation, society tends to forge nearly unbreakable inner constraints. Kingston's aunt did not kill herself because she had violated her deepest conscience or sinned against her holy God. She killed herself because she had shamed her family and so made life in their midst impossible. To prohibit adultery and the social chaos it can wreak, Chinese villagers would ostracize the whole clan of an adulteress (an adulterer, being less visible, got much less severe treatment, if any punishment at all). The clan in turn would cut the offending woman off without a word, a memory, a marker in the family cemetery. Few traditional personalities were strong enough, "modern" enough, to buck this tremendous social pressure. Most individual psyches caved in under the strain and found suicide a relief.

In such tragedies lie some of the most sober questions the religions have to face. At what point do customs, mores, ethical laws become ungodly in their psychic demands, demonic in their rigidity? What analogues in Muslim, Christian, and other religious codes could write similar stories of ruin, victimizations parallel to that of Kingston's aunt? Traditional China seldom asked such modern questions, as traditional Europe and India seldom did. Traditional China gave its social codes divine sanctions, spirit-driven powers,[11] as did most other countries. Traditionally, society has held together by the will of its ultimate realities. For good and bad, traditional social thought has given the tribe life-and-death powers over the individual, sanity and insanity powers over the psyche.

SELF

Among the villagers, who have predominated in Chinese history, the self was first of all a member of a clan. The clan lineage stretched back many generations, providing a sizeable list of ancestors who deserved veneration, and stretched to the side in many collateral branches. What individuality a person achieved depended upon the clan as its context or matrix. The Confucian hierarchies strictly subordinated women to men, younger siblings to elder, peasants to the gentry who employed them. Within these many constraints, individual talent could bring a person considerable progress or prominence; distinctive personality traits could arise but seldom with the sort of freedom that modern Western individualism has promoted. Through most of Chinese history, the many greatly predominated over the one.

For men with education and middle- to upper-class opportunities, the sage was the cultural ideal. By study and meditation, a man could aspire to a sagacity that would bring him both personal peace and the respect of his community. As one recent commentator has put it:

At the center of the Confucian tradition stands the sage, who has centered himself in the ways of Heaven. Sagehood for the Confucian is a complex goal. It is something that everyone by nature is said to possess, yet in daily life the realization of the goal is distant. Learning and self-cultivation are directed toward the realization of sagehood, a process of recovering man's true nature or sagely intention. There is an emphasis upon "measuring up" in this process of learning, that is, emulating those who have gone before and adjudicating one's own life in the light of the previous experiences of others. Thus the sense of self for the Confucian is tempered by the a priori model of the sage.[12]

After Confucius himself, the sage most admired by the Confucians was Mencius (ca. 390–305 B.C.E.). The book that bears Mencius' name is much like the *Analects* of Confucius: sayings and maxims that show the Master applying the Way of the ancients to problems of current times. Mencius sought the same ends as Confucius: Goodness (jen) and Justice. However, he was more optimistic about human nature, thinking that of itself human nature is set for Goodness and Justice. One of the most famous stories in which he couched this teaching is called Bull Mountain:

Mencius said, "Bull Mountain was once beautifully wooded. But, because it was close to a large city, its trees all fell to the axe. What of its beauty then? However, as the days passed things grew, and with the rains and the dews it was not without greenery. Then came the cattle and goats to graze. That is why, today, it has that scoured-like appearance. On seeing it now, people imagine that nothing ever grew there. But this is surely not the true nature of a mountain? And so, too, with human beings. Can it be that any man's mind naturally lacks Humanity [jen] and Justice? If he loses his sense of the good, then he loses it as the mountain lost its trees. It has been hacked away at—day after day— what of its beauty then?"[13]

The encouragement that Mencius gave those seeking sagely perfection stemmed mainly from this notion that, were people to avoid impeding the mind, the mind would unfold toward humanity and justice. As Confucius had implied that jen was an extraordinary achievement, something gained only by the very rare, Mencius suggested that anyone could make great progress because human nature was on the side of jen and would find virtue congenial if properly exposed to it. As anyone would rush to save a child from falling into a well, spontaneously seeking the child's good, so anyone would want to live midst humanity and justice, if given half a chance.

Most Chinese women have had to make their own opportunities for influence, if not virtue, since the going social structures have accorded them only a second-class citizenship. As one Western missionary wrote in 1899:

To defend herself against the fearful odds which are often pitted against her, a Chinese wife has but two resources. One of them is her mother's family, which, as we have seen, has no real power. . . . The other means of defense which a Chinese wife has at her command is—herself. If she is gifted with a fluent tongue, especially if it is backed by some of the hard common sense which so many Chinese exhibit, it must be a very peculiar household in which she does not hold her own. Real ability will assert itself, and such light as a Chinese woman possesses will assuredly permeate every corner of the domestic bushel under which it is of necessity hidden. If a Chinese wife has a violent temper, if she is able at a moment's notice to raise a tornado about next to nothing, and to keep it for an indefinite period blowing at the rate of a hundred miles an hour, the position of such a woman is almost certainly secure. The most termagant of mothers-in-law hesitates to attack a daughter-in-law who has no fear of men or of demons and who is full equal to any emergency. A Chinese woman in a fury is a spectacle by no means uncommon. But during the time of the most violent paroxysms of fury, Vesuvius itself is not more unmanageable by man.[14]

Needless to say, this sort of fury did not fit the model of the Confucian sage. On the other hand, it gave many women leverage against would-be sages, allowing them, too, a little space in which to grow an estimable self.

ULTIMATE REALITY

For the classical Confucians, the Way of the ancients led to harmony with "Heaven," the overarching ultimate reality. The emperor was the "Son of Heaven," and his rule was good as long as he held the "mandate of heaven." In effect, this meant that the demise of humanity and justice opened the door to revolution. The mandate of heaven having passed out of a degenerate emperor's hands, others could rise up to claim it. The Taoists made the Way itself the ultimate reality, taking it as both a first principle and a sort of motherly love.[15] Chuang-tzu added nuance by speaking of the Great Clod one could join by walking in the Tao properly. The Great Clod was the whole of nature from which we come and to which we return. The Buddhists spoke of nirvana and the bodies of the Buddha (earthly body, celestial body, and teaching body) as ultimate, contributing the sense that what we perceive are but empty and passing forms of an ineffable state of unconditionedness.

In the twelfth century C.E. system of the Neo-Confucian Chu Hsi, China's greatest synthesizer, ultimate reality had sharply cosmological overtones. Chu was a philosopher of nature, as well as an ethician, and his sense of nature's ultimate reality fused Confucian and Buddhist ideas:

At the beginning of things Chu Hsi puts the idea of wu-chi, *a term which literally means "non-existence," "absolute non-existence," but which in this system really stands for potential existence, universal virtuality, or as this school describes it, the "Great Void" (*t'ai-hsu*). It is in fact from* wu-chi *that there emerges* t'ai-chi, *the principle of all things, which for Chu Hsi, as for his predecessors, is the keystone of the system. According to his definitions of it, this first principle is pure, infinite, eternal and absolute being, substance in its completeness, the principle of the world and cause of all things. Therefore it is said to be "extremely lofty, extremely excellent, extremely subtle and extremely spiritual." Although it can be regarded as spiritual, yet once located, it is located in matter. It is, if you like,*

spirit, but not spirit distinct from matter; it is one with matter, infused into the mass which it animates and organizes.[16]

By understanding the composition of ultimate reality, the sage could win a balanced, poised view of life. As he gained seasoning, fewer and fewer things could surprise him or take away his peace. His regular meditations provided the chance to root himself in the ultimate build of nature; his participation in the official ceremonies made the entire traditional sense of order beautifully compelling. H. G. Creel concludes his study of Chinese thought by linking such balance and ceremony:

Balance, poise, is the hallmark of the Chinese who has been reared in the tradition of his nation's culture. This is true whether he is a scholar who studied the classics in the traditional manner, or a farmer or coolie who grew to manhood in a part of China untouched by the storms of "Westernization." It shows itself in a quiet assurance that has none of the assertiveness that goes with what we all call "pride," and an affability that is quite imperturbable. It is an enviable quality. Where does it come from? Not just from moral maxims; this is not merely a way of thought but a way of life. And that way of life comes from the practice of li, *which Confucius taught twenty-five hundred years ago and the Chinese have continued to cultivate to our own century.*

Li *is (in part) ceremony. Most of us in the modern West have little use for ceremony: we think it is mostly foolishness. Undoubtedly it can be overdone, as Confucius himself realized. But ceremony of a commonsense variety is simply a means of imparting rhythm to life. When we play tennis or golf we recognize that rhythm is essential, but we live most of our lives at a jerky pace. The result is to injure our digestions, our nervous systems, and even our productivity. The traditional Chinese habit is to live in a more ordered way. Of course, ceremony sometimes involves inconvenience. I used to wonder why it was that in imperial China court was always held at dawn—a horrible hour to get people out of bed. And I thought it still stranger that, even in the time of Confucius, when matters of the gravest importance were to be discussed, those taking part in the conference were supposed to sit up the whole night before; this seemed nothing but a primitive religious ritual. Then I had the opportunity to attend a sacrifice at the temple of Confucius in Peking.*

It was held at dawn, and I had to get out of my bed at two a.m.—how willingly you can imagine. For most of the long ride to the temple I felt very sorry for myself. Gradually, however, the impressiveness of the situation and the magnificence of my surroundings took me out of myself. The sky was a deep, luminous blue that was quite unbelievable. The temples and pine trees had indeed passed before my eyes on other occasions, but my senses were so sharpened by the dawn that I now realized that I had never before really seen, much less appreciated them. After many years I can still see the details of that ceremony much more clearly than I see the room about me. And I now understand why the Chinese held court at dawn. If it had been my business to deliberate about affairs of state, I would have done a far better job of it that morning than I could ever do it over a luncheon table, or drowsing in midafternoon.[17]

Thus ritual supported the Chinese ideal of balance by setting affairs of state and personal matters in the beautiful context of nature's dawn, nature's surround, nature's depth. When such a context took hold of the traditional Chinese, they felt at one with ultimate reality, in their rightful place at the center of the world.

MAO TSE-TUNG

Among the recent leaders transforming Chinese culture, Mao Tse-tung (1893–1976) stands out as by far the most influential. Born to lower middle-class parents in Hunan province in east-central China, Mao threw off the Buddhist faith of his mother and the Confucian classics of his meager schooling to read his way into the Communism of Marx and Lenin. His career in war and politics led to a ruthless, pragmatic focus on what he thought necessary to free China first from native imperial rule, then from foreign powers such as Japan and the West, and finally from the various "backwardnesses" that kept the vast majority of China's huge population desperately poor. Among these backwardnesses Mao numbered the traditional religious and social structures, so he determined to root them out in the name of Communist progress.

Something of Mao's approach to "progress" comes through in "The Foolish Old Man Who Removed the Mountains," a story of his that became one of the three "oft-read" articles the Chinese people were encouraged to ponder regularly:

There is an ancient Chinese fable called "The Foolish Old Man Who Removed the Mountains." It tells of an old man who lived in northern China long, long ago and was known as the Foolish Old Man of North Mountain. His house faced south and beyond his doorway stood the two great peaks, Taihang and Wangwu, obstructing the way. He called his sons, and hoe in hand they began to dig up these mountains with great determination. Another greybeard, known as the Wise Old Man, saw them and said derisively, "How silly of you to do this! It is quite impossible for you few to dig up these two huge mountains." The Foolish Old Man replied, "When I die, my sons will carry on; when they die, there will be my grandsons, and then their sons and grandsons, and so on to infinity. High as they are, the mountains cannot grow any higher and with every bit we dig, they will be that much lower. Why can't we clear them away?" Having refuted the Wise Old Man's wrong view, he went on digging every day, unshaken in his conviction. God was moved by this, and sent down two angels, who carried the mountains away on their backs. Today, two big mountains lie like a dead weight on the Chinese people. One is imperialism, the other is feudalism. The Chinese Communist Party has long made up its mind to dig them up. We must persevere and work unceasingly, and we, too, will touch God's heart. Our God is none other than the masses of the Chinese people. If they stand up and dig together with us, why can't these two mountains be cleared away?[18]

Mao's attack on feudalism included broadsides against the Confucian tradition. Indeed, the whole culture that hierarchized society and kept so many from sharing in the common wealth had to be razed; therefore, the philosophical and religious underpinnings of the culture were special targets. During the revolutionary war Mao did not hesitate to deal with his enemies ruthlessly, and after the Communist victory he did not scruple to eliminate further opposition. When religious groups seemed to represent or aid such opposition, they too were persecuted. The only God Mao bowed before was his image of the Chinese people. To his mind improving their lot was an end justifying any means, a work sanctifying all who joined it.

As many commentators have pointed out, Mao's attacks on religion did not mean the end of ritual or belief. Not only did many old religious ways continue underground among large portions of society, but the Communists themselves developed rituals and memorial ceremonies. As a description published in 1977 puts it:

Ritual is part of the lifestyle in China today. Great rallies are held not only in the Tiananmen Square in Peking, but in most major cities on festive occasions such as National Day (October 1) and Labor Day (May 1). The study of Mao's writings also has a ritualistic flavor at times. The purpose of ritual is to give expression to group solidarity and to arouse enthusiasm for common tasks. A family might gather around a portrait of Chairman Mao, read some quotations and sing a revolutionary song before starting the day's work. In the evening they may again gather and discuss the day's activities in light of Mao's teachings about service and struggle. In such family meetings current events and news documents are sometimes studied. Family problems are also discussed. . . . Part of the purpose of ritual is also to recall the past and to affirm the revolutionary effort to move beyond those bitter days. The "meal of bitter remembering" is an almost sacramental ritual.[19]

In the meal of bitter remembering older people would try to teach younger people how miserable the pre-Communist days had been. The dinner would consist of such nearly inedible fare as wild vegetable soup, steamed bran, and husks. The emotion with which the older people reenacted their past poverty and suffering usually moved the younger people deeply. The new regime, whatever its faults, was trying to give all people decent food, clothing, shelter, and medical care. It was trying to destroy once and for all the class differences that in the past had let a few people live luxuriously by forcing most people to live wretchedly. In the days when Mao ruled China people saluted his portrait, read his speeches and poems, and sent him letters expressing their deepest thanks, problems, or hopes because he personified the new opportunities they saw opening up, the life of comradeship they hoped was dawning.

SUMMARY

We began our study of Chinese religion by attending to the paramount traditional sages, Confucius and Lao-tzu. Confucius emphasized Goodness (jen) and the way of the ancients. If a person was willing to work hard, he or she might develop the humaneness, sympathy, and firm grounding in the Way that Goodness connoted. To such a person, the traits of other people would become attractive, and life would seem very much worth living. The *Analects* makes so much of jen that it becomes more than pragmatic, almost a synonym for ultimate reality or godliness. The best way to progress in jen is to immerse oneself in li (ritual or protocol). Confucius hoped that such an immersion would lead to rulers exercising power through moral example rather than force. Developing the rich implications that ritual or ceremony can have for humanizing social relations, Herbert Fingarette has characterized Confucius as a profound ancient thinker whose ideas are germane and applicable to present times.

Lao-tzu stands to Confucius as poet to political scientist. Although Lao-tzu is keenly interested in reforming political life, his instinct is to center all reforms in a return to the Tao, a mystic entity best approached in a simple, "uncarved" mentality. It is when life is primitive (uncorrupted by social artifice), that the Tao holds sway. The Tao is far too profound, far too rich, for superficial conventions to capture. Following it makes one dark where ordinary people are bright, blank where ordinary people are clear. Were leaders to follow this sort of "unknowing" back to its source, they might fashion a society too simple to promote thievery, too humane to care about profit. Then leaders could guide affairs by wu-wei: smoothly, easily, with a touch of nature's grace.

Chinese views of nature have built on an ancient heritage. Since perhaps 500 years before Confucius, yin-yang theory has shaped the traditional cosmology. The five hsing also had a venerable history, as did the divination theory upgraded by the I Ching. One might therefore speak of a Chinese protoscience alert to the constant interactions among nature's qualities. Feng-shui or geomancy was another Chinese outlook influential into the present century. Unless the force of feng-shui favored one's home or office, one was in a perilous state. Chinese social thought found equal peril in disgracing one's clan. For such violations of the clan ethic as adultery one might feel forced to suicide. The villagers were always watching to see whether one kept the common mores, and such pressure suggests the destructive character that religion can assume when conformity to group tradition becomes a rigid absolute.

Psychologically, the clan predominated over the self not only through ethics but also through social stratifications. If one was female or peasant, one's self ran in quite narrow tracks. For educated males the major personal ideal was sagehood on the Confucian model. Trying to emulate wise men such as Mencius, the aspirant sought goodness and justice through meditation and ritual. Regarding ultimate reality, the Neo-Confucians conceived a cosmology with such basic principles as void and spirit. In tune with these, the mature personality could gain the vaunted Chinese balance and imperturbability. Ceremonies at dawn helped statesmen apply their balance to practical problems, setting everything in the wider context of nature's serene beauty. Mao Tse-tung tried to substitute Marxist-Leninist notions for these traditions, stressing above all the will and good of the masses. Mao's own person and ideas, however, became the subject of at least quasi-religious rituals, as the masses tried to put past sufferings behind them and move ahead to a new Communist order.

STUDY QUESTIONS

1. Why does Goodness lead the sage to dislike no one?

2. How might a Confucian appreciation of ritual improve contemporary American culture?

3. Why is Lao-tzu's mind blank and muddled?

4. Explain the symbolism of the uncarved block.

5. Explain the configuration dark-cold-female.

6. Why would traditional Chinese villagers consider adultery a deep threat?

7. What is the permanent truth in Mencius' story about Bull Mountain?

8. Is what one sees at dawn more ultimate than what one sees at mid-afternoon? Why?

9. Explain Mao's saying, "Our God is none other than the masses of the Chinese people."

NOTES

1. Confucius, *Analects*, 4: 1–5; in Arthur Waley, trans., *The Analects*. New York: Vintage Books, n.d., pp. 102–3.

2. Confucius, *Analects*, 2:3.

3. Herbert Fingarette, *Confucius—The Secular As Sacred*. New York: Harper & Row, 1972, pp. 42–43.

4. *Tao Te Ching*, 1; in D.C. Lau, trans., *Lao Tzu: Tao Te Ching*. Baltimore: Penguin, 1963, p. 57.

5. Ibid., 20:47; Lau, pp. 76–77.

6. Ibid., 19; in Wing-Tsit Chan, trans., *The Way of Lao Tzu*. Indianapolis: Bobbs-Merrill, 1963, p. 132.

7. Ibid., 63; in Chan, p. 212.

8. Laurence G. Thompson, *Chinese Religion: An Introduction*, 3d ed. Belmont, Calif.: Wadsworth, 1979, pp. 3–4.

9. Jack Potter, "Wind, Water, Bones and Souls: The Religious World of the Cantonese Peasant," in Laurence G. Thompson, ed., *The Chinese Way in Religion*. Encino, Calif.: Dickenson, 1973, pp. 220–21.

10. Maxine Hong Kingston, *The Woman Warrior*. New York: Alfred A. Knopf, 1977, pp. 3–5.

11. See C.K. Yang, *Religion in Chinese Society*. Berkeley: University of California Press, 1961.

12. Rodney L. Taylor, "Journey Into Self: The Auto-Biographical Reflections of Hu Chih," *History of Religions*, 21/4 (May 1982), pp. 337–38.

13. *Mencius*, 6A.8; in W.A.C.H. Dobson, trans., *Mencius*. Toronto: University of Toronto Press, 1963, p. 141.

14. Arthur Smith, *Village Life in China*. New York: n.p., 1899, pp. 303–5 quoted by Margery Wolf, "Chinese Women: Old Skills in a New Context," in *Women & Culture*, ed. M. Z. Rosaldo and L. Lamphere. Stanford, Calif.: Stanford University Press, 1974, p. 159.

15. See Ellen Marie Chen, "Tao as the Great Mother and the Influence of Motherly Love in the Shaping of Chinese Philosophy," *History of Religion*, 14/1 (August 1974), pp. 51–64.

16. René Grousset, *The Rise and Splendour of the Chinese Empire*. Berkeley: University of California Press, 1953, p. 215.

17. Herrlee G. Creel, *Chinese Thought From Confucius to Mao Tse-tung*. Chicago: University of Chicago Press, 1953, pp. 260–61.

18. Mao Tse-tung, *Selected Works*, vol 3. Peking: People's Publishing House, 1961, p. 322, quoted by Donald E. MacInnis, *Religious Policy and Practice in Communist China*. New York: Macmillan, 1972, pp. 15–16.

19. Raymond L. Whitehead, *Love and Struggle in Mao's Thought*. Maryknoll, N.Y.: Orbis, 1977, p. 93.

CHAPTER

14

Japanese Religion

CHRONICLES: EARLY SHINTO

The genius of Japanese religion goes back to pre-Chinese days, before the influx of Confucian, Taoist, and Buddhist philosophies. The native Japanese tradition, which under the competitive pressure of these imports expressed itself as *Shinto* ("the Way of the Kami"), stressed the beauty of the Japanese islands. The ancient mythology contained in the *Kojiki* and the *Nihongi* (chronicles composed about 712 and 720 C.E.) tells stories of the ancestors of the Japanese people and the creation of the lovely islands. The primal human couple, Izanagi and Izanami, descendents of several generations of gods, receive the task of solidifying the land and inhabiting it. They erect a pillar toward heaven (a favorite shamanic symbolism) and give birth to various islands and children. In their first try at procreation Izanami, the female, speaks before Izanagi, the male. Because of this violation of "proper" order they suffer an imperfect birth and must redo the nuptial ceremony. (Some of these details remain in the modern Shinto marriage ceremony.)

The genealogical interests of the early chronicles reflect the people's desire to connect their present social order with the pristine time of creation. If they could show a link between their current rulers and social organization, the eighth century (as we now call it) would be in harmony with the pattern the gods had laid out in the beginning. For the early Japanese, then, as for many other archaic peoples, the cosmological myth was all-important. The way the gods had made the Japanese islands; the sword, beads, mirror, and other imperial regalia given to the first parents; and the other creational symbols showed how present times could still move by the power of the original act that made Japan the navel point of reality.

As Shinto came to reflect on its earliest traditions, it spoke of the *kami*, the forces moving through rocks and trees, seas and souls. Anything striking, powerful, giving rise to fear or awe might be a kami. The kami preferred rough nature to pacified villages, came to ecstatics more than staid and ordinary people; they were everywhere, applying or expressing the divine powers of creation, the godlike forces that originally had formed the islands and the people. Out of this

---

Japanese Religion: Twenty-Five Key Dates

CA. 4500–250 B.C.E.   Jomon Period: Hunting and Gathering

CA. 660   Jimmu, Traditional First Emperor

CA. 250 B.C.E.–250 C.E.   Yayoi Period: Blending of Ethnic Groups

5 C.E.   Building of National Shrine at Ise

285   Confucianism Introduced

CA. 550   Buddhism Introduced

594   Buddhism Proclaimed State Religion

645   Taika Reform Remodels Japan on Chinese Lines

712–720   Completion of Shinto Chronicles

805–806   Introduction of Tendai and Shingon Buddhist Sects

890   Cultural Renaissance: Novels, Landscape Painting, Poetry

1175–1253   Introduction of Pure Land, Zen, and Nichiren Buddhist Sects

1333   Civil War

1549   Francis Xavier Arrives in Japan

1600–1867   Tokugawa Era: Confucianism Prospers, Buddhism Controlled by State

1646–1694   Basho, Leading Buddhist Poet

1650   Beginning of Popular Literary Culture

1730–1801   Motoori Norinaga, Leader of Shinto Renaissance

1850   New Religions Emerge

1854   Admiral Perry Forces Trade with West

1868–1871   Meiji Persecution of Buddhism; Shinto Brought under State Control

1894–1905   Successful Wars with China and Russia

1899   Religion Forbidden in Public Schools

1939   Department of Education Controls All Religious Bodies

1945   Japan Surrenders in World War II; Shinto Disestablished

---

heritage comes Japan's great love of nature, which has determined that the main line of Japanese religion would be esthetic as much as theological. Because of the kami, the harmony and peace of quiet woods and still ponds has had as much influence as social ceremonies.

The early chronicles also personify the forces of nature. For example, the Sun Goddess Amaterasu (the ancestor of all later emperors) stands in tension with the Wind God Susanoo. In the background of the stories about the conflicts between these two stand the antagonisms between social forces (for example, the force of ceremonial and the force of unbridled freedom) as well as natural. A brief excerpt captures the flavor:

After this Susa-no-o Mikoto's behavior was exceedingly rude. In what way? Amaterasu ... had made august rice fields of Heavenly narrow rice fields and Heavenly long rice fields. Then Susa-no-o, when the seed was sown in spring, broke down the divisions between the plots of rice, and in autumn let loose the Heavenly piebald colts, and made them lie down in the midst of the rice fields. Again, when he saw that Amaterasu was about to celebrate the feast of first-fruits, he secretly voided excrement in the New Palace. Moreover, when he saw that Amaterasu was in her sacred weaving hall, engaged in weaving garments of the Gods, he flayed a piebald colt of Heaven, and breaking a hole in the roof-tiles of the hall, flung it in. Then Amaterasu started with alarm, and wounded herself with the shuttle. Indignant of this, she straightway entered the Rock-cave of Heaven, and having fastened the Rock-door, dwelt there in seclusion. Therefore constant darkness prevailed on all sides, and the alternation of night and day was unknown.[1]

Susanoo is what comparativists call a *trickster*. In

157

Freudian terms he expresses the impulsive *id*. Amaterasu stands for royal culture and order, closely tied in with the light and regularity of the sun. Beneath its entertainment the story is pondering over the variety of forces in human nature as well as cosmic. How do order and disorder correlate? How much ceremonial disciplining of impulse is necessary to make human beings worthy of the lands and traditions the gods have given them? How much stultifies creativity? Amaterasu, the Sun Queen, has feminine sensibilities. Susanoo's breaking of her orderly rows and rules has overtones of a fractious child trying to upset a mother usually quite calm. When the child goes too far—desecrating the palace and disrupting the weaving of the gods' clothing—the lights go out, the rule of the mother finally asserts itself.

CHRONICLES: STORIES

The chronicles detail further adventures of Susanoo and other kami. One of the most famous stories concerns the fated marriage of Princess Yamato and Prince Plenty. The Prince, who was a kami, never showed himself in the daytime. Always he came to the Princess at night. This troubled the Princess, so she begged him to delay one morning, that she might behold his face. He agreed, saying that the following morning he would enter her toilet case. However, he warned her not to be alarmed at his looks. This caused the Princess to wonder in her heart.

At daybreak the Princess looked into her toilet case. There she saw a beautiful little snake, about the size of the cord that goes round a woman's robe. Frightened, she cried out. This shamed the god, so he changed himself into human form. Speaking harshly to the Princess, he told her that as she had shamed him so he would shame her. Walking on the Great Void, he ascended to Mount Mimoro, departing from his bride. The Princess, overcome with remorse, stabbed herself in the womb with chopsticks and died. People therefore called her tomb the Chopstick Tomb, and they said that while human beings worked on it by day the gods finished it at night.

The great imperial shrine of Shinto, foremost among the many hundreds of Shinto shrines scattered throughout the islands, stands at Ise, on the east coast of Honshu near Osaka. The Nihongi (Chapter 1, verses 175–176) records the enshrinement of Amaterasu at Ise by the Princess Yamato-hime no Mikoto. The goddess directed the Princess to this spot, calling it the place of the divine wind, the land to which the waves

of the eternal world return. Liking its seclusion and beauty, the goddess chose it for her own special shrine.

Through the centuries thousands of pilgrims have made their way to Ise. The sort of emotions many of them no doubt felt come through clearly in the following excerpt from a monk's diary:

When on the way to these Shrines one does not feel like an ordinary person any longer but as though reborn in another world. How solemn is the unearthly shadow of the huge groves of ancient pines and chamaecyparis, and there is a delicate pathos in the few rare flowers that have withstood the winter frosts so gaily. The cross-beams of the Torii or Shinto gate way is without any curve, symbolizing by its straightness the sincerity of the direct beam of the Divine promise. The shrine-fence is not painted red nor is the Shrine itself roofed with cedar shingles. The eaves, with their rough reed-thatch, recall memories of the ancient days when the roofs were not trimmed. So did they spare expense out of compassion for the hardships of the people. Within the Shrine there are many buildings where the festival rites are performed, constructed just like those in the imperial Palace. Buddhist monks may go only as far as the Sacred Tree known as the Cryptomeria of the Five Hundred Branches. . . .

And particularly it is the deeply-rooted custom of this Shrine that we should bring no Buddhist rosary or offering, or any special petition in our hearts and this is called "Inner Purity." Washing in sea water and keeping the body free of all defilement is called "Outer Purity." And when both these Purities are attained there is then no barrier between our mind and that of the Deity. And if we feel to become thus one with the Divine, what more do we need and what is there to pray for? When I heard that this was the true way of worshipping at the Shrine, I could not refrain from shedding tears of gratitude.[2]

The account obviously comes from a time when Buddhism had made strong inroads into Japanese piety. In fact, Shrine officials seem to discriminate against Buddhists, trying to maintain a Shinto purity about the grounds and those who walk them. Even for the pilgrim of Buddhist convictions, the Shrine grounds inspire religious awe. Passing through the Torii takes the visitor out of the profane world, into a precinct sacred to the kami. It is like being reborn into another world. Especially impressive are the tall trees, dark groves, and (almost as counterpoint) delicate flowers. Everything suggests the honesty of nature, its lack of artifice. (To this day Ise remains simple, with little adornment. At first one who comes to it after visiting other shrines wonders why the most famous should be so understated. Then it dawns that the understatement or roughness is in fact an eloquent sermon all its own. Like the simplicity of certain Japanese gardens or pieces of pottery, the effect is a diminution of egocentricity, an objective focus on what is basic and valuable.)

The pilgrim's account underscores the Shinto concern for purity. Many Japanese have retained the customs of taking a pinch of salt to purify themselves and taking steaming baths and plunges into the sea to cleanse body and spirit alike. The sense that the kami are physical presences stimulates a desire to make the body-spirit composite as open to the divine nearness as possible. When there is no barrier between our mind and that of the Deity, we have reached the goal of religious striving, the heart of traditional Japanese culture. The pilgrim's tears show the peculiar power of religious purity, its tendency to break out in what those who experience it claim is an unearthly joy. That there should be such beauty, that we should be able to become one with it, and that this union should fulfill the deepest yearnings of our hearts is so good it makes the pilgrim's cup overflow.

NATURE

Shinto mythology, as we have seen, personified the great forces of nature such as the sun and the wind. Other kami were less clearly personal, more simply the power of an arresting shape or a beautiful sound. Some of these less personal kami had erotic overtones, in that stones shaped like phalluses or vulvas might be considered "bodies" of kami. Others were simply gigantic or unusual. Thus the Japanese approach to nature stood open to revelations. The force that kept things going might break out at any time, in any place. In 1976 we met a middle-aged Japanese man who explained to us the traditional notion that there are 800,000 gods. He was in the Meiji gardens of Tokyo, come for his noonday swim. "You," he said, "have one God. We Japanese have 800,000." He did not render a theological explanation of this difference, but the sweep of his hand across the Meiji landscape suggested that some of the 800,000 gods graced each compass direction. The flowers, trees, and pools might each have their kami. The world was charged with divine forces. Appreciating them was mainly a matter of becoming attuned.

Were one to apply a little theology to the man's religious sensibilities, the "coincidence of opposites" might emerge. Is the One God of the Western Bible absolutely different from the 800,000 Japanese gods? Or does the Bible try to point beyond this-worldly realities by way of radical simplification, as the Japanese tradition tries to point beyond by way of almost unlimited multiplication? Eight-hundred thousand is not a huge number to people whose national debt runs into the trillions, but it is more than any of us can clearly imagine. Thus it seems to be saying that just about anything in nature can manifest the divine. Indeed, it may even be saying that nothing in nature (or anywhere else) subsists apart from the divine. True, the man himself did not say this, and we should not put words into his mouth. On the other hand, the cultural conflict between East and West did not seem to trouble him at all, perhaps because some deep part of him sensed a coincidence of opposites.

Whatever their theology, many Japanese have betaken themselves to nature for peace of soul. On the way, they have faced many splendid vistas of mountains and seas, as well as many small-scaled beauties. In the Heian Shrine of Kyoto, for example, one comes upon a middle-sized pond with cherry trees along its bank and a wooden bridge crossing its center. Standing on the bridge, one notices loaves of bread for sale. The bread is for feeding the carp that have been bred to dazzling colors. Gold and red and multicolored, spotted and striped and waved, they churn the water and draw the eye. When the sun strikes their gorgeous scales, a kaleidoscope of colors flashes forth.

Is this merely another tourist attraction? Should one think of it as just a tour de force of marine biology? Or are the fish and all other things in the shrine beautiful to a purpose? Is the point that beauty, like music, soothes the savage breast, draws forth the deeper humanity latent in us all? Most religions have linked such latent humanity with theophanies: manifestations of the divine. Japan seems often to have linked them with what we might call *kalophanies*: manifestations of the beautiful. Indeed, much of Japanese esthetics has taken unsullied nature as its model. In fusing Chinese and native Shinto influences, gardens, flower arrangements, architectural ideals, and the like have married the esthetic and the religious.

Concerning Japanese gardens Robert S. Ellwood writes:

Virtually any album of the beauties of Japan will give prominent place to photographs of the traditional gardens of the island nation, especially those austere yet somehow unforgettable rock, moss, and gravel landscapes that are the pride of certain great Zen temples. Like most traditional arts of Japan, they have both aesthetic and spiritual meaning. Also like most tra-

ditional Japanese arts, they have two sources, native and Chinese.

The idea of a special set-apart place with gnarled old trees and large stones can be traced back to ancient Shinto. Though it is misleading to call Shinto "nature worship" as is often done—the kamis' role as patrons of clans and families was and is more important than their relation to particular natural phenomena—it is true that its shrines often hallow sites of great natural beauty. These are places where, for both spiritual and aesthetic reasons, one would come to breathe an atmosphere of purity and rejuvenation. Countless Japanese—and foreigners—have felt this atmosphere in the classic gardens of Zen temples and imperial villas.

The transition from outdoor shrine to Zen garden, however, required a massive infusion of Chinese culture. The Chinese garden, most faithfully reproduced in the landscaping of the Heian shinden, *endeavored to reproduce the islands and grottoes of the immortals of Taoist mythology or of the Buddhist Pure Land. The gardens were sited by geomancy and gave appropriate place to* yang *and* yin *elements. A high* yang *boulder was counterbalanced by a* yin *pond; lines were curved rather than straight; waterfalls were introduced to represent life and bamboo to symbolize strength.*[3]

Thus modern Japanese gardens and the modern Japanese approach to nature overall have tamed some of Shinto's preference for roughness.

SOCIETY

As Ellwood's reference to the place of the kami in clan life suggests, Japanese religion has also tended to invest the family line with a religious aura. The emperor, descended from the Goddess Amaterasu, originally was the head of the most powerful family, and most other Japanese traditionally have taken their identities from their past ancestors and present relatives. Generally, the group has predominated over the individual, and much of the individual's sense of honor and ethics has derived from a strong need not to disgrace the clan. In medieval times samurai warriors so fully submitted themselves to their lords that if they came into disfavor in the lord's eyes they usually would offer to commit suicide. In recent times the business corporation has taken on many attributes of a clan. For example, the corporation generally promises to care for the individual worker through both career and retirement, and the individual worker pledges strong loyalty to the corporation and submission to its overall needs.[4]

The basic unit in Japanese society has been the *ie*, or family household. Usually this is an extended family: The eldest son and his wife live with the son's parents, while younger sons set up branch houses nearby. When several such households develop, they constitute a larger family unit. This larger grouping of several *ie* usually celebrates the New Year together and cares for a family cemetery grounds. Ancestral tablets usually record the names of past family members in a Buddhist temple, but the family may also maintain a Shinto shrine. The larger family also will arrange suitable marriages for its young adults. Outside the whole system fall Japan's outcastes, many of whom perform works (such as slaughtering) offensive to traditional Buddhist sensibilities.[5]

The earliest strata of Japanese culture reflect a clan orientation. For example, the Kofun period (about 250–600 C.E.) takes its name from the large tombs built during its years. Like the Chinese, the Japanese have long venerated their ancestors and taken great pains to try to assure them a peaceful afterlife. One contemporary scholar understands this attitude as a basic strand in the weave of Japanese religion:

From the earliest records of human life, human beings have shown a religious attitude toward the dead, since they recognize the passage from earthly life to a form of spiritual existence. The early Japanese were no exception, for they practiced several types of burial. The first evidence of intentional burials is the simple burial of bodies in a flexed position or covered with red ochre and stones. During the Yayoi period [about 250 B.C.E. to 250 C.E.], the dead were interred in jars. This custom originated in Korea. Gradually the jars were covered with stone slabs (dolmen burial). This seems to have been the forerunner of the large mausoleums called kofun. *These tombs are often huge mounds covering a stone chamber, all of which is surrounded by a moat. Boat-shaped coffins of wood and stone in the tombs may have been for the voyage of the soul to the next world. In general, with the passage of time, there was an increasing concern for the ritual disposal of the dead: All these practices indicate religious passage to an afterlife. The transition to agriculture in Yayoi times probably led to a higher valuation of burial in the earth; the erection of tombs probably was the result of an abrupt intrusion from the Asian continent.*

How can we interpret all these concerns for the dead and afterlife? The initial Western scholarship on Japanese religion was confused in asking whether the origin of Japanese religion was ancestor worship or nature worship; there was also the confused controversy as to whether ancestor worship was truly indigenous to Japan or was a Chinese importation. But there is no single origin of Japanese religion. The evidence suggests that the Japanese people have always shown a reverent concern for the dead and that this concern has assumed diverse forms, not only in prehistoric but also in historic times. Much of the archeological evidence for understanding Japanese religion is found in burials, especially in the elaborate tomb burials of the Kofun period. In later periods the religious significance of the dead is expressed in Buddhist funeral and memorial services.[6]

For our interests in wisdom or sagacity, Japanese sociology underscores the religious importance of group solidarity. The funeral customs that prevailed in most historical periods served to keep individuals closely tied to the history of the clan. The Confucian mores that Japan adopted provided a strong reverence for parents, a tight organization of the extended family. Joined with the Shinto divinization of the emperor as a descendent of the Sun Goddess, this sociological intensity served to make the Japanese quite cohesive. Little notion of a melting pot infiltrated the ideals of Japanese culture. During most periods immigrants were resisted, foreigners kept at arms length. In fact, during the Tokugawa regime (1600–1868) Japan completely closed itself to Western influences. Despite intense missionary activity, it has remained quite content with its native traditions. True, a genius at adapting other people's ideas has made Japan a leading technological power. However, an intense love of its own land and traditions also has kept the Japanese well rooted and unified, even after the traumas of World War II.

SELF

If the Shinto and Confucian strands in Japanese culture made the individual subordinate to the clan or family, the Buddhist strands pushed the question of the self in the direction of ultimate reality. However, Buddhism has tended to conceive of the ultimate reality that gives the individual its meaning as empty: beyond all form or conditioning. This conviction emerges quite clearly in the following discussion by a contemporary Buddhist philosopher, Abe Masao:

Zen is also deeply concerned with the question "What am I?" asking it in a way peculiar to Zen, that is: "What is your original face before you were born?"

Science seeks for the origins of our existence in a temporal and horizontal sense—a dimension which can be pushed back endlessly. To find a definite answer to the question of our origin we must go beyond the horizontal dimension and turn to the vertical dimension, i.e., the eternal and religious dimension. Saint Paul once said, "For in him [the Son of God] all things were created . . . and in him all things hold together" (Col. 1:16–17). In Christianity it is through creation, as the eternal work of the only God, that all things hold together. Zen, however, raises a further question. It asks, "After all things are reduced to oneness, to what must the One be reduced?" Sunyata or nothingness in Zen is not a "nothing" out of which all things were created by God, but a "nothing" from which God himself emerged. According to Zen, we are not creatures of God, but manifestations of emptiness. The ground of my existence can and should not be found in the temporal dimension, not even in God. Although this groundlessness is deep enough to include even God, it is by no means something objectively observable. On the contrary, groundlessness, realized subjectively, is the only real ground of our existence. It is the ground to which we are "reconverted" or turned back by a negation of negation.[7]

Many of the dialogues between Zen masters and their disciples play out this Buddhist interest in the ground of the self. Of course, Buddhism finally says that there is no self, in the sense of a permanent personal identity. What makes any of us be recedes out of sight, is part and parcel of the overall no-thing-ness of the universe. Only when we sense our connection with this overall, most-basic reality will our "selfhood" come into clear focus. The empty character of the most basic reality will then soften our rigidities, loosen our graspings. At the edge of reason, going as far as the imagination can picture and the mind can conceptualize, Zen speaks of a groundless ground. We might, in Western terms, call this the ultimate Mystery of existence.

When we "come to ourselves," as the classical descriptions of conversion sometimes put it, we discover that our identities cannot be separated from the ultimate Mystery. But a true conversion, one that brings us into the heart of Buddhist wisdom, denies that the ultimate is negative. If we have only sensed the ultimate by pushing away the things that we experience, denying that the ultimate is like minerals, animals, vegetables, human beings, or anything else limited by space and time, we have gone but half the journey. We must also deny this sort of denial, negate this sort of negation. The ultimate that gives us our truest names is a groundless ground, a full emptiness, a present absence. It is ineffable, something we better apprehend by silence than speech.

We have encountered this sort of reasoning before, in our discussions of Nagarjuna. Japanese Buddhism, and through Japanese Buddhism Japanese culture as a whole, has used the negation of negation to rivet the question of the self on the here and now. One of the famous teaching stories that made this point was the parable of Yajnadatta.[8] Yajnadatta was a handsome young man who used to admire himself in the mirror each morning. One day, however, he looked into the mirror and found no one looking back, only a blank glass. His reaction was to think that he had lost his head. Terribly upset, he searched every corner of his house, sure that the missing head had to be behind the chair or under a mat. But his searches were to no avail. He was very worried, and so he had to ponder the meaning of his head very carefully. So doing, he finally realized that he was more the person who searched than the head being sought. Later it dawned on him that he had been looking at the back of the mirror, so of course he had seen no head reflected back to him. But from the time he focused on the source of his searching, he determined not to seek his identity or joy outside himself.

Zen makes this story a parable about the nature of personal reality. We will find who we are by searching the originating parts of our consciousness, not by searching among the data of sense or the objects we encounter in the outside world. If we persist in asking about our asking, trying to find who it is that raises these problems, thinks these thoughts, feels these feelings, we start on the path to enlightenment. As we progress, the coincidence of our personal identity with the ground, the empty basis, of all realities will become clearer and clearer. We cannot adequately define ourselves, know ourselves, appreciate ourselves apart from the emptiness or nirvana that gives us our selves. When we realize that who and what we are is a manifestation of emptiness, we shall drop all ego and distance from things as they truly are. In many times and places, this self-effacement has been a powerful Japanese ideal.

ULTIMATE REALITY

The various Japanese Buddhist schools placed different nuances on ultimate reality. For Zen Buddhists it was the groundless ground or inmost Buddhanature one best reached by meditation. For devotional schools the ultimate reality was a personification of Buddhan-

ature to whom one could pray as a child or a servant would. For philosophical schools it was the far side of the near-far reality that is both samsara and nirvana. Reasoning dialectically, most such schools imitated Nagarjuna in moving away from reifications. Last, imaginative schools such as Shingon took over the tantric tradition and used mandalas to symbolize the way to enlightenment.

Among the common people, shamanistic and Shinto notions filled the world with ghosts and spirits. Bodhisattvas and kami tended to run together, Shintoists speaking of the founders of the Buddhist sects as kami and Buddhists acknowledging the spiritual significance of clan heroes and striking natural sites. Most villagers attended many ceremonies to celebrate the clan, placate malign forces, and augment the forces of good. Amulets, shrines, and prayers all served a desire for protection, purity, and peace. Usually this popular religion was vivid and colorful.

Among the modern educated classes, the tradition has apparently become muted, expressing itself more in a sensitivity to natural beauty or social dislocation than in explicitly religious terms. The following description from a modern Japanese novel dramatizes such sensitivity:

He thought he could detect a dripping of dew from leaf to leaf. Then he heard the sound of the mountain. . . . The sound stopped, and he was suddenly afraid. A chill passed over him, as if he had been notified that death was approaching. He wanted to question himself, calmly and deliberately, to ask whether it had been the sound of the wind, the sound of the sea, or a sound in his ears. But he had heard no such sound, he was sure. He had heard the mountain. It was as if a demon had passed, making the mountain sound out.[9]

The middle-aged man who has these sensations and thoughts is full of a deep dread. As though he can find no center, no keystone to hold his arch, he fears an unknown void, an unknown greater reality, that seems capable of seizing him at any time. The mountain is what is should be, a simple mound of earth. But it refuses to be just that. In the dead of night it gives out warnings, soundings, moanings. The man trembles before such communications. The last thing he wants is a world full of dark mysteries, a constant reminder of his mortality. Yet another part of him is fascinated by the intimations he receives. Even though they seem more threatening than soothing, they make his life interesting and keep his spirit alert. It is hard to say how typical of traditional Japanese culture these feel-

*Figure 14   Torii (sacred gateway) to National Shinto Shrine at Ise.
Photo by J. T. Carmody.*

ings are. Probably the trauma of World War II, which is never explicitly mentioned but always lies just under the surface, shapes them significantly. Still, they depend on the traditional Japanese discipline that has attuned generations to the slightest movement in their natural environment. And they are of a piece with the long Japanese traditions of lovely gardens, hallowed ceremonies, and appreciation of pottery or painting.

The Japanese ultimate reality supported the clan structure, urged the individual to find harmony with nature, and made nature a privileged form of its presence. However, it also overspilled these sociological, psychological, and ecological categories, taking form in the 800,000 Shinto gods, crooking a finger in the 800,000 hints the sensitive person received of an otherness both dreadful and fascinating. Normally, such otherness has not been physically remote. Apart from the tendency of devotional Buddhists to picture a Pure Land, most Japanese religionists have riveted the ultimate onto proximate, this-worldly realities. Thus it has whispered in weird moments when mountains rumbled, comforted in quiet times of unexpected peace.

A peculiar emptiness, no doubt much shaped by Buddhist convictions, has hollowed the Japanese psyche. Thus the disquiet and sadness of the man troubled by the mountain seems quite revealing, at least in the context of modern Japan. In Japan as well as China, the Taoist tradition of retirement has offered a counterweight to Confucian business. In the retirement of a garden or a floral arrangement, the modern Japanese man or woman might ponder a bittersweet sense that very old ways were suffering serious assault. The beauty of these old ways kept them sweet. A mere look in the garden, smell of the flowers, confirmed their rightness. But their vulnerability to the rush and pollution of modern times made their contemplation sad. Under such heat they were almost sure to wilt. So having worried in the dead of night about the rumbles of his mountain, the man goes on to remember a recent conversation with a geisha. She had told him she planned to commit suicide, and he could see again the packets of poison she had laid on the table.

YASUNARI KAWABATA

The man who wrote *The Sound of the Mountain* himself committed suicide in 1972. This was but four years after he had received the Nobel Prize for Literature, a writer's greatest honor. Apparently Yasunari Kawabata felt he could no longer go on. The encroachment of old age, or the confusions of the times, or his own sense of honor determined that it was time to end his journey. His striking novels somewhat portend such a finish. Consistently they brood about the disconnections among people, the many ways the times are out of joint. But they also convey a wonderful appreciation of the Japanese cultural tradition, rich in esthetics, keen as a knife about honor. The tradition that formed Yasunari Kawabata proposed that life should be an art form. One was to expect little, to try to do much. If the mind was alert and the spirit well trained, any of the traditional Japanese disciplines might mold a strong, impressive personality.

Among such traditional disciplines was the game of *Go*, a complicated board-game on the order of chess. Kawabata has depicted the demise of the last great master of Go, in whom the fusion of art and life may have achieved its last masterpiece:

It may be said that the Master was plagued in his last match by modern rationalism, to which fussy rules were everything, from which all the grace and elegance of Go as art had disappeared, which quite dispensed with respect for elders and attached no importance to mutual respect as human beings. From the way of Go the beauty of Japan and the Orient had fled. Everything had become science and regulation. The road to advancement in rank, which controlled the life of a player, had become a meticulous point system. One conducted the battle only to win, and there was no margin for remembering the dignity and the fragrance of Go as an art. The modern way was to insist upon doing battle under conditions of abstract justice, even when challenging the Master himself. The fault was not Otake's [the challenger's]. Perhaps what had happened was but natural, Go being a contest and show of strength.

In more than thirty years the Master had not played Black [moved first]. He was first among them all, and brooked no second. During his lifetime no one among his juniors advanced as far as the Eighth Rank. All through the epoch that was his own he kept the opposition under control, and there was no one whose rank could carry across the gap to the next age. The fact that today, a decade after the Master's death, no method has been devised for determining the succes-

sion to the title Master of Go probably has to do with the towering presence of Honnimbo Shusai. Probably he was the last of the true masters revered in the tradition of Go as a way of life and art.[10]

Of the several striking passages in this quotation perhaps the most significant is: "From the way of Go the beauty of Japan and the Orient had fled." The *way* of Go clearly was more than a game, let alone a secular profession. It was a method for organizing one's life, tempering one's spirit, becoming the refined yet powerful personality the tradition idealized. Above all, Go had been a thing of beauty, a discipline conducing to grace, intelligence, and strong character.

The Master totters and cannot follow through. At sixty-four he no longer has the strength to ward off the new generation. But the reader senses that the opponent (Otake) across from him, for all his personal brilliance, is but an instrument of the new times. The Master has had the misfortune to fall into a chasm of history. The end of his era points to the beginning of a new age, but there are large cracks between the two epochs.

Although Kawabata acknowledges the arrogance and injustice in the old regime of Masters such as Shusai, his sympathies obviously lie with the past. In the past, Go and other such elegant arts were practiced mainly for their own sake. Around them grew up an etiquette, a protocol, both grave and lovely. *How* one did things was as important as *what* one did. Being was more important than doing, doing well more important than achieving much. And so the old regime encouraged excellence, a full-bodied immersion in Go that could make one's person and game style unique. The reader suspects that the other disciplines Japan has nurtured as "ways"—the martial arts, the tea ceremony, swordsmanship, archery, flower arrangement, and the rest—used to partake of the same rationale. Even without the competitive dimension of Go, they came most alive when one invested in them a whole self, tried to fuse one inmost soul with their serious, exacting demands.

The picture of Yasunari Kawabata on the back of *The Master of Go* suggests a man who tried to live the high esthetic that shapes so many of his novels. The face is almost solemn. A shock of white hair caps a high forehead. Strong brows and black eyes challenge the spectator. The lips are closed, almost pursed. One's main impression is of a dignified strength. The eyes suggest an arrogant youth. The visage in older age stays just this side of arrogance, reined in by regret and realism. Kawabata is not a man one would approach lightly. Fools and babblers quickly would get the gate. But he is a man from whom one might learn much about Japanese mastery. He is an aesthetic sage, a person wise in the ways of beauty and sadness.[11]

SUMMARY

The roots of Japanese wisdom lie in the earliest Shinto chronicles, whose written form derives from the eighth century c.e. There primal myths such as the story of Izanagi and Izanami told the Japanese people that the origin of their lovely islands was divine and the gods had organized the traditional social relations purposefully. The kami were the dominant forces in traditional Japanese religion, shaping both a deep veneration of nature and a strong clan allegiance. In the stories of Amaterasu and Susanoo, one sees an ancient attempt to depict the balance of nature's forces and objectify the human psyche's inner tensions. Stories about the origin of the imperial shrine at Ise illustrate a strong desire to root Shinto piety in divine commands, as the reports of pilgrims to Shinto shrines suggest the emotional appeal of the Japanese ideals of purity and harmony with nature.

Nature has been a central interest throughout Japanese religious history. The 800,000 gods of Shinto suggest the spread of divinity through nature as well as society; the many lovely Japanese shrines show the fusion of a naturalistic piety with an esthetic demand for beauty. From both native and Chinese influences, the Japanese have made gardens, pools, grottoes, and other naturalistic settings the privileged foci of their religion. Along with the intensely clannish structure of Japanese society, nature has placed the individual in a wide field and discouraged excessive self-concern. Japanese burial customs have formed people in the same direction, reminding them that the clan stretches far back into the past. To preserve the honor of the clan, prove oneself worthy of one's elders and ancestors, has stood high on the list of societal motivations.

Perhaps Zen has most dramatically attacked the problem of the self. Spotlighting the originating force in our lives, the one who asks the many questions preoccupying us, Zen has taught the Japanese to sense the emptiness in which all individual selves stand. As the parable of Yajnadatta suggests, as long as we seek peace or self-understanding in externals, we are like people who have lost their heads. Only the groundless ground within us can reveal the faces we had before our parents were born. This groundless ground has been one of Japan's deepest intuitions about ultimate reality, but other intuitions have also left their stamp. In addition to the Shinto desire to multiply the divine presences, Buddhist schools other than Zen have stressed devotional, imaginative, and intellectual aspects of Buddhanature. As well, shamanistic strands and folk religion have populated the world with ghosts and varied spirits.

Among the modern educated classes, a haunting sense that ultimate reality can rumble ominously has sobered many sensitive psyches. As masterfully displayed in the novels of Yasunari Kawabata, modern Japanese culture stands alienated from its estheticoreligious traditions, imbued with a great sense of loss. Kawabata felt that the disciplined ways that had served so many so well were sure to fall victim to modern technology and bustle. The ascendancy of the old masters was at an end, and it had not yet appeared what new wisdom might take their place.

STUDY QUESTIONS

1. What is the psychological significance of Susanoo?

2. Explain the purity that dominates the pilgrim's recollections of Ise.

3. How has Japan related the beautiful and the holy?

4. What do Japanese burial customs say about the sociology of Japanese religion?

5. Who is the "I" looking for its lost head?

6. What might traditional Japanese religion tell people about the sound of the mountain?

7. How could a game such as Go focus Japanese religious ideals?

NOTES

1. Nihongi, I: 40–45; in Ryusaku Tsunoda et al., eds., *Sources of Japanese Tradition*, vol. 1. New York: Columbia University Press, 1964, p. 27.

2. A. L. Sadler, *The Ise Daijingu Sankeiki or Diary of a Pilgrim to Ise*, quoted in H. Byron Earhart, ed., *Religion in Japanese Experience*. Encino, Calif.: Dickenson, 1974, pp. 25–26.

3. Robert S. Ellwood, Jr., *An Invitation to Japanese Civilization*. Belmont, Calif.: Wadsworth, 1980, pp. 120–21.

4. See William Ouchi, *Theory Z*. Reading, Mass.: Addison-Wesley, 1981.

5. See Ellwood, *An Invitation*, pp. 23–24.

6. H. Byron Earhart, *Japanese Religion: Unity and Diversity*, 3d ed. Belmont, Calif.: Wadsworth, 1982, p. 25.

7. Abe Masao, "God, Emptiness, and the True Self," in Frederick Franck, ed., *The Buddha Eye*. New York: Crossroad, 1982, pp. 71–72.

8. Ibid., p. 72.

9. Yasunari Kawabata, *The Sound of the Mountain*. Tokyo: Tuttle, 1971, p. 8.

10. Yasunari Kawabata, *The Master of Go*. Tokyo: Tuttle, 1973, pp. 52–53.

11. See Yasunari Kawabata, *Beauty and Sadness*. Tokyo: Tuttle, 1975.

15

Greek Rationalism

Homer
Socrates
Plato
Aristotle
Nature
Society
Self
Ultimate Reality
Einstein
Summary
Study Questions
Notes

HOMER

Biblical revelation and Greek philosophy are two of the main pillars by which Western culture has long stood. Insofar as biblical revelation and Greek philosophy have become transformed into Marxist politics and Einsteinian science, they have recently become two of the main waves of the global culture we can see advancing on the horizon. To be sure, it is some distance from the biblical prophets to Marx, from Aristotle to Einstein. Nonetheless, there would have been no Marx without Amos, no Einstein without Aristotle. In the present chapter we study the religious aspects of the Greek rationalism that has long undergirded Western politics and science. That rationalism never dominated Greek religion, moved outside of Greece, and underwent many changes, but much of its religious import stands clear in its classical origins. As they pondered the significance of their discovery of *mind*, the

Greeks opened the door to the later Western sense that the Creator has a special presence in human reason and guarantees the world an intelligible order.[1]

The first great deposit to the Greek account of reason was made by Homer. Indeed, for the Greek philosophers and political scientists who followed him, Homer was much like the Shinto Chronicles: a collection of the earliest sapiential lore. Little in the *Iliad* or the *Odyssey* escaped later criticism, but overall these epics served as a common cultural foundation. In Eric Voegelin's reading, the Homeric epics focus on the causes of cultural decline:

The epics are not concerned with causes and effects on the level of pragmatic history but with the phenomenon of decline itself. The Homeric society is disordered inasmuch as on decisive occasions the conduct of its members is guided by passion rather than by reason and the common good. The blinding through passion, the ate, *is not the cause of disorder, it is the disorder itself. Something is badly wrong with the leading Homeric characters; and under one aspect, therefore, the* Iliad *is a study in the pathology of heroes.*[2]

For Socrates, Plato, Aristotle, and much of later Christian reflection, the pathology of all human beings, peasants as well as heroes, was a central concern. Why did human beings let themselves be led by passion rather than reason? How could they ignore the common good for the sake of personal trifles? The Greek discovery of mind was not at all a denial of emotion, an excision of passion. Traditional Greek wisdom was well aware that full human vitality demands the marriage of reason and passion. The question, though, was which partner would predominate. Were reason not to rule, the household would surely come to grief. So from its earliest ruminations on the causes of wars and disorders, the Greek tradition spotlighted the vagaries of passion. And in the light of that focus it became increasingly clear that the first mastery wisdom required was mastery of oneself. The voice of the Delphic oracle that declaimed "Know Thyself" was but a main singer in a Pan-Hellenic chorus. One had to know oneself in order to master oneself. No lover of wisdom could be a plaything of his or her passions.

In this context, an abiding Greek interest from the time of Homer was the phenomenon of knowledge. How does it come about that we see the light, find our way disclosed? The development of Greek epistemology took the form of a progressive sophistication:

On a first level there was the literary revelation of man to himself. Homeric simile drew on the characteristics of inanimate nature and of plants and animals to illuminate and objectify and distinguish the varied springs of action in the epic heroes. The lyric poets worked out expressions of personal human feeling. The tragedians exhibited human decisions, their conflicts and interplay, and their consequences. Within the literary tradition there occured reflection on knowledge. For Homer, knowledge comes by perception or by hearsay. Man's knowledge is always partial and incomplete. But the Muses are omnipresent. They perceive everything. They are the ones that enable the bard to sing as if he had been present or as if he had heard the tale from an eyewitness. But for Hesiod the Muses do not inspire but teach; and they are far less trustworthy than Homer claimed. They may teach the truth but they may teach plausible falsehood. They singled Hesiod out on Mount Helicon and taught him not to repeat the folly and lies of his predecessors but to tell the truth about the struggle in which man ekes out his livelihood.[3]

Parallel to this sophistication was a purification of the Homeric gods. As Hesiod, Xenophanes, Hecataeus, and the other post-Homerians made progress, the passionate excesses of Zeus and the other Olympian gods became less and less acceptable.

SOCRATES

Socrates (470?–399 B.C.E.) was the figure who changed Greek religion decisively, by dying for his convictions about the truth. In Plato's dialogue the *Apology* the case of Socrates moves at three different levels. First, there is a report of the trial at which Socrates was condemned to death for impiety. Second, there is the deeper meaning of this trial, which is that Athens has shown itself unworthy of the man who might have been its savior. Third, there is the paradox of Socrates' going to his physical death because of his surpassing spiritual life.

The report of the trial features Socrates' defense, in which he refutes the charge of impiety by arguing that his whole life has been a mission to reform the disorder of the Athenian city-state by the inspiration of the god of Delphi. If his life's work has been a religious mission, how can any fair assessment find him impious? His method in carrying out his mission has been simply to question the wisdom that others claim to possess. An inner voice has always steered him away from prideful or irreligious actions, and this voice has never told him to desist from questioning the opinions of other people. It has, however, kept him from seeking to bring the city-state to order by winning political office. Indeed, he would have been dead long ago had he gained political office, since the other officeholders have been so corrupt they would never have suffered someone who would have refused to cooperate with their crimes. What an irony: that the only man who consistently obeyed a divine counsel should be on trial for irreligion!

Of the 500 jurors, 281 voted for Socrates' conviction, so legally his defense failed. Probably he had offended too many powerful people for it to have been otherwise. When the Oracle had proclaimed him the wisest man in Athens, he had been puzzled. He knew that he understood very little. Then it dawned on him that minimal wisdom was realizing one did not know very much. In fact, compared to those who think they know much but actually know little, to know one does not know would be a mark of rare distinction. Socrates was well aware that his willingness to show other people their ignorance had often upset them badly. Thus the verdict of guilty can have come as no surprise to him. But as he had felt it necessary to defend the integrity of his life, the rightness of his obedience to the gods, so he felt it necessary in the second part of his trial to argue that he should receive the highest honors the city-state could bestow on a faithful citizen, rather than the death penalty. In making this case Socrates proceeds calmly, detached from the clash of passions on the human level, almost amused by the ironies of the situation:

Well, what penalty do I deserve to pay or suffer, in view of what I have done? I have never lived an ordinary quiet life. I did not care for the things that most people care about—making money, having a comfortable home, high military or civil rank, and all the other activities, political appointments, secret societies, party organizations, which go on in our city. I thought that I was really too strict in my principles to survive if I went in for this sort of thing. So instead of taking a course which would have done no good either to you or to me, I set myself to do you individually in private what I hold to be the greatest possible service. I tried to persuade each of you not to think more of practical advantages than of his mental and moral well-being, or in general to think more of advantage than of well-being in the case of the state or of anything else. What do I deserve for behaving in this way? Some reward, gentlemen, if I am bound to suggest what I really deserve, and what is more, a reward which would be appropriate for myself. Well, what is appropriate for a poor man who is a public benefactor and who requires leisure for giving you moral encouragement? Nothing could be more appropriate for such a person than free maintenance at the state's expense.[4]

This somewhat ironic proposal, along with Socrates' second suggestion (that he pay an insignificant fine), is rejected and the death penalty imposed. On the way to his death, Socrates faces his jurors with the consequences of their action. They will be known as the people who condemned Socrates. Now they and he come to a parting of the ways. He goes to die while they continue to live. The implication is that the true lover of wisdom always has before him or her the prospect of death. Living with death in mind, true philosophers feel a salutary pressure to make all their thoughts and actions able to withstand death's assessment. Only the freedom from human opinions that nearness to death provides can keep one faithful to the philosophic vocation.

Moreover, at the judgment bar of death verdicts often turn over. Then "dying" may appear to be living without reflection, as the majority of people do. Then "living" may appear to be the following one's conscience whatever the outcome, in hope that the light of conscience will prove divine and so immortal. Thus Socrates can honestly tell his jurors that he cannot say whose fate is better. Only the gods know whether his dying for conscience is better or worse than his jurors' living after their condemnation of him.

In Socrates, the pregnant theme that the individual conscience is the site of God-given wisdom gave birth to a new morality. Ever after, the love of wisdom whispered to the West that death was the only vantage point for judging the worth of a life, the guiding voice of one's god the only ruler deserving full obedience.

PLATO

Through his various dialogues, Plato pursued the implications of the life and teachings of Socrates. Among the most crucial of these implications is the **conversion** that wisdom requires. To portray such conversion concretely, Plato uses a parable about people imprisoned in the darkness of a cave. To them any talk of a realm of light will seem foolish. So it is with the life of the spirit, the life of spiritual light. To people mired in merely sensual knowledge, living deep in the pit of their passions, the values of the lover of wisdom will seem pure folly. The idea of the good, which dominates the ethics of the lover of wisdom, is beyond the appreciation of those who live mainly by their senses. Still, the idea of the good is worth the struggle to attain it, for its attainment brings into focus the full range of reality.

Plato's conclusion to the main theme of the parable runs as follows:

This image, then, dear Glaucon, we must apply as a whole to all that has been said, likening the region revealed through sight to the habituation of the prison, and the light of the fire in it to the power of the sun. And if you assume that the ascent and the contemplation of the things above is the soul's ascent to the intelligible region, you will not miss my surmise, since that is what you desire to hear. But God knows whether it is true. But, at any rate, my dream as it appears to me is that in the region of the known the last thing to be seen and hardly seen is the idea of good, and that when seen it must needs point us to the conclusion that this is indeed the cause for all things, of all that is right and beautiful, giving birth in the visible world to light, and the author of light and itself in the intelligible world being the authentic source of truth and reason, and that anyone who is to act wisely in private or public must have caught sight of this.[5]

Several points in the quotation are worth noting. First, there is the Platonic sense that the love of wisdom involves the ascent of the soul to an intelligible region above the level of sense life. Second is the dominant Platonic symbolism of light. In its ascent, the soul pursues the light, seeks the dawn of truth that will make reality clear. Third, the ethical cast of Plato's thought shows in the character of the idea that he finds shedding the greatest light: the idea of the good. When people pursue the truly good, their souls open to the spiritual light that gives order and fulfillment. Without the pursuit of the good, the soul's passionate desire for goodness, the light of wisdom will never shine.

As Plato's meditations on goodness, light, and order grew richer, a philosophy of history developed. The philosopher's vocation is to open the soul to reality and thereby show history its god-given shape. The shape of history is an In-Between. Human knowledge of time's story moves between the poles of the divine One, the mind at the top of consciousness, and the Unlimited of prime matter at the bottom. Beyond either the One or the Unlimited, human beings are not competent to go. The greatest human achievement is to open oneself to the luminosity that the divine gives in time for time's direction. The meaning of history takes shape only when people see that advance is greater awareness of the divine light, and regress is lesser awareness. Such awareness comes through the converse, the dialogue, that the human spirit can have with its divine ground. When the human spirit becomes aware of being moved by the divine, being enlightened by the divine, it has the chance to realize the proper structure of its life. Then it will neither aspire to the power and knowledge of divinity nor despair before the impenetrability of the Unlimited.

The value of this grasp of the field of human knowledge as an In-Between becomes clearer when one knows the history of human beings' attempts to situate themselves in the world. In that history there are two main ways of coming to grief. Most frequently, human beings despair of gaining a firm hold on "reality," because of the overwhelming number of things "reality" seems to contain. Situating themselves close to the Unlimited, near the bottom pole of their consciousnesses, the majority fall into a careless relativism. To them it doesn't matter what opinion about reality they follow, since no opinion accounts for the whole better than another. Less frequently, people err in the other direction, fixating on the upper pole of the One and thinking they have clear access to the divine mind. In that case the whole of history becomes falsely simple; no mystery remains. From there it is a short step to trying to eliminate whatever does not fit one's simplistic (but supposedly divinely sanctioned) vision. The

great butchers who have murdered millions in the name of such visions show the diabolical dangers of excess at the top. Excess at the bottom is the sensual immersion of the people in the cave, unaware of the light at the top of their minds. Their sins are usually smaller, but collectively they produce the great inertia that keeps human progress, human awareness of the meaning of history, so retarded.

The In-Between is the postion of delicate balance. This stance reconciles the knowledge that divine light is the core of being human with the realization that the inreach of the divine light does not make human beings God. The human vocation is merely to follow the light, to try to aid the light's wider and deeper diffusion. Doing this, one learns that the light finally is too bright for human comprehension. Then it is clear that the full meaning of history recedes from sight, resting in a divine Mind human beings will never plumb.

ARISTOTLE

By the end of Plato's career, the classical Greek understanding of reason was well formed.[6] The In-Between amounted to a balanced position, in which human materiality and human spirituality both received their due. Aristotle further refined this balance, bringing the classical Greek achievement to a high polish. In epistemology, metaphysics, and ethics, he found wisdom to be a golden mean, virtue to stand in the middle.

Aristotle's epistemology pivoted on the act of understanding. Realizing that understanding is an interaction of sensation and intellection, he stressed the grasp of form in *phantasms*. By this image he meant that our understanding is a matter of seeing the point in diagrams, images, or symbols. Take the number series 2, 4, 8, 6, 3, 5, 10, 8, __. Assume it has a pattern. When you grasp the pattern, you know the form or intelligibility that makes the matter (the previously random numbers) an ordered whole. Then, expressing this grasp, you have the concept or formula that allows you to predict the future numbers in the series. The formula is $+ 2 \times 2 - 2 \div 2$. The blank number therefore is 4. The next batch of numbers would be 6, 12, 10, 5. When you understand this, or any other problem, your matter and spirit cooperate to render the matter and spirit (form, intelligibility) of reality itself.

So much for a small sample of the Aristotelian the

ory of knowledge and metaphysics. Both find a duality in the human being's self and world. One could say that the hinge of the duality is the act of knowing, in which spirit sheds light on matter. Then Aristotle would focus the range of Plato's In-Between, from the One above to the Unlimited below, at the central area where the light ultimately derived from the One gives some illumination of the many derived from the unlimited. For example, the light or significance of the originally discrete numbers, which becomes apparent in the flash of understanding their pattern, brings their multiplicity into a kind of unity. One could in theory deal with thousands of such numbers through the single formula.

This view suggests that the reality most proportioned to human beings is sense-oriented, since our knowing begins with sensation. But we human beings have a drive to go beyond sensible multiplicity. We are more than our sensation. Because of our participation in the divine light, we can grasp the unities of material multiplicities. We can even move beyond matter to think about immaterial realities: beauty, being, God.

In ethical matters Aristotle argued that virtue means doing what is reasonable. Broken down, this position entailed contemplation of unchangeable truths and the art, developed through experience, of applying unchangable truths to particular circumstances. Somewhat as Plato did, Aristotle emphasized the part of human beings that is drawn to the light. But Aristotle described contemplation of truth in the context of the natural world, rather than apart in a realm of its own. Still, there is seldom any doubt that the reasonable or lightsome part is Aristotle's favorite. The best virtues are intellectual and the highest activity is the contemplation of immaterial, unchanging truths:

> *The wholly rational part of the soul is the province of "intellectual virtue," and it is itself twofold inasmuch as one part of it is concerned with the contemplation of unchangeable truths and the other with truths and objects which are subject to change. The virtue of the first part is* sophia, *or theoretical wisdom, and that of the second is* phronesis, *or practical wisdom. It is* phronesis *which discovers what is right in action and so makes it possible for desires to conform to reason by discovering ends and then relating means to ends. But the ultimate end for man, which is living well (*eudaimonia*), is not a matter of deliberation or choice—it is, rather, something given in the nature of man. This is something which could vary, although it is clear that Aristotle does not suppose that in fact it does vary. The highest of the virtues is, however, theoretical wisdom, and this is an activity of which man is capable*

> *because of something divine in his nature—in its exercise he approximates to the life of God; and for man, as for God, his highest function is thought. This thought will be about objects which cannot be other than they are and so never change.*[7]

This description stresses the upper pole of Aristotle's thought, the divine light in us. The lower pole receives more emphasis in Aristotle's treatises on natural science. Overall, the ethical position is similar to Plato's. Human beings receive their order, their proper way of living, by letting reason predominate over—and direct—sensation and desire. Reason is the most divine part of human nature. Indeed, reason is the light of the Divine Mind flashing in limited beings. The greatest good is to enlarge the power and the province of this light. Thus the best life is that of *theoria* (contemplation), which maximizes one's study of the eternal reasons that give the world its shape. Still, Aristotle never denies the material fundament that even theoria depends upon. However rational, human beings remain animals, intrinsically dependent upon matter. The great struggle in human maturation is so to discipline one's passions and sensations that they serve one's rational ends. The mature, reasonable person is not a caricature, not a being with only a head, but an integrated, graceful whole of matter directed by spirit. Such a well-matured personality is like a great work of art, its materials perfectly expressing the idea or form its maker had in mind when fashioning it.

NATURE

The Aristotelian scheme described nature in terms of **hylomorphism**: a fusion of matter and form. As material, it was proportioned to our animality, available through our senses. As formed, it bore an intelligibility that patient study might grasp. Aristotle thought that all human beings naturally desire to know. To be human is to wonder, question, probe. In fact, the unexamined life is not worth living. Not to think, to raise one's sights toward the unchanging reasons of things, is to default on one's very construction. So Aristotle himself took the whole world for his province of study. What we today call physics, biology, mathematics, political science, aesthetics, logic, and philosophy all came under his scrutiny. However, perhaps his most potent contribution in the realm of natural science came through his logical works. By perfecting the syllogism he gave reasoning a sharper precision than previously it had had. Aristotle did not appreciate the random, statistical dimension of nature. He did not grasp the novelty of historical situations nor the full significance of the contingent (nonnecessary) act of existence. But the power of his reasoning entered the treasury of Western methodology, furnishing later natural science with an ideal of strict inference from the patterns of sensible data.

Overall, classical Greek culture tended to think of nature as eternal and cyclic. The pre-Socratic philosophers who probed the constitution of nature anticipated some of Aristotle's stress on form or intelligibility. Pythagoras, in fact, thought that all natural entities were ruled by numbers. This rational strain of high Greek culture stood at some remove from the mentality of most of the populace, for whom nature was full of spirits, so that the personification of gods of the sea and the storm made good sense. Insofar as nature seemed to be a realm of corruption, always changing and decaying, many Greeks yearned for a freedom from material nature, an afterlife purely spiritual. Thus the notion of an immaterial, immortal soul gained considerable currency. Not only was the immortality of the soul a tenet of Plato and Aristotle, but it also influenced the Greek **mystery religions**, many of whose rites were designed to convince members they were destined for a blissful afterlife as freed spiritual beings.

Among the Stoic philosophers who followed Plato and Aristotle, natural law was a major interest. Such philosophers speculated that human beings might have laws much like those that govern rocks, trees, and cows to guide their behavior. The Stoics' reasonings about such laws tended to be abstract and general, but they did advance the classical confidence that reason can find the final, efficient, material, and formal causes of beings and thus determine much of their nature.

By *final causes* the Greek tradition meant the ends for which a being or action labors. In constructing a house, the end would be the goal that the builders, architects, and prospective owners intend: the completed mansion or shack. The good of such completed products is the reason why constructions are undertaken. Analogously, people marry in order to share life and produce children, people run schools in order to turn out educated students, people write books in order to put their ideas into available form. One could add further ends or final causes (money, fame, keeping busy) to any of these processes, but the multiplicity of such ends does not detract from the value of analyzing a process in terms of its final cause(s).

Indeed, Aristotle said that the final cause is the first in the order of causation, implying that the most important thing one can know about a process is the goal it has in mind. The *efficient cause*—the one who puts the process in motion (the sculptor swinging the chisel, the contractor directing the building)—takes aim from the final cause; the stuff from which the construct is to be made (*material cause*) and the shape in which it is to be cast (*formal cause*) mediate between the final and the efficient causes.

Obviously this scheme of causation suffers serious limitations, not the least of which is a heavy dependence on the model of rational human proceeding. Still, it helped the Greeks launch a careful study of natural processes, and it slowly revealed, through the Christian Middle Ages, the need for more empirical and mathematical methods. Throughout it kept the processes of the human mind in close connection with the processes of nature, tending to project nature as the material work of a divine mind filled with ends and forms. Some philosophers and historians of science have argued that Christian revelation added a more coherent rationale for scientific study, since its notion of a purposeful Creator God bolstered the confidence of scientists that nature did indeed run in intelligible patterns,[8] but this argument need not deny the classical Greek contribution.

The legacy of the classical Greek wisdom regarding nature reposes in its stress on intelligibility. Greek experience suggested that the human mind is isomorphic to natural reality: so patterned to nature that nature yields sense to those who probe it carefully. As well, those who conjecture about nature, proposing creative hypotheses about its construction, may well find their bright ideas verified. It is worth a chance. The power of the human mind should not be underestimated. Western science drew a great deal of its motivation and form from these Greek attitudes.

SOCIETY

The classical Greek philosophers gave politics a high status. Plato's *Laws* and *Republic* are major treatises on politics, and they comprise about 40 percent of the Platonic corpus. Aristotle's *Nicomachean Ethics*, a foundational text in the West, put reason to work on the problem of social order, producing such apparently dry but actually explosive paragraphs as this:

If then, there is some end of the things we do, which we desire for its own sake (everything else being desired for the sake of this), and if we do not choose everything for the sake of something else (for at that rate the process would go on to infinity, so that our desire would be empty and vain), clearly this must be the good and the chief good. Will not the knowledge of it, then, have a great influence on life? Shall we not, like archers who have a great mark to aim at, be more likely to hit upon what is right? If so, we must try, in outline at least to determine what it is, and of which of the sciences or capacities it is the object. It would seem to belong to the most authoritative art and that which is most truly the master art. And politics appears to be of this nature; for it is this that ordains which of the sciences should be studied in a state, and which each class of citizens should learn and up to what point they should learn them; and we see even the most highly esteemed of capacities to fall under this, e.g. strategy, economics, rhetoric; now, since politics uses the rest of the sciences, and since, again, it legislates as to what we are to do and what we are to abstain from, the end of this science must include those of the others, so that this end must be the good for man. For even if the end is the same for a single man and for a state, that of the state seems at all events something greater and more complete, whether to attain or to preserve; though it is worth while to attain the end merely for one man, it is finer and more godlike to attain it for a nation or for city-states. These, then, are the ends at which our inquiry aims, since it is political science, in one sense of that term.[9]

The end of things we do is their final cause: the good that they, or we using them, seek to bring about. But in human affairs there must be some chief, ultimate good that grounds the whole process. Otherwise human affairs would be an endless chain of things dependent on other things, a process with no ground or final meaning. Knowing this chief good would enable us to set the whole of life in order. For Aristotle such knowledge is political science. When politics takes aim at the overall good of society, it reaches for a worldview that might coordinate all other human knowledge: economics, rhetoric, and the rest.

Clearly, this is a view of politics that largely has passed from the modern scene. Modern politics tends to doubt that there is any final, ordering good; in practice it prescinds from long-range, philosophical questions. In its defense modern politics could point out that the classical Greek political science easily might become thought control, and that such political science reflects the stratified society of fourth century B.C.E. Athens, in which many were slaves and only a few participated in civic affairs. Moreover, modern politics might note in the paragraph a rather jumbled logic that seems to assume, rather than demonstrate, that politics is "the most authoritative art" and that never says clearly what the overarching, directive good

actually is. However, the disarray of modern politics argues that the rational schemes of the classical Greeks at least deserve a hearing.

As we shall see in the next section, the classical Greek view of society often assumes that the city-state (**polis**) is but the individual writ large. Were a state to order itself by reason, as a strong individual does, it would surely come to good health. Thus Plato dreamed of a philosopher-king, who might unite wisdom and power. Thus most who read Plato and Aristotle carefully store away a fond hope that one day a long-range, unemotional understanding of the true nature and goods of social existence may dominate their leaders. Insofar as modern political science, both Liberal (individualistic) and Marxist (socialistic), has lost the classical Greek appreciation of contemplative reason, it has offered the world only a truncated view of what social life ought to be.[10] Moreover, it has left the contemporary world nearly defenseless against the storms of words, the uncontrolled rhetoric, that buffet today's citizens.

Doris Lessing makes this last point throughout her many-volumed *Canopus in Argos*, a work that has the appearance of science fiction but in substance is a long meditation on political science. A major theme in Volume 5 is the difficulty reason has making itself heard amidst the clamor of emotional outbursts. What Klorothy, the representative of a rational regime sent to observe an emotional regime, says to his superior, Johor, could come straight from Plato or Aristotle:

Is it possible, Johor, that we sometimes tend—I put it no stronger than that—to overestimate the forces of reason? . . . I must tell you that I was affected myself [by the fervent rhetoric]. Oh, how small and meagre and pitiful suddenly seemed to me all our efforts, above all our language, so cool and measured and chosen. *I saw myself as, I knew, those miners saw me at that moment: a figure apart from them, their lives, their efforts, an alien figure sitting quietly on a bench, indifferent and passionless.*[11]

SELF

The person wise by Greek standards finds many occasions for such ironic musings. Sweet reason so seldom rules public affairs that those who believe in reason's therapies find themselves the most frustrated of physicians. Thus they either develop a strong sense of humor or they risk despair at life's tragic flaws. The Greek tradition did tend to find life tragic, as the clas-

Figure 15   The Parthenon, remains of a prime symbol of Athens' golden age. Photo by J. T. Carmody.

sical dramas suggest. But the greatest Greek tragedians and philosophers found strong counterweights to despair in their very experiences of reason.

Because human beings can recognize that they are irrational, they can learn to be rational. As long as the light shines in the darkness, darkness does not completely vanquish human hopes. This is true both epistemologically (in terms of the theory of knowledge) and ethically. Epistemologically, the occurrence of light, insight, shows that human beings are knowers and the world is knowable. Pondered, this can lead one to see that disorder depends upon order, nonbeing depends upon being, evil depends upon good. We would not be able to understand, were disorder, nonbeing, and evil foundational. We do understand, so they must be derivative—privations of what is primordial and basic. The same holds ethically. We cannot act except to try to gain some good. We never intend evil or chaos as such. The goods we pursue may be specious—stupid and false. Ethical maturation demands our coming to love goods that are true. But even for the ethically weak goodness is basic, and the wellspring of action is positive. Even the thief pursues happiness, as the adulterer dreams of beauty. Human nature is on the side of reason and goodness. Health is as near as becoming what we are.

Such a philosophy of human nature ruled the classical Greek view of wisdom, and long after pagan Greece had passed from the historical scene such philosophy shaped Western culture. Thus one finds Greek reason living on in Jewish philosophers such as Philo, Maimonides, and Spinoza. Muslim philosophers such as Avicenna, Averroes, and Al-Ghazali owe Aristotle a sizeable debt. Augustine stands in the Platonic tradition, Aquinas depends upon Aristotle, and popes such as John XXIII use the Greek tradition of natural law. Modern science develops tools created by the classical Greeks, and the creative reason of an Einstein updates the Greek tradition. For example, when Einstein said that God does not play dice (with the world), he placed himself with the Greeks who insisted that nature is intelligible. When Alexsandr Solzhenitsyn said that one word of an artist's truth is more powerful than the massive lies of tyrannies like the Soviet, he placed himself with the Greek philosophers of light. The Johannine Gospel that made the light that shines in the darkness the splendor of the divine Logos depended on Hellenistic conceptualization. Groups like Amnesty International who shake up international politics simply by publicizing the truth about political prisoners are worthy children of Plato.

The Greek self is lightsome: centered in reason. It can divide itself, succumb to passion, generate disorder in a thousand ways. But its core quality, the virtue that is its signature, is its movement toward the light. In contrast to Hebrew wisdom, Greek wisdom does not speak much of sin. The person who does not do the good must not really know it. Therefore education becomes a major battleground, as the Platonic dialogues make clear. Again and again we see a war between the true teachings of lovers of wisdom such as Socrates and the false, merely rhetorical teachings of sophists. The lovers of wisdom seek what is real and true, letting the chips fall where they may. The sophists are whoring speech makers selling their persuasive skills to the highest bidder. Where the lovers of wisdom seek to judge, to determine what is fair and true, the sophists seek to persuade, to win an argument.

What does it imply to describe a self in which judgment stands front and center? It implies making the self responsible for what it thinks and does, responsible for its "reality." Human beings have the capacity to conceive how things may hang together and to test such conceptions. In a wide range of matters, from experimental science to household finance, adulthood should find them realizing that patient, sober testing is the only way to personal wisdom. Thus the scientist knows that the only hypothesis worth a damn is proved valid by experiment. The mature householder knows that the only budget for financial peace is the one that leaves wide safety margins, depends on no windfalls. What *may* occur is legion. Anything that is not self-contradictory is possible. What is so, or is likely to happen, is quite restricted. When experience is our guide, when we brush away fantasies and deal with actualities, we become sober and judicious. Sobriety and judiciousness are not stuffiness or constipation. They are not the crabbed caution of our worst bankers and bureaucrats. They are simply listening carefully to the dictates of reason and conscience, waiting faithfully on the demands of the light.

According to the Greeks, we have within us a light, a voice that we can trust to be a faithful guide. Like Socrates listening to his **daimon**, we can know whether we are overreaching ourselves: going beyond the evidence, playing fast and loose with the implications. To go beyond oneself was the great Greek sin of *hubris*: pride, refusal to acknowledge one's limitations. To go beyond oneself is the great sin causing so much suffering today: contemporary wars, economic chaos, family life in disarray. To be sure, one can err by defect as well as excess. There are selves wrecked by sloth and cowardice as well as selves wrecked by hubris. For the classical Greeks sweet reason was a golden mean; virtue always lay in the middle. Thus the ideal classical Greek self was happy in the In-Between, peaceful because strong in self-knowledge.

ULTIMATE REALITY

The many savior gods that characterized Greek religion during Hellenistic times seemed to offer their devotees a way out of their world of suffering and death. In classical times, however, the religious atmosphere was much cooler. For Plato the ultimate reality illuminating the spiritual realm was the idea of the Good. For Aristotle the divinity at the beginning of the chain of efficient causes was an Unmoved Mover, a self-sufficient being that was Pure (unlimited) Act. Aristotle's was the more influential theology. Developed, it yielded the idea that a fullness of intelligence and being stands ready to satisfy the human mind's quest for explanation. If one starts asking about the origin of things—from child to parents, from parents to grandparents, from close human grandparents to distant simian great-grandparents, from apes to animal life, from the beginnings of animal life to the start of life itself, from simple life to complex inanimate matter, from complex inanimate matter to the first presence of simple matter—one either regresses infinitely or comes to a "beginning" that is of another order: uncaused, self-sufficient. That beginning is Aristotle's Unmoved Mover: a Fullness of Being and Light.

This conceptualization has shaped a great deal of Western philosophical theology. Modern philosophy has had differences with it, and it differs in many ways from Buddhist philosophy, but it continues to have considerable power. For if we assume that there must be a reason for things to exist as they do (a large assumption, many people would say), Aristotle's line of argument makes sense. What is required to make such an assumption? At the least, one must find the world (being) intrinsically intelligible and find the human mind intrinsically intelligent. These two findings, Aristotle implied, occur in judgment, the act of reflective understanding in which we assert that something is or is not so. The reasonable ultimate reality of the Aristotelians therefore depends upon a positive elucidation of human judgment, an exegesis of our de facto assertions of truth that finds us identified with objective reality as knowers fused with the known.[12]

But can even a positive elucidation of human judgment find Being of a different order, make the move from finite, potential beings to Infinite Pure Act? It is a difficult move, since even the most confident defender of human reason has to acknowledge many frailties. The most that human reason can do is show the likelihood of an Infinite Perfection, its consistency with the intelligible build of reality. Then, meditating on the relation between our human experience of truth and goodness and the intimations of Truth and Goodness that such experiences carry, one may sense something of the inreach of the divine reason that Plato and Aristotle felt.

Eric Voegelin, who has devoted years to such meditation, thinks that Aristotle finally found human consciousness itself to be shaped by the inreach of the divine mind:

Consciousness is the area of reality where the divine intellect (nous) moves the intellect of man (nous) to engage in the search of the ground. Aristotle has carefully analyzed the process in which the divine and human intellect (nous) participate in one another. In his language, man finds himself first in a state of ignorance (agnoia, amathia) concerning the ground (aition, arche) of his existence. Man, however, could not know that he does not know, unless he experienced an existential unrest to escape from his ignorance (pheugein ten agnoian) and to search for knowledge (episteme).[13]

In other words, the structure of human awareness leads inevitably to the search for an explanation of our human state. We have a tension, a restlessness, to understand how the world fits together, what is the whole of things. For Voegelin's Aristotle, our movement from oblivion to awareness that we are ignorant, and then from ignorance to knowledge depends on the igniting of our minds by the divine mind. For the light to shine enough for us to realize that we are ignorant is already the active presence in us of the divine mind. In fact, our minds participate in the divine mind. The light in us has to rest in the matrix of the divine light. This is true of scientific light, the insights that slowly move the researcher through her problem in the laboratory. It is true of existential light, the groping of artists and people with no art for a "philosophy," a way of understanding the world, that feels solid and rings true. Indeed, this groping process is our inmost vocation as human beings. We are not primarily college students, accountants, homemakers, Elks, Shriners, or other odd fellows. We are primarily beings lured by the light, beckoned by the Mystery of life to find some solid ground, some rock and salvation to quiet our fears.

Moreover, the "ground" of which the passage speaks is, as the Greek words *aition* and *arche* suggest, a "cause" and "first" that might support both the structure of human consciousness and the whole reality onto which human consciousness opens. Until we develop a love of wisdom, make progress toward Ultimate Reality, we are ignorant of the basis, the cause and first principle, of our very selves. When we recognize this state, we feel an increasing unease, a growing hunger to know. The desire to know reverses the flight into distraction that is the will not to know. By fleeing ignorance, we allow ourselves to be drawn to the light; the quest for light dominates the personality, defining who we want to be. At that point, we have made the ground our sober passion, entered on the Greek wisdom way. As "pilgrims of the Truth," or "wayfarers toward the Light," we recognize time because it is a chance to study the eternal, the no-thing that invites us to commune beyond the world.

EINSTEIN

Of the two greatest Greek lovers of wisdom, Plato was the more poetic, Aristotle the more scientific. Thus the mystical classical Greek approach to the divine ground appears most clearly in Plato's myths, as the inferential, step-by-step rational approach is represented by Aristotle's analyses. Insofar, however, as they shared a conviction that human beings live in the In-Between, Plato and Aristotle agreed that the questing character of human intelligence is a movement toward the divine ground that the divine ground itself initiates.

From the Greek characterization of the span of human reason as an In-Between, much subsequent Western wisdom drew a sense that the divine is an act of unlimited understanding both beyond our comprehension and more intimate to us than we are to ourselves. As intimate to us and our world, the Greek analysis of ultimate reality supported a nature we could profitably investigate. As beyond our comprehension, Being rather than a being, the Greek ultimate reality set limits to hubris, demonstrated that we cannot measure the final reason of things.

In the Protestant Reformation, the age of revolution, and the romantic eras of modernity, the Greek sense of the In-Between came under serious assault: Biblical truths were more holistic, passions of human beings more politically significant; analysis of reality was less important than feeling and changing it. When critical history, relativity theory, quantum mechanics, indeterminism, psychoanalysis, evolution, and a host of other new viewpoints came charging into the twenteith century, it appeared that Greek rationality was completely routed. Two World Wars completed the volcanic outburst, leaving reason in full disarray. The biblical doctrine of sin stood more than vindicated. The time for *theoria* and *phronesis* (speculative and practical wisdom) seemed long ago and far away.

Nonetheless, through the past five hundred years creative intelligence, in the persons of such giants as Newton and Einstein, has continued to do the things that Greek epistemology said it must. For instance, if we follow Einstein's advice not to understand creative science one must look at what creative scientists *do* rather than at what they *say*, we find a combination of mysticism and empirical hardheadedness reminiscent of the philosophers of the In-Between. (They, however, would assure us it could not be otherwise.)

For example, Einstein's various moves beyond "normal" imagination, his theories surpassing then-current evidence, illustrate the isomorphism of mind and physical reality. As Einstein's work demonstrates strikingly that isomorphism, or parallelism, often shows itself as a hunger for elegance, a drive for the straightforward formula that is most "fitting." Einstein, like all who pursue reason was not simply a human computer. His creativity was a passionate fusion of mind, imagination, and esthetic wonder. In thinking beyond ordinary sensation, coming to space that is curved, time that is a fourth dimension, Einstein developed an intimate dialogue with nature, a state of mutual openness. Being intimate with nature's ways through long and highly personal study, individuals governed by the rational let their minds be stripped of preconceptions, giving nature more spirit to teach and to lead on. Thereby, they persuade nature to reveal more of itself, to be unusually susceptible to study.

At work in the depths of the creative scientist, as Einstein knew from within, is a feeling one can only liken to religion:

You will hardly find one among the profounder sort of scientific minds without a peculiar religious feeling of his own. But it is different from the religion of the naive man. For the latter God is a being from whose care one hopes to benefit and whose punishment one fears; a sublimation of a feeling similar to that of a child for its father, a being to whom one stands to some extent in a personal relation, however deeply it may be tinged with awe. But the scientist is possessed by the sense of universal causation. The future, to him, is every whit as necessary and determined as the past. There is nothing divine about morality, it is a purely human affair. His religious feeling takes the form of a rapturous amazement at the harmony of natural law, which reveals an intelligence of such superiority that, compared with it, all the systematic thinking and acting of human beings is an utterly insignificant reflection. This feeling is the guiding principle of his life and work, in so far as he succeeds in keeping himself from the shackles of selfish desire. It is beyond question closely akin to that which has possessed the religious geniuses of all ages.[14]

Clearly, this religious feeling can never substitute for hard thinking. In the middle of the In-Between we must reason, pore over data, make our connections step by step. But the drive to understand, the universal causation at the top of our span that lures us on, fires the creative scientist with a passion for the light, a deep reverence for the "mind" behind the universe. In fact, as the quotation shows, sensitive scientists come to fear that selfishness will taint the pure consciousness they need to appreciate the divine intelligence. Of course, Plato and Aristotle would have argued that morality, rightly plumbed, also reveals the divine. Their followers would make more distinctions among myth, science, philosophy, and religion. But Plato and Aristotle would have seen Einstein as one of their own, another lover of wisdom drawn by the divine mind.

SUMMARY

We began our survey of the classical Greek species of wisdom with Homer, the writer on whom all the subsequent masters drew. In the *Iliad* and the *Odyssey*, Homer sang of the problem of cultural decline. His conclusion was that blinding comes through inordinate passion. In the wake of this insight, Greek culture, and much of Western culture generally, probed the relation between reason and passion. At the same time, the Greeks made unprecedented advances in understanding the human mind, gradually delineating the structure of human reason and so the basic build of the human world.

Socrates showed the moral and inspirational sides of human reason, dying for his convictions and forcing Athens to see the falsity of its unquestioned "religion." As the Delphic Oracle had described him, Socrates was the wisest man in Athens because he knew what he didn't know. This "agnostic" quality became an important motif in Greek wisdom, in large part because it was such a strong defense against hubris. Socrates also made Athens uncomfortably aware that mental and moral well-being ought to count more than practical advantage.

For Plato mental and moral well-being took one toward the idea of the Good. Freed from the cave of sensual bondage, the human spirit could progress to the point where it discovered its vocation to interact with the divine ground. There it would be clear that human consciousness has the structure of an In-Between and that human virtue consequently is a matter of balance. Aristotle specified these propositions more exactly, riveting onto the interplay of imagination and intellect and developing a hylomorphic view of reality. In ethics Aristotle lauded the contemplative life, showing the place of both theoretical and practical wisdom.

The Greek penetration of nature laid the foundations for later Western science, above all by showing the isomorphism between the physical world and the human mind. Aristotelian logic was a powerful tool for working out complex problems; the scheme of the four principal causes suggested that nature is a construct of the divine mind. In political theory Aristotle stressed the need to order social affairs under the ultimate good, a view that contrasts tellingly with most modern political theories.

The self to be fitted into the polis was most distinguished by its reason. The light that de facto occurs in human beings was the center of the classical anthropology. Reasoning from this light, one could build a very positive, intelligible worldview. Where sophists sought only temporary victories, true lovers of wisdom would strive to grasp the inner build of such an intelligible worldview. By listening to the voice of conscience, following the inner light, one could recognize in human consciousness the presence of the divine mind. The unrest characterizing awakened human beings, the desire to escape ignorance and to find the ground of their lives, is a quest for the ultimate light.

Scientists such as Einstein exemplify intellect that is complemented by a passionate response to the appeal of reason. In the search for truth that motivates scientific research, they verify the classical notion that consciousness is an In-Between, both reasoning carefully over empirical details and opening their souls to wonder at a Mind that passes beyond the top of their span.

STUDY QUESTIONS

1. Explain the Homeric notion that social disorder mainly derives from the dominance of passion over reason.

2. What is the main lesson in the fate of Socrates?

3. How could the idea of good be "the cause for all things of all that is right and beautiful"?

4. Why does *phronesis* depend upon a rich fund of experience?

5. Why is the final cause the first in the order of causation?

6. What is the chief good that ought to determine the shape of politics?

7. How valid is the Greek view that the self pivots on the act of judgment?

8. How do the divine and the human relate in the In-Between?

9. Why was "the harmony of natural law" so important to Einstein?

NOTES

1. See Bruno Snell, *The Discovery of Mind.* New York: Harper & Row, 1960.

2. Eric Voegelin, *Order and History*, vol. 2. Baton Rouge: Louisiana State University Press, 1957, p. 83.

3. Bernard Lonergan, *Method in Theology.* New York: Herder & Herder, 1972, pp. 90–91.

4. Plato, *Apology*, 36b-e; in Edith Hamilton and Huntington Cairns, eds., *Plato: Collected Dialogues.* Princeton, N.J.: Princeton University Press/Bollingen, 1961, pp. 21–22.

5. Plato, *Republic*, 517b-c; in Hamilton and Cairns, *Plato*, pp. 749–50.

6. See Eric Voegelin, *Anamnesis.* Notre Dame, Ind.: University of Notre Dame Press, 1978, pp. 89–115.

7. C. B. Kerferd, "Aristotle," in *The Encyclopedia of Philosophy*, vol. 1, ed. Paul Edwards. New York: Macmillan, 1967, pp. 161–62.

8. See Stanley Jaki, *The Road of Science and the Ways to God.* Chicago: University of Chicago Press, 1978.

9. Aristotle, *Nicomachean Ethics*, 1094a-b; in Richard McKeon, ed., *Introduction to Aristotle*, 2d ed. Chicago: University of Chicago Press, 1973, p. 347.

10. See Eric Voegelin, *The New Science of Politics.* Chicago: University of Chicago Press, 1966.

11. Doris Lessing, *The Sentimental Agents*. New York: Alfred A. Knopf, 1983, pp. 41, 45.

12. See Bernard Lonergan, *Insight*. New York: Philosophical Library, 1957.

13. Eric Voegelin, *Order and History*, vol. 4. Baton Rouge: Louisiana State University Press, 1974, pp. 189–90.

14. Albert Einstein, *The World as I See It*. Secaucus, N.J.: Citadel Press, 1979, pp. 28–29.

16

Wisdom Among Shamanic Peoples

THE AGED

Shamanic peoples generally revere wisdom and tend to think of it as the fruit of a long experience with the ways of the tribe, the vagaries of nature, the comings and goings of the spiritual powers. Insofar as the oldest members of a tribe are apt to have the richest experience, they usually become the keepers of tribal wisdom. As long as a tribe can meet its material needs without great trouble, its aged people are not burdens but special resources. They assume the roles of teachers, counselors, and models of the tribe's mores. In times of trouble, however, when food and resources are scarce, or the tribe is suffering the onslaughts of modern Western culture, the aged may be considered more trouble than they are worth. This, however, is a rupture of the traditional shamanic pattern.

The traditional culture of the Coast Salish Indians of western Washington and British Columbia, for example, made old age the best time in the life cycle. People became "old" when they could no longer per-

form the roles prescribed by their sex or youthful talents. Thus when men could no longer hunt effectively or women could no longer gather they would yield those tasks to younger replacements and assume new responsibilities. This changeover usually occurred between ages forty-five and fifty. In their new status as aged people, without reproductive and economic duties, Coastal Salish elders gained considerable freedom. For example, they could have sanctioned love affairs. Indeed, Coastal Salish culture found affairs between older and younger tribal members romantic, so many elders, both men and women, took new partners.

As well, taboos lessened and spiritual powers grew:

Many of the taboos that applied to people in their youth and maturity were waived for the elderly. Women past child-bearing age could no longer pollute hunters or their gear, nor would they contaminate the berry patches or offend the salmon. Old men no longer had to observe the disciplines of sexual abstinence and fasting that were incumbent on active hunters and fishermen. Certain foods forbidden to the young were reserved to the old. With the raising of these restrictions new avenues of spiritual power opened up to both men and women. The old often were caretakers for people in dangerous liminal states—successful spirit questers, girls at menarche, women in childbirth, warriors returned from battle, mourners, and the recently dead. A grandmother was an ideal attendant for a girl at her first menstruation, because she was not only wise, experienced, and concerned about her granddaughter but also impervious to the girl's sacred contagion.[1]

Among the Coastal Salish young people therefore were taught to be courteous to their elders, in part because long life was thought to evidence a powerful supernatural helper (who would avenge any insult). Most religious specialists—shamans, mediums, or people who knew spells—were old, and old people usually led the most important annual ceremonies. The Coastal Salish elders also kept the traditional myths: "In a preliterate society, old people are almost always the repositories of important cultural traditions. They not only transmit traditional information and beliefs, they also contribute their own insights to a living and growing corpus. The Coastal Salish elders, too, were the keepers and creators of traditional lore in the form of genealogies, family histories, and myths."[2]

One of the first connotations of *wisdom* among shamanic peoples, then, is "the traditional lore that old people have assimilated and tested." In this sense wisdom is both historical and pragmatic. It comes from the past, to which the elderly are the best link, and it teaches the proven ways of getting along with nature, keeping peace in the tribe, and so on. Particular colorings of this general description will vary from tribe to tribe, depending upon individual customs and beliefs, but generally the content of the elders' wisdom will range from stories (myths) depicting the tribal worldview to specific techniques for fishing, weaving, dancing the harvest dance, or the like.

One might therefore see in shamanic cultures a reflection of the Aristotelian distinction between theoretical and practical wisdom. Few shamanic tribes would care to develop such a distinction into separate treatises on metaphysics and folk ways, but most would agree that the aged—those with the deepest roots in the past—often are the most helpful both in clarifying the tribal world and in practicing the arts (of healing, woodworking, predicting the weather, and so forth) that make daily life run smoothly. Since old people usually have had the time and inclination to bring the past to bear on the present, they have tended to assume the roles of historians and teachers quite willingly,

perhaps from an instinctive awareness that those who neglect the past are condemned to repeat its follies.

ECOLOGY

The content of shamanic wisdom often is largely what we might call ecological. All in all, the main purpose of much traditional lore is to help the tribe live in harmony with the natural powers. For in the typical shamanic worldview nature and divinity or ultimate reality compenetrate, even collapse into one another. To be a full self is to be integrated into the social group, and to be a healthy social group is to be integrated into a sacral nature. Until we students make an imaginative effort to understand what it was like to live in a world thoroughly subject to nature's caprice, we cannot understand the shamanic perspective. What only happens to the contemporary citizen of an industrialized culture occasionally—in times of flood, tornado, earthquake, serious illness—happened to the tribal person every day. Every day the individual felt, or feels, the dominance of the natural world, the powers of sun, storm, and rain. And this "feeling" was not a mild enjoyment of a sunset, a bittersweet walk in the rain. It was a sense of dependence and vulnerability rooted deep in the soul.

To be sure, tribal peoples have varied in their manifestations of this sense of dependence. Eskimos, living in hazardous conditions most of the year, have exhibited more sober respect than Indians or Africans living in a lush forest. The forest has its demands and dangers, but they tend to be considerably less stark than the Eskimos' snow and ice. Still, both Eskimo and forest dweller have met nature much more directly, much more nakedly, than citizens of industrialized cultures. As a result, their sense of ecology has not been merely scientific or esthetic, but a straightforward consequence of the reality with which tribal cultures must contend daily.

Thus the following portion of an anthropological assessment of the traditional worldview of the Cahuilla Indians of southern California could describe countless other tribal peoples:

Another assumption and a corollary of the postulate of ?iva?a [a power or energy source] was that man was an integral part of nature, and that most of the universe was an interacting system. Man was seen as one of a number of cooperating beings, who, together with his fellow Cahuilla, shared in the workings of the universe. Thus, an ecological ethic existed which assumed that any action affected other parts of the system. It was a reciprocal process, therefore man had an obligation to the rest of the universe. For instance, permission had to be granted from pemtexweva, *whose role it was to provide the Cahuilla with game, to exploit the food resources such as deer, mountain sheep, and antelope. The reciprocal obligations were that the deer allowed themselves to be caught, while man was careful not to overkill or waste the products provided by the deer.[3]*

The myths and ceremonies of the shamanic tribe typically sought the people's acceptance of such an ethic, their understanding and embrace of the network of reciprocal obligations in which they stood. Shamans drew on the power running through this network, often employing personal spirit-helpers. Aged people could probe such a worldview after many years of experience and find it both orderly and challenging. As the "interconnectedness" of all living things grew richer and deeper, a mature reverence or piety could emerge. How wonderful that things should interrelate, conspire, so intricately! How bountiful of the source of the world to provide such profusion!

One of the most famous Amerindian statements of the characteristic tribal ecology came from Smohalla, a Wanapum living on the Columbia River in the mid-1880s. Note the opposition Smohalla finds between his people's ways and the ways of the invading whites, and his personification of the earth as a venerable mother:

All these [whites, blacks, Chinese] are new people; only the Indians are of the old stock. After awhile, when God is ready, he will drive away all the people except the people who have obeyed his laws. Those who cut up the lands or sign papers for lands will be defrauded of their rights, and will be punished by God's anger. Moses was bad. God did not love him. He sold his people's houses and the graves of their dead. It is a bad word that comes from Washington. It is not a good law that would take my people away from me to make them sin against the laws of God. You ask me to plough the ground! Shall I take a knife and tear my mother's bosom? Then when I die she will not take me to her bosom to rest. You ask me to dig for stone! Shall I dig under her skin for her bones? Then when I die I can not enter her body to be born again. You ask me to cut grass and make hay and sell it, and be rich like white men, but how dare I cut off my mother's hair? It is a bad law and my people can not obey it. I want my people to stay with me here. All the dead men will come to life again; their spirits will come to their bodies again. We must wait here, in the homes

of our fathers, and be ready to meet them in the bosom of our mother.[4]

CEREMONIES

Shamanic peoples generally have inculcated their ecology through comprehensive ceremonies. Geared to the annual turn of the season, such ceremonies have preached that nature's holiness is alive and rhythmic. At key times in the ordinary life cycle, they have dramatized how human time can be an ongoing initiation into the mysteries of the cosmos, the depth and richness of nature's powers. As explained by Black Elk, the Oglala Sioux system of ceremonies is a good illustration of the tribal wisdom that all nature's directions and times can be significant, if we but open our spirits to their power.

Unifying the seven major rites of the Oglala Sioux was the sacred pipe that a mysterious woman gave the people early in their history. The smoke of the pipe rising to God would carry all the people's prayers. When she gave the pipe to the Sioux chief, the mysterious woman said:

"Behold this and always love it! It is lela wakan *[very sacred], and you must treat it as such. No impure man should ever be allowed to see it, for within this bundle there is a sacred pipe. With this you will, during the winters to come, send your voices to* Wakan-Tanka, *your Father and Grandfather. With this sacred pipe you will walk upon the Earth; for the Earth is your Grandmother and Mother, and She is sacred. Every step that is taken upon Her should be as a prayer."[5]*

The seven rites at which the Oglala Sioux smoked the pipe and celebrated their life with their Grandfather the Great Spirit and their Grandmother the Earth were a ceremony to purify the dead, a ceremony for purification in the sweat lodge, a ceremony for crying for a vision, the sun dance, a ceremony for making relatives of people of other nations, a ceremony to prepare girls for womanhood, and a sacred ball game. Some of these ceremonies apparently predated the introduction of the sacred pipe, but from the time of its introduction all the ceremonies used the pipe. Not only had the mysterious woman commanded this, but also the pipe clearly fit all the ceremonies. For each of the ceremonies was but an expression of the tribe's ongoing and basic effort to consecrate itself and all of nature to the Great Spirit, thereby repairing or strengthening its harmony with the living whole of the cosmos.

We could use any of the seven rites to illustrate the Oglala Sioux, or the general shamanic, wisdom that human beings hunger for union with a sacral world. Perhaps *inipi*, the ritual of the sweat lodge, will provide the simplest example. As Black Elk emphasized, inipi used all the powers of the universe: the earth and all the things that grow from the earth; water, fire, and air. The lodge was made from twelve to sixteen young willows, set so that they marked the four quarters of the universe. The rocks represented Grandmother Earth and the fire represented Wakan-Tanka. The door faced the east, whence comes the light of wisdom. The fireplace stood at the center of the lodge, symbolizing Wakan-Tanka's position at the center of the universe. Persons undergoing the ceremony prayed to each of the symbolic elements and directions, asking to be centered by its power, reminded of their frail place in the total scheme. Smoking the pipe to prepare themselves, they would walk outside the lodge and place the pipe with its stem slanting to the east.

For the purification the door was closed, making the lodge completely dark. This action represented the ignorance that the ceremony had to purify away. The water poured on the hot rocks would fill the lodge with steam. As they perspired, the participants could feel their impurities oozing away. Each moment and gesture oriented the participant's spirit to holy things, invoking their aid. Then came a crucial time in the ceremony:

The leader now sprinkles water on the rocks, once for our Grandfather, Tunkashila, *once for our Father,* Ate, *once for our Grandmother,* Unchi, *once for our Mother,* Ina, *the Earth, and then once for the sacred pipe; this is done with a sprig of sage or sweet grass, so that the steam will be fragrant, and as it rises and fills the little lodge, the leader cries: "O Wakan-Tanka, behold me! I am the people. In offering myself to You, I offer all the people as one, that they may live! We wish to live again! Help us!"*[6]

Although all traditional peoples have prayed to receive the light from their God, few have ceremonialized their desire as beautifully and thoroughly as the Oglala Sioux.

MYTHS

As the story of the mysterious woman who gave the Oglala Sioux their sacred pipe suggests, most tribal peoples have expressed their worldviews in terms of stories. Stories dealing with supernatural powers or stepping outside profane time to deal with events "in the beginning" are *myths*. And just as the Oglala Sioux wove their myths into their ceremonies, making the ceremonies enactments of the worldview expressed in the myths, so most other tribal peoples have coordinated their myths and ceremonies. On the whole, rituals or sacred ceremonies have been but dramatic enactments of the myths by which tribal peoples have situated themselves in the world. If the myths that the old people or shamans guard form the people's imaginations in terms of accounts of creation or the origin of tribal customs, the ceremonies draw the people into an active re-presentation or real-ization of the mythic truths.

This religious usage is not peculiarly shamanic. When Jews celebrate Passover with a full investment in the myth of the Exodus, or Christians celebrate Easter with a full investment in the myth of the Resurrection, they too become active participants. Were their participation to become as physical as tribal peoples', through long dances, songs, fastings, and purifications, they too would feel the transforming power of symbols that have seized the full personality: mind and emotion, heart and subconscious.

In contrast to the Amerindian examples presented, let us consider some examples of African mythological wisdom. The first, exemplifying the rich traditions of African tribes such as the Dogon, comes from the teachings of Ogotommeli, a blind Dogon elder who in 1947 consented to initiate Marcel Griaule, a French anthropologist, into the mysteries of his people's ancient worldview.

Griaule recorded thirty-three days of instruction. Day One was for meeting the master and getting a first sense of his personality. When the guide brought Griaule to Ogotemmeli's door, they were met by a striking person:

At last there appeared a brown tunic, drawn in at the seams and frayed by long use like the standards of the warriors of old. Then a head bent beneath the lintel of the door, and the man stood up to his full height, turning towards the stranger a face that no words can describe. "Greetings!" he said, "Greetings to those who are athirst!" The thick lips spoke the purest Sanga language. So alive were they that one saw nothing else. All the other features seemed to be folded away, particularly as, after the first words, the head had been bent. The cheeks, the cheekbones, the forehead and the eyelids seemed all to have suffered the same ravages; they were creased by a hundred wrinkles which had caused a painful contortion as of a face exposed to too strong a light or battered by a hail of stones. The eyes were dead.[7]

By the seventeenth day the initiation was well under way, right in the middle of the Dogon mythological system. At that time Griaule and Ogotemmeli were discussing the symbolism of the paintings that adorned the temples of Ogotemmeli's region. The serpents, crocodiles, patches of color, and the rest laid out the Dogon world system. Painted in millet-gruel and rice, the paintings had a very practical purpose: " 'And what, you ask, is the use of the paintings?' said Ogotemmeli. 'It is this: they help the plants to grow, they promote germination. The day before the sacrificer wets his brushes, the ears for the sowing are spread out on the roof, the symbol of the primal field.' In this way, at the start of the cycle of vegetable growth, the still unfertilized seeds are taken and incorporated in the universal cycle, in the general movement of clouds and men."[8]

The stories of the different animals represented in the temple paintings were part of a vast cycle of tales in which the Dogon laid out the history of the world. But this "history" was no sterile documentation of the dead past, because the characters in the stories influenced such present Dogon activities as planting and weaving. Members of the Dogon tribe varied in the number of stories they knew and in the depth of their understanding. In his area Ogotemmeli was the master mythologist, revered for his unparalleled depth and breadth of understanding. In his mind the myths made the whole world fraught with symbols: the earth was the wife of God, water was the Divine seed, and divine offspring of God were always present in the fiber skirts of the women, which were full of water and words.

On the thirty-third and last day, having gone through such key myths as the First Word, Weaving, the Granary, the Drums, Cultivation, the Smithy, the Temple, Women, Circumcision, the Cult of the Dead, Fire, and the Signs of the Zodiac, Ogotemmeli sent the European on his way with a sacrifice.

Ogotemmeli offered prayer. He called the heavens to witness; he made resounding channels ready for the flow of grace. He paid his debt to the Powers of Water, of whom he had perhaps spoken too freely to the stranger from the northern lands. He asked for a happy issue to the long homeward journey that the stranger was about to undertake. He turned his face to the north, to the land where the Europeans were said to live. It was a propitious hour, the hour when the shadows move upwards in the courtyards and outline the smallest recesses of the roofs, and when the sun, its force abated, drinks the blood on the altars less quickly than the thirsty souls.[9]

DIVINITY

In concrete myths and prayers, African tribal societies have worked out rich conceptualizations of divinity. John S. Mbiti, a prominent scholar of African religions, finds a great coherence among the many tribes' views of God. For example, he finds it commonly accepted, even among peoples who speak of God anthropomorphically, that God is Spirit:

One of the most explicit descriptions of God as Spirit occurs in a traditional Pygmy hymn which says: "In the beginning was God, today is God, tomorrow will be God. Who can make an image of God? He has no body. He is as a word which comes out of your mouth. That word! It is no more, it is past, and still it lives! So is God." In a Shona traditional hymn, God is addressed as "the Great Spirit" who piles up rocks to make mountains, causes branches to grow and gives rain to mankind. Thus, God is pictured as an active and creative Spirit.[10]

Mbiti's style is to connect different tribes' notions, weaving them into unified statements on different religious topics. In their own thought context, the majority of African tribes' concepts seem more concrete, embedded in myths and prayers. The myths feature spirits other than God, and frequently they make such spirits the most prominent religious foci. That is the case in Ogotemmeli's teaching, where the Nummo, or divine spirits, predominate over the rather distant creator God. In fact, the frequent distance of the creator God has led some scholars to speak of the African High God as a *Deus Otiosus*: a God who has little effect on daily life (literally: who is leisurely or idle). But this may misunderstand the significance of having an ultimate referent that need not be called into every affair but always is available as a last resort.

Supporting this more positive interpretation of the African High God are the various prayers that reach out, in times of distress, to the Great Spirit or Lord. For example, the prayer of a !Kung bushman forthrightly pleads and reflects: "Gauwa must help us that we kill an animal. Gauwa, help us. We are dying of hunger. Gauwa does not give us help. He is cheating. He is bluffing. Gauwa will bring something for us to kill next day, after he himself hunts and has eaten meat, when he is full and is feeling well."[11] The Ruanda-Urundi, who usually pray to the god Ryangombe, reach out to Imana, the Great Creator, when they are in dire straits:

O Imana of Urundi (Ruanda), if only you would help me! O Imana of pity, Imana of my father's house (or country), if only you would help me! O Imana of the country of the Hutu and the Tutsi, if only you would help me just this once! O Imana, if only you would give me a rugo *[home] and children! I prostrate myself before you, Imana of Urundi (Ruanda). I cry to you: give me offspring, give me as you give to others! Imana, what shall I do, where shall I go? I am in distress, where is there room for me? O Merciful, O Imana of mercy, help me this once!*[12]

One sees, then, that group ceremonial and private, solitary prayer are not incompatible. At times of distress, when particular problems are overwhelming, an individual may go apart from the crowd and cry all the pain out to God. God can care. All tribal theologies assume that rituals and prayers can make a difference. *How* they can make a difference, what the Creator may choose to do, is never certain. But *that* divine intervention is possible is always certain, since it is a direct inference from creation itself: If God once chose to make the world, organize the tribe, God now can choose to help the tribe or individual in pain.

Because of this merciful possibility, as well as the Creator's other splendors, the Mashona of Southern Rhodesia would pray:

Great Spirit! Piler up of rocks into towering mountains! When thou stampest on the stone, the dust rises and fills the land. Hardness of the precipice; waters of the pool that turn into misty rain when stirred. Vessel overflowing with oil! Father of Runji, who seweth the heavens like a cloth; let him knit together that which is below. Caller forth of the branching trees: Thou bringest forth the shoots that they stand erect. Thou hast filled the land with mankind, the dust rises on high, oh Lord! Wonderful One, thou livest in the midst of the sheltering rocks, thou givest of rain to mankind: We pray to thee, hear us, Lord! Show mercy when we beseech thee, Lord.[13]

POWER

The wisdom of nonliterate peoples frequently took them into the mysteries of the High God. At the top of the span of human understanding, they confessed that the total scheme of things escaped their ken. Nonetheless, they were equally convinced that some ways of dealing with the inscrutable High God, and with nature and one another, were better than others. The signs of such effective religious ways were ecological harmony, tribal prosperity, and peace. Hunger, bad luck, or strife signified that the people were out of

phase with the ultimate powers. Betaking themselves to their myths and ceremonies, consulting the most experienced members of the tribe, shamanic peoples tried to purge themselves of the faults (violations of taboos, moral failings) that might have been responsible for such disharmony. For without the power of ultimate reality on their side, they were vulnerable, ill at ease, out of sorts. Religion, then, has long had a close relation with power: the creative force behind the world, the ultimate energy by which the world stands, the source of human exhilaration. Traditionally, to be religious was not to dampen one's enthusiasms but to ignite them, not to turn eros into a dray horse but a thoroughbred.

Early theoreticians such as G. Van der Leeuw, who pondered the reports of missionaries, made a great deal of the power (*mana, orenda, wakanda*) that the missionaries found at the center of such peoples' religions:

One may possess either great or limited mana; *two magicians may attack each other by employing two sorts of* mana. *Power enjoys no moral value whatever.* Mana *resides alike in the poisoned arrow and in European remedies, while with the Iroquois* orenda *one both blesses and curses. It is simply a matter of Power, alike for good or evil. Codrington's [the missionary who first described the Melanesian* mana*] discovery was followed by others in the most diverse parts of the world. The* orenda *of the Iroquois has just been referred to; "it appears that they interpreted the activities of Nature as the ceaseless strife between one* orenda *and another." The Sioux Indians, again, believe in* wakanda, *at one time a god of the type of an originator, at another an impersonal Power which acquires empirical verification whenever something extraordinary is manifested.*[14]

Subsequent anthropological and religious scholarship has added considerable nuance to this idea that power is central to non-literate religions, but much in Van der Leeuw's description is useful. The shaman is a seeker of power. The shamanic tribe evaluates the efficacy of its leaders, myths, and ceremonies in terms of their power to bring prosperity and peace. So the vision quest of many American Indians had a strong dimension of power. One sought a revelation, a personal spirit-helper, and a new name to *empower* the rest of one's life. So the rites for healing that shamans have employed both exercised and sought the power to cure. The shaman would draw on her or his personal power, step out into trance to seek the power of the spirits or gods, and try to muster the bodily and spiritual powers of the patient.

In the imaginative worldview of most shamanic tribes, where vivid symbols could take root in fertile, well-disposed psyches, great power frequently did flash forth. Vision quests brought young warriors the revelations of guardian eagles or bears. Dying children revived when aged shamans sang over them. The fertility power of women consecrated at the menarche produced the miracle of new human life. The killing power of hunters overcame the mighty buffalo.

And so it went in other parts of the shamanic world. The nourishing power of corn, gift of the corn maiden, sustained the people year after year. The power of Mother Earth, Father Sky, and all the directions of the compass laid the foundation of thousands of tribes' worlds. As later philosophers spoke of *being*, and later theologians spoke of *grace*, earlier peoples spoke of *power*: to endure, see, enjoy the world, and die bravely. Less concerned with material possessions than we, more concerned with personal spiritual power and wisdom, tribal peoples evolved views of the world and ethical systems significantly different from those of Western people.

Tribal ways have sustained the human race for at least 99 percent of our history (from circa 98,000 B.C.E. to 1000 C.E.). Our modern ways have brought unimagined material prosperity, but also the first real threat of racial suicide. As a result, it is now common to look at tribal peoples' ecological sensitivity with envy. Unfortunately, it is not at all common to re-evaluate the spiritual basis of shamanic life, its rich imagination and ecstatic power, and to consider how it might move us away from our lethal technology, toward fulfillments neither polluting nor destructive. Shamanic wisdom recognized that the first test of power is survival. Whether we shall be as wise remains to be seen.

SUMMARY

Shamanic wisdom often has reposed in the aged. Among the Coastal Salish Indians, for example, old people were free of many taboos and acted as caretakers for people in transition states because of their greater access to spiritual powers and greater learning in tribal traditions. Generally, tribal wisdom has swung between the venerable worldview the elders preserved and the practical skills needed in everyday life. In its entire span, however, shamanic or tribal wisdom has sought an ecological harmony with nature. As the Cahuilla Indians illustrate, being human has meant being part of a natural system of reciprocal rights and
duties. The famous statement of Smohalla put a personal face on this "ecology": for Smohalla's people the earth was a holy mother.

Ceremonies and myths inculcated the ecology of shamanic wisdom. Black Elk's description of the seven main rites of the Oglala Sioux demonstrates the complexity and pervasiveness of one tribal ceremonial. Drawing all parts of nature into their spiritual lives, the Oglala Sioux sought acceptance from Father Spirit and Mother Earth, purity of mind and purity of heart. As the ritual of the sweat lodge makes plain, shamanic wisdom was thoroughly psychosomatic or holistic. In cleansing the body one cleansed the spirit, and vice versa. Interwoven with tribal ceremonies were myths like the Dogon stories that Ogotemmelli preserved. In painting mythical animals on a local temple, a Dogon priest expected to aid the harvest, for the stories the animals recalled were charged with power.

The divinity of most African tribes was spiritual in the sense of removing the High God from daily affairs. Thus everyday events usually were shaped by second-order divinities or spirits. However, in times of special need some African tribes cast their prayers toward the High God, believing he could arise and give them help. From the frank !Kung prayer that admits Gauwa may be bluffing, to the lyric Mashona hymn that praises God as an overflowing vessel, Africans regularly put this theology to the test. Like traditional peoples everywhere, they finally thought that divinity should show itself in power. Past theoreticians of religion may have overemphasized certain aspects of such power, but the general significance of mana or wakanda seems plain. Shamans used ecstacy to gain power. Mothers and warriors exhibited striking power. To be in harmony with nature and the gods was to benefit from the power running the cosmic system; to be out of harmony was to risk such power's running amok.

In our dialogues with shamanic wisdom today, we might do well to stress the power of survival. As we stand close to the threshold of racial suicide, shamanic wisdom can point to tens of thousands of years of survival power.

STUDY QUESTIONS

1. Why was a Coastal Salish grandmother an ideal attendant for a girl at her first menstruation?

2. In what sense were Smohalla's laws ecological?

3. Describe what an Oglala Sioux likely experienced in the sweat lodge.

4. What is the "universal cycle" into which the Dogon unfertilized seeds would be taken?

5. Write a response for Gauwa.

6. Why could shamans gain special powers?

NOTES

1. Pamela T. Atmoss, "Coastal Salish Elders," in *Other Ways of Growing Old*, ed. Pamela T. Atmoss and Stevan Harrell. Stanford, Calif.: Stanford University Press, 1981, p. 231.

2. Ibid., p. 232.

3. Lowell John Bean, *Mukat's People*. Berkeley: University of California Press Pb, 1974, p. 165.

4. Sam Gill, ed., *Native American Traditions*. Belmont, Calif.: Wadsworth, 1983, p. 157.

5. Black Elk, *The Sacred Pipe*, ed. Joseph Epes Brown. Baltimore: Penguin, 1971, pp. 5–7.

6. Ibid., p. 38.

7. Marcel Griaule, *Conversations with Ogotemmeli*. New York: Oxford University Press, 1965, p. 12.

8. Ibid., p. 112.

9. Ibid., p. 219.

10. John S. Mbiti, *African Religions and Philosophy*. Garden City, N.Y.: Doubleday, 1970, pp. 44–45.

11. Mircea Eliade, *From Primitives to Zen*. New York: Harper & Row, 1967, p. 268.

12. Ibid., pp. 268–69.

13. Ibid., p. 269.

14. Geradus Van der Leeuw, *Religion in Essence and Manifestation*, vol. 1. New York: Harper & Row, 1963, p. 26.

CHAPTER
17

Wisdom in
Prophetic Societies

Israelite Priests
Jewish Rabbis
Christian Priests
Christian Teachers
Muslim Mullahs
Muslim Theologians
Zoroastrians
Summary
Study Questions
Notes

ISRAELITE PRIESTS

The general function of the priest in the history of religion is to mediate between the people and Ultimate Reality, above all by offering sacrifice. In the Hebrew Bible priests have an ancient status and several important functions. According to the Pentateuch (five books of Moses), priests derive from the clan of Aaron, behind whom stands Levi, one of the twelve sons of Jacob and twelve tribes of Israel. The older texts of the Hebrew Bible distinguish at least three priestly tasks: giving oracles (Deut. 33:7–11), instructing in the law (Deut. 33:10), and offering sacrifice (Deut. 33:10). In the view of some scholars, instruction in the law grew out of giving oracles. If so the movement was from a charismatic or shamanistic beginning (receiving the communication of the divine Spirit) to a systematic or reasoned (sapiential) instruction in the divine will. The prophetic quality of biblical religion showed itself

in both phases of such a priestly development, since both oracles and more formalized instruction sought the people's conformity to the divine will, but by the later biblical period instruction in the law had become a prime priestly duty:

"So shall you know that I have sent this command to you, that my covenant with Levi may hold, says the Lord of hosts. My covenant with him was a covenant of life and peace, and I gave them to him, that he might fear; and he feared me, he stood in awe of my name. True instruction was in his mouth, and no wrong was found on his lips. He walked with me in peace and uprightness, and he turned away from iniquity. For the lips of a priest should guard knowledge, and men should seek instruction from his mouth, for he is the messenger of the Lord of hosts. But you have turned aside from the way; you have caused many to stumble by your instruction; you have corrupted the covenant of Levi, says the Lord of hosts, and so I make you

despised and abased before all the people, inasmuch as you have not kept my ways but have shown partiality in your instruction. (Mal. 2:4–9)

In this conception of the responsibilities of the Levites, the priest was to proffer knowledge and instruction in religious matters. He could not do this were he not in awe of God, his life not upright and his lips not clean. His true function was to be a messenger of the Lord (a function not very different from that of the prophet). Were he to stumble, turning aside from true religion, many others would stumble in his wake, because they would not receive the good instruction necessary for strong faith. One sees, therefore, the Hebrews' unwillingness to separate mind and will. People cannot know the will of the biblical God, discern the pathways of biblical religion, without wisdom and understanding. Thus they need a teacher learned in the holy tradition. On the other hand, the mental aspect of learning and teaching is not enough. Unless wisdom and understanding proceed from the heart, expressing a core personality that trembles before the awesome reality of the divine, teaching will not produce religious prosperity. The teachers of Israel therefore had to be holy, not just tellers of the law but doers.

This explains much of the biblical legislation regarding priestly matters. The book of Leviticus, highly revered because traditionally considered one of the five books written by Moses himself, reflects the ritual interests of the Israelite priests. Chapters 1 to 7 deal with laws governing the sacrifice, chapters 8 to 10 with installing the Aaronic priesthood, chapters 11 to 15 deal with laws of cleanliness and uncleanliness, chapter 16 with the ritual for the Day of Atonement, chapters 17 to 26 with the holiness code (ancient materials expressing the need for Israelites to be like their holy God), and chapter 27 with votive offerings and dues. None of this legislation is disinterested or very speculative. All of it is instruction and law aimed at bringing home the implications of the covenant, the demands of sharing life with the holy God. We might express the wisdom of such teaching in the proposition that God demands holiness. To prosper in the only way that is ultimately important, people must discipline themselves to purity and obedience.

The concluding portion of Leviticus 16, dealing with the ritual for the Day of Atonement, encapsules many of these priestly themes:

"And it shall be a statute to you for ever that in the seventh month, on the tenth day of the month, you shall afflict yourselves, and shall do no work, either the native or the stranger who sojourns among you;

for on this day shall atonement be made for you, to cleanse you; from all your sins you shall be clean before the Lord. It is a sabbath of solemn rest to you, and you shall afflict yourselves; it is a statute for ever. And the priest who is anointed and consecrated as priest in his father's place shall make atonement, wearing the holy linen garments; he shall make atonement for the sanctuary, and he shall make atonement for the tent of meeting and for the altar, and he shall make atonement for the priests and for all the people of the assembly. And this shall be an everlasting statute for you, that atonement may be made for the people of Israel once in the year because of all their sins." And Moses did as the Lord commanded him. (Lev. 16:29–34)

JEWISH RABBIS

From 586 to 538 B.C.E. most Jews were in exile in Babylonia. In the mid-fifth century, under the leadership of Ezra and Nehemiah, the small community that had returned to Palestine almost a century before found a new foundation. In Babylonia study had become more egalitarian, no longer limited to the priestly class.

In the beginning of the period following the return, the priests probably continued to dominate the process of teaching the Law, as they had in the past (Malachi 2:7). But now, participation in Torah study became a matter of choice and ability unrelated to lineage or rank among the people. Ezra's role in this process is crucial (Ezra 7:10). Upon his return to Judea in 444, Ezra arranged for a major convocation of the people (Nehemiah 8) in which the Law was read and explained. From this we may assume that he reflected, at least to some extent, ideas and developments that were current in the exile experience.

Moreover, the Law took on a new importance and became the constitution of the Jewish people, to be studied and expounded as the normative guide for living. All future generations saw the Law as the source of Jewish life. The study of Torah took on a greater importance, and all of the sacred literature that developed in later years was directly or indirectly seen as nothing but a commentary on the "constitution."

This development in Jewish life also marked the end of prophecy among the Jews. In the past, God's will was believed to be made known to the people through the prophets; now it was seen as being directly available to them through the Torah. With the Torah becoming paramount in Jewish religion, the need for teachers of the Law replaced the need for charismatic "voices of God."[1]

If one defines prophecy in terms of charismatic inspiration, then prophecy did indeed die out among the Jews after the return from exile (the mystics are an exception as are the writers of apocalyptic.). Then the type around which Judaism clustered was a sapiential figure, who eventually became the rabbi. In the development of Talmudic Judaism, where the rabbis extended the Torah to every nook and cranny of daily life, the charism most prized was legal learning. After their expulsion from Jerusalem in 70 C.E., when the second temple was destroyed, Jews no longer offered sacrifices. The rabbis continued to study and develop sacrificial laws, but the sacrifice itself yielded primacy to religious ethics. As priests had sacrificed, rabbis studied. In fact, study became a primary way of offering oneself to God, even a form of prayer.

To develop their wisdom, to extend the wisdom of the Torah, the rabbis wrote commentaries on both the Scriptures and the teachings of their predecessors. Often their style was concrete, occasionally even piquant:

Our masters have taught: For two years and a half there was a difference between the school of Shammai and the school of Hillel. The one school said: It were better for a man not to have been created than to have been created. And the other school said: It were better for a man to have been created than not to have been created. They voted and concluded: It were better for a man not to have been created than to have been created; now that he has been created, let him search his deeds.[2]

Hillel (about 73–4 B.C.E.) was a Pharisee who used biblical interpretation to justify the oral law. He stressed social justice, ritual piety, and the strenuous study of Torah. Shammai, his contemporary, perhaps was more conservative, and more literal in matters of biblical interpretation. Shammai also advocated diligent study of Torah. At issue in the little story is a sapiential question: Would it have been better for human beings not to have been created? Why might the later rabbis have judged it better for human beings not to have been created? Perhaps because they had seen the sufferings caused by the expulsion from Jerusalem in 70 C.E. Or perhaps because the difficulties of being holy like their God constantly weighed upon them. For whatever reason, since human beings had been created, the rabbis urged them to make their lives as good as possible. If a person were to "search his deeds," he would find much room for progress.

The rabbis' study of Torah, then, was quite practical, quite action-oriented (as the biblical prophets' teachings had been).

The result of the rabbis' labors was the vast Talmudic corpus, layer upon layer of commentary. Of the tendency to describe this Jewish wisdom as "encyclopedic" Judah Goldin has said:

To speak of it as an encyclopedia ... is perhaps useful to suggest its catholicity of interests; but the character of its discussions is as unlike an encyclopedia as is a round-table conversation unlike a polished essay. Once one has said that the Talmud is unique, it is futile of course to search for comparisons. It is not a museum, it is not church minutes, it is not an anthology, it is not an encyclopedia. But even stammering efforts to describe it may not be entirely useless. They may warn us of the dangers in applying literary canons from other genres to such a work. And they may refresh the metaphor which the Sages themselves employed when they contemplated the Talmud. To them it was a sea, full of life and action, with deeps and shallows; skill was indispensable to navigate it; but the expanse was wide and the horizon rich and the voyage rewarding. And because the waters never stood still, they never grew stagnant.[3]

CHRISTIAN PRIESTS

The first followers of Jesus broke with the Old Testament view of priesthood. In their eyes Jesus was the unique and definitive high priest, who had offered himself as a perfect sacrifice. Thus Hebrews writes of Jesus:

The former priests were many in number, because they were prevented by death from continuing in office; but he holds his priesthood permanently, because he continues for ever. Consequently he is able for all time to save those who draw near to God through him, since he always lives to make intercession for them. For it was fitting that we should have such a high priest, holy, blameless, unstained, separated from sinners, exalted above the heavens. He has no need, like those high priests, to offer sacrifices daily, first for his own sins and then for those of the people; he did this once for all when he offered up himself. Indeed, the law appoints men in their weakness as high priests, but the word of the oath, which came later than the law, appoints a Son who has been made perfect for ever. (Hebrews 7:23–28)

Behind this new interpretation of priesthood lies the Christian faith in Jesus' death and resurrection. Hebrews sees Jesus as a heavenly being, eternal and perfect, who came to earth and died to expiate human sins. As the divine Son, Jesus could make a perfect sacrifice. Once, and for all humankind, he expiated sins or made atonement. The oath to which the passage refers comes from Psalm 110:4: "The Lord has sworn and will not change his mind, 'You are a priest for ever after the order of Melchizedek.'" (Melchizedek was a biblical priest-king who reminded Christians of Jesus because he appeared without beginning or end.)

With this notion of Jesus as their high priest, the Christians tended to focus the priesthood on the sacrifice memorialized in their eucharistic ceremony. Although all members of the Christian community shared in the priesthood of Christ, to whom they were joined as branches to the vine, a special class arose with the direct responsibility to keep liturgical and political order. When pressed for the basis of this development, churches such as the Roman Catholic have tended to speak of the ordained priesthood as part of Christ's will for his Church: "We speak of a priestly office and call its authority the 'power of order' (as contrasted with the 'power of jurisdiction' by which the Church is externally governed), because it is Christ's will that within the priestly body of the faithful there be a governing body charged by Christ's authority with celebrating the Eucharist, administering the sacraments, and transmitting the power to do these things."[4]

The functions of priests (or ministers), who have been the most prominent sacral figures in Christianity, expanded through the centuries, so that ritual leadership, political power, and teaching authority all came to be vested in their ranks. Bishops, as the foremost priests, were the prime local authorities, and their power was held to derive from the apostles who had been the first companions of Jesus. If such early Christian writers as James are representative, the wisdom of the first Christian leaders was not speculative but practical:

Who is wise and understanding among you? By his good life let him show his works in the meekness of wisdom. But if you have bitter jealousy and selfish ambition in your hearts, do not boast and be false to the truth. This wisdom is not such as comes down from above, but is earthly, unspiritual, devilish. For where jealousy and selfish ambition exist, there will be disorder and every vile practice. But the wisdom from above is first pure, then peaceable, gentle, open to reason, full of mercy and good fruits, without uncertainty or insincerity. And the harvest of righteousness is sown in peace by those who make peace. (Jas. 3:13–18)

Priests and bishops therefore seldom were sapiential figures in the Aristotelian sense, lost in contemplative rumination. Ideally, they were servants of the upbuilding of the Church, people wise in the ways of the Spirit that conduced to religious growth. Such learning as they possessed amounted to a grasp of the Christian tradition, a formation in the "mind of Christ." Thus their political power was supposed to be almost accidental, the result of a primacy in service. They only existed to further the common good of Christ's followers, without whom they had no reason to be:

The position of Church officials (if we may be pardoned the comparison) is like that of officials in a club of professional chess-players: their functions cannot be discharged by individual players. But their functions have only one ultimate purpose—that excellent chess be played. This purpose accounts for the activities of the club and gives them meaning. Similarly it is the function of the priestly office to serve the universal priesthood of those who believe and love, are sealed by God's Spirit and redeemed, who unconditionally surrender themselves to God in Christ—which in the last analysis is the higher good. But even in its possessor, official priesthood refers back to faith, grace and love. For if it is to be rightly used it requires the Spirit who is poured forth upon all members of the Church.[5]

In such an understanding of the Christian priesthood, one finds both sapiential and prophetic elements. Church officials are supposed to have the wisdom to facilitate the good living of Christian faith, but they will only have such wisdom, and so carry out their special tasks, if they follow the divine Spirit (much as the biblical prophets did).

CHRISTIAN TEACHERS

The Christian bishops who guided the development of the Church in the early centuries C.E. were the young community's foremost theologians. Such talented men as Augustine in the West and the Cappadocians (Basil, Gregory of Nyssa, and Gregory of Nazianzus) in the East led many battles against deviant doctrine. In the process they hammered out the theses about the Trinity, the Incarnation, and grace that became the innermost core of Christian doctrine. For such Church Fathers, teaching and doctrine were central parts of a bishop's pastoral task. Unless the people clung to the same faith as their forebears, they would wander from the path of salvation. True, what the Scriptures taught, and the sacraments enacted, presented many problems. How God might be both three persons and one nature, or how Christ might have two natures but be only one person, was a genuine mystery. But one could always better grasp the inner sense of such a mystery, always develop a keener sense of its religious import. Primary among the ways to such development were deep prayer and devout reading of the Scriptures and the works of holy Fathers. (Many of the great Christian theologians were monks.) Those who took up the pages of God's revealed Word, praying that the Spirit would give them wisdom and understanding, could always hope to learn more of the breadth and height and depth of God's plan of salvation.

Through the Middle Ages theology became an academic enterprise. Bishops continued to safeguard the faith, but a new class of Church professionals took up the work of studying faith systematically. In the West many such teachers made use of the newly recovered works of Aristotle, giants such as Anselm and Aquinas building impressive theological constructs. The general motto in such building made theology "faith seeking understanding." Faith came first, furnishing theologians what they were to try to understand. But reason had its usefulness, since any new insight into the divine mysteries was precious. So the hallmark of the Western medieval thinkers' achievement was a balance between faith and reason. In the East Byzantine theology remained fairly conservative, convinced that the Fathers had laid down a patrimony not easily exhausted.

The sixteenth-century Protestant reformers brought a new teaching style. Probably the most impressive theologian among them was John Calvin, and the doctrinal school that developed after him illustrates some of the pecularities of Christian sagehood.

According to Calvin the Bible contains all that is necessary to know God and our duties towards Him and our neighbour. . . . All human works outside the Christian faith are sins; and even the good works of Christians are intrinsically evil, though covered and not counted as sins through the imputed merits of Christ. This trust ("faith" in the Protestant sense) extends not only, as in Lutheranism, to the certitude of having obtained justification but to the perfect assurance of eternal salvation, and from this follows the specifically Calvinist doctrine of the inadmissibility of grace [its quality of not being able to be lost].[6]

The **Calvinist** stress on biblical revelation reflects the Reformers' distrust of medieval **scholasticism**. For the Reformers the late medieval Church had wandered away from true faith and the only way back was through the Bible. The Spirit would inspire the devout reader with a sense of what the Bible truly taught. In the Calvinist reading of the Bible, prior to the Fall Adam and Eve had enjoyed the power to gain full happiness. Through their Fall into sin, however, they lost both their innocence and their power to do what was pleasing to God. Thus they and their descendants have constantly been displeasing to God. Without the faith in Christ that can repair this disastrous situation, all human actions would be damning. Only the merits of Christ, which extend to his followers as a sort of shield, keep away the wrath of God. Still, believers can trust the merits of Christ completely. Indeed, they can rest assured of eternal salvation, since the grace of Christ that saves them from hell cannot be lost.

Of course, this is only one version of Christian doctrinal wisdom, and many non-Calvinist teachers would dissent from large parts of it. But it sheds light on why many Christians grow up convinced that they are intrinsically sinful, and why many churches prohibit self-confidence and merrymaking. The power of this theology comes from its deep sense of God's grandeur. Because God is utterly holy and powerful, the failings of human beings stand revealed as a deep ungodliness. On the other hand, Calvinism seems to miss some of the humanism in Jesus' teaching. Often Jesus' God seems to care less about people's sins than about their renewal in love. Indeed, sometimes Jesus implies that people will only do what is right, stop their sinning, when they realize that God's love makes them valuable, intrinsically good. As long as they think themselves worthless sinners, they will have little reason to believe they can live righteously.

MUSLIM MULLAHS

The wisdom of the prophetic religion of Islam often has been mediated through the *mullah* (a Persian form of the Arabic word *mawlawi*, "a learned person or scholar"). The Shiites use the term to designate a scholar of the religious law (Shariah), who may also perform such functions as leading prayer in the mosque, teaching the Koran, preaching, and telling stories of the different *imams* (spiritual leaders descended from the Prophet). How, then, do most mullahs regard the Law that they study and expound?

H. A. R. Gibb has suggested that they regard it as the constitution of the Muslim Community:

To regard the Shari'a, *however, as merely a complicated system of legal rules and discussions is entirely inadequate. It is the constitution of the Muslim Community, the pattern of its communal order. As the political government of the Community more and more manifestly failed to fulfil its organized function by its divisions and its growing secularization, it became the task of the religious leaders to make or remake the communal life and order of all Muslims, in every land and under every form of government, in the image of its true pattern, and thus to preserve and to reinforce the unity of the Muslim Community in the terms of its divine constitutions, homogeneous in social practice and ethical ideals. And it is the fact of this millennial and never-completed endeavour, in the face of long-established and resistant local custom among the diverse Muslim populations, which has given the Muslim world that psychological unity which it continues to display down to the present time, and which, in their common Koranic basis, embraces (if more loosely) the Shi'a and Khawarij [an ancient deviant group] as well as the four Sunni schools.*[7]

In rural Iran, where the local mullah often is the most important religious authority, much Muslim teaching expresses prejudice against women, concludes Erika Friedl.[8] For example, at a village gathering an elderly man told a largely female audience the following story about Adam and Eve. Eve had been sulking ("as women always do"). God took pity on Adam, who was lonely and neglected, opening the door to paradise just enough for Adam to get a peek. Eve, who was nosey ("like all women") peeked in too. What she saw—beautiful *houris* [maidens] waiting to serve the men who would come to paradise—made her run back to Adam eager to please.

Another story with the same chastening intent concerned the Prophet's daughter Fatme. One day the Prophet sent Fatme to visit a woman whom he described as the best wife in her town. When Fatme arrived the woman would not admit her, because the woman's husband was not home. She asked Fatme to come back the next day, after the husband had given permission for the visit. The next day Fatme brought along her little son. The woman again refused to receive her, because the husband had only given permission for Fatme to visit, not the son. The third day Fatme brought both her sons. Again she was kept out, because the new permission had only been for herself and one son. Finally, on the fourth day, Fatme gained entrance. She found the woman sitting in the courtyard near the door with her skirts gathered, a stick nearby, a cup of water standing in the sun, and some dry bread in her lap. The woman explained that she ate only bread and water because her husband, a shepherd, had nothing better in his fields. The stick lay nearby in case the husband, finding something wrong, should want to beat her. She gathered her skirts to facilitate sexual intercourse, should her husband feel desire when he saw her from the gate.

The "wisdom" in these stories is quite dubious, from our contemporary Western perspective, but it is the sort of folkloric teaching that mullahs (and their counterparts in Judaism, Christianity, and other religions) have created or repeated for centuries. The general point in such teaching is to reinforce the tribes' sense of values. In the rural Iranian tribe that Friedl was studying, women ranked considerably lower than men. This has hardly been a unique phenomenon. In some epochs of the Christian Middle Ages, priests could quote local town law to the effect that husbands had the right to beat their wives for transgressions, buttressing such law with biblical texts. In many small Jewish towns, the local rabbi held a similar power, his interpretations of Torah and Talmud sanctioning or vetoing a dozen matters in business, family, and synagogue life. Like the medieval priest and the rural mullah, the small-town rabbi often did much of his teaching by stories and proverbs.

Thus the "little tradition" presided over by the main functionaries of the prophetic cultures could have a "wisdom" quite different from the official doctrine or theology being taught at the top. What the elite prescribed was not always what the majority heard. Sometimes it was more rigorous; other times it was more flexible. Generally, however, the offical or scholarly teaching was more closely connected to the pure streams of the tradition, whether Biblical or Koranic. Among village teachers, more legend and local custom were apt to creep in. As a result, teachers with some understanding of both the pure tradition and the local customs became "interpreters." Often the mullah's task was to prevent the ignorant from distorting the Shariah utterly.

MUSLIM THEOLOGIANS

To represent the high tradition of Muslim teaching, we draw upon a creedal statement attributed to Ahmad ibn Hanbal (d. 855 C.E.), the founder of one of the four great Sunni schools of jurisprudence. One of the major debates raging in Hanbal's time concerned the relation between faith and works. Hanbal went to the core of the issue, pointing out that even one's faith (obviously one's works) depends completely on the mercy of God:

And when a man is asked, are you a believer? he should say, I am a believer, if God wills; or I am, I hope; or he should say, I believe in God, His angels, His Books and His Messengers. ... Man's destiny is from God, with its good and evil, its paucity and abundance, its outward and inward, its sweet and bitter, its liked and disliked, its good and bad, its first and last. ... It is a decree that He has ordained, a destiny that He has determined for men. No one ever will go beyond the will of God (may He be glorified), nor overstep His decree. Rather, all will attain the destiny for which He has created them, applying themselves to the deeds which He has determined for them in His justice (may our Lord be glorified). ... [9]

We sense in this passage a wisdom similar to Calvin's. Hanbal is so impressed by the sovereignty of God that he places all happenings in God's hands. This does not necessarily deny human freedom. God's will and power can be the foundation or enablement of human freedom. But it does underscore the overwhelming primacy of the Creator. If there is a God like the Allah of the Koran, He is Lord of *everything*. Nothing happens without His permission. All places and times stand before His mind. The believer may quake at such a theology or derive from it great peace. The Lord of the World knows all and could condemn much. Yet Koranic revelation insists that Allah is merciful, compassionate, fully just. He did not send Muhammad so much from wrath as from a desire to warn humankind, to give them a chance to repent and gain bliss in the Garden.

The religious wisdom of Hanbal probably is most impressive when it elucidates the believer's abandonment of self to God. The consistent implication of a theology of divine providence or predestination as deep as Hanbal's is that one must surrender all ego to the Creator of the worlds. Shariah, then, could become but a means of self-surrender. Although some people might get lost in the letters, others could use the many prescriptions of the Law to give themselves over completely to the divine will. When such a use steered a middle path between rigor and laxity, hopelessness and presumption, it displayed a very mature Muslim faith.

For then everything that one experienced—the good and the bad, the sweet and the bitter—could be given its properly Godward orientation. One could still fight the evil and second the good, but now in the wider perspective of God's mystery. In God's mystery, many things turn out to be complicated, much "good-ness" and "evil" is hard to judge. Indeed, a great deal of the meaning of what happens to us depends on our attitude. Devout Muslims would say that when we remain honest about this mysteriousness, admitting that our fates wholly repose in God, we approach a position in which we cannot lose. If things go well, we can praise the divine goodness. If things go badly, we can beg the divine help. Our transgressions can bring us a deeper sense of God's patience. Our joys can light the sky with a parent's smile.

As Muslim wisdom wrestled with these and other aspects of the relation between the divine and the created, some of its best theologians verged on a "negative theology" like that of many Hindu and Christian mystics. Stressing the divine distance from everything created, such theologians wanted God to be "beyond," nothing we might take for granted. The following series of questions and answers drives this point home:

QUESTION: What does it mean to believe in the existence of God Most High? ANSWER: It means to believe that God Most High exists and that He exists by virtue of His essence, not by virtue of any intermediary, and that His existence is necessary ... not affected by non-existence. ... QUESTION: What does it mean to believe in the infinite anteriority of God? ANSWER: It means to believe that God is pre-existent. We mean by this that He existed before everything, that at no time was He non-existent, and that His existence had no beginning. QUESTION: What does it mean to believe in the infinite continuance of God (may He be praised and exalted)? ANSWER: It means to believe that God (may He be praised and exalted) is permanently existent, that His permanence has no end, that He will never cease to exist, and that nonexistence can never come to Him. QUESTION: What does it mean to believe that God Most High is dissimilar to contingent beings, that is, to creatures? ANSWER: It means to believe that nothing is like God Most High, neither in His essence, nor in His attributes, nor in His acts. QUESTION: What does it mean to believe that God (may He be praised and exalted) is dissimilar in His essence to creatures? ANSWER: It means to believe that the essence of God (may He be praised and exalted) does not resemble creatures in any way. Whatever you might conceive in your mind, God is not like that, "Like Him there is naught." (Surah 42:9) [10]

The theologians who discoursed in this manner moved Islam close to the sapiential style of the Greeks and the Indians. For such theologians, questions of being and questions of action greatly overlapped. To think correctly about God was very important, because what one thought would shape how one prayed, kept the Five Pillars, followed the Shariah. Realizing that God is completely Other, one might pray and act mystically, as though, despite all His invisibility, God's otherness made Him as near as the pulse at one's throat.

ZOROASTRIANS

Zoroaster (ca. 628–551 B.C.E.) was the Iranian prophet, long antedating Islam, who, along with the Hebrew prophets, ushered in the "axial age" when the human personality came to know its individual structure:

It was concern with the private individual as personal, as independent in some degree from the group of which he formed a part, that increasingly exercised the great prophets who arose in the Axial Age, notably Zarathustra (Zoroaster) in Iran and the Biblical prophets among the Hebrews. The prophets spoke to human beings in the name of a supreme and unique God, not reducible within any image, visible or mental, but expressing a moral dimension in the cosmos; they demanded unconditional allegiance from each person to this transcendent vision. Zarathustra and his successors preached the duty of each individual personally to take part in a cosmic struggle between good and evil, justice and injustice, light and dark; a struggle in which finally light and truth must be victorious.[11]

Shortly after the Muslim invasions of the seventh century C.E., the Zoroastrian church, trying to regroup, summarized the teachings it had received from Zoroaster and developed for over a millennium. Known both as "Selected Counsels of the Ancient Sages" and "The Book of Counsel of Zartusht," this catechism brought together the essentials of faith that every fifteen-year-old was expected to know before being invested with the sacred girdle and so officially coming of age. The text begins with a series of questions:

In conformity with the revelation of the Religion the ancient sages, in their primeval wisdom, have said that on reaching the age of fifteen every man and woman must know the answer to these questions: "Who am I? To whom do I belong? From whence have I come? and whither do I return? From what stock and lineage am I? What is my function and duty on earth? and what is my reward in the world to come? Did I come forth from the unseen world? or was I (always) of this world? Do I belong to Ohrmazd [the good Spirit]

or to Ahriman [the Devil]? Do I belong to the gods or to the demons? Do I belong to the good or to the wicked?[12]

These are good questions, and the ability to answer them would prove anyone's maturity. Perhaps the most central question, however, is: "What is my function and duty on earth?" Studying the answer that the young initiate was supposed to give may show us the core of Zoroastrian sagehood.

The answer has several parts. First, the devout Zoroastrian's primary duty on earth is to confess the faith, practice it, take part in its worship, and live it well. Living it well entails ever keeping Ohrmazd in mind, distinguishing profit and loss, and marking the difference between sins and good deeds. From the outset, then, the wise Zoroastrian thinks of life as a battleground between good and evil. Ohrmazd and Ahriman are fighting it out, so one must constantly choose one's allegiance. The second duty incumbent upon all the faithful is marriage and procreation. The fight between light and darkness is quite physical, a question of powers that shape the earth. By begetting earthly offspring the believer builds up the forces of good, increases the power of life and vitality.

The third duty runs in the same vein: The believer is to cultivate and till the soil. Whatever brings fruitfulness and growth is part of the weaponry of Ohrmazd. Physical vigor and natural bounty bespeak the Good Spirit; decay and barrenness are the ways of the Evil Spirit. The fourth duty, expressed somewhat strikingly, extends this principle to the animal kingdom. The believer is to "treat all livestock justly." Since animals are an important part of the reality being contested between the two great powers, bringing animals into the fold of Ohrmazd, and expressing one's faith in His lordship over them, is a religious act.

The fifth and last duty divides believers' time into thirds. One third of their nights and days are to be spent attending the seminary and consulting the holy sages. Another third are to go for tilling the soil and making it fruitful. The final third are to be spent in eating, rest, and enjoyment. Such a division of life time is intriguing. Study, work, and recreation emerge as equally valuable. All of life comes under the sway of the Good Spirit, and this division of life time would make people pleasing to the Good Spirit by developing their learning, prosperity, and health. One keeping this discipline could expect to pass the Judgment and come to the Final Resurrection, when the Light of Paradise would begin to shine. For the prophetic religion of Zoroastrianism, then, wisdom has been knowing which of life's two primordial paths leads to bliss and walking it steadfastly.

SUMMARY

To indicate the sapiential dimension of representative prophetic societies we dealt with Jewish, Christian, Muslim, and Zoroastrian figures and teachings. For Israelite priests, instruction in the Law was a prime duty. This instruction, and the study it assumed, were quite practical, as the legislation in such priestly books as Leviticus suggests. The goal of Israelite priestly lore was a holiness worthy of the holy God. Among the rabbis the goal did not change but the focus shifted from sacrifice and ritual to study. After the return from exile in Babylon the Torah became the community's mainstay. Those learned in the Torah became the heroes of faith, and through Talmudic times the implications of the Torah extended until they became a great sea.

Christian priests stood in the lineaments of Jesus, the great high priest who had sacrificed himself for his people's salvation. Thus the Christian ordained have had a sharply liturgical orientation. The wisdom for which they have been trained is that which would preserve the traditional faith and build up the vitality of the Church. Christian teachers such as the Fathers, medieval scholastics, and Reformers slowly developed a scholarly theology. In Calvin's view of creation, the Fall, and salvation, the Bible was the great authority and wisdom was accepting one's predestined fate from God.

The Muslim mullahs who mediated Shariah to the common people were perhaps the most popular exponents of Islamic wisdom. In their view the Law or Faith was the constitution of the community, its divinely given blueprint. Often the local mullahs instructed through folkloric means, as did the local Christian priests and rabbis. The misogynism afflicting rural Iranian religion in recent times shows some of the dangers in all the religions' popular wisdoms, as the teachings of great theologians such as Hanbal represent impressive achievements. Hanbal's sense of God's overwhelming priority anticipated Calvin's. Muslim questions and answers about the divine essence and otherness show a negative theology far removed from popular corruptions.

Zoroastrianism suggests a final transmutation of prophecy into wisdom. The dualism of the Iranian prophet became the serious catechetical questioning of people trying to live for Ohrmazd rather than Ahriman. In teaching their young people who they were, where they came from, how they were to live, and the rest, traditional Zoroastrians developed a corps of believers dedicated to fighting on the side of life and light.

STUDY QUESTIONS

1. How did Israelite priests think about atonement?

2. To what degree was the disagreement between Hillel and Shammai sapiential?

3. How wise is the view that Christian Church officials should be as instrumental as officials in a chess club?

4. How does the Calvinist reliance on the interior persuasion of the Holy Spirit blur the distinction between prophecy and wisdom?

5. Why does local teaching often resort to stories?

6. What is the religious implication of the Koranic verse "Like Him there is naught" (Koran 42:9)?

7. Evaluate the Zoroastrian division of life time into thirds.

NOTES

1. Samuel T. Lachs and Saul P. Wachs, *Judaism.* Niles, Ill.: Argus, 1979, p. 9.

2. Nahum N. Glatzer, ed., *Hammer on the Rock: A Midrash Reader.* New York: Schocken, 1962, p. 13.

3. Judah Goldin, "The Period of the Talmud," in *The Jews,* ed. Louis Finkelstein. New York: Schocken, 1970, p. 189.

4. Karl Rahner and Herbert Vorgrimler, *Theological Dictionary.* New York: Herder & Herder, 1965, p. 377.

5. Ibid.

6. F. L. Cross, ed., *The Oxford Dictionary of the Christian Church.* London: Oxford University Press, 1966, p. 220.

7. H. A. R. Gibb, "Islam," in *The Concise Encyclopedia of Living Faiths.* Boston: Beacon, 1967, p. 182.

8. Erika Friedl, "Islam and Tribal Women in a Village in Iran," in *Unspoken Worlds,* ed. Nancy Falk and Rita Gross. San Francisco: Harper & Row, 1980, pp. 159–73.

9. Kenneth Cragg and Marston Speight, eds., *Islam From Within.* Belmont, Calif.: Wadsworth, 1980, pp. 119–20.

10. Ibid., p. 137.

11. Marshall G. S. Hodgson, *The Venture of Islam,*

vol. 1. Chicago: University of Chicago Press, 1974, p. 115.

    12.   R. C. Zaehner, *The Teachings of the Magi.* New York: Oxford University Press, 1956, pp. 20–21.

CHAPTER

18

Conclusion

Stages on Life's Way
Contemporary Shamanism
Contemporary Prophecy
Contemporary Wisdom
Dinah Howell Revisited
Summary
Study Questions
Notes

STAGES ON LIFE'S WAY

The religious figures and ideas we have studied collect both sociological and psychological energies. Shamans, prophets, and sages have all functioned as central religious resources for their societies, but they also represent psychological potentialities that cut across sociocultural boundaries. In light of today's interest in personality development, these psychological potentialities take on some interesting overtones. As theoreticians such as Erik Erikson, Lawrence Kohlberg, James Fowler, Robert Kegan, and Carol Gilligan show, life time tends to unfold in stages.[1] Is it possible, then, that shamans, prophets, and sages emerge at different stages of the evolution of the religious personality?

It is indeed possible. In fact, there are quite apparent correlations between our three central religious types and the crises and virtues Erikson finds in adolescence, adulthood, and old age. Since Erikson makes it plain that early characteristics continue in later life and later virtues are anticipated in early life, such correlations need not imprison any religious type in a particular personality stage. In fact, central religious functionaries in nonliterate, Western, and Eastern cultures have tended to display many of the strengths of all the stages of the life cycle. But the similarities between shamanic initiation and the adolescent identity crisis, prophetic willfulness and the adult crisis of generativity, and sagacious understanding and the crisis of integrity in old age are quite arresting.

Shamans tend to gain their vocations at the transition from childhood to adulthood. Whether through the initiatory death-resurrection of the Siberian ecstatic or the vision quest of the American Indian, the goal is an intense experience that changes the person's images of both self and world. Typically, animals and plants become more vivid. The world stands fraught with powers the shaman can tap, voices offering guidance. Through such an initiation, the tribal member becomes an exceptional adult. Their visionary experiences give shamans a solid, powerful identity. Ever after, asking who the shaman is leads back to the images that crystallized in the initiation. Like the adolescent who comes together in the more or less dramatic experience of finding a work, a social role, or a comfortable persona, shamans are integrated by their initiations. Later life may deepen or even alter this integration, but the work of shamanizing depends on the first solutions of an indentity crisis.

We have described prophets in terms of will, stressing their vocation from God to present their society a Word that would transform its behavior. However dazzling the prophet's visions, this ethical Word dominates the prophet's general role. From the cauldron of prophetic experience a divine imperative bubbles forth: Do what is right! To a world stripped of idols, bent low to worship One Lord, the prophet delivers a message insisting on justice and obedience. Typically, this message has little patience with ambiguity. The Law that codifies the Word easily becomes an absolute. True, the Law usually gains nuance and subtlety, as later teachers try to extend it to all of life. But in itself the prophetic word holds small brief for confusion. God has set before human beings only two ways: death and life. The way of death is disobedience. The way of life is following the Torah, the Gospel, or the Koran. The Prophet, like the adult, is nearly obsessed with generativity (gaining life). Because prophets care for life so passionately, all the institutions necessary for life draw prophets' criticism. Any stagnation, weakness of faith, or moral fatigue that threatens life feels the prophetic lash.

The sage tends to move beyond imperatives and clarities to simple being and unknowing. For the sage the mystery of the Way, the Buddhanature, or Brahman is so absorbing that lesser matters lose their urgency. Sages may strongly support their peoples' traditions. Much of their reflection can be political. But the wisdom to love life in face of death, the strength to end one's years whole rather than despairing, only comes from having gone beyond laws, customs, traditions and the rest to deal with the ground-level mystery. Communing with the darkness of our origin, the darkness of our term, sages detach themselves from the preconceptions and obsessions that blind the rest of us. More and more the wondrous aspect of people and stars, animals and sunsets dominates their interest. So sages, like typically successful older people, let go of themselves, accepting a mystery they finally realize they can never dominate, one they must accept and accommodate as a spouse.

CONTEMPORARY SHAMANISM

When we turn from the forms of tribal shamanism to the imaginative power it displays we discover many correlations between shamanism and religious art. Indeed, it becomes clear that the power shamanic rituals seek has strong affinities with the therapies of drama and the ecstasies of literature, music, and painting.

Then a film such as *We of the Never Never* becomes a variation on the shamanic theme of death and resurrection. Although the landscape is the Australian outback, rather than the mountains or steppes of Central Asia, the plot is similar. A woman finds she must die to the civilities of middle-class society, suffer even the death of her beloved husband, to learn the life of the beautiful land, the strength of an unspoiled child. Or listening to *A Prairie Home Companion* one is seized by the melodies of Ukrainian folk song. They are so pure, so spirited, that one soars in flights of fantasy. Or musing over a novel one leaves weekday imagination and takes a sabbath journey, finding roots in Africa that tangle with the roots of suffering peoples everywhere.

Art is ecstatic, and religious art doubly so. It is shamanic, in that it sparks the imagination to flights that bring power, opens the soul to forces that integrate and heal. Consider the following dialogue:

Here's the thing, say Shug. The thing I believe. God is inside you and inside everybody else. You come into the world with God. But only them that search for it inside find it. And sometimes it just manifest itself even if you not looking, or don't know what you looking for. Trouble do it for most folks, I think. Sorrow, lord. Feeling like shit. It? I ast. Yeah, It. God ain't a he or a she, but a It. But what do it look like? I ast. Don't look like nothing, she say. It ain't a picture show. It ain't something you can look at apart from anything else, including yourself. I believe God is everything, say Shug. Everything that is or ever was or ever will be. And when you can feel that, and be happy to feel that, you've found It.

Shug a beautiful something, let me tell you. She frown a little, look out cross the yard, lean back in her chair, look like a big rose. She say, My first step from the old white man was trees. Then air. Then birds. Then other people. But one day when I was sitting quiet and feeling like a motherless child, which I was, it come to me: that feeling of being part of everything, not separate at all. I knew that if I cut a tree, my arm would bleed. And I laughed and I cried and I run all around the house. I knew just what it was. In fact, when it happened, you can't miss it. It sort of like you know what, she say, grinning and rubbing high up on my thigh. Shug! I say. Oh, she say. God love all them feelings. That's some of the best stuff God did. And when you know God loves 'em you enjoys 'em a lot more. You can just relax, go with everything that's going, and praise God by liking what you like.

God don't think it dirty? I ast. Naw, she say. God made it. Listen, God love everything you love—and a mess of stuff you don't. But more than anything else,

God love admiration. You saying God vain? I ast. Naw, she say. Not vain, just wanting to share a good thing. I think it pisses God off if you walk by the color purple in a field somewhere and don't notice it. What it do when it pissed off? I ast. Oh, it make something else. People think pleasing God is all God care about. But any fool living in the world can see it always trying to please us back.[2]

The God described in the dialogue is close and natural. In religious ecstasy, which is quite like sexual ecstasy, the person stripped of other comforts feels the nearness of what is ultimate. Then trees, air, flowers, and other people become presences of God. God is not separate from ordinary pains and joys. God loves what human beings love, wants appreciation for all that is beautiful. So the outgoing of the shaman, the religious visionary, or the artist brings a homecoming that makes the physical world sacred. The struggle to overcome everydayness and to reach a point of view that gives things meaning culminates in a return to everydayness. What builds up life and goodness in nature and among people is good. What destroys life and goodness in nature or among people is bad. Racism and sexism, the glaring evils with which the novel contends, only grow worse by this criterion. Shug's theological confession clarifies their unnatural, arbitrary character. Having looked at the world with fresh eyes, Shug sees the poverty of imagination in evil. People step on one another because they are too stupid or lazy to admire the good things God has made.

So one way to make shamanism contemporary is to expose oneself to good art. Going with something that's going beautifully, imaginatively, we step out of the dullness and hopelessness that refuse to let the world shine. Thereby, we contemplate possibilities much realer than our previous dead ends. Religiously, Shug's vision is far more powerful than the blindness of the culture that puts her down. The strength she has gained from suffering is far stronger than the strength of those who bully her racially, sexually, or economically. She is a person of valor and deep humanity; her oppressors are people of little account, because ecstasy has not raised them out of self-centeredness.

CONTEMPORARY PROPHECY

No doubt artists such as the author of the novel we quoted want the world to change. No doubt their visions of what ought to be, truly could be, make them

feel responsible for social change. Still, their style of address is more imaginative than volitional. In the foreground are the characters and visions they may have been inspired to create. Social changes, conversions, and fresh dedications to justice are in the background.

One of the exceptions to this characterization is Elie Wiesel. For although Wiesel is an estimable artist, well acquainted with shamanic flights of imaginative creativity, the core motivation or passion of his life and work is prophetic. Robert McAfee Brown's recent study makes this point early on, comparing Wiesel to the prophet Jeremiah.

Brown draws this comparison from Wiesel's own problems with Job, the innocent sufferer to whom many of Wiesel's readers likely would compare him. As Job suffered without any guilt, so Wiesel suffered the loss of his family in the Nazi concentration camps through no fault of his own. But in the Bible Job finally capitulates to God, agreeing that he has no basis for questioning the divine ways. Wiesel, however, has continued to challenge God to explain His role in the holocaust. Thus in his own interpretation of Job Wiesel makes the capitulation insincere, a ploy by which to mock the supposedly just deity:

Wiesel would have preferred another ending in which Job remained a fighter. And he salvages the biblical text only by ingeniously suggesting that Job's pious assertions at the end were spoken in a mocking tone, their very orthodoxy suggesting—on the lips of one like Job—that their content is spurious, and that "in spite or perhaps because of appearances, Job continued to interrogate God."[3]

Brown goes on to express many parallels between Wiesel and the biblical prophet Jeremiah. Both were victims of injustice by virtue of their origin, Wiesel because he was a Jew living in a Hungarian town that lay in the path of the Nazi onslaught. Both were survivors, witnesses who felt compelled to tell the world of the evil they had seen. After a ten-year, self-imposed moratorium, Wiesel seared the world with some of the first lessons of "holocaust literature" in his devastating novel *Night*. Like Jeremiah, Wiesel would force the world to look at what it refuses to see, shattering its serenity. Jeremiah complained that the wicked prosper while the good suffer. Wiesel has greatly magnified this complaint, by simply reporting what "humanity" became in the death camps.

Jeremiah finally taught his contemporaries that a time comes when we must turn from reviewing the ways of death to affirm the ways of life. By the time of his fourth novel, Wiesel had married, fathered a child, and a little light had relieved the darkness of his nightmarish visions. As Jeremiah felt terribly alone, because most people would not hear his speech, so Wiesel has felt alone, depressed by how little has changed, even after a full publication of the events of the holocaust. Both prophets came to feel an obligation to stop an obscene forgetfulness by forcing people to remember the covenant, the Law, and the moral thrust of Israel's existence. Both pondered the possibility that God too suffers and is in exile, and both underscore how we are responsible for our fate. As the biblical prophet came to see a connection between the fate of Israel and the fate of all nations, so has Wiesel. Both have felt they had no choice but to testify, could not do otherwise. Each uses a style that is simple, deceptively so. Both pack their opening statements with most of the message that is to follow. They consider transmission more important than invention. Each would have given a great deal, all that he had, to be able to tell a different tale, speak a normal message.

The point to Brown's characterization of Wiesel in terms of (Brown's understanding of) the prophet Jeremiah is not to present an item-by-item parallelism. The purpose is to express the anguish that both messengers have felt at having to bear words of lamentation and accusation born of a horrifying encounter with human beings' resistance to God. When profound prophets long to be ordinary people, neither especially gifted nor expecially burdened, God or history may single them out for commissions they cannot avoid. Their unpleasent task is forcing their contemporaries, any within sound of their voice, to hear words of judgment, cries that things must change. Today Elie Wiesel, using his biblical and Hasidic heritage, cries out that the points of view, aggressions, and madnesses that produced the holocaust of six million Jews are still with us, above all in the buildup of nuclear arms. Despite Nazism's object lesson in dehumanization, we still hold views of other human beings, indulge amnesias about past policies and brutalizations, that bear bloody similarities to the Nazi perversions. So, out of the depths, Wiesel writes "memoranda": works that say, "You will not forget; I force you to remember."

CONTEMPORARY WISDOM

Novelists such as Alice Walker and Elie Wiesel offer us visions and memoranda that would make us much wiser. In presenting human experiences of God, evil, joy and sorrow, they draw us out of our ordinary torpor, force us to face harder and better things. None-

theless, their view of overall reality, their philosophy or comprehensive vision, tends to be inchoate rather than fully developed, implicit rather than laid out at length. The imagination and will that they employ are crucial faculties, absolutely necessary if the world is to know health and hope. But because they often lack the comprehensive, dispassionate, intellectual elaboration of the total scheme of things, their works may leave us without the full gift that "wisdom" connotes. This is no crushing criticism, of course. It is enough for them to be contemporary shamans and prophets. People's gifts differ, and we—so much less gifted than Walker or Wiesel—ought mainly to be grateful that they have given us so much. Nonetheless, we may still wish that some sage would provide us the gift of wisdom, a view of the whole.

Eric Voegelin seems to be a sage who applies classical Greek understanding of final causes to contemporary problems. Agreeing with Aristotle that an indefinite chain of causes and effects leaves human meaning up in the air, Voegelin shows that virtually no one actually lives without assuming that his or her time makes sense:

How does Aristotle proceed? What is the detailed argument in such matters? He starts from common-sense observations as all good philosophers do, especially the classic philosophers. One should be aware that we always act as if we had an ultimate purpose in fact, as if our life made some sort of sense. I find students frequently are flabbergasted, especially those who are agnostics, when I tell them that they all act, whether agnostics or not, as if they were immortal! Only under the assumption of immortality, of a fulfillment beyond life, is the seriousness of action intelligible which they actually put into their work and which has a fulfillment nowhere in this life however long they may live. They all act as if their lives made sense immortally, even if they deny immortality, deny the existence of a psyche, deny the existence of a Divinity—in brief, if they are just the sort of fairly corrupt average agnostics that you find among college students today. One shouldn't take their agnosticism too seriously, because in fact they act as if they were not agnostics![4]

Voegelin is saying that both Aristotle's commonsensical method and his insistence on ultimate causes remain valid today. In analyzing human existence, we should not let ourselves be mesmerized by what people say. Whether people are intellectuals or barflies, we should mainly attend to what they do, how they live. Not one in a thousand of them lives as though nothing made any difference. At work, with their children, taking a stroll, almost all of them use their imaginations and wills as though honesty, dependability, or appreciation were important. De facto, therefore, such people are not agnostics. De facto, they live their lives as though something in them reached out to transcend the grave. Human life does not explain or justify itself. The individual deeds we perform at work or in our families presuppose significance from a whole or higher power that we ourselves but dimly sense. Still, this dim sensing is sufficient to keep most people going. Hoping, struggling, preserving some remnants of integrity, most people heed the voice of conscience that tells them to try to do a good job, try not to injure their children. Were we to ponder this common phenomenon, the superficial agnosticism mouthed in our colleges would stand revealed as largely a sham, as would the superficial certainties mouthed in our churches.

The fact is, we human beings are complex entities, integrating several levels of being. The ordering of these levels, however, depends upon the primacy of reason, which in return depends upon the divine being that is reason's ground:

Man belongs to inorganic being; with a part of his existence he belongs also to the existence of the psyche; man also has a life of the spirit, a life of reason. The question then simply is: by what is man distinguished from animals, from plants, from inorganic matter? The answer is: by his life of reason. Therefore, conformity to the life of reason is what is best for man in order to live out his nature. It is the life of reason, in the sense of a differential criterion of man, that gives the guide for preferences. All preferences on the merely biological level of instincts and urges, or on the merely psychological level of hedonism or satisfactions, or pleasures, or on the merely metabolistic level of having good food, are on a lower level which is not worth being considered as the ultimate purpose. The ultimate purpose is the life of reason itself. . . .

But now comes a question: what is this nature of man which is briefly formulated as "the life of reason"? For expressing the life of reason we have quite a vocabulary already developed by the classic philosophers, which in part is identical with the Christian vocabulary and has remained a constant through the history of mankind. Here comes now that question of the ground.

The ground of existence is an experienced reality of a transcendent nature towards which one lives in a tension. So, the experience of the tension towards transcendent being is the experiential basis for all analysis in such matters. For the expression of this tension, a vocabulary has been developed. Already

Heraclitus knew three variants or nuances of the tension: love, hope and faith. Where love towards a Divine Being is experienced, where hope for fulfillment in relation to such a Being is experienced as the point of orientation in life—where these experiences are present, there is that openness of the soul in existence which is an orienting centre in the life of man.[5]

DINAH HOWELL REVISITED

For Voegelin, wisdom depends upon an open soul. When we appropriate our tension toward the divine ground, we see that nothing finite or temporal need hold us in sway. Living out of time, toward eternity, we experience the "immortalizing" that Aristotle underscored. This immortalizing makes us free and joyous, fulfilled in our inmost depths. We have begun to fall in love with the Mystery of ultimate reality, which alone can secure us beyond evil and death. Giving our lives over into this Mystery's trust, we begin to live as though ultimate reality were parental, a benevolent light in which there is no darkness at all. Of course, we never apprehend this light fully. Always we suffer the limits of an embodied spirituality. Voegelin is not a Gnostic, telling us we can shed our flesh. He is, however, a mystic philosopher, a lover of wisdom who insists that the primary terms of our right ordering are matters we can experience.

In the beginning of our survey of the world religions' main personality types, we described Dinah Howell, a fictitious everywoman, asking how her struggles for meaning and happiness might strike the great shamans, prophets, and sages. Dinah stood for ourselves: the groping mass of those who are not sure, who want to walk the right way but cannot find it. At the end of our survey, let us try to boil the various functionaries' messages down into a program that Dinah might understand and use. We shall do this in terms of **mysticism** and **sanctity**.

The great figures in the world religions all verify Voegelin's thesis that the primary terms that can give human beings right order are matters of experience. Shamans, prophets, and sages all point to specific times and places when the power of Wakan-Tanka, or the Word of God, or the light of realization came upon them. Thereafter, they spoke of what they had learned directly, personally, as a matter of indisputable experience. Black Elk saw a hopeful future for the Oglala Sioux; Muhammad received the message of the angel Gabriel; the Buddha understood the cause of suffering: All these heroes of religion were mystics, people who had experienced ultimate reality directly. In Voegelin's terms, all were moved by the ground of being to open their imaginations, wills, and minds to a new ordering. Ever after their formative experiences, they dealt with ultimate reality as an intimate. Converted, with their consciousness rearranged, they knew that human beings are not the measure of things. The measure of things is the holy ultimate reality toward which we are in tension, after which we grope.

To Dinah Howell, or to any of us, the mystics offer a remedy: Follow the tension of your being toward the divine ground. Accept faith, hope, and love as guides. Continue to live as though you were immortal. Those who say that this world is all there is cannot guide you. If you will consider your own depths, quiet your senses, and discover the structure of your self, you will learn that holy reality has always been ahead of you, securing your being and laying out your path. It is your nature to commune with this holy reality and nothing less will quiet your restless heart. So learn to meditate, contemplate, pray. Following your thoughts, descending to your heart, you will lose a thousand superficial tyrannies. Slowly but steadily, a unique peace and joy will arise. When you love your God with whole mind, heart, soul, and strength, you will glimpse what seized the souls of the mystics, East and West.[6]

Mysticism, then, is one characteristic of all religions' archetypal figures. The other is sanctity. The preeminent shamans, prophets, and sages have embodied the visions, justice, and wisdom they proclaimed. They have not just spoken of holy things; they have done holy things. Their performance is impressive, but, so is their being. Ultimately, such being must be characterized as "goodness." The archetypal religious personalities were good people, people who brought out the best in those they met. They challenged the laziness of their people but supported their spirit. They demanded conversation, yet they stirred up faith, hope, and love. Although they counseled solitude for meditation and prayer, they addressed society by resolutely opposing injustice. Although they loved quiet communion with the One, they felt strong impulses to succor the many, the suffering and poor. In this sense, their love of their neighbors was as important as their love of their God. They were not just enlightened but compassionate. Their social contacts sent them deeper into contemplation, and their contemplation sent them out on errands of mercy. They followed their tension toward the ground of being, yet they never lost their balance and stumbled into gnosticism.

SUMMARY

The shamans, prophets, and sages we have studied show interesting correlations with the crises of adolescence, adulthood, and old age that developmental psychologists recently have been studying. As teenagers or young adults must find a vision that gives them an identity, pass an initiation into new social and personal roles, so shamans typically gain a new identity at the beginning of their careers. Similarly, the moralistic concerns of prophets parallel the crises of adult generativity in work and family life. Finally, the crises of old age, when people of rich experience must find ways to appreciate life in the face of death and to end their years with integrity, parallel the interests and struggles of sages. This is not to say that wisdom cannot appear early on, nor that shamanism has no lessons for the elderly. It is simply to suggest that the imaginative, volitional, and intellectual emphases that characterize our three archetypical religious functionaries bear intriguing resemblances to typical stages on life's way.

In this perspective, contemporary examples of shamanism, prophecy, and wisdom may take on more resonant tones. The work of contemporary artists such as Alice Walker, author of *The Color Purple,* may seem shamanic in its flights of imagination. When the novel's two main characters focus their image of God, they gain an adult identity, find a religion they can use. The art of Elie Wiesel shares such shamanic virtues, but its more central thrust is prophetic. With his soul in cinders from the holocaust, Wiesel chronicles injustice so that it cannot be forgotten or ignored. The old images that he interprets and the new images that he suggests challenge our will. Such genocidal evil must never happen again, Wiesel avows, and he writes to bind his readers to his resolution. In this he is like the biblical prophet Jeremiah, who felt fated to assault his listeners (and God) with accusations of injustice.

Eric Voegelin, who exemplifies contemporary wisdom, emphasizes the experience of tension toward the divine ground. Here, in the core of our rationality, he finds the Archimedian lever that might order the world. De facto, most people lean unconsciously toward God. Unthinkingly, we presume that we are immortal. Wisdom is taking this given dynamic to heart, making it conscious and loved. If we do, we become mystic philosophers on a small scale. Contemplating the movements of our spirits, we sense the Mystery that gives them rest. In the joy and peace of this tension, ultimate reality opens the self, showing the source of meaning.

For ordinary people, for ourselves and Dinah

Howell, such mysticism is the first approach to spiritual and mental health. We can proceed from there by commitment to the sort of sanctity—goodness toward other people—that the great religious figures have displayed. As they have been mystics communing with the ultimate, so they have also been benefactors of their fellow human beings, people committed to the works of justice and love. The choice to follow them is always before us. No one can keep Dinah Howell miserable but herself. True, mysticism and sanctity are not easy. In the end, though, they may hurt less than confusion and boredom.

STUDY QUESTIONS

1. How is prophecy similar to the challenges of adulthood?

2. Why should God love admiration?

3. Why do the wicked prosper?

4. What is the question of the ground?

5. How might mysticism and sanctity summarize the religion of the archetypal figures we have studied?

NOTES

1. See Erik H. Erikson, *The Life Cycle Completed.* New York: W. W. Norton, 1982; Lawrence Kohlberg, *Collected Papers On Moral Development and Moral Education.* Cambridge, Mass.: Center for Moral Education, 1976; James W. Fowler, *Stages of Faith.* New York: Harper & Row, 1981; Robert Kegan, *The Evolving Self.* Cambridge, Mass.: Harvard University Press, 1982; Carol Gilligan, *In A Different Voice.* Cambridge, Mass.: Harvard University Press, 1982.

2. Alice Walker, *The Color Purple.* New York: Washington Square, 1982, pp. 177–78.

3. Robert McAfee Brown, *Elie Wiesel: Messenger to All Humanity.* South Bend, Ind.: University of Notre Dame Press, 1983, pp. 12–13. Wiesel himself has said, "I believe that the purpose of literature is to correct injustice." *Responses to Elie Wiesel*, ed. Harry James Cargas. New York: Persea Books, 1978, p. 10.

4. Eric Voegelin, *Conversations With Eric Voegelin.* Montreal: Thomas More Institute, 1980, p. 6.

5. Ibid., pp. 7–8.

6. See Rudolf Otto, *Mysticism East and West.* New York: Macmillan, 1970; R. C. Zaehner, *Hindu and Muslim Mysticism.* New York: Schocken, 1969.

A

Appendixes

The following appendixes are brief expositions of the main historical and philosophical features of the traditions we have treated typologically. They represent another, perhaps more standard way of dealing with the major world religions. Because our focus has been on key personality types, we have only alluded to the historical or philosophical context in which particular shamans, prophets, or sages have worked. Now we briefly attend to such contexts, in effect going back over the phenomena of shamanism, prophecy, and sagehood from another point of view.

Our hope is that these appendixes will satisfy the need students and teachers have for background on the world religious traditions. The materials are excerpts from our introductory text, Ways to the Center, 2d ed. (Belmont, Calif.: Wadsworth, 1984). Ways lays out historical and philosophical aspects of the major traditions at some length, and these appendixes are condensations or abstracts of the chapters in Ways. [Teachers and students who aren't especially interested in further historical and philosophical summaries can, of course, simply ignore these materials. But we have been convinced by several readers of our manuscript that it would be useful to offer the option of filling out our typology with standard materials. We hope they will seem a bonus, not a further burden.]

1

Religions of Nonliterate Peoples

In this section, we examine four contemporary non-literate peoples from different parts of the world: American Indians, Eskimos, Africans, and Australians. Each area has many cultural subgroups, so what we can say about each group as a whole is limited. Nonetheless, this chapter should give us a better understanding of how the ancient religious mind has endured down to the present.

AMERICAN INDIANS

Today, because of their contact with white culture, which has altered their reality markedly, few American Indians live as their great-grandparents did. However, on the western reservations enough of the old traditions and native mentality remains to distinguish Indian children from those of other ethnic groups. At least, that is what child psychiatrist Robert Coles concluded after extensive contacts with Pueblo and Hopi children of New Mexico.[1] They showed an instinctive reverence for the land, a living relationship with their departed ancestors, and a revelatory dream life that he had not found in black, white, or Chicano children. All these characteristics indicate ancient beliefs, but the most significant is the orientation to the land.

For our purposes, these attitudes link contemporary American Indians with their most ancient forebears, who probably came from Siberia across a land bridge at the Bering Strait as much as 30,000 years ago. Upon contact with Europeans in the fifteenth century, native North Americans comprised several distinct geographical groups.[2] In the East were woodland tribes, who both hunted and planted. Southeastern tribes cultivated the land extensively, midwestern Plains tribes were primarily buffalo hunters, and southwestern tribes lived in pueblos or were nomads. Along the Pacific Northwest coast, fishers predominated. In each case, the tribal economy determined the life-style. Depending on the buffalo meant a life quite different from that which depended on salmon or corn. Nonetheless, scholars think that some basic attitudes were held by all North Americans.[3]

At the core of these attitudes lay belief in a primary holy force. For the Sioux it was *wakan*; for the Algonquin, *orenda*. Other tribes gave it other names. But shamans throughout the continent agreed that a holy force held all things together. North American Indian life largely revolved around this force. It made nature alluring and intimidating, a source of parental influences that on occasion turned severe. Perhaps the key goal of these tribes was to keep harmony with such holy natural power, to move with its cosmic pulse. Harmony was the way to fertility of both tribe and field, to success in both hunting and war, to a full life. By contrast, disharmony led to disaster: ruined crops, sickly children, defeat in war.

As noted, these ideas originated many millennia in the past. In fact, many of the myths, rituals, and beliefs of the native North Americans resemble those of Siberian tribes, and the two groups share numerous physical characteristics. The North Americans' original myths, rituals, and beliefs likely developed in a culture centered on hunting, warfare, and shamanistic activities, which North Americans pursued until recent times.[4] Even today Navaho ritual attempts cures by singing, and Zuñi ritual shows traces of hunting ceremonies (though the Zuñi have been settled agriculturalists for some time).

Divinity

For the most part, ancient North Americans did not worship a supreme "God." For them, the categories "nature" and "divinity" were largely indistinguishable. Some of the agricultural tribes thought of a supreme power associated with the sky or the sun, but most peoples worshipped several powers. For instance, scholars studying Indian myths find a variety of creator spirits. Earth Diver (an animal or bird who brings the earth up out of the water) is a common one, but the Zuñi tell of numerous workers who disappeared once the world was organized.

Less revered than deities are the myths' culture heroes, whose function is to socialize the tribe. Often they are twins to whom the people trace their arts and crafts. Another superhuman figure in many tribal mythologies is the spirit who owns the animals. Unless the people reverence this spirit, they will not have good hunting or fishing. A third character in North American mythology is the antihero called Trickster. He is both a cunning person and a dupe, a principle of both order and disorder, the founder of convention and yet its chief defier. Typically, he has enlarged intestines, an insatiable appetite, and an extended, uncontrolled penis that goes off on adventures of its own. Trickster will not control his bowels or bladder, and he makes practical jokes and humbles the haughty. In short, he is human impulsiveness, the psychoanalytic id, set free as an entertainer.[5]

These native divinities, of course, were not principally ideas. If we imply that they are philosophical conclusions or abstract inferences, we misrepresent them. Rather, they have been the stuff of story telling, song, and dance. North Americans lived with them, spoke to them from the heart, and sought access to their sacredness through traditional ceremonies. Perhaps such ceremonies are the best introduction to the American Indians' religious sense of both society and self.

Ceremonies

Some ceremonies, which we might call negative, emphasized the dangers of falling out of harmony with sacred power. For instance, warriors and homicides had to be purified, lest they infect the tribe; relatives of dead persons had to be protected against ghosts. Even scalping ceremonies were negative, insofar as they were efforts to tame and tap the male spirit power, which resided in the head. Death, then, was a time of crisis demanding ritual protection to restore the harmony it had upset.

Much other Native American ritual, however, was positive, aiming at intimacy with a benevolent supernatural power. A good example of this is the vision quest. Many North American Indians strenuously sought a vision of a guiding spirit. (South Americans accepted visions that came but tended not to pursue them.) The vision quest became a rite of passage, a threshold to maturity. Without a vision as a guiding experience, one could not walk with direction or live with full purpose. If a young man's vision quest failed, he might become a tribal marginal, forced to dress in women's clothing and barred from male roles. Girls could quest until puberty, when a different kind of power came, the power of motherhood.

As Charles Eastman, a Santee Sioux, tells it, a young man would begin the vision quest with a steam bath, putting off all worldly thoughts. Then he would ascend the most commanding summit, strip to his moccasins and breechcloth, and stand erect and motionless for several days.[6] To prove his sincerity, he might cut off his little finger or offer strips of flesh from his arm. When his vision came, it usually included a promise for his tribe, a glimpse of a tutelary animal (often a wolf or eagle), and a token (perhaps a feather or hair), which became his most prized possession. Finally, the youth would also receive his song—the particular chant that he alone could sing on important occasions. If he had other visions in the future, he could accumulate a "medicine bundle" of tokens. Often shamans who were great healers relied on them to work cures.

An important variation on this vision theme was the Hopi representation of spirits through ceremonial masks. In that tribe, children up to eight or nine believed the *kachinas*, or masked dancers, to be real spirits in their midst. The crisis of the Hopi passage to adulthood occurred when the dancers dropped their masks, for then the young person had to accept that the reality of the *kachinas* was not physical but completely spiritual.[7]

Largely through their visions, Native American shamans functioned as healers, prophets, and diviners. As healers, they tended to suck from victims' bodies objects thought to be the tools of witches or ghosts. Shamans from Navaho and other tribes of the Southwest stressed healing by ritual singing, while holy people of planting tribes specialized in spells for crop fertility. The Pueblos of New Mexico were agriculturalists who shifted from shamanist, rather individualistic, ceremonies to more formalized, priestly rituals. However, even their lengthy chants for healing and fertility retained ecstatic elements from a preagricultural, nomadic past.

Among hunting tribes, the concept of the self or soul was not well defined. Humans were thought to have several souls, one or more of which might live on after death. In fact, the Sioux were exceptional in not fearing the dead. Other tribes would have a child "adopt" a deceased relative to tame the relative's loosed soul. Reincarnation was a common belief, and the Hopi buried dead infants in the hope that their souls would return in future children. The Pueblos had a singularly clear and happy conception of the afterlife. For them the dead would either join the *kachinas* or become rain clouds. More typical was the Hopis' muted hope—they buried women in their wedding dresses, anticipating the women's passage to the next world.

Despite the importance of these notions, Native Americans were less concerned with salvation in a future heaven than with a good life in the present. Happiness or success was to enjoy the beautiful land, to have many children, and to know the spirits intimately. Our modern notions of getting ahead would have meant little to a traditional Native American. Far more important than possessions was the power to see.

Recent Movements

In the nineteenth century, a pantribal movement called the Ghost Dance responded to Indians' depression and temporarily lifted their spirits. It was a cult based on trance and a spiritual message promising that if the Indians renewed the old ways and danced the new dance, they would defeat the whites and witness the return of the buffalo. In 1886 a Paiute named Wowoka rallied hundreds of Paiutes, Kiowas, and Cheyenne in Nevada. By 1890 the Sioux, who had lost 9 million acres of their best land, turned to the Ghost Dance as a last resort. Across the country, Indians sang of the message brought by a spotted eagle: The dead are returning; the nation is coming; the Father will return the elk, the deer, and the buffalo. But the whites killed Sitting Bull, and the movement ended in the tragedy of Wounded Knee.[8]

Today one of the most interesting Native American religious movements is the Peyote religion. It was introduced in the late nineteenth century by Apaches, who traded for peyote across the Mexican border. Slowly a body of rituals developed, many of them from the Plains Indians, until there was a complete ceremonial of confession, singing, drumming, and praying. The movement incorporated some Christian elements, reached many tribes of the Plains and the Southeast, and filled some of the void left by the Ghost Dance. Today, incorporated as the Native American Church, the Peyote religion offers Indians the legal right to take peyote as their ritual sacrament.

In these and other ways, some of the tribes are preserving their traditions. Pueblos, Navahos, and Hopis have retained some of their rituals, while in the Plains the Sun Dance ceremony of dedication and endurance is being revived. On the reservations, though, the main heritage seems to be the intimacy with nature that Coles witnessed and the concern for living at the center of nature that has so impressed Christian observers.[9] With the native American understanding of suffering,[10] this heritage makes for a powerful, underappreciated religious resource. American scholars still have a hard time appreciating the holistic, more-than-rational character of American Indian religion.[11] Perhaps for that reason, foreign scholars have worked more vigorously to show the importance of American Indian religion.[12] But a desire for greater intimacy with earth powers has brought feminist writers such as Margaret Atwood to an American Indian psychology,[13] and ecological concerns may bring more of us to it in the future.[14]

ESKIMOS

Far north of the American Indians, but having some contact and a common Siberian past, have lived the Eskimos, our next ancient religious group. The Eskimo groups differ significantly, especially the coastal and inland groups. However, most of the 50,000 or so who call themselves "Inuit" understand one another. From Greenland, across Canada and Alaska, and to the Bering Strait, their life has traditionally revolved around fishing and hunting. Naturally, their culture is most shaped by their environment. Because sheer survival is a formidable feat, Eskimo children learn to disregard egocentric or self-indulgent impulses. From their earliest years, they are part of a group dominated, regulated, and challenged by the wind, the river, the tundra, and, above all, the snow and ice. They see the harshness of life so clearly that the behavior demanded by their parents makes sense. Furthermore, the opportunities to express kindness and friendliness are all the more precious. Wary yet full of grace, children may grow up and carve wonderful seals or spirits in ivory or stone. Or, they may grow up and try to drown their pain in alcohol.[15]

The Supernatural

The full history of the Eskimos' habitation in the far north is beyond recovery. Their location, physical characteristics, and culture argue for a North Asian origin. Like that of traditional, shamanist Siberian tribes, traditional Eskimo life was dominated by the supernatural. Spirits and powers were as real as ice and snow. Eskimo notions of creation, however, were rather vague. North Alaskans held that when Great Raven was sitting in darkness, he came to consciousness and was moved to create trees and humans.[16]

Eskimos of northern Canada had a myth of Sedna, goddess of the sea and source of the sea animals. Originally, Sedna was a handsome girl who proudly spurned prospective suitors. One spring a fulmar flew in from across the ice and wooed her; his song described the soft bearskins she would rest on and the good food she would never lack were she to become his wife. However, the new bride found herself in the most wretched conditions, bitterly lamenting her rejection of previous human suitors. To avenge her, Sedna's father killed the lying fulmar, but he and Sedna then became objects of the other fulmars' wrath. While Sedna and her father were fleeing from an attack, a heavy storm arose, and the father decided to surrender Sedna to the birds by throwing her overboard. She clung to the side of the boat, but he cut off her fingers. The first joints became whales, the second joints became seals, and the stumps became ground animals. The storm subsided and Sedna returned to the boat with a fierce hatred for her father. While he was sleeping she had her dogs gnaw off his feet and hands. He cursed her, the dogs, and himself, whereupon the earth opened and swallowed them all. Ever since, they have lived in the nether world, where Sedna is mistress of sea life.[17]

In a Greenland version of this myth, Arnaquagsaq, the old woman living in the ocean depths, sits in her dwelling in front of a lamp and sends out the animals that Eskimos hunt. Sometimes, however, parasites settle on her head, and in her anger she keeps back the game. Then the *angakoq* (shaman) must brave the way to her and remove the parasites. To do this, he must cross a turning wheel of ice, negotiate a kettle of boiling water, skirt terrible guardian animals, and finally navigate a bridge as narrow as a knife's edge.[18] He narrates this journey to the community, who follow the tale breathlessly in their mind's eye.

On traditional Eskimo earth live the goblin people—dwarfs, giants, trolls, shadows, and the like—who can help travelers or carry them off to torture. Below the earth is an underworld—a warm, comfortable place where the dead can enjoy what they liked in life. The sky is usually considered a good place, too, although western Greenlanders pictured it as being cold and deserted. When the northern lights appeared in the sky, the dead were believed to be playing football with a walrus head.[19]

Eskimos traditionally regarded rocks, animals, food, and even sleep as alive. Their whole world was alive, though only humans and animals had true souls. The basic image for those souls was either a shadow or a breath. The souls were miniatures of what they animated; thus, they were pictured as tiny humans, tiny caribou, and so on. A child was named for a dead person in the belief that he or she inherited that person's soul and qualities. For that reason, the Caribou Eskimo called a child who had inherited an ancestor's name "grandmother" or "grandfather." Many Eskimos also believed in animal reincarnation. For instance, the fish soul was thought to dwell in the intestines, so they threw fish intestines back into the water to replenish the schools.

The most general Eskimo religious conception, however, was "Sila." Najagneq, a shaman whom the explorer Knud Rasmussen met in Nome, described Sila as "a great spirit, supporting the world and the weather and all life on earth, a spirit so mighty that his utterance to mankind is not through common words, but by storm and snow and rain and the fury of the sea; all the forces of nature that men fear."[20] On the other hand, Sila could also express himself gently, by sunlight or calm of the sea. Frequently, he spoke to small children. Since many of his messages warned of danger, children were directed to alert the shaman. When all was well, Sila dwelt in endless nothingness, apart from everything. He was a mystery, whether he was close or far away. Thus Najagneq concluded, "No one has ever seen Sila; his place of being is a mystery."[21]

The Shaman

Normally, the shaman mediates between Sedna or Sila and the tribe. Another of Rasmussen's informants, Igjugarjuk, said this about shamanist power: "All true wisdom is only to be learned far from the dwellings of men, out in the great solitudes; and is only to be attained through suffering. Privation and suffering are the only things that can open the mind of man to those things which are hidden from others."[22] The hidden powers themselves choose the persons who are to deal with them, often through revelations in dreams.

Igjugarjuk, for instance, became a shaman because of strange visions he had at night, which marked him as a potential *angakoq*. He was therefore given an instructor. In the dead of winter, his instructor placed him in a tiny snow hut and left him without food or drink. His only provision was an exhortation to think of the Great Spirit. Five days later the instructor returned and gave him some lukewarm water. Again he exhorted him to think of the Great Spirit and left. Fifteen days later, the instructor gave Igjugarjuk another drink of water and a small piece of meat. After ten more days—a total of thirty days of nearly complete solitude and fasting—Igjugarjuk saw a helping spirit in the form of a woman. For five months after this he was kept on a strict diet and forbidden sexual intercourse to consolidate his new power. Throughout his later career, he fasted whenever he wanted to see his spirit and gain her help.

Other Eskimo shamans have reported initiations involving being shot through the heart or drowned. One who was drowned described being tied to a pole and carried out onto a frozen lake. His instructor cut a hole in the ice and thrust him into it, so that he stood on the bottom with his head under water. He claimed to have been left in this position for five days, and when he was hauled up, his clothes were not wet. He had overcome death and become a great wizard.[23]

In these accounts, we can see that the Eskimo shaman's way to power is through an initiatory ordeal that often has a death-resurrection motif. Eliade's materials on Eskimo shamans detail other initiatory techniques.[24] For instance, a neophyte may have to rub stones over and over until helping spirits come, or an older shaman may extract the neophyte's soul from his eyes, brain, or intestines, so that the spirits may determine what is best in him. Through this process, the neophyte learns how to draw out the soul himself, so as to travel on mystical journeys. Still another initiatory motif focuses on sudden illumination. In the shaman's brain flashes a sort of searchlight or luminous fire that enables him to see in the dark, perceive coming events, or read others' secret thoughts. Finally, Iglulik Eskimos speak of the shaman's ability to see himself as a skeleton, all of whose parts he can name in a special language. The skeleton represents elementary human stuff, that which can best resist sun, wind, weather, and even death. By going in spirit to his skeleton, the shaman strips himself of perishable flesh and blood and readies himself to deal with the holy.

Traditional Eskimo society focused on survival: gaining shelter against the cold and obtaining the seal, fish, or deer that furnished food and clothing. The basic social unit was the married couple, and the male hunted and the female sewed. Both the hunting and the sewing took place in the midst of complex taboos. As interpreted by the shaman, these taboos formed a system for dealing with the spirits. Shamanist ecstasy, then, served social as well as individual ends. The shaman fasted, danced, or ingested tobacco to gain for the tribe access to the control center of the natural world.

This culture may go back beyond the Bronze Age.[25] Since that time, Eskimos have been hunters, and the elaborate taboo system that they developed seems designed to conciliate the game who had to suffer so that the Eskimos could live. As one Iglulik shaman put it, "Life's greatest danger lies in the fact that man's food consists entirely of souls."[26] Therefore, great precautions were taken to placate the spirits of the game and avoid their anger. For instance, Eskimos poured water on the snout of the ringed seal when they killed it, because it lived in salt water and was thirsty.

Many analyses of Eskimo culture linger somewhat pruriently over marriage.[27] According to Freuchen, Eskimo marriage began by the man's "capturing" the woman (carrying her off more or less against her will). It was not sexually exclusive, for a man might offer his wife to a visiting friend, regularly arrange to share her with other men, take another man's wife on a hunt with him if his own were pregnant, and so on. Some groups practiced polygamy, and the general attitude was that sexual desire is just another appetite like hunger.

In part, these marital arrangements usually reflected a shortage of women. Fathers prized male children, and many female infants were killed by strangling or exposure because raising them and providing a dowry loomed as too great a burden. In daily life, however, women were indispensable. They cooked the food and made all the clothing, often chewing for hours on an animal skin to soften it for sewing. Women went on dogsled trips, and some could handle the dogs better than men. Eskimo men feared menstrual blood, so women were forbidden contact with game. For the same reason, men isolated women who were in labor. In fact, both birth and death were awesome events involving dangerous forces. A new mother was restricted in what she could eat, whom she could see, what clothing she could wear, and more. Only certain persons could touch the dead, and, if possible, a person died outdoors. If death occurred indoors, everything in the house had to be destroyed.[28]

The "spirit songs" recorded by Rasmussen offer our final glimpse into the Eskimo mind.[29] They breathe both loneliness and sensitivity. Fighting their vast, barren land, Eskimos remind us about how many trials ancient peoples endured. Their lives were short, their labors heavy. Eskimo children often died in birth, and Eskimo hunters were frequently lost at sea or frozen in storms. Nonetheless, the Eskimo human spirit devised implements for building igloos at breakneck speed and for hunting, fishing, and traveling by sled. It also produced a somber yet poetic thought world. Although that world was poorer mythologically than those of the American Indian or African, it was equally impressive in imagining life's elemental forces. Sitting on their ice floes and working animal skins, Eskimo men and women did what had to be done to survive. Their wisdom about Sila was no cheap grace; Sila was in both storm and quiet. It moved the bear as well as the child. Knowing Sila, one could call life good. Knowing Sila, one could be glad to be an Eskimo.

AFRICANS

The Africa most germane to our study in this chapter is south of the Sahara.[30] In the north, Islam is now the major influence, while in the south, ancient religion mingles with Christianity. A 1980 census estimated that 200 million Africans were Christians, 190 million were Muslims, and 65 million adhered to traditional ancient ways.[31] However, those figures are deceptive. Ancient notions persist so strongly that African Islam and Christianity differ markedly from their counterparts elsewhere.[32]

Because they were oral peoples, no materials are available for a history of the cultural development of traditional Africans. Still, some analysts of African mythology find indications of very ancient thought patterns, as well as of extensive cross-cultural influences. For instance, one analyst sees in Dogon thought evidence of a time of hunting and gathering, a time of early land cultivation, a time of grain cultivation, and a time of contact with Hellenistic culture.[33] Another analyst, in a famous study of Near Eastern kingship, draws extensive parallels between Egyptian notions more than 4,000 years old and twentieth-century African views.[34] A third, like scholars of ancient peoples generally, underscores the conservatism and tenacity of oral traditions. Some African tribes have kept a ritual language that is different from contemporary speech and that goes back countless generations, just as liturgical Latin or Old Slavonic does.[35]

World View

In analyzing traditional African religion, one first notes that most tribes have had a Supreme Being. In East Africa, its most common name has been Mulungu, which connotes an impersonal spirit that is far away.[36] Mulungu is creative, omnipotent, and omnipresent. It may be heard in thunder and seen in lightning. Originally Mulungu was intimate with the world, but in later days it withdrew. When personified, Mulungu is envisioned as having a wife and family. He molds human bodies and gives all life its breath.

Under Mulungu are subordinate powers.[37] Africans reverence both these powers and their own departed ancestors. The most important of the subordinate natural powers are the spirits of the storm, but earth spirits, water spirits, and spirits associated with crafts (such as blacksmithing and weaving) exert considerable influence, as do gods associated with divination.

West Africans have families of gods and build temples. They tend to pray every day, using simple, personal words, and frequently they pray at one of the many shrines that dot the countryside. Usually their prayers are quite practical—petitions for health, security, good farming, or safe travel. They commonly sacrifice something to a god, usually offering a liquid or cereal.[38]

Through many images, then, traditional Africans made their world sacred. It was a living whole, not our science's objective collection of matter. Perhaps relatedly, African art tends to avoid representing the supreme God. Indeed, there are numerous myths of his withdrawal to the distant heaven. One myth says that originally God's heaven was just above their heads, but children came to wipe their hands on it, women hit it when pounding grain, and finally a woman with a long pole hit heaven in the eye. God then moved away. The Burundi of central Africa say that God went off because a crippled baby was born, and some humans wanted to kill God, whom they held responsible. In African mythology, God often leaves by climbing a spider's thread. If there were a great emergency, humans might to able to find the thread and obtain God's help again. The African God, then, is both far and near, both inscrutable and able to be petitioned. In general, he is considered kind and good, a father or friend. He creates and sustains all things, but no one has ever seen him.

Overall, Africans seem to experience nature as being bountiful and good, unlike the Eskimos. Perhaps as a result, Africans show little tendency toward asceticism. God's heavenly world is but a larger and happier version of their present good life. Many tribes hope that after death there will be a rebirth from the world of ghosts into another part of the sunlit earth.

Because nature is bountiful, natural processes, including sex, are accepted without great question. The Ashanti of Ghana say that sexual knowledge came when the python sent man and woman to lie together. Consequently, many Ashanti thank the python for their children. If they find a dead python, they sprinkle it with white clay and give it a ritual burial. Africans tend to fear abnormal births, however, and disfigured persons become outcasts. Twins are regarded differently by different tribes. Some tribes expose them to die, but others welcome and honor them. Like Eskimos, Africans think that souls are numerous, that the world is alive, and that a new child may inherit a soul from an ancestor.

Traditionally Africans also emphasize rites of passage, investing birth, adolescence, marriage, and death with religious significance and giving the self a sense of development. Usually these rites are performed at home under the guidance of a family elder. At a birth, the family will make offerings to the ancestors. They will also divine to which deity the child should be dedicated. Adolescent ceremonies stress endurance. They are ordeals designed to toughen children into adults and to impart adult sacred lore. Frequently they take the form of circumcision or clitoridectomy.

Many tribes are polygynous, and so African women often are co-wives. As the operation of a women's society such as the Sande of Sierra Leone shows, one of the purposes of clitoridectomy is to develop deep sisterly ties, lest husbands play women off against one another. Thus, the painful excision of the initiate's clitoris is performed amid strong group support; other women console the initiate with food, songs, and dances, promising her that her present suffering will ensure her future fertility and be a sign to her husband of her moral and religious maturity. It is also likely that clitoridectomy is thought to remove any maleness (since the clitoris is perceived as a penislike organ), allowing the woman to fit into her female social status more easily.[39] Anthropologists furnish similarly interesting accounts of African circumcision.[40]

Almost all Africans consider marriage a sacred duty, and children are a great blessing. For that reason, the menarche (first menstruation) can be a time of tribal rejoicing and such celebrations as the Pygmies' *elima* feast for young women. Indeed, female fertility is linked directly to tribal prosperity. With no Social Security system, African parents see many children as their hedge against old age. Thus, polygyny and large families are frequent. Westerners trying to lower the birthrate find themselves upsetting an old economic system.[41]

Funeral rites are intended to separate the dead from the living without offense. One must perform them most carefully, for they can influence the dead person's peace in the spirit world. Funerals keep the living in view, too, stirring up consoling memories and reminding the bereaved that all life is fleeting.

Divination

The African religious functionary who merits most attention is probably the diviner. One scholar has suggested that there are several levels of African divination, and that the diviner at the deeper levels is equivalent to a profound shaman.[42] The two polar categories this scholar uses are "possession" and "wisdom." In possession, the diviner is filled by a spirit that reads omens, interprets movements of sacred animals, and so on. In wisdom, the spirits, gods, and the diviner's own personality are subordinate to the cosmic order. Thus, wisdom is a protoscience or cosmology—an effort to set the facts of nature and experience into some overarching scheme. Often through wisdom the diviner arrives at the notion of a Supreme Being who intelligently controls all cosmic flux. In other words, the diviner of wisdom is an intellectual, not an ecstatic or spirit-possessed functionary. His or her religious talent is to conceive a comprehensive view of how all events fit into a sacred scheme.

However, possession and wisdom are not clearly differentiated. Intermediate forms lie between them. The Mwari cultists of the Matopo Hills of Zimbabwe, for instance, believe that God speaks through mediums whom he possesses deep in certain caves, and that these messages give a comprehensive view of his operations in the world.

Another evidence that African world views reflect centuries of cultural exchange is the common divinatory systems that stretch from Zaire to South Africa. In one system, for example, a basket containing 205 pieces of bone or wood represents all reality. To answer a question, the diviner shakes the basket and analyses the pattern into which the pieces fall. The possible combinations are enormous, so students travel long distances to study with famous teachers. In effect, the basket and its pieces are a microcosm of the African world's social institutions and forces. The diviner can feed into this system the problem at hand and then read out an answer. As with the shaman's report from the gods, the diviner's answer often becomes a means to healing or reconciliation.

With the witch doctor, who is a sort of physician,

the diviner supports the forces of good, just as witches (to be distinguished from witch doctors) and sorcerers are agents of evil. Most tribes think that witches work at night, are usually women, and inherit or buy from demons a power to inflict harm.[43] The sorcerer taps the power that witch doctors use, but turns it to harm. He or she may make potions, cast spells, or put pins in an image of the victim. Needless to say, sorcerers and witches are greatly feared and hated.[44]

AUSTRALIANS

Historically, the Australian aborigines probably migrated from Southeast Asia (southern India and Sri Lanka) about 50,000 years ago. They spread throughout the continent and were isolated from outside influences until the arrival of Europeans in the eighteenth century. From the time of Cook's voyage interest grew, and in 1778 the British settled a penal colony in the area that is now Sydney. At the time of European contact, the aborigines probably numbered about 350,000. Some aspects of their culture suggest that they had had contact with peoples of Melanesia and New Guinea. Presently they number about 120,000, and about 45,000 are of pure stock. In the semidesert northern region, they maintain much of their original culture, which is based on hunting and gathering and which was fairly uniform across the numerous tribes.

World View

The secrecy and foreignness of much Australian lore have made it hard for Western investigators to penetrate its history or philosophic structure. Nevertheless, E. A. Worms has suggested a list of the original religion's essential features, which include the belief in a personal sky being, belief in helping spirit beings, belief in holy, powerful objects left by the sky being, ritual drama to renew divine creativity, initiation rites for both sexes, sacrifice and prayer, and a medicine man leader.[45]

T. G. H. Strehlow has complemented this list by sketching the beliefs that were held over the entire continent.[46] According to Strehlow, most tribes believed in eternal supernatural beings, whom they linked with totemic animals, plants, or natural phenomena. In fact, the concept of totem came into religious studies largely as a result of research in

Australia.[47] As Webster defines it, a totem is "an animal, plant, or other object serving as the emblem of a family or clan." The eternal supernatural beings were therefore ancestors and clan founders.

In the beginning, many tribes say, these supernatural beings slept under the earth's crust. Time began when they were "born out of their eternity" and burst to the surface. According to the Unambal of northwestern Australia, in the beginning Ungud lived in the earth as a snake, while in the sky was Wallanganda, the Milky Way. During the night they created everything through a creative dream. Ungud transformed himself into the beings that he dreamed; Wallanganda threw out a spiritual force, shaped it into images, and projected them onto the rocks of the present landscape.[48] Next, spirits arose, shaped as either animals or humans and based on Wallanganda's images. In turn, they shaped the rest of the earth—mountains, sand hills, plains, and so on. The ancestors were also responsible for the aborigines' sacred songs and rituals, which were preserved with great care.

The ancestors were restrained only by a vague superior force that could punish any crimes, although they were also subject to age, sickness, and decay. Eventually they sank back into their first state of sleep, having produced the sun, moon, stars, death, labor, and pain. In the Northern Territory, scholars have found cults and art honoring the ancestors' fertility. In other regions, natives venerate rocks, trees, and *tjurunga* (distinctive slabs of wood) as sites where ancestors left supernatural powers.

Thus, Australians parceled divinity among several supernatural figures. Central Australians believed that human beings came into existence as semiembryonic masses that were joined together by the hundreds. The totemic ancestors then sliced these masses into individual infants. The traces of these masses left in the landscape became a principle of human life, for pregnant women would receive them and pass them on to the unborn. In other words, a soul could enter the fetus from a certain point in the landscape. It would be an immortal gift from one of the ancestors, the ancestor's own reincarnation. The newborn was thus a being of high dignity. Also, the newborn had strong links to a particular rock or tree, since from it had come the ancestor's spirit.

Now mortal, humans pass through a temporal circuit. Life begins when one's parent perceives the coming of the ancestor's spirit to the womb. This most often occurs in a dream but may be prompted by morning sickness or even birth pangs. During initiation into maturity, one partially reenters the dream time—the time when he or she originated out of eternity. Adult life means returning deeper and deeper into this time through religious ceremonies. At death one crosses the final threshold and again becomes a sacred spirit in the sky.[49]

Ritual

Puberty rites were a crucial occasion. Scholars first thought that they existed only for men, but more recent scholarship suggests that menstruation and childbirth were ritualized as religious experiences.[50] Puberty rites took place in considerable secrecy on sacred ground. Often this sacred ground represented the world as it was in the beginning, for in the puberty ceremonies the participants relived the time of creation.

One tribe, the Kurnai, separated adolescent boys from their mothers matter-of-factly, but most tribes even today begin the ceremonies with much weeping and lamentation. Initiates may vary in age from six to fourteen, and they undergo various bodily operations. Most ceremonies follow a regular pattern of segregation of the initiates, instruction, bodily operations, revelation of some sacred objects and ceremonies, washing, and returning to ordinary life.[51] The dominant symbolism of the entire ceremony is death and resurrection. The novice dies to the child's world of irresponsible ignorance and is reborn as a mature, spiritual being. Supposedly the mothers take the death motif literally. Thinking hostile supernatural beings have killed their sons, they mourn as at a funeral. When the boys return, the women treat them as new beings, quite different from what they were.

During the ceremony, the boys are covered with branches or rugs. They may not use words, only sounds and signs. In the ritual operations deadly supernatural beings act upon them. When the bullroarer (a slat of wood tied to the end of a thong that roars when whirled) is sounded, the supernatural beings may knock out a tooth, pull out hair, or scar the body. Circumcision is the key act, however, because it is a direct slash at a life source.

Six months to three years after circumcision, many tribes perform a second operation called subincision. Students of Australian religion debate its significance. Subincision involves slitting the underside of the penis and permanently opening the urethra. Some tribes give it overtones of bisexuality, likening the wound to a vulva. In that case, it may represent males' efforts to arrogate powers of mothering. Supporting this is the sociological fact that the boys pass from female to male control at this time. Other evidence indicates that subincision is a way to gather blood, which is needed for

other ceremonials. From this perspective the act approximates menstruation.

Girls' initiations are tailored more for the individual, since they are triggered by the onset of menstruation. Older women teach the girl songs and myths relating to female dignity and duties in seclusion. After this instruction, they lead the young woman to a fresh lagoon for a ritual bath and then display her to the community as an adult. In some tribes, a girl's initiation includes defloration with some sort of dildo, followed by ritual intercourse with a group of men. No doubt this act has more than a sadistic or carnal motive, but its exact religious significance is unclear. Certainly ancient peoples treat sexuality as a dimension of tribal life, so perhaps this aspect of the ceremony is a way of tying the potential mother to the gods' and tribe's forces.

The female puberty rite is only the first rite in an Australian woman's life. Marriage, childbearing, menopause, and old age occasion further instruction in the nature of the sacred. As the revelations become more profound, the ceremonies become more secret. Westerners have found a pattern in the women's rituals similar to that in the men's—the reenactment of mythical events from the time of creation.

In early times, women apparently played important parts in the men's rituals. Myths speak of female ancestors who were more powerful than male ancestors and of men stealing songs, powers, and artifacts that had belonged to the women. The bullroarer is one of the artifacts that the men supposedly stole. Women may have originally functioned in the male circumcision rites, for among some tribes today the initiate gives his foreskin to his sister, "who then dries it, anoints it with ochre, and suspends it from her neck."[52] No myth speaks of women stealing important religious items or doctrines from men. Most likely, then, in earlier times religious collaboration between the sexes was greater than it has been recently. In modern times, women have not been privy to male lore. For that reason, men say that women do not progressively reenter the sacred dream time—that female ceremonies are not a steady return to spiritual existence in the sky.

The Medicine Man

The principal figure in Australian ritual life is the medicine man, who derives his healing powers from visionary contacts with supernatural beings. Usually he possesses magical items that symbolize these powers: quartz crystals, pearl shells, stones, bones, or the like.

Mircea Eliade has described the ecstatic, highly imaginary making of a medicine man among the Wiradjuri of southeastern Australia.[53] First his father places two large quartz crystals against the boy's breast. They disappear into his body, making him clever and "able to bring things up." These crystals feel warm, but other ones that the boy drinks look like ice and taste sweet. From this time on, the boy can see ghosts.

During the boy's puberty rites, after a tooth has been knocked out, he learns to go down into the ground and bring up quartz crystals. The initiators take him to a grave, where a dead man rubs him to make him clever. The dead man also gives him a personal totem, a tiger snake. By following the snake, the boy and his father find the living places of various gods. At the initiation's climax, they climb a thread to Baiame's place in the sky. Baiame looks like an old man with a long beard, and from his shoulders extend two great quartz crystals.

Evidently, the medicine man is a sort of shaman whose healing powers derive from his ability to "travel to heaven." They are represented by his quartz crystals, which are part of divinity itself, and his animal spirit, the tiger snake, helps him in his tasks. An Unmatjera medicine man from central Australia reported that an old doctor threw crystals at him during his initiation and then cut out his insides. He was dead until the old man put more crystals in his body, covered it with leaves, and sang over him. The singing caused him to swell up. Then the old man gave him new internal organs and brought him back to life. From that time the medicine man was able to produce quartz crystals within himself at will, and they gave him the power to heal.

Thus, Australian ancient religion bound people to the land and to one another through imaginative myths and rituals that brought them into contact with ancestral totemic spirits or divinities. Its basic goal was to keep harmony with these powers. By integrating with them through ritual, a person supported nature as well as personal and tribal life. Death broke one's ties with the supernatural beings, so funeral rites had two functions—consoling the bereaved and helping the deceased to find his or her new station. The Aranda believed that finding one's new station entailed the immortal soul's going back to the place where it first passed into the fetus. The dead person's second, mortal soul turned into a ghost and was capable of malicious acts. Consequently, the mourning ceremonies tried to mute any anger that the deceased might have borne against relatives and friends. After a stated time, the ghost was incapable of mischief, because it departed for other haunts or faded away.

NOTES

1. Robert Coles, *Children of Crisis,* vol. 4, *Eskimos, Chicanos, Indians* (Boston: Little, Brown, 1977).

2. Weston La Barre, "Amerindian Religions," in *Historical Atlas of the Religions of the World,* ed. I. al Faruqi and D. Sopher (New York: Macmillan, 1974), pp. 51–57.

3. J. R. Fox, "Religions of Illiterate People: North America," in *Historia Religionum, II,* ed. C. J. Bleeker and G. Widengren (Leiden: E. J. Brill, 1971), pp. 593–608.

4. A. Clos, "Religions of Illiterate People: Asia," in *Historia Religionum, II,* ed. C. J. Bleeker and G. Widengren (Leiden: E. J. Brill, 1971), pp. 573–592.

5. Paul Radin, *The Trickster: A Study in American Indian Mythology* (New York: Philosophical Library, 1956).

6. Charles A. Eastman, *The Soul of the Indian* (Boston: Houghton Mifflin, 1911), pp. 6–8.

7. Emory Sekaquaptewa, "Hopi Indian Ceremonies," in *Seeing with a Native Eye,* ed. Walter H. Capps (New York: Harper & Row, 1976), p. 39.

8. Dee Brown, *Bury My Heart at Wounded Knee* (New York: Holt, Rinehart and Winston), 1971.

9. Carl F. Starkloff, *The People of the Center: American Indian Religion and Christianity* (New York: Seabury, 1974).

10. Åke Hultzkrantz, "The Contribution of the Study of North American Indian Religions to the History of Religions," in *Seeing with a Native Eye,* ed. Walter H. Capps (New York: Harper & Row, 1976), pp. 86–106.

11. Sam D. Gill, "Native American Religions," *Council on the Study of Religion Bulletin,* 1978, 9(5):125–128.

12. Åke Hultzkrantz, "North American Indian Religion in the History of Research: A General Survey," *HR,* 1966, 6(2):91–107; 1967, 6(3):183–207; 1967, 7(1):13–34; 1967, 7(2):112–148.

13. Margaret Atwood, *Surfacing* (New York: Popular Library, 1976).

14. N. Scott Momaday, "Native American Attitudes to the Environment," in *Seeing with a Native Eye,* ed. Walter H. Capps (New York: Harper & Row, 1976), pp. 79–85.

15. See Coles, *Children of Crisis,* vol. 4, pp. 216–217.

16. Kaj Birket-Smith, *The Eskimos* (London: Methuen, 1959), p. 161.

17. Franz Boas, *The Central Eskimo* (Lincoln: University of Nebraska Press, 1964), p. 175.

18. Ibid, pp. 178–179.

19. Birket-Smith, *The Eskimos.*

20. Knud Rasmussen, *Across Arctic America* (New York: Putnam's, 1927), p. 385.

21. Ibid, p. 386.

22. Ibid, p. 81.

23. Ibid, p. 86.

24. Mircea Eliade, *Shamanism* (Princeton, N.J.: Princeton University Press, 1964), p. 58.

25. Clos, "Religions of Illiterate People: Asia," p. 576.

26. Birket-Smith, *Eskimos,* p. 166.

27. Peter Freuchen, *Book of the Eskimos* (Cleveland: World, 1961).

28. Boas, *Central Eskimo,* p. 201.

29. Rasmussen, *Across Arctic America,* p. 261.

30. John Mbiti, "Traditional Religions in Africa," in *Historical Atlas of the Religions of the World,* ed. I. al Faruqi and D. Sopher (New York: Macmillan, 1974), pp. 61–68.

31. David B. Barrett, ed., *World Christian Encyclopedia* (New York: Oxford University Press, 1982), p. 782.

32. For moving literary presentations, see Hamidou Kane, *Ambiguous Adventure* (New York: Collier Books, 1969) on Islam, and Chinua Achebe, *No Longer at Ease* (New York: Fawcett, 1969) on Christianity.

33. Evan Zuesse, "Divination and Deity in African Religions," *HR,* 1975, *15*(2):167, note 15.

34. Henri Frankfort, *Kingship and the Gods* (Chicago: University of Chicago Press, 1978), pp. 33–34. (Originally published 1948.)

35. Geoffrey Parrinder, *African Traditional Religion,* 3rd ed. (New York: Harper & Row, 1976), p. 17.

36. Geoffrey Parrinder, "Religions of Illiterate People: Africa," in *Historia Religionum, II,* ed. C. J. Bleeker and G. Widengren (Leiden: E. J. Brill, 1971), p. 556.

37. John Mbiti, *African Religions and Philosophy* (Garden City, N.Y.: Doubleday, 1969), p. 67.

38. Parrinder, "Religions of Illiterate People: Africa," p. 561.

39. This paragraph is adapted from Denise Lardner Carmody, *Women and World Religions* (Nashville: Abingdon, 1979), p. 34. See Carol P. MacCormack, "Biological Events and Cultural Control," *Signs,* 1971, *3*(1):93–100; also Mbiti, *African Religions and Philosophy,* pp. 165–171.

40. Colin Turnbull, *The Forest People* (New York: Simon & Schuster, 1963), p. 217.

41. See Ian Barbour, ed., *Finite Resources and the Human Future* (Minneapolis: Augsburg, 1976), especially pp. 55–114.

42. Zuesse, "Divination and Deity," pp. 158–182.

43. See Parrinder, *African Traditional Religion,* p. 124.

44. This is dramatically portrayed in the anthropological novel by Elenore Smith Bowen, *Return to Laughter* (Garden City, N.Y.: Doubleday, 1964).

45. See Mircea Eliade, *Australian Religions* (Ithaca, N.Y.: Cornell University Press, 1973), p. 194.

46. T. G. H. Strehlow, "Religions of Illiterate People: Australia," in *Historia Religionum, II,* ed. C. J. Bleeker and G. Widengren (Leiden: E. J. Brill, 1971), pp. 609–628.

47. Emile Durkheim, *The Elementary Forms of the Religious Life* (New York: Free Press, 1965).

48. Eliade, *Australian Religions,* p. 68.

49. Mircea Eliade, *From Primitives to Zen* (New York: Harper & Row, 1967), p. 162.

50. Rita M. Gross, "Menstruation and Childbirth as Ritual and Religious Experience in the Religion of the Australian Aborigines," *JAAR,* 1977, *45*(4): 1147–1181.

51. Eliade, *Australian Religions,* p. 88.

52. Ibid, p. 122.

53. Eliade, *From Primitives to Zen,* p. 424.

2

Judaism

Judaism is the oldest of the three major prophetic religions. The founding and development of Christianity and Islam could not have occurred without the preexistence of Judaism.

INTRODUCTION

In the beginning, the Jews were most likely a loose collection of seminomadic tribes that wandered in what is today Israel, Jordan, Lebanon, and Syria. They may have cultivated some crops, but their self-designation was "wandering Aramaeans" (Deut. 26:5). Thus, when scouts returned from Canaan (present-day western Israel) with grapes, pomegranates, and figs (products of settled cultivators), they caused quite a stir.[1]

Members of an extended family tended to worship their particular "god of the father," defining themselves largely in terms of their patriarch and his god. The cult therefore centered on clan remembrance of this god, who wandered with the tribe in its nomadic life. The common name for such a clan divinity was *el*. Before their settlement in Canaan, the people seem to have worshipped a variety of *els:* the god of the mountain, the god of seeing, the god of eternity, and so on. Usually they worshiped at altars constructed of unhewn stones, which they considered to be the god's house. In addition to the "els" were household deities and minor divinities and demons of the desert. In later orthodox Jewish interpretation, Abraham drew on whatever sense there was of a unity among these "els" or of a supreme "el" over the others to dedicate himself to a God who was beyond nature. That God, the creator of the world, Abraham called Yahweh.[2]

For later orthodoxy, Abraham became the "Father" of the Jews and his God Yahweh became their God. In that sense, Judaism began with Abraham. Abraham lived around 1800 B.C.E. From about 1650 to 1280, the people of Abraham, then known as Hebrews, were in Egypt, subjects of the Egyptian kingdom.[3] Their leader at the end of their stay in Egypt was Moses. In later Jewish theology, Moses functioned as the founder of the Jewish people, because God revealed through Moses his will to strike a covenant and fashion himself a people. In the incident at the burning bush, Jewish faith said, Moses experienced God's self-revelation. God commissioned Moses to lead the people out of Egypt, giving as his authoritative name only "I am who I am" (or "I am whatever I want to be").

Moses then led the Jewish people out of Egypt. In the most significant episode in that exodus, Egyptian pursuers drowned in the sea. Free of them, the Israelites (the descendants of Jacob, Abraham's grandson) wandered in the desert until they entered the homeland that God had promised them. The deliverance from Egypt through the unexpected event at the Reed Sea (not the present-day Red Sea) marked all subsequent Jewish faith. Looking back to this event, later generations clung to the belief that their God ruled history and would continue to liberate them from oppression.

In the desert, Moses and the people tested the meaning of their exodus experience. They came to believe, through what the Bible pictures as God's miraculous speaking to them, that they were bound to God by a covenant.[4] In this compact, based on the relation between an overlord and a vassal, God pledged care and the people pledged fidelity. The commandments accompanying this covenant gave the binding relationship (which the Bible saw as prefigured in Adam, Noah, and Abraham) an ethics. They became the basis of the Law and the revelation that bound the people together.

When the Israelites finally settled in Canaan (in the latter half of the thirteenth century B.C.E. under Moses' successor Joshua),[5] they changed from a nomadic to an agricultural people. They were still a group of confederated tribes, but in settlement their bonds tended to loosen, as each group kept to its own area and developed its own ways. Only in times of common danger would the groups weld together. Settlement also meant religious changes, as local sanctuaries replaced the wandering ark of the covenant as the house of God. A somewhat professional priesthood apparently developed around the sanctuaries, and as the Israelites conquered Canaanite temples, they took over the scribal schools attached to the temples. These schools were probably the first sources of written Hebrew religious literature. In addition, the Canaanite religion itself was a great influence on the Israelites. Before long it produced a conflict between Israelites who favored the older God Yahweh—the God of Abraham, Moses, and the covenant—and those who favored the agricultural gods (baals) of the Canaanites.

KINGS AND PROPHETS

From about 1200 to 1000 B.C.E. the Israelites had a government by "judges"—charismatic leaders who took command in times of common danger. However, they eventually adopted monarchical rule, organizing a sturdy little kingdom under David at a new capital: Jerusalem. This kingdom unified the tribes of both north and south, and under Solomon, David's son, it had a brief but golden age of culture and empire.

Following Solomon's death, the northern and southern portions of the kingdom split apart. The north (Israel) lasted from 922 to 722 B.C.E. when it fell to Assyria. The south (Judah) lasted until 586, when it fell to Babylon. (Both Assyria and Babylon lay to the northeast.) These were centuries of great political strife. They also spawned a series of important religious "prophets," who dominate the next phase of biblical history. Greatest of the early prophets was Elijah, who preached in the north against the corrupt kings Ahab and Ahaziah and the queen Jezebel. The legendary stories about Elijah portray him as a champion of Yahweh and of true prophecy against the false prophets of the Canaanite baals. What is clear from these stories is the influence at the time of charismatic personalities who felt that God inspired them to stand up for the old religious ways—even if doing so infuriated the establishment.

Around 750 B.C.E. the northern prophet Amos, who was the first of the writing prophets, issued a clarion call for justice. Changing the notion that Yahweh was simply Israel's protector, Amos made his divine blessings dependent on repentance from sin. His God was clearly in charge of nature, but the key access to him was social justice. In other words, he was a God of people and history, especially concerned that humans deal with one another fairly.

Hosea, another northern prophet, also spoke up for mercy and justice (and for nonidolatrous cult), but he expressed God's attitude as that of a spouse willing to suffer infidelity, unable to cast off his beloved (the people covenanted to him). In the south, the successors to these northern prophets were Isaiah, Jeremiah, and "Second Isaiah" (the source of Isaiah, chapters 40–55). They made the same demands, but with greater stress on punishment by foreign powers. Reading the signs of the times, they thought that God would subject his people to captivity because they had not relied on him in pure faith. However, both Jeremiah and Second Isaiah held out hope for a new beginning, assuring Judah that a remnant of the people would keep faith.

Prophecy, which often distinguishes Western religion from Eastern wisdom religion, is not so much the predictions that appear on today's tabloids as a discernment of what the divine spirit is saying to the people of God. The great biblical prophets analyzed the state of faith and, from that analysis, shrewdly estimated political or military fortunes. A goodly portion of such recorded prophecy was, of course, written after the fact. No portion of respectable prophecy, though, pries into the divine mystery. God remains God; the prophet has only the word that God deigns to speak. The establishment of Moses as the supreme prophet testifies to the social utility that Jews have expected communication with God to bear. They expected such communication to result in communal renovation, strengthening, and redirection. Prophecy was not a display of individual virtuosity or a matter involving crystal balls.

As prophecy intimates, the ultimate bonding agent of Jewish society has been God; only the atypical, modern secular Jew would dispute this. Through history the master of the universe, the Adonai that all prayers bless, has bound Jews together as his people. Physically and legally one is a Jew if one is born of a Jewish mother; spiritually one is a Jew if one identifies oneself with the people fashioned at Sinai, framed by the Torah, and covenanted to God. To be sure, many problems attend election as God's people, and Jews have not been unmindful of them. Indeed, the relations between the chosen people and the Gentile nations has been a constant topic for Jewish meditation. In good times, such meditation has turned over history's mysteries gratefully: Why were we chosen when we show no special merits? What are our obligations to the nations?

Indubitably, the Gentile nations were under God's direction, too. It could not be that God had no fulfillment in store for them. So Jewish thinkers worked out the notion of the Noachian covenant: God made a pact with the Gentile nations modeled after the promise he made to Noah, in which he stressed the need for human beings to respect life, especially by avoiding bloodshed. The Bible sees the rainbow as a symbol of God's fidelity to this pact: He will never destroy humanity, never again allow it to suffer as it did in the flood. Yet God could well have more in store for the nations than this Noachian covenant, and Israel's vocation was to be a light unto the nations—to provide them with a greater knowledge of God. In that way, being the chosen people became less a matter of honor than of responsibility.

In bad times, however, reflection on being chosen by God had to probe darker mysteries. For instance, the prophets almost fixated on the horror that Israelites refused their election. Such people wanted kings like the nations had, cults like those to Baal, fertility from the land rather than from the covenant. With some deliberateness, many Jews turned their backs on God because they could not endure living in faith; "I am whatever I want to be" was too much for them. For the prophets, this was the deepest sickness of the soul, the most debilitating sin, as well as a rejection of Israel's better self. The worst of biblical times, then, occurred when people left the covenantal faith.

During the reign of the southern king Josiah (640–609 B.C.E.), there was a religious reform that scripture scholars see as the source of the "Deuteronomic" recasting of the early Jewish tradition. It shaped not only the book of Deuteronomy but other historical writings as well. Among the influential ideas were that Yahweh had elected Israel to be his people; that observing the covenant laws was necessary for religious prosperity; that Jews ought to repudiate contacts with foreigners and foreign gods; that the cult should be consolidated in Jerusalem; and that Israel ought to rely only on Yahweh, since he controls history and oversees nature. Both the prophets and the Deuteronomic historian-theologians, therefore, testify to the dangers to survival that Jews of that time felt.

From their exile to Babylon in the sixth century Jews thought they had learned a capital lesson. They now viewed their history as one of wavering fidelity to the covenant, and this view suggested to them that infidelity to religious law led to national disaster. God had chosen them by covenanting with them in a special way, and unless they responded with signal fidelity, they would reap not blessing but judgment. Consequently, the returnees stressed their isolation and uniqueness. Still, historical experience also suggested, at least to some prophets and religious thinkers, that God himself was universal, Lord of all peoples. His dominion included the foreign nations, for they had obviously served as his instruments for chastening Israel. He had punished through the Babylonians and freed through the Persians.

As a result, exile and return made Jews focus more and more on Jerusalem and its cult as the source of their identity. At the same time, they clarified their ideas about God's worldwide outreach, finally realizing that God had to be the creator of all things. Views of the covenant changed somewhat, but the predominant view was that God would punish Israel for infidelity and reward it for standing firm. However, God was not bound to be merciful. Mercy, rather, was an outflow of his unpredictable, unmeasurable goodness. Somehow, despite all human weaknesses, God would give a new future. Often the Jews envisioned this future as messianic—coming through a holy ruler anointed by God.

The wisdom literature that dominated the last eras of the Hebrew Bible helped the people to contend with first Greek (Hellenic) and then Roman rule. Still, foreign rule chafed, especially when it threatened Jewish religious practice.

RABBINIC JUDAISM

The forces who urged revolt against the Romans suffered a crushing defeat in 70 C.E., when Titus destroyed the Temple in Jerusalem and cast out most of the Jews into the Diaspora (in this context, *Diaspora* refers to the settlement of Jews outside Palestine). The Pharisees and their successors, the doctors of the law, picked up the pieces. They originated with the lay scribes (lawyers) who arose in the postexilic Hellenistic period, but they did not organize themselves as a distinct party until the Maccabean revolt.[6] The Pharisees stood for a close observance of the covenant law, applying it in all aspects of daily life. This belief had come to dominate the scribes who preceded the Pharisees, and it dominated the rabbis (teachers) who came after them.

In the Diaspora these rabbis became the center of

communal life. The Temple had fallen and with it the cultic priesthood. So the alternative to cultic sacrifice—an alternative that had begun in Babylonian exile, when Jerusalem and the Temple were far away—filled the religious void. This alternative was the synagogue—the gathering place where the community could pray and hear expositions of the Torah. The synagogue became the central institution of Judaism in exile, and the study necessary to expose the Torah well made Judaism an intellectual powerhouse.

What we call rabbinic Judaism focuses on the synagogue, legal exposition, and study that emphasize the teacher (the rabbi). Increasingly, the teachers wanted to base their expositions on the teachings of their eminent predecessors, so they gathered a great collection of commentaries. Eventually, this collection became the Talmud ("the Learning"), a vast collection of the oral law that was composed of the Mishnah (itself a collection of interpretations of biblical legal materials) and the Gemara (commentaries on the Mishnah).[7]

Perhaps the best-known portion of the Talmud is the *Pirke Avot* ("Sayings of the Fathers").[8] It contains opinions of some of the oldest and most influential rabbis, but it is especially valuable for the spirit, the animating love, with which it infuses both the study of the Torah and the ethical life that the Torah should inspire. The Talmud is a "fence" for Torah—a protective device to keep people from violating the Law on which their identity and survival depend.

The rabbis called the legal portion of the Talmud *halakah*. Through reason, analogies, and deep thought, it made the most minute applications of the Torah. For instance, halakah concerned itself with the dietary laws intended to keep the Jews' eating practices clean or fitting *(kosher)*. It also went deeply into the laws for the observance of the Sabbath. For centuries such laws, in their biblical forms (for example, Leviticus and Numbers), had kept the Jews separate from their neighbors. As the scribes, Pharisees, and then the Diaspora rabbis concentrated their legal expertise, however, halakah became very complex. Certainly in the Roman Empire, non-Jews strongly associated the Jews with their laws. Thus, halakah partly contributed to anti-Semitism, insofar as it stressed the sense of "otherness" that often is used to justify bigotry.

Balancing the strictly legal teaching and lore, however, was the looser, more folkloric *haggadah*. This was a treasury of exegetical and homiletic (explanatory and preaching) stories that applied biblical passages to a congregation's present circumstances.[9] Where halakah reasoned closely, haggadah was apt to employ mythic devices, including paradigmatic figures and symbols. Haggadah drew much of its authority from the fact that Jewish theology had always held (at least in the ultimately dominant Pharisaic opinion) that an oral Torah accompanied the written Law of Moses (the Pentateuch, or first five books of the Bible) and the other books of the Hebrew Bible. Haggadah shows unscientific but pious reflection over traditional passages, especially those of scripture, that pictured God in his holy freedom—God at work creating this world in which we live.

For rabbinic Judaism, the Law helped to ease the problem of bad faith. Without abandoning their ideal of the perfect faith outlined in Maimonides' thirteen articles, the rabbis focused more on performance than on motivation or thought. What one believed about God, within broad limits, was less important than keeping the Sabbath and fulfilling one's communal obligations. This attitude encouraged considerable intellectual freedom, including lively debate, tolerance, and theological ambiguity. As well, it prevented the establishment of a clear-cut religious authority and dogma, such as that encountered by Roman Catholics in the magisterium of their councils and popes. The Law, which seemed so specific, had dozens of interpreters. On and on the Talmud grew, because most interpreters had insights worth preserving.

The result was a subtle but significant shift in the notion of the faith requisite for community membership. It was expressed in action, not in speculation or confession. How one used one's body, money, and time was more important than how one used one's mind or tongue. Such a practical view of faith meant that the community could bind itself through rituals, ethics, and laws without excessive concern about their meaning (although the rabbis did not ignore their meaning or the proper motivation behind actions).

This emphasis on action relates to the Jewish refusal to separate mind and body and to the Jewish commitment to hallowing life. One obeyed the Law to express and learn that God, who is holy, wants holy people. Through the quite overt keeping of the Law, Jews reminded themselves that they were the people called to sanctify God's name. A Jew knew that his neighbor accepted this identity because he could see that his neighbor obeyed the Law. Not accidentally, withdrawal from the Law and from the traditional God whom the Law hallowed have gone hand in hand in modern times.

Talmudic Religion

In terms of theology proper, the Talmud clung to scriptural faith.[10] Its central pillar was the Shema (Deut.

6:4): "Hear, O Israel: The Lord our God is One Lord." (A second pillar was the biblical notion of election.) The Talmudic view of the Shema was practical rather than speculative. That is, the rabbis did not spend much energy probing the unity of God, the confluence of the divine attributes, or the like. The oneness of God meant to them God's sole dominion over life. He was the Lord of all peoples, the world's only source and guide.[11] The most practical of God's attributes were his justice and his mercy, but how they correlated was not obvious. Clear enough, though, were the implications for ethics and piety: A person ought to reckon with God's justice by acting righteously and avoiding condemnation. A person also ought to rely on God's mercy, remembering that he is slow to anger and quick to forgive.

Through such righteous living, a person could look forward to God's kingdom, which would come through the Messiah. The Messiah would rejuvenate or transform this earthly realm, which is so often a source of suffering. Of the Messiah, Isadore Epstein says, "At the highest the Messiah is but a moral leader who will be instrumental in fully rehabilitating Israel in its ancient homeland, and through a restored Israel bring about the moral and spiritual regeneration of the whole of humanity, making all mankind fit citizens of the Kingdom.[12] This description rejects the Christian tendency to equate the Messiah with a divine son and also provides a foundation for the Zionistic fervor to return to the land. The concept of God's kingdom eventually included a supernatural dimension (heaven), but Judaism rather distinctively emphasizes that personal fulfillment comes through daily life.

The thrust of the Talmud, therefore, is not so much theological as ethical. The rabbis were more interested in what one did than in how one spoke or thought. So they balanced considerable theological leeway with detailed expectations of behavior. One could hold any opinion about the subtleties of God's nature, but how one observed the Sabbath was clearly specified.[13] A major effect of this ethical concern was the refinement of the already quite sensitive morality of the Hebrew Bible. For instance, the rabbis wanted to safeguard the body against even the threat of mortal injury, so they called wicked the mere raising of a hand against a person.

The spirit of talmudic ethics, thus, is both precise and broad. The Talmud goes to extreme detail, but it applies to all humanity. According to the Talmud, the great vices are envy, greed, and pride, for they destroy the social fabric. Anger is also socially destructive, so the rabbis lay great stress on self-control. On the other hand, self-control should not become gloomy asceticism. Generally speaking, the Talmud views the goods

of the earth as being for our enjoyment. We should fear neither the body nor the world.

In fact, God, who gives us both the body and the world, obliges us to keep them healthy and fruitful. To spurn bodily or material goods without great reason, then, would be to show ingratitude to God—to withdraw from the order God has chosen to create. Wealth and marriage, for instance, should be viewed as great blessings that should be accepted with simple thankfulness. For the truest wealth, finally, is to be content with one's lot. In faith, the pious Jew tried to raise his sights beyond everyday worries to the master of the universe, from whom so many good things flow. The ultimate purpose of religious life was to sanctify this master's name—to live in such love of God that his praise was always on one's lips.

Hallowing Time

Through religious observances the Talmudists set the social program for inculcating their ethical ideals. In practice, every day was to be hallowed from its beginning. At rising the faithful Jew would thank God for the night's rest, affirm God's unity, and dedicate the coming hours to God's praise. He was supposed to pray at least three times each day: upon rising, in midafternoon, and in the evening. Ritual washings, as well as the kosher diet, reminded the faithful of the cleanliness that dedication to God required. Prayer garments such as the fringed prayer shawl; the phylacteries, or *tefelin* (scriptural texts worn on the head and the arm); and the head covering reinforced this cleanliness. The mezuzah (container of scriptural texts urging wholehearted love of God) over the door was a reminder to the entire home to adopt this attitude. Home was to be a place of law-abiding love. When possible, Jews would say their daily prayers together in the synagogue.

The synagogue, of course, was also the site of congregational worship on the Sabbath and on the great feasts that punctuated the year. Primary among them were (and still are) Passover, a spring festival that celebrates the exodus of Israelites from Egypt; Shavuot, a wheat harvest festival occurring seven weeks after Passover; Booths (Sukkoth), a fall harvest festival whose special feature is the erection of branch or straw booths that commemorate God's care of the Israelites while they were in the wilderness; the New Year; and the Day of Atonement (*Yom Kippur*).

The last is the most somber and solemn of the celebrations: the day on which one fasts and asks for forgiveness of sins. It is a time when estranged members of the community should make efforts to reconcile their differences, and when all persons should rededicate themselves to the holiness that God's covenant demands. There are other holidays through the year, most of them joyous, and collectively they serve the several purposes of a theistic cult: recalling God's great favors (anamnesis), binding the community in common faith, and expiating offenses and restoring hopes.

In the home, celebration of the Sabbath did for the week what the annual feasts did for the year. It gave time a cycle with a peak that had special meaning. From midweek all looked forward to the Sabbath joy, preparing the house and the food for God's bride. When the mother lit the candles and the Sabbath drew near, even the poorest Jew could feel that life was good. Special hospitality was the sabbath rule; rest and spiritual regeneration were the Sabbath order. Regretful as all were to see the Sabbath end, a glow lingered that strengthened them so that they could return to the workaday world.[14]

The principal rites of passage were circumcision, through which males entered the covenant community on their eighth day; bar mitzvah, to celebrate the coming of age; marriage; and burial. Through communal celebration, these rites reinforced the faith that life is good, the Torah is life's crown, marriage is a human's natural estate, and death is not the final word.

In the perspective of Jewish faith, circumcision is not a matter of hygiene. It is a sign of the pledge made between Abraham and God, a sign in the very organ of life. For the rest of his life, the man signed this way stands out from the rest of unsigned humanity. Naked, the Jewish man is clearly a Jew.

The circumcision ritual is called a *bris*, the Hebrew word for covenant. When most children were born at home, the bris meant a family feast, with crowds of relatives and friends, learned speeches, and general merrymaking. Each step of the ceremony was something to be stored in the memory for later meditation. Contemporary ceremonies retain what they can of this tradition, gathering relatives and friends to celebrate the new birth. The bris intensifies the ordinary joy parents feel at the gift of a child, by emphasizing that the covenant community is being extended another generation.

With the rise of a Jewish feminist consciousness have come rituals for bringing girls into the covenant and adulthood. Thus Judith Plaskow, a prominent Jewish feminist and theologian, has written a bris ceremonial for a girl. From various scriptural passages, Plaskow weaves together a celebration of a girl's entrance into community life parallel to that for a boy.[15]

Following circumcision, the next rite of passage for the Jewish child is the *bar mitzvah* or ceremonial accession to adulthood. The religion tradition behind the bar mitzvah assumes that a child does not develop the capacity to grasp the concepts of Judaism, nor to fulfill Judaism's disciplines, until the age of thirteen. Before that time, the father is responsible for the child. The bar mitzvah makes the child's transition to personal responsibility. In recent times, there has arisen the "bas mitzvah" ceremony for girls, an improvised way to ritualize girls' graduation from Sunday-school training and to recognize their new status as adults.

Jews, like all other peoples, have persisted in marrying, generation after generation, for better or worse, for richer or poorer. Traditionally, their marriages have taken place under a canopy (*huppah*) supported by four poles, the original purpose of which was to provide the ceremony a sacred space. The day itself usually entailed a fast, and other similarities to the Day of Atonement, in the belief that on their wedding day God forgives a couple all their past sins, so that they may begin their life together afresh.

Funeral rites, the last stage on life's way, have involved Jews in a final confession of faith. Ideally the dying person said, "Understand, O Israel, the Lord our God is One. I acknowledge before Thee, my God, God of my fathers, that my recovery and death are in your hand. May it be your will to heal me completely, but if I should die, may my death be an atonement for all sins that I have committed." After death there was a ritual washing of the body, a funeral dominated by the recitation of psalms, a ritualized burial, a meal for the mourners, and then the *shivah*, a seven-day period of mourning, during which friends were expected to visit and a *minyan* (quorum of ten) was to gather each day. The mourning period has concluded with visiting the synagogue the first Sabbath after the shivah.

THE MEDIEVAL PERIOD

Returning to our historical sequence, we can note that at the end of the first millennium of the common era, Jews emigrated to Europe, North Africa, and Egypt, taking with them the scholarship of the talmudic school to which they felt the closest ties. The Babylonian traditions were more popular, but in countries such as Italy, which had close ties with Palestine, Palestinian influence was great. In Europe, of course, the Jews were largely under Christian rule, although southern Spain and southern France were under Muslim rule.

The two great Jewish traditions, the Sephardic (Iberian) and the Ashkenazi (East European) can be characterized by their subjugation under either Muslim or Christian rule, respectively. The two traditions shared more than they held separately because of the Talmudists, and their different sytles in intellectual matters and in peity largely derive from the different cultures in which they evolved. In the tenth and eleventh centuries, the Sephardim in Spain developed a golden culture, with philosophy, exegesis, poetry, and scientific learning at their peak. Toledo and Cordoba were great centers of learning, but so were Avila and Lisbon.

Whereas for the Talmudist study of the Torah was the highest activity, many of the medieval philosophers considered the contemplation of God's eternal forms (through which he had created the world) as such. Maimonides became the prince of Jewish philosophers largely because he was also learned in the talmudic tradition and so could reconcile the old with the new. For him philosophical contemplation did not take one away from the Torah, because the proper object of philosphical contemplation is the one Law we find in both scripture and nature.

A key teaching in Maimonides' system was divine incorporeality. God had to be one, which he could not be if he occupied a body, since matter is a principle of multiplicity. To rationalize the anthropomorphic biblical descriptions of God, where he has bodily emotions if not form, Maimonides allegorized as Philo had done. The dynamic to his system, however, was the conviction that philosophical reason can provide the key to scripture. As his own *Guide for the Perplexed* puts it, "This book will then be a key admitting to places the gates of which would otherwise be closed. When the gates are opened and men enter, their souls will enjoy repose, their eyes will be gratified, and even their bodies, after all toil and labor, will be refeshed.[16]

Maimonides has probably been most influential through the thirteen articles in which he summarized Jewish faith, and which even today are listed in the standard prayer book. They are: (1) the existence of God, (2) God's unity, (3) God's incorporeality, (4) God's eternity, (5) the obligation to worship God alone, (6) prophecy, (7) the superiority of the prophecy of Moses, (8) the Torah as God's revelation to Moses, (9) the Torah's immutability, (10) God's omniscience, (11) reward and punishment, (12) the coming of the Messiah, and (13) the resurrection of the dead.[17] In this summary a philosopher gave the key headings under which reason and biblical revelation could be reconciled.

In medieval Germany a movement arose among people called the Hasidim, who upheld a relatively new spiritual ideal. Biblical religion had spoken of the poor of God (*anawim*), and from biblical times a *hasid* was one who piously devoted himself to God. The medieval expression of this piety, in which intellectualism was subordinate to devotion, contested rabbinic learning. What characterized the truly pious person, this movement argued, was serenity of mind, altruism, and renunciation of worldly things. The asceticism, especially, ran counter to traditional Judaism, for it seemed to entail turning away from the world. Indeed, Hasidic speech relates to the reality that has always drawn mystics and caused them to neglect the world—the reality of glimpsing the divine being itself, of experiencing the biblical "goodness of the Lord." This divine love exalts the soul and seems far more precious than anything the world can offer.

Hasidism in its medieval, Germanic form is not the direct ancestor of the modern pietism that goes by this name. Intervening between Hasidism's two phases was a most influential Jewish mysticism, that of the Cabala. *Cabala* means "tradition," and the Cabalists sought to legitimize their movement by tracing it back to secret teachings of the patriarchs and Moses.

The paramount book of the Cabalistic movement, and the most representative of its symbolism, was the *Zohar*—the "Book of Splendor." From 1500 to 1800, the *Zohar* exerted an influence equal to that of the Bible and the Talmud. Analysis of the work suggests that it was written in Spain at the end of the thirteenth century, most likely by Moses de León.[18] The *Zohar* is similar to haggadic materials in that it interprets scriptural texts symbolically and in pietistic fashion rather than in the legal manner of halakah. For instance, the *Zohar* turns over each word of Genesis, searching for hidden clues to the divine plan. It concerns itself with the numerical value of the words' letters (for example, a = 1) and correlates clues in Genesis with clues from other visionary parts of the Hebrew Bible, such as Ezekiel, chapter 1, and Isaiah, chapter 6. To align its interpretation with respectable past commentary, it cites traditional rabbis, but the *Zohar's* immediate concern is not the rabbis' interest in ethics but an imaginative contemplation of divinity and the divine plan.

THE MODERN PERIOD

If the mark of modernity is a turn from rather mythical religious authority to human authority and self-reliance, modernity did not begin for Judaism until the end of the eighteenth century. In fact, thorough exposure to a secularized, technological culture did not come to most of the rural population of the eastern European *shtetls* (villages) until close to World War II. Until that time enlightenment and reform made little impact, for talmudic and Hasidic orthodoxy kept the traditions basically unchanged.[19] Jacob Neusner attributes the breakup of traditional Judaism in the modern period to two factors, the Enlightenment and Hasidism.[20] The Enlightenment, whose main feature according to Kant was the realization that humanity should be guided by its own reason and not by institutional authorities, in effect attacked the legal and philosophical underpinnings of traditional Judaism. By extending political rights to Jews ("Emancipation"), the Gentile thinkers of the Enlightenment took away the basis of the Jewish community—it was no longer a ghetto or a world set apart from the national mainstream.

By its philosophical turn to individual reason, the Enlightenment attacked the talmudic assumption that traditional law and its interpretation by the Fathers are the best guides for life. Thus, intellectual Jews who accepted the ideals of the Enlightenment tended to abandon talmudic scholarship (or at least deny that it was the most important learning) and devote themselves to secular learning. This movement spawned the distinguished line of Jewish scientists, social thinkers, and humanists, but it meant that the Jewish community lost some of its best talent. It also meant intellectual warfare between the advocates of the new learning and the defenders of the old.

The relation of Hasidism to traditional, talmudic Judaism is more complex. Modern Hasidism begins with Israel Baal-Shem-Tov (1700–1760). Baal-Shem-Tov and his followers taught a religious inwardness, a joyous communion with God.[21] They sought to restore the traditional faith, which they saw as endangered by false messianism, arid intellectualism, and talmudic legalism. Hasidism did not attack the Law and traditional practice itself. Rather, it shifted Jewish religious focus from the "scientific" rabbinic leader to the gifted Hasid or holy person, who manifested divine wisdom and joy. The movement quickly caught fire in eastern Europe, and thousands rushed to the Hasidic "courts." In their vivid portrait of *shtetl* life, Zborowski and Herzog[22] have shown the attraction that the Hasidim exerted in the typical village. Many of the villagers (usually men) yearned to go off to the courts for spiritual refreshment, and many would leave their families for substantial periods of time.

Hasidism ran the danger of irrationalism and an intolerance of anything modern, but for discerning contemporary Jews such as Martin Buber[23] and Abraham Heschel,[24] it became a valuable resource. Although large portions of the educated, who were desirous of a Jewish enlightenment and emancipation from Christian discrimination, strongly opposed Hasidic piety, it remained vigorous in the villages well into the twentieth century. There it tended to commingle with talmudic faith, blending legal observance with emotional fervor. Jewish village life hinged on the Sabbath (in the time-organizing way described above) and on three blessings: the Torah, marriage, and good deeds.

The Torah meant God's revelation and Law. In practice, it meant the exaltation of learning. *Shtetl* parents hoped that they would have learned sons, well versed in the Law, who would bring glory to the family. Thus, the ideal son was thin and pale, a martyr to his books. From age five or so he marched off to a long day of study, beginning his education by memorizing a Hebrew that he did not understand and then progressing to subtle talmudic commentaries. The Torah shaped the economic and family lives of *shtetl* Jews, because men tried to free themselves for study, placing the financial burdens on women. The poor scholar, revered in the *shul* (synagogue school) but master of a threadbare family, exemplified the choices and values that the Torah inspired.

Many men did work in trades (the state usually prevented Jews from owning land and farming), but even they would try to gain dignity by devoting their spare time to learning. Glory for women came from caring for the home, the children, and often a little shop. So much were those responsibilities part of religion for women that no commandments prescribed for them exact times for prayer, fasting, synagogue attendance, charitable works, or the like. Women's three principal *mitzvot* (duties) out of the traditional 613 were to bake the Sabbath bread, to light the Sabbath candles, and to visit the ritual bath (*mikvah*) after menstruation.

In the *shtetl*, marriage was the natural human situation and children were its crown. Father and mother were obligated to create a home steeped in Torah and good deeds (fulfillment of the *mitzvot* and acts of charity). In semiserious popular humor, nothing was worse than an old maid, while an unmarried man was pitied as being incomplete. Of course, kosher rules and keen legal observance marked the devout home, which was but a cell of the organic community. That community supported needy individual members with material goods, sympathy in times of trouble, and unanimity in religious ideals. One had to share one's wealth there, whether wealth of money or wealth of mind, and the seats of honor in the synagogue went to the learned and to the community's financial benefactors.

The community exacted quite a toll through the

pressure it exerted to conform with its ideals and through the gossip and judgment that ever circulated. Nevertheless, most Jews gladly accepted being bound by the common laws and custom, and few Jews could avoid being bound by the equally overt and common suffering. The urban populations in the Russian and Polish ghettos shared an almost paranoid spiritual life, with pogroms (persecutions) a constant specter, while the rural populations of eastern Europe never knew when some new discrimination or purge would break out. In both situations, Jews' mainstay was their solidarity in faith. Consequently, we can understand how threatening movements to change the faith, such as the Reform or Enlightenment (described below), must have been. The old ways had been the foundation of Jewish sanity. New conditions, as in Germany and the United States, seemed much less solid than long familiar suffering and endurance.

Reform

Thus, the traditional legal authority crumbled because of the new secular learning. From within, Judaism succumbed to a desire for more emotionally or spiritually satisfying evidence of God's helpfulness. In response to this crisis of the tradition came a "Reform" of orthodox conceptions. On a popular level (though we are still speaking of the relatively educated), Reform meant an effort to accept modern culture and still remain a Jew. In other words, it meant searching for new definitions of Jewishness that would not necessitate alienation from the intellectual and political life of Gentile fellow nationalists.

The stress of Reform was ethical. Reform Jews saw their tradition as offering all peoples a moral sensitivity, a concern for the rights of conscience and social justice, which derived from the prophets and the great rabbis but that could serve the dawning future age of equality, political freedom, and mutual respect. In part, this ethical stress was the result of wishful thinking. Reform Jews tended to be talented people who were either formally or informally excluded from national and university life. As a result, their visions of a new day led them to stress what in their own religious past might abet equal opportunity.

A response to Reform within Judaism was a self-conscious "Orthodoxy." It tended to recruit those who shared many of the Reformers' perceptions but who disagreed with their reinterpretation of the tradition. Instead, Orthodoxy insisted that the Torah be the judge of modernity and not vice versa. Positively, however, the Orthodox conceded the possibility that living with

Gentiles might be a good, God-intended arrangement. No doubt, the breakup of Christian control over culture that marked the Western shift from medieval to modern times played a strong role in this reevaluation. That is, the Orthodox realized that, despite its evident dangers to faith, living among Gentiles might free Jews of the prejudice endemic in medieval Christian faith. (In its most virulent form, that prejudice branded all Jews as "Christ killers.")

In their contests with the Reformers, the Orthodox could draw on factors that tradition had driven deep into the Jewish psyche. First, there was the conservatism that was almost intrinsic to a faith built on teaching "fathers" and the father-figure of the family. Such conservatism made it difficult for the younger generation to convince the older. Second, the Orthodox could claim, much more plausibly than the Reformed, that they represented the wisdom and experience of the past by which the people had survived. Third, the Orthodox were more genuinely religious than the Reformed; although the virtuosi wanted to develop faith, the majority of reformers were secularly minded, drawn by goods outside the traditional culture. Last, the combination of these factors gave Orthodoxy the advantage of appearing safer and surer than Reform.[25]

Conservative Judaism represented an effort to find a centrist position, between Reform and Orthodoxy. Its founder was Rabbi Zecharias Frankel (1801–1875), chief rabbi of Dresden and later head of the Breslau Theological Seminary in Germany. Frankel's position was that Judaism should change slowly, remaining true to its traditional character and only allowing slight modifications of traditional practice. In the United States, Solomon Schechter of the Jewish Theological Seminary of America was the central promoter of Conservative Judaism.

Presently Conservative Judaism is the largest of the three main groups of American Jews. Its intellectual center is the Jewish Theological Seminary in New York, its rabbinical assembly numbers more than one thousand members, and its league of synagogues (the United Synagogue) numbers more than one thousand congregations. The Conservative worship service has introduced family pews, developed a modernized liturgy in the vernacular, and allows women a fuller role in the congregation's ritual life.

Zionism

The movement most responsible for the establishment of the state of Israel is Zionism. Most of the medieval piety movements anticipated Zionism insofar as their messianism regularly involved the notion of returning to the ancestral land (and to the holiest of cities, Jerusalem). The greatest impetus to Zionism, however, was the persecutions that convinced European Jews they were in peril on the Continent: pogroms in Russia from 1880 to 1905, Ukranian massacres from 1917 to 1922, persecutions in Poland between 1922 and 1939, and above all, the Nazi persecution that began in 1933 that culminated in the Holocaust. Jewish commentators have no consensus on what recent history means. For Richard Rubenstein, it means the death of the traditional God.[26] For Emil Fackenheim, it means a call to hold together both evil and divine providence.[27] For Hanna Arendt, it shows that history can make evil utterly commonplace or banal.[28] Such commentators do agree that we must not ignore, deny, or explain away the evil of the Holocaust. As Elie Wiesel has said, it is better to keep silent than to depreciate the suffering of so many innocent victims with "explanations."[29] By 1948 about 650,000 Jews lived within the British Mandate of Palestine, and at the birth of Israel many hundreds of thousands more emigrated from Europe and from Arab lands (where, after the 1948 war, conditions were difficult). The main ideologist for the movement was a Viennese named Theodor Herzl. His witness of anti-Semitism during the Dreyfus affair in France at the end of the nineteenth century convinced him and many other Jews that only by having their own nation could Jews be free of constant persecution.

Today Judaism is most vital in Israel and the United States, and in both places the battles over what it means to be a Jew in the modern world continue unabated. Israel has become the spiritual center of Judaism, and what faith can mean after Auschwitz and the Holocaust has become the prime topic of theological discussion.[30] Because of its vigorous intellectual tradition, Judaism disproportionately contributes to the debates about the value of modernity, and its voice is now influencing many Christian thinkers.[31]

NOTES

1. Herbert May, ed., *Oxford Bible Atlas*, 2nd ed. (New York: Oxford University Press, 1974), p. 57; G. Widengren, "Israelite-Jewish Religion," in *Historia Religionum, I,* ed. C. J. Bleeker and G. Widengren (Leiden: E. J. Brill, 1969), p. 226.

2. Isadore Epstein, *Judaism* (London: Penquin, 1959), pp. 12–14; Eric Voegelin, *Order and History I, Israel and Revelation* (Baton Rouge: Louisiana State University Press, 1956), pp. 188–195.

3. I. al Faruqi and D. Sopher, eds., *Historical Atlas of the Religions of the World* (New York: Macmillan, 1974), p. 286.

4. John L. McKenzie, S. J., *Dictionary of the Bible* (Milwaukee, Wis.: Bruce, 1965), pp. 153–157.

5. William Foxwell Albright, "The Biblical Period," in *The Jews: Their History*, ed. Louis Finkelstein (New York: Schocken, 1970), pp. 15–19.

6. Joseph Fitzmyer, "A History of Israel," in *The Jerome Biblical Commentary*, vol. 2, ed. R. Brown, J. Fitzmyer, and R. Murphy (Englewood Cliffs, N.J.: Prentice-Hall, 1968), p. 692; Judah Goldin, "The Period of the Talmud," in *The Jews: Their History*, ed. Louis Finkelstein (New York: Schocken, 1970), pp. 121–129.

7. *Encyclopedia Judaica*, s.v. "Talmud, Babylonia." See Jacob Neusner, "Form and Meaning in Mishnah," *JAAR*, 1977, 45(1):27–54; "History and Structure: The Case of the Mishnah," *JAAR*, 1977, 45(2):161–192.

8. R. Travers Herford, *Pirke Aboth: The Ethics of the Talmud* (New York: Schocken, 1962).

9. Renée Bloch, "Midrash," in *Approaches to Ancient Judaism*, ed. William Scott Green (Missoula, Mont.: Scholars Press, 1978), pp. 19–50; Nahum N. Glatzer, ed., *Hammer on the Rock* (New York: Schocken, 1962).

10. Epstein, *Judaism*, pp. 121–194. On the Talmud's view of prophecy (which its law was somewhat trying to replace), see Nahum N. Glatzer, "A Study of the Talmudic-Midrashic Interpretation of Prophecy," in his *Essays in Jewish Thought* (University: University of Alabama Press, 1978), pp. 16–35.

11. See Jacob Neusner, ed., *The Life of Torah: Readings in the Jewish Religious Experience* (Encino, Calif.: Dickenson, 1974), pp. 17–24.

12. Epstein, *Judaism*, p. 140.

13. See Robert Goldenberg, *The Sabbath Law of Rabbi Meir* (Missoula, Mont.: Scholars Press, 1978), pp. 159–264.

14. For a contemporary view of the Sabbath, see Richard Siegel et al., *The Jewish Catalogue* (Philadelphia: Jewish Publication Society of America, n.d.), pp. 103–116.

15. Judith Plaskow, "Bringing a Daughter into the Covenant," in *Womanspirit Rising*, ed. Carol P. Christ and Judith Plaskow (San Francisco: Harper & Row, 1980), p. 181.

16. Moses Maimonides, *The Guide for the Per-*

plexed, 2nd ed., trans. M. Friedlander (New York: Dover, 1956), p. 11.

17. R. J. Zwi Werblowsky, "Judaism, or the Religion of Israel," in *The Concise Encyclopedia of Living Faiths*, ed. R. C. Zaehner (Boston: Beacon Press, 1967), pp. 45–48.

18. See Gershom G. Scholem, ed., *Zohar: The Book of Splendor* (New York: Schocken, 1963), pp. 12–21.

19. Jacob B. Argus, *The Meaning of Jewish History*, vol. 2 (New York: Abelard-Schuman, 1963), pp. 300–485; Cecil Roth, *A History of the Jews* (New York: Schocken, 1961), pp. 235–424.

20. Jacob Neusner, *The Way of Torah*, 2nd ed. (Encino, Calif.: Dickenson, 1974), pp. 68–71.

21. See Elie Wiesel, *Souls on Fire* (New York: Vintage, 1973).

22. Mark Zborowski and Elizabeth Herzog, *Life Is with People* (New York: Schocken, 1962).

23. Martin Buber, *Hasidism and Modern Man* (New York: Harper Torchbooks, 1966).

24. Abraham J. Heschel, *Man's Quest for God* (New York: Scribner's, 1954), *God in Search of Man* (New York: Farrar, Straus & Giroux, 1955).

25. On this conflict in the United States, see Sydney Ahlstrom, *A Religious History of the American People* (New Haven, Conn.: Yale University Press, 1972), pp. 969–984; also Neusner, *Life of Torah*, pp. 156–203.

26. Richard L. Rubenstein, *After Auschwitz* (Indianapolis, Ind.: Bobbs-Merrill, 1966).

27. Emil Fackenheim, *God's Presence in History* (New York: New York University Press, 1970).

28. Hannah Arendt, *Eichmann in Jerusalem* (New York: Viking, 1965).

29. See Elie Wiesel, *The Oath* (New York: Random House, 1973).

30. Eva Fleischner, "A Select Annotated Bibliography on the Holocaust," *Horizons*, 1977, *4*(1):61–83.

31. See, for example, Rosemary Ruether, *Faith and Fratricide* (New York: Seabury, 1974).

3

Christianity

If we gather all its parts, Christianity is the largest religion in the world. What began as a Jewish sect has carried its version of the Torah and prophecy around the globe.[1]

INTRODUCTION

Christianity developed from the life and work of Jesus of Nazareth,[2] as Buddhism developed from the life and work of Gautama. Jesus (whose historical reality is attested to by such non-Christian authors as Josephus, Tacitus, Suetonius, and Pliny the Younger) was born about 4 B.C.E. (by current calendars) in Palestine. We know little about his youth except through Gospel stories, such as those of his circumcision and his dialogues with religious teachers. (The stories of his birth are probably legendary, in the service of the various New Testament authors' theologies.[3]) We assume that he grew up as a Jewish youth of his times. About the year 27 C.E. he started from his native Galilee on a career as an itinerant preacher.

While Jesus' message has been interpreted in very different ways, certain essentials seem quite clear. Joachim Jeremias's careful study argues that Jesus' own voice echoes in the New Testament parables, riddles, discussions of the reign of God, the peculiar use of *amen*, and the peculiar use of *Abba* (Father) for God.[4] On etymological and historical grounds, these are the safest leads to how Jesus himself preached (with concrete, lively language) and to what he had to say (that a new time was dawning and that God is intimately parental). Jesus' main theme was an announcement that the reign of God was at hand in his (Jesus') own person.[5] That reign or kingdom was a new beginning, a time of justice and holiness.

According to the New Testament writers, this theme meant that Jesus had fulfilled Jewish religion and superseded it. Jesus himself solicited a radical commitment to the new opportunties that God's reign offered, which included intimacy with God and friendship with other persons. The morality that Jesus anticipated in the Kingdom[6] is most graphic in his Sermon on the Mount. There the evangelists have him bless those who are poor, gentle, mourning, hungry and thirsty for what is right, merciful, pure in heart, peacemaking, and suffering for the cause of justice. They are the citizens of the Kingdom; dispositions or circumstances like theirs render human beings open to divine love. The gist of Jesus' own life, according to the New Testament, was just such love.

Information on Jesus' public life and ministry remains imprecise (because of the limited sources). Apparently he linked his work with that of John the Baptist, his message raised oppostion from the religious establishment, he worked out only some of the particulars for living in the kingdom, and he predicted woe to those who rejected his program. Furthermore, he planted at least the seeds of the Christian Church by gathering disciples and co-workers, and he gained a reputation as a healer. His death came by order of the Roman procurator Pontius Pilate on the dubious grounds that he threatened the peace.

Interpretations

Beyond this bare outline, historical and theological interpretations diverge. According to the New Testament and the orthodox faith of later centuries, the old reign of Satan and sin died with Jesus. Furthermore, after death Jesus was raised (resurrected) and was disclosed to be "Lord" or ruler of humanity. More tersely, Jesus was the divine Son whose dying and rising brought the world salvation. This interpretation thus stresses a twofold quality in Jesus: He was both human and divine. The councils that specifically discussed and defined Jesus' being found this interpretation to be the intent of the Gospel and Epistle writers.

Another interpretation of the New Testament is that Jesus was the Messiah—the anointed king of the age of grace, where *grace* came to mean not just peace and material plenty but intimacy with God and sharing in divine life. From the titles that the New Testament gives to Jesus, his own reported claims, and the miracles (healings, raisings from the dead, and so on) that the New Testament attributes to Jesus, we can conclude that the New Testament writers found him most remarkable—so remarkable that he had to be more than human. For them he was the bringer of salvation,[7] God's Word incarnate, the Christ (Messiah), and the divine Son.

In the earliest portions of the New Testament, the Epistles, Jesus is a living spiritual reality. The assumption behind Paul's directions for Church life, for instance, is that "the Lord" lives in Christians' midst. After Jesus' death, his followers apparently thought that his movement was finished, but the events of the ressurrection convinced them that he had assumed a new form of existence. They stayed together in Jerusalem; at Pentecost (fifty days after Passover, when Jesus had died), they experienced what they called the Holy Spirit, whom they thought Jesus and the Father had sent. The Spirit charged them to go out and preach about Jesus. Thus, the early Christians proclaimed that Jesus' life and death were the definitive act of salvation. The disciples also preached that Jesus was the Messiah. As such he was in accordance with Jewish tradition and yet responsible for its transformation. From a historical perspective, then, the first Christians appear as sectarian Jews—Jews with a new interpretation of messianism.

It took some time for the first interpretations of Jesus to sift out and clarify, and a principal catalyst in that process was Paul. From the accounts in Acts and his own writings, Paul was Pharisaic Jew whose conversion on the road to Damascus (Acts 9:3–9) was quite dramatic. After his conversion he tried to show his fellow Jews that Jesus was their Messiah, but their opposition to his preaching, plus his own further reflection on Jesus' life and death, led Paul to think that in Jesus God had opened the covenant to all persons—Gentiles as well as Jews.

Consequently, Paul made the Gospel (good news) about Jesus a transformation of the Torah. Because God had fulfilled in Jesus the intent of the Law, the Law's many detailed prescriptions were passé. Adherence to an external code could not make one righteous (on even terms with God). Only by opening to God's love and healing could one stand before him acceptably. Paul called that opening "faith." For him Jesus was the agent of a shift from the Torah to the Gospel, from works to faith. The way to become right with God was to commit oneself to Jesus. Thus, for Paul, Jesus represented the kingdom, embodied God's grace. As Paul's vision spread, he saw Jesus' transition from death to life as the climax of salvation history. Jesus the Christ was a new Adam, a new beginning for the human race. All who clung to him, who used him to interpret their lives, became members of his "body." Christ and the Church formed a living entity.

Paul's interpretation of Jesus was the key to early Christianity developing into a universal religion. By dropping the requirements of the Jewish Law and extending membership to all who would base their lives on Jesus, the early Church broke with Judaism irreparably.

At first the Christians expected the future to be short. Jesus would soon return in power and glory to consummate his work. As the years went by, the beliefs shifted. Jesus had accomplished the essentials of salvation through his death and resurrection. However long it took in God's dispensation for Jesus' salvation to work itself out, there was no doubt of the final success. The faithful would just have to endure. Living in faith and hope, they were to preach the good news to all whom they could reach.

THE APOSTOLIC AGE

The Gospel writers—Mark, Matthew, Luke, and John—all interpreted the life of Jesus.[8] Even in the most journalistic portions of the New Testament, they have cast Jesus' sayings and doings in terms of their own theologies. Matthew, for instance, works largely with Jewish notions, trying to show that Jesus is the successor to Moses, the Gospel is the successor to the Torah, and so on. The other Gospels, as well as Hebrews and Revelation, are similarly theological. John arranges Jesus' public life around a series of signs giving him a sacramental glow and making him a thaumaturgist (wonder worker). The second half of John's Gospel concentrates on Jesus' "glory": his intimacy with the heavenly Father and his victorious death and ressurrection. Hebrews tries to show that Jesus fulfilled

Jewish types of sacrifice, while Revelation is a Christian apocalypse (disclosure) designed to shore up faith against Roman persecution.

By the end of the first century, then, the Church had a variety of theologies. The majority were extensions of Jewish religion in the light of Jesus as the Messiah. The "apostolic age" is the period of elaboration of what Jesus meant and how the Church was to organize itself. It embraces roughly the first three centuries, and a central concern was authority. For the early Church, an *apostolos* was a person to whom God delegated Church authority. However, balancing this apostolic, "offical" authority was a looser, charismatic leadership expressed through prophecy, teaching, speaking in tongues, and so on. The earliest Church preaching was intended to show that Jesus fulfilled the promises of Jewish scripture. In their teaching, the apostles relied on oral tradition about Jesus' person and words.

During the second century the leadership of the Church passed from those who had seen Jesus themselves to those who had received the gospel from eyewitnesses but had not themselves known the Lord. The "fathers" who led the second-century Church are therefore apostolic in the sense that they had direct contact with the twelve. Writers from the early second century[9] reveal something of the young Church's internal and external problems. Internally, keeping discipline was obviously a major difficulty. As Christ's return was delayed, human weaknesses and individualism asserted themselves. Externally, from the time of Nero (54–68), the Church was ever liable to persecution by the Roman authorities.

Gnosticism

More potentially destructive than Rome were the Gnostic heresies. Their teachings varied considerably, but their common element was heterodox Judaism under the influence of Hellenistic and Iranian thought. In essence most Gnosticism involved a dualistic mythology. Matter, the negative principle, came from a Demiurge—subordinate divinity whom the Father God begot as Wisdom but who fell from grace. Divinity itself was a *pleroma* (fullness) of times and levels. Gnosticism offered a revelation to certain "elect" persons: if they would hate this lower world of material creation (which was under the fallen Demiurge) and believe in a higher spiritual and divine realm, they might return to glory with God.

To explain their revelation, the Gnostics taught that each of the elect had a hidden spark from God's eternal world. The sparks fell into matter because of a heavenly war between darkness and light (or, in other versions, because of an accident during the production of the divine emanations). The jealous, inferior god who clumsily fashioned the material realm, which is subject to time and fate, was born in the same accidental process. He was the author of carnal humanity, in which the divine spark was a prisoner. Higher beings would one day dissolve this fallen world, but in the meantime they call to our hidden sparks by means of saviours, revelations, and rites of baptism.[10]

Gnosticism blended the Hellenistic notion of divine emanation, mystery religion notions about salvation through sacramental rites, and Jewish notions of sin and redemption. It stressed the division between this world and heaven, the evil of matter and the flesh, and the need for asceticism (celibacy and bodily discipline) to gain freedom from matter.

Only a thin line separates the apostolic fathers from the conciliar fathers and the great theologians of the "patristic" age (age of the Fathers), for the three centuries after the deaths of the Twelve were characterized by a continuity of theological themes. First, there was the task of defending Church discipline and morality against both laxness and rigorism. Second, Church leaders had to walk a middle way between inspiration through charismata and institutional authority. Against Gnostics, the Church had to affirm the goodness of material creation. Against those who denied Jesus' humanity (the Docetists), it had to maintain that he was fully human and had really suffered and died. The Christian Church had little power in the secular world until the conversion of Constantine (312), so even when it was not suffering active persecutions, it was not very influential. Church leaders continued to reflect on the relation between Jesus and Judaism, as well as on conceptions of Jesus and God that would make most sense to educated Hellenists.

The apostolic Church developed a rule by local bishops. They became the primary teachers of doctrine, the primary defenders of orthodox (straight) belief. The bishops led the common worship, settled community disputes, and, to the extent that their talents allowed, fought heresies through sermons and writings. They were the main line of Fathers around whom the early Church arranged itself. The great heroes, as we mentioned, were the martyrs, and the life of the community took its liturgical pattern from the Eucharist (communal meal) and baptism (rite of entry into the Church). Forgiving sins raised questions of moral theology, for after baptism all were supposed to keep their faith pure, but gradually the Church allowed sinners to return to their community after they did penance. In the first three centuries, then, the Church established elements of the character that it has borne ever since.

THE CONCILIAR AGE

During the fourth and fifth centuries, a number of meetings (councils) of Church leaders were held that formally established the discipline and official doctrine (dogma) that any group in union with the apostolic Church had to adopt.[11] From those meetings came the name for the next period of the Christian history. Above all, the meetings dealt with the central issues of the Christian creed, hammering out the dogmas about God, Jesus, salvation, and the like that became the backbone of Christian theology. Various controversies made Church leaders realize that it was imperative to determine which apostolic sources were genuine expressions of faith and which were not. That imperative resulted in the establishment of a Christian scriptural canon.

Three main factors determined the final canon: whether the writing in question came from an apostle or a close associate of an apostle, whether it was accepted by the Church at large, and whether its contents were edifying for faith.[12] As early as 170, leaders in Rome had determined a canon of authoritative books. In the early decades of the fourth century, Bishop Eusebius of Caesarea (perhaps the first significant Church historian) divided candidate books into three categories: acknowledged, disputed, and spurious. The acknowledged and the disputed books constitute the twenty-seven books of today's New Testament. In 367 Athanasius of Alexandria published a "Festal Letter" that listed these twenty-seven books.

The first great dogmatic council occurred at Nicaea in 325. It produced the Nicene Creed (statement of belief) that was especially important for clarifying Jesus' divine status as Logos or Son. Before Nicaea, most Churches had been content to repeat what scripture (Jewish and Christian both) said about God and Jesus. However, Church theologians did not know how to respond to questions that scripture did not address. One such question came from Arius, a priest of Antioch, who proposed that Jesus, as the Logos of God (the divine Son) is subordinate to the Father. In short, Arius' proposition was that if one drew a line between created beings and the uncreated divine substance, the Logos would fall on the side of created beings, because "there was a then when he was not." Athanasius, drawing on the Alexandrian tradition, assaulted Arius' argument. Speaking for what he held

to be orthodoxy, he said that the Logos was of the same substance as the Father, possessing the single divine nature. Nicaea agreed with Athanasius, making his position dogma.

Trinitarian Doctrine

Athanasius also perceived that the canonical literature gave the Holy Spirit divinity equal to that of the Father and the Son. Therefore, he extended the meaning of his word *homoousion* (of one stuff) to include the Holy Spirit and so set the lines of what would become, at the Council of Constantinople in 381, the doctrine of the Spirit's divinity. That completed the doctrine of the Trinity: one God who is three equal "persons," each of whom fully possesses the single divine nature.

Christology

The councils not only set the pattern of Trinitarian faith that dominated the following centuries but also dealt with a host of problems that arose when people started to think about Jesus as the divine Word. Nestorius, from Antioch, and Cyril, from Alexandria, squared off in Christological controversy, and again Alexandria won. Nestorius stressed the unity of the Christian God, though he affirmed Christ's two natures (human and divine). Cyril thought that Nestorius' affirmation was not strong enough to safeguard the single personhood of Jesus Christ the God-man, so he pressed for a "hypostatic" (personal) union of the two natures. Councils of Ephesus (431) and Chalcedon (451) affirmed Cyril's doctrine of one "person" and two "natures." Later Christological development affirmed that Jesus had a rational soul, two wills, and two sets of operations. This orthodox Christology resulted from trying to systematize the scriptural teaching about God and Jesus. It stressed that only the union of the divine with the human in Jesus could save human beings from sin and give them divine life. Orthodoxy cast many groups in the shade, branding their positions as heretical, but it also developed Christ's meaning considerably.

The conciliar definitions gave Christian faith considerably more precision and at least tacitly encouraged theologians to study and speculate further on the doctrinal tracts that they had laid out. The conciliar age was also fraught with the intrusions of secular leaders, for after Constantine and his successors made Christianity the favored imperial religion, the emperors assumed that they had the right, even the pious duty, to intervene in Church affairs. Thus, the tension between Church and State, as we now call it, started its long and tangled history in the conciliar age.

In fact, the councils were the spearhead of the advances that the Church and State made into one another's affairs.[13] No longer were Christians under the constant threat of persecution and martyrdom. They could enter worldly occupations, including government service—a situation that both weakened their faith and made it more realistic. As a result, the original feeling of urgency gave way to the realization that the Lord's return might be far down the road.

Monasticism

Such worldliness stimulated new religious movements within the Church that opposed the laxness or "accommodation" that worldly success easily begot. The most important reforms generated interest in monasticism and virginity (which overlapped, insofar as monks took vows of celibacy). Both males and females found a monastic life of dedication to prayer and charitable works a way of maintaining their martyrlike intensity of faith. Theirs was a "white" martyrdom, not the red one of blood, and many found that it led them to the desert for solitude and asceticism.

Partly because of the dangers of the desert solitude, many monks soon formed communities, and before long these communities admitted women (nuns). So the dedication that had previously been an informal option (largely in terms of virginity or widowhood) took institutional form. Thenceforth monasteries were powerhouses of Christian faith that laity and clerics alike viewed as centers of holiness. That, too, was an innovation added to the New Testament religion, which had no monastic life. The Church's decision that monastic life was truly in keeping with New Testament religion was analogous to the decision to coin new doctrinal concepts. Quite consistently, the Protestant reformers of the sixteenth century opposed the development of monasticism (as being unbiblical), just as they opposed the development of the Catholic notion of authority.

EASTERN CHRISTIANITY

From the ninth to the fifteenth centuries, a complicated, still quite obscure process of alienation between Byzantine (Eastern) Christianity and Roman Christi-

anity resulted in their separation. Each group finally rejected the other, charging it with having broken the traditional faith. Some of the factors in the separation were the fall of the eastern Roman Empire, the failure of the Crusades, the growing antagonism of Islam, the growth of the papacy, the stirrings of Protestant reactions against the papacy, and the rivalry between Russia and western Europe.[14] These factors take us to the beginning of modernity in Eastern Christendom, explaining why East and West have remained divided to the present.

Thus, the break between Eastern and Western Christianity owed a great deal to political and cultural conflicts. Although separating these conflicts from theological differences is virtually impossible, we can delineate some of the more clearly religious issues. For instance, the patriarch Photius, who presided at Constantinople from 858 to 886, drew up a list of what Byzantines considered to be Latin (Western) errors in faith. This list reveals how the two portions of Christendom had developed different understandings of Orthodoxy. In this list Photius cited irregularities in the observance of Lent (the period of penance before Easter), compulsory celibacy for the clergy, denying priests the power to administer confirmation (the Christian sacrament of adulthood), and false teaching about the Holy Spirit. Clearly, the list concentrates on points of Church discipline and administration.

The most acute point of theological difference between the East and the West was what came to be known as the *Filioque*. According to the Nicene Creed, within the life of the Trinity the Holy Spirit proceeds from the Father. The Western Council of Toledo (589) made an addition to the Nicene Creed: The Holy Spirit proceeds not just from the Father but also from the Son (*Filioque* means "And from the Son"). Each tradition became attached to its Trinitarian formula, and so the *Filioque* became a sharp bone of contention. The East claimed that it was heretical; the West claimed it merely articulated a tacit understanding of traditional faith that Nicaea had assumed. The practical significance of the difference is not clear, but it probably shows the East's tendency to appreciate the Father's primal mystery—the Father's status as a fathomless source from which *everything* issues.

In response to Photius, Latin theologians composed their own list. In their view the Eastern discipline that allowed clerics to marry, that baptized by immersion, that celebrated the Eucharist with leavened bread, and that had different rules for fasting deviated from tradition. The debate even descended to such details as whether bishops should wear rings, whether clergy should wear beards, and whether instrumental music was valid at the liturgy. However, the main theological issue continued to be the *Filioque*, while the main political issue emerged as the difference in the churchs' understanding of authority. The Eastern church's tradition was a loose federation of bishops, all of whom were considered successors of the apostles. The Eastern church also stressed the rights of individual churches and ethnic groups. The Western tradition was a "monarchical" leadership by the bishop of Rome. As successor to Peter, he claimed primacy over the other churches.

Separation

The pivotal movement in the East-West division was the mutual excommunications of 1054. In the opinion of many contemporary theologians and historians the division between the Eastern and Western branches of the Church was a tragic accident. (Historians now say much the same of the sixteenth century Reformation split in Europe.) The sticking point through those centuries was a main factor in the East-West division—papal authority. Recently some ecumenical theologians have suggested ways that Protestant and Orthodox churches might acknowledge certain papal powers, but full accord remains quite distant.

Thus, the Orthodox church represents an understanding of Christianity somewhat different than that of Western Christianity.[15] It numbers perhaps 75 million persons, depending on the estimates used for Russia, and within the family of Christian churches it stresses the conciliar tradition, the federation of local churches in geographical families, and a lofty theology of the Trinity, Christology, and grace. As we noted, the liturgy is its center, and it has a rich sacramental life.[16] In its baptism and confession of sins, Orthodoxy's accent is sharing God's life—beginning divine life in baptism or repairing it in penance. Overall, Orthodoxy places the mystery of the Christian God to the fore. For the East, God is less a lawgiver or a judge than a spiritual power operating through creation. Creation ought to respond to God's power and beauty, so the Divine Liturgy becomes a song of praise, a hymn to the goodness and love that pour forth from the Father of Lights. Orthodoxy especially venerates Mary, the Mother of God, for her share in the "economy" of salvation—her share in the design of grace that raises humans to participate in the divine immortality.

THE MEDIEVAL PERIOD

In discussing the medieval period of Christanity, we shift focus from the East, where Orthodox faith took shape, to the European West. Evangelization (missionizing) of Europe progressed steadily from the time of the councils, most of it presuming somewhat vaguely that the bishop of Rome was preeminent among the Church's episcopal leaders. During the fifth and sixth centuries, Christian missionaries made considerable inroads among the Germanic tribes. Frequently they would convert tribal leaders from paganism or Arianism, and then the entire tribe would convert. However, Western state leaders tended to think that the Church was something for them to control. That tendency, plus problems of Church discipline, made the Western situation confusing. From the tenth century, however, there were efforts to reform the Church and increase its spiritual vitality.

As well, individual Church leaders found that they could increase their freedom from local secular rulers by increasing their allegiance to the bishop of Rome. The friction between Church and State therefore shifted to the interaction between the pope and the Germanic emperor. A key issue was who should appoint local bishops. The investiture controversy, as it is called, was solved in a compromise in the Concordat of Worms (1122). Secular rulers had to recognize the independence of the local bishop by virtue of his loyalty to the pope, and the pope had to consult the emperor and appoint bishops acceptable to him.[17]

During the twelfth century the Crusades to the holy sites in Palestine riveted the Christian imagination, but they tended to increase the alienation between Eastern and Western Christendom. When the Fourth Crusade (1204) conquered Constantinople, set up a Western prince, and tried to Latinize the Eastern church, relations deteriorated to their lowest point.

Scholasticism

The thirteenth century was the high point of medieval intellectual life, and the movement known as Scholasticism reaced its peak then. The Scholastics systematized the conciliar and patristic (the Fathers') theological doctrines.[18] Though they accepted the disciplines of tradition and the Church's teaching office, the medieval theologians seized the right to develop reason and use it to illumine the realities of faith. Thomas Aquinas, who most carefully related reason and faith, gained the greatest following. Just as conciliar theology had moved beyond scriptural ideas (in order to illumine scripture), so Aquinas' Scholastic theology moved beyond conciliar theology in order to illumine it through Greek philosophy. For Aquinas, philosophy was the wisdom available to reason. It was a universal basis for discussion, regardless of religious allegiance. Jews, Muslims, Christians, and pagans all had reason, and so all could philosophize. Theology, which rested on divine revelation, perfected philosophy, taking it into realms that it could not penetrate on its own.

Hierarchy

Aquinas' hierarchy had counterparts in the medieval Church structure. The clergy had separated themselves from the laity, and within the clerical order there were numerous ranks: monks, priests, canons, bishops, abbots, archbishops, cardinals, and more. The papacy had a considerable bureaucracy and wielded great secular power. Because the general culture had a Christian world view, heaven and hell had a vivid reality. Thus, the papal power to bar persons from Church membership and so from heaven made people fear the pope greatly. Considerable worldliness entered into the papal use of excommunication, interdict, and the like, because by medieval times the Church had forgotten the *parousia* (second coming of Christ) and was concentrating on shaping daily life.

The unsurpassed literary rendition of medieval Christianity is Dante's *Divine Comedy*. It shows the medievals' hierarchical thinking, their concern with heaven, hell, and purgatory, the venality of many medieval clergy, the infusion of pagan learning into medieval culture, and the sophistication of medieval moral theology, which catalogued virtues and vices quite precisely. Another wonderful source of insight into medieval Christianity is Chaucer's *Canterbury Tales*, which describes the daily habits of representative social types and the unconscious ways in which faith wove through medieval culture. From Dante and Chaucer one gathers that intellectuals of the late medieval period, especially nonclerical intellectuals, found many defects in the hierarchical Church, yet they basically accepted the terms of Christian faith. Their criticism focused on the discrepancy between the values that the Church professed and the all-too-human way in which it conducted itself.

The medieval cathedrals also exhibited hierarchy through their stretching from earth toward heaven. The basic architectural thrust is toward heaven, as all commentators point out, yet within the cathedrals are windows and statues that bring God down into daily life. Most cathedrals were built over centuries, and sometimes the townspeople contributed free labor, as if they wanted the cathedral to praise God doubly. Significantly, Chartres and Notre Dame de Paris both bear Mary's name. As the Virgin Mother of God, Queen of Heaven, and recourse of weak human beings, Mary was a mainstay of medieval faith.

In their battles with the Arians during the fifth and sixth centuries, Church leaders had necessarily stressed Jesus' divinity, which the Arians denied. Consequently, the Roman liturgy had come to place Christ and the action of the Mass apart from the people (as befit Christ-God). The size of the cathedrals, the inability of many people to see the ceremonies, the inability of many people to understand the Latin in which the ceremonies were conducted—all these factors prompted devotion to Mary and the infant Jesus, which brought God closer and made faith more human.

Around the cathedral walls, in wonderful stained glass, were biblical scenes, pictures of saints, and the like that told even the illiterate what faith meant. With the statues of the Virgin and Jesus, they gave comfort to the person who slipped into the cathedral's darkness to pray. In its majestic space, one gained a proper perspective on one's problems. At a time when hard work, early death, and many sufferings were the rule, the cathedrals were for many a great support.

THE PERIOD OF REFORM

During the late fourteenth and the fifteenth centuries, the papacy was in great disarray. At one point there were two claimants to the chair of Peter, one in Rome and one in Avignon.

The spark that set the Reformation blazing was Martin Luther (1483–1546), an Augustinian monk whose study and spiritual searches had convinced him that the heart of the gospel is the Pauline justification by faith (the belief that only faith makes one right with God). Only by reviving this Pauline theme could Christianity regain its pure beginnings. Justification by faith meant the fall of the whole system of "works" that the Catholic church had developed by late medieval times—the Mass, the sacraments, the rosary, and so forth.

Luther was prompted by the prevailing practice of indulgences (papal remissions of purgatorial punishment due for sins), which one could obtain for various good deeds, including almsgiving. Behind this practice lay some simple economics. The popes had spent lavishly in their Renaissance enthusiasm for art and culture. Leo X, for instance, was perhaps 125,000 ducats in debt at the time that he endorsed the preaching of Johann Tetzel, Luther's first adversary,[19] which included granting an indulgence for a contribution to the building of St. Peter's in Rome. To Luther the whole system—the pope's extravagance, his pretension to control a treasury of merits generated by the saints, out of which he might draw "credits" to cover sinner's debts, and his focusing his economics on the Mass—was blasphemous. On October 31, 1517, Luther nailed his ninety-five Theses to the door of the castle church at Wittenberg, which amounted to a formal challenge to the system.

Many Germans who for political or religious reasons had grievances against Rome supported Luther. As his thought expanded, he made scripture the sole arbiter of Christian faith, declared the primacy of individual conscience, upgraded the status of the layperson, and urged the use of the vernacular rather than Latin. Luther also stressed the uniqueness of Christ's death on the cross and so taught that the Eucharist prinicipally commemorates the Last Supper, rather than representing Christ's sacrificial death. On the basis of scripture, he judged the doctrine of purgatory unfounded and the practice of monastic life an aberration. Because Luther was a fine preacher, he made these ideas matters for discussion in the marketplace. By translating the Bible into German, he put the central basis for his reform within reach of all literate people (and just about standardized High German in the process). Finally, Luther's departure from monastic life and subsequent marriage led thousands more to leave their monasteries and convents.

Luther's reform in Germany quickly generated uprisings elsewhere. In Switzerland, Ulrich Zwingli (among the German speaking) and John Calvin (among the French speaking) led movements with similar themes. In England, Henry VIII and Thomas Cranmer separated their church from Rome.

Catholic Reform

The Catholic response to the Protestant Reformation took place at the Council of Trent (1545–1563). Trent affirmed the reliance of the Church on both scripture and tradition, the effective power of the sacraments, the need for humans to cooperate in the work of justification (that is, no justification by faith alone), and the possibility of sin after justification. It also provided for reforms in clerical education and a general housecleaning to remove the laxness and venality that had made the Reformers' charges more than credible. Probably the most powerful single agent of the Catholic Reformation was the Society of Jesus (the Jesuits), which Pope Paul III approved in 1540. Its founder was Ignatius of Loyola, a Basque.

From the middle of the sixteenth to the middle of the seventeenth century, religious wars ravaged much of Europe. In France they subserved civil frictions. The Edict of Nantes (1598) preserved the status quo: Protestant areas would remain Protestant, Catholic areas (the majority) would remain Catholic. Germany was the most furious battlefield. Until the Peace of Münster (1648) there was constant carnage. The upshot in Germany was the famous dictum *"Cujus regio, ejus religio"*: Each area would follow the religion of its prince.

How inherently wicked or good the self is was an important question in the Reformation debates between Protestants and Catholics. Protestants, following Luther's stress on justification by faith and Calvin's stress on God's sovereignty, tended to emphasize the corruption of human nature through sin. Catholics, partly in reaction to that Protestant position and partly from their own emphasis on the sacraments and the Incarnation, saw an essential goodness in human nature (though they spoke of sin as darkening the mind and weakening the will). Clearly, though, Christianity made the West suspicious of human instincts.

On the other hand, a certain realism about worldly life, in which imperfection if not sin was inevitable, tended to soften this rigorism. Christian moral theologians have usually taught that sins of the flesh are less grievous than sins of the spirit (such as pride, anger, or hatred).

The Pauline discussion of sin and grace in terms of "flesh" and "spirit" focused Christian discussion of the self as embodied. That Paul's original language did not intend a matter-spirit dualism was almost forgotten after Christianity took up Greek thought. As a result, extremists tended to deprecate the body, marriage, and the world of human affairs as fleshly pursuits. In response to the Manichaean and Albigensian heresies, the Catholic Church affirmed the goodness of the body, but the Church's general orientation toward heaven, its introduction of celibacy for holders of high Church offices, and its preference for ascetic saints tended to make the average person regret his or her flesh. For women this caused considerable suffering, because the male Church teachers often projected their sexual problems onto women. In that case, women became wanton, seductive, and dangerous. Moreover, the Reformation did not relieve women's plight. Luther thought that woman's vocation was to "bear herself out" with children, while John Knox trumpeted against "petticoat" power in the Church. Reformation biblicism, then, meant merely a return to the patriarchy of the scriptures.

Christian Rituals

By means of its sacramental system, the Christian Church has ritualized its members' passage through the life cycle. The system has begun with baptism, the sacrament designed to celebrate a person's birth into divine life and church membership.

The second sacramental rite in the normal Western life cycle was confirmation, the Christian celebration of coming-of-age. (The Eastern Christians celebrated along with baptism a rite called "chrismation" that bestowed the gift of the Holy Spirit.) The main motif in this celebration was asking God to give the candidate further strength from the Holy Spirit, in view of the services that adult life would require him to perform.

The Holy Eucharist has been the principal sacrament in the majority of the Christian traditions, and the ritual for the Eucharist has begun with a Liturgy of the Divine Word. Overall, the Church celebrated the Eucharist as both a memorial of Jesus' death and a memorial of his last meal, when he gave himself to his friends under the signs of bread and wine. Since Jesus' death and resurrection were the central events in the Christian reading of history, each Eucharistic memorial laid before the Christian faithful an epitome of their sense of reality. In Jesus' death and resurrection stood revealed the meaning and destiny of each human life.

Moreover, by receiving Jesus' body and blood, the believer was nourished in the divine life that Jesus' death and resurrection had made available. The Eucharist therefore was like the messianic banquet that Jews of Jesus' time had believed would accompany God's definitive victory.

The person who found baptism, confirmation, and the Holy Eucharist insufficient to keep him from sin could have recourse to sacramental rites of penance, which were designed to reconcile him with God and the rest of the community.

When the time has come to marry, Christians have been expected to celebrate their union through a marriage ritual. The theology of marriage likens the conjunction of man and woman in matrimony to the union between Christ and the Church. A Christian marriage is meant for both the mutual comfort of the spouses and the procreation of children.

A sixth sacramental ritual deals with the ordination of the Church's ministers. In churches with several ranks of ministers, the bishop presides at the ordination.

Many churches also celebrate sacramental rituals for the healing and consolation of the sick and the dying. The last stage on the Christian's life way is the burial rite, which usually focuses the Holy Eucharist for the occasion of death and burial. The Liturgy of the Word features psalms and scriptural passages concerned with death and the Christian hopes for resurrection, and the person is buried in consecrated ground with prayers for forgiveness and the life of the blessed in heaven.

The Christian sacramental system is the basic framework of the traditional Christian's church life. While many churches of the Protestant Reformed tradition came to downplay the sacraments that Catholics and Eastern Orthodox celebrated, Protestants still assemble for baptism, a liturgy of the scriptural Word, and to solemnize such occasions as marriage, ordination, and Christian burial. Whatever reservations they have about the Catholic and Eastern Orthodox development of almost sumptuous rituals, Protestants retain the Christian conviction that God uses material things (if only words and music) to draw human beings to himself in spirit and truth. The churches of the Catholic and Orthodox traditions extend this principle to bread and wine, oil and wax, and various "sacramentals" (signs, such as holy water and ashes, meant to solemnize smaller occasions). The result is a counterbalance to any Christian overemphasis on sin or unbridled condemnation of the world. If God's own Word has taken flesh, the body and the world has to be basically good. All of life, therefore, has "sacramental" possibilities. As the Holy Eucharist shows the deepest potentialities of an ordinary meal, so the union of Christ with the Church shows the deepest potentialities of ordinary sexual intercourse. Not every generation of Christians preaches this sacramentalism boldly, but it always lies ready to hand in the mainstream tradition.

As Robert McAfee Brown has shown,[20] the spirit of Protestantism that has come down from the sixteenth century stresses, first, the notion of reform itself—of always having to renew one's faith because of one's sure distance from God's holy will. Second, it stresses God's sovereignty, the authority of scripture, the priesthood of all believers, and the vocation of the laity to exercise their faith in the midst of the secular world.

The Reformation left Protestants and Catholics at odds, and the conflict has abated only in recent years. Today they seem to agree (despite such throwbacks as Northern Ireland) that the Reformers had legitimate grievances and that the Reformers' return to scripture renewed faith. On the other hand, Protestant and Catholic scholars also agree that many of the defects in modern Christianity result from its lacking the sense of a catholic tradition and common authority. The ecumenical task for the future, they would say, is for Christians to put their humpty-dumpty together again.

MODERNITY

The religious life of the West changed dramatically in the modern period. It had to contend with new political, philosophical, and scientific thought. More profoundly, for the first time it met a passionate counterfaith, for modernity opposed deep commitment to humanity's own powers to reliance on God.

The Enlightenment thinkers saw themselves as part of a movement for progress, the watchword of which was criticism. They took as their enemy ignorance, intolerance, and repression, vowing to attack all their manifestations in national culture. Furthermore, it assumed that both creation and human nature were essentially good, thus producing an expectation of great progress. Things would improve and freedom would increase as trustworthy critical reason expressed trustworthy human nature in a quite trustworthy natural order.

Quite obviously, the Enlightenment view of human nature clashed with that of traditional Christianity. Although reason held an important place in the medieval Scholastic synthesis, the medieval mind never doubted that human nature is only perfectible through divine grace. In Reformation thought, Protestant and Catholic alike, both human reason and human love suffer the effects of sin, with the result that only God can give the fulfillment they seek. The Enlightenment contested the beliefs of both periods.

The principles of Reformation and modernity have worked for more than four and a half centuries since Martin Luther. The reforming spirit continued both within and without Lutheranism and Calvinism, simplifying Christianity to yield a stark biblical faith and worship. Thus, Puritanism, Methodism, and Baptist religion moved Protestantism farther from Catholic dogmatic and sacramental theology. In reacting to this trend, Anglo-Catholicism tried to mediate between the ancient Catholic tradition and the Protestant instinct for the new religious needs of post-Renaissance society. However, the tide of the Protestant sectarians brought waves of individual, enthusiastic experience, which in turn promoted preaching, revivalism, and biblical literalism. Meanwhile, traditional Catholic authority fought modernity tooth and nail, only accepting modern scholarship and modern conceptions of human rights in the twentieth century.

During the nineteenth century, the Enlightenment meant liberalism in religious matters. Christianity was adapted to the needs of the day, which liberals thought were primarily humanistic in character. Adolf Harnack's slogan that the Christian essence is "the fatherhood of God and the brotherhood of man" encapsules much of the liberal spirit.

On occasion, both liberals and evangelicals (people rooted in the gospel) pressed for social change. The industrial revolution produced some abysmal working conditions, and Christian exponents of the "social gospel" agreed with Karl Marx that such conditions destroyed human dignity. In the "liberation theology" of recent years, this kinship has become explicit, and many liberation theologians are combining Marxist economic analyses with Christian beliefs. The most eloquent are Latin Americans,[21] but thought like theirs has penetrated the counsels of both Geneva and Rome. Recently Latinos, blacks, Asians, and feminists in North America who want to promote social change through radical Christian faith have rallied around liberation theology.[22]

NOTES

1. For a brief study of Christianity that includes fine maps of its spread, see Gerald Sloyan, "Christianity," in *Historical Atlas of the Religions of the World*, ed. I. al Faruqi and D. Sopher (New York: Macmillan, 1974), pp. 201–236.

2. One of the most thorough recent treatments of the critical and theological issues concerning Jesus is Edward Schillebeeckx, *Jesus* (New York: Seabury, 1979).

3. See Raymond E. Brown, *The Birth of the Messiah* (New York: Doubleday, 1977).

4. Joachim Jeremias, *New Testament Theology: The Proclamation of Jesus* (New York: Scribner's, 1971), pp. 29–36.

5. Karl Rahner and Herbert Vorgrimler, *Theological Dictionary* (New York: Herder and Herder, 1965), pp. 236–241.

6. A succinct discussion of New Testament ethics is J. L. Houden, *Ethics and the New Testament* (New York: Oxford University Press, 1977).

7. Jeremias, *New Testament Theology*, pp. 250–257.

8. Reliable and readable is Stephen Neill, *Jesus through Many Eyes* (Philadelphia: Fortress, 1976). For a literary stress, see Leonard L. Thompson, *Introducing Biblical Literature* (Englewood Cliffs, N.J.: Prentice-Hall, 1978), pp. 213–307.

9.   See Maxwell Staniforth, trans., *Early Christian Writings* (Baltimore: Penguin, 1968).

10.   J. Doresse, "Gnosticism," in *Historia Religionum, I*, ed. C. J. Bleeker and G. Widengren (Leiden: E. J. Brill, 1969), pp. 536–537.

11.   See Jaroslav Pelikan, *The Christian Tradition, 1: The Emergence of the Catholic Tradition* (Chicago: University of Chicago Press, 1971).

12.   J. G. Davies, "Christianity: The Early Church," in *The Concise Encyclopedia of Living Faiths*, ed. R. C. Zaehner (Boston: Beacon Press, 1967), pp. 60–69.

13.   William A. Clebsch, *Christianity in European History* (New York: Oxford University Press, 1979), pp. 29–84; Stephen Reynolds, *The Christian Religious Tradition* (Encino, Calif.: Dickenson, 1977), pp. 35–77.

14.   Donald W. Treadgold, *The West in Russia and China*, vol. 1 (Cambridge: Cambridge University Press, 1973), pp. 1–23.

15.   On classical Eastern theology, see Jaroslav Pelikan, *The Christian Tradition, 2: The Spirit of Eastern Christendom* (Chicago: University of Chicago Press, 1974); see also G. P. Fedotov, *The Russian Religious Mind* (Cambridge, Mass.: Harvard University Press, 1966).

16.   See Timothy Ware, *The Orthodox Church* (Baltimore: Penquin, 1964).

17.   C. W. Monnich, "Christianity," in *Historia Religionum, II*, ed. C. J. Bleeker and G. Widengren (Leiden: E. J. Brill, 1971), p. 65.

18.   Jaroslav Pelikan, *The Christian Tradition, 3: The Growth of Medieval Theology* (Chicago: University of Chicago Press, 1978), pp. 268–307.

19.   Owen Chadwick, *The Reformation* (Baltimore: Penguin, 1964), p. 41.

20.   Robert McAfee Brown, *The Spirit of Protestantism* (New York: Oxford University Press, 1965).

21.   The breakthrough work was Gustavo Gutierrez, *A Theology of Liberation* (Maryknoll, N.Y.: Orbis, 1973). Especially provocative is Jose Miranda, *Marx and the Bible* (Maryknoll, N.Y.: Orbis, 1974). A fine survey that brings liberation thought to the United States is Robert McAfee Brown, *Theology in a New Key* (Philadelphia: Westminster, 1978).

22.   See Sergio Torres and John Eagleson, eds., *Theology in the Americas* (Maryknoll, N.Y.: Orbis, 1976).

APPENDIX

4

Islam

The prophetic religion that began with Israel and took a new turn in Christianity gained a further career in Islam. Islam, which is the world's fastest growing religion today, arose from the visions of the prophet Muhammad. At its height, Islam stretched from India to western Spain.[1] Today it is a great force in Africa, a middling presence in China and the Soviet Union, a shareholder in the petropolitics of the Middle East, a huge presence in Indonesia, and the religion of more than 6 million North Americans.

INTRODUCTION

Islam stems directly from the two precepts contained in the profession of faith. "There is no God but God, and Muhammad is his Prophet." Allah (the Muslim term for God) is the ultimate agent of Islamic revelation and religion, but he chose to work through Muhammad. Thus, Muhammad was the spokesman, the medium, of a definitive message and book (the Qur'an). Through it God expressed once and for all the divine mercy and judgment.

Muhammad was born in 570 C.E. in Mecca, which is in present-day Saudi Arabia. Around 610, he began to receive revelations. At that time, the religious milieu of the Arabian Peninsula was a mixture of polytheism, polydemonism, and animistic nature worship. Most of the people identified with one of the nomadic tribes that lived in the area. Mecca was a religious and commercial center, where people came to venerate the Black Stone, set in what is known as the Kaaba. Today scholars surmise that the stone was a meteorite. Whatever its origin, it served as a rallying point for local

soothsayers and poets, who dominated the Arab religion that Muhammad witnessed as a youth. Among the Arabs there, a difficult social transition was under way from a nomadic society, in which loyalty was to one's clan, to a mercantile society, in which loyalty was to one's business partners (or simply to profit). The result was considerable upheaval. Before that time persons such as orphans and widows, who fell outside of nuclear families and trading groups, could find support in their larger clans, but the social change destroyed this support. Muhammad grew up as an orphan, so he must have felt some of the suffering experienced by such persons. Indeed, much of the social reform in his early message was to provide a religious basis for a unity extending beyond the clan that would prompt concern for orphans, widows, and the poor.

Muhammad grew up in a branch of the ruling Kuraish family under the care of his uncle, and he probably entered his family's caravan trade as a youth. In adulthood he married a wealthy widow, Khadija, who was some years older than he and who had been his employer. They had six children, of whom four daughters survived. Whether from personal troubles, challenges in the social situation, or a positive desire to understand the world more deeply, Muhammad developed the habit of going off to the hills nearby. There, in a cave, he enjoyed meditative solitude and began to have visions. His first visions, according to the Qur'an (53:1–18, 81:15–25) were of someone "terrible in power, very strong."[2] That person hovered near him on the horizon and imparted a revelation.

At first, he wondered if he was going crazy. However, Khadija encouraged him to believe in the revelations, and as his thought clarified, he attributed them to the angel Gabriel. Muhammad continued to

239

receive revelations for the rest of his life (over twenty years), and these messages, which either he or early disciples wrote down on "pieces of paper, stones, palm-leaves, shoulder-blades, ribs and bits of leather,"[3] formed the basis of the Qur'an.

From what scholars conjecture to be the early revelations, five major themes emerge: God's goodness and power, the need to return to God for judgment, gratitude and worship in response to God's goodness and pending judgment, generosity toward one's fellow human beings, and Muhammad's own vocation of proclaiming the message of goodness and judgment.

Muhammad's proclamation met with considerable resistance, principally because it threatened some powerful vested interests. First, the absoluteness of Allah threatened the traditional polytheism. However, it was much more than a challenge to custom and traditional religion—it was a challenge to the commerce that had grown up around the Kaaba. The livelihoods of the merchants who sold amulets, the soothsayers who sold fortunes, and the semiecstatic poets who lyricized the old gods were all imperiled.[4] Second, Muhammad's call for social justice implied a revolution—if not in contemporary financial arrangements, at least in contemporary attitudes. Third, the message of judgment was hardly welcome, for no age likes to find itself set before divine justice, hell fire, or the sword of retribution. Last, many Meccans ridiculed Muhammad's notion of the resurrection of the body.

The first converts to Muhammad's revelations came from within his own family. When he started to preach publicly, around 613, the leaders of the most powerful clans opposed him vigorously. He thus tended to be most successful among the low-ranking clans and those with young leaders ripe for a new order. Also, those who were considered "weak" (without strong clan protection) found the new prophecy attractive. Muhammad was proposing a religious association based on faith in Allah that transcended clan allegiances and so might make the weak stronger.

In 619 Muhammad suffered a personal crisis. His wife and uncle, who had been his foremost supporters, both died. Muslims ("submitters" to his God) were slowly increasing in number, but the future was very uncertain. In 622 he left Mecca and went to Yathrib, to the north, to arbitrate a long-standing dispute between two leading tribes. He settled there, and the town became Medina, the town of the Prophet. Muslims call Muhammad's departure or flight from Mecca the *Hejira*, and they view it as the turning point in the history of early Islam. Annemarie Schimmel interprets the Hejira as the complete breakup of Muhammad's relations with his own tribe—a definitive break with the old order,[5] which was a virtually unheard-of act in the clan-based society of the time.

One problem for Muhammad in Medina was the local Jewish community, who refused to accept him as a genuine prophet and ridiculed his interpretation of Jewish scripture. Apparently Muhammad either drove them out of Medina or had them killed or sold into slavery.[6] After consolidating his power base and building support among the neighboring bedouin tribes, Muhammad started to challenge the Meccans. He disrupted their trade in an effort to overthrow the city's commercial base, and in 624 his vastly outnumbered troops won a surprising victory at Badr. Finally, after several further skirmishes, Muhammad won a decisive victory at the Battle of the Ditch.

Muhammad's greatest triumphs came through diplomacy among the tribes, however. Mecca finally fell in 630 without the stroke of a single sword. In control, Muhammad cleansed the Kaaba of pagan idols. In the two remaining years of his life, Muhammad further developed the educational program that he had set up in Medina. "The centre of all his preoccupations was the training, educating, and disciplining of his community."[7]

Muhammad demonstrated an abundant humanity. In addition to his religious sensitivity and his political and military skills, Muhammad manifested a notable sympathy for the weak, a gentleness, a slowness to anger, some shyness in social relations, and a sense of humor.[8] According to the *Hadith* (tradition), for instance, the Prophet's second in command, Abu Bakr, started to beat a pilgrim for letting a camel stray. Muhammad began to smile and then indicated to Abu Bakr the irony that a pilgrim like Bakr (a pilgrim through life) should beat a pilgrim to Mecca.

In glimpses obtained from the Qur'an and the earliest levels of the tradition, Muhammad seems to have been an ordinary man whom God singled out to receive revelations. Muhammad's virtue was to accept his commission and keep faith with it until death. The emphasis in the Prophet's own preaching on the sovereignty of God and on the divine authority for the Qur'anic message led him to stress his own ordinariness, his liability to error, and the like. He made no claim to miraculous power. The central miracle was the Qur'an itself—a message of such sublimity and eloquence that it testified beyond doubt to a divine source. In keeping with Muhammad's own humility, orthodox Islam has condemned any move to exalt Muhammad above ordinary humanity or worship him.

Nonetheless, popular Muslim religion sometimes seized on hints in the Qur'an and made Muhammad superhuman. The most famous of its images is Muhammad's "night journey" to Jerusalem, after which he ascended to Paradise, talked with the prophets who preceded him, and experienced an ineffable vision of God. This story became so popular that it finally entered orthodox faith. Later religious faith also elaborated on Muhammad's preaching of the coming Last Judgment and tended to think of the Prophet as its shield and intercessor on the Last Day.

QUR'ANIC RELIGION

After Muhammad's death, his followers collected the texts of his revelations and established the orthodox version during the rule of Othman (644–656). The present version of the collection follows the editorial principle that the chapters (suras) should be ordered in decreasing length. The result is that the present text tells the reader nothing about the chronology of the revelations. For our purposes it is enough simply to accept the fact that Muhammad's revelations were written down and that he used them as the basis of the program that he urged on his listeners. Among the earliest themes of his preaching were the sovereignty of God, the imminence of judgment, and the need for fraternal charity.

The later passages of the Qur'an, those that likely were written in Medina, concern more practical affairs. As the head of an established political and religious community, Muhammad had to deal with questions of law and order. Thus, we can find the seeds of later Islamic law on inheritance, women, divorce, warfare, and the like. These seeds, plus the *Hadith*, which contain what the Prophet himself taught and judged,[9] are the primary sources of Islamic law. Generally, Muhammad's law and social teaching were advances on the prevailing mores. They improved the lot of the downtrodden and humanized both business and war. For instance, Muhammad made widows and orphans the prime beneficiaries of the *zakat* (almsgiving) required of all the faithful. Two points on which outsiders frequently fault Muhammad and the Qur'an are the doctrines of holy war (jihad) and polygamy. Nevertheless, they were improvements on the pre-Muslim practices and improved treatment of both women and prisoners of war.

The Five Pillars

On the basis of the Qur'an's prescriptions for a true Islam, a true religion of submission of the will of Allah,

Muslims have elaborated five cardinal duties known as the "pillars" of true faith. They are: witnessing to faith (proclaiming the creed), ritual prayer, fasting during the lunar month of Ramadan, almsgiving, and pilgrimage to Mecca. The witness to faith epitomizes the Muslim's orientation in the universe. There is no God but God, and Muhammad is his Prophet. Allah is the only fit object of worship, and Muhammad is the last of the prophets—the "seal."

What a comparitivist might call the rigorous monotheism of Islam has both negative and positive aspects. Negatively, in what amounts to an attack on false religion, Islam makes idolatry (associating anything with Allah) the capital sin. At the outset, then, Muhammad's revelation implied an attack on the prevailing Arab religion. Later it led to a polemic against Christian Trinitarianism and a check on worldly pride or mammon that might dimish God's sovereignty. Positively, Islamic monotheism generated great praise for the "Lord of the Worlds"[10]—the Creator who guides all things, who is the beauty and power by which the world moves. For the Muslim mystics, the words of the creed swelled with hidden meaning. Like the Cabalists, some Muslim mystics assigned each letter a numerical value and then composed numerological accounts of how the world hangs together. Many Muslim mystics pushed the concept of divine sovereignty so far that they denied the existence of anything apart from Allah. Not only was there no God beside him, there was no being apart from his Being. While the orthodox Muslims found such pantheism blasphemous, the mystics tended to stress the oneness of the Lord's domain.[11] Last, rigorous monotheism implied that Muhammad himself was not divine. His high status was to be the *rasul*—the prophetic mouthpiece.

The second pillar of faith is prayer, which has worked out as an obligation to pray five times daily. Authoritative authors such as al-Ghazali went to great lengths to specify the postures, words, number of bows, and proper places and times for prayer,[12] but the primary effect of the second pillar on the common people was to pace them through the day in the great Muslim practice of remembrance *(dhikr)*. At each call from the minaret, they were to remember the one God whom they serve—remember his compassion, his mercy, and his justice. Ideally, by praying fervently at the appointed hours, one can forge a chain that links together more and more moments of remembrance, so that God progressively comes to dominate all one's thought, action, and emotion. Experiencing Muslim prayer is impressive. The slow chant of the Qur'anic words becomes haunting, stirring even the non-Arabist. The voice (usually recorded today) is passionate—a lover's near sob, a tremulous witness to God's grandeur.

Third, what the prayer times are to the day, the holy month of Ramadan is to the year. Ramadan is the month of fasting and (interestingly enough) of celebration. Through all the hours of daylight (from the time that one can distinguish a black thread from a white), no food or drink is to pass the lips. Thereby, the Muslim learns discipline, sacrifice, and the price that divine treasures cost.[13] Against the secular succession of months, in which no time is more significant than any other, the religionist erects special times like Ramadan. These times opppose the flux, fence off a portion of time as sacred.

Fourth, Islam develops a similar paradigm for space by praying toward Mecca and by the obligation to make a pilgrimage to Mecca at least once in one's lifetime. For Muslims, Mecca is the center, the *omphalos* (navel) where the world was born. It is the holy city where Qur'anic revelation was disclosed to the world. Thus, the psychodynamics of the pilgrimage run deep. Without doubt, devout pilgrims feel that they are going to the holiest spot in creation.

On pilgrimage, Muslims dress alike, go through the same traditional actions, and often experience an exhilarating sense of community.

The fifth pillar, almsgiving, focuses this sense of community in a practical, economic way. By insisting that all contribute to the support of the poor (often one-fortieth of their wealth annually), Qur'anic religion gives its community *(Ummah)*[14] food and clothing. The Muslims alms, then, is more than a tiny dole or act of charity—it is an act of social, corporate responsibility. Furthermore, it reminds the advantaged that they are one family with the disadvantaged and that the stern Judge will demand a strict account of what they have done with his gifts.

Tradition says that the Qur'an teaches that the Prophet and his successors bore a theocratic power. That is, they had authority in both the religious and the secular spheres, because Islam does not distinguish the two. Due to the concept of the Ummah, Muslims had to fight for brethren in other places who suffered tyranny (Qur'an 4:75). For Muslim leaders, the consensus of the community was an important goal, for they wanted a single divine rope to bind the Ummah together. Strong faith was to create an equality among all believers, and God would reward every man and woman who was faithful through difficulties and trials.

Human Destiny

The destiny of the human being, as we have seen, was either the Fire or the Garden. Islam did not consider man and woman to be laboring under a "fallen" human nature, for Muslims did not regard the sin of Adam and Eve as being contagious or passed on to their offspring. Thus, Islam did not speak of redemption. The Prophet was a revealer or a medium of revelation; he was not a ransom, a victim, or a suffering servant. Instead of sin (in the deep sense of alienation from God by irrational actions), Islam tended to stress human forgetfulness (of God's goodness). Human nature was weak—prone to a kind of religious amnesia. In the Prophet's own conception of human destiny, men and women have a common responsibility to remember God's goodness and to respond by fulfilling his will. Originally, both men and women were to offer prayer and alms; however, in later times women's status deteriorated, and they did not have this obligation.

In the Qur'an there is some basis for sexual equality: Reward and punishment in the afterlife depend on deeds, not gender; marriage and conjugal life are precious; women have dowry rights in some divorces, inheritance rights, rights to remarry, and rights to protection in time of pregnancy and nursing. However, women's rights were not equal to those that the Qur'an gave males in either divorce or inheritance. Moreover, the Qur'an does not even consider the possibility that women might assume leadership roles in the community, receive an education equal to that of males, teach law or theology, or engage in polygamy (as males could).

Another revealing view of women in Islamic society comes from the imagery of the Garden.[15] For many men, the best part of the heavenly Garden was the *hur:* dark-eyed, buxom virgins. In addition to his earthly wife, each male in heaven could expect to have seventy *hur.* They would never be sick, menstruating, pregnant (unless he wished), bad-tempered, or jealous. He would be able to deflower a thousand each month and find them all intact when he returned to them. In descriptions of the Judgment scene, one sees the reverse of this fantasy: Women are in charge of men, which is a sure sign of disorder.

In fairness, Islam improved the lot of Arab women considerably, and certain parts of the community allowed women a function in the *Hadith,*[16] in scholarship, and in saintliness.[17] Also, many modern Muslims deplore the injustices that women have suffered in the past, interpret Qur'anic religion in a way that gives women great dignity, and bitterly oppose the drive of fundamentalists to return to such traditions as marrying girls off when they reach thirteen.

The self that was faithful to the identity set by the community could expect to gain Paradise. God would forgive sins (violations of religious law), so they did not mean a loss of community membership. What separated one from the Ummah in the orthodox view was to deny that the injunctions of the Qur'an came from God and thus were eternally binding. Among the Shia, who predominate in Iran, faith also included acknowledging the mystical imam of the time—the hidden successor to Ali whom the Shiites expect to come as the Messiah. By uniting with this hidden imam, one partook of salvation.

Historically, the major theoretical question concerning the self was the relation of human freedom to divine will. At least in the Meccan sections, the Qur'an takes human freedom for granted. Muhammad's call and his preaching make no sense without a capacity to respond. Similarly, the scenes of Judgment Day assume that human beings have been responsible for their actions—that they could have done otherwise than they did. However, later Qur'anic passages emphasize God's omnipotence. As a result, the question arises, Does God lead some persons astray—or at least leave them in error?

In the Umayyad period (ca. 661–749) a group of strict predestinarians (the Jabriya) stressed God's complete control. Opposing them were the Qasriya, who defended human responsibility. The Mutazilites defended both human freedom and God's perfect justice. Still another position, that of al-Ashari, satisfied many people with the following formula: "God creates in man the will to act and the act, and man acquires the act by performing it." To say the least, the issue vexed Islam. In later times the common person frequently felt that life was fated—that it was out of his or her hands. Among the few monistic mystics, human freedom was lost in the divine nature.

In summary, Islam has given the self rather complex directives. The core message is that membership in the Prophet's community and submission to God fulfill the human duties. The way to realize oneself is to follow the community law. In the present, such self-realization means spiritual security; in the future, it will mean Paradise. While waiting for Paradise, one can work the earth, trade, fight, or enjoy the pleasures of the senses, so long as the chosen activity does not divert one from the ultimate reality of God. If one is submissive to God, most things are licit. More things are licit for men than for women, as we have seen, but the Qur'an did improve the Arab woman's lot considerably.

Ritual

Like all religious traditions, Islam ritualizes the main events of the life-cycle. However, more than most other religions, Islam allows the ceremonies of entrance into the Ummah, marriage, and burial to be shaped by the prevailing culture or earlier religious customs of the land. An example of this is the Yoruba Muslims of West Africa.[18]

The life cycle of the Yoruba Muslim begins on the day he becomes a member of the worshiping community. This may be the day when, as an adult, he formally converts to Islam, or the eighth day after his birth, when he receives his name. The major action in the adult conversion ceremony is an ablution, to symbolize the pure life the convert is entering upon. For the naming ceremony of a newborn child, the presiding cleric receives money in a covered dish. The cleric prays for the child, preaches a solemn sermon (often in Arabic), and then gives the child its name. Some West African Muslims also sacrifice a sheep or cut the infant's hair. (The Yoruba practice circumcision, as well as the drawing of tribal marks on the face or body. Apparently Islam did not introduce these customs but rather gave them a new interpretation.)

The second major stage on the Yoruba Muslim's way is marriage. The presiding cleric must divine that the proposed match is a good one and pray for the marital partners. Before the wedding, the groom has to pay the bride's family several monies and gifts. During the wedding ceremony the cleric quotes the Qur'an (4:34), to the effect that one of the signs God has given human beings is creating mates for them, that they may find quiet of mind. Putting love and compassion between these mates, God gives reflective people a sign of his goodness and care. The presiding cleric also asks the bride questions, including whether she will love, honor, and obey her husband. He repeats most of the quotation from the Qur'an, and reminds the bride that "the good women are therefore obedient, guarding the unseen as Allah has guarded." The ceremony concludes with prayers to Allah that he bless this wedding. (Most of the West African Muslim community supports the traditional polygyny.)

Funeral rites complete Islam's ritual impact on the Yoruba life cycle. When a person has died the neighbors come together and dig a grave. They then wash the corpse, repeating the ablutions of the conversion ceremony. They dress the corpse in a white cap, loin cloth, and sewn sheet, and then put it into the grave and cover it with earth. The presiding cleric prays for the deceased person, that God may forgive her sins. The dead person's family is expected to pay the cleric handsomely, with food as well as money. Some modernized sects hold a second ceremony, on the eighth day after the burial, with readings from the Qur'an, a sermon, and a eulogy of the deceased.

For Yoruba Muslims (and all Muslims), Friday is

the center of the weekly cycle, when all good Muslims are supposed to gather at noon in the main mosque for communal worship. In the large towns the mosques are crowded with male worshipers. (A smaller number of women are allowed to worship, segregated from the males, at the back of the mosque.) The service begins with the call to prayer and then has a sermon in the vernacular.

After the sermon comes the heart of the Friday service, the communal *salat* or ritual prayer. Together the group go through the actions of the fivefold daily prayer—bowing, kneeling, and touching their foreheads to the ground. Muslim prayer is essentially this doing, this performative act. So "a mosque in the last resort is not a building. It is a place of prostration and any patch of ground in ritual purity suffices where a human frame may stretch itself—a fact about Islam which accounts in large measure for the naturalness of its occasions and the contagion in its expansion. A faith that does not need to house its worshipers has no walls to hide its creed."[19]

THE AGE OF CONQUEST

At Muhammad's death in 632 most of Arabia had accepted Islam, though often the allegiance was superficial. Some tribes took the occasion of the Prophet's death to attempt a revolt. General Khalid al-Walid, who served the first caliph (leader) Abu Bakr, crushed them within a year. Thus, when Abu Bakr died in 636, Arabia was united and poised for adventure. The obvious foes were Byzantium and Persia, which threatened Arabian prosperity and were ripe for religious and military conquest. The Muslim armies were amazingly effective. By 636 they controlled both Damascus and Jerusalem. As important in this lightning conquest as their military skill, though, was the unrest of the peoples they conquered. Those peoples "welcomed the Muslims as kin-liberators from Byzantine politics, economic exploitation, Church persecution, and social tyranny."[20] On the eastern frontier, by 649 all of Persia was in Arab hands.

The quick conquest of Syria released men for further expeditions in the West; by 640 there were conquests in Egypt. Cairo and Alexandria soon fell, and the Arabs established themselves as a marine power operating from the southeastern Mediterranean. By 648 they had conquered Cyprus; by 655 they were in charge of the waters around Greece and Sicily. On land in North Africa, the Muslims conquered the Berber region of Tripoli in 643 and then proceeded to Carthage. Soon Muslims were as far away as China, India, and western Europe. By 699 Islam occupied Afghanistan, while various campaigns south of the Caspian and Aral seas brought Armenia, Iraq, Iran, and eastern India into the Muslim fold by 800.

At the beginning of the ninth century, Arab rule along the southern Mediterranean stretched from Palestine to the Atlantic. Muslims controlled three-quarters of the Iberian Peninsula, and most Mediterranean traffic had to reckon with Muslim sallies. European campaigns had brought Arab soldiers as far north as Orleans.

In the ninth century, from their positions in southeastern France, they pushed northeast as far as Switzerland. Muslim expansion ended after 1050 and by 1250 Islam's European presence had weakened considerably. However, Islam had spread through all of Persia, crossed northern India, and reached the western Chinese border. In East Asia, it had a discernible presence in Sumatra, Borneo, and Java. All of North Africa was securely Muslim, while down the East African coast as far as Madagascar it exerted a strong influence. In many of these regions, of course, substantial portions of the populations remained non-Muslim.

Historians debate the motivation for all this expansion, and we can safely say that it was complex. The Arabs were likely suffering from population pressures on the Arabian Peninsula, which incited many of them to search for more land. Symbolically, religion served as a rallying point for the Arab cause. It stressed common bondage to a single Lord, and it dignified the Arab movement with a sort of manifest destiny. Certainly the generals who dominated the era of conquest were as accomplished in worldly affairs as they were in religious.

The Muslims grouped most of the conquered non-Muslims together as *Dhimmis*—members of religions that Arab law tolerated. As "peoples of the book," Jews and Christians were *Dhimmis*, with title to special respect. There were nevertheless frictions, especially if Jews or Christians were blatantly derogatory of the Prophet and his Book, but usually people were not compelled to convert to Islam.

Internal Strife

Despite its enormous outward success in the age of conquest, the Islamic community suffered notable internal divisions. With the exception of Abu Bakr, the first caliphs, known as the *Rashidun* (rightly guided), all left office by murder. Ali, the fourth caliph, was the center of a fierce struggle for control. His main opponent was Muawiya, the head of a unified stronghold in Syria. Muawiya maneuvered to have the legitimacy of Ali's caliphate called into question. As a result, Ali lost support in his own group, and dissidents called Kharijites appeared who had a hand in many later conflicts. A Kharijite killed Ali in 661, and the caliphate passed to the Umayyad dynasty—the followers of Muawiya.

However, Ali's influence did not end with his assassination. In fact, his assassination became part of Islam's deepest division, the one between the Shia (party), who were loyalists to Ali, and the Sunni (traditionalists). The "party" supporting Ali believed that the successors to Muhammad ought to come from Muhammad's family—in other words, that Islamic leadership should be hereditary. This conviction was supported by certain verses of the Qur'an, in which the Prophet supposedly indicated that Ali would be his successor. The Shia therefore consider the first three caliphs, who preceded Ali, as having been usurpers. After Ali's death, they took up the cause of his sons, Hasan and Husain.

The word that the Shia gave to the power that descended through Muhammad's family line was *imamah* (leadership). Through its history, the Shia has made it a cardinal doctrine that Muhammad's bloodline has an exclusive right to *imamah*. The slaughter of Husain in Iraq in 680 was an especially tragic event, and the Shiites have come to commemorate it as the greatest of their annual festivals. It gives their Islam a strong emphasis on sorrow, suffering, and emotion that quite distinguish it from Sunni piety.[21]

THE GOLDEN CIVILIZATION

In his history of science, Stephen Mason states that Muslim scientific culture began in the era of the Umayyads.[22] The Umayyads had been auxiliaries of the Romans in Syria, so when they established the caliphate in Damascus in 661, they brought an enthusiasm for Hellenistic culture. In particular, they became patrons of the sciences. For example, in 700 they founded an astronomical observatory at Damascus. However, the Umayyads fell to the Abbasids in 749. The Abbasids set their caliphate in Baghdad and turned to Persian rather than Hellenistic culture, supporting the Persian specialities of medicine and astronomy. Al-Mansur, the second Abbasid caliph, was also devoted to learning, bringing Indian astronomers and doctors to Baghdad and having many Indian scientific treatises translated.

Under his successors, translation continued to be a major project. As a result, many Greek treatises (for example, those of Galen and Ptolemy) became available to Muslims. Partly because of Babylonian and Zoroastrian influences, the Baghdad caliphs deemed astronomy especially important. They imported Indian mathematicians to help in astronomical calculations and made Baghdad a center of astronomical learning.

From 970, the Spanish branch of the Muslim Empire had a distinguished scientific center in Cordoba. Similarly, the religious authorities patronized science, especially medicine and astronomy, at Toledo from the early eleventh century. The Spanish Muslims tended to be critical of Ptolemy and to favor Aristotelian doctrines. Averroës (1126–1198) was a great Aristotelian synthesizer who composed a full philosophical corpus.

Albert Moore has shown the effects of Islam's monotheism in the field of art, arguing that it led to a classical concentration on the architecture and ornamentation of the mosque.[23] Moore indicates that paintings of hunting and of love scenes were permitted in private Muslim homes. Nonetheless, the preponderance of Muslim art during the golden age was nonpictorial, including rugs, vases, lamps, and mosques.

A distinctively Islamic calligraphy developed from the trend to decorate pages from the Qur'an. A favorite subject for embellishment has been the *Bismallah*, the prefix to the Qur'anic suras ("In the name of God"). Through an extension of calligraphic swirls and loops, Muslims developed an ingenious ability to suggest flowers, birds, lions, and so on. The Sufi interest in numerology also encouraged artistic work.

Law

Within the inner precincts of Islam, neither science nor art constituted the main cultural development. Rather, the most important flowering of Qur'anic faith was the law *(Sharia)*.[24] As the opening verses of the Qur'an suggest, a fundamental concern in Islam is guidance, and Islam went to lawyers, not to scientists, poets, or even mystics, for its most trustworthy guidance. In fact, Islam obtained little guidance from philosophical theology, which began a most promising career but foundered on the shoals of sectarian controversy and debates about the relation of reason to faith. Although numerous schools of law developed, the differences among them were relatively slight, and they usually left little place for innovative reason. Thus, the authorities accounted them more trustworthy than philosophical theology—better cement for Muslim society.

The early theological discussions dealt with the nature of faith. Idolatry and unbelief were the major evils for the Qur'an, so it was important to understand them well. The types of sins were also an important early theological focus. Later debates focused on the unity of God (in the context of discussing the divine attributes) and on the relation of the divine sovereignty to human freedom. While there was a full spectrum of opinions, in Sunni quarters the more moderate positions tended to win favor. Before long, however, Islam effectively curtailed speculation, favoring instead careful efforts to ascertain what legal precedents any *practical* problem had in the *Hadith* of the Prophet, the Qur'an, community consensus, or analogous situations.

To be sure, Muslims did not view religious law as a human creation. Rather, it was divine guidance, the expression of God's own will. The goal of the lawyers was to offer comprehensive guidance for all of life— much as the rabbis' goal was to apply the Torah to all of life. In practice, the lawyers tended to divide their subject matter into obligations to God (for example, profession of faith and performance of prayer) and obligations to other human beings (for example, individual and social morality, such as not lying and not stealing). The lawyers classified theology under the first set of obligations, for theology was the science of right belief, and right belief was primary among the things that human beings owed to God. As they refined their science, the lawyers also distinguished all human actions according to five headings: obligatory, recommended, permitted, disapproved, and forbidden. Thus, one had to confess the unity of God and the Prophethood of Muhammad, one was counseled to avoid divorce, and one was forbidden to eat pork. Since Muslim society was a theocracy, *Sharia* was the code of the land. While that made for a certain unity and order, it also prepared the way for the Sufi emphasis on personal devotion.

THE PERIOD OF DIVISION

A minor source of division within the Muslim community was the differences in law developed by the various schools. Given the four recognized legal schools of Sunni, the large Shia minority, which had its own legal schools, and the division of the Islamic Empire into eastern and western parts centered at Baghdad and Cordoba, respectively, one can see that religious and political unity was less than perfect. Still, Muslims holding to the five pillars and the Qur'an had

more in common with one another than they had with any non-Muslim peoples. Thus, legal or creedal differences did not divide Muslim religion severely. In contrast, different devotional styles, such as Sufism, caused considerable hubbub.

Sufism

Opinions about the merits of Sufism differ. Fazlur Rahman, commenting especially on the work of al-Ghazali (1058–1111), speaks of the "fresh vitality" that al-Ghazali's devotionalism infused into the Muslim community.[25] Isma'il al Faruqi, on the contrary, cites Sufism as the first step in Islam's decline from its golden civilization.[26] It is true that al-Ghazali was not a typical Sufi (he had great learning as well as great piety), and that al Faruqi's sympathies lie with the reforming Wahabis (see below), for whom Sufism was an abomination. Still, a survey of studies shows quite mixed reactions to Sufism. Most commentators agree that its initial centuries (the ninth through thirteenth) were more creative and positive than its later ones.

At the outset, Sufism (the name likely comes from the Arabic word for wool, which Sufis wore as a gesture of simplicity),[27] stood for reform and personal piety. In a time when political and military success tempted Islam to worldliness, and the rise of the law brought the dangers of legalism, the Sufis looked to the model of Muhammad at prayer, communing with God. For them the heart of Islam was personal submission to Allah, personal guidance along the straight path. In later centuries, through its brotherhoods and saints, Sufism set a great deal of the emotional, anti-intellectual, and antiprogressive tone of an Islam that had lost its status as a world power.

Several cultural streams ran together to form the Sufi movement. First was the ascetic current from traditional desert life, which was basic and simple—a daily call for endurance. Out of a keen sense of the religious values in such a harsh life, Abu Dharr al-Ghifari, a companion of the Prophet, chastised the early leaders who wanted to lead a sumptuous court life after their conquests. Second, many of the Sufi ecstatics drew on the Arab love of poetry. Their lyric depictions of the love of God, coupled with Qur'an's eloquence, drew sensitive persons to the side of a living, personal faith that might realize the beauties of Islam.

Third, the more speculative Sufis drew on Gnostic ideas that floated in from Egypt and the Fertile Crescent. By the ninth century, Sufi contemplatives (especially the Persian Illuminationists) were utilizing those ideas to analyze the relations between divinity and the world. (The Sufis seem to have found the emanational ideas—the theories of how the world flowed out of the divine essence—rather than the dualistic theories of good and evil most attractive.) This kind of understanding, along with the alchemical interests noted previously, was the beginning of the esoteric and sometimes magical lore for which the orthodox theologians and lawyers held Sufis suspect. Last, Indian (especially Buddhist) thought apparently influenced the eastern portions of the Muslim realm, and it perhaps was a source of the tendencies toward self-annihilation that became important in Sufi mystical doctrine.

Taken at their own word, the Sufis desired to be faithful followers of Muhammad and the Qur'an. The more honored among them never intended any schismatic or heretical movements. At their creative best, they fashioned stories to carry their messages about the paradoxes of the spiritual life, the need for being focused and wholehearted, the way that God comes in the midst of everyday life. In these stories, the poor man turns out to be rich; the fool turns out to be truly wise. Like their counterparts in other traditions, the Sufis left no doubt that riches and prestige tend to be obstacles to spirituality.

Predictably, this challenge to the expectations of society, of the religious authorities, and of the literally minded won the Sufis no love. Perhaps to intensify their opposition, some Sufis became even more poetic, challenging the establishment and suggesting that its religion was little more than dead convention. An example of this is a story of a dervish who meets the devil. The devil is just sitting patiently, so the dervish asks him why he is not out making mischief. The devil replies, "Since the theoreticians and would-be teachers of the Path have appeared in such numbers, there is nothing left for me to do."[28]

Decline

By the beginning of the fourteenth century, the age of some of the greatest Sufi figures was over; Sufism started to decline, and with it much of Islam's religious vitality. The orders continued to multiply, and many princes and sultans continued to patronize them, but abuse, scandal, and superstition became more and more common. Still, the Sufis played a considerable role in the expansion of Islam, largely by serving as models of piety for the common people and giving them hopes of wonder working.

The organizations of Sufi influence were the Sufi orders, or brotherhoods. The first seems to date from the twelfth century. Typically, at the order's local lodge, a small number of professionals resided to teach and lead worship. Most members were (and are) lay adherents who came for instruction when they could and who supported the lodge by contributing money, manual labor, and so on. Each order tended to have its own distinctive ritual, whose purpose was usually to attain ecstatic experience. The ritual was the group's interpretation of the general virtue of *dhikr* (remembrance) that all Muslims seek. For instance, whirling dances characterized many of the Mevlevi dervish meetings, while Saadeeyeh Sufis developed a ceremony in which the head of the order rode over prone devotees on horseback.

LATE EMPIRE AND MODERNITY

During the period of empire (the Ottoman Empire of Turkey and the Middle East, Persia,[29] and the Mogul dynasty in India,[30]) at least three general changes occurred in Muslim society. The first was the transformation of the Islamic Near East from a commercial economy based on money to a feudal economy based on subsistence farming. The second was the replacement in positions of authority of Arabic-speaking peoples by Turks. The Arab tribes retained their independence in the desert regions, where they held out quite well against Turkish rule. In the cities and cultivated valleys (the plains of Iraq, Syria, and Egypt), however, the Arabs became completely subjected, and the glorious language that had been the pride of Islam became the argot of an enslaved population. The third change was the transfer of the seat of Islam from Iraq to Egypt.

By the eighteenth century, however, the Ottoman Empire was in decay—corrupt, anarchic, and stagnant. The principal religious form of revolt during this period was Sufism. At first Sufism was mainly an escape for oppressed individuals, but with the organization of more brotherhoods, it became a social movement that was especially powerful among the artisan class. The long centuries of stagnation finally ended, however, with increased contact with the West. From the beginning of the sixteenth century, European expansion brought some of the new learning of the Renaissance and the Reformation. The French in particular had considerable influence in the Middle East, and Napoleon's easy conquest of the Ottoman Turks at the end of the eighteenth century was the final blow to Islamic military glory.

The Wahabis

Also during the time of Napoleon arose an Islamic reform that was designed to check Sufism.[31] One of the first leaders in this reform was a stern traditionalist named Muhammad ibn Abd al-Wahab, whose followers came to be known as Wahabis. They called for a return to the doctrines and practices of the early generations, of the ancestors whom they venerated.

An immediate effect of the Wahabi movement was great hostility toward the Sufi brotherhoods. In fact, Muslims interested in renovating orthodoxy singled out the Sufis as their great enemies, although they also attacked the scholasticism of such theological centers as al-Azhar in Cairo. One of the leaders of the nineteenth-century reform was the apostle of Pan-Islam, Jamal al-Din al-Afghani, who proposed the political unification of all Muslim countries under the caliphate of the Ottoman sultans. While Pan-Islam has never been realized, it stimulated the widespread search for an effective Muslim response to modernity. In India and Egypt, conservative groups arose that gravitated toward the Wahabi position. Many of the Sufi organizations lost their strength, and those that survived tended to back away from gnosis and return to a more traditional theology.

The organizations that have grown up in recent times, such as the Association for Muslim Youth and the Muslim Brotherhood, seem in good measure an effort to fill the void created by the demise of the brotherhoods. The new groups differ by operating primarily in pluralistic cultures, while the Sufi orders drew on the ardor of a homogeneous culture that was secure in its unchallenged faith.

Western Influence

A characteristic of Islamic modernity was the invasion of Western secular ideas. These ideas came on the heels of modern Western takeovers in the Middle East, at first through the administrations of the Europeans who governed the newly acquired territories and then through the educational systems, which were Westernized. The new classes of native professionals—doctors, lawyers, and journalists—frequently trained abroad or in native schools run by Westerners. One political effect of such training was to raise Muslim feelings of nationalism and to provoke cries for Westernized systems of government. The new ideas challenged the *madrasas*, or religious schools, too, for it was not immediately apparent that these new ideas could be taught along with traditional theories of revelation and Qur'anic inspiration.

Controversy over societal matters has been more heated than that over theology because the guidance provided by the traditional legal schools diverged more sharply from Western mores than Muslim theology diverged from Western theology. Slowly Islamic countries have developed civil codes and separated civil courts from religious courts. In the mid-nineteenth century, the Turkish Republic breached the wall of tradition when it abolished the authority of the *Sharia* in civil matters. In other countries the *Sharia* has remained the outer form, but new legislative codes direct the interpretations. The tactic has been to invoke the Qur'an, the *Hadith*, and the traditions of the schools but to leave the legislators and judges free to choose the authority that is most appropriate. Specifically, the legal reforms have applied primarily to marriage contracts (protecting girls against child marriage), divorce proceedings, and polygamy—central factors in the traditional family structure.

Finally, Islamic secularism is less advanced than Western secularism. True, fundamentalism attracts a noteworthy number of Christians and Jews, but their cultures more clearly differentiate the civic realm, the realm shared with citizens of other religious convictions (or of none), than Islamic countries do. Conversely, Islam has kept the sacred and the secular more tightly conjoined than Christianity or Judaism has. It professes that there is no secular realm—that everything lives by the will and touch of Allah, who is as near as the pulse at one's throat.

NOTES

1. There are good maps on the spread of Islam in Geoffrey Barraclough, ed., *The Times Atlas of World History* (Maplewood, N.J.: Hammond, 1979), pp. 104–105, 134–135, 138–139; see also I. al Faruqi and D. Sopher, eds. *Historical Atlas of the Religions of the World* (New York: Macmillan, 1974), pp. 237–281.

2. We have used the translation by A. J. Arberry, *The Koran Interpreted* (New York: Macmillan, 1973).

3. W. Montgomery Watt, *Muhammad: Prophet and Statesman* (New York: Oxford University Galaxy Books, 1974), p. 7.

4. On the pre-Islamic background, see Ignaz Goldziher, *Muslim Studies,* vol. 1 (Chicago: Aldine, 1967), pp. 11–44; Marshall G. S. Hodgson, *The Venture of Islam,* vol. 1 (Chicago: University of Chicago Press,

1974), pp. 103–145; M. M. Bravmann, *The Spiritual Background of Early Islam* (Leiden: E. J. Brill, 1972).

5. Annemarie Schimmel, "Islam," in *Historia Religionum, II*, ed. C. J. Bleeker and G. Widengren (Leiden: E. J. Brill, 1971), p. 129.

6. Charles J. Adams, "The Islamic Religious Tradition," in *Judaism, Christianity and Islam*, ed. J. O'Dea, T. O'Dea, and C. Adams (New York: Harper & Row, 1972), p. 166.

7. H. A. R. Gibb, *Mohammedanism*, 2nd ed. (New York: Oxford University Press, 1962), p. 30.

8. See Watt, *Muhammad*, pp. 229–231.

9. On the development of the *Hadith*, see Ignaz Goldziher, *Muslim Studies*, vol. 2 (Chicago: Aldine, 1975), pp. 17–251.

10. Kenneth Cragg, *The House of Islam*, 2nd ed. (Encino, Calif.: Dickenson, 1975), pp. 30–34; Arberry, *Koran Interpreted*, pp. 5–18.

11. See Martin Lings, *A Sufi Saint of the Twentieth Century*, 2nd ed. (Berkeley: University of California Press, 1973), pp. 121–130; R. C. Zaehner, *Hindu and Muslim Mysticism* (New York: Schocken, 1969), pp. 86–109.

12. W. Montgomery Watt, *The Faith and Practice of al-Ghazali* (London: Allen & Unwin, 1953), pp. 90–130.

13. See Cheikh Hamidou Kane, *Ambiguous Adventure* (New York: Collier, 1969).

14. Cragg, *House of Islam*, pp. 73–108; Frederick Mathewson Denny, "The Meaning of *Ummah* in the Qur'an," *HR*, 1975, *15*:34–70.

15. Jane I. Smith and Yvonne Haddad, "Women in the Afterlife: The Islamic View as Seen from the Qur'an and Tradition," *JAAR*, 1975, *43*: 39–50.

16. See Goldziher, *Muslim Studies*, vol. 2, pp. 366–368.

17. On scholarship and saintliness, the Sufis somewhat sponsored women, though their overall view of women was ambivalent; see Annemarie Schimmel, *Mystical Dimensions of Islam* (Chapel Hill: University of North Carolina Press, 1975), pp. 426–435.

18. This section adapts Patrick J. Ryan's *Imale: Yoruba Participation in the Muslim Tradition* (Missoula, Mont.: Scholars Press, 1978), pp. 249–270.

19. Cragg, *House of Islam*, p. 60.

20. al Faruqi, "Islam," in *Historical Atlas*, p. 248.

21. See W. Montgomery Watt, *The Formative Period of Islamic Thought* (Edinburgh: University Press, 1973), pp. 253–278.

22. Stephen F. Mason, *A History of the Sciences*, rev. ed. (New York: Collier, 1962), p. 95; see also A. I. Sabra, "The Scientific Enterprise," in *Islam and the Arab World*, ed. Bernard Lewis (New York: Knopf, 1976)), pp. 181–200; G. Anawati, "Science," in *The Cambridge History of Islam*, vol. 2, ed. P. M. Holt et al. (Cambridge: University Press, 1970), pp. 741–779.

23. Albert C. Moore, *Iconography of the Religions: An Introduction* (Philadelphia: Fortress, 1977), pp. 213–225; see also Richard Ettinghausen, "The Man-Made Setting," in *Islam and the Arab World*, ed. Bernard Lewis (New York: Knopf, 1976), pp. 57–88; G. Fehervari, "Art and Architecture," in *The Cambridge History of Islam*, vol. 2, ed. P. M. Holt et al. (Cambridge: University Press, 1970), pp. 702–740.

24. See J. Schacht, "Laws and Justice," in *The Cambridge History of Islam*, vol. 2, ed. P. M. Holt et al. (Cambridge: University Press, 1970), pp. 539–568.

25. Fazlur Rahman, *Islam* (Garden City, N.Y.: Doubleday, 1968), p. xxii.

26. al Faruqi, "Islam," in *Historical Atlas*, p. 267.

27. Martin Lings, *What Is Sufism?* (Berkeley: University of California Press, 1977), pp. 45–46; A. J. Arberry, *Sufism* (New York: Harper Torchbooks, 1970), p. 35.

28. Idries Shah, *The Way of the Sufi* (New York: Dutton, 1970), p. 169.

29. Roger M. Savory, "Land of the Lion and the Sun," in *Islam and the Arab World*, ed. Bernard Lewis (New York: Knopf, 1976), pp. 245–272.

30. S. A. A. Rizi, "Muslim India," in *Islam and the Arab World*, ed. Bernard Lewis (New York: Knopf, 1976), pp. 301–320; see also I. H. Qureshi et al., "The Indian Sub-Continent," in *The Cambridge History of Islam*, vol. 2, ed. P. M. Holt et al. (Cambridge: University Press, 1970), pp. 1–120.

31. See Rahman, *Islam*, pp. 237–260.

5

Hinduism

PRE-VEDIC INDIA

Before the first invasions of Aryans from the northwest around 2000 B.C.E., an impressive Indian culture already existed. Its beginnings stretch back to the second interglacial period (400,000–200,000 B.C.E.), and its earliest religion, on the basis of ancient peoples living in India today, was shamanist, focusing on the worship of nature—especially on the life force. In 1924 excavations at two sites along the Indus River, called Harrapa and Mohenjo-daro, furnished the first extensive evidence of a high ancient Indian culture. This culture, called the Harrapan or Dravidian, stretched over about 500,000 square miles[1] and was distributed in small towns between the two "capitals" of Harrapa and Mohenjo-daro.

Some of the most significant remains from the Harrapan culture are small sandstone seals, engraved with a pictorial script and apparently used to mark property. They are decorated with various animals, both real and imaginary, and indicate a modest economic and artistic life. Other interesting finds include a small bronze statue of a dancing girl, lithe and graceful, and a red sandstone sculpture of the torso of a young man, also artistically impressive. Some scholars hypothesize that these finds indicate creative potential that was stifled by conservative forces, but others logically suggest that these artifacts are the only remains we have of a rather vigorous art whose other products perished.

By about 1500 B.C.E. the Harrapan culture was destroyed, after perhaps a millennium and a half of existence. (Most scholars postulate a long growth period before the 400 years of prosperity.) The destructive Aryan conquerers were a pastoral and nomadic people who loved fighting, racing, drinking, and other aspects of the warrior life. They probably came from the north, where the cooler climate favored such vigor, and they thought of themselves as the salt of the earth—their name means "from the earth" or "noble." (This name survives in *Iran* and *Eire*; in addition, all European languages save Finnish, Hungarian, and Basque are related to the Aryans' language.)

The Aryans had fair skin and pointed noses, a fact responsible for their hostile reaction to the dark, snub-nosed Dravidians. They moved by horse, ate meat, and hunted with bow and arrow. There is no evidence that they ever learned to navigate or sail, and they produced no striking art, although they did know iron and fashioned good weapons. Like many other warrior, nomadic peoples (for example, the Celts), they loved story telling and singing. Indeed, their culture and religion were highly verbal. Their society was male dominated, with a primarily patriarchal family structure, priesthood, and cast of gods.[2]

Two peoples thus contributed to the beginnings of Hindu culture. If the Harrapan culture was representative, the people who came before the Aryans in the Indus Valley were stable, even conservative city dwellers who nevertheless developed (or took from earlier peoples) important fertility rites. The Aryans were a rough, fighting people who had a much simpler technology than the Harrapans but whose poetry and religion were more imaginative. These Aryans became the dominant force militarily and politically, imposing their will and their gods on the subjugated Dravidian natives.

However, Indian culture never lost its Dravidian features. At most they were dormant for a while. After the demise of Vedic culture, Dravidian interests in fertility reemerged (the Aryans had their own fertility interests). The complex devotionalism of later Hinduism is best explained in terms of many non-Aryan factors.

VEDIC INDIA

By Vedism most scholars mean the culture resulting from the mixture of Aryans, Harrapans, and other peoples of the Indus and Ganges valleys. This culture expressed itself in the earliest Indian writings, which are a collection of religious songs, hymns, spells, rituals, and speculations called the Vedas. It is convenient to consider them as representing the first stages of Hinduism, for although later India abandoned many of the Vedic gods and practices, the Vedas retained scriptural status throughout the later centuries, weaving themselves deeply into India's fabric.

The word *veda* means "wisdom" (cognates are the English *wit* and the German *wissen*). To the traditional Hindu, the Vedic literature represents the highest intuitive knowledge that the *rishis* (holy persons or seers) had attained.[3] The technical term denoting such a state of wisdom is *shruti*, which translators often render as "revelation." *Shruti* does not connote that divinities outside the human realm broke through the veil separating heaven and earth in order to impart light from above; as we shall see, Hinduism does not have such an exalted view of the gods. Rather, *shruti* implies that the eminent holy person has perceived certain things in peak experiences (often induced by the ritual drink soma). Therefore, Vedic literature, representing what the *rishis* had seen, was considered the best and holiest presentation of knowledge.

The Vedas consist of four separate collections of materials. Together, these four collections are known as the *Samhitas. Samhitas* therefore is a synonym for Vedas. The individual collections are called the *Rig-Veda, Sama-Veda, Yajur-Veda,* and *Atharva-Veda.* The *Rig-Veda* is the oldest, largest, and most important. It contains more than a thousand *suktas* or individual units, which are hymns to the gods, magical poems, riddles, legends, and the like. They show considerable learning and poetic skill, which argue against their being the spontaneous poetry of freewheeling warriors or rude peasants. More likely, they represent the work of priestly leaders—the careful creation of an educated class concerned with regulating contact with the gods and maintaining its own social status.

Most of the *Rig-Veda*'s hymns have two purposes. First, they praise the god being addressed; second, they ask the god for favors and benefits. Though this praise-and-plead purpose is the most usual, the *Rig-*

Veda has other functions. For instance, it includes petitions for forgiveness of sins, such as having wronged a brother, cheated at games, or abused a stranger, which indicate a developed moral sense. Although the *Rig-Veda* may not separate itself completely from an ancient world view, where being out of phase with the cosmic processes is almost physically dangerous, it provides solid evidence of religion centering on free, responsible choices made for good or evil. As well, some of the hymns of the *Rig-Veda* are philosophical, wondering about the first principle behind the many phenomena of the world. A famous philosophical text is 10:129, where the poet muses about the creation of the world. At the beginning there was no being and no nonbeing, no air and no sky beyond. It was, in fact, a time before either death or immortal life had begun. Then only the One existed, drawn into being by heat that interacted with the primal waters and the void. However, from desire the One started to think and emit fertile power. Thus, impulse from above and energy from below began to make the beings of the world. But, the hymn asks in conclusion, who knows whether this speculation is valid? Even the gods were born after the world's beginning, so who can say what happened? Only one who surveys everything from the greatest high heaven knows, if indeed even that being knows.

The Vedic Gods

A study of the Vedic gods shows what the earliest Hindus thought about the deepest forces in their world. The gods are many and complex (tradition said there were 330 million), but of course a few stand out as the most important. By textual analysis, scholars have uncovered different generations of the Vedic gods. The oldest group consists of the gods of the sky and the earth. The second oldest group generally represents earthly and especially heavenly forces. Indra (storm), Mithra (sun), Agni (fire), and Soma (ritual drink) are examples. The third generation of gods includes Brahma, Vishnu, and Shiva. They arose after the Aryans arrived in India and so perhaps indicate Dravidian influences. The Hindu trinity of Brahma, Vishnu, and Shiva stands for creation, preservation, and destruction. Finally, the fourth generation, which comes to the fore in the philosophical texts called the Upanishads, comprises abstract deities such as One God, That One, Who, and the Father of Creation (Eka Deva, Tad Ekam, Ka, and Prajapati).[4] Upanishadic seers had become dissatisfied with the concrete, world-affirming outlook at the core of the *Rig-Veda* and searched for simpler, more spiritual notions.

Brahmanism

In the early Vedic period, the sacrifice was quite simple. It required no elaborate rituals, no temples, no images—only a field of cut grass, some ghee (clarified butter) for the fire, and some soma (some poured onto the ground for the gods and some drunk by the participants). Later the sacrifice became more elaborate, involving the chanting of magical sounds, reenacting the world's creation, and slaying a variety of animals.[5] Since this elaboration went hand in hand with the increasing importance of the priest (*brahmin*, or brahman), commentators often refer to sacrificial Vedic religion as Brahmanism.

Brahmanism reached its greatest elaboration with the horse sacrifice, a ceremony that lasted more than a year. In the first step of this complicated ritual, attendants bathed a young white horse, fed it wheat cakes for three days, consecrated it by fire, and then released it and let it wander for a year. Princes and soldiers followed the horse, conquering all territory through which it traveled. After one year, servants brought the horse back to the palace. During the next new moon, the king shaved his head and beard. After an all-night vigil at the sacred fire, the queens went to the horse at dawn, anointed it, and decorated it with pearls. A sacrifice of 609 selected animals, ranging from the elephant to the bee (and sometimes a human), followed.

The sacrifice reached its climax after attendants slaughtered the horse itself and placed a blanket over it. The most important queen then slipped under the blanket to have (simulated?) sexual intercourse with the horse, while the other queens and the priests shouted obscene encouragements. After this, participants ate the horse in a ritual meal. The entire ceremony fits the pattern of ancient celebrations of the new year, which often involved sacrifices and orgies designed to renew the world's fertility.

The Upanishads

Before the end of the Vedic period, Brahmanism declined for at least two reasons. First, common sense dictated that society had more to do than listen to priests chant all day. The texts imply that even during the times of the *Rig-Veda*, people were unhappy with the priests' constant prating. A satire in 7:103, for instance, likens them to frogs croaking over the waters. Second, intellectuals desired something more satisfying than magic. The Upanishads reveal the intellec-

tuals' turn to interiority, which resulted in sacrifice becoming less a matter of slaughter, ritual, and words and more a matter of soul cleansing and dedication to the divine powers.

The word *Upanishad* connotes the secret teaching that one receives at the feet of a guru. Out of hundreds of treatises (over the period from 800 to 300 B.C.E.), a few Upanishads came to the fore.[6] They show that the intellectuals embraced a variety of styles and ideas and that their movement was poetic as much as philosophical. Whether poetic or philosophical, though, the movement's goal was quite religious: intuitive knowledge of ultimate truths, of the unity behind the many particulars of reality.

The Upanishads themselves do not agree on whether the unity behind everything is personal, impersonal, or a mixture of the two. However, they do tend to use two words in discussing it, both of which are more impersonal than personal. The first word is *Brahman*, which generally means the first principle, cause, or stuff of the objective world. Brahman, in other words, is the final answer for the Upanishadic thinkers who wondered about how things are founded—especially things in the material world.

The second word, *atman*, means the vital principle or deepest identity of the subject—the soul or self. Probing this reality by thought and meditation, the Upanishadic seers moved away from Vedic materiality to spirituality. The internal world, the world of atman and thought, was a world of *spirit*.

Combining these new concepts of Brahman and atman, some of the Upanishadic seers found a coincidence—the basic reality within and without, of self and the world, is the same. Atman is Brahman. So in the Chandogya Upanishad (6.1.3), the father Uddalaka teaches his son Shvetaketu that Shvetaketu himself is, most fundamentally, Brahmanic ultimate reality: *Tat tvam asi* ("That thou art"). The soul and the stuff of the world are but two sides of the same single "being" or "is-ness" that constitutes all existing things.

For the Upanishadic thinkers, this realization was liberating because it avoided the priests' multiplicity, externalism and materialism that had sickened their souls. Though sacrifice and the gods continued to have a place in Upanishadic religion, they were quite subordinate to monism.

In addition, the Upanishadic thinkers felt an urgent need for salvation, unlike the Vedists. Perhaps echoing Buddhist beliefs, the writers of the Upanishads worked with experiences that they found more dismal, depressing, and afflicting than the first Aryans had. Whereas those vigorous warriors had fought and drunk, living for the moment, these later meditative sages examined the human condition and found it sad.

To express their beliefs, they fashioned the doctrines of samsara and karma, which did not appear in the early Vedas.

Samasara (the doctrine of rebirths) implies that the given world, the world of common sense and ordinary experience, is only provisional. It is not the ultimate existence. To take it as ultimate or fully real, therefore, is to delude oneself and thus to trap oneself in a cycle of rebirths. Only when one penetrates Brahman, the truly real, can one escape this cycle. Otherwise, one must constantly travel the scale of animal life (up or down, depending on one's advances or backslidings in wisdom).

Karma is the law that governs advancement or regression in the samsaric life of deaths and rebirths. Essentially, it is the law that all acts have unavoidable consequences. In an almost physical way, they determine one's personality. Karma also explains one's status: A person's present life is shaped by that person's past lives. The only way to escape the round of rebirths, the pain of samsara, is to advance by meritorious deeds and be saved or freed. (Hinduism chooses to live with the illogic of a law both necessary and capable of being undercut by freedom.)

THE PERIOD OF NATIVE CHALLENGE

From about 600 B.C.E. to 300 C.E. the Vedic religion, including its Upanishadic refinements, was seriously challenged by some Indians.

Materialistic, Jain, and Buddhist challenges to Vedism first arose in northeastern India, where warrior tribes were more than ready to contest the priest's pretensions to cultural control. By this time (600 B.C.E.), the Aryans had settled in villages, and India was a checkerboard of small kingdoms, each of which controlled a group of such villages. Some intellectuals, radically opposed to the Vedas, strongly attacked the Vedic belief that there is a reality other than the sensible or material. It is hard to know precisely what these materialists taught, because few of their writings have survived, but Buddhist literature reports that Ajita, a prominent materialist thinker, said that earth, air, fire and water are the only elements—the sources of everything in the universe. According to Ajita, the differences among things just reflect different proportions of these elements. Human beings are no exception, and at death they simply dissolve back into these four elements. There is no afterlife, no reincarnation, no soul, and no Brahman. During the brief span of her life, a person should live "realistically," enduring pain and pursuing pleasure. Nothing beyond the testimony of the senses is valid knowledge, and what the senses reveal is what is real.

Jainism was a very different challenge that grew from the struggles for enlightenment of Vardhamana, called the Jina (conqueror) or Mahavira (great man). He was born to wealth but found it unfulfilling, so he launched a life of asceticism. After gaining enlightenment by this self-denial, he successfully preached his method to others. The Jina opposed both the ritualism and the intellectualism of the Vedic tradition. The only significant sacrifice, he said, is that which conquers the self. Similarly, the only worthy knowledge is that which enables the personality to gain full freedom.[7]

The Jina's followers became opponents of all forms of violence and pain. Consequently, they opposed the Vedic sacrifice of animals, calling it an assault on life that opposed true religion. Also, Jains became critical of matter. Their "karma" was a semisolid entity that attached itself to the spirit through acts involving material objects.[8] In memory of the Jina, whom they considered to be a great *tirthankara* ("crosser of the stream of sorry life"), Jains eschewed eating meat, harming anything believed to have a soul, and physical activity. Since total avoidance of these activities was practically impossible, Jains tried to balance any injury that they inflicted or bad karma that they generated by acts of self-denial or benevolence.

Today there are about 2 million Jains in India (the largest cluster is in Calcutta), who, through their discipline and their specialization in business, have become quite prosperous. In their temples one can see pictures of nude, ascetic saints who represent an ideal of complete detachment, and the Jain doctrine of *ahimsa* (noninjury) has made a permanent impression on Indian culture.[9]

Since we discuss Buddhism at length in the next appendix, we note here only that from a Hindu perspective, Buddhism arose, much like Jainism, as an anti-Vedic protest in the sixth century B.C.E. It was another stimulus to Hindu reform, another attack on both the Vedic sacrifices and their Brahmanistic rationale.

Bhagavata

Especially in western India, movements arose that, unlike materialism, Jainism, and Buddhism, forced changes from within Hinduism. A collective word for these movements is Bhagavata (devotionalism), which connotes an emotional attachment to personal gods such as Krishna and Shiva. Devotees (*bhaktas*) continue to claim that such devotion is a way of salvation or self-realization that is superior to sacrifice or intellectual meditation.[10]

The premier work of the Bhagavata tradition is the *Bhagavad Gita*, in which Krishna is the featured god. The *Gita* offers ways of salvation to all types of persons, but *bhakti* (devotional love) appears to be its highest teaching.[11] In what seems to be the work's climax, Krishna announces that the best "way" (*marga*) is love of Krishna and that he, Krishna, loves his devotee in return. In other words, there is a divine love for humanity as well as a human love for divinity. This final teaching, probably even more than the *Gita*'s catholic offering of many religious ways, has made it Hinduism's most influential text.

In later Hindu theology, Krishna became an avatar, or manifestation, of Vishnu, whom we discuss shortly. However, let us first describe the beginnings of a devotional cult to Shiva. This cult, too, was a reaction against the Vedic religion, and one of its fascinating texts is the Shvetashvatara Upanishad. For the devotees of Shiva, this text serves as the *Bhagavad Gita* serves Krishnaites—as a gospel of the personal god's love. It is unique among the Upanishads for its theism (focus on a personal god), yet it shares with the monistic Upanishads an effort to think logically.

The author begins by asking momentous questions: What is Brahman? What causes us to be born? Then the author rejects impersonal wisdom, materialism, and pure devotion as being inadequate answers. His own answer is to interpret Brahman (the ultimate reality) as a kind of god, who may become manifest if one meditates upon him. According to the Shvetashvatara Upanishad, Shiva is in everything. He has five faces and three eyes, which show his control of all directions and all times (past, present, and future). The devotee of Shiva therefore deals with a divinity as ultimate and powerful as Krishna but whose destructive capacities are more accentuated.

Devotion to Krishna (Vishnu) or Shiva, then, satisfies the person who wants religious feeling and a personal god with whom to interact. Probably this sort of person predominated in Hindu history. From the legends about the gods and from the epics (especially the *Mahabharata* and the *Ramayana*), the *bhaktas* found models for religious love and for faithful living as a good child, husband, wife, and so on.

Smriti

During this period of challenge to Vedic authority, one other development merits attention because it was responsible for a great deal of Hindu religious literature. This movement was commentary on the Vedic literature that was intended to make it more comprehensible, practicable, and contemporary. The authority of this commentary movement is described by the word *smriti* (tradition).

By the end of the third century C.E., the *smriti* tradition had developed some very important and common ways of understanding the Vedic heritage that greatly shaped Hindu social life.

The great social development of the *smriti* period was the caste system. The Vedas (for example, *Rig-Veda* 10:90) had spoken of the creation of humanity in terms of the four ranks: priests, warriors, merchants, and workers. In the original sacrifice Purusha, the primal man, gave his mouth, arms, thighs, and feet to make those four ranks. However, law codes such as Manu's were required to justify casteism.[12] Apparently, casteism precedes the Aryan subjugation of the native Indians, but whether it was first based on color, occupation, tribe, or religious beliefs is unclear.[13]

In practice castes subdivide into about 25,000 occupational *jatis*, which have made Hindu social life a jigsaw puzzle. These societal distinctions have spawned some social customs peculiar to the eye of the outside. For instance, fishermen who weave their nets from right to left do not speak to fishermen who weave from left to right, and coconut harvesters do not associate with coconut cultivators. Furthermore, members of one *jati* often cannot marry members of another. Modern India has tried to de-emphasize these customs, but they remain influential. Modern India has also tried to improve the lot of the untouchables, who lie outside the caste system, but they still exist. Even now, only certain groups of people carry garbage, clean homes, work in banks, and so on.

Personal Life

From the *smriti* elaboration of Vedic tradition came another influential doctrine, that of the four legitimate life goals. These were pleasure (*kama*), wealth (*artha*), duty (*dharma*), and liberation (*moksha*). *Kama* was the lowest goal, but it was quite legitimate. *Kama* meant sexual pleasure but also the pleasure of eating, poetry, sport, and so on. *Artha* was also a legitimate goal, and around it developed learned discussions of ethics, statecraft, manners, and the like.[14] Because the person of substance propped society, wealth had a social importance and was thus more significant than pleasure.

Dharma, or duty, was higher than pleasure or

wealth. It meant principle, restraint, obligation, law, and truth—the responsible acceptance of one's social station and its implications. So in the *Bhagavad Gita*, Krishna appeals to Arjuna's dharma as a warrior: It is his duty to fight, and better one's own duty done poorly than another's done well. *Moksha* meant liberation, freedom, and escape. It was the highest goal of life, because it represented the goal of one's existence: self-realization in freedom from karma (the influences of past actions) and ignorance. The concept of *moksha* meant that life is samsaric—precarious and illusory. It also meant that pleasure, wealth, and even duty all could be snares.

As a complement to its exposition of life goals, *smriti* also analyzed the stages in the ideal unfolding of a life.[15] For the upper classes (excluding the workers), the four stages, or *ashramas*, were student, householder, hermit, and wandering mendicant. In a 100-year life, each would last about 25 years. In studenthood, the young male would apprentice himself to a guru to learn the Vedic tradition and develop his character. Depending on his caste, this would last 8 to 12 years and dominate the first quarter of his life. Then he would marry, raise children, and carry out social responsibilities. Hindu society honored marriage, and the economic, political, and social responsibilities of the householder gave him considerable esteem.

When the householder saw his children's children, however, *smriti* urged him to retire from active life and start tending his soul. He could still give advice and be helpful in secular affairs, but he should increasingly detach himself from the world. Finally, free of worldly concern, seeking only *moksha*, the ideal Hindu would end his life as a poor, wandering ascetic. Thereby, he would be an object lesson in the true purpose of human life, a teacher of what mattered most.

In effect, this scheme meant an ideal development (not often realized but still influential) of learning one's tradition, gaining worldly experience, appropriating both tradition and experience by solitary reflection, and finally consummating one's time by uniting with ultimate reality. From conception to burial, numerous ceremonies have paced the Hindu through this cycle. The most important were adornment with the sacred thread (signaling sufficient maturity to begin studying the Vedas), marriage, and funerary rites.

Women have fallen outside this scheme. During most of Hindu history, their schooling, such as it was, took place at home, and they were not eligible for *moksha*.[16] A major reason for this was the lowering of the marriage age from fifteen or sixteen years to ten or even five. This both removed the possibility of education (and consequently religious office) and fixed women's role to being wife and mother. In fact, in later Hinduism being a wife was so important that a widow was prohibited from mentioning any man's name but that of her deceased husband. Even if she had been a child bride or had never consummated her marriage, the widow was not to violate her duty to her deceased husband and remarry. If she did, she would bring disgrace on herself in the present life and enter the womb of a jackal for her next rebirth.

Thus, the widow was the most forlorn of Hindu women. Without a husband, she was a financial liability to those who supported her. If menstruating, she could be a source of ritual pollution. If barren, she was useless to a society that considered women essentially as child producers. In such a social position, many widows must have felt that they had little to lose by throwing themselves on their husband's funeral pyre.[17] (Even suttee, though, was not simple. If the widow did not burn herself out of pure conjugal love, her act was without merit.)

THE PERIOD OF REFORM

From about 300 to 1200 C.E., the various movements that criticized or amplified the Vedic heritage resulted in a full reform of Hinduism. The criticisms of materialists, Jains, and Buddhists (all of whom rejected the Vedas) prodded Hinduism's growth. The elaborations of bhakti cults and *smriti* (tradition) likewise changed Hinduism. Similarly, the development of philosophical schools and the rise of the major Hindu sects effectively revamped Hinduism. The orthodox philosophies (*darshanas*) were conceived as explanations of *shruti* (Vedic revelation).

There are six such philosophies or schools: Mimamsa, Samkhya, Yoga, Nyaya, Vaisheshika, and Vedanta.[18] We can content ourselves with explaining Vedanta, the most celebrated *darshana*.

Shankara, the greatest of the Vedanta thinkers, was a Malabar brahmin of the ninth century who tried to systematize the Upanishads in terms of "unqualified nondualism" (*advaita*). In other words, he tried to explain the basic Upanishadic concepts of Brahman and atman with consistency and rigor. To do this, Shankara first esablished that there are two kinds of knowledge, higher and lower. Lower knowledge is under the limitations of the intellect, while higher knowledge is free of such limitations.

Higher knowledge comes by a direct perception that is free of either subjective or objective limitations.

In practice it is the direct vision that the seers who produced the Vedas enjoyed—*shruti*. Quite likely, therefore, Shankara assumed that the Vedanta philosopher practices a yoga like that of the ancient sages. If so, he assumed that the Vedanta philosopher experiences a removal of the veil between the self and Brahman (with which the self is actually identified). According to Shankara, all passages of the Upanishads that treat Brahman as *one* derive from higher knowledge; all references to Brahman as *many* or dual derive from lower knowledge.

Shankara's core affirmation in his philosophical construction was that reality within is identical with reality without: Atman is Brahman. In other words, when one realizes through revelation, or higher knowledge, that there is no change, no space-time limitations, no cause-effect qualifications to the real, one then discovers that there is no self. Rather, there is only the Self, the Brahman reality that one directly perceives to be the ground of internal and external being.

From the perspective of lower knowledge, there is, of course, a personal, separate, changing self. In absolute terms, though, there is one indivisible reality that is both subjectivity and objectivity, that is atman-Brahman. Since we rarely perceive directly, we often live and move in maya (illusion). The world of maya is not unreal in the sense that there are no elephants in it to break your foot if you get in the way of a circus parade. The elephants in the world of maya are substantial, their dung is mighty, and their step will crush your foot. But this viewpoint has limited validity. From a higher viewpoint, all that goes on in maya has no independent existence. The elephants' movement is a "play" of the only reality that exists independently—that is uncaused, unconnected, sovereign, and fully real.[19]

Vaishnavism and Shaivism

The more popular reformations of Vedism were theistic movements that brought the energies of Bhagavata (devotionalism) back into the Vedic fold. Two principal such movements centered on Vishnu and Shiva.

The theistic religion centered on Vishnu (Vaishnavism) got its impetus from the patronage of the Gupta kings in the fourth century C.E. Perhaps the most winning aspect of Vaishnavite doctrine, though, was its notion that the god is concerned about human beings, fights with them against demon enemies, and sends incarnations of himself (avatars) to assist humans in troubled times. In one traditional list there are ten

avatars, the most important being Rama (the hero of the epic *Ramayana*), Krishna, Buddha(!), and Kalki (who is yet to come).

Vaishnavism promoted itself in several ways. Two of the most effective tied Vishnu to the Bhakti cult. Between the sixth and the sixteenth centuries, the *Puranas* (legendary accounts of the exploits of gods and heroes) pushed Vishnu to the fore. The *Bhagavata Purana*, perhaps the most influential, was especially successful in popularizing the avatar Krishna. In fact, the tenth book of the *Bhagavata Purana*, which celebrates Krishna's affairs with the girls who tended cows (*gopis*), mixes erotic entertainment with symbolism of the divine-human relationship. As the cowgirls were rapt before Krishna, so could the devotee's spirit swoon before god. When one adds the stories of Krishna's extramarital affairs with Radha, his favorite *gopi*, the religious eros becomes quite intense. The *Puranas* were thus the first vehicle to elevate Vishnu and his prime avatar to the status of bhaki (devotional) gods.

Vaishnavite bhakti was promoted in southern India during the seventh and eighth centuries.[20] There Tamil-speaking troubadours called *alvars* ("persons deep in wisdom") spread devotion to Vishnu by composing religious songs. However, their wisdom was simply a deep love of Vishnu, a love that broke the bonds of caste and worldly station. The constant theme of the songs was Vishnu's own love and compassion for human beings, which moved him to send his avatars. The *alvars* were so successful that they practically ousted Buddhism from India, and they were the main reason that Vishnu-Krishna became the most attractive and influential Hindu god.

Vaishnavism also had the good fortune of attracting the religious philosopher Ramanuja,[21] who is now second only to Shankara in prestige. Ramanuja lived in the eleventh century, and his main accomplishment was elaborating on the Upanishadic doctrine in a way that made divinity compatible with human love. For Ramanuja, Brahman consisted of three realities: the unconscious universe of matter, the conscious community of finite selves, and the transcendent lord Ishvara.

Furthermore, Ramanuja held that the Upanishadic formula "This thou art" meant not absolute identity between atman and Brahman but a relationship: the psychological oneness that love produces. The highest way to liberation was therefore loving devotion to the highest lord who represented Brahman. Knowledge and pure action were good paths, but love was better. By substituting Vishnu or Krishna for Brahman or Ishvara, the Vaishnavites made Ramanuja a philosophical defender of their bhakti. For those who wanted to reformulate revealed doctrine through love, Ramanuja was the man.

Contending with Vaishnavism was Shaivism—devotion to Shiva. Shankara had been a Shaivite, but his intellectualism hardly satisfied the common person's desires for an emotional relationship with divinity. Shiva was the Lord of the Dance of Life and the Destroyer who terminated each era of cosmic time. From the earliest available evidence, Shaivism was a response to this wild god. It was frequently a source of emotional excesses, and its tone always mixed love with more fear and awe than Vaishnavism did.[22]

For example, one of the earliest Shaivite sects taught that to end human misery and transcend the material world, one had to engage in such rituals as smearing the body with cremation ashes; eating excrement, carrion, or human flesh; drinking from human skulls; simulating sexual intercourse; and frenzied dancing. Members of other sects, such as the eleventh-century Kalamukha (named for the black mark they wore on their foreheads), became notorious as drug adicts, drunkards, and even murderers.[23] Even when Shaivites were thoroughly respectable, their religion was more fiery and zealous in its asceticism than that of the love-struck but more refined Vaishnavites. Shaivite priests tended to come from the lower, non-Brahmin classes, and Shaivite followers often regarded the *lingam* (phallus) as Shiva's main emblem. Parallel to the Vaishnavite *alvars* were the Shaivite *adiyars*, whose poetry and hymns were a principal factor in Shiva's rise to prominence, especially in southern India.

The worshiper of Shiva grew conscious that he or she was a sinner through mysterious rituals and Shiva's own symbols of fire and a skull. As a result, there was little equality, little of the lover-beloved relationship, between the devotee and Shiva. The Shaivite deprecatingly referred to himself or herself as a cur. That the god would come to such a person was pure grace. Worship, then, was essentially gratitude that the tempestuous god chose to forgive rather than destroy.

Shaktism

A last reformulation of the Hindu tradition came through movements that scholars group as Shaktism or Tantrism.[24] This sort of Hinduism focused on secret lore whose prime objective was to liberate the energies of imagination, sex, and the unconscious. It is hard to know exactly what *Shakti* sects believed and practiced, because most of their rites were secret, but one of their main beliefs was that the union of coitus is the best analogy for the relationship between the cosmos and its energy flow. This belief seems to have spawned a theory of parallels or dualisms, in which male-female, right-left, and positive-negative pairings all had highly symbolic aspects.

One of the many Tantrist rituals for gaining *moksha* was called *chakrapuja* (circle worship). In it men and women (Tantrist groups tended to admit members without regard for sex or caste) used a series of elements (all having Sanskrit names beginning with the letter *m*) that might facilitate union with Shakti: wine, meat, fish, parched rice, and copulation. In right-hand Tantrism these elements were symbols. Left-hand Tantrism used the actual elements [not hedonistically but with ritual discipline, to participate in *lila* (reality's play)]. Other Tantrist practices involved meditation to arouse the *kundalini*—the snake of energy lying dormant at the base of the spine.[25]

Overall, the reformation of the Vedic tradition meant expanded roles for some Vedic gods and a shift of popular religion from sacrifice to devotional, theistic worship. The reformers tried to defend and extend their ancient heritage, allowing people to respond to any part of it that they found attractive. In this way, the reformers created an eclectic religion that is tolerant of diversity in religious doctrine and practice.

Hinduism explicitly recognized that people's needs differed by speaking of four *margas* that could lead to fulfillment and liberation. Among intellectuals, the way of knowledge was prestigious. In this *marga* one studied the classical texts, the Vedic *shruti* and commentators' *smriti*, pursuing an intuitive insight into reality. Shankara's higher knowledge is one version of this ideal. If one could gain the viewpoint where Brahman was the reality of everything, one had gained redeeming wisdom.

But philosophy patently did not attract everyone. Therefore, the way of *karma* (here understood as meaning works or action) better served many people. The *Bhagavad Gita* more than sanctioned this way, which amounted to a discipline of detachment. If one did one's daily affairs peacefully and with equanimity of spirit, then one would not be tied to the world of samsara. Doing just the work, without concern for its "fruits" (success or failure), one avoided bad *karma* (here meaning the law of cause and effect). Gandhi, who was much taken with this teaching of the *Gita*, used spinning as an example of *karma marga*.

A third *marga* was meditation (*dhyana*), which was usually based on the conviction that one can reach the real self by quieting the senses and mental activity to descend without thinking to the personality's depths. For the many who meditated, the way of *dhyana* usually meant peace, a great sensitivity to body-spirit relationships (through, for example, posture and breath control), and a deepening sense of the oneness of all reality.

Finally bhakti had the status of a *marga*, and, according to the *Bhagavad Gita*, it could be a very high way. Of course, *bhaktas* ran the gamut from emotional hysteria to lofty mysticism. The *Gita* qualified the self-assertiveness justified by bhakti, however, by making its final revelation not human love of divinity but Krishna's love for humans. On the basis of such revelation, the *bhakta* was responding to divinity as divinity had shown itself to be.

THE PERIOD OF FOREIGN CHALLENGE

From about 1200 C.E. on, Hinduism increasingly contended with foreign cultures, rulers, and religions. Islam and Christianity both made serious impacts on Indian life, and their presence is felt to this day.

One definite result of Islam's presence in India was a new religion, Sikhism. Traces of it were found among Hindus who considered aspects of Islam very attractive, but it actually began as a result of the revelations of the prophet Nanak, a Punjabi born in 1469. Nanak's visions prompted him to sing the praise of a divinity that blended elements of the Muslim Allah and the Hindu trinity of Brahma, Vishnu, and Shiva. This God he called the True Name. The religious prescriptions for serving the True Name that he set for his followers were rather severe and anticeremonial, steering away from Hindu pilgrimages and devotions and favoring compassion and neighborly good deeds. The Sikhs developed into a small but hardy religious band, and on numerous occasions they proved to be excellent warriors. They number about 6 million in India today, and their great shrine remains in Amritsar in the northwest. Many of the other holy Sikh sites, however, are now in Pakistan because of the 1947 partition.[26]

Christianity has been present in India since the first century C.E. according to stories about the apostle Thomas's adventures there. It is more certain that a bishop of Alexandria sent a delegation to India in 189 and that an Indian representative attended the Council of Nicaea (325). Only in the sixteenth century, however, did the Christian missionary presence become strong. The Christian impact, as distinguished from the Western impact, has not been impressive statistically. According to 1980 census figures, only 3.9 percent of all Indians considered themselves Christians. Nevertheless, Christians opened hundreds of charitable institutions, especially schools, and were responsible for the first leprosaria. They also promoted hospital care for the tuberculous and the insane. Mother Teresa of Calcutta continues that tradition today.

MODERNITY

After the reformation of the ancient tradition, Hinduism increasingly focused on bhakti, moving away from Vedic orthodoxy. The singers of bhakti cared little whether their doctrines squared with the Upanishads or the great commentators. The notions of *shruti* or *smriti*, in fact, meant little to them. They thought that the love they had found undercut traditional views of social classes, sex, and even religions. The god of love was no creator of castes, no despiser of women, no pawn of Hindus against Muslims. With little concern for intellectual or social implications, the singers and seers who dominated modern bhakti gave themselves over to ecstatic love.

Perhaps the greatest representative of bhakti was Chaitanya, a sixteenth-century Bengali saint whom his followers worship as an avatar of Krishna.[27] His followers see his unbounded religious ecstasy as the ideal communion of divinity and humanity. He was the major figure in the devotional surge toward Lord Krishna that produced some remarkable Bengali love poetry during the sixteenth and seventeenth centuries.[28] His movement continues, with a rather high profile, in the United States through the work of Swami Prabhupada. The swami's monks in saffron robes who chant on street corners, and his numerous publications,[29] have made "Hare Krishna" part of our religious vocabulary.

Partly in opposition to the excesses of bhakti and partly because of the influence of Western culture, a group of Bengali intellectuals in the early nineteenth century began to "purify" Hinduism by bringing it up to the standards that they saw in Christianity. The first such effort was the founding of the group Brahmo Samaj by Rammohan Roy in 1828. Roy was a well-educated brahmin whose contacts with Islam and Christianity led him to think that there should be only one God for all persons, who should inspire social concern.

God should, for example, oppose such barbarism as suttee (*sati*), the Hindu practice in which a widow climbed on her husband's funeral pyre and burned with him.[30] In 1811 Roy had witnessed the suttee of his sister-in-law, whom relatives kept on the pyre even though she was screaming and struggling to escape. He knew that in Calcutta alone there were more than 1,500 such immolations between 1815 and 1818. Roy pressured the British to outlaw the practice, and in 1829 a declaration was issued that forbade it (though it did not completely stamp it out). Members of the Brahmo Samaj thought this sort of social concern was essential to pure religion.[31]

TAGORE AND GANDHI

In the twentieth century, these currents of domestic and foreign stimuli to religious and social reform inevitably affected the controversies over Indian nationalism and independence.

Rabindranath Tagore (1861–1941), modern India's most illustrious writer, won the Nobel Prize for literature in 1913. His life's work was a search for artistic and educational forms that would instill Indians with a broad humanism. In Tagore's renewed Hinduism, India would give and receive—give resources for individual creativity and receive Western energies for using that creativity to improve society.

Mohandas Gandhi (1869–1948) was a political genius who made some of Tagore's vision practical. He trained as a lawyer in England and found his vocation as an advocate of the masses in South Africa, where he represented "colored" minorities. In India Gandhi drew in part on a Western idealism that he culled from such diverse sources as the New Testament, Tolstoy's writings on Christian socialism, Ruskin's writings on the dignity of work, and Thoreau's writings on civil disobedience. He joined this Western idealism with a shrewd political pragmatism of his own and Indian religious notions, including the *Bhagavad Gita's* doctrine of karma-yoga (work as a spiritual discipline) and the Jain-Hindu notion of *ahimsa* (noninjury). Gandhi's synthesis of these ideas resulted in what he called *satyagraha* (truth force). To oppose the might of Britain he used the shaming power of a simple truth: Indians, like all human beings, deserve the right to control their own destinies. In Gandhi himself one can see the conflicts, confusions, and riches of the Hindu tradition in the mid-twentieth century, for he called himself such a seeker of *moksha*, just a servant of the one God found whenever we harken to truth.[32]

NOTES

1. Troy Wilson Organ, *Hinduism* (Woodbury, N.Y.: Barron's, 1974), p. 40; see also Thomas Hopkins,

The Hindu Religious Tradition (Encino, Calif.: Dickenson, 1971), pp. 3–10; A. L. Basham, *The Wonder That Was India* (New York: Grove Press, 1959), pp. 10–30.

2. On the earliest history and religion of the Indian Aryans, see Mircea Eliade, *A History of Religious Ideas*, vol. 1, *From the Stone Age to the Eleusinian Mysteries* (Chicago: University of Chicago Press, 1978), pp. 186–199.

3. See Edward C. Dimock, Jr., et al., *The Literature of India: An Introduction* (Chicago: University of Chicago Press, 1978), pp. 1–2. Also Satsvarupta dasa Gosvami, *Readings in Vedic Literature* (New York: Bhaktivedanta Book Trust, 1977), pp. 3–4. For an overview of Vedic literature, see James A. Santucci, *An Outline of Vedic Literature* (Missoula, Mont.: Scholars Press), 1976.

4. See Organ, *Hinduism*, p. 66.

5. Hopkins, *Hindu Religious Tradition*, pp. 19–35.

6. Robert Ernest Hume, *The Thirteen Principal Upanishads* (New York: Oxford University Press, 1971), pp. 5–13.

7. See Mircea Eliade, *Histoire des croyances et des idées religieuses*, vol. 2, *de Gautama Bouddha au triomphe de Christianisme* (Paris: Payot, 1978), pp. 151–153.

8. Heinrich Zimmer, *Philosophies of India* (Princeton, N.J.: Princeton University Press, 1969), pp. 227–234.

9. For a brief summary of Jainism, see Carlo Della Casa, "*Jainism," in *Historia Religionum, II*, ed. C. J. Bleeker and G. Widengren (Leiden: E. J. Brill, 1971), pp. 346–371; see also A. L. Basham, "Jainism," in *The Concise Encyclopedia of Living Faiths*, ed. R. C. Zaehner (Boston: Beacon Press, 1967), pp. 261–266.

10. See S. N. Dasgupta, *Hindu Mysticism* (New York: Frederick Ungar, 1959), pp. 113–168.

11. Franklin Edgerton, *The Bhagavad Gita* (New York: Harper Torchbooks, 1964), p. 105; see also R. C. Zaehner, *The Bhagavad-Gita* (New York: Oxford University Press, 1973), pp. 1–41; Ann Stanford, *The Bhagavad Gita* (New York: Seabury, 1970), pp. vii–xxvii; Juan Mascaró, *The Bhagavad Gita* (Baltimore: Penquin, 1962), pp. 9–36; Gerald James Larson, "The *Bhagavad Gita* as Cross-Cultural Process," JAAR, 1975, *43*(4):651–669.

12. See Sarvepalli Radhakrishnan and Charles A. Moore, eds., *A Sourcebook in Indian Philosophy*

(Princeton, N.J.: Princeton University Press, 1957), pp. 184–189.

13. On the "tripartite Indo-European ideology" (priests-warriors-farmers) that George Dumézil has found at the root of Aryan society, see Eliade, *History of Relgious Ideas*, vol. 1, pp. 192–195.

14. See Radhakrishnan and Moore, *Sourcebook in Indian Philosophy*, pp. 193–223.

15. Sudhir Kakar, "The Human Life Cycle: The Traditional Hindu View and the Psychology of Erik H. Erikson," *Philosophy East and West*, 1968, *18*:127–136; see also Basham, *Wonder That Was India*, p. 158.

16. Basham, *Wonder That Was India*, pp. 177–188.

17. See Basham, *Wonder That Was India*, pp. 186–188.

18. On the six orthodox schools, see Radhakrishnan and Moore, *Sourcebook in Indian Philosophy*, pp. 349–572; Zimmer, *Philosophies of India*, pp. 280–332 (Samkyha and Yoga), 605–614.

19. See Zaehner, *Hinduism*, pp. 36–56; see also R. C. Zaehner, *Hindu and Muslim Mysticism* (New York: Schocken, 1969), pp. 41–63.

20. Glenn E. Yocum, "Shrines, Shamanism, and Love Poetry," *JAAR*, 1973, *61*(1):3–17.

21. See Zaehner, *Hindu and Muslim Mysticism*, pp. 64–85.

22. On the Puranic Shiva, see Cornelia Dimmitt and J. A. B. van Buitenen, eds., *Classical Hindu Mythology* (Philadelphia: Temple University Press, 1978), pp. 59–146. On Shiva in the Tamil literature, see Glenn E. Yocum, "Manikkavacar's Image of Shiva," *HR*, 1976, *16*(1):20–41.

23. Organ, *Hinduism*, p. 288.

24. See Zimmer, *Philosophies of India*, pp. 560–602; see also Kees W. Bolle, *The Persistence of Religion* (Leiden: E. J. Brill, 1965); Mircae Eliade, *Yoga: Immortality and Freedom* (Princeton, N.J.: Princeton University Press, 1970), pp. 200–273.

25. Ernest Wood, *Yoga* (Baltimore: Pelican, 1962), pp. 140–147; see also Eliade, *Yoga*, pp. 244–249.

26. For a brief survey of Sikhism, see Kushwant Singh, "Sikhism," in *Historical Atlas of the Religions of the World*, ed. I. al Faruqi and D. Sopher (New York: Macmillan, 1974), pp. 105–108; see also John Noss, *Man's Religions* (New York: Macmillan, 1974), pp. 226–235.

27. Nervin J. Hein, "Caitanya's Ecstasies and the Theology of the Name," in *Hinduism: New Essays in the History of Religions*, ed. Bardwell L. Smith (Leiden: E. J. Brill, 1976), pp. 15–32; Joseph T. O'Connell, "Caitanya's Followers and the Bhagavad-Gita," in *Hinduism*, pp. 33–52.

28. See Edward C. Dimock, Jr., and Denise Levertov, trans., *In Praise of Krishna* (Garden City, N.Y.: Doubleday, 1967).

29. Following are some representative works: Swami Prabhupada, *The Nectar of Devotion* (Los Angeles: Bhaktivedanta Book Trust, 1970); *Krishna: The Supreme Personality of Godhead,* 3 vols. (Los Angeles: Bhaktivedanta Book Trust, 1970). On the Hare Krishna movement, see J. Stillson Judah, *Hare Krishna and the Counterculture* (New York: Wiley, 1974).

30. Radical feminist Mary Daly has exposed the full horror of suttee; see Mary Daly, *Gyn/Ecology* (Boston: Beacon Press, 1979), chap. 3.

31. For brief selections from the leading Indian voices of the past century, see Ainslee T. Embree, *The Hindu Tradition* (New York: Vintage, 1972), pp. 278–348.

32. See Mohandas K. Gandhi, *An Autobiography: The Story of My Experiments with Truth* (Boston: Beacon Press, 1957).

APPENDIX

6

Buddhism

THE BUDDHA

The Buddha was born about 560 B.C.E. outside the town of Kapilavastu in what is now part of Nepal just below the Himalayan foothills. His people were a warrior tribe called Sakyas and his clan name was Gautama. The religious climate in which he grew up was quite heated. Some objectors were challenging the dominance of the priestly brahmin class. The writers of the early Upanishads reveal the dissatisfaction with sacrifice that was burning among intellectuals, while the accounts of the Mahavira are evidence of the ascetic movement that also challenged the priestly religion of sacrifice. In secular culture, the sixth century B.C.E. saw a movement from tribal rule toward small-scale monarchy, a growth in urban populations, the beginnings of money-based economies, the beginnings of government bureaucracies, and the rise of a wealthy merchant class.[1] Thus, the Buddha grew up in a time of rapid change, when people were in turmoil over religion and open to new teachings.

Religious faith heavily embellishes the accounts of the Buddha's birth and early life, so it is difficult to describe this period accurately. Legend has it that his father, Suddhodana, was a king, who received a revelation that his child would be a world ruler if the child stayed at home but a spiritual saviour if the child left home. According to other legends, the Buddha passed from his mother's side without causing her any pain, stood up, strode seven paces, and announced, "No more births for me!"[2] In other words, the child would be a spiritual conquerer—an Enlightened One.

As the Buddha grew, his father surrounded him with pleasures and distractions, to keep him in the palace and away from the sights of ordinary life. When the Buddha came of age, the father married him to a lovely woman named Yasodhara. So Sakyamuni ("sage of the Sakyas") lived in relative contentment until his late twenties. By the time of his own son's birth, however, the Buddha was restless. [He named the child Ruhula (fetter).]

What really precipitated Sakyamuni's religious crisis, though, was an experience he had outside the palace. On several outings he met age, disease, and death. They shocked him severely, and he became anxiety ridden. How could anyone take life lightly if these were its constant dangers? Meditating on age, disease, and death, the young prince decided to cast away his round of pleasures and solve the riddle of life's meaning by becoming a wandering beggar. Renouncing his wife, child, father, and goods, he set off to answer his soul's yearning.

The teachers to whom the Buddha first apprenticed himself specialized in meditation and asceticism. Their meditation, it appears, was a yogic pursuit of enlightenment through *samadhi* (trance). From them the Buddha learned much about the levels of consciousness but was not fully satisfied. The teachers could not bring him to dispassion, tranquillity, enlightenment, or nirvana (a state of liberation beyond samsara). In other words, the Buddha wanted a direct perception of how things are and a complete break with the realm of space, time, and rebirth.

To attain these goals, Sakyamuni turned to asceticism to such a degree that he almost starved himself. The texts claim that when he touched his navel, he could feel his backbone. In any event, asceticism did not bring what Sakyamuni sought either. (Because of this, he and his followers have always urged moderation in fasting and bodily disciplines. Theirs, they like to say, is a middle way between indulgence and severity

261

that strives to keep the body healthy, as a valuable ally should be, and to keep the personality from excessive self-concern.)

What liberated the Buddha, apparently, was recalling moments of peace and joy from his childhood, when he had sat in calm but perceptive contemplation. According to the traditional accounts, Mara, the personification of evil or death, tried to tempt Buddha (who sat meditating under a fig tree) away from this pursuit.[3] First, he sent a host of demons, but the Buddha's merit and love protected him. Then, with increased fear that this contemplator might escape his realm, the evil one invoked his own power. However, when Mara called on his retinue of demons to witness his power, the Buddha, who was alone, called on mother earth, which quaked in acknowledgment. As a last ploy, Mara commissioned his three daughters (Discontent, Delight, and Desire) to seduce the sage. But they, too, failed, and Mara withdrew. (Psychological interpretation can illuminate the details of this legend when they are considered as symbols of dramatic changes in the personality—the challenges, fears, resistance, and final breakthrough. Then Mara would stand for the dread of conversion to a radically new path.)

Enlightenment

The *enlightenment* (realization of the truth) itself occurred on a night of the full moon. According to tradition, Buddha ascended the four stages of trance. In later times these four stages were considered as a progressive clarification of consciousness: (1) detachment from sense objects and calming the passions; (2) nonreasoning and "simple" concentration; (3) dispassionate mindfulness and consciousness with bodily bliss; and (4) pure awareness and peace without pain, elation, or depression.[4]

According to tradition, then, one progressed in a contemplative sitting by moving from confusion and sense knowledge to pure, unemotional awareness. The assumption was that this progress facilitated direct perception of reality—seeing things as they really are. It might bring in its train magical powers (the ability to walk on water, to know others' minds, or to remember one's previous lives, for instance), but its most important achievement was to eliminate desire, wrong views, and ignorance, which are the bonds that tie one to samsara. To break them is therefore to free consciousness for nirvana.

Another traditional way of describing the Buddha's enlightenment is to trace his progress through the night. During the first watch (evening), he acquired knowledge of his previous lives. This is a power that some shamans claim, so it is not Buddha's distinguishing achievement. During the second watch (midnight), he acquired the "divine eye" with which he surveyed the karmic state of all beings—the dying and rebirth cycle that is their destiny. With this vision he realized that good deeds beget good karma and a move toward freedom from this destiny, while bad deeds beget bad karma and a deeper entrenchment in samsara. The second achievement made Buddha a moralistic philosopher, insofar as he saw the condition of all beings as a function of their ethical or unethical behavior.

During the third watch (late night), the Buddha reached the peak of perception, attaining "the extinction of the outflows" (the stopping of desire for samsaric existence) and grasping the essence of what became the Four Noble Truths: (1) All life is suffering; (2) the cause of suffering is desire; (3) stopping desire will stop suffering; and (4) the Eightfold Path (explained below) is the best way to stop desire.

The Eightfold Path outlines the life-style that Buddha developed for people who accepted his teaching and wanted to pursue nirvana. As such, it is more detailed than a description of what Buddha directly experienced in enlightenment—something that he probably elaborated on later. The explanation of reality that Buddha developed out of enlightenment, which became known as the doctrine of dependent coarising, also came later. It explains the causal connections that link all beings.

Enlightenment seems to have been the dramatic experience of vividly perceiving that life, which Sakyamuni had found to consist of suffering, had a solution. One could escape the terror of aging, sickness, and death by withdrawing one's concerns for or anxieties about them—by no longer desiring youth, health, or even life itself. By withdrawing in this manner, one lessened the bad effects of karma, for desire was the means by which karma kept the personality on the wheel of dying and rebirth. Removing desire therefore took away karma's poison. To destroy desire for karmic existence, though, one had to penetrate the illusion of its goodness. That is, one had to remove the ignorance that makes sensual pleasures, financial success, prestige, and so on, seem good. Buddha designed the Eightfold Path and the doctrine of dependent coarising to remove ignorance and rout desire.

Dependent Coarising and the Eightfold Path

Often Buddhists picture dependent coarising as a wheel with twelve sections or a chain with twelve links (the first and the last are joined to make a circuit).[5] These twelve links explain the round of samsaric existence. They are not an abstract teaching for the edification of the philosophical mind, but an extension of the essentially therapeutic analysis that the Buddha thought would cure people of their basic illness.

The wheel of dependent coarising turns in this way: (1) Aging and dying depend on rebirth; (2) rebirth depends on becoming; (3) becoming depends on the appropriation of certain necessary materials; (4) appropriation depends on desire for such materials; (5) desire depends on feeling; (6) feeling depends on contact with material reality; (7) contact depends on the senses; (8) the senses depend on "name" (the mind) and "form" (the body); ((9) name and form depend on consciousness (the spark of sentient life); (10) consciousness shapes itself by samsara; (11) the samsara causing rebirth depends on ignorance of the Four Noble Truths; and (12) therefore, the basic cause of samsara is ignorance.

One can run this series forward and back, but the important concept is that ignorance (of the Four Noble Truths) is the cause of painful human existence, and aging and dying are its final overwhelming effects and the most vivid aspects of samsara. Thus, the chain of dependent coarising is a sort of practical analysis of human existence.

In the Buddha's enlightenment, as he and his followers elaborated on it, there is no single cause of the way things are. Rather, all things are continually rotating in this twelve-stage wheel of existence. Each stage of the wheel passes the power of movement along to the next. The only way to step off the wheel, to break the chain, is to gain enlightenment and so detach the stage of ignorance. If we do detach ignorance, we stand free of karma, karmic consciousness, and so on, all the way to aging and rebirth.

The result of enlightenment, then, is no rebirth, which is the implication of nirvana. Nirvana is the state in which the chain of existence does not obtain—in which desire is "blown out" and one escapes karma and samsara. Thus, nirvana begins with enlightenment and becomes definitive with death. By his enlightenment, for instance, the Buddha had broken the chain of dependent coarising; at his death his nirvana freed him from rebirths.

The Eightfold Path (which is the Fourth Noble Truth) details how we may dispel ignorance and gain nirvana[6] by describing a middle way between sensuality and extreme asceticism that consists of (1) right views, (2) right intention, (3) right speech, (4) right action, (5) right livelihood, (6) right effort, (7) right mindfulness, and (8) right concentration. "Right views" means knowledge of the Four Noble Truths. "Right intention" means dispassion, benevolence, and refusal to injure others. "Right speech" means no lying, slander, abuse, or idle talk. "Right action" means not taking life, stealing, or being sexually disordered. "Right livelihood'" is an occupation that does not harm living things; thus, butchers, hunters, fishers, and sellers of weapons or liquor are proscribed. "Right effort" avoids the arising of evil thoughts. In "right mindfulness," awareness is disciplined so that it focuses on an object or idea to know its essential reality. "Right concentration" focuses on a worthy object of meditation.

The first two aspects of the Eightfold Path, right views and right intention, comprise the wisdom portion of the Buddhist program. If we know the Four Noble Truths and if we orient ourselves toward them with the right spiritual disposition, then we are wise and come to religious peace. Tradition groups aspects three, four, and five under morality.[7] To speak, to act, and to make one's living in wise ways amount to an ethics for nirvana, a morality that will liberate one from suffering. Finally, aspects six, seven, and eight entail meditation. By setting consciousness correctly through right effort, mindfulness, and concentration, one can perceive the structures of reality and thus personally validate the Buddha's enlightened understanding.[8]

The three divisions of the Eightfold Path compose a single entity, a program in which each of the three parts reinforces the other two. Wisdom sets up the game plan, the basic theory of what the human condition is and how one is to cope with it. Morality applies wisdom to daily life by specifying how one should speak, act, and support oneself. Regular meditation focuses one on the primary truths and the reality to which they apply. In meditation the Buddhist personally appropriates the official wisdom, personally examines the ethical life. As a result, meditation builds up the Buddhist's spiritual force, encouraging the peaceful disposition necessary for a person to be nonviolent and kindly.[9]

THE DHARMA

Buddhists have seen in Sakyamuni's enlightenment the great act centering their religion. The Buddha is worthy of following because in enlightenment he became shining with knowledge *(bodhi)*. Buddha himself apparently debated what to do after achieving enlightenment. On the one hand, he had this dazzling light, this potent medicine, to dispense. On the other hand, there was dreary evidence that humanity, mired in its attachments, would find his teaching hard to comprehend and accept.[10] Legend says that the god Brahma appeared to the Buddha and pleaded that the Enlightened One teach what he had seen for the sake of wayward humanity. Out of compassion (which became the premier Buddhist virtue), the Enlightened One finally agreed to Brahma's request.

What Buddha first preached was the Four Noble Truths, but he apparently prefaced his preaching with a solemn declaration of his authority as an immortal enlightened one. From this preface Buddhists have concluded that one must have faith in the authority behind the *dharma* (the teaching) if the dharma is to have its intended effect.

The Buddha's preaching won him innumerable converts, men and women alike, many of whom decided to dedicate their lives to following him and his way. A great number entered the *sangha*, or monastic order, assuming a life of celibacy, poverty, and submission to rules of discipline.[11] Other followers decided to practice the dharma while remaining in their lay state, and they frequently gave the Buddha and the Buddhist community land and money.[12] In both cases people became Buddhists by taking "refuge" in the three "jewels" of the Enlightened One's religion: the Buddha himself, the teaching (dharma), and the community (*sangha* can mean either the monastic community or the entire community of Buddhists, lay and monastic, past and present).[13]

In time a catechism developed to explain the Buddha's teaching. One of the catechism's most important notions was the "three marks" of reality. Together with the Four Noble Truths and dependent coarising, the three marks have helped countless Buddhists hold the dharma clearly in mind. According to this conception, all reality is painful, fleeting, and selfless. This formula adds something to the insights of the Four Noble Truths. That all life or reality is painful is the first truth: the reality of suffering. By this Buddhists do not mean that one never experiences pleasant things or that one has no joy. Rather, they mean that no matter how pleasant or joyous one's life, it is bound to include disappointment, sickness, misunderstanding, and finally death. Since the joyous things do not last, even they have an aspect of painfulness.

Second, all life is fleeting, or passing. Everything changes—nothing stays the same. Therefore, realistically there is nothing to which we can cling, nothing that we can rely on absolutely. In fact, even our own realities (our "selves") change. On one level, we move through the life cycle from youth to old age. On a more subtle level, our thoughts, our convictions, and our emotions change.

Third, there is no self. For Buddhists, the fleetingness of our own consciousness proves that there is no atman—no solid soul or self. In this the Buddhists directly opposed Hinduism as well as common belief. All people, it seems, naturally think that they have personal identities. Buddhists claim that personalities consist of nothing solid or permanent. We are but packages of physical and mental stuff that is temporarily bound together in our present proportions.

The tradition calls the component parts of all things *skandhas* (heaps), which number five: body, feeling, conception, karmic disposition, and consciousness. Together the *skandhas* make the world and the person of appearances, and they also constitute the basis for clinging to existence and rebirth. To cut through the illusion of a (solid) self—Buddhists do not deny that we have (changing) identities—is therefore the most important blow that one can strike against ignorance. This is done by being open to the flowing character of all life and decisively pursuing nirvana.

The early teachers described the realms of rebirth to which humans were subject and in so doing developed a Buddhist version of the Indian cosmic powers and zones of the afterlife. Essentially, the Buddhist wheel of rebirth focuses on six realms or destinies. Three are lower realms, which are karmic punishment for bad deeds. The other three are higher realms in which good deeds are rewarded. The lowest realm is for punishing the wicked by means befitting their particular crimes. However, these punishments are not eternal; after individuals have paid their karmic debt, they can reenter the human realm by rebirth. Above the lowest realm is the station of the "hungry ghosts," who wander the earth's surface begging for food. The third and least severe realm of the wicked is that of animals. If one is reborn in that realm, one suffers the abuses endured by dumb beasts.

The fortunate destinies reward good karma. The human realm is the first, and in it one can perform meritorious deeds. Only in the human realm can one become a buddha. The two final realms are those of demigods (Titans) and the gods proper. Both include a variety of beings, all of whom are subject to rebirth. Since even the Buddhist gods are subject to rebirth, their happiness is not at all comparable to the final bliss of nirvana. Better to be a human being advancing toward enlightenment than a divinity liable to the pains of another transmigratory cycle. Perhaps for that reason, the Buddhist spirits and divinities, as well as the Buddhist ghosts and demons, seem inferior to the human being. Apparently Buddhism adopted wicked and good spirits from Indian culture without much thought. In subjecting these spirits to the powers of an *arhat* (one who achieves nirvana), however, Buddhists minimized their fearsomeness.

Despite its sometimes lurid description of the six

realms, the dharma basically stated that each individual is responsible for his or her own destiny. The future is neither accidental, fated, nor determined by the gods. If one has a strong will to achieve salvation, a day of final triumph will surely come. As a result, karma is less an enslavement than an encouragement.

For about forty-five years after his enlightenment, the Buddha preached variants on his basic themes: the Four Noble Truths, dependent coarising, and the three marks. His sangha grew, as monks, nuns, and laypersons responded to his simple, clear message. At his death he had laid the essential foundation of Buddhism—its basic doctrine and way of life. Thus, his death *(parinirvana)* came in the peace of trance. The physical cause of his death was either pork or mushrooms (depending on which commentator one reads), but in the Buddhist view the more profound cause was the Buddha's sense of completeness. When he asked his followers for the last time whether they had any questions, all stood silent. So he passed into trance and out of this painful realm. According to legend, the earth quaked and the sky thundered in final tribute.

After the Buddha's death his followers gathered to codify the dharma, which he had said should be their leader after him. According to tradition, they held a council at Rajagraha during the first monsoon season after the *parinirvana* to settle both the dharma and the Vinaya (the monastic rules). The canon of Buddhist scriptures that we now possess supposedly is the fruit of this council. However, textual analysis suggests that the dharma was transmitted orally for perhaps three centuries.

Within 100 years of the Buddha's death, dissensions split the sangha.[14] These first schisms prefigured later Buddhist history. New schools have constantly arisen as new insights or problems made old views unacceptable. As a result, the sangha has not been an effective centralized authority or a successful source of unity. Nonetheless, it has given all Buddhists certain essential teachings (almost all sects would agree to what we have expounded of dharma so far). Also, it has fostered a very influential monastic life. The monastic order, which has always been the heart of Buddhism (monks have tended to take precedence over laity as an almost unquestioned law of nature), has been a source of stability in Buddhism. We therefore describe the lives of Buddhist monks and nuns.

Monasticism

A major influence on the Buddhist monastic routine has been Buddha's own life. According to Buddha-ghosa, a Ceylonese commentator in the fifth century C.E., the Buddha used to rise at daybreak, wash, and then sit in meditation until it was time to go begging for food. He stayed close enough to a village (wandering from one to another) to obtain food, but far enough away to obtain quiet. Usually devout laity would invite him in, and after eating lightly he would teach them the dharma. Then he would return to his residence, wash, and rest. After this he would preach to the monks and respond to their requests for individual guidance. After another rest he would preach to the laity and then take a cool bath. His evening would consist of more individual conferences, after which, Buddhaghosa claims, he would receive any deities who came for instruction.[15]

The Vinaya established rules that would promote such a steady life of meditation, begging, preaching, and counsel. Originally the monks always wandered except during the rainy season, but later they assumed a more stable setting with quiet lands and a few simple buildings. From the Vinaya's list of capital offenses, though, we can see that a monk's robe did not necessarily make him a saint.

The four misdeeds that merit expulsion from the order are fornication, theft, killing, and "falsely claiming spiritual attainments." Committing any of thirteen lesser misdeeds led to a group meeting of the sangha and probation. They included sexual offenses (touching a woman, speaking suggestively to a woman, urging a woman to gain merit by submitting to a "man of religion," and serving as a procurer), violating the rules that limited the size and specified the site of a monk's dwelling, falsely accusing other monks of grievous violations of the rule, fomenting discord among the monks, or causing a schism. With appropriate changes, similar rules have governed the nuns' lives.

Nuns had varying degrees of freedom to run their own affairs in the monasteries, but they were regularly subject to monks. Women never gained regular access to power over males, either in Buddhism's conception of the religious community or in its conception of marriage. Insofar as celibacy became part of the Buddhist ideal, marriage became a second-class vocation and women became a religious danger.[16] By opening a religious life to Indian women, Buddhists gave them an option besides marriage and motherhood—a sort of career and chance for independence. No longer did a girl and her family have to concentrate single-mindedly on gathering a dowry and arranging a wedding. Morever, by offering an alternative to marriage, Buddhism inevitably gave women more voice in their marriage decisions and then in their conjugal lives. Finally, Buddhist widows could enter the sangha, where they might find religious companionship, or they could stay in the world, remarry, inherit, and manage their own affairs.

The Laity

From earliest times, Buddhism encouraged its laity to pursue an arduous religious life. Though his or her white robe never merited the honor that a monk's colored robe received, a layperson who had taken refuge in the three jewels and contributed to the sangha's support was an honorable follower. Early Buddhism specified morality *(sila)* for the laity in five precepts. The first of these is to refrain from killing living beings. (Unintentional killing is not an offense, and agriculturalists have only to minimize their damage to life.) The second is to refrain from stealing. The third precept deals with sexual matters. It forbids intercourse with another person's wife, a nun, or a woman betrothed to another man. It also urges restraint with a wife who is pregnant, nursing, or under a religious vow of sexual abstinence. Apparently relations with courtesans were licit, and the commentators' explanation of this precept assumes that it is the male's duty to provide control in sexual matters (because females are by nature wanton). The fourth precept imposes restraint from lying, and the fifth precept forbids drinking alcoholic beverages.

This ethical code has been the layperson's chief focus. Occasionally he or she received instruction in meditation or the doctrine of wisdom, and later Mahayana sects considered the laity fully capable of reaching nirvana. (In the beginning only monks were so considered; nuns never had the status of monks, in part because of legends that the Buddha established nunneries only reluctantly.) The principal lay virtues were to be generous in supporting monks and to witness to Buddhist values in the world. The financial support, obviously enough, was a two-edged sword. Monks who put on spiritual airs would annoy the laity who were sweating to support them. On the other hand, monks constantly faced a temptation to tailor their doctrine to please the laity and so boost their financial contributions. The best defenses against such abuses were monasteries in which the monks lived very simple, poor lives.

Other practices that devout laity might take up have included regular fasting, days of retreat for reading the scriptures, praying, hearing sermons, giving up luxurious furniture and housing, abstaining from singing, dancing, and theater, and decreasing their sexual activity. Clearly, such practices have further advanced the pious layperson toward a monastic sort of regime and have often smacked of puritanism.

Scholars suggest that early Buddhism did not develop many new ceremonies or rites of passage; instead it integrated local celebrations and customs into its practices. To this day, birth and wedding ceremonies do not involve Buddhist priests very much, but funeral services do. In early times, the Indian Buddhists likely celebrated the New Year and a day of offering to the ancestors, both of which were probably adopted from Hinduism. In addition, Indian Buddhists commemorated the Buddha's birthday and the day of his enlightenment. Robinson and Johnson suggest that cults of trees, tree spirits, serpents, fertility goddesses, and funeral mounds all came from preexisting Indian religious customs.[17] However, the Bodhi Tree under which the Buddha came to enlightenment prompted many Buddhists to revere trees. Such trees, along with *stupas* (burial mounds) of holy persons, were popular places of devotion.

The worship of statues of the Buddha grew popular only under the influence of Mahayana thought after 100 C.E., but an earlier veneration of certain symbols of the Buddha (an empty throne, a pair of footprints, a wheel or lotus, or a bodhi tree) paved the way. These symbols signified such things as Buddha's presence in the world, his royal renunciation, and the dharma he preached. The lotus became an especially popular symbol, since it stood for the growth of pure enlightenment from the mud of worldly life.

Meditation

A central aspect of early Buddhist life was meditation, which has remained a primary way to realize the wisdom and to inspire the practice that lead to nirvana. Meditation *(dhyana)* designated mental discipline. For instance, one could meditate by practicing certain devotional exercises that focused attention on one of the three jewels—the Buddha, the dharma, or the sangha. These would be recalled as the refuges under which one had taken shelter, and the meditator's sense of wonder and gratitude for protection would increase his or her emotional attachment. Thus, such meditative exercises were a sort of bhakti, though without sexual overtones.

Indeed, both the saints *(bodhisattvas)* and the Buddha could become objects of loving concentration. However, such devotion was not meditation proper, for *dhyana* was a discipline of consciousness similar to yoga. As is clear from the story of his own life, Buddha's enlightenment came after he had experienced various methods of "mindfulness" and trance. It is proper, then, to consider Buddhist meditation a species of yoga.[18]

The mindfulness of Buddhists was usually a control of the senses and imagination geared to bringing "one-pointed mental consciousness" to bear on the truths of the dharma. For instance, one fixed on mental processes to become aware of their stream and the *skandhas* and to focus on the belief that all is fleeting, painful, and selfless. In addition, meditation masters sometimes encouraged monks to bolster their flight from the world by contemplating the contemptibleness of the body and its pleasures.

MAHAYANA

In the development of Buddhist sects, which reached its most important point in the years 100 B.C.E. to 100 C.E. with the rise of the Mahayana, wisdom, meditation, and mortality were all important to all parties. However, the saintly ideal and the place of the laity differed among Theravadins and Mahayanists. Even more, the notion of the Buddha and the range of metaphysics varied considerably. The rise of Mahayana was the first major change in Buddhism.[19] Before its emergence, early Buddhism was fairly uniform in its understanding of Buddha-dharma-sangha and wisdom-morality-meditation. (Theravada has essentially kept early Buddhist beliefs, so the description of Buddhism thus far characterizes Theravada.)

The hallmark of Mahayana was its literature, which placed in the mouth of the Buddha sutras describing a new ideal and a new version of wisdom. *Mahayana* means "great vehicle," symbolizing a large raft able to carry multitudes across the stream of samsara to nirvana. *Hinayana* is the term of reproach that Mahayanists used to characterize those who rejected their literature and views. It means "lesser vehicle," symbolizing a small raft able to carry only a few persons across the samsaric stream. Theravadins, pointing with pride to the antiquity of their traditions and claiming to have preserved the original spirit of Buddhism better than the innovating Mahayanists, do not refer to themselves as Hinayanists. Today Theravada Buddhism dominates Sri Lanka, Thailand, Burma, and Laos. Other Asian countries are dominated by Mahayana Buddhism. Tibet has been dominated by Vajrayana or Thantra.

Let us deal first with two innovative teachings of the Mahayana schools, emptiness and mind-only, and some implications of the notions of nirvana and samsara. Finally we will consider the Mahayana views of the Buddhist ideal and of the Buddha himself.

Emptiness

Emptiness *(sunyata)* is a hallmark of Mahayana teaching. In fact, the Mahayana sutras known as the *Prajnaparamita* ("wisdom-that-has-gone-beyond") center on this notion. By the end of the Mahayana development, emptiness had in effect become a fourth mark of all reality. Besides being painful, fleeting, and selfless, all reality was empty. Thus, further rumination on the three marks led Mahayana philosophers to consider a fourth mark, emptiness, as the most significant mark of all reality. No reality was a substance, having an "own-being." Obviously, therefore, none could be an atman, be constant, or be fully satisfying.

The word *sunya* conveys the idea that something that looks like much is really nothing. Etymologically it relates to the word *swelled*. As a swelled head is much ado about nothing, so things that are *sunya* appear to be full, solid, or substantial but actually are not. The spiritual implication of emptiness *(sunyata)* is that the world around us should not put us in bondage, for it has nothing of substance with which to tie us. Philosophically the word implies *anatman* (no-self), that there is nothing independent of other existents. For the Mahayana, all dharmas (here meaning items of existence) are correlated, and any one dharma is void of classifying marks.

Mind-only

Emptiness was the special concern of the Madhyamika Mahayana school.[20] The second major Mahayana school, the Yogacara, which became influential from about 300 C.E. on, proposed another influential teaching on ultimate reality, mind-only.[21] Like the teaching on emptiness, it went beyond early Buddhist teaching, and the Theravadins rejected the sutras that attributed this teaching to the Buddha. The teaching of mind-only held that all realities finally are mental.

One of the principal Yogacarin sutras, the *Lankavatara*,[22] described a tier of consciousnesses in the individual culminating in a "storehouse" consciousness *(alayavijnana)* that is the base of the individual's deepest awareness, the individual's tie to the cosmic. The storehouse consciousness is itself unconscious and inactive, but it is the repository of the "seeds" that ripen into human deeds and awareness. Furthermore, Yogacarins sometimes called the storehouse consciousness the Buddha's womb. Thereby, they made the Buddha or Tathagata (Enlightened Being) a metaphysical principle—a foundation of all reality.

From the womb of the Buddha issued the purified

thoughts and beings of enlightenment. The symbolism is complex (and interestingly feminine, suggesting a Buddhist version of androgyny or primal wholeness). Its main point, though, is clear: The womb of the Buddha *(Tathagata-garbha)* is present in all living beings, irradiating them with enlightenment.

Samsara and Nirvana

As the intellectuals and contemplatives worked further with immaterial consciousness and its philosophical consequences, they changed the relationships between samsara and nirvana. In the beginning, Buddhism thought of samsara as the imperfect, illusory realm of given, sense-bound existence. The Buddha himself exemplified this view when he urged his followers to escape the world that is "burning" to achieve nirvana. His original message regularly said that spontaneous experience makes one ill, and that health lies in rejecting attachments to spontaneous experience. With time, however, the philosophers, especially the Mahayanists, came to consider the relations between nirvana and samsara as being more complex. From analyzing the implications of these concepts, the philosophers determined that nirvana is not a thing or a place. The Buddha realized this, for he consistently refused to describe nirvana in detail. But while the Buddha's refusal was practical (such a description would not help solve the existential problems of being in pain), the refusal of the later philosophers was largely epistemological and metaphysical. That is, they thought that we cannot think of such a concept as nirvana without reifying it (making it a thing), and that the reality of nirvana must completely transcend the realm of things.

Mahayana Devotion

It was not philosophy that brought Mahayana popular influence, however, but its openness to the laity's spiritual needs, its devotional theology. Early Buddhism held monks in greater regard than laity. Consequently the laity considered themselves to be working out a better karma, so that in their next lives they might be monks (or, if they were women, so that they might be men).

Mahayana changed this view of the laity. Stressing the Buddha's compassion and his resourcefulness in saving all living creatures, it gradually qualified the Theravadin ideal of the arhat (saint) and fashioned a new, more socially oriented ideal. Mahayana thereby prepared the way for later schools that were in effect Buddhist devotional sects, such as the Pure Land sect. Such sects believed that through graceful compassion, a Buddha or bodhisattva only required that one devoutly repeat his name and place full trust in him for salvation. In this "degenerate age," the difficult paths of wisdom and meditation were open only to the few. Therefore, the Enlightened One had opened a broader path of devotion, so that laity as well as monks might reach paradise and nirvana.

Mahayana did not destroy monastic dignity. Rather, it just stressed the social side of the ideal. The Mahayanists saw the Hinayana arhat as too individualistic. To pursue one's own enlightenment and salvation apart from those of other living beings seemed selfish. So the Mahayanists began to talk of a bodhisattva, a being who is enlightened but postpones entrance into nirvana to labor for the salvation of all living things. Out of great compassion *(mahakaruna)*, he remains in the samsaric world for eons if need be, content to put off final bliss, to help save other living beings.

Finally, Mahayanists began to contemplate the Buddha's preexistence and the status he had gained as a knowledge being. In this contemplation, his earthly life receded in importance, so much that some Mahayanists began to say that he had only apparently assumed a human body. Then, linking this stress on the Buddha's metaphysical essence with the Indian doctrine of endless kalpas of cosmic time and endless stretches of cosmic space, Mahayanists emphasized the many Buddhas who had existed before Sakyamuni and the Buddhas who presided in other cosmic realms.

In this way the notion of Buddhahood greatly expanded. First it was the quality shared by many cosmic beings of wisdom and realization. Later, in East Asian Mahayana, Buddhahood became the metaphysical notion that *all* beings are in essence enlightenment beings. Enlightenment, therefore, is just realizing one's Buddha-nature. It is the beginning of nirvana, the break with samsara, and the achievement of perfect wisdom all in one.

Buddhahood thus became complex and many-sided. The Buddha came to have three bodies: The dharma body, in which he was the unmanifest aspect of Buddhahood or Enlightenment-being; the human body in which he appeared on earth; and the glorification body, in which he was manifest to the heavenly beings, with all his marks and signs. Moreover, the distinction between Buddhas and great bodhisattvas blurred and largely dissolved in the popular mind, giving Buddhist "divinity" a full spectrum of holy beings. Citing the Mahayana understanding of divinity, therefore, is the surest way to refute claims that Buddhism is not a religion. Whatever merit the position that Buddhism is not a religion has rests in the strictly human experiences that *may* have been the core of the historical Buddha's enlightenment. By the fifth or sixth century after the Buddha's death, the hills were alive with chants to a variety of divine figures.

TANTRISM

We have seen the Hindu mixture of occult and erotic practices called Tantrism or Shaktism. Indian Buddhism helped create this trend and incorporated many of its notions. Tantrism had antecedents in both Buddha's teaching and in the surrounding Hindu Brahmanism. Buddha appears to have allowed spells, and the canon contains reputed cures for snakebite and other dangers.

Buddhist Tantrists took over such sacred sounds as "om," as well as esoteric yogic systems, such as *kundalini*, which associated sacred syllables with force centers *(chakras)* in the body. They also used mandalas (magic figures, such as circles and squares) and even *stupas* (shrines). The Buddhist Tantrists were thus hardly bizarre or innovative, mainly developing ancient Hindu esoteric practices in a new setting.

What novelty the Tantrists did introduce into Buddhism came from their creative use of rites that acted out mandalas and esoteric doctrines about bodily forces. Perhaps under the influence of Yogacara meditation, which induced states of trance, the Tantrists developed rituals in which participants identified with particular deities.

A principal metaphysical support of Tantrism was the Madhyamika doctrine of emptiness, which the Tantrists interpreted to mean that all beings are intrinsically pure. Consequently, they used odd elements in their rituals to drive home the truths of emptiness, purity, and freedom. For the most part, these ways did not become public, since the Tantrists went to considerable pains to keep their rites and teachings secret. In fact, they developed a cryptic language that they called "twilight speech," in which sexual references were abundant.[23] For instance, they called the male and female organs "thunderbolt" and "lotus," respectively. As with Hindu Tantrism, it is not always possible to tell whether such speech is symbolic or literal. Some defenders of Tantrism claim that it tamed sexual energy in the Indian tradition by subjecting it to symbolization, meditative discipline, and moral restraints. Other critics, however, view Buddhist Tantrism as a corruption of a tradition originally quite intolerant of libidinal practices. For them the Tantrist explanation that, since everything is mind-only, the practice of erotic rites means little is simply a rationalization.

In a typical Tantrist meditation, the meditator would begin with traditional preliminaries such as seeking refuge in the three jewels, cleansing himself of sins (by confession or bathing), praying to past masters, or drawing a mandala to define the sacred space of the extraordinary reality that his rite was going to involve. Then the meditator would take on the identity of a deity and disperse all appearances of the world into emptiness. Next, using his imagination, the meditator would picture himself as the god whose identity he was projecting.

So pictured, he and his consort would sit on the central throne of the mandala space and engage in sexual union. Then he would imagine various Buddhas parading into the sacred space of the mandala and assimilate them into his body and senses. In that assimilation, his speech would become divine, he could receive offerings as a god, and he could perform any of the deity's functions. So charged with divinity, he would then return to the ordinary world, bringing back to it the great power of a Buddha's divine understanding.[24]

The relation of the master (guru) and the disciple was central in Tantrism, because the master represented the tradition. (Zen has maintained this stress on the master.) The Tantrist gurus occasionally forced their pupils to engage in quite bizarre and painful practices to teach them to examine the mirror of their minds, to learn the illusory character of all phenomena, and to stop the cravings and jealousies that clouded their mirror.[25] Pronouncing the death of old judgments and the birth of new ones of enlightenment, the guru might confuse the pupil, punish him, and push him to break with convention and ordinary vision. When Buddhism had become vegetarian, some Tantrist masters urged eating flesh. When Buddhism advocated teetotalism, some urged intoxicating spirits. In such ways, Tantrist wisdom could become paradoxical and eccentric.[26]

THE DEMISE OF INDIAN BUDDHISM

Buddhism declined in India after the seventh century, only in part because of Tantrist emphases. Invaders such as the White Huns and the Muslims wrecked many Buddhist strongholds, while the revival of Hinduism, especially of Hindu bhakti sects of Vishnu and Shiva, undermined Buddhism. Mahayana fought theistic Hinduism quite fiercely, not at all seeing it as equivalent to the Buddhist theology of bodhisattvas and Buddhas, but Hinduism ultimately prevailed because of its great ability to incorporate other movements. Indeed, Buddha became one of the Vaishnavite avatars.

Early missionary activity had exported it, however, and Buddhism proved to be hardier on foreign soil than on Indian. So Hinduism, which has largely been confined to India, became the native tradition that opposed the Muslims, while Buddhism became an internationalized brand of Indian culture.[27]

CONTEMPORARY BUDDHIST RITUALS

To fill out our historical account, let us focus on how contemporary Buddhist piety actually functions in such disparate locales as Burma and California, remembering that a similar ritualism has been important throughout all of Buddhist history.

Pious Burmese Buddhists who met in the 1950s and early 1960s began and ended the day with devotions performed in front of a small household shrine. This shrine usually consisted of a shelf for a vase of fresh flowers and a picture of the Buddha. It was always located on the eastern side of the house (the most auspicious side) and placed above head level (to place the Buddha below head level would be insulting). During the time of devotions, householders would light candles and place food offerings before the Buddha.

Coming before this shrine, the householders would petition to be freed from the four woes (rebirth in hell, as an animal, as a demon, or as a ghost), from the three scourges (war, epidemic, and famine), from the eight kinds of unfortunate birth, from the five kinds of enemy, from the four deficiencies (tyrannical kings, wrong views of life after death, physical deformity, and dull-wittedness), and from the five misfortunes, that they might quickly enter nirvana. They would end the morning prayer by reciting the five precepts, pledging to abstain from taking life, from stealing, from drinking intoxicants, from lying, and from sexual immorality. In the evening many Burmese, especially the elderly, would conclude a similar session of homage, petition, and rededication by praying a rosary. The Buddhist rosary consisted of 108 beads, one for each of the 108 marks on the feet of the Buddha (which, in turn, represent his 108 reincarnations). While fingering a bead the devotee usually would say either "painful, selfless, fleeting" or "Buddha, dharma, sangha" three times.[28]

Since 1970 there has been a successful Buddhist monastery near Mount Shasta in northern California.[29] The central occupation of the monastery is *zazen*, or sitting in meditation. Most members of the monastery spend two to three hours in meditation each day. During the morning service, the trainees make three bows and offer incense to the celebrant, Kennett-Roshi. The community then intones and recites portions of the Buddhist scriptures. There are three more bows, and then the community processes to the founder's shrine, where they recite more scriptures. During the evening ceremony, in addition to the scripture recitations, there is a reading of the rules for *zazen*. At meals someone recites portions of the scriptures while the food is passed, to help community members increase their sense of gratitude for what they are about to receive. Vespers finish the evening service, and through the day monks say prayers before such activities as shaving their heads and putting on their robes. At Mount Shasta there are regular periods throughout the year when the monks concentrate on meditation almost full-time, making a strong effort to come closer to enlightenment.

The recitation of the Buddhist scriptures potentially has the effect of reciting mantras, for when sounds enter consciousnesses that have been purified by discipline and made alert by meditation, they can develop almost mesmerizing cadences. The ritual bows, use of incense, use of flowers, and the like help to engage all the senses and focus all the spiritual faculties, so that the prayer or meditation to be performed can be wholehearted.

A major difference between the monastic ritualism of Mount Shasta and the lay ritualism of the Burmese Buddhism we described is the stress the lay ritualism placed on petitioning the Buddha for protection against misfortune and help with worldly needs. Part of this difference stems from the greater stress that Theravada lay doctrine places on gaining merit. Whereas the monastic doctrine of Soto Zen stresses the enlightenment nature of all reality, the Burmese Buddhists live in a thought-world filled with ghosts and gods that constantly make them aware of a need to improve their karmic state. In both cases, however, Buddhist rituals set believers to worship, the central religious act, as other religions' rituals set their adherents to worship. In both cases, the rituals teach the believers to collect themselves, praise what they take to be ultimate reality, and gain the spiritual aid they need.

NOTES

1. Richard H. Robinson and Willard L. Johnson, *The Buddhist Religion* (Encino, Calif.: Dickenson, 1977), p. 13; see also Trevor Ling, *The Buddha* (London: Temple Smith, 1973), pp. 37–83; Mircea Eliade, *Histoire des croyances et des ideés religieuses*, vol. 2, *De Gautama Bouddha au triomphe de Christianisme* (Paris: Payot, 1978), p. 174.

2. Edward Conze, *Buddhist Scriptures* (Baltimore: Penguin, 1959), p. 34; see also Eliade, *Histoire des croyances.*

3. Conze, *Buddhist Scriptures*, pp.48–49; see also Lowell W. Bloss, "The Taming of Mara," *HR*, 1978, *18*(2):156–176.

4. Robinson and Johnson, *Buddhist Tradition*, p. 28.

5. Ibid. p. 31; see also Edward J. Thomas, *The History of Buddhist Thought* (New York: Barnes & Noble, 1951), pp. 58–70; Henry Clarke Warren, *Buddhism in Translations* (New York: Atheneum, 1973), pp. 202–208.

6. See William Theodore de Bary, ed., *The Buddhist Tradition* (New York: Vintage, 1972), pp. 15–20; see also Edward Conze, *Buddhism: Its Essence and Development* (New York: Harper Torchbooks, 1959), pp. 43–48; I. B. Horner, "Buddhism: The Theravada," in *The Concise Encyclopedia of Living Faiths*, ed. R. C. Zaehner (Boston: Beacon Press, 1967), pp. 283–293.

7. See Winston K. King, *In the Hope of Nibbana: Theravada Buddhist Ethics* (LaSalle, Ill.: Open Court, 1964).

8. Texts on wisdom, morality, and meditation are available in Stephen Beyer, *The Buddhist Experience* (Encino, Calif.: Dickenson, 1974); see also Conze, *Buddhist Scriptures.*

9. Edward Conze, *Buddhist Meditation* (New York: Harper Torchbooks, 1969); see also Nyanaponika Thera, *The Heart of Buddhist Meditation* (London: Rider, 1969).

10. John Bowker discusses this rather creatively; see Bowker, *The Religious Imagination and the Sense of God* (Oxford: Clarendon Press, 1978), p. 244; see also Willis Stoesz, "The Buddha as Teacher," *JAAR*, 1978, *46*(2):139–158.

11. See I. B. Horner, "The Teaching of the Elders," in *Buddhist Texts through the Ages*, ed. Edward Conze (New York: Harper Torchbooks, 1954), pp. 17–50. Also Warren, *Buddhism in Translations*, p. 392; Charles S.

Prebish, ed. *Buddhism: A Modern Perspective* (University Park: Pennsylvania State University Press, 1975), pp. 16–26, 49–53; Conze, *Buddhism: Its Essence and Development*, pp. 58–69; Beyer, *Buddhist Experience*, pp. 65–73.

12. On the laity, see Conze, *Buddhism: Its Essence and Development*, pp. 70–88.

13. See Conze, *Buddhist Scriptures*, pp. 182–183.

14. See Prebish, *Buddhism: A Modern Perspective*, pp. 29–45; see also Edward Conze, *Buddhist Thought in India* (Ann Arbor, Mich.: Ann Arbor Paperbacks, 1967), p. 121; Janice J. Nattier and Charles S. Prebish, "Mahasamghika Origins: The Beginnings of Buddhist Sectarianism," *HR*, 1977, *16*(3):237–272.

15. Robinson and Johnson, *Buddhist Religion*, p. 77; see also John S. Strong, "Gandhakuti: The Perfumed Chamber of the Buddha," *HR*, 1977, *16*(4):390–406.

16. See Nancy Falk, "An Image of Woman in Old Buddhist Literature: The Daughters of Mara," in *Women and Religion*, rev. ed., ed. J. Plakow and J. A. Romero (Missouli, Mont.: Scholars Press, 1974), pp. 105–112.

17. Robinson and Johnson, *Buddhist Religion*, p. 81.

18. Mircea Eliade, *Yoga: Immortality and Freedom* (Princeton, N.J.: Princeton University Press, 1969), pp. 162–199; see also S. N. Dasgupta, *Hindu Mysticism* (New York: Frederick Ungar, 1959), pp. 85–109.

19. For general overviews of Mahayana, see Edward Conze, "Buddhism: The Mahayana," in *The Concise Encyclopedia of Living Faiths*, ed. R. C. Zaehner (Boston: Beacon Press, 1967), pp. 296–320; also Edward Conze, ed., *Buddhist Texts through the Ages* (New York: Harper Torchbooks, 1954), pp. 119–217.

20. See Conze, *Buddhist Thought in India*, pp. 238–244; see also Prebish, *Buddhism: A Modern Perspective*, pp. 76–96; T. R. V. Murti, *The Central Philosophy of Buddhism* (London: Allen & Unwin, 1955).

21. See Conze, *Buddhist Thought in India*, pp. 250–260; Prebish, *Buddhism: A Modern Perspective*, pp. 97–101; Thomas, *History of Buddhist Thought*, pp. 230–248.

22. D. T. Suzuki, trans., *The Lankavatara Sutra* (London: George Routledge, 1932).

23. Beyer, *Buddhist Experience*, pp. 258–261; Eliade, *Yoga*, pp. 249–254.

24. Robinson and Johnson, *Buddhist Religion*, p. 120.

25. Herbert Guenther, trans., *The Life and Teachings of Naropa* (New York: Oxford University Press, 1971), p. 43; see also W. Y. Evans-Wentz, ed., *Tibet's Great Yogi Milarepa* (New York: Oxford University Press, 1969), p. 93.

26. See Beyer, *Buddhist Experience*, pp. 174–184, 225–229, 258–261.

27. There are major qualifications to this statement, of course. On Hinduism in Southeast Asia, see Robinson and Johnson, *Buddhist Tradition*, pp. 129–136; on Hinduism in Indonesia, see Clifford Geertz, *Islam Observed* (Chicago: University of Chicago Press, 1968), pp. 29–43.

28. Melford Spiro, *Buddhism and Society* (New York: Harper & Row, 1970), pp. 209–214.

29. Charles S. Prebish, *American Buddhism* (North Scituate, Mass.: Duxbury Press, 1979), p. 164.

7

Chinese Religion

PREAXIAL CHINESE RELIGION

Philosopher Karl Jaspers has spoken of an "axial period" of human civilization, during which the essential insights arose that spawned the great cultures.[1] In China the axial period was the sixth and fifth centuries B.C.E., and the two most important figures were Confucius and Lao-tzu, whose Confucianism and Taoism, respectively, formed the basis for all subsequent Chinese culture. Before them, however, were centuries, perhaps even millennia, of nature and ancestor-oriented responses to the sacred, when the ancient mind dominated the Chinese people.

In China, for instance, divination mixed with the Confucian ethical code, so that the prime divinatory text, the *I Ching*, became one of the Confucian classics. As the popular Chinese folk novel *Monkey*[2] shows, other ancient attitudes were alive well into the sixteenth century C.E. So the preaxial world view that we now sketch was a constant feature throughout Chinese religious history.

First, though, we must qualify the concept of Chinese religion. China, like most ancient cultures, did not develop religion as a separate realm of human concern. The rites, sacred mythology, ethics, and the like that bound the Chinese peoples were simply their culture. These cultural phenomena were not distinguished from the daily routine. So, what we underscore here for our purposes is not necessarily what the Chinese underscored. Second, the Chinese attitude toward ultimate reality stressed nature—the physical world. Nature was the (sacred) essential context of human existence, and there was no clear creator outside nature.

Of course, nature appeared to be both constant and changing. The cosmos was always there, but it had seasons and rhythms, as well as unexpected activities such as storms and earthquakes. To explain this tension between stability and change, the Chinese of the Han period thought in terms of a union of opposing basic forces. Yang was the force of light, heat, and maleness. Yin was the balancing force of darkness, cold, and femaleness. The changes in the relations between yang and yin accounted for the seasons, the moon's phases, and the tides.

Another aspect of nature was the mixture or proportions of the five vital forces (water, fire, wood, metal, and earth) at any given time. They were the qualities that activated nature—that gave particular things and events their character. Together, the yin-yang theory and the theory of the five vital forces formed the first Chinese explanation of nature.[3]

Above the system, not as its creator from nothingness but as its semipersonal overlord, was the heavenly ruler. His domain was human and natural behavior. The heavenly ruler probably was the first ancestor of the ruling dynasty. That is, the Chinese first conceived him as the clan head of the ancient ruling house of Shang.[4] Later they modified this anthropomorphic conception to heaven, a largely impersonal force. Then the emperor became the "Son of Heaven," not in the sense that he was the descendant of the first ancestral leader of the ruling clan but in the sense that he represented the force that governed the world.[5]

Another name for the director of the natural system was *Tao*. Essentially, *Tao* meant "way" or "path." The Confucians spoke of the *Tao* of the ancients—the customs or ethos that prevailed in the golden beginning times. Similarly, the Chinese Buddhists described their tradition as the "Way of the Buddha." However, the Taoists most directly appropriated the naturalistic overtones to *Tao* and focused on nature's directing path. For them the *Tao* was an ultimate reality, both within the system and beyond it.

Within the natural system, however, the prehistoric Chinese stressed harmony. That is, they tended to think that trees, rivers, clouds, animals, and humans compose something whole. As a result, natural phenomena could be portents, while human actions, whether good or evil, influenced both heaven and earth. So the oldest Chinese were citizens of nature, not a species standing outside and apart from it. Consequently, they did not consider human beings apart from the other creatures of the cosmos.

When Chuang-tzu spoke of reentering the Great Clod,[6] he spoke from this ancient conviction. To die and return to the material world, perhaps to be a tree or a fish in the next round, was natural and right. With some qualifications that we shall mention, the Chinese have favored long life rather than immortality, enlightenment that polishes worldly vision rather than enlightenment that draws one out of the world.

The Peasant Heritage

The vast majority of China's billions have been peasants, who, with relatively few changes, continued to stress animistic forces, amulets, and divination rites up to the beginning of the twentieth century (if not right up to the present).

Folk religion is always an effort to explain nature, but it employs a logic that is more symbolic than that of yin-yang, the five dynamic qualities, or *Tao*. Rather, it emphasizes similarities and differences, whether in shapes, sizes, or names. As close to dreaming as to science, folk religion easily allows the subconscious great influence. So, for instance, diviners thought they had a key to nature in the cracks of a baked tortoise shell, or the flight patterns of birds, or the broken and unbroken lines that the *I Ching* interpreted as ratios of yin and yang. It was but a small step to use these interpretational techniques to control nature—to use them as magic.

One functionary who has specialized in this symbolic magic is the practitioner of *feng-shui*.[7] *Feng-shui* is the study of winds and water, or geomancy. Essentially, it involves how to position a building most auspiciously. In a convoluted symbolism involving dragons and tigers, it has tried to make the living forces of nature yield good fortune by figuring out the spiritual lay of the land. What nature disposed, according to *feng-shui*, architecture could oppose or exploit. For instance, straight lines are believed to be evil influ-

ences, but trees or a fresh pond can ward them off. Consequently, the basic design of Chinese villages has included trees and ponds for protection. Similarly, a winding approach to a house has diverted evil forces. The *feng-shui* diviner plots all the forces, good and evil, with a sort of compass that marks the different circles of power of these forces. *Feng-shui* has prevailed well into modern times, a fact attesting to its perceived importance.

Other important ancient functionaries were the mediums and the shamans. The Chinese shaman (or shamaness) was perhaps less ecstatic than the Siberian, more a subject of possession or a medium than a traveler to the gods.[8] More importantly, the existence of the shaman shows that ancient China believed in a realm of personified spirits.[9] These spirits could come to susceptible individuals with lights and messages or be the spirits of departed ancestors speaking through a medium who was in trance. If one did not revere them, speak well of them, and give them gifts of food, the ancestor spirits could turn nasty.

In later times, ordinary people thought that the ancestor spirits lived in a spiritual equivalent of the human world, where they needed such things as food, clothing, and money. Thus, pious children would burn paper money to send assistance to their departed parents.[10] In fact, one's primary obligation of a religious sort was just such acts of commemoration, reverence, and help. This ancestor veneration so impressed Western missionaries that they fought bitterly among themselves about its meaning. Some missionaries found ancestor rites idolatrous, while others found them praiseworthy expressions of familial love.[11]

CONFUCIANISM

Confucius (551–479 B.C.E.) became the father of Chinese culture by transforming the ancient traditions into at least the beginnings of a code for directing social life. More than two centuries passed before his doctrine became the state orthodoxy (during the Han dynasty, 206 B.C.E.–220 B.C.E.), but from the outset it had a healing effect on Chinese society. Confucius lived during a warring period of Chinese history, an epoch of nearly constant social disorder. For Master K'ung (the original name of Confucius), the way from such disorder toward peace was obtained from the ancients—the venerable ancestors who were closer to the beginning and wiser than the people of the present age. What the ancestors knew, what made them wise, were the decrees of heaven. As we have seen, heaven meant nature's overlord. Thus, Confucius accepted the ancient, preaxial notion that nature has some order. In his view, the way to a peaceful and prosperous society was to adapt to that order. People could do that externally through sacrificial rites and hierarchical social relationships. Internally, one had to know the human mind, and the human mind had to be set in *jen* (fellow feeling or love).[12]

For external order, the emperor was paramount. As the Son of Heaven, he conveyed heaven's will to earth. In other words, the China of Confucius's time held the notion that the king was the sacred intermediary between the realm of heaven and the realm modeled upon it, earth. What the king did for human society, then, was both priestly and exemplary. By officiating at the most important rites, through which his people tried to achieve harmony with heaven, the king represented society before the ultimate judge of society's fate.

Confucius approved of the model leadership of the legendary kings, and he also approved of the notion that ritual makes a sacrament of the vital flow between heaven and earth. One focus of this teaching, then, was historical: He concentrated on how the ancients reportedly acted. Another focus was liturgical. He was himself a master of court ritual, and he thought that proper sacrifice and etiquette were very important.

Having had little success in public affairs (he never obtained high office or found a ruler willing to hire his counsel), he turned to teaching young men wise politics and the way to private virtue. In other words, he became the center of an academic circle, like that of Plato, which had ongoing dialogues about the good life, political science, private and public morality, and so on. The *Analects* are a collection of fragments from the Master. In them we can see why Confucius impressed his followers, who finally made him the model wise man. (After his death, Confucius gained semidivine status and became the center of a religious cult.)[13]

For Confucius, the Way manifests itself as a golden mean. It opens a path between punctiliousness and irregularity, between submissiveness and independence. Most situations are governed by a protocol that will yield graceful interactions if it is followed wholeheartedly. The task of the gentleman is to know that protocol, intuit how it applies in particular cases, and have the discipline to carry it out. The death of a parent, for instance, is a prime occasion for a gentleman to express his love and respect for that parent. According to the rites of mourning, he should retire from public affairs, simplify his living arrangements, and devote himself to grieving (for as long as three years).

As that example suggests, filial piety was a cornerstone of Confucianism. If the relations at home were correct, other social relationships would likely fall in line. The Confucian classic *The Great Learning*[14] spells out this theory, linking the individual in the family to the order of both the state and the cosmos. Moreover, the family circle was the training ground for a gentleman's lifelong dedication to humanity (*jen*) and ritual propriety (*li*). When a man developed a sincere love for his parents and carried out his filial duties, he rooted himself firmly in both *jen* and *li*. (We consider the place of women below.)

Different followers developed different aspects of Confucius's teaching. Mencius, for instance, changed the Master's view of *jen*, drawing it down from the almost divine status accorded it by Confucius and making it a real possibility for everyman.[15] For Mencius human nature was innately good. We are evil or disordered only because we forget our original nature. Like the deforested local hill, the typical human mind is so abused that we cannot see its spontaneous tendency toward altruism and justice. If we would stop deforesting it with vice, we would realize that virtue is instinctive. Just as anyone who sees a child at the edge of a well rushes to save the youth, so anyone educated in gentlemanliness will rush to solve civic problems.

Thus, Mencius centered Confucius's teaching on the goodness of human nature. Living two centuries after the Master, Mencius tried to repeat Confucius's way of life. So, he searched for an ideal king who would take his counsel, but he had to be satisfied with having a circle of young students. Mencius, though, somewhat lacked Confucius's restraint in discussing heavenly things (Confucius considered the human realm more than enough to master). According to Lee Yearley,[16] Mencius practiced a disciplined religion to increase physical vigor by acting with purity of heart, and he was willing to die for certain things such as justice and goodness. So, just as one can consider some of Confucius's sayings as quite religious (for example, "It is not better to pay court to the stove than to heaven"), one can view Mencius as having transcendent beliefs. Both Confucian thinkers, we believe, appealed to more than human prudence.

Mencius also proposed an ultimately religious theory that history moves in cycles, depending on how a given ruling family handles the *te* (the power to govern well) that heaven dispenses.[17] The sharpest implication of this theory was that an unjust ruler might lose the mandate of heaven—that a revolutionary might properly receive it. Furthermore, Mencius advanced the view that the king brought prosperity only when he convinced the people that the things of the state were their own. This view was in part shrewd psychology: A people who have access to the royal park will think it small even if it is 100 miles square; a people denied access to a royal park one mile square will complain that it is far too vast. As well, however, it brought Confucius's stress on leadership by example and virtue up to date. Only if the king demonstrates virtue can he expect the people to be virtuous.

In summary, then, the hallmarks of the original Confucians were a reliance on ancient models, a concern for the golden mean between externalism and internalism, a stress on filial piety, and a deep respect for the ruler's connection with heaven. These socially oriented thinkers emphasized breeding, grace, and public service. Their goal was harmony and balance through a hierarchical social order.[18] They gave little attention to the rights of peasants or women, but they did prize ethical integrity, compassion, and learning. Against the blood and violence of their times, they called for a rule through moral force. This was their permanent legacy: Humanity is fidelity to virtue.

NEO-CONFUCIANISM

During the Sung dynasty (960–1279 C.E.), the axial Confucian thought that lay in the teachings of Confucius, Mencius, and others grew into a full-fledged philosophy that included metaphysical interpretations of nature and humanity.

The neo-Confucian philosophy of nature that gained the most adherents involved the interaction of two elements, principle and ether. Ether, or breath, was the basis of the material universe. All solid things condensed out of ether and eventually dissolved back into it.[19] In the dynamic phases of this cycle, ether was an ultimate form of yang. In the still phases, it was the ultimate form of yin. The neo-Confucian view of material nature therefore preserved the tension of dualities—of hot and cold, male and female, light and dark—that had always fascinated the Chinese. One reason for the acceptance of neo-Confucianism, in fact, was that it appeared as just a modern version of the ancient patrimony. The second element in nature's dualism, principle, etymologically related to the veins in jade or the grain in wood. It was the *pattern* running through all material things, their direction and purpose. If you opposed principle (went against the grain), all things became difficult. In terms of cognitional theory, the neo-Confucians invoked principle to explain the mind's ability to move from the known to the unknown. They also used it to ground the mind's appreciation of the connectedness of things. Principle was considered to be innate in human beings—it was

nature's inborn guidance. The main task of human maturation and education was to remove the impediments that kept people from perceiving their principle. This task implied a sort of asceticism or moral diligence, sometimes involving meditation and self-denial.

Despite these metaphysical developments, neo-Confucianism retained a commitment to the traditional Confucian virtues associated with character building. The paramount virtue continued to be *jen*. The ideogram for *jen* represented a human being: *jen* is humaneness—what makes us human. We are not fully human simply by receiving life in a human form. Rather, our humanity depends upon community, human reciprocity.[20] *Jen* pointed in that direction. It connected with the Confucian golden rule of not doing to others what you would not want them to do to you. Against individualism, it implied that people have to live together helpfully, even lovingly. People have to cultivate their instinctive benevolence, their instinctive ability to put themselves in another's shoes. That cultivation was the primary educational task of Confucius and Mencius.

The neo-Confucians also kept the four other traditional virtues: *yi, li, chih,* and *hsin. Yi* meant duty or justice, and it signified what is right, what law and custom prescribe. Its context, therefore, was the Chinese culture's detailed specification of rights and obligations. Where *jen* undercut such formalities, giving justice its heart, *yi* took care of contractual exactitudes.

Li, which meant manners or propriety, was less exact than *yi.* To some extent it depended on learning, so Confucius tried to teach by word and example what a gentleman would do in various circumstances, but it also required instinct, breeding, or intuition. Handling authority over household servants, men in the fields, or subordinates in the civil service involved *li.* So, too, did deference to superiors, avoidance of ostentation, and a generally graceful style. *Li* therefore was the unguent that soothed all social friction. In a society that prohibited the display of hostile emotion, that insisted on a good "face," *li* was very important.

Chih (wisdom) was not a deep penetration of ultimate reality like the Buddhist *Prajna-paramita*; it depended on neither enlightenment nor mystical union with *Tao.* Rather, it was a prudent sense of right and wrong, decent and indecent, profitable and unprofitable that one could hope to gain by revering the ancients and attentive living. *Hsin* meant trustworthiness or good faith. It was related to *jen* insofar as what one trusts in another is his or her decency or humanity, but it pertained more to a person's reliability or dependability. A person of *hsin* was not flighty or capricious.

TAOISM

The classical, axial-period Taoists responded to the troubled warring period quite differently from the Confucians. They agreed that the times were disordered and that the way to set them straight was by means of the ancients' *Tao*. But the great Taoist thinkers, such as Chuang-tzu and Lao-tzu, were more imaginative and mystical than the Confucians. In their broad speculation, they probed not only the natural functions of the Way and the interior exercises that could align one with it but also the revolt against conventional values that union with *Tao* seemed to imply. Of the two great Taoists, Chuang-tzu is the more poetic and paradoxical. His stories stress the personal effects of living with *Tao*. Lao-tzu's orientation is more political. For him *Tao* gives a model for civil rule, lessons in what succeeds and what brings grief. Insofar as Chuang-tzu is more theroetical and less concerned with political applications, he enjoys a certain logical priority over Lao-tzu.[21]

Chuang-tzu

What impressed Chuang-tzu most was the influence of one's viewpoint. The common person, for example, can make little of the ancients' communion with nature, unconcern for human opinion, and freedom. Such things are like the great bird flying off where the sparrow has never been. Yet if one advances in the "fasting of the spirit" that the ancients practiced, their behavior starts to make sense. Apparently such "fasting of the spirit" was a meditative regime in which one laid aside distractions and let simple, deep powers of spiritual consciousness issue forth.

Chuang-tzu pictured those powers rather dramatically: They can send the sage flying on the clouds or riding on the winds, for they free the soul so that it can be directed by *Tao* itself. *Tao* is the wind blowing on the ten thousand things, the music of the spheres. With little regard for petty humankind, it works nature's rhythms. The way to peace, spiritual ecstasy, and long life is to join nature's rhythms. But by joining nature's rhythms, one abandons social conventions. *Tao* throws off our human judgments of good and bad, right and wrong. Thus, the true Taoist becomes ec-

centric with respect to the rest of society, for he (or she, though women seldom participated in Chinese society) prefers obscure peace to troubled power, leisurely contemplation to hectic productivity.

In rather technical terms, Chuang-tzu attacked those who thought they could tie language directly to thought and so clarify all discourse. If *Tao* touches language and thought, he showed, they become highly symbolic. Moreover, Chuang-tzu made his attack on conventional values and language into simple good sense. It is the worthless, cast-off, unpopular trees and people that survive. Those who would be prominent, who would shine in public, often end up without a limb (as punishment for crime or disfavor). When he was asked to join the government, Chuang-tzu said he would rather drag his tail in the mud like a turtle. When his wife died, he sang and drummed instead of mourning: She was just following *Tao*, just taking another turn. Puncturing cant, deflating pomposity, excoriating our tendency to trade interior freedom for exterior position, Chuang-tzu ridiculed the sober Confucians. They, like other prosaic realists, seemed too dull to be borne—too dull for a life of spiritual adventure, for a *Tao* as magnificent as the heavens and as close as the dung.

Lao-tzu

Thomas Merton has published a delightful interpretation of Chuang-tzu that relates him to the contemplative spirit of Western poets and monks.[22] No one has done quite the same thing for Lao-tzu or the *Tao Te Ching*, perhaps because Lao-tzu's style is more impersonal. The *Tao Te Ching (The Way and The Power)*,[23] like the *Chuang-tzu* (the book left by Chuang-tzu and his school), is of undetermined origin. Its author's existence is more uncertain than that of the *Analects*. But the book itself has become a world classic, in good measure because of its mystic depth (and vagueness). In it a very original mind meditates on *Tao*'s paradoxical qualities to glean lessons about human society. Interpreters vary in the weight they give to the mystical aspects of the *Tao Te Ching*,[24] but in any interpretation Lao-tzu thought that Tao holds the secret to good life.

Consequently, a major concern of the *Tao Te Ching* is to elucidate just how nature does operate and how society should imitate it. Its basic conclusion, presented in a series of striking images, is that *Tao* moves nature through *wu-wei* (active not-doing). Three of the principal images are the valley, the female, and the uncarved block. Together, they indicate *Tao*'s distance from most human expectations. The valley symbolizes *Tao*'s inclination toward the lowly, the underlying, rather than the prominent or impressive. Lao-tzu's female is a lesson in the power of passivity, of yielding and adaptability. She influences not by assault but by indirection, by nuance and suggestion. The uncarved block is human nature before society limits it. These images all show *wu-wei*.

Wu-wei is also shown in the power of the infant, whose helplessness can dominate an entire family. It is in the power of water, which patiently wears away rock. Wryly Lao-tzu reminds us of the obvious: A valley resists storms better than a mountain, a female tends to outlive a male, an infant is freer than a king, and a house is valuable for the space inside it. Such lessons underscore a reality that common sense tends to ignore because it tends to notice only what is prominent. In contrast, *Tao* moves nature by a subtle, elastic power. Were rulers to imitate *Tao*, moving others by *wu-wei* rather than *pa* (violent force), society might prosper.

Wu-wei, it follows, tries to shortcircuit the law of the human jungle, the round after round of tit for tat.[25] But to gain *wu-wei*, human nature must become like an uncarved block, which is perhaps the most important of Lao-tzu's symbols. (Holmes Welch, who argues that we can read the *Tao Te Ching* on several levels, makes the uncarved block its key.[26]) It symbolizes the priority of natural simplicity over social adornment. A block of wood or jade, before it is carved, has infinite potential, but once we have made it into a table or a piece of jewelry, its use is fixed and limited.

Impressed by the limitless creativity of nature, Lao-tzu wanted to recover human nature's originality. In his eyes, the Confucians tended to overspecialize human nature. A society with fewer "modern" advances, less technology, and more spontaneous interaction with nature and fellow humans would be much richer than the Confucians'.[27] The Taoists, who took their lead from Lao-tzu and Chuang-tzu, tried to show how less could be more, how neglect could be cultivation. If people would shut the doors of their senses and thus cut off distractions, how less can be more would be obvious. The good life is not found in having but in being. By being simple, whole, alert, and sensitive in feeling, one finds joy.

Throughout history, many commentators have criticized Lao-tzu and his followers for both naiveté and obscurantism. They have especially jumped on the Taoist precept that a good way to promote peace and simplicity is to keep the people ignorant. Taoists believed that by not knowing and therefore not having many desires, a populace is quite docile. Critics maintain that it is but a short step from such docility to sheephood and being at the mercy of evil rulers.

However, a close reading of the *Tao Te Ching* shows that *wu-wei* is quite different from mindless docility or even complete pacifism. Rather, it includes the regretful use of force to cut short greater evil. As well, *wu-wei* is not sentimental, which further distinguishes it from most Westerners' view of "the people." As easily as nature itself, *wu-wei* discards what is outworn, alternating life with death. Because of this objectivity, Taoism can seem inhuman. For a people close to nature, though, humaneness is a less anthropocentric virtue than it is for ourselves. It is less personal and more influenced by the belief that self-concern is folly.

Religious Taoism and Aesthetics

Two great consequences of the school in which Chuang-tzu and Lao-tzu predominated had considerable influence through subsequent Chinese history. One consequence was religious Taoism, which was considerably different from the philosophical Taoism of the founding fathers in that it employed their symbolism literally and turned to quests for extraordinary powers and immortality.[28] A second consequence was aesthetic: Chinese art became heavily Taoist.

The religious Taoists formed a "church," generated a massive literature complete with ritualistic and alchemical lore, and earned the wrath of modern educated Chinese, who considered religious Taoism a bastion of superstition. Also, religious Taoists became embroiled in politics and sponsored violent revolutionary groups.[29] Their rituals and revolutionary politics went together, because from their rituals they derived utopian visions of what human society ought to become.

The religious Taoists sought physical immortality by diverse routes.[30] Some sponsored voyages to the magical islands in the East, where the immortals were thought to dwell. Others pursued alchemy, not to turn base metal into gold but to find the elixir of immortality. A third Taoist interest was hygiene. The two favorite regimes were breathing air and practicing a quasi-Tantric sexual yoga. Along with some dietary oddities, some religious Taoists counseled trying to breathe like an infant in the womb, so as to use up the vital force as slowly as possible. Adepts would lie in bed all day, trying to hold their breath for at first a hundred and eventually a thousand counts. Perhaps some became euphoric through carbon dioxide intoxication. The yogis of sex practiced retention of the semen during intercourse, thinking that this vital substance could be rechanneled to the brain and thereby enhance one's powers and longevity. In these exercises, the proximate goal was prolonging physical life, and the ultimate goal was a full immortality.

Religious Taoism also developed regimes of meditation, which it coupled with a complicated roster of gods. The basic assumption behind this venture was that the human body is a microcosm—a miniature world.[31] Within it, certain gods preside over particular organs and functions. By visualizing one of these gods, Taoists thought, one could identify with its powers of immortality.[32]

Taoism had as strong an impact on Chinese aesthetics as it did on Chinese popular religion.[33] As a guide to creativity, it stressed spontaneity and flow. Largely because of Taoist inspiration, calligraphy, painting, poetry, and music ideally issued from a meditative communion with the nature of things.

BUDDHISM

Buddhism may have entered China as early as the beginning of the first century B.C.E. and almost certainly established itself by the middle of the second century C.E.[34] From this beginning, Buddhism slowly adapted to Chinese ways. Most of the preachers and translators who worked from the third to the fifth centuries C.E. favored Taoist terminology. This was especially true in the south, where the intelligentsia created a market for philosophy. In the less cultured north, Buddhism made progress by being presented as a powerful magic.[35] By the middle of the fifth century, China had its own sectarian schools, comparable to those that had developed in India.

In general, Mahayana attracted the Chinese more than Theravada and so the native schools that prospered developed Mahayana positions.

The Chinese brought to Buddhism an interest in bridging the gap between the present age and the age of the Buddha by constructing a line of masters along which the dharma passed intact. The Master was more historical than timeless scriptural texts were, and the authority-minded Chinese were more concerned about history than the Indians had been.

Indeed, conflicts over the sutras were a sore problem for the Chinese, and in trying to reconcile seemingly contradictory positions, they frequently considered one scripture as being authoritative. A principal basis for the differences among the burgeoning Chinese Buddhist sects, therefore, lay in which scripture the sect's founder had chosen as most authori-

tative. (The notion of sects is distinctively Chinese, since it is based on the old concept of the clan. Chinese culture venerated its ancestors, and each Chinese Buddhist school accordingly had its dharma founder or patriarchal teacher.)

Buddhist Sects

The most popular sects were the Ch'an and Ching-t'u, which devoted themselves to meditation and the Pure Land, respectively.

According to legend, Bodhidharma, an Indian meditation master devoted to the *Lankavatara*, founded Ch'an in the fifth century C.E. Paintings portray Bodhidharma as a fierce champion of single-mindedness, and he valued neither pious works nor recitations of the sutras. Only insight into one's own nature, which was identical with the dharma-nature of all reality, was of signficance; only enlightenment justified the Buddhist life. Tradition credits Bodhidharma with developing the technique of "wall gazing," which was a kind of peaceful meditation—what the Japanese later called "just sitting" (*shikan-taza*).

Probably the most eminent of the Ch'an patriarchs who succeeded Bodhidharma was the sixth patriarch, Hui-neng. According to the *Platform Sutra*, which purports to present his teachings, Hui-neng gained his predecessor's mantle of authority by surpassing his rival, Shen-hsiu, in a demonstration of dharma insight. Hui-neng is regarded as the authoritative spokesman for the southern Ch'an school which held that enlightenment comes suddenly. Because all Buddha-nature is intrinsically pure, one need only let it manifest itself. The northern school held that enlightenment comes gradually and thus counseled regular meditation. (Hui-neng himself probably would have fought any sharp distinction between meditation and the rest of life. In wisdom all things are one and pure.) The southern school finally took precedence.[36]

Pure Land Buddhism (Ching-t'u) derived from T'an-luan (476–542). He sought religious solace from a grave illness, and after trying several systems, he came to the doctrine of Amitabha Buddha and the Pure Land. Amitabha is the Buddha of Light, devotion to whom supposedly assures one a place in the Western Paradise. T'an-luan stressed faith in Amitabha and the recitation of Amitabha's name as ways to achieve such salvation. This, he and his successors reasoned, was a doctrine both possible and appropriate in the difficult present age. The Pure Land sect greatly appealed to the laity, and it developed hymns and graphic representations of paradise to focus its imagination. In stressing love or emotional attachment to Amitabha (called A-mi-t'o fo in China), it amounted to a Chinese Buddhist devotionalism. By chanting "na-mo a-mi-t'o-fo" ("greetings to A-mi-t'o fo Buddha"), millions of Chinese found a simple way to fulfill their religious needs and made A-mi-t'o fo the most popular religious figure of Chinese history.[37]

Medieval Buddhism

The T'ang dynasty (618–907) followed on the Sui (589–618), under which North and South China had been reunited. Buddhism had made steady gains in China even before this reunification, but after reunification it grew by leaps and bounds. A major reason for this growth was the perception of both the Sui and the T'ang rulers that Buddhism could help them knit together the northern and southern cultures.

On the other hand, both the Sui and the T'ang rulers feared the power of the sangha and took steps to limit its influence. Thus they insisted on regulating the admission, education, and ordination of the Buddhist clergy and on licensing the Buddhist temples. As well, the emperors put pressure on the sangha to enforce the Vinaya strictly, for these rules governing monastic life tended to restrict the clergy's economic enterprises. Such imperial efforts to control Buddhism were only partly successful, for many medieval empresses and wealthy merchants saw to it that temple wealth grew. Still, the golden age that Buddhism enjoyed in these dynasties flowed from the positive support the emperors gave it. For all their care that Buddhist fervor not become subversive of their own rule, the Sui and T'ang leaders made Buddhist ritual an important part of the state ceremony.

At the great capital of Ch'ang-an, Buddhist art dominated a vibrant cultural life. The architecture of the pagodas and temples gracefully blended Indian and native Chinese elements, producing a distinctively Chinese Buddhist appearance. The images and paintings that adorned the temples drew on the full range of sources with which the great Chinese Empire came in contact. Thus there were not only native Chinese art forms but also Indian, Persian, Greco-Roman, and Central Asian. Similarly, the T'ang dynasty was a high point in the history of Chinese poetry, and the moving forces behind this poetry were the two congenial streams of Buddhist and Taoist philosophy.

Medieval Buddhism also permeated the life of the common people, including the village peasantry, for the government developed a network of official temples that linked the provinces to the capital. On official feast days, ceremonies held throughout the land reminded the people that they shared a uniform religious faith. The provinces also used the Buddhist temple grounds for their fairs, thereby making them the centers of the local social, economic, and artistic life. The great feast days were the Buddha's birthday and the Feast of All Souls, when large crowds would gather to honor the Buddhist deities, listen to the sutras, or hear an accomplished preacher expound the dharma.

The state and the sangha therefore had a symbiotic relationship throughout the Sui and the T'ang dynasties. Whether pulling in the same direction or wanting to go opposite ways, they were mutually influential. One place where Buddhist views considerably modified traditional Chinese customs was the penal codes. The traditional customs were quite cruel, so the Buddhist ideals of compassion and respect for life served as a mitigating influence. Both the Sui and the T'ang rulers granted imperial amnesties from time to time, and when the rulers remitted death sentences they often justified their actions in terms of Buddhist compassion or reverence for life. Specifically, both dynasties took up the custom of forbidding executions (indeed, the killing of any living thing) during the first, fifth, and ninth months of the year, which were times of Buddhist penance and abstinence. It is somewhat ironic, therefore, that through the centuries, Buddhism's major impact in the public sphere was its control of burial rites.

MERCANTILE RELIGION

By the fourteenth century C.E., guilds of artisans and businessmen had developed, and folk religiosity in China had become more mercantile. The guild became a sort of family or clan and had its patron gods and rituals. People now invoked the spirits who were the patrons of good selling, and a folk mentality affected the examinations that were part of the way to civil office. For instance, masters of the Confucian classics who did well in the examinations and secured good jobs took on an aura of religious power. As well, numerous stories were told of scholars who received miraculous help from a patron deity, and these scholars gave the Confucians their own measure of magic and mystery.[38]

The common people also went to a great variety of shrines and temples to find out their futures. In addition, students prayed for success in their examinations, travelers prayed for safe journeys, and young people prayed for good marriages. Popular Chinese religion thus became almost economic. Gods and powers were the foci of business—a business of getting along well with an unseen world of fate and fortune. Confucianism, Taoism, and Buddhism all were mixed into this economic popular religion, but its base was preaxial closeness to nature.

WOMEN'S STATUS

Among the Confucians, a peasant or a woman was unlikely to find honor simply through interior excellence. In fact, of the three Chinese traditions, Confucianism was the most misogynistic. The woman's role in Confucianism was to obey and serve her parents, husband, and husband's parents. She was useless until she produced a male heir, and her premarital chastity and marital fidelity were more important than a man's. In some periods, obsession with female chastity became so great that society insisted on total sexual segregation.[39]

Since a Chinese woman's destiny was early marriage, childbearing, and household duties, her education was minimal. She was not necessarily her husband's friend, confidante, or lover—males and courtesans could fulfill these roles. A Chinese woman was primarily her husband's source of sons. They were the reason for her marriage—indeed, for her sex. As a result, the ideal Chinese woman was retiring, silent, and fertile. Custom severely curtailed her freedoms, but never more cruelly than through foot binding. Mary Daly recently described this custom in graphic terms: "The Chinese ritual of footbinding was a thousand-year-old horror show in which women were grotesquely crippled from very early childhood. As Andrea Dworkin so vividly demonstrates, the hideous three-inch-long 'lotus' hooks—which in reality were odiferous, useless stumps—were the means by which the Chinese patriarchs saw to it that their girls and women would never 'run around.' "[40] However, there is anthropological evidence that many Chinese women overcame their submissive role by cleverly manipulating gossip so that abusive husbands or mothers-in-law would lose face.[41] Still, until the Communist takeover, women had no place in the political system and did very well if they merely outwitted it.

The Taoists were kinder to women and to the socially downtrodden generally. They were responsible for curtailing the murder of female infants by exposure, and their more positive regard for female symbols as examples of how the *Tao* worked upgraded femininity.[42] This was not an unmixed blessing, since it involved the "strength" of the one who was submissive and the manipulative power of the one who got herself mounted. Still, by bestowing feminine or maternal attributes on the *Tao* itself, the Taoists made femininity intrinsic to ultimate reality.[43]

The Buddhist sangha also improved the lot of women. It offered an alternative to early marriage and the strict confinement of the woman's family role. In the sangha a woman did not have full control of her life, but she did often have more peer support and female friendship than she could have in the outside world. In fact, Confucian traditionalists hated Buddhist nuns for their influence on other women. By telling women there were alternatives to wifely subjection, the nuns supposedly sowed seeds of discontent.

THE COMMUNIST ERA

For more than two millennia, the ideas and beliefs that we have described prevailed in China with amazing stability and consistency. Despite new dynasties, wars, changing artistic styles, and even dramatic new religions such as Buddhism and Christianity, the general culture perdured. In the family, the government bureaucracy, and the villages, the folk/Confucian tradition was especially solid.

However, that changed in the early twentieth century. From without, Western science and Western sociopolitical thought dealt it heavy blows; from within, the decay of the imperial government led to the birth of the Republic in 1912. Belatedly, China entered the modern world. In the twentieth century, its ancient culture showed cracks and strains everywhere. As a result, Chinese religious traditions, especially Confucianism, came under strong attack. Identified with the old culture, they seemed out of place in the modern world. Since the "cultural renaissance" of 1917, China has tried to cast off its Confucian shackles; since the Communist takeover of 1949, China has espoused a program of ongoing revolution.[44]

The paramount figure in this program, of course, was Mao Tse-tung. Mao was born in 1893 in Hunan (a south-central province) of a "middle" peasant family (that is, not one of abject poverty). His father had little culture or education, and his mother was a devout Buddhist. Mao himself received a traditional primary school education, whose core was memorizing the Confucian classics. (As a result, he developed a profound distaste for Confucius.) He had to leave school when he was thirteen to work the land, but prompted by his desire for more education, he ran away and enrolled in a modern high school. There he first encountered Western authors who challenged traditional Chinese culture.

Slowly Mao adopted a more positive program as a result of increased engagement with the developing Chinese Communist party, increased knowledge of developments in Russia, and then years as a guerrilla soldier. Before long, Mao was a convert to Marxism-Leninism. He joined the Chinese Communist party in 1921, took part in the Communist collaboration with Chiang Kai-shek's Kuomintang party until 1926, and then led Communist forces that opposed Chiang. By 1935 Mao was in charge of the Communist party and engaged in what became his legendary "long march." Through World War II the Communists and the Kuomintang collaborated uneasily against the Japanese; after the war the final conflict with Chiang led to the Communist takeover in 1949. Throughout this period Mao pursued the twofold career of military general and political theoretician. While gaining power he collaborated with the Russians, but he eventually decided that China had to go its own way. The result was a massive experiment in agrarian reform, enfranchising the lower classes, and trying to control economics by Marxist-Leninist and Maoist dogma.

The reason for this brief biographical sketch of Mao is that he was the most important figure in China's break with tradition and plunge into modernity. Influenced by the Confucian classics and Buddhism, he nevertheless repudiated them both. On the surface at least, Maoism took shape as a secular humanism—a system that referred to nothing more absolute than "the people." Some of its doctrines and programs dramatically changed the life of the people. The women's movement, for instance, and the related changes in the marriage law raised an entire segment of the population from subjection to near equality.[45] By stressing agricultural production, local health care, and "cellular" local government, Chinese Communism has become an even more grandiose socialist experiment than the Soviet.

As part of the program instituting these changes, Mao's party denounced religion. Instead of gods and sacrifices, it offered self-reliance, hard work, and the mystique that the people united are invincible. Temples became government property, religious professionals were persecuted, and religious literature was derided or proscribed. The party likewise attacked the Confucian classics, virtues, and traditions. Throughout, its goal was to destroy the old class society and make a new people with one will and one future.

However, as one might expect, religion and tradition died harder than the Communists had hoped. In the rural regions, peasant traditions continued to have great influence. Among the intellectuals, conforming to the party line resulted in rather wooden, if not second-class, philosophy, science, and art.

Since the death of Mao Tse-tung, China has opened to the West. The "four modernizations" (in industry, science and technology, agriculture, and military affairs) urged by Mao's successors aimed at bringing China into the modern world. "To 'handle the problem of religion' correctly, the regime has recently convened 2 major study conferences: the China Atheistic Seminar (Nanking, December, 1978) calling for scholarly research on atheism, and the National Planning Conference on Religious Studies (Kunning, February, 1979) calling for scholarly research on religions from the Marxist standpoint. On 15 March 1979, the regime promulgated a new policy statement entitled 'Religion and Superstition,' re-establishing the pre-1966 religious policy as 'correct.' The Religions Affairs Bureau in Peking formally resumed operation the next day. Open persecution of believers is now expected to decline, but authentic legal toleration remains unlikely."[46]

Before 1966 the policy, expressed in article 88 of the Constitution of 1954, had been that the people of the People's Republic enjoy freedom of religious belief. During the Cultural Revolution of 1966–69 the policy was to promote atheism. The Constitution of 1975 stipulated in article 28 that citizens have the freedom to practice a religion, and the freedom not to practice a religion and to propagate atheism. In mid-1980 the demographic results of these policies were estimated as follows: nonreligious Chinese, 527 million people or 59 percent of the population; folk-religionists, 179 million people or 20 percent of the population; atheists, 107 million people or 12 percent of the population; Buddhists, 53 million people or 6 percent of the population; Muslims, 21 million people or 2.4 percent of the population; Christians, 1.8 million people or 0.2 percent of the population.[47]

NOTES

1. Karl Jaspers, *The Origin and Goal of History* (New Haven, Conn.: Yale University Press, 1953), p. 2.

2. Arthur Waley, trans., *Monkey* (New York: Grove Press, 1958).

3. Lawrence G. Thompson, *The Chinese Religion: An Introduction*, 2nd ed. (Encino, Calif.: Dickenson, 1975), pp. 3–15; Joseph Needham, *Science and Civ-*

ilisation in China, vol. 2 (Cambridge: University Press, 1969), pp. 216–345.

4. David N. Keightley, "The Religious Commitment: Shang Theology and the Genesis of Chinese Political Culture," *HR*, 1978, *17*(3–4):213.

5. Hans Steininger, "The Religions of China," in *Historia Religionum, II*, ed. C. J. Bleeker and G. Widengren (Leiden: E. J. Brill, 1971), pp. 479–482.

6. *Chuang Tzu*, sec. 6; see Burton Watson, trans., *Chuang Tzu: Basic Writings* (New York: Columbia University Press, 1964), pp. 76, 81.

7. Thompson, *Chinese Religion: An Introduction*, 3rd ed. (Belmont, Calif.: Wadsworth, 1979), pp. 22–24; Needham, *Science and Civilisation*, pp. 354–363.

8. Eliade, however, stresses the Chinese shaman's magical flight. See Mircea Eliade, *Shamanism* (Princeton, N.J.: Princeton University Press, 1972), pp. 448–457.

9. On the ritualistic side of early Chinese shamanism, see Jordan Paper, "The Meaning of the 'T'ao-T'ieh,'" *HR*, 1978, *18*(1):18–41.

10. Anna Seidel, "Buying One's Way to Heaven," *HR*, 1978, *17*(3–4):419–431.

11. Donald W. Treadgold, *The West in Russia and China*, vol. 2 (Cambridge: University Press, 1973), pp. 20–26.

12. Arthur Waley, trans., *The Analects of Confucius* (New York: Vintage, 1938), pp. 27–29.

13. Laurence G. Thompson, ed., *The Chinese Way in Religion* (Encino, Calif.: Dickinson, 1973), pp. 139–153.

14. Wing-Tsit Chan, *A Source Book in Chinese Philosophy* (Princeton, N.J.: Princeton University Press, 1963), pp. 84–94.

15. W.A.C.H. Dobson, trans., *Mencius* (Toronto: University of Toronto Press, 1963), p. 131.

16. Lee H. Yearley, "Mencius on Human Nature," *JAAR*, 1975, *43*:185–198.

17. See Eric Voegelin, *Order and History*, vol. 4 (Baton Rouge: Louisiana State University Press, 1974), pp. 272–299.

18. On this period, see Werner Eichhorn, *Chinese Civilization* (New York: Praeger, 1969), pp. 43–85; H. G. Creel, *The Birth of China* (New York: Reynal and Hitchcock, 1937), pp. 219–380.

19. A. C. Graham, "Confucianism," in *The Concise Encyclopedia of Living Faiths*, ed. R. C. Zaehner (Boston: Beacon Press, 1967), p. 370.

20. Thaddeus Chieh Hang T'ui, "*Jen* Experience and *Jen* Philosophy," *JAAR*, 1974, *42*:53–65.

21. H. G. Creel, *What is Taoism?* (Chicago: University of Chicago Press, 1970), pp. 37–47.

22. Thomas Merton, *The Way of Chuang Tzu* (New York: New Directions, 1968).

23. Arthur Waley, trans., *The Way and Its Power* (New York: Grove Press, 1958).

24. Waley stresses the mystical; Wing-Tsit Chan's *The Way of Lao Tzu* (Indianapolis, Ind.: Bobbs-Merrill, 1963) stresses the pragmatic.

25. Denise Lardner Carmody, "Taoist Reflections on Feminism," *Religion in Life,* 1977, *44*(2):234–244.

26. Holmes Welch, *Taoism: The Parting of the Way* (Boston: Beacon Press, 1966), pp. 35–49.

27. For a sketch of a utopia that is Taoist in spirit if not in origin, see Ernest Callenbach, *Ecotopia* (New York: Bantam, 1977).

28. Current scholarly opinion, however, associates religious Taoism with preaxial religion. See *Encyclopaedia Britannica* 15th ed., s.v. "Taoism," "Taoism, History of"; N. Sivin, "On the Word 'Taoist' as a Source of Perplexity," *HR*, 1978, *17*(3–4):303–330.

29. Werner Eichhorn, "Taoism," in *The Concise Encyclopedia of Living Faiths*, ed. R. C. Zaehner (Boston: Beacon Press, 1967), pp. 389–391; Welch, *Taoism*, pp. 151–158.

30. Welch, *Taoism*, pp. 130–135; K'uan Yu, *Taoist Yoga* (New York: Samuel Weiser, 1973).

31. Kristofer Schipper, "The Taoist Body," *HR*, 1978, *17*(3–4):355–386.

32. Edward H. Schafer, "The Jade Woman of Greatest Mystery," *HR*, 1978, *17*(3–4):393–394.

33. Chang Chung-yuan, *Creativity and Taoism* (New York: Harper Colophon, 1970), pp. 169–238; Albert C. Moore, *Iconography of Religions* (Philadelphia: Fortress, 1977), pp. 170–180; Raymond Dawson, *The Chinese Experience* (New York: Scribner's, 1978), pp. 199–284.

34. For overviews, see R. H. Robinson, "Buddhism: In China and Japan," in *The Concise Encyclopedia of Living Faiths*, ed. R. C. Zaehner (Boston: Beacon Press, 1967), pp. 321–344; C. Wei-hsun Fu, "Mahayana Buddhism (China)," in *Historical Atlas of the Religions of the World*, ed. I. al Faruqi and D. Sopher

(New York: Macmillan, 1974), pp. 185–194. Space forbids consideration of the history of Buddhism in the many other Asian lands that it influenced. For treatments on this subject, see Charles S. Prebish, ed., *Buddhism: A Modern Perspective* (University Park: Pennsylvania State University Press, 1975). On contemporary issues, see Heinrich Dumoulin, ed., *Buddhism in the Modern World* (New York: Macmillan, 1976).

35. On Buddhist beginnings in China, see Arthur F. Wright, *Buddhism in Chinese History* (Stanford, Calif.: Stanford University Press, 1959), pp. 21–41. Also Kenneth K. S. Ch'en, "The Role of Buddhist Monasteries in T'ang Society," *HR*, 1976, *35*(3):209–230.

36. Dumoulin, *History of Zen Buddhism*, p. 88; P. Yampolsky, *The Platform Sutra of the Sixth Patriarch* (New York: Columbia University Press, 1967).

37. Beatrice Lane Suzuki, *Mahayana Buddhism* (New York: Macmillan, 1969), pp. 63–65; T. O. Ling, *A Dictionary of Buddhism* (New York: Scribner's, 1972), pp. 15–16.

38. C. K. Yang, *Religion in Chinese Society* (Berkeley: University of California Press, 1970), pp. 265–272.

39. Vern L. Bullough, *The Subordinate Sex* (Balitmore: Penguin, 1974), p. 249.

40. Mary Daly, *Gyn/Ecology* (Boston: Beacon Press, 1979), chap. 4. The reference to Dworkin is to her *Woman Hating* (New York: Dutton, 1974), p. 103.

41. Magery Wolf, "Chinese Women: Old Skills in a New Context," in *Woman, Culture, and Society*, ed. M. Z. Rosaldo and L. Lamphere (Stanford, Calif.: Stanford University Press, 1974), pp. 157–172.

42. Denise Lardner Carmody, *Women and World Religions* (Nashville: Abingdon, 1979), pp. 66–72.

43. Ellen Marie Chen, "Tao as the Great Mother and the Influence of Motherly Love in the Shaping of Chinese Philosophy," *HR*, 1974, *14*(1):51–63.

44. See Thompson, *Chinese Way*, pp. 231–241; Donald E. MacInnes, *Religious Policy and Practice in Communist China* (New York: Macmillan, 1972). See also Yang, *Religion in Chinese Society*, pp. 341–404.

45. Elisabeth Croll, ed., *The Women's Movement in China* (London: Anglo-Chinese Educational Institute, 1974).

46. *World Christian Encyclopedia*, ed. David B. Barrett (New York: Oxford University Press, 1982), p. 234.

47. Ibid., p. 231. Figures have been rounded.

8

Japanese Religion

THE ANCIENT-FORMATIVE PERIOD

According to ethnologists, the people we now call the Japanese perhaps are a mixture of an indigenous people (the Ainu) and peoples from the Asiatic mainland and the southern islands. This mixture is one clue to the composite character of Japanese religion as well as to the general tolerance that has historically marked Japanese culture. The native religion goes back to the Japanese prehistoric period, which lasted until the early centuries of the Common Era. Clay figurines that archeologists have excavated from this earliest Jomon period indicate a special concern with fertility.[1] As the hunting and gathering culture of the earliest period gave way to agriculture and village settlement, religious practices came to focus on agricultural festivals, revering the dead, and honoring the leaders of the ruling clans. According to the primitive mythology, which existed long before the written versions that date from the eighth century, such leaders were descendants of the deity—once again a version of sacred kingship.

However, the mythology and cult surrounding the ruling family were but part of the earliest Japanese religion. Research suggests that in the villages outside the leading families' influence, people probably conceived of a world similar to that of Siberian shamanists. The world has three layers. The middle is the realm of humans, where we have a measure of control, but the realms above and below, which spirit beings control, are far larger. The kami dwell in the high plain of heaven and are the objects of cultic worship; the spirits of the dead live below, condemned to a filthy region called Yomi.[2] (In some versions, the dead go to a land beyond the sea.) Apparently Yomi was es-

pecially important for the aristocrats' cult, which suggests not only a connection between folk and imperial religion but also indicates why Shinto came to stress ritual purification, especially from polluting contacts with the dead.

The Kami

The kami represented the sacred power involved in the principal concerns of prehistoric Japanese religion (kingship, burial of the dead, and ritual purification).[3] They were rather shadowy figures or spiritual forces who were wiser and more powerful than humans. From time to time, kami would descend to earth, especially if a human called them down and helped them assume a shape (in their own world the kami were shapeless). They were called down by means of *yorishiro*—tall, thin objects that attracted the kami. Pine trees and elongated rocks were typical *yorishiro*, and they suggest that the kami had phallic connotations. To a lesser extent, rocks of female shape also attracted the kami, and relics from the great tombs of the third and fourth centuries—a profusion of mirrors, swords, and curbed jewels—suggest that these artifacts also drew the kami. (Such objects became part of the imperial regalia.)

Because the kami held key information about human destiny, it was important to call them down into human consciousness. That occurred through the kami's possession of shamans or mediums. Most of the early shamans (*miko*) were women, and they functioned in both the aristocratic and the popular cults. Ichiro Hori has shown that female shamans persisted throughout Japanese history.[4] The *miko* were quite important to society. They tended to band together and travel a circuit of villages, primarily to act as mediums for contact with the dead but also to serve as diviners and oracles. They also ministered to spiritual and physical ills, which popular culture largely attributed to malign spirits. As a result, the *miko* developed both a poetic and a pharmacological lore. In composing songs and dances to accompany their ministrations, they contributed a great deal to the formation of traditional Japanese dance, theater, balladry, and puppetry.

Essentially, the kami were the forces of nature. They impressed the Japanese ancient mind, as they impressed the ancient mind elsewhere, by their striking power. Sensitive individuals could contact them, but the kami remained rather wild and unpredictable. Later, Shinto shrines stressed natural groves of tall trees and founders of religious cults were often possessed by spirits. As the early mythology shows, however, the kami remained in charge.

As the eighth-century chronicles, the *Kojiki* and *Nihon-shoki*, have preserved it, Japanese mythology adapted to Chinese influences early on. For example, redactors regularly changed the Japanese sacred number 8 to the Chinese sacred number 9,[5] and they were influenced by the Chinese cosmogonic myths. The result was a creation account in which the world began as a fusion of heaven and earth in an unformed, egg-shaped mass that contained all the forces of life. Gradually the purer parts separated and ascended to heaven, while the grosser portions descended and became the earth.

Shinto Mythology

Chinese influence disappears when the chronicles come to the myths of the kami's origin and to the related question of how the Japanese islands came to be. The first kami god was a lump that formed between heaven and earth; he established the first land. Six generations later, the divine creator couple, Izanagi and Izanami, arose by spontaneous generation. They married and produced the creations that followed.

For instance, heaven commanded Izanagi and Izanami to solidify the earth, which hitherto had been only a mass of brine. Standing on a bridge between heaven and the briny mass, they lowered a jeweled spear and churned the brine. When they lifted the spear, drops fell, solidified, and became the first island. The couple descended to this island, erected a heavenly pillar (the typical shamanistic connector to heaven), and proceeded to procreate.

In tortuous logic, the myth describes the fate of the first two. Izanami died giving birth to fire, and Izanagi followed her to the underworld. Izanagi then produced many deities in an effort to purify himself of the pollution of the underworld. By washing his left eye he produced the sun-goddess Amaterasu, and by washing his right eye he produced the moon-god. When he washed his nose he produced the wind-god Susanoo. In this story of descent to the underworld and divine creation, scholars see an expression of the aboriginal Japanese rites of purification and fears of death. The sun-goddess, who became the supreme being of the Yamato clan, a powerful Japanese family, and the focus of the clan's cultric center at Ise, presided over the land of fertility and life. Opposing her was the domain of darkness and death. Rituals were performed to keep darkness and death from afflicting sunny fertility—harvests, human procreation, and so on. As Izanagi purified himself of death by plunging into the sea, the Japanese throughout their history have used salt as a prophylactic. People will scatter it around the house after a funeral, place it at the edge of a well, set a little cake of it by a door jamb, and even scatter it before the bulging sumo wrestler as he advances toward his opponent.[6]

In subsequent myths, Amatersau and Susanoo have numerous adventures arising from the antagonism between the life-giving sun and the withering wind. These figures also demonstrate the trickster and noble sides of natural divinity. Susanoo, the trickster, committed "heavenly offenses" that later became a focus of ritual purification. He broke the irrigation channels for the imperial rice field that Amaterasu had set up; he flayed a piebald colt and flung it into the imperial hall; and, worst of all, he excreted on the goddess's imperial throne. Unaware, she "went straight there and took her seat. Accordingly, the Sun Goddess drew herself up and was sickened."[7] These offenses reflect practical problems of an agricultural society (respecting others' fields), cultic problems (a sacrificial colt was probably supposed to be of a single color and not be flayed), and speculation on the tension between divine forces of nature.

From these and other materials in the earliest chronicles, it is clear that the ancient-formative period of Japanese history centered on natural forces, some of which were anthropomorphized. In the background were the kami, whom we may consider as foci of divine power. Anything striking or powerful could be a kami. To relate themselves to the natural world, the early Japanese told stories of their love for their beautiful islands (worthy of being the center of creation) and of the divine descent of their rulers. The fact that Amaterasu is a sun-goddess suggests an early matriarchy, as does the fact that kingship only came with the

Taika reforms of 645 C.E. Shinto maintained the divinity of the emperor until the mid-twentieth century, when the victorious allies forced the emperor to renounce his claims.

BUDDHISM

Buddhism infiltrated Japan by way of Korea during the second half of the sixth century C.E. It first appealed to members of the royal court as a possible source of blessing and good fortune. Also, it carried overtones of Chinese culture, which had great prestige. The Japanese rulers, in the midst of trying to solidify their country, thought of the new religion as a possible means, along with Confucian ethics, for unifying social life. So, during the seventh century, emperors built shrines and monasteries as part of the state apparatus. In the eighth century, when the capital was at Nara, the Hua-yen (called Kegon in Japan) school established itself and began to exert great influence. The government ideologues expediently equated the emperor with the Hua-yen Buddha Vairocana, and they made the Hua-yen realm of "dharmas not impeding one another"[8] a model for Japanese society. Kegon has survived in Japan to the present day, and it now has about 500 clergy and 125 temples.

At Nara, Buddhism had considerable influence on the arts and crafts, but when the imperial seat moved to Kyoto, it had even more. In the early ninth century, under the monk Saicho, Mount Hiei became an immensely successful center of T'ien-t'ai (Japanese "Tendai"). In its heyday this center had more than 3,000 buildings and 30,000 monks.[9] Also in the ninth century the religious genius Kobo Daishi established a school (Shingon) that eventually overtook Tendai in popularity. It was a form of Tantrism that focused on Vairocana as the cosmic Buddha, and it won great favor because of its colorful rituals and Kobo Daishi's political flair.[10] Buddhism of the Heian period (794–1185) finally grew rather corrupt, however, because of the collusion between the monks and the ruling families. When power passed to the military and the court moved to Kamakura, the time was ripe for more popular and native forms of Japanese Buddhism.

Kamakura Buddhism[11]

In many scholars' opinion, the rise of the Pure Land, Nichiren, and Zen Buddhist sects during the Kamakura dynasty (1185–1333) produced one of Japan's most distinctive religious achievements. Pure Land Buddhism, which focused on Amida, the bodhisattva of light, became the most influential form of devotional Buddhism. It was popularized by evangelists such as Ippen (1239–1289) who encouraged songs and dances in honor of Amida. Ippen taught that devotion to Amida and the holy realm where Amida presided was "the timely teaching" suitable for a degenerate age. By practicing the *nembutsu* or recitation of "homage to Amida Buddha," followers could gain great merit or even full salvation (entry to the Pure Land). This prescription was simple, practicable, and available to all. It did not require deep philosophy or meditation, simply faith. The laity found Ippen's message very appealing.

As one of Ippen's devotional works makes clear, he encouraged followers of Pure Land with a steady stream of moralistic advice. Verse after verse, the work tells devotees to adore the glory of God, not ignore the Buddha's virtue, revere the three jewels, not forget the power of faith, devoutly practice the *nembutsu*, forget other religious practices, trust the law of love, not denounce the creeds of other people, promote a sense of equality, and avoid discriminatory feelings. They were to awaken a sense of compassion, be mindful of the sufferings of other people, cultivate amiability, not display an angry countenance, preserve a humble manner, and not arouse a spirit of arrogance. It is as though Ippen found all the traits of a good character to flow from faith in Amida. Were the faithful to yearn for the bliss of the Pure Land, and not forget the tortures of hell, they would lead wonderfully meritorious lives.

Honen (1133–1212) was more insistent on the singularity of the *nembutsu*, in effect separating Pure Land Buddhism from other sects and making the *nembutsu* the be-all and end-all of the middle way. Honen personally suffered persecution for his position and for his success in winning converts. In a letter written to the wife of the ex-regent Tsukinowa, Honen described the essentials that a convert to Pure Land would have to embrace. The gist of his exposition is that the *nembutsu* is the best way to rebirth in the Pure Land, because it is the discipline described in Amida's own vow to become a bodhisattva and open salvation to all creatures. Indeed, the earthly Buddha Sakyamuni entrusted the *nembutsu* to his disciple Ananda, that Ananda might make it Sakyamuni's main bequest to posterity. Finally, all the Buddhas of the six quarters of the world endorse the *nembutsu*. So while other religious practices, such as meditations or ritual ceremonies, have considerable value, only the *nembutsu* has the highest stamp of authority. What does it matter than some critics claim the *nembutsu* is too easy, fit only for simpletons? Amida and Sakyamuni have endorsed it; would one rather stand with earthly critics or heavenly masters?

Shinran (1173–1262), Honen's most successful disciple, came to feel that the successful propagation of the *nembutsu* depended on the clergy's closer identification with the laity. He therefore urged breaking with the tradition of clerical celibacy and he himself took a wife. So strong was his conviction that salvation depends purely on the grace of Amida that he rejected practices such as monastic vows and disciplines as possible impediments to genuine faith. Whereas some conservative Pure Land preachers urged a continuous recitation of the *nembutsu*, Shinran thought that a single invocation of Amida Buddha, if filled with loving faith, would suffice for salvation. Shinran's hymns ring with this loving faith: Amida endlessly sends forth his pure, joyous, wise, universal light. It is brighter than the sun and the moon, illumining numberless worlds. Sakyamuni came into the world only to reveal Amida's vow and the primacy of faith in Amida's grace. By faith even the worst of sinners will come to Amida's mercy, as surely as all mountain water finally comes to the ocean. Eventually, Amida's faith in the disciple will make things right.

Pure Land has the effect of providing Japan a very appealing form of Buddhist devotionalism. The mercy of Amida rang true to the Japanese tendency to seek a God who shows signs of maternal kindness. Nichiren (1222–1282) agreed with the Pure Land Buddhists that simple devotional forms like the *nembutsu* were desirable, but he found their stress on Amida unwarranted. For Nichiren, the be-all and end-all of Buddhist faith was the Lotus Sutra. He considered this scripture the final teaching of Sakyamuni, in which his three bodies (historical, doctrinal, and blissful) came together in a marvelous unity. Other schools had overlooked one or more of these three aspects, slighting either the historical life of the Buddha, his existence as the dharma giving all reality its true form, or his existence as the perfection of salvation (the center of the abode of the blessed). Devotion to the Lotus Sutra assured that a balance would be restored. Thus Nichiren urged the practice of chanting homage to the Lotus Sutra. In rather uncompassionate style, he called Amida Buddhism a hell and Zen a devil. Today there are many subsects of Nichiren Buddhism that together make this school second only to Pure Land in popularity.

Two of the great pioneers who launched Ch'an on its illustrious career in Japan were Eisai (1141–1215) and Dogen (1200–1253). Eisai studied Ch'an in China and then established himself in Kamakura, the new center of Japanese political power. His teaching won special favor among the hardy warlords who were coming to dominate Japan, and from his time Zen and the samurai code had close bonds. For Eisai mind was greater even than heaven. Buddhism, which concentrated on the mind, had known great success in India and China. Among the different Buddhist schools, the one founded by Bodhidharma especially riveted onto mastering the mind. From Bodhidharma's missionary ventures in China, Zen had made its way to Korea and Japan. Now it was time for Japan to capitalize on Zen's great potential.

By studying Zen, one could find the key to all forms of Buddhism. By practicing Zen, one could bring one's life to fulfillment in enlightenment. To outer appearances, Zen favored discipline over doctrine. Inwardly, however, it brought the highest wisdom, that of enlightenment itself. Eisai was able to convince some of the Hojo regents and Kamakura shoguns to become patrons of Zen, and so he planted it solidly in Japan.

If Eisai proved to be a good politican, able to adapt to the new Kamakura times and to benefit from them, Dogen proved to be the sort of rugged, uncompromising character Zen needed to deepen its Japanese roots and gain spiritual independence. After studying at various Japanese Buddhist centers without satisfaction, he met Eisai and resolved to follow in his footsteps and visit China. After some frustration in China, Dogen finally gained enlightenment when he heard a Zen master speak of "dropping both mind and spirit" (dropping dualism). Returning to Japan, he resisted the official pressures to mingle various forms of Buddhism and would only teach Zen. Nonetheless, within Zen circles Dogen was quite flexible, teaching, for example, that study of the Buddhist scriptures (scholarship) was not incompatible with a person-to-person transmission of the truth (the guru tradition).

Within Zen circles, Dogen also distinguished himself for his worries about the use of koans. The Rinzai school of Ch'an that Eisai had introduced to Japan stressed the use of these enigmatic sayings as a great help to sudden enlightenment. In Dogen's opinion, the Chinese Soto school was more balanced and less self-assertive. He therefore strove to establish Soto in Japan, teaching a Zen that did not concentrate wholly on the mind but rather on the total personality. This led him to a practice of simple meditation *(zazen)* that ideally proceeded without any thought of attaining enlightenment and without any specific problem in mind. Disciplining the body as well as the mind, Dogen aimed at a gradual, lifelong process of realization.

In some of his "conversations," Dogen movingly expressed his great faith in the power of Zen Buddhism. Quoting Eisai, he spoke of a monk's food and clothing as gifts from heaven. The teacher is but an intermediary between the pupil and heaven. Heaven gives each of us what we need for our allotted life span, and we should not make a fuss over these things. The student should direct his gratitude to heaven, much more than to his master, opening himself to all of heaven's gifts. The greatest of heaven's gifts is truth, and it is the good fortune of monks to be able to pursue truth full time. The difficulties monks or any of us face in securing life's practical necessities should not obscure this central point. Such difficulties should merely make us serious, willing to sacrifice for being able to pursue the truth. If monks lived utterly leisurely lives under full patronage, they likely would grow lazy and selfish. If, on the contrary, they live in poverty, begging for their food or working the land, they likely will grow hardy in spirit.

Dogen's compassion was equal to his faith, for he also liked to tell his disciples the story of Eisai's decision to give some copper to a destitute man who had come to the monastery begging help for his wife and children. The copper had been destined to make a halo for a statue of the Buddha. When some of Eisai's monks complained that he had forgotten this lofty destination, Eisai agreed that ideally the copper would have gone into a halo for the Buddha's statue. But Buddha's own example of spending himself for the sake of needy human beings had urged Eisai to be generous, sacrificing some of the monastery's goods for the lives of fellow human beings.

Both Pure Land and Zen made their great impressions on Japanese culture largely in terms of the goodness they encouraged. From its deep faith in the goodness of Amida Buddha, Pure Land taught the Japanese people Shinran's concern for sinners, outcastes, men and women tending to doubt their own worth. From its deep experiences of self-realization, Zen matured a gratitude for all of creation that easily became a great compassion for all creatures suffering pain. Situating themselves within the common Buddhist tradition, the Kamakura schools suggested that faith and insight, devotion and practical charity, are not antagonistic but complementary. If one goes deeply enough into faith, one reaches a gratitude that is almost identical with the gratitude that rushes forth in enlightenment. If one goes deeply enough into meditational insight, one reaches a gratitude that is almost identical with the wholehearted faith that Amida Buddha is utterly trustworthy and good. The legacy of the Kamakura schools, finally, was their depth. Shinran and Dogen were such heroes of the spiritual life that all subsequent Japanese aspirants to sanctity or wisdom saw in them clear models of the way.

Francis Cook has summarized the Japanese innovations of traditional Buddhism.[12] First, the Japanese tended not to adhere to traditional codes of conduct, whether for laity *(sila)* or for monks *(vinaya)*. Eventually, priests were able to marry, eating meat and drinking alcoholic beverages were allowed, and monks could have more than a spare robe. Second, Japanese Buddhism tended to move religious activity from the temple to the home. As a result, emphasis was shifted to the laity, and monks or priests were relegated to the care of temples and the performance of ceremonies (especially funerals). Caring for temples frequently came to be a family affair, as fathers passed a priesthood on to their sons.

Third, after the Kamakura period several sects promulgated the notion that one practice summarized Buddhism. In that they were to a degree reacting against the syncretism of the Shingon and Tendai sects. As we have seen, Honen made chanting Amida's name (a practice known as *nembutsu*) the only way to be reborn in the Pure Land. Dogen thought that meditative sitting summarized everything essential. Nichiren, finally, insisted that chanting "homage to the Sutra of the Lotus of the True Law" was the way to identify with the Buddha.

Buddhism sometimes eclipsed Shinto, but the native tradition always lay ready to reassert itself. Whenever there was a stimulus to depreciate foreign influences and exalt native ones, Shinto quickly bounced back. Also, Shinto only defined itself in the seventh century, when Buddhism, Confucianism, and Taoism started to predominate. In crystallizing, it acquired Buddhist philosophy, Confucian ethics, and Taoist naturalism. The result was a nature-oriented worship with special emphasis on averting pollution. Shinto domesticated Buddhism as a religion of kami-bodhisattvas, and it topped Confucian social thought with the emperor's divine right.

THE MEDIEVAL-ELABORATIVE PERIOD

Earhart defines the medieval-elaborative period of Japanese history as the years 794 through 1600.[13] This stretches from the Heian era, when the court at Kyoto had a glorious culture, though the Kamakura and Muromachi eras, and ends with the fall of the Momoyama dynasty. During the Heian era, court life developed a sophisticated aesthetic sense; by the Kamakura era the warrior estates had assumed power and made the emperor merely a puppet. As noted below, the Buddhist sects of Shingon and Tendai, which dominated the Heian era, were esoteric, comprehensive systems that tried to accommodate a variety of interests. Though they later lost influence to Zen and Pure Land, they began Buddhism's penetration of the lower classes. For its own part, Shinto kept pace with Buddhism by organizing itself.

In the Kamakura period (1185–1333), Buddhism responded to the increasing importance of the warrior class. Zen especially became a central part of the warrior's discipline, furnishing spiritual resources for his ideal of fearlessness and spontaneous action. Among the common people, devotional Buddhism—Pure Land and Nichiren—gained favor. They affected the final domestication of Buddhism, making it serve the lower classes in their search for prosperity and a good afterlife.

Shinto

While Japan worked its changes on Buddhism, Shinto was liberally borrowing from the foreign traditions. Since it represented the oldest native traditions, the result was a great enrichment, or at least a great complication, of what constituted Shinto. From Buddhism, Shintoists developed the notion that the kami were traces of the original substances of particular Buddhas and bodhisattvas. As a result, Buddhist deities were enshrined by Shintoists (and kami by Buddhists). So thoroughly did Buddhism and Shinto combine that Dengyo Daishi and Kobo Daishi, the founders of Tendai and Shingon, thought it natural to erect shrines to honor the kami of the mountains of their monastic retreats.

From Shingon, Shintoists absorbed certain esoteric practices, such as using mandalas to represent the basic dualities of mind-matter, male-female, and dynamic-static.[14] Because of such dualism, people began to call Shinto "Ryobu," which means "two parts" or "dual." In one of its most dramatic actions, dualistic Shinto gave the Ise shrine an inner and an outer precinct to make two mandalas that would represent the two sides of Amaterasu. She was the sun-goddess of the ancient traditions, but she was also Vairocana, the shining Buddha of Heaven.

Later in the medieval period, a number of Shinto scholars took issue with syncretism.[15] Some of them just wanted to upset the evenhandedness that had developed, so that the kami would predominate over the bodhisattvas or so that Amaterasu would predominate over Vairocana. Others wanted to rid Shinto of its syncretions and return to its original form. The most important of these medieval Shinto reformers were Kitabatake and Yoshida, who worked in the fourteenth

and fifteenth centuries. They drew from writings of Ise priests, who wanted to give Shinto a scripture comparable to that of the Buddhists. Another step in the consolidation of Shinto's position was the organizing of its shrines, which began in the tenth century and continued through to the twentieth. The resulting network provided every clan and village with a shrine to represent its ties with the kami.

Christianity

In the mid-sixteenth century Christianity came to Japan in the person of the charismatic Jesuit missionary Francis Xavier. It flourished for about a century, until the Tokugawa rulers first proscribed it and then bitterly persecuted it. The first Western missionaries made a great impact because Japan was used to religions of salvation. Pure Land Buddhism, for instance, was then popular among the common people. By impressing the local warrior rulers (often by holding out prospects of trade with the West), the Christians gained the right to missionize much of Japan and made some lasting converts. Western artifacts fascinated the Japanese as well, and for a while things Western were the vogue.

However, before the missionaries could completely adapt Christianity to Japanese ways, the shoguns became suspicious that they had political and economic designs. The shogun Ieyasu (1542–1616) killed many who had converted to Christianity, and after his death Christianity's brief chapter in Japanese history came to a bloody close. Shusaku Endo's recent novel about the Christians' persecution, *Silence,*[16] caused a stir among the contemporary Japanese Christian community because of its vivid description of the trials (in faith as well as body) that the missionaries underwent.

At the end of the medieval period of elaboration (around 1600), then, five traditions were interacting. Buddhism brought Japan a profound philosophy that stressed the flux of human experience, the foundation of is-ness, and death. In return, it was revamped to suit Japanese tastes. Confucianism furnished a rationale for the state bureaucracy and for social relationships. It stressed formality and inner control, which especially suited merchants and government officials, and one can see its imprint in the Bushido Code, which prevailed during the Tokugawa period.[17] Taoism most influenced folk religion, while, as we have seen, Shinto developed a rationale for the kami and a strong shrine system. Christianity came to represent foreign intrusion, but since it converted perhaps 500,000 Japanese, it also satisfied a hunger for other ways to salvation. Probably the average person mixed elements from these traditions with folk beliefs to fashion a family-centered religion that would harmonize human beings with the forces—kami, bodhisattvas, and evil spirits—that presided over good fortune and bad.

THE MODERN-REFORMATIVE PERIOD

During the Tokugawa shogunate (military dictatorship), which lasted from 1600 to 1867, Japan experienced peace and stability. The Tokugawa rulers expelled the Christian missionaries and severely limited contacts with the West. The biggest shift in the social structure was the rise of the merchant class, which went hand in hand with the growth of cities.

Regarding religion, the Tokugawa shoguns made sure that all traditions served the state's goals of stability. In the beginning of the seventeenth century those goals had popular support because the preceding dynasties had allowed great civil strife. Buddhists had to submit to being an arm of the state. Neo-Confucianism eclipsed Buddhism in state influence, perhaps because it was less likely to stir thoughts of independence or individualism. Shinto suffered some decline in popular influence but retained a base in folk religion. As well, Shinto generated a clearer rationale for separating from Buddhism.

Finally, during the Tokugawa period the first new religions arose. They were eclectic packagings of the previous, medieval elements, and they drew their success by contrasting favorably with the highly formal, even static, culture that prevailed in the early nineteenth century. The new religions usually sprang from a charismatic leader who furnished a connection with the kami—indeed, whom his or her followers took to be a kami. By personalizing religion and addressing individual faith, the new religions stood out from the dominant formalism and offered something attractively dynamic.

The Bushido Code provides a good summary of the religious and ethical values that formed the Japanese character through the late medieval and early modern period. Bushido was the "way of the warrior," whether he be a samurai (warrior) in fact or only in spirit. For Japanese women, the Bushido concern for honor focused on chastity. Manuals instructed young girls who had been compromised how to commit suicide (with the dagger each girl received when she came of age), including details of how, after plunging in the blade, she should tie her lower limbs together so as to secure modesty even in death. When a pow-

erful lord would not stop his advances, the noble Lady Kesa promised to submit if he would kill her samurai husband first. The lord agreed, and she told him to come to her bedroom after midnight and kill the sleeper with wet hair. Then she got her husband drunk, so that he would sleep soundly, washed her hair, and crept under the covers to await her fate.[18] This was not typical, but it is instructive.

From the close of the Tokugawa period in 1867 to World War II, Japan was in transit to modernity. It abolished the military dictatorship and restored the emperor. It also changed from a largely decentralized feudal society into a modern nation organized from Tokyo. Japan made astonishing strides in education and culture, assimilating Western science and again opening itself to the outside world (at first under duress, due to Admiral Perry and the U.S. gunboats during 1853 and 1854, then voluntarily). Success in two major wars with China and Russia between 1895 and 1905 gave the Japanese great confidence, and the first third of the twentieth century was a time of increasingly strident nationalism.

During this period Buddhism lost its official status as a branch of the government, Shinto was established as the state religion, and Christianity was reintroduced. In addition, more new religions appeared, which, like Buddhism and Shinto, took on nationalistic overtones.

For our interests, the modern period, beginning with the Meiji Restoration (of the emperor) in 1868, is most significant because of the revival of Shinto. This was largely a political operation, designed to glorify the imperial family and to unify the country around its oldest traditions. Edwin Reischauer has described the widespread changes in secular life that the Meiji leaders introduced.[19] Japanese cities were revamped, and Western ideas of individual rights and responsibilities that are part of a modern state were brought in. H. B. Earhart provides documents of the propaganda that Meiji leaders generated to link the nation with religion and reestablish Japan's sense of divine mission.[20] "The Imperial Rescript on Education" (1890),[21] for instance, explicitly linked the imperial throne ("coeval with heaven and earth") with filial piety to make nationalism the supreme personal virtue. To bring their tradition up to date and do what their revered ancestors had done, the modern Japanese had only to be utterly loyal to the emperor.

The New Religions

Since the government was pushing Shinto, the new religions tended to join the nationalistic trend. Tenrikyo and Soka Gakkai both owe as much to Buddhist as to Shinto inspiration, but other new religions found it useful to shelter under the nationalistic umbrella. Tenrikyo sprang from a revelation that its founder, Nakayama Miki, had in 1838.[22] She had been a devout Pure Land Buddhist, but while serving as a medium in a healing ceremony for her son, she felt a kami possess her—the "true, original kami Tenri O no Mikoto" ("God the Parent"). Miki embarked on a mission to spread her good news, healing sick people and promulgating the recitation of "I put my faith in Tenri O no Mikoto." The Tokugawa authorities harassed her somewhat, but in time a large number of followers accepted her as a living kami. Her writings became the Tenrikyo scripture, her songs became its hymns, and her dances shaped its liturgy. Recalling the creation myth of Izanagi and Izanami, she built a shrine "at the center of the world," where the first parents had brought forth the land. The shrine had a square opening in its roof and a tall wooden column—ancient symbolism for the connection to heaven.

Miki's teachings stress joyous living. In the beginning God the Parent made humans for happiness, but we became self-willed and gloomy. By returning to God the Parent and dropping self-concern, we can restore our original joy. The way to return is faith in God the Parent and participation in Tenrikyo worship. Earhart has suggested that Tenrikyo's success comes in part from its return to peasant values.[23] By stressing gratitude for (sacred) creation, social rather than individual good, hard manual work, and the like, this sect has generated great popular enthusiasm. By the end of the nineteenth century, Tenrikyo claimed more than 2 million members, testifying to the power of combining old, shamanistic elements with new organizational forms and liturgies. Tenrikyo even revived the ancient Shinto concern for purification by focusing on an interior cleansing of doubts and untoward desires.

Soka Gakkai derives from Makiguchi Tsunesaburo (1871–1944), who preached a new social ethic based on three virtues: beauty, gain, and goodness.[24] Makiguchi found Nichiren Buddhism attractive, so he worked out his ethics in terms of the Lotus Sutra: Beauty, gain, and goodness came from faith in the Lotus. During World War II the leaders of Soka Gakkai refused the government's request that all religionists support the military effort, arguing that compliance would compromise the truth of the Lotus Sutra (by associating Soka Gakkai with other Buddhist sects and with Shintoists). For this they went to prison. Makiguchi died in prison, but his movement revived after the war through the efforts of Toda Josei. By 1957 Toda had reached his goal of enrolling 750,000 families, largely through his fine organizational abilities and his shrewd use of enthusiastic youths. As well, Soka Gakkai capitalized on the frustration of Buddhists committed to the Lotus Sutra but alienated by the bickering among the various Nichiren groups. In a time of national confusion, Soka Gakkai's absolutism (all other religious options were held to be false) held great appeal. According to Soka Gakkai, commitment to the Lotus Sutra (and to itself) would dissolve all ambiguities.

Recent History

Japan's defeat in World War II produced great national trauma, prompting the success of hundreds of new religions. Culturally, defeat meant a shattering of national pride; religiously, it meant a body blow to state Shinto. The Western conquerors, led by Douglas MacArthur, force-fed the Japanese democracy and the concept of individual liberties. On its own, Japan rebuilt with incredible speed, soon becoming the economic giant of Asia. The new constitution disestablished Shinto and allowed complete individual religious freedom. The older traditions, which people identified with the national self-consciousness of prewar times, were shattered, and the new religions rushed in to fill the void. In the past two decades or so, the older traditions have regrouped, especially Buddhism, but secularism has been a strong trend. Caught up in its technological spurt, Japan has seemingly put aside nationalistic and cultural issues, preferring to let the traumas of the war heal by benign neglect.

Today the Japanese religious picture is quite complicated. The culture is secularistic, at least outwardly, but in the alleyways Buddhism and Christianity struggle to revive themselves. Confucian and Taoist elements remain part of the Japanese psyche, but in rather muted voice. Strangely, perhaps, it is Shinto—the ancient version rather than the state—that is the strongest religious presence. Divinity in nature, which Japanese religion has always stressed, continues in the shrines that connect present times to the aboriginal kami.

This interest in nature is religious in the sense that nature has regularly represented to the Japanese something ultimate. Thus, concern for nature has often been an ultimate concern—a stance before the holy. This stance seldom involved violent beliefs. The major prophetic figures do not tell tales of burning bushes or theologize out of mysteriously parted seas. Rather, the predominant mood has been peaceful.[25] Japanese religion tries to gain access to the core of the personality, where the personality touches nature's flow. It tries, probably semiconsciously, to let the moss and rocks work their influence. These objects can summarize existence, giving messages from mind only. Such Buddhist ideas suggest emptiness—the strangely satisfying "no-thing-ness" that the spirit disgusted with ideas, the spirit more holistically inclined, often finds in open space or the sea.

The religious veneration of nature, or even the religio-aesthetic use of nature for soothing the soul, implies an impersonal ultimacy. Furthermore, it implies that humanity, as well as divinity, is more at one with nature than over or against it. Religion based on nature, in fact, tends to collapse humans and gods into nature's forces or nature's flows. As a result, Japan has not seen the world as created by a transcendent force. Rather, Japan has let nature somewhat suppress knowledge and love of divinity, subordinating them to energy and flow. Human beings have been encouraged not to exploit nature (though recent technological changes qualify this statement). Through most of Japanese history, one would prune or rake nature rather than lay waste to it, at least in part because human beings did not have a biblical writ to fill the earth and subdue it.[26] Rather, they had a call to live with nature. Today we might hear that as a call to be ecological, grateful, and thus graceful.

For many Japanese, the most beautiful views have opened onto exquisite gardens. The Shinto roots of the gardening tradition stressed gnarled old trees and large rocks in places set aside for the kami. When Chinese culture began to shape Japanese tastes, Taoist and Buddhist influences become important. Traditional Chinese gardens sought to reproduce the islands and grottoes of the Taoist immortals or the beauty of the Buddha's Pure Land. Chinese geomancy set many of the stylistic ideals, and harmony between yin and yang forces was a high requirement. Thus a large yang boulder would be counterbalanced by a low yin pool. Waterfalls represented life and bamboo represented strength.

Once again, Zen was the native Japanese development that most directly varied the Chinese model. In the case of gardening, Zen pushed the designs in a more abstract and asymmetrical direction. In the Zen scheme, gardens were not so much places for leisurely strolling as places for meditation. Translating many notions from Sung landscape painting, the Zen gardeners stressed emptiness and the lack of human or emotional touches. So the Zen gardens tended to have no benches or wine cups. Instead of showy flowers they stressed moss or rocks. The Ryoanji or Rock Garden Monastery of Kyoto, built around 1500, epitomizes this abstract style. There are no ponds or streams, only white gravel raked to resemble eddies— phenomenal reality playing on the surface of emptiness.

The tea ceremony was one of several rituals the Japanese developed to beautify each part of daily living. Often it would take place in the teahouse of a shrine garden. Indeed, many Zen Buddhists came to consider the tea ceremony a sort of sacrament, symbolizing the grace, austerity, and concentration that good living requires. While the core of the ceremony was simply making and sipping whipped green tea, the teahouse, the utensils, and the manner of serving all played important parts. Ideally there would be lovely surroundings: a garden of great beauty, flowers, a *suiboku* painting or a scroll of elegant calligraphy. Afficionados paid special attention to the bowl in which the tea was served, and master potters often strove to produce simple, elegant tea vessels. Although the upper classes sometimes embellished the tea ceremony with ostentatious displays, the protocol developed by Sen no Rikyu, the greatest of the tea masters, stressed "poor tea": absolute simplicity and ordinariness.

Flower arrangement *(ikebana)* brought aesthetic refinement home to many Japanese family circles. In a sense, the goal of flower arrangement was to make a miniature garden, and so a miniature, domestic paradise. Like the tea ceremony, flower arrangement became a "way": an avocation both refreshing and disciplining. In flower arrangement the great virtues were simplicity, asymmetry, and form (color was secondary). The preferred forms were understated rather than obvious, subtle rather than bold. The ideal was to hint at a mysterious meaning and suggest old, somewhat formal ways.

Throughout all their arts, the Japanese have tried to express and develop their sense of emptiness, form, the changeableness of human beings, and the primacy of nature. Rarely did a Japanese art form flourish without close ties to religion. In the tea and flower ceremonies, for instance, one is hard pressed to say where art leaves off and religious contemplation begins. A certain blankness signals the touch of Buddhist emptiness. A certain austerity signals the touch of Shinto antiquity, when life was close to nature, unemotional and strong.

Women's Status

It is ironic that a culture that has been considered feminine has been almost oppressively male dominated. Although there are traces of an early matriarchy and strong influences from female shamans and their successors in the new religions, women have regularly occupied a low position in Japanese society. Of course, women's influence in the traditional home and even the modern office is stronger than superficial sociology suggests.[27] Expert in the very refined Japanese tact, wives and mothers have found ways of influence despite their institutionalized powerlessness. Officially, however, Japan accepted Confucian notions of social relationships (no doubt because they fit traditional predilections), so the female was almost always designated as the underling.

The important religious roles played by females in Japanese history should be further discussed. Perhaps their phallic overtones made it fitting that the kami should possess females. Or perhaps shamanism offered the powerless a chance to gain attention and influence. Whatever the reasons, women were the prime contact with divinity in folk Shinto, despite strong menstrual taboos. As well, they were the prime contact with the spirits of the dead and so were central in maintaining the clan. The figurines from the prehistoric Jomon period suggest that women were originally considered awesome because of their power to give birth. The difficulty of the women's liberation movement in contemporary Japan suggests that the powers of women represented by these former roles have long been suppressed.

For reasons of psychological convenience as well as self-interest, the men dominating Japanese society have found it advantageous to place religion and femininity in opposition to warfare and business. As the recourse to nature (retirement) has been in contrast to things official, so the recourse to monasteries, female shamans, and even geishas has been in contrast to workaday life. In part, of course, this contrast links religion with recreation, art, and family life. (In modern Japan a man identifies as much with his job and company as with his family.) Thus, nature, religion, and women are considered surplus commodities and yet especially valuable ones: surplus in that they do not figure much in modern work, but valuable in that work alone does not constitute a complete existence.

Clan Emphasis and Ethics

The modern stress on a man's work, identifying him with his corporation, is the result of the group structure of Japanese business. Consequently, the typical businessman takes much of his recreation with his fellow workers apart from his family. Considered in the con-

text of Japanese religious history, this situation is somewhat anomalous. Earhart, for instance, has gathered documents that testify to the religious significance of family life,[28] showing the sense of clan that has predominated. (In fact, the modern corporation exploits this sense of clan loyalty.)

Moreover, a characteristic of the traditional family was concern with the dead. As in China, ancestor veneration was a significant portion of the average person's religious contacts with ultimate powers. Originally, the Japanese probably believed that the departed continued to hover around the places where they had lived. The Japanese tended to associate their ancestors with kami and bodhisattvas after these figures were introduced by Shinto and Buddhism. Therefore, in its petitions and venerations, the clan reminded itself of its own identity (the function that some sociologists, such as Durkheim, have considered the main rationale for religion) and kept attuned to the natural forces of life and death.

Thus, the family tended to be the locus of daily worship, and the family shrine tended to predominate over the village or national shrine. Still, there was not a sharp division between the family clan and the national clan. The emperor was often considered the head not only of his own line but also of the entire Japanese people; the gods of Shinto mythology were the gods of the collective Japanese group; and national shrines such as Ise were the site of ceremonies performed on behalf of the entire nation.

This historical sense of clan was accompanied by certain ethical assumptions that were immensely influential in shaping the Japanese conscience. The medieval samurai felt that his life belonged to his feudal lord. If he failed his lord, by being defeated or less than fully successful, he was expected to offer to commit ritual suicide—to petition his lord for this "favor," so that he might mend the honor he had violated. In contemporary Japan, the individual worker is supposed to promote the honor of his bosses above all. He is to assume any failures by his group and to attribute any successes to the group's leader. Thus, the boss (or at most the group as a whole) always gets credit for a bright idea or increased productivity. If the worker does not rock the boat, the corporation will take care of all his needs until he dies.

Overall, Japan is not a place where Whitehead's definition of religion (what a person does with his or her solitude) is very helpful.[29] Although standing alone before the Golden Pavilion has shaped for many Japanese a sense of ultimacy,[30] group activities—at home, in war, or at work—have been the crucial factors in developing such a sense.

NOTES

1. Johannes Maringer, "Clay Figurines of the Jomon Period," *HR*, 1974, *14*:128–139.

2. Carmen Blacker, "The Religions of Japan," in *Historia Religionum, II,* ed. C. J. Bleeker and G. Widengren (Leiden: E. J. Brill, 1971), p. 518.

3. H. Byron Earhart, *Japanese Religion: Unity and Diversity*, 2nd ed. (Encino, Calif.: Dickenson, 1974), pp. 11–16.

4. Ichiro Hori, *Folk Religion in Japan* (Chicago: University of Chicago Press, 1968), pp. 181–251. See also Carmen Blacker, *The Catalpa Bow* (London: Allen & Unwin, 1975).

5. G. Bownas, "Shinto," in *The Concise Encyclopedia of Living Faiths*, ed. R. C. Zaehner (Boston: Beacon Press, 1967), p. 349

6. Ibid., p. 357.

7. Ibid.

8. For an introduction to Hua-yen metaphysics, see Francis H. Cook, *Hua-yen Buddhism* (University Park: Pennsylvania State University Press, 1977).

9. Richard J. Robinson and Willard L. Johnson, *The Buddhist Religion* (Encino, Calif.: Dickenson, 1977), p. 175.

10. Francis H. Cook, "Heian, Kamakura, and Tokugawa Periods in Japan," in *Buddhism: A Modern Perspective*, ed. Charles S. Prebish (University Park: Pennsylvania State University Press, 1975), p. 223.

11. The section adapts materials from Ryusaku Tsunoda et al., *Sources of Japanese Tradition*, vol. 1 (New York: Columbia University Press, 1964), pp. 184–260.

12. Francis H. Cook, "Japanese Innovations in Buddhism," in *Buddhism: A Modern Perspective*, ed. Charles S. Prebish (University Park: Pennsylvania State University Press, 1975), pp. 229–233.

13. Earhart, *Japanese Religion*, pp. x–xi.

14. Ibid., p. 73.

15. See Tsunoda et al., *Sources of Japanese Tradition*, pp. 261–276.

16. Shusaku Endo, *Silence* (Rutland, Vt.: Tuttle, 1969).

17. Robert N. Bellah, *Tokugawa Religion* (Boston: Beacon Press, 1970), pp. 90–98.

18. Denise Lardner Carmody, *Women and World Religions* (Nashville: Abingdon, 1979), p. 84.

19. Edwin O. Reischauer, *Japan Past and Present*, 3rd ed. rev. (Tokyo: Tuttle, 1964), pp. 108–141.

20. H. Byron Earhart, ed., *Religion in the Japanese Experience: Sources and Interpretations* (Encino, Calif.: Dickenson, 1974), pp. 201–210; see also Tsunoda et al., *Sources of Japanese Tradition*, vol. 2 (New York: Columbia University Press, 1964), pp. 131–210.

21. Earhart, ed., *Religion in the Japanese Experience*, p. 204.

22. See Blacker, *Catalpa Bow*, pp. 130–132.

23. Earhart, *Japanese Religion*, p. 112.

24. Ibid., pp. 114–117.

25. See Blacker, *Catalpa Bow*, and Hori, *Folk Religion in Japan*, for the shamanistic exceptions to this statement.

26. See Lynn White, Jr., "The Historical Roots of Our Ecological Crisis," in *Ecology and Religion in History*, ed. David and Eileen Spring (New York: Harper Torchbooks, 1974), pp. 15–31. The other articles in this volume suggest the sort of qualifications one would expect in discussing Japanese ecology. See especially Yi-Fu Tuan, "Discrepancies between Environmental Attitude and Behaviour," pp. 91–113.

27. On contemporary professional and business life in Japan, see Ichiro Kawasaki, *Japan Unmasked* (Rutland, Vt.: Tuttle, 1969); Nobutaka Ike, *Japan: The New Superstate* (Stanford, Calif.: Stanford Alumni Association, 1973).

28. Earhart, ed., *Religion in the Japanese Experience*, pp. 145–159.

29. Alfred North Whitehead, *Religion in the Making* (New York: Meridian, 1960), p. 16.

30. Yukio Mishima has brought this lovely Zen temple into recent Japanese religious consciousness. See his *The Temple of the Golden Pavilion* (Rutland, Vt.: Tuttle, 1959).

9

Greek Religion

GREECE

Greece dazzles both world historians and historians of religion with its cultural diversity and splendor. Like classical Egyptian and classical Iranian religious culture, classical Greek religious culture has passed from the scene. Its influence in modern Greece lies under the surface of Eastern Orthodox Christianity, much as classical Egyptian religion lies under present-day Egyptian Islam and classical Zoroastrianism lies under present-day Iranian Islam. It is dead, but not without its influence.

Moreover, the influence of classical Greek religion is active in a sense different from that of its Egyptian or Iranian counterparts. Through the philosophy, science, literature, politics, and art that it nurtured, classical Greece became tutor to the West. For example, it furnished Christianity and Islam with many of their intellectual categories. Insofar as those categories have been developed in modern science and technology, classical Greece has been absolutely instrumental in shaping the present global society.

In his world history, Arnold Toynbee locates the beginnings of Greek culture about the middle of the third millennium B.C.E., when Sumerian and Egyptian influences apparently stimulated civilization in Crete.[1] Sir Arthur Evans, the foremost archeologist of ancient Crete, called the Bronze Age culture that had developed by 2000 B.C.E. "Minoan" after Minos, the legendary king of Crete. By about 1700 B.C.E. the Minoans had a linear script, and in the period 1580–1450 B.C.E. a splendid civilization flourished. The first true Greeks, called Minyans, were Aryan-speaking Indo-Europeans. They established relations with Minoan Crete, and between 1450 and 1400 B.C.E., at which time they were

known as Mycenaeans, the Greeks had settled at the capital city of Knossos. The Mycenaean period (1400–1150 B.C.E.) constituted Crete's last glory; the Dorians invaded from northern Greece and cast a "dark age" over the Aegean from 1100 to 650 B.C.E.

During that period, literacy largely passed from the Greek scene. Consequently, much of our knowledge of Minoan religious culture comes from archeological excavations. These reveal that caves were great cultural centers from Neolithic times, serving as dwellings, cemeteries, and churches all in one. (Insofar as they gave rise to the mythic labyrinth, Cretan caves influenced the Greek religious psyche permanently.[2]) As the archeological excavations show quite clearly, the foremost deity of Cretan cave religion was a goddess, whose primary features were fertility and mastery of animals. This corresponds with remains found on Cretan mountains, where Minoans also celebrated fertility.

However, the goddess cult probably did more than simply venerate natural life. The many burial remains, symbols of butterflies and bees (change-of-state beings), and other artifacts suggest a complex veneration of life, death, and rebirth. Probably participants underwent initiation into these mysteries, much as ancient Africans or Australians have long done. The remains of or artistic representations of bull horns, double axes, trees, animals, cosmic pillars, and blood sacrifices testify to a particularly rich Neolithic agricultural goddess religion.

In light of later Greek initiations—for example, those of the Eleusinian and Orphic mysteries—it is likely that the Minoan goddess cult aimed at ensuring a happy afterlife.[3] If so, it probably had conceptions of immortality that continued through the dark age and served as a counterpoint to Zeus and the Olympian gods. In the Olympian scheme, the afterlife was only a shadowy, dismal existence. The mystery religions that offered a more hopeful view may well have derived from the Cretan earth goddess.

At any rate, as the script that archeologists have discovered and called Linear B shows, people spoke Greek on Crete from 1400 B.C.E. By that time, Minoan and Mycenaean cultural forces were interacting. One important effect was that later Greek religious culture appropriated Minoan Crete as its golden age. For instance, according to Olympian legend, Zeus was born on Crete, and Apollo, Heracles, and Demeter (and even the non-Olympian Dionysis) performed prodigies or had high adventures in Crete. Crete thus became the *omphalos*, the navel or birth center, of the classical Hellenic world. At the end of his life and literary career, when he composed his masterpiece the *Laws*, Plato placed his characters on Crete, walking from Knossos into the hills to the temple cave of Zeus.

Olympian Religion

The Cretan or Minoan strand of Greek religious history wove itself deep into the Hellenic fiber. The Mycenaean strand, however, was throughout more predominant. Linear B shows that the people who invaded Crete were Indo-Europeans—the people that shaped both Iran and India. One of the outstanding characteristics of Indo-European religion was its interest in sky phenomena—storms, wind, lightning, the sun, and stars. Zeus, the prime Greek Olympian god, is a close relative of both Vedic and Iranian sky-gods. (In proto-Indo-European religion, Mother Earth was polar to Father Sky but less powerful.) Furthermore, the Indo-Europeans were much concerned with the human word—in sacrifices, chanting, spells, and sagas. Their traditions were largely oral, and they opposed writing when they first encountered it among Near Eastern peoples. It is worth underscoring that they had a powerful, double sense of the sacred—the sacred was both charged with divine presence and forbidden to human touch. Throughout its later development, Greek religion never lost this sense of awe-filled untouchability. Last, Indo-Europeans divided their society and gods into three groups. As a result, Vedic India, Aryan Iran, and preclassical Greece all thought in terms of priests, warriors, and commoners (though in Greece the priestly class was underdeveloped), as did Celts and Romans.

If both Crete and mainland Greece maintained earlier traditions during the dark age,[4] we can assume that the emergence of Homeric, Olympian religion was quite slow. By the time of Homer, however, the Indo-European religion had a distinctively Greek flavor. For instance, Zeus had acquired a mythological lineage. According to Hesiod's *Theogony*, he was born in the third generation of gods, after the original period of Earth and Heaven and the second period of the Titans. When Zeus overthrew his father Kronos, the present world resulted. (Eliade sees in the rather violent mythology of the *Theogony* a Greek account of creation. Heaven and earth separate; nature's forces assume their present order.)[5]

Zeus came to preeminence slowly. Most likely, his many liaisons with local goddesses represent a religious and political takeover, as a unified Greek culture emerged out of local traditions. These local traditions did not disappear, but instead entered the larger complex of Greek religious notions, enriching both Greek mythology and religious practices. For instance, the local Cretan dances of armed youths during their initiation ceremonies became part of the colorful story of the infant Zeus' birth in Crete. The noise of the youths' clashing shields drowned out the infant's cries, and so saved him from Kronos, who wanted to devour him. Furthermore, the Cretan Zeus merged with the child and lover of the Cretan goddess, linking him to the island's Neolithic past.

In classical Greece, Zeus was first among the gods dwelling on Mount Olympus, as Homer portrayed him. He was the father of humans, the ruler of their destinies, and, despite his own moral waywardness, the ultimate upholder of justice. In addition to Zeus, the roster of the foremost Olympian gods includes Hera, Zeus's wife; Poseidon, god of the sea; Hephaestus, the divine blacksmith; Apollo, god of law and order; Hermes, the divine messenger; Artemis, mistress of wild beasts; Athena, patroness of feminine and practical arts; and Aphrodite, goddess of love.

Of these gods and goddesses, Apollo deserves special mention, because he came to symbolize many virtues that seem typically Greek, such as serenity, harmony, balance, and order.[6] Through his oracle at Delphi, Apollo gave counsel on matters of liturgical propriety and ritual purification. For example, Apollo had charge of purifying homicides, who had to cleanse themselves of their "pollution." One would take serious matters needing counsel to Apollo's pythia (priestess) at Delphi. In trance, she would exclaim the wisdom with which Apollo filled her. The origins of the pythia's exclamation may lie in shamanism, but by classical times Apollonian wisdom had distanced itself from the emotional and irrational, becoming primarily intellectual *theoria*—relatively serene religious contemplation. As epitomized in the Delphic oracle's command "Know thyself," Apollonian religion deified thought and spirit. For that reason, it encouraged science, art, philosophy, and music.

Somewhat the antithesis of Apollo was Dionysus, an eccentric among the gods of the Olympian period. A son of Zeus by a mortal woman, Dionysus apparently always remained an outsider. His cult was not native to central Greece, while psychologically its concern with the irrational and emotional made many fear it. In his well-known study *The Greeks and the Irrational*, E. R. Dodds associates Dionysus with "the blessings of madness."[7] Unlike the ecstasy of the Apollonian pythia, that of the followers of Dionysus (for example, of the women called maenads)[8] was wild, frenzied, and orgiastic. Such ecstasy represented the enthusiasm (being filled with divine force) that could come from dancing and wine drinking.

For Eliade, Dionysus conjures up "the totality of life, as is shown by his relations with water and germination, blood or sperm, and by the excess of vitality manifested in his animal epiphanies (bull, lion, goat)."[9] Finally, Dionysus was a god of vegetation who would disappear to the underworld and then spring back to life. The most influential literary source on the Dionysian cult, Euripides' play the *Bacchae*, portrays the god's followers as wildly joyous. If the play is accurate, their mountain revels culminated in tearing apart live animals and eating their flesh raw (so as to commune with the god of animal life).

Strangely enough, the Greeks recognized something essential in Dionysus. Call it the need for madness, reverence for the life force, or the value of temporarily escaping one's mortal bonds—they blessed it and called it good. As a result, Apollo vacated Delphi during the three winter months and allowed Dionysus to reign.

Earthly Religion

However, the sky-oriented Olympian religion never was the whole story. From the Minoans and the psyche came an earthly religion to balance the sky. Certainly the Dionysian cult was a major manifestation. So, too, were the many mother goddesses. Hera, Artemis, and Aphrodite, for example, all relate to fertility and mother earth. In Hesiod's *Theogony*, Gaea (earth) actually precedes and produces heaven. In popular religion, Demeter and Persephone were very influential. In fact, Demeter's search for Persephone in the underworld was a major theme of the Eleusinian mysteries, which are described below.

The result of this earth-oriented counterweight to the somewhat overbearing Olympians was a view that humans should aim to become, in Plato's phrase, "as much like God as possible." Through contact with the forces of life and fertility (in the Eleusinians' case) and with the forces of intellectual light (in the philosophers' case), the limits of mortality were challenged. "No," many Greeks said, "we are made for more than a few days in the sun. If we truly know ourselves, we can find undying life."

The Eleusinian mysteries were practiced in Athens from about 600 B.C.E. on, though they clearly originated much earlier. They evolved from the myth of Demeter's search for Persephone in the underworld,[10] which included a subplot about Demeter's unsuccessful (because of human folly) attempt to make Demophoon, the infant prince of Eleusis, an immortal. Thus, the mysteries consisted of rites and revelations that gave initiates precious knowledge in this life and bliss in the world to come.

We do not know the particulars of the mysteries, which were strictly secret, but the mysteries probably grafted Neolithic agricultural ideas onto the Olympian theme that the gods are immortal. If so, the mysteries moved beyond the myths of the Hainuwele type, in which agriculture entailed ritual murder and gods that die. The result was a new, powerful synthesis of sexuality and death (as reflected in Persephone being carried to the underworld by Pluto) and of agriculture and a happy existence beyond the grave (as in Demeter representing mother earth). This religious synthesis made Eleusis an important cultic center for almost 2,000 years. Adherents to the Eleusinian mysteries lived in all parts of the Greek world and came from all social classes. Anyone who spoke Greek and had "clean hands" (including women, children, and slaves) could take part. Poets of the stature of Pindar and Sophocles praised the mysteries, and they were a powerful force in Greek life.

The background of the Orphic rites was a mythology somewhat like that of Demeter and Persephone.[11] Orpheus was a prominent Thracian hero, the son of Calliope by Apollo. His great gift was for music—when he played the lyre wild beasts grew calm, trees danced, and rivers stood still. Orpheus married the nymph Eurydice, who died from snakebite while fleeing Aristaeus, another son of Apollo. Orpheus could have regained Eurydice from the underworld if he had been able to resist looking at her. But he had to wander inconsolably until followers of Dionysus tore him apart (because of his devotion to Apollo). From this background Guthrie concludes: "The story throws light upon the Orphic religion because that is exactly what, in its main features, it stood for, a blend of the Thracian belief in immortality with Apolline ideas of *katharsis* [purification]. From the one it took *ekstasis*, enthusiasm, and a deep spiritual hope; from the other a for-malizing influence, an almost legal atmosphere of rules and regulations."[12]

The direct basis for the doctrines elaborated in the Orphic rites, however, was another myth, that of Dion-ysus Zagreus, the son of Zeus and Persephone. Zeus proposed to make Dionysus ruler of the universe, but the Titans were so enraged that they dismembered and devoured him. Athena saved Dionysus' heart and gave it to Zeus, who swallowed it and then destroyed the Titans with lightning. Dionysus Zagreus was born anew from that heart, while from the ashes of the Titans came the human race, which was thus part divine (from Dionysus) and part evil (from the Titans). Conse-quently, the Orphics believed in the divine origin of the human soul but also in the need to leave behind the soul's Titanic inheritance through ritual initiation and reincarnation.

For eternal blessedness, Orphics preached, one had to follow a strict moral code, abstain from the flesh of living creatures, and cultivate the Dionysian part of human nature. When fully pure, the soul would be reincarnated no more. No more would it drink of the spring of Lethe (forgetfulness), but, light as air, it would live in union with the divine mind. The Orphics ap-pealed to persons of refinement, and Orphism cer-tainly influenced Plato, the natural philosopher Empedocles, and the Roman epic poet Vergil.

Both the Eleusinian mysteries and the Orphic rites sought immortality, the one by a profound ritualization of the life force, the other by purifying the divine soul. Together, they were a strong counterforce to the pes-simism fostered by heaven-oriented Olympianism. An-other counterforce to the sky was the *chthonioi*, the spirits who lived in the dark recesses of the earth.[13] Though they were hardly mentioned in Homer, in popular religion they tended to spell out the twofold function of mother earth: fertility and rule of the dead. For the most part, the *chthonioi* were local spirits, concerned with a particular town's crops or deceased. Sometimes their cult blended with the cult of a local hero. Other times sacrifices to the *chthonioi* had over-tones of devotion to Gaea, Demeter, Pluto, or Tro-phonious—divinities of fertility or Hades. Whether the *chthonioi* were gods or shady figures imagined to pop-ulate the afterlife is not clear. Regardless, they elicited considerable fear, and the common people tried not to offend them.

Philosophy

The common people did not build Athenian culture or make the breakthrough called philosophy. Rather,

an aristocratic elite, working for several centuries, slowly distinguished the realms of myth and reason and in so doing wrote a pivotal chapter in the history of human consciousness. Before philosophy, the con-cept of reason was vague. We have seen the prehistoric suspicion that something can travel in dreams, rise in shamanist flight, and survive the grave. In Egypt, the Amon hymns exhibited a strong sense of transcend-ence—of the human mind pressing beyond materiality to divine mystery itself. In Iran, Zoroaster's interior dualism (the battle between Truth and the Lie) re-vealed a striking grasp of the abstract spirit.

Although many cultures thus showed some aware-ness of reason and spirit, the culture of the Greek city-state identified reason and controlled it. Only the line of pre-Socratic thinkers—most prominently, Pytha-goras, Xenophanes, Parmenides, and Heraclitus—so disciplined their dissatisfaction with Olympian culture that they saw human mind *(nous)* itself as being divine and real. India approached this belief but never came away with Greece's balancing belief in the material world.

The story of the pre-Socratics, which weaves into that of the dramatists and Sophists (teachers of shallow philosophy), is a fascinating chapter in religion.[14] Partly from interior experimentation and partly from an em-pirical study of nature, the early philosophers moved beyond what most previous peoples had meant by the word *god*. As we have seen, peoples believing in the cosmological myth considered the world to be a living whole. With the rise of civilized religion, Mesopota-mians, Egyptians, Iranians, and others focused on the political aspect of the cosmos. In other words, divinity to them was in good part a symbolic representation of their own society. Even Ahura Mazdah had a strong political function. For Darius I, Ahura Mazdah sanc-tioned the building of an empire of Truth.

Out of its dark age, Greek creativity produced a pantheon—a roster of gods—that was neither natural nor political. The Olympians were anthropomorphic, evidencing human aspects. To be sure, Zeus was a sky-god and Athena fought for Athens. But although nature and politics played important roles, they did not make the Olympians distinctive. What made the Olympians distinctive was the rich, anthropomorphic mythology surrounding them. In these divine characters or per-sonalities, human passions were blown up to divine stature. Contemplating such divinity, ruminating on the Olympian mythology, the Greek geniuses clarified where and how *mythos* shatters on *logos*—where story must yield to analytic reason.

Of course, this realization was prompted by his-torical events. It did not spawn at a seaside resort. Looking around them, the Greek geniuses of the fifth and fourth centuries B.C.E. saw a succession of empires. The decline of Babylon, Egypt, and Persia evoked the question, "What is the meaning of history's process?" As a result, historians such as Herodotus and Thucydides wanted a break with myth, an explanation of the flux in political affairs.[15] As a result, Socrates, Plato, Aristotle labored heroically to produce such a break.

When the Athenians sentenced Socrates to death for impiety, they shocked Plato to the depths of his soul. If Athens could reject the one wise person who might save it, what chance did truth have?[16] Eventually Plato correlated the Athenian city-state experience with the flux of empires and came to wonder about the possibility for human order. The *Republic* and *Laws*, which constitute about 40 percent of Plato's writings, testify to how long and deeply problems of political order absorbed him. His great problem, in fact, was the disorder of most humanity—citizens, empire builders, the great and small alike. Grappling with this problem, Plato saw that all order—personal, sociopolitical, and historical—depends on a truth only luminous from God. Since Plato's great problem remains our own, we do well to attend to his insight.

From instinct, observation, and reflection, Plato decided that history means more than wars and power struggles. Restricted to that level, history is literally absurd—a cause for despair—and yields no ordering truth (except negatively as an analysis of cultural destruction).

Rather, we must become aware of a reality that is not distorted by our lusts; divine mystery must shine forth an ordering light. Where warmongers and powerbrokers close themselves, philosophers must be receptive and willing to change. Where politicians restrict reality to money and influence, philosophers must go to the center of things—to the soul's passion for justice and love. Like a new Prometheus firing humanity's soul, the Platonic lover of wisdom made justice and love humanity's great passion. The presence or absence of that passion makes health or disease. Plato minces no words: One either admits divine mystery or faces disaster.

The fire and order of the Platonic soul clarified human reality. From Plato's time, some persons have realized that the meaning of their existence was to move through experience toward the intellectual light of God. Thus, the process of human questioning—human searching for flashes of insight and then sustained visions—has been a primary task for those seriously religious since Plato. The Western development of science, philosophy, and the humanities was made possible by the Greek consecration of this task.

Plato himself used myth and symbols to suggest the psychology, politics, and natural philosophy of the newly clarified human consciousness. These uses were deliberate, calculated attempts to keep touch with the whole field of human awareness, to keep from getting lost in abstraction. Aristotle, more prosaic, commonsensical, and scientific than Plato, analyzed the new clarification of consciousness in drier, more technical terms.[17] As he saw it, a person first experiences ignorance about the meaning of human existence. This ignorance, however, is peculiar: It is knowing that one does not know—being aware that one is in the dark. Instinctively we seek release from the tension that this realization produces. Aware of our confusion, upset that we do not know how our lives make sense, we are moved to clarify things. If distractions, whether personal or social, do not interfere, we will pursue enlightenment, and our search will become inner directed. We will grope forward by an intuition or foreknowledge of what we seek, just as we work a math problem by a knowing ignorance that enables us to recognize when our answer is correct.

Likewise, in the profound problem of human understanding that Aristotle was working on, there is a sense of the answer or goal from the beginning. Looking for the reality that will order both ourselves and our world, questioning and following the thoughts of our mind, we slowly advance toward the divine light, the divine mind, the divine being. Indeed, divinity itself, Aristotle finally realized, had been attracting him from the beginning. From the first, his glimmerings of light, of intellectual understanding, had been sharings in God. Developing this Platonic and Aristotelian insight, the Christian theologians Augustine and Aquinas wrote a new treatise on the image of God, stating that our intellectual light is a share in the activities of the Father, the Son, and the Holy Spirit.[18]

The Hellenistic Religions

Following the cultural flowering of Greek religion in drama and philosophy, the Hellenistic religions dominated. This period resulted from Alexander the Great's conquests (*Hellenism* is the term for his vision of an ecumenical, transnational culture). The Hellenistic era extended from Alexander (who died in 323 B.C.E.) well into the Roman and Christian periods. According to historians who love classical Greek culture, it was not a time of glory. Gilbert Murray, for instance, speaks of a "failure of nerve," while E. R. Dodds speaks of a "fear of freedom."[19] From our standpoint, perhaps the most significant feature of Hellenistic religion was its syncretism. In an imperial area populated by numerous ethnic groups, many different gods, beliefs, and rituals all became alike. We can conclude our historical survey of Greek religion by describing the most important aspects of this syncretism.

Alexander himself was something of a visionary, for what lured him to empire building was the idea of an ideal realm in which conquered peoples "were to be treated not as uncivilized and barbarous members of subject races but as equals with whom one must live in concord."[20] Before Alexander, the Greeks had some knowledge of foreign religions through travel and trade, but, in general, oriental deities had made little impact on their own piety. [One exception might be Cybele, a mother goddess imported from Phrygia (central Turkey), who was identified with Rhea, the mother of Zeus.] However, from the time of the Diadochi, Alexander's successor rulers, oriental cults began to spread. By the beginning of the second century B.C.E. they were predominant. The most popular gods were Cybele, Isis, and Serapis. In the later Roman period, Mithra also flourished.

As noted, Cybele was a mother goddess (and mistress of the animals). Usually she was accompanied by her young lover, Attis. (We may hypothesize that to the Greeks Cybele and Attis echoed the Minoan cave goddess and her consort.) She was severe and vengeful, and accompanied by lions. When Attis was unfaithful, she drove him insane. Eventually Cybele became a maternal deity like Demeter, Hera, and Aphrodite— a patroness of life, protectress of particular cities, and defender of women.

In her ceremonies devotees reenacted Attis' insanity and consequent self-castration. They would take the pine tree (Attis' symbol), bury it, mourn for the dead god, and then observe his resurrection. Resurrected, Attis would rejoin Cybele, which was cause for great feasting. The cult seems to have promoted fertility, and its rituals have overtones of the vegetative cycle and sexuality. Celebrants went to emotional extremes, dancing, scourging themselves, and even on occasion imitating Attis' castration. We could say that the worship of Cybele attracted Dionysian energies.

In ancient Egypt, Isis was the wife of Osiris and the mother of Horus. In the Hellenistic period she achieved a wider influence, often in the company of Serapis. Serapis was an artificial creation, the result of the Greeks' aversion to the Egyptian tendency of worshiping gods in animal form. Fusing Osiris with his symbol (Apis, the bull), the Greeks made a new god: Serapis. He was bearded and seated on a throne, like Zeus, Hades, and Asclepius, some of whose functions he shared (such as rule of the sky, rule of the underworld, and healing). Joined with Isis, Serapis was primarily a fertility god, bedecked with branches and fruit.

Isis rather overshadowed Serapis, for she became a full-fledged, several-sided deity. As the consort of Osiris-Serapis, she was the heavenly queen of the elements, the ruler of stars and planets. Because of such power, she could enter the underworld to help her devotees or to stimulate the crops. Indeed, as a vegetative goddess she blended with Demeter and also the moon-goddess Selene. Perhaps her most important role, though, was to represent feminine virtues. In distress, she had sought the slain Osiris and brought him back to life. Sensitive and compassionate, she would do the same for her followers. As the mother of Horus (she was often represented as suckling him), she would help women in childbirth and with child raising. Unlike Cybele, the Hellenistic Isis was soft and tender. Yet, as recent scholarship has shown,[21] her devotees assumed a code of high ethics and her cult was strikingly upright.

Like those for Cybele and Attis, the ceremonies for Isis and Osiris-Serapis amounted to a cycle of mourning and rejoicing. Mourning, followers reenacted Isis' search for Osiris and her discovery of his dismembered parts. Rejoicing, they celebrated Osiris' resurrection and the return of Isis' joy. Apuleius' famous account gives some of the details of the rituals, which included bathings, ten days of abstinence from sex, "approaching the gates of death," and entering the presence of the gods.[22] Clearly, the ceremonies were elaborate and effective, much as the Eleusinian mysteries must have been. Through the cycle of Osiris' death and resurrection, followers would gain confidence that their own lives were in good hands. Through the dramatic symbolization of the afterlife, they could anticipate security and bliss.

Mithra, whom we know from Iran, never took strong hold among the Hellenistic Greeks, but he did become important among the Romans influenced by Hellenism, especially the Roman soldiers. Indeed his transformation illustrates almost perfectly the religious amalgam that cross-cultural contact produced at this time. In Mithra's Romanization, Jupiter (Zeus) took on attributes of Ahura Mazdah and became a great champion of Truth. Mithra, in turn, became Jupiter—Ahura Mazdah's faithful helper in the battle against the Lie. In this later mythology, Mithra was born of a rock (symbol of the celestial vault), and from birth carried a bow, arrows, and dagger (much like a Persian noble). He shot the arrows into the heavens from time to time to produce a heavenly spring of pure rain water. Very important was his sacrifice of the bull, from whose blood sprouted the corn (symbol of vegetation).

Thus, Mithra was both a celestial deity (later associated particularly with the sun) and a fertility god. His followers would trace his circuit through the sky, reenact the mythology of his birth, and celebrate a bull sacrifice in his name. After the sacrifice they would feast together, believing that the bull's meat and blood contained the substance of eternity. As the Mithraic doctrine developed, it generated a complicated astrology, by which the progress of initiates' souls through the heavens was shown. At its peak, Mithraism ran underground "churches" and schools. Today excavations under Christian churches, including St. Clement's in Rome, reveal statuary, classrooms, and altars used by Mithraists.

In summary, the Hellenistic period was a time of profuse religious activity. Onto Greek and then Roman religious culture, a cosmopolitan era grafted elements from the Egyptians, Persians, Phrygians, and others. [We have not even mentioned the Syrian cults of the mother goddess Adonis and of various baals (Canaanite and Phoenician local deities), which constituted another strand of Hellenistic fertility religions.][23] Beyond doubt, a certain cultural confusion underlay all this excitement. Thrown into close contact with foreigners, all persons in the new empires had to face new divinities and beliefs. Partly as a result, many persons felt great need for signs of salvation or assurances of a happy afterlife. The upshot was a frenzy of mysteries through which devotees could feel stirring emotions or see marvelous sights. With a rush of sorrow, sexual excitement, or hope for rebirth, an initiate would feel passionately alive. In a time of disarray and ceaseless warfare, when the city-state or clan no longer offered security or guidance, such a sense of vitality was more than welcome.

Religious Implications

Nature and divinity run together in Greek religion. Throughout its history, the Greek religious mind associated all major natural phenomena with particular gods. As noted, the sky, sea, and earth were powerful deities. The major stress was on fertility (which was the focus of most local festivals), perhaps due to the poor quality of the rocky Greek soil. The Homeric hymns, for instance, sing praise to mother earth, who feeds all creatures and blesses humans with good crops. Relatedly, they make the man with good crops a symbol of prosperity. The earth, mother of the gods and wife of the starry heavens, has blessed him—his children can play merrily.[24] As a result of its prehistoric roots, then, Greece saw much divinity in natural growth.

In social terms, Greek religious culture reflects the ethical ideas that bound first the early clanspeople and then the citizens of the city-state. The ethics of the early historical period evolved from the extended family. There was no money, and banditry was rife, so a man's great virtue was to provide food, shelter, and defense—whether by just means or otherwise. Consequently, most men (it was a patriarchal culture) petitioned the gods for material prosperity and success in arms. They called one of their number good *(agathos)* and praised him for excellence *(arete)* if he was a survivor. The more elevated notions of justice later developed by philosophers clashed with the less moral tradition. Since early Greek religion did not associate godliness with justice, the philosophers called for its overthrow.

Another primitive concept that died hard was "pollution." This was the dangerous state of being unclean, or at odds with the natural powers because of some dread deed. Homicide was especially polluting, but incest, contact with a dead person, or even a bad dream or childbirth could also be polluting, each in varying degrees. Washing in a spring would cleanse away a bad dream; purification by fire and the offering of pig's blood cleansed a homicide. The concept of pollution seems to have been a way for the Greeks to deal with dreadful, amoral happenings that might bring destructive contact with the sacred, even though they were unintentional. Since polluted persons could contaminate others, they were often banished.

Greek cults used magical formulas, prayers, sacrifices, dances, and dramatic scenes—a wealth of creative expressions. Magical formulas probably were most prominent in agricultural festivals, where peasants mixed models of snakes and phalluses with decomposing, organic materials, such as pine branches and remains of pigs, to excite powers of fertility. Greek prayers would recall a god's favors and the sacrifices that the praying person had offered previously. This implied a sort of barter: We will honor you and offer a sacrifice if you give us success in crops (or war, or family life, or whatever). Occasionally texts indicate pure admiration for divine power or beauty, but the ordinary attitude was quite practical. Since the gods were not necessarily rational or holy, they had to be cajoled. Indeed, a Greek tended to pray and sacrifice rather parochially, addressing the family Apollo or Athena, who might remember fat sacrifices offered in the past. Each family or city-state had its own traditions, customs, myths, and gods, which served both to bind the members together and to maintain the splintering among the different tribes.

Sacrifice was a primary way to keep local religion in good health. By giving the local god good things, one could expect prosperity in return. (Significantly, this implied that the gods blessed those who were wealthy and had good things to sacrifice and that those who sacrificed and met bad luck had secret sins or wicked ancestors. Either way, human success and goodness were rather arbitrary.) In a sacrifice, usually parts of an animal were offered and the rest was consumed. According to a Homeric account, for instance, a pig was cut up, pieces of each limb were wrapped in fat and thrown on the fire, and barley grains were sprinkled on the fire. The meal that followed was a mode of communion with the deities.

Greek cults produced many priests, but their status and functions were limited. In principle, any person could pray and sacrifice to any god, so priests had no monopoly. They tended to be limited to particular temples and were seldom organized into bands or hierarchies. A large clan might have its own officiating priest, and the priest of a prosperous temple might make a good living from sacrifice fees. Otherwise, priesthood was not a road to status or wealth. Priests seldom gave instruction or performed divinations, though some priests in the mystery rites did both.

Many Greek religious authors were rather harsh on women. Hesiod, for instance, reported the myth of Pandora and the box of evils, which made woman the source of human woes. In other places he called woman "that beautiful evil," the "snare from which there is no escaping," and "that terrible plague."[25] Socrates, when asked about the advisability of marriage, balanced the boon of heirs against the woes of a wife: "One quarrel after another, her dower cast in your face, the haughty disdain of her family, the garrulous tongue of your mother-in-law, the lurking paramour."[26] In Plato's *Republic*, women were to be equal to men socially and sexually, having rights to education and rule. Nonetheless, Plato tended to consider women less independent than men, in good part because of their physique: "The womb is an animal that longs to generate children." Aristotle, however, was the most unequivocal misogynist. To him women were simply inferior, both intellectually and morally. In his matter-and-form theory, women supplied only the matter for human reproduction, men supplying everything effective and active.

Women did have legal rights in Athenian society, but their lives were largely circumscribed by male control. Their basic function was to bear children. The playwright Euripides summarized the impact of this socialization, putting into the mouths of the women of his *Andromache* such self-evaluations as: "There's a touch of jealousy in the female psyche"; "For nature tempers the souls of women so they may find a pleasure in voicing their afflictions as they come"; "A woman even when married to a cad, ought to be deferential, not a squabbler"; and "And just because we women are prone to evil, what's to be gained from perverting men to match?"

On the other hand, we have seen that Greek divinity frequently was powerfully feminine. In the Minoan-Mycenaean period, a great goddess was the prime deity. In the Olympian period, Demeter, Hera, Athena, Artemis, and Aphrodite all exerted great influence. In the Hellenistic religions, Cybele and Isis more than equaled Mithra. Psychologically, then, Greek culture never doubted the divinity of the feminine. More than Israelite, Christian, or Muslim culture, Greek divinity was androgynous. Furthermore, certain religious groups offered women escape from social oppression, such as the Eleusinian and Dionysian sects. There, in a sort of utopean free zone, women could experience equality and dignity. Although these cults never compensated for women's lack of dignity or status in ordinary life, it was an implicit admission that ordinary life was quite imperfect.

The personal side of Greek religion is perhaps most manifest in myths dealing with human creation. In the most famous collection of myths, Hesiod's *Works and Days*, ancient Greeks read that they were the last and lowest in a series of human generations. During the first ages, races of gold, silver, and bronze flourished, but they came to various bad ends. A flood intervened, followed by the age of the heroes. Finally the present iron people arose. In other words, Hesiod's myth put into Greek form the widespread belief in a golden age or a previous paradise, with the accompanying message that the present age was a low point.

Partly from this religious heritage, the prevailing mood of many Greek writers was pessimistic. As Sermonides, a writer of the seventh century B.C.E. put it, "There is no wit in man. Creatures of a day, we live like cattle, knowing nothing of how the god will bring each one to his end."[27] Others echoed Sermonides: Human beings have only a short time under the sun; their powers fade quickly, their fortunes are uncertain. By comparison, Delphic wisdom was more positive: Gain self-knowledge and moderation. Self-knowledge, above all, was accepting one's mortality. By moderation, one could avoid hubris and tragedy. There were overtones of jealousy in this advice from Apollo, however, as though the god feared humans' yearning for immortality or resented their craving a life of passion.

Indeed, passion was ever a danger, for the Greeks were competitive and lusty. In the end, they would not give up their dreams of immortality. So becoming godlike became a central theme of philosophy and mystery religion. Empedocles, for instance, thought that his wisdom made him a god among mortals. Plato taught that the soul is divine and deathless. The common person would more likely find divinity in one of the mystery rites, through a union with Demeter or a knowledge from Isis, either of which could bring victory over death.

The personal implications of Greek religion were greatest in the philosophers' clarification of reason, universal humanity, and the participation of divinity in human thought. As we have noted, the poets, dramatists, and early philosophers slowly clarified the nature of human reason, separating it from myth. By focusing on the mind *(nous)* and its relations with being *(ousia)*, the pre-Socratics prepared the way for Plato and Aristotle, who realized how mind and being coincide. Moreover, this work did not take the Greek intellectuals away from either religion or politics. Rather, it introduced them to an order that set all the fundamentals—nature, society, self, and divinity—in harmony. In other words, it took them to the heart of what it means to be human.

Finally, the philosophers' order meant a new perspective on death. In early times, death was shadowy. For Homer, the dead had only a vague existence around their graves or in the underworld. There was no judgment or punishment for injustice towards one's fellows. Only those who had directly affronted the gods had to suffer. The mystery cults said one could conquer death by union with an immortal divinity, and their great popularity indicates the hold that death had on Greece starting in the sixth century B.C.E. The philosophers spoke of judgment and punishment because they were acutely aware that justice rules few human situations. In quite deliberate myths, Plato symbolized the inherent need we have for a final accounting. Without it, he suggested, reason would lose balance.

There is no need to review the status of divinity in the Greek world view, since we have traced its development in our history. In the eyes of many scholars, the Greeks were among the most religious of ancient peoples. From heaven to under the earth, from crude emotion to the most refined spirituality, their great culture put a religious shine on everything. Today, if we find the world "sacred" (deeply meaningful) through science or art, if we find the human being "sacred" (deeply valuable) through medicine or philosophy, if we find the political order alive with counsels both good and bad—if we ever think in these ways, it is largely because of the Greeks. They made the "transcendental" qualities—unity, truth, goodness, and beauty—part of Western religion. Finally, in the Greek discovery of reason, human beings glimpsed the possibility that divinity is eminently rational, the sacred is a holy word. That glimpse changed the history of Western religion and now is rewriting the history of the entire world.

NOTES

1. Arnold Toynbee, *Mankind and Mother Earth*, (New York: Oxford University Press, 1976), pp. 77–78.

2. Phillipe Borgeaud, "The Open Entrance to the Closed Palace of the King: The Greek Labyrinth in Context," *HR*, 1974, *14*(1):1–27; Raymond Christinger, "The Hidden Significance of the 'Cretan' Labyrinth," *HR*, 1975, *15*(2): 183–191.

3. Mircea Eliade, *A History of Religious Ideas*, vol. 1, *From the Stone Age to the Eleusinian Mysteries* (Chicago: University of Chicago Press, 1978), p. 136; K. Kerenyi, "Voraussentzungen in der Einweihung in Eleusis," in *Initiation*, ed. C. J. Bleeker (Leiden: E. J. Brill, 1965), pp. 59–64; M. Mehauden, "Le secret central de l'initiation aux mysteres d'Eléusis," in *Initiation*, ed. C. J. Bleeker (Leiden: E. J. Brill, 1965), pp. 65–70.

4. B. C. Dietrich, *The Origins of Greek Religion* (New York: de Gruyter, 1974), pp. 191–289.

5. Eliade, *History of Religious Ideas*, vol. 1, pp. 247–250.

6. W. K. C. Guthrie, *The Greeks and Their Gods* (Boston: Beacon Press, 1955), pp. 73–87.

7. E. R. Dodds, *The Greeks and the Irrational* (Berkeley: University of California Press, 1966), pp. 76–82.

8. Ibid., pp. 270–282.

9. Eliade, *History of Religious Ideas*, vol. 1, p. 360.

10. H. J. Rose, *A Handbook of Greek Mythology* (New York: Dutton, 1959), pp. 91–94.

11. Edith Hamilton, *Mythology* (New York: New American Library, 1942), pp. 103–105.

12. Guthrie, *Greeks and Their Gods*, p. 318.

13. Ibid., pp. 217–253.

14. See Eric Voegelin, *Order and History, II: The World of the Polis* (Baton Rouge: Louisiana State University Press, 1957), pp. 203–331.

15. Ibid., pp. 332–373; Eric Voegelin, *Order and History, IV: The Ecumenic Age* (Baton Rouge: Louisiana State University Press, 1974), pp. 178–183.

16. John Carmody, "Plato's Religious Horizon," *Philosophy Today*, 1971, *15*(1):52–68.

17. Voegelin, *Order and History, IV*, pp. 187–192; Werner Jaeger, *Aristotle* (New York: Oxford University Press, 1962), pp. 366–406.

18. Bernard Lonergan, *Verbum* (Notre Dame, Ind.: University of Notre Dame Press, 1967).

19. Murray, *Greek Religion*, pp. 119–165; Dodds, *Greeks and the Irrational*, pp. 236–269.

20. M. J. Vermaseren, "Hellenistic Religions," in *Historia Religionum, I*, ed. C. J. Bleeker and G. Widengren (Leiden: E. J. Brill, 1969), p. 495.

21. Sharon Kelly Heyob, *The Cult of Isis among Women in the Graeco-Roman World* (Leiden: E. J. Brill, 1975), pp. 111–127.

22. See Vermaseren, "Hellenistic Religions," pp. 522–533.

23. Ibid., pp. 523–528.

24. See Mircea Eliade, *From Primitives to Zen* (New York: Harper & Row, 1968), p. 55.

25. See Eliade, *History of Religious Ideas*, vol. 1, p. 256.

26. Vern L. Bullough, *The Subordinate Sex* (Baltimore: Penguin, 1974), p. 59.

27. Eliade, *From Primitives to Zen*, p. 540.

GLOSSARY

Adonai Jewish term for God or Lord

ahimsa Hindu nonviolence or noninjury

alienation separation from nature, society, self or God; estrangement

Allah Muslim God

amulet a charm thought to protect the wearer against evil

anatman Buddhist no-self

apocalypse revelation concerning the end of the world or consummation of salvation

Aryans self-designated noble race that dominated ancient India and Iran

Astarte feminine nature deity of the ancient Canaanites

atman Buddhist and Hindu term for self or substantial entity

autonomy independence; self-rule

avatar incarnate form of a Hindu deity

axis mundi pole or pillar that connects earth to heaven

baal masculine nature deity of ancient Canaanites

Baal Shem Tov founder of modern Jewish Hasidism (1700–1760)

belief system worldview; conception of ultimate reality

bhakti Hindu term for devotion

bodhisattva Mahayana Buddhist term for saint or enlightened one

bon ancient Tibetan shaman

brahman (or **brahmin**) Hindu priest

Brahman Hindu term for ultimate reality

Buddhanature ultimate reality as intrinsically enlightened

caliph Muslim head of state

Calvinist pertaining to the thought of John Calvin (1509–1564), a leading Protestant Christian reformer

canon rule, law or official collection, e.g., the *canon* of scriptural books

canon law Christian church legislation

charism gift or talent thought to come from God

Common Era period shared by Christians and Jews (A.D.)

contemplation simple, direct consideration from one's center

contingency state of being dependent, caused by another

covenant compact or contract, especially that between God and Israel

conversion turning around, having a deep change of heart

cosmological myth the storied belief that all beings share in and express a single ultimate substance

cosmology the study of the natural whole of the world

Creator the Divine as having made the world from nothingness

cult (1) worship; (2) an unorthodox religious group

daimon Greek term for inner spirit of conscience

dharma (1) Buddhist term for ultimate particle of reality; (2) Hindu term for class or caste responsibility

Dharma Buddhist and Hindu term for Teaching or Doctrine

dhikr Muslim term for recollection or remembrance (of God)

diaspora Jewish term for dispersion or exile from Israel

dissociation psychological term for personality split that separates one from reality

divination art of discerning future events

Dravidian pertaining to the native Indians who pre-dated the Aryan invaders

dualism a system that poses two principles or powers (e.g., light and darkness) in opposition to one another

ecology study of the network of natural correlations

ecstasy stepping outside ordinary consciousness, usually in joy and power

emptiness Buddhist notion that no entity has a sub-stance or "own-being"

enlightenment Buddhist term for realization of the truth or attainment of the goal

enstasis self-collection; autonomy

evangelicals those who base their lives on the Chris-tian gospel

faith belief; commitment or assent beyond factual surety or proof

Fathers the Christian leaders and teachers of the sec-ond to fifth century C.E. who formed classical doctrine

Freudian deriving from the theories of Sigmund Freud (1856–1939), the pioneer analyst of the for-mation of the psyche in childhood

geomancy the practice of discerning and employing the psycho-physical forces of the earth

God the Supreme Being; usually considered per-sonal in the West

gospel Christian glad tidings or joyous message of salvation

grace divine favor or free help

guru spiritual guide or teacher

hadith Muslim traditions about Muhammad

haggadah Jewish stories or lore

hagiography writing about saints

hajj Muslim pilgrimage to Mecca

halakah Jewish legal tradition

hesychaism an Eastern Christian school of spiritu-ality that stressed breathing exercises and the Jesus Prayer

Hinayana older Buddhist sects that arose in India in the first four centuries after Buddha's death; "smaller vehicle"

hope virtue or power to anticipate a good future

hylomorphism Aristotelian theory that considered reality as a composite of matter and form

iconoclasm tendency to smash idols or icons

ideology a set of ideas advanced to defend one's interests rather than to disclose truth

imagination faculty by which we depict things in our mind's eye

jen ("run") Confucian virtue of humaneness

kalpa Indian unit of cosmic time

kami Shinto gods or spirits

karma Hindu and Buddhist term for the physical law of cause and effect

karma-yoga Indian discipline to purify work by strip-ping oneself of attachment to success or failure

koan Zen puzzle used in the pursuit of enlightenment

kosher fit or proper; suitable according to Jewish law

lama Tibetan Buddhist monk

Li Confucian term for propriety and ritual protocol

liturgy formal religious ceremony

magic attempts to control divinities for one's own use

Mahayana branch of Buddhism that arose in the schism of the second century after the Buddha's death and came to dominate East Asia; "greater vehicle"

maya Hindu term for illusory quality of common person's "reality"

merkabah chariot of *Ezekiel* 1:22–28, which became a major interest of Jewish mystics

Messiah the anointed one expected by Jews to bring peace and salvation

metaphysics philosophical study of underlying causes

midrash Jewish exegesis of scripture

moksha Hindu term for release or liberation

monism a system of thought that finds reality to be one, not multiple

morality ethics; concern for good behavior

mullah Muslim (especially Shiite) teacher and prayer leader

mystery   something that has not been explained or cannot be explained

mystery religions   ancient Greek cults that promised immortality through secret ceremonies

mysticism   experience of direct communion with ultimate reality

myth   explanatory story, usually traditional

nirvana   Buddhist goal of liberation or fulfillment

nonliterate   using no writing or reading

occult   concerning hidden, supernatural, or paranormal matters

omphalos   navel or birth-center of the earth

ontology   the study of being or existence

orgiastic rites   socially sanctioned descent into disorder and promiscuity, for the sake of creativity

pantheism   view that God is in all things and all things are God

pantheon   roster or assembly of the gods

Passover   Jewish liturgical feast commemorating the exodus from Egypt under Moses

patristic   relating to the Church fathers

peace   tranquillity of order

pietism   Seventeeth-century German Lutheran movement that stressed the religious emotions

polis   Greek city-state

pollution   state of alienation from the sacred

pranayama   Indian breath control

prophet   spokesperson for God or a divinity

purdah   Muslim seclusion of women

rabbi   Jewish title for teacher of oral Torah

rasul   Muslim prophet or messenger

religion   communion with, service of, or concern for ultimate reality

revelation   disclosure (of sacred truth)

rishis   Vedic seers

rita   Vedic concept and deity of cosmic order

ritual   prescribed, formalized religious action or ceremony

rubric   liturgical instruction or directive

sages   wise people

samadhi   Indian term for highest state of meditation or yoga

samsara   Hindu and Buddhist term for the state of continual rebirths

sanctity   holiness, special goodness

Sangha   Buddhist term for the community (especially of monks)

satori   Zen term for enlightenment

satyagraha   M. K. Gandhi's notion that truth has its own power

scholasticism   tendency to refine a body of knowledge more than is fruitful

scholastics   medieval Christian teachers who reasoned very closely

shaman   ancient specialist in techniques of ecstasy

shariah   Islamic law or teaching

Shekinah   Jewish term for Divine presence

Shia   sectarian Islam that opposed the Sumni orthodoxy

Sikhism   Indian religion that synthesizes Islam and Hinduism

shirk   Muslim term for idolatry

sila   Buddhist term for ethics or morality

sin   offense against God; moral (culpable) error or misdeed

soothsayer   speaker of truth or wisdom

sorcery   witchcraft; the use of occult forces to do evil

suchness   Buddhist term for reality plain and simple

Sunni   majority denomination of Islam

suttee   Indian practice of having widows burn themselves

synod   meeting of Church leaders; council

synoptic   relating to the three gospels that run parallel and so can be taken in "at a glance" (Matthew, Mark, Luke)

talisman   charm for averting evil; amulet

Talmud   primary source of Jewish law and rabbinic learning; Mishnah plus Gemara

tantra   Hindu and Buddhist term for ritual manual;

approach to liberation through ritualistic, symbolic, or magical means

Tao   Chinese term for cosmic and moral "Way" or "Path"

theocentric   God-centered

theocracy   political rule by religious leaders

theophany   manifestation of the Divine

Torah   Jewish revelation or law

totem   animal, plant, or other object that serves as a clan emblem

transcendent   that which is beyond (human grasp)

transmigration   passing of the life force from one entity to another

typology   characterization in terms of ideal figures

Vajrayana   Buddhist school using Tantric techniques; most influential in Tibet

Vedas   prime Hindu scriptures

wisdom   wholistic understanding

worship   praise and petition of the deity

yang   Chinese principle of nature that is positive, light, and male

yin   Chinese principle of nature that is negative, dark, and female

yoga   Hindu and Buddhist term for discipline, especially that which is interior and meditative

yogins   those who practice yoga

Yom Kippur   solemn Jewish holiday, Day of Atonement

zaddik   Jewish (especially Hasidic) saint

Zen   Japanese school of Buddhism that stresses meditation

Zionism   Jewish movement to secure a state in Palestine

Zoroastrianism   religion founded by Iranian prophet and dualist Zoroaster (ca. 628–551 C.E.)

FURTHER READINGS

Alexander, Hartley Burr, *The World's Rim*. Lincoln: University of Nebraska Press, 1967. A lyric study of American Indian rituals and customs.

Andrae, Tor, *Mohammed: The Man and His Faith*. New York: Harper & Row, 1960. A psychological approach, interpreting Mohammad's personality and faith.

Auel, Jean, *The Clan of the Cave Bear*. New York: Bantam, 1981. A fascinating novel that recreates Neanderthal life.

Babbitt, Irving, trans., *The Dhammapada*. New York: New Directions, 1965. A clear translation of one of Buddhism's most beloved religious guides.

Baeck, Leo, *The Essence of Judaism*. New York: Schocken, 1961. A clear presentation of the main ideas and characteristics, from a survivor of the Nazi camps.

Basham, A. L., *The Wonder That Was India*. New York: Grove, 1959. A classical presentation of Indian culture before the Muslims, full of fascinating details.

Beyer, Stephen, ed., *The Buddhist Experience*. Encino, Calif.: Dickenson, 1974. A good reader, stressing the existential, even quirky sides of lived Buddhist faith.

Black Elk, *The Sacred Pipe*. Ed. Joseph Epes Brown. Baltimore: Penguin, 1971. A beautiful presentation and explanation of Sioux rituals.

Boas, Franz, *The Central Eskimo*. Lincoln: University of Nebraska Press, 1964. A somewhat dry anthropological study that lays out the main physical and cultural details.

Bolshakoff, Sergius, and Pennington, M. Basil, *In Search of True Wisdom*. Garden City, N.Y.: Doubleday, 1979. A warm account of the convictions and ways of life of Russian and Greek Christian spiritual masters.

Bowker, John, *The Sense of God*. Oxford: Clarendon, 1973. A brilliant study of the implications of recent social studies for religious understanding.

Brown, Joseph Epes, *The Spiritual Legacy of the American Indian*. New York: Crossroad, 1982. A good summary statement by a long-time student of American Indian culture.

Brown, Robert McAfee, *Creative Dislocation—The Movement of Grace*. Nashville: Abingdon, 1980. A moving autobiographical account that captures much of the change on the American religious scene since the 1960s.

Brown, Robert McAfee, *Elie Wiesel*. Notre Dame, Ind.: University of Notre Dame Press, 1983. A thorough and admiring presentation of the main literary motifs of the most influential of the holocaust writers.

Brueggemann, Walter, *The Land*. Philadelphia: Fortress, 1977. Interesting observations on the biblical notions of how the land figures in the promises to Israel.

Carmody, Denise L., and Carmody, John T., *Christianity: An Introduction*. Belmont, Calif.: Wadsworth, 1983. An undergraduate text presenting doctrine, history, and contemporary trends.

Carmody, John, *Ecology and Religion: Toward A New Christian Theology of Nature*. Ramsey, N.J.: Paulist, 1983. An overview of the whole question that uses the methodology of Bernard Lonergan to move from dialectics to ethics and spirituality.

Carmody, John, *Reexamining Conscience*. New York: Seabury, 1982. A practical spiritual regime that fuses mysticism and sanctity.

Castaneda, Carlos, *Tales of Power*. New York: Simon & Schuster, 1974. Interesting literary use of Yaqui shamanic ideas.

Chan, Wing-Tsit, *A Source Book in Chinese Philosophy*. Princeton, N.J.: Princeton University Press, 1969. A fine collection of basic texts from the whole span of Chinese history.

Chang, Chung-yuan, *Creativity and Taoism*. New York: Harper & Row, 1970. Explains the Taoist spirit behind much East Asian art and spirituality.

Conze, Edward, trans., *Buddhist Scriptures*. Baltimore: Penguin, 1959. A good collection of much-revered texts from different Buddhist schools.

Cragg, Kenneth, and Speight, Marston, eds., *Islam From Within*. Belmont, Calif.: Wadsworth, 1980. Good primary sources that show something of the inner pulse of Islam.

Creel, Herrlee G., *Chinese Thought from Confucius to Mao Tse-tung*. Chicago: University of Chicago Press, 1953. A lucid interpretation by a long-time scholar of Chinese culture.

Crim, Keith, ed., *Abingdon Dictionary of Living Religions*. Nashville: Abingdon, 1981. Perhaps the best single-volume reference tool.

David-Neel, Alexandra, *Magic and Mystery in Tibet*. New York: Dover, 1971. Somewhat dated but interesting observations from an early twentieth-century tourist and student.

Dodds, E. R., *The Greeks and the Irrational*. Berkeley: University of California Press, 1951. A famous study of the wild side of Greek culture.

Donner, Florinda, *Shabono*. New York: Delacorte, 1982. A beautiful, interesting account of an anthropologist's stay with a South American shamanic tribe.

Donohue, John J., and Esposito, John L., eds., *Islam in Transition: Muslim Perspectives*. New York: Oxford University Press, 1982. Muslim voices speak out on a variety of socio-political questions.

Earhart, H. Byron, ed., *Religion in Japanese Experience*. Encino, Calif.: Dickenson, 1974. A useful collection of primary sources that show Japanese religion evolving over the centuries.

Einstein, Albert, *The World As I See It*. Secaucus, N.J.: Citadel Press, 1979. Brief occasional essays on a variety of topics by one of the most fascinating modern minds.

Eliade, Mircea, *From Primitives to Zen*. New York: Harper & Row, 1967. A useful collection of primary texts from across the full range of the religious traditions (somewhat strangely arranged).

Eliade, Mircea, *A History of Religious Ideas*. Chicago: University of Chicago Press, 1978. The masterwork of the preeminent historian of religion in our time.

Eliade, Mircea, *Shamanism: Archaic Techniques of Ecstasy*. Princeton, N.J.: Princeton University Press/Bollingen, 1972. The outstanding monograph on the subject.

Ellwood, Robert S., Jr., *An Invitation to Japanese Civilization*. Belmont, Calif.: Wadsworth, 1980. A readable and brief introduction to Japanese history and viewpoints.

Embree, Ainslie T., ed., *The Hindu Tradition*. New York: Vintage, 1972. A good short collection of primary sources displaying something of the rich variety in Hinduism.

Erikson, Erik, *The Life Cycle Completed*. New York: W. W. Norton, 1982. A tight summary statement from the prime theoretician of the life cycle.

Falk, Nancy, and Gross, Rita, eds., *Unspoken Worlds*. San Francisco: Harper & Row, 1980. A good collection of relatively first-hand accounts of women's experiences in the non-Western religious traditions.

Fingarette, Herbert, *Confucius—The Secular as Sacred*. New York: Harper & Row, 1972. A stimulating brief study that stresses the Confucian genius with ritual.

Finkelstein, Louis, ed., *The Jews*. New York: Schocken, 1970. A useful collection of essays by the leading scholars of the past generation.

Franck, Frederick, ed., *The Buddha Eye*. New York: Crossroad, 1982. Primary sources from the Kyoto school, one of the most influential in recent Buddhist philosophy.

Gill, Sam D., *Beyond the Primitive*. Englewood Cliffs, N.J.: Prentice-Hall, 1982. An interesting presentation from the standpoint of cultural anthropology.

Gill, Sam D., *Native American Religions*. Belmont, Calif.: Wadsworth, 1982. An undergraduate text, from a leading American scholar.

Glatzer, Nahum, ed., *Hammer on the Rock: A Midrash Reader*. New York: Schocken, 1962. A good brief sampler of Talmudic voices.

Griaule, Marcel, *Conversations with Ogotemmeli*. New York: Oxford University Press, 1965. A riot of imaginative invention, as anthropology reproduces the rich mythology of the Dogon.

Halifax, Joan, *Shamanic Voices*. New York: E.P. Dutton, 1979. A nice collection of first-person testimonies and renditions of shamanic experience.

Hamilton, Edith, and Cairns, Huntington, eds., *Plato: Collected Dialogues*. Princeton, N.J.: Princeton University Press/Bollingen, 1961. The complete works of the thinker to whom all the rest of Western philosophy is a footnote.

Harner, Michael, *The Way of the Shaman*. San Francisco: Harper & Row, 1980. An interesting interpretation, spiced with personal experience and suggestions for the reader's shamanic practice.

Hodgson, Marshall G. S., *The Venture of Islam*. Chicago: University of Chicago Press, 1974. The masterwork on Islamic history.

Hori, Ichiro, *Folk Religion in Japan*. Chicago: University of Chicago Press, 1968. A full treatment of Japanese folk customs and shamanism.

Hultzkrantz, Åke, *The Religions of the American Indians*. Berkeley: University of California Press, 1979. A useful but somewhat overly structured view of the whole.

Kakar, Sudhir, *Shamans, Mystics, and Doctors*. New York: Alfred A. Knopf, 1982. Very interesting interviews and reflections on Indian folk medicine.

Kelsey, Morton, *Discernment*. Ramsey, N.J.: Paulist, 1978. Interesting essays on the charismatic dimension of Christianity.

Kinsley, David R., *The Sword and the Flute*. Berkeley: University of California Press, 1975. A fine study of Kali and Krishna.

Kurtèn, Björn, *Dance of the Tiger*. New York: Berkeley, 1981. An intriguing novel of prehistoric life.

Léon-Dufour, *Dictionary of the New Testament*. San Francisco: Harper & Row, 1980. A somewhat technical word book.

Levin, Meyer, *Classic Hasidic Tales*. New York: Penguin, 1975. Engaging stories from the Ba'al Shem Tov and his successors.

Lewis, I. M., *Ecstatic Religion*. Baltimore, Penguin, 1971. A solid sociological study of shamanism and the ecstatic.

Lings, Martin, *A Sufi Saint of the Twentieth Century,* 2d ed. Berkeley: University of California Press, 1973. A surprisingly dry study of an absorbing mystical figure.

Lonegran, Bernard, *Insight*. New York: Philosophical Library, 1957. A full study of understanding, in the Aristotelian-Thomist tradition.

Marshack, Alexander, *The Roots of Civilization*. New York: McGraw-Hill, 1972. The symbolic and time-factored aspects of earliest intelligence.

Marshall, George N., *Buddha: The Quest for Serenity*. Boston: Beacon, 1978. A readable biography.

Mbiti, John, *African Religions and Philosophy*. Garden City, N.Y.: Doubleday, 1970. A good thematic study, dealing with the main topics and resting on a broad base of data.

McKeon, Richard, ed., *Introduction to Aristotle,* 2d ed. Chicago: University of Chicago Press, 1973. A good selection of primary texts.

Naipaul, V. S., *Among the Believers*. New York: Vintage Books, 1982. A perceptive and critical journalist's account of encounters with contemporary Muslim regimes.

Naipaul, V. S., *India: A Wounded Civilization*. New York: Vintage Books, 1978. Strong and perceptive cultural criticism.

Neusner, Jacob, *The Way of Torah,* 3d ed. Belmont, Calif.: Wadsworth, 1979. A slim and readable undergraduate text.

Otto, Rudolf, *Mysticism East and West*. New York: Macmillan, 1970. A comparison of Shankara and Meister Eckhart.

Perrin, Norman, and Duling, Dennis, *The New Testament: An Introduction*, 2d ed. New York: Harcourt Brace Jovanovich, 1982. A challenging interpretation of the basic issues.

Radhakrishnan, Sarvepalli, and Moore, Charles A., eds., *A Source Book in Indian Philosophy*. Princeton, N.J.: Princeton University Press, 1957. A good collection of central primary sources.

Rahman, Fazlur, *Islam*. Garden City, N.Y.: Doubleday, 1968. A standard but somewhat dry historical treatment.

Rahner, Karl, and Vorgrimler, Herbert, *Theological Dictionary*. New York: Herder & Herder, 1965. Two Roman Catholic philosophical theologians' reflections on primary Christian notions.

Ray, Benjamin, *African Religions*. Englewood Cliffs, N.J.: Prentice-Hall, 1976. A good introduction to the main notions.

Schillebeeckx, Edward, *Jesus*. New York: Seabury, 1979. A quite technical and thorough study of problems of the historical Jesus.

Scholem, Gersham G., *Major Trends in Jewish Mysticism,* 3d ed. New York: Schocken, 1963. The standard beginning place for Jewish mysticism.

Smart, Ninian, and Hecht, Richard D., eds., *Sacred Texts of the World*. New York: Crossroad, 1982. An excellent collection of primary sources for all of the traditions.

Sproul, Barbara, *Primal Myths.* New York: Harper & Row, 1979. A good selection of myths of creation from around the world.

Suzuki, Shunryu, *Zen Mind, Beginner's Mind.* New York: Weatherhill, 1970. A set of poetic conferences from a contemporary Soto Zen master.

Thompson, Laurence G., *Chinese Religion: An Introduction*, 3d ed. Belmont, Calif.: Wadsworth, 1979. A clear undergraduate introduction.

Thompson, Laurence G., *The Chinese Way in Religion.* Encino, Calif.: Dickenson, 1973. A good collection of original sources.

Trepp, Leo, *Judaism: Development and Life*, 3d ed. Belmont, Calif.: Wadsworth, 1982. A warm overview of the whole.

Tsunoda, Ryusaku, et al., eds., *Sources of Japanese Tradition.* New York: Columbia University Press, 1958. A fine assembly of original sources.

Turnbull, Colin, *The Forest People.* New York: Simon & Schuster, 1962. A charming account by an anthropologist accepted into the tribe.

Turnbull, Colin, *The Mountain People.* New York: Simon & Schuster, 1972. A disturbing view of a people rendered inhumane by their dislocations.

Van der Leeuw, Geradus, *Religion in Essence and Manifestation.* New York: Harper & Row, 1963. A standard phenomenology of the whole of religious experience.

Voegelin, Eric, *Anamnesis.* Nortre Dame, Ind.: University of Notre Dame Press, 1978. Essays on the structure of reason and history.

Voegelin, Eric, *Conversations with Eric Voegelin.* Montreal: Thomas More Institute, 1980. Informal manifestations of great learning and profound cultural interpretation.

Walker, Alice, *The Color Purple.* New York: Washington Square, 1982. A lovely novel, warm and deep.

Warren, Henry Clarke, trans., *Buddhism in Translations.* New York: Atheneum, 1973. A good collection of Theravada texts.

Weitzmann, Kurt, et al., *The Icon.* New York: Alfred A. Knopf, 1982. A beautiful art book, with interpretive essays.

Welch, Holmes, *Taoism: The Parting of the Way.* Boston: Beacon, 1966. History and interpretation, with special emphasis on the *Tao Te Ching*.

Yang, C. K., *Religion in Chinese Society.* Berkeley: University of California Press, 1961. A rather dry but informative sociological survey.

Zaehner, R. C., *The Teachings of the Magi.* New York: Oxford University Press, 1976. A good brief collection of Zoroastrian texts.

Zborowski, Mark, and Herzog, Elizabeth, *Life Is with People.* New York: Schocken, 1962. A wonderful source of insight into Eastern European Jewry before World War II.

Zimmer, Heinrich, *Philosophies of India.* Princeton, N.J.: Princeton University Press/Bollingen, 1969. A solid, somewhat difficult study of the main Indian systems.

Index